• BANTAM AIR & SPACE SERIES •

23

William S. Phillips's great painting of General Jimmy Doolittle's raiding planes has been made available as a limited-edition print signed by both the artist and General Doolittle.

The painting appearing on the cover of this edition is used by courtesy of The Greenwich Workshop.

PRELUDE TO GLORY

That morning I had an early breakfast with Joe and packed my B-4 bag. I told her, "I'll be out of the country for a while. I'll be in touch as soon as I can."

She knew nothing about what I had been doing over the past few weeks at Eglin and McClellan. When I was working in industry I always kept her informed of my itinerary during my many trips. But when I put the uniform on, she always believed that a military man's wife, family, and friends have "no right or need to know" official secrets. I always appreciated her attitude about that, but know how difficult it is for any wife to accept not knowing where her husband is going or when he'll be back.

We had had many separations before in our lives together, but I had the feeling she knew this departure was different. I kissed her tenderly. She held back her tears, but I'm sure she thought it was going to be a long time before she saw me again. I wondered if we would ever see each other again.

I Could Never Be So Lucky Again

GENERAL JAMES H. "JIMMY" DOOLITTLE

with Carroll V. Glines

FALCON ™

BANTAM BOOKS

NEW YORK • TORONTO • LONDON • SYDNEY • AUCKLAND

I COULD NEVER BE SO LUCKY AGAIN

A Bantam Falcon Book

PRINTING HISTORY

Bantam hardcover edition published September 1991

Bantam paperback edition / August 1992

Grateful acknowledgment is made for permission to reprint the following: Excerpt from THE SPIRIT OF ST. LOUIS by Charles A. Lindbergh reprinted with permission of Charles Scribners Sons, an imprint of Macmillan Publishing Company. Copyright © 1953 Charles Scribners Sons; copyright renewed © 1981 Anne Morrow Lindbergh. Excerpt from Thirty Seconds Over Tokyo by Ted W. Lawson, copyright © 1943, 1953 and renewed 1971 by Ted Lawson and Robert Considine. Reprinted by permission of Random House Inc. Excerpt from The Tibbets Story, copyright © 1978 by Paul W. Tibbets. Originally published by Stein & Day, Inc., reprinted with permission of Scarborough House, Publishers. Excerpt from the Drew Pearson syndicated column reprinted by permission of UFS, Inc.

FALCON *and the portrayal of a boxed "f" are trademarks of Bantam Books, a division of Bantam Doubleday Dell Publishing Group, Inc.*

Library of Congress Catalog Card Number: 91-3353.

ISBN 0-553-29725-2

Published simultaneously in the United States and Canada

Bantam Books are published by Bantam Books, a division of Bantam Doubleday Dell Publishing Group, Inc. Its trademark, consisting of the words "Bantam Books" and the portrayal of a rooster, is Registered in U.S. Patent and Trademark Office and in other countries. Marca Registrada. Bantam Books, 666 Fifth Avenue, New York, New York 10103.

PRINTED IN THE UNITED STATES OF AMERICA

RAD 0 9 8 7 6 5 4 3 2 1

To Joe

FOREWORD

One of the valued honors of my life is preparing this foreword for Jimmy Doolittle's memoirs. It's an honor because I consider him to be one of the greatest Americans we have had in our history.

Jimmy has been my hero since my teenage years of the 1920s when he thrilled the world with his daring aerobatics and set many speed records. His winning of the Thompson Trophy in the Gee-Bee racer that had earned such a bad reputation especially caught my imagination. Everything he did thereafter seemed to make news and I followed his exploits in the papers and on radio as avidly as other kids followed stories about sports heroes like boxers Gene Tunney and Jack Dempsey and the great baseball players of the day, Ty Cobb and Babe Ruth.

Like many other kids of my generation, Jimmy's aerial escapades and fearless racing inspired me to take up flying. I wanted to be a pilot like Jimmy Doolittle and earn my wings in the Army Air Forces. I did, eventually, in a roundabout way. He's still my hero not only because of his activities as a pilot, but because of the many lasting contributions he has made to flying and to our way of life.

You will find out in these pages from Jimmy himself that he enjoyed raising a bit of hell in an airplane in his early days. He had forced landings and crashes, many of them, but learned something valuable each time. He bailed out three times to save himself. He became a test pilot. And in those days, before aeronautical engineers and high-speed wind tunnels could give us a fair idea of how much an airplane could stand before disintegrating, that meant he found out personally by flying them to near destruction. He was a daredevil as far as his public image was concerned, but few know that he was one of the first, if not the first, to earn a doctorate in the aeronautical sciences. And from MIT, no less. His doctorate provided him with the knowledge that enabled him to help develop high-octane fuel. Without this, our defeat of Germany in the air may not have been possible. He taught us how to get more mileage out of a tank of fuel.

Perhaps most Americans remember Jimmy for leading the surprise raid on Japan of April 18, 1942. No one, especially not the Japanese, thought anyone could fly heavily loaded land-based medium bombers off a carrier's deck. Jimmy and his Tokyo Raiders did and taught the Japanese an important lesson: America could and would retaliate for the attack on Pearl Harbor. It was a psychological blow more than a destructive one, but it gave Americans the morale boost we so desperately needed at that time.

Such a daring flight was typical of Jimmy. By that time he had become known as the master of the calculated risk, a hard-earned title that came about because although he took great personal risks he always did so by first thinking through the variables involved and allowing himself better than fifty-fifty odds of survival.

Jimmy's greatest contributions to aviation were the 1929 experiments with instrument flying that led to his being the first pilot ever to fly completely "blind" from takeoff to landing. All of us flying today are the beneficiaries of his skill, foresight, and persistence in seeking the solution to all-weather flying.

Jimmy Doolittle is too modest to say these things, but as you read this book, you will see how this former boxing champion matured as a leader of men and took on successively more difficult jobs during World War II. Along with Generals "Hap" Arnold, "Tooey" Spaatz, and Ira Eaker, Jimmy pioneered strategic bombing and laid the groundwork for victory in Europe.

Jimmy's extraordinary energy, common sense, and faith in his people made him one of the most revered generals in our history. In North Africa, he chose to fly on the most difficult missions because he wanted to see firsthand what the enemy defenses and fighter tactics were. His dedication and single-minded enthusiasm to get any job assigned to him completed successfully were infectious and earned him increasing responsibilities. His leadership of the famous 8th Air Force is a classic case of superb management of men and their machines to help bring about success in war.

As you will note, Jimmy did not fade away when the war was over. He has probably served on more federal boards and commissions than any other American. His contributions to knowledge and to the progress of aeronautics and astronautics have earned him more awards, honors, citations, plaques, and trophies than anyone else I know of. Yet he has remained modest, unassuming, and amazed that what he has done should continue to gain such enthusiastic accolades.

In 1985, I thought the time had come to promote Jimmy Doolittle and Ira Eaker from the rank of lieutenant general to full general. Both of them had made outstanding contributions to our national defense during their long lifetimes. I introduced a joint resolution in the United States Senate authorizing the President to promote both of them on the Air Force's retired list. Such a promotion would carry no increase in compensation or benefits but would be a way to honor two very deserving former military leaders.

I thought the resolution would sail through the Senate and House without argument or objection. It was passed unanimously by the Senate, but certain young individuals in the House gave me a hard time. If I really wanted this joint resolution to go through, they said, they would vote for approval provided I went along with certain political tradeoffs they had in mind.

I was furious and said so with expletives undeleted. They had no conception of what Jimmy and Ira had done for this nation and they wanted to make these promotions a political issue. Honoring brave men who had served with total dedication as these two had done should not be based on politics. I refused to trade these promotions for my vote on the boondoggling projects of a bunch of rookie congressmen.

There was one way around these scoundrels. I marched up Pennsylvania Avenue to the White House and asked President Ronald Reagan to make a formal request of the Senate for the promotions. Military promotions are made by the president as commander in chief with the advice and consent of the Senate. President Reagan, who admires Jimmy as much as I do, signed the nominations immediately and the Senate approved. No one in the House wanted to go public with any objections.

But that's not the end of the story. We thought both men

should have their stars pinned on simultaneously in a Washington ceremony. Although grateful to be accorded the honor, Jimmy objected. "Ira outranks me," he said. "I think he should get it first because of his long, uninterrupted military service. I was a reserve officer with a ten-year break in service."

We honored Jimmy's wish. Ira received his four stars first on April 26, 1985, and Jimmy received his a short time later. In 1989, Jimmy also received the Presidential Medal of Freedom from President George Bush for his extraordinary contributions to aerospace progress and his extensive service in the nation's interest.

You will not find stories like this in the following pages because Jimmy Doolittle never engages in self-praise. He does not ask favors and always keeps his promises and commitments, no matter how much it may inconvenience or cost him. He dislikes the use of the vertical pronoun but realizes it is difficult to tell one's life story without it.

This is a story of one uncommon man's adventures, daring, honesty, and dedicated service to his country. It is about a man who spent 71 happy years with his one-and-only sweetheart, whom we all knew as "Joe." It is the story of a unique American whose life spans the entire history of heavier-than-air aeronautics and our ventures into space and who has contributed immeasurably to both. There will never be another like him.

BARRY M. GOLDWATER
SCOTTSDALE, ARIZONA

PREFACE

For a long time I have resisted all requests to write my memoirs. I have always felt an autobiography would seem too self-serving. However, at the behest of family and friends, I decided to acquiesce.

I have been joined in this effort by Colonel Carroll V. Glines, USAF (retired), a pilot and an award-winning author, who interviewed me on many occasions for four books about certain aspects of my life: *Doolittle's Tokyo Raiders*, *Four Came Home*, *The Doolittle Raid: America's Daring First Strike Against Japan*, and *Jimmy Doolittle: Master of the Calculated Risk*.

Since we gradually lose our ability to recall as we grow older, in the interest of accuracy, I have relied heavily on the voluminous correspondence in my personal files, interviews I granted many writers and historians through the years, my military and civilian records, and official histories of the Air Force and the corporations that employed me. The memoirs and biographies of my military contemporaries have been especially helpful in providing their viewpoints concerning actions, decisions, and situations in which I was involved.

I have always tried to be truthful in my dealings with my fellow human beings. If I have erred in the following pages, I offer my sincere apologies and promise to make any corrections of fact in subsequent editions of this work. No doubt there will be honest differences of opinion in regard to the rightness or wrongness of decisions I made in the past, especially during my years in uniform. I respect the right of others to differ and hope that those who dispute my judgments will appreciate my viewpoint in the context of the time in which they were made.

My life has spanned the history of successful controlled flight from the Wright brothers to the astronauts. I have been blessed with an understanding family who tolerated my all-too-frequent absences from home. I have survived many mishaps in the air. I have participated in some historical developments that have made contributions to aeronautical progress, and have been privileged to serve my country in many different and fulfilling ways. And I have been honored many times over, far more than I deserve.

As I reflect on more than nine decades of life on this planet, I realize I have been luckier than the law of averages should allow. I could never be so lucky again.

JAMES H. DOOLITTLE
PEBBLE BEACH, CALIFORNIA

ACKNOWLEDGMENTS

We wish to express our gratitude to all those who helped on these memoirs. We are especially indebted to John Doolittle, his devoted wife, Priscilla, and Celeste Ventura for their never-faltering encouragement and their efforts in locating background materials that facilitated recall of many of the incidents and experiences related here. Their editorial suggestions and those of Mary Ellen Glines provided a very helpful review throughout the writing process.

We are also grateful for the assistance rendered by the curators at the Library of Congress, the National Air and Space Museum, the Air Force Academy, the Arizona Historical Society, and Western Reserve University, and the personnel of the Office of Air Force History who made appropriate files and photographs available for study. Of special help was Duane J. Reed of the Air Force Academy, who provided access to the Doolittle family photo albums donated to the academy library, and William Madsen, retired public affairs specialist, for his photocopying work.

The public relations staffs of TRW, Aerospace Corporation, Space Technology Laboratories, and Mutual of Omaha responded promptly and efficiently to our requests for background information. So did General Larry D. Welch, chief of staff of the U.S. Air Force, and Admiral James B. Busey, administrator of the Federal Aviation Administration, when we requested copies of military and civilian pilot files. And we appreciate the interest taken by many former Air Force personnel who provided materials and anecdotes, especially Lieutenant Colonel George M. Epperson, a former intelligence officer in the 8th Air Force during World War II.

Special thanks are reserved for Senator Barry M. Goldwater for continually encouraging the writing of these memoirs and for granting an interview while he was recovering from his fourth hip operation.

JAMES H. DOOLITTLE
AND CARROLL V. GLINES

I Could Never Be So Lucky Again

CHAPTER 1

April 18, 1942

The 16-ship Navy task force centered around the aircraft carriers *Hornet* and *Enterprise* had been steaming westward toward Japan all night. I had given my final briefing to the B-25 bomber crews on the *Hornet* the day before. Our job was to do what we could to put a crimp in the Japanese war effort with the 16 tons of bombs from our 16 B-25s. The bombs could do only a fraction of the damage the Japanese had inflicted on us at Pearl Harbor, but the primary purpose of the raid we were about to launch against the main island of Japan was psychological.

The Japanese people had been told they were invulnerable. Their leaders had told them Japan could never be invaded. Proof of this was the fact that Japan had been saved from invasion during the fifteenth century when a massive Chinese fleet set sail to attack Japan and was destroyed by a monsoon. From then on, the Japanese people had firmly believed they were forever protected by a "divine wind"—the *kamikaze*. An attack on the Japanese homeland would cause confusion in the minds of the Japanese people and sow doubt about the reliability of their leaders.

There was a second, and equally important, psychological reason for this attack. America and its allies had suffered one defeat after another in the Pacific and southern Asia. Besides the devastating surprise attack on Pearl Harbor, the Japanese had taken Wake Island and Guam and had driven American and Filipino forces to surrender on Bataan. Only a small force of Americans was left holding out on the island of Corregidor. America had never seen darker days. Americans badly needed a morale boost. I hoped we could give them that by a retaliatory surprise attack against the enemy's home islands launched from a carrier, precisely as the Japanese had done at Pearl Harbor. It would be the kind of touché the Japanese military would understand. An air strike would certainly be a blow to their national morale and, furthermore, should cause the Japanese to divert aircraft and equipment from offensive operations to the defense of the home islands.

The basic plan for the raid against Japan was simple. If the Navy task force could get us within 400 to 500 miles of the Japanese coast, the B-25 medium Army bombers aboard the *Hornet* would launch, with carefully trained crews, against the enemy's largest cities. Although the carrier's deck seemed too short to allow the takeoff of a loaded B-25 land-based Army bomber, I was confident it could be done. Two lightly loaded B-25s had made trial takeoffs the previous February from the *Hornet* off the Virginia coast before the carrier had joined the Pacific fleet. All of the pilots had practiced a number of short-field takeoffs at an auxiliary field near Eglin Field, Florida.

I would take off first so as to arrive over Tokyo at sunset. The other crews would leave the carrier at local sunset and head for their respective targets. I would drop four 500-pound incendiary bombs on a factory area in the center of Tokyo. The resulting fires in the highly inflammable structures in the area would light up the way for the succeeding planes and steer them toward their respective targets in the Tokyo-Yokohama area, Nagoya, and the Kobe-Osaka complex. The rest of the B-25s would be loaded with four 500-pound bombs each—two incendiaries and two demolition bombs. After launching the B-25s, the Navy task force was to retreat immediately and return to Hawaii.

We would not return to the *Hornet*. After bombing our targets, we were to escape to China. The planes would be turned over to the new Air Force units being formed in the China-Burma-India theater.

There were five crew members in each airplane—pilot, copilot, bombardier, navigator, and gunner. One crew had a physician aboard—Dr. (Lieutenant) Thomas R. White—who had volunteered and qualified as a gunner so he could go. This was a fortuitous choice, as it turned out, for four members of another crew.

The State Department had tried to get permission from the Soviets for us to land in Soviet territory for refueling. This flight would have been an easy 600 miles or so after bombing the Japanese targets. But permission was denied because the Soviets were neutral vis-à-vis Japan and did not want to have another Axis power at their back door invading their country from that direction.

Therefore, after dropping its bombs, each plane was to head generally southward along the Japanese coast, then westward to Chuchow, located about 70 miles inland and about 200 miles south of Shanghai. After refueling there, we were to proceed to Chungking, 800 miles farther inland. The greatest in-flight distance we would have to fly was 2,000 miles. With the fuel tank modifications we had made and extra gas in five-gallon cans, there was enough fuel on board to fly 2,400 miles, provided the crews used the long-range cruising techniques we had practiced.

Our planes had been positioned on the deck for takeoff the evening before. The mechanics had run up their engines and made last-minute adjustments. I wanted the crews to get a good night's sleep, but few heeded the advice of an oldster who, at 45, was twice the age of most of them. Some of the officers played poker with the Navy pilots who had been unable to fly since leaving California because our planes took up all the space on the deck. The Navy pilots and our crews wanted to recoup their individual losses before we left.

The *Enterprise* launched scout planes at daybreak for 200-mile searches, and fighters were sent up as cover for the task force. The weather, which had been moderately rough during the night, worsened. There was a low overcast and visibility was limited. Frequent rain squalls swept over the ships, and the sea began to heave into 30-foot crests. Gusty winds tore off the tops of the waves and blew heavy spray across the ships, drenching the deck crews. At 6:00 A.M., a scout plane returned to the *Enterprise* and the pilot dropped a bean bag container on the deck with a message saying he had sighted a small enemy fishing vessel and believed he had been seen by the enemy.

Admiral William F. Halsey immediately ordered all ships to swing left to avoid detection. Had the enemy vessel seen the aircraft? No one knew. The question was answered about 7:30 A.M. when another patrol vessel was sighted from the *Hornet* only 20,000 yards away. A Japanese radio message was intercepted by the *Hornet*'s radio operator from close by. One of the scout planes then sighted another small vessel 12,000 yards away. A light could be seen bobbing in the rough sea. Halsey ordered the cruiser *Nashville* to sink it.

Unknown to us, the Japanese had stationed a line of radio-equipped picket boats about 650 nautical miles out from the coast to warn of the approach of American ships. I went to the bridge where Captain Marc A. Mitscher briefed me on what had happened. "It looks like you're going to have to be on your way soon," he said. "They know we're here." I shook hands with Mitscher and rushed to my cabin to pack, spreading the word as I went.

Some of the B-25 crews had finished breakfast and were lounging in their cabins; others were shaving and getting ready to eat; several may have still been dozing. A few had packed their bags, but I think many were completely surprised because they thought they would not be taking off until late afternoon.

At 8:00 A.M., Admiral Halsey flashed a message to the *Hornet*: LAUNCH PLANES X TO COL DOOLITTLE AND GALLANT COMMAND GOOD LUCK AND GOD BLESS YOU.

The ear-shattering klaxon horn sounded and a booming voice ordered: "Now hear this! Now hear this! Army pilots, man your planes!"

The weather had steadily continued to worsen. The *Hornet* plunged into mountainous waves that sent water cascading down the deck. Rain pelted us as we ran toward our aircraft. It was not an ideal day for a mission like this one.

The well-disciplined Navy crews and our enlisted men, some of whom had slept on deck near their planes, knew what to do. Slipping and sliding on the wet deck, they ripped off engine and gun turret covers and stuffed them inside the rear hatches. Fuel tanks were topped. The mechanics pulled the props through. Cans of gasoline were filled and handed up to the gunners through the rear hatches. Ropes were unfastened and wheel chocks pulled away so the Navy deck handlers could maneuver the B-25s into takeoff position.

Meanwhile, the *Hornet* picked up speed as best it could in the rough sea and turned into the wind. The 20-knot speed of the carrier and the 30-knot wind blowing directly down the deck meant that we should be airborne safely and quickly. This ability of an aircraft carrier to turn its "airfield" into the wind is a distinct advantage. Rarely do Navy pilots have to worry about cross-wind takeoffs and landings. However, a rough sea such as the one in front of us could ruin a pilot's day if he ignored the signals of the deck officer and tried a takeoff when the bow of the ship was heading into the waves. It was like riding a seesaw that plunged deep into the water each time the bow dipped downward.

Lieutenant Henry L. "Hank" Miller, the naval officer assigned to us at Eglin Field, Florida, to teach us how to take off in minimum distances, said good-bye to each crew. He told us to watch a blackboard he would be holding up near the ship's "island" to give us last-minute instructions and the carrier's heading so our navigators could compare our planes' compasses with the ship's heading and set their directional gyros. The navigators were very concerned about our magnetic compasses. After more than two weeks on the carrier, they would be way off calibration, especially on those planes that were tied down close to the carrier's metal structure. With an overcast sky, the navigators wouldn't be able to take shots of the sun or stars with their sextants. It would be dead reckoning all the way to the Japanese coast. A check on the accuracy of the compasses was essential.

My crew emerged quickly from their quarters below decks. Sergeant Paul J. Leonard, our crew chief, was one of those skilled mechanics who knew instinctively what to do. He already had his barracks bag and toolbox stowed in the rear and was helping the deck crews get our ship into takeoff position. In the air, he would be the top turret gunner. During our training at Eglin, he had proven he was a marksman with the twin .50s. Born in 1912, he had dropped out of high school in Roswell, New Mexico, and enlisted in the Army Air Corps in 1931, at the start of the Depression. He was one of those rare individuals who applied himself and became one of the most outstanding mechanics with whom I ever served. Men like him were the backbone of the nation's air service when war began and were highly regarded for their dedication and expertise. They set high standards for the enlisted men who served with them.

Sergeant Fred A. Braemer, of Seattle, Washington, was another "old-timer." He had joined the infantry in 1935 and transferred to the Air Corps in 1939. He had completed both bombardier and navigator training but was serving on our crew as the bombardier.

Our copilot was Lieutenant Richard E. "Dick" Cole, from

Dayton, Ohio, who had completed pilot training in July 1941. Dick was a quietly competent pilot who had attended Ohio University for two years before enlisting as a Flying Cadet. If anything happened to me, I was confident that he would take over the controls of the aircraft and the leadership of the crew without hesitation.

Lieutenant Henry A. "Hank" Potter, of Pierre, South Dakota, was our navigator. Like so many young men in those days, he had also completed two years of college, the minimum for entry into flying training, and had graduated from navigator school in 1941.

I was proud of my crew and all the other volunteers who were willing to lay their lives on the line for a risky mission that I could not tell them about until we were on the carrier. Every man had proven his competence during our training at Eglin. I felt completely comfortable and confident as our B-25 was placed in takeoff position and the wheels chocked.

I knew hundreds of eyes were watching me, especially those of the B-25 crews who were to follow. If I didn't get off successfully, I'm sure, many thought they wouldn't be able to make it either. But I knew they would try.

I started the engines, warmed them up, and checked the magnetos. When satisfied, I gave the thumbs-up sign to the deck launching officer holding the checkered flag. As the chocks were pulled, he looked toward the bow and began to wave the flag in circles as a signal for me to push the throttles forward to the stops. At the instant the deck was beginning an upward movement, he gave me the "go" signal and I released the brakes. The B-25 followed the two white guide lines painted on the deck and we were off with feet to spare as the deck reached its maximum pitch.

We left the *Hornet* at 8:20 A.M. ship time. The carrier's position was about 824 statute miles from the center of Tokyo. Its position: latitude 35°43′N, longitude 153°25′E.

I signaled Dick for wheels up and as the plane gained flying speed, I leveled off and made a 360-degree turn to come over the carrier. This gave Hank Potter a chance to compare the magnetic heading of the carrier with our compass and align the axis of the carrier with the drift sight. The course of the *Hornet* was displayed in large figures from the gun turret near the island. Through the use of the airplane's compass and directional gyro, we were able to set a fairly accurate course for Tokyo.

As we headed toward Japa
how easy the takeoff had bee
tions, they should have no trou
been easy and practicable. That
port to Washington when I got
future operations.

I began to wonder about the a
alissimo Chiang Kai-shek, China's
land in China after bombing Japan
tion against his people by the Japane
na's coastal areas and Manchuria for ese
had been slaughtered by the thousands rauding Jap-
anese troops invaded an area. Americ military personnel in
China reported that leaks of classified information were common; we were told that secrecy was almost impossible to maintain in Chiang's headquarters. As a result, it was decided in Washington that he would not be informed of our plans until we were at sea and the mission could not be recalled.

As we droned on at about 200 feet above the water, Dick Cole and I took turns at the controls. We were all concerned about gas consumption, and everyone on the flight deck was continually checking the gauges against our estimates. A half hour after takeoff we were joined by the second B-25 to depart, which flew a loose formation with us. It was piloted by Lieutenant Travis Hoover. About an hour later, we sighted a camouflaged Japanese ship that we thought might be a light cruiser. About two hours out we flew directly under an enemy flying boat that just loomed at us suddenly out of the mist. We don't think they saw us. It was heading directly toward the task force.

The weather improved gradually as we got closer to Japan. We changed course briefly several times to avoid various civil and naval surface craft until we made landfall north of Inubo Shima, about 80 miles north of Tokyo. This was the first time Hank Potter was able to get an accurate fix on our position. Trav Hoover promptly turned off toward his target area.

Since we were somewhat north of our desired course, I decided to take advantage of our position and approach the target area from a northerly direction, thus avoiding anticipated antiaircraft batteries and fighter planes located in the western part of the city. We stayed as low as we could and saw many flying fields interspersed among the beautiful scenery. People on the

There were many planes in the air, mostly pparently trainers.

hortly after noon in Tokyo. About 10 miles north we saw nine enemy fighters in three flights of three. ole kept Paul Leonard advised of the enemy aircraft he d see ahead and at one time counted 80. The fighters didn't ttack us, but flak from antiaircraft ground batteries shook us up a little and might have put a few holes in the fuselage.

When we spotted the large factory buildings in our target area, I pulled up to 1,200 feet and called for bomb doors open. Fred Braemer toggled off the four incendiaries in rapid succession. It was 12:30 P.M. Tokyo time.

I dropped down to rooftop level again and slid over the western outskirts of the city into low haze and smoke, then turned south and out to sea. We saw many barrage balloons over east central Tokyo and passed over a small aircraft factory with a dozen or so completed planes on the flying line. Unfortunately, we had no bombs left and I didn't want anyone to do any strafing with our machine guns. If we had done that and were downed for any reason, we would surely have been dealt with severely by our captors.

As we sped toward the coast, we saw five fighter planes converging on us from above. There were two little hills ahead. I swung very quickly around the hills in an S turn. The fighters turned also, but apparently they didn't see the second half of my S. The last time I saw them, they were going off in the opposite direction from us.

We stayed low off the coast and Hank Potter plotted a perfect course to Yaku-shima. The ceiling gradually lowered along the route and got down to about 600 feet. We then turned west over the China Sea and encountered a headwind. Hank Potter estimated we would run out of gas about 135 miles from the Chinese coast. We began to make preparations for ditching. I saw sharks basking in the water below and didn't think ditching among them would be very appealing. Also saw three naval vessels and many small fishing vessels. None of them fired, so they probably didn't see us.

Fortunately, the Lord was with us. What had been a headwind slowly turned into a tailwind of about 25 miles per hour and eased our minds about ditching. Trav Hoover had followed us nearly all the way to the Chinese coast. However, he left us as the weather deteriorated and it began to get dark. Visibility was reduced drastically by fog and light rain. As we crossed the Chinese coast, I went on instruments and pulled up to 8,000 feet through the overcast. Our maps showed the mountains to be about 5,000 feet above sea level, but the maps were probably inaccurate. We saw dim lights below occasionally through cloud breaks but had to remain on instruments.

We tried to contact the field at Chuchow on 4495 kilocycles. No answer. This meant that the chance of any of our crews getting to the destination safely was just about nil. Chuchow was situated in a valley about two miles wide and 12 miles long. Without a ground radio station to home in on, there was no way we could find it. All we could do was fly a dead-reckoning course in the direction of Chuchow, abandon ship in midair, and hope that we came down in Chinese-held territory.

When the gas gauges read near zero, I put the B-25 on automatic pilot and told the men in which order to jump: Braemer, Potter, Leonard, and Cole. If we all jumped in a straight line, it would be easier to find one another when we got on the ground. As Dick Cole left, I shut off both gas valves and squeezed quickly after him through the forward hatch. It was about 9:30 P.M. ship time. We had been in the air for 13 hours. We might have had enough fuel left for about another half hour of flight, but the right front tank gauge showed empty, and fuel gauges, even today, are notoriously inaccurate when registering near the zero mark. We had covered about 2,250 miles, mostly at low speed, but about an hour at moderate high speed had more than doubled the consumption during that time.

As I dropped into the rainy darkness, I suddenly realized that I should have put the flaps down before we bailed out. It would have slowed down the landing speed, reduced the impact, and shortened the glide.

This was my third parachute jump to save my hide. It was impossible to see anything below, so all I could do was wait until I hit the ground. My concern as I floated down was about my ankles, which had been broken in South America in 1926. Anticipating a sudden encounter with the ground, I bent my knees to take the shock. When I hit, there wasn't much impact. I had landed in a rice paddy and fallen into a sitting position in a not-too-fragrant mixture of water and "night soil."

I stood up, unhurt and thoroughly disgusted with my situation and the smell, unhooked my parachute harness, and looked around. I saw a light and approached what looked like a small farmhouse. I knocked on the door and shouted, "*Lushu hoo megwa fugi*" ("I am an American"). This was the Chinese phrase we had been taught aboard the carrier by Lieutenant Commander Stephen Jurika, who had served in the Far East before the war. But I must have used the wrong dialect. I heard movement inside, then the sound of a bolt sliding into place. The light went out and there was dead silence.

It was cold and I was shivering. I stumbled on in the darkness and came to a sort of warehouse. Inside, two sawhorses held a large box that was occupied by a very dead Chinese gentleman. It must have been the local morgue. I left and found a water mill, which got me out of the rain, but I was thoroughly chilled. I lay down but couldn't sleep, so spent most of the night doing light calisthenics to stave off the cold. I stayed there until dawn and then followed a well-worn path toward a small village, where I came upon a Chinese who spoke no English. I drew a picture of a train on a piece of paper. He smiled, nodded, and started off. I followed him to a military headquarters where a Chinese major who spoke a little English gestured for me to hand over my .45-caliber automatic pistol. I refused and explained that I was an American and had parachuted during the night into a rice paddy nearby. He didn't seem to believe me, so I told him that I would take him to the spot and show him the parachute.

The officer, surrounded by about a dozen armed soldiers, escorted me to the rice paddy where I had landed, but the 'chute was gone. I said the people in the house must have heard our plane and could verify that I had knocked on their door the night before. However, when the farmer, his wife, and two children were questioned, they denied everything. The major said, "They say they heard no noise during the night. They say they heard no plane. They say they saw no parachute. They say you lie."

The soldiers started toward me to relieve me of the .45. It was not a comfortable situation. I protested and was saved from having to tussle with them when two soldiers emerged from the house with the parachute. The major smiled and extended his hand in friendship, and I was thus admitted officially to China. He led me back to his headquarters for a warm meal and a much-needed bath. I dried out my uniform but the stench remained intact.

Meanwhile, the major's men found all four of my crew. It was a relief to see that they were in reasonably good shape. The only minor injury was suffered by Hank Potter, who had sprained an ankle on the bailout.

When the soldiers found our plane, Paul Leonard and I went to the crash site to see what we could salvage. There is no worse sight to an aviator than to see his plane smashed to bits. Ours was spread out over several acres of mountaintop. I fished around the debris for my belongings and found my oil-stained uniform blouse. Some enterprising scavenger had already stripped it of all the brass buttons. There was nothing left of our personal belongings that was worth carrying away.

I sat down beside a wing and looked around at the thousands of pieces of shattered metal that had once been a beautiful airplane. I felt lower than a frog's posterior. This was my first combat mission. I had planned it from the beginning and led it. I was sure it was my last. As far as I was concerned, it was a failure, and I felt there could be no future for me in uniform now. Even if we had successfully accomplished the first half of our mission, the second half had been to deliver the B-25s to our units in the China-Burma-India theater of operations.

My main concern was for my men. What had happened to my crew probably had happened to the others. If so, they had to be scattered all over a considerable area of China. How many had survived? Had any been taken prisoner by the Japanese? Did any have to ditch in the China Sea?

As I sat there, Paul Leonard took my picture and then, seeing how badly I felt, tried to cheer me up. He asked, "What do you think will happen when you go home, Colonel?"

I answered, "Well, I guess they'll court-martial me and send me to prison at Fort Leavenworth."

Paul said, "No, sir. I'll tell you what will happen. They're going to make you a general."

I smiled weakly and he tried again. "And they're going to give you the Congressional Medal of Honor."

I smiled again and he made a final effort. "Colonel, I know they're going to give you another airplane and when they do, I'd like to fly with you as your crew chief."

It was then that tears came to my eyes. It was the supreme compliment that a mechanic could give a pilot. It meant he was so sure of the skills of the pilot that he would fly anywhere with him under any circumstances. I thanked him and said that if I ever had another airplane and he wanted to be my crew chief, he surely could.

While I deeply appreciated Paul's supportive remarks, I was sure that when the outcome of this mission was known back home, either I would be court-martialed or the military powers that be would see to it that I would sit out the war flying a desk. I had never felt lower in my life.

CHAPTER 2

Looking back over more than nine decades it is difficult to recall names and incidents of my very early childhood with much certainty. Unfortunately, I never knew my grandparents on either side, but my mother was a good photographer and it is through the many photographs in the albums she maintained for me that I am able to bring back memories of distant times and places.

Our branch of the Doolittle family is believed to have originated in France, relocated to England, then migrated to this country in the late 1600s or early 1700s. My grandfather, Augustus Albertus Doolittle, was born in East Canaan, Connecticut, in 1844. He was a carpenter and married my grandmother, Margaret Hobson, in the 1860s.

My father, born in 1869, was Frank Henry Doolittle. It isn't certain whether he was born in Connecticut or Massachusetts. A restless, ambitious man who was smitten with wanderlust, he was an excellent carpenter. In his early thirties, he sailed around the Horn from Massachusetts, arrived in San Francisco, and settled down across the bay at Alameda to practice his craft. He met and married my mother, Rosa Ceremah Shephard, in the early 1890s. I came along on December 14, 1896, an only child.

I regret deeply that I cannot recall much about my mother's family background. I know she was of sturdy pioneer stock, strong-willed yet compassionate, intent upon keeping me on a straight-and-narrow path, but a firm disciplinarian when I strayed. She guided me safely through those early years and managed somehow to see to my needs. I owe her more than I can ever express.

I guess they didn't know what to name me for a while, since my birth certificate recorded me simply as "Doolittle." The "James" and "Harold" were added later and I have no idea where they came from. I have never been particularly happy about my middle name.

In the summer after I was born, my father joined the thousands of dreamers and adventurers who stampeded to the Klondike in search of gold. He took his bag of carpenter's tools with him and sailed by boat to Seattle and then to Skagway, Alaska. Then he trekked over the Chilkoot Pass to the Klondike gold fields near Dawson. Doubtless he prospected, but since gold was elusive, he kept body and soul together with his carpentry skills. However, he lost his tools in a boat accident as he traveled down the Yukon River to Norton Sound.

In 1899, my father worked his way around to St. Michael where he got a job with the Alaska Commercial Co., a supplier of tools and mining equipment for the prospectors. Still hoping to make his fortune, he pushed on to the Seward Peninsula and finally Nome when the news spread that gold had been discovered on the beaches and was easy pickings.

Once he got to Nome, my father wanted us to join him. On one of the last ships to leave before the winter freeze, he sent a letter to my mother asking her to bring me with her the following spring. So in June 1900, my mother, her sister Sarah, and I sailed on the SS *Zealandia* and arrived in Nome two weeks later. It was just one of the 30 steamers that carried nearly 10,000 people to Nome that month.

Contrary to popular conception, the Klondike River and the gold district named for it are in Canada, not Alaska. The real gold rush stampede to Alaska was not to the Klondike. It was to the sandy beaches of Nome, a thousand miles to the west, during that summer of 1900. It could be reached only by dog sled or boat; therefore, most took the latter course so they wouldn't have to climb mountains, run river rapids, or backpack their own supplies to get there.

A Dawson City newspaper warned its readers, "The gold fever is no respecter of persons. Like the dew of heaven it falls with absolute impartiality upon the just and the unjust alike. Its germs once planted in the system, take root and thrive so vigorously that it dominates its victim like an all-consuming passion for drink.''[1]

Gold had been found in September 1898 along the Snake River near where Nome now stands. Three Swedes were the first to stake claims and took out about $2,000 in gold that year. The Cape Nome Mining District was organized and claims were staked out and recorded. That autumn about 40 men filed claims to 7,000 acres of prospecting ground. Late in June 1899, when the ice broke in the Bering Sea, several vessels reached the settlement that was growing up along Anvil Creek where about 400 people were living in tents and crude driftwood cabins.

A man named John Hummel, who was ailing and could not work much, is generally believed to have been the first to discover gold along the beach. As soon as the news got out, the miners working a few miles inland along the creeks rushed to the beaches. The strike was unquestionably the greatest poor-man's diggings ever found. Within a short time, 2,000 miners were at work sifting the sand. Within two months, using simple hand rockers to sift the sand, the miners had taken out about $750,000 in gold dust.

When the steamers returned to the States that autumn, stories of the gold find spread around the world. Interest in ''the gold sands of Nome'' grew rapidly. Many thought the gold in the beach would be inexhaustible because, supposedly, the supply was being constantly renewed by the waves from the ocean bottom. It wasn't true, but the stampede began in the spring of 1900 when the first ships left ports on the West Coast and made their way through the Aleutian Islands and the Bering Sea ice fields to this paradise of riches. The ice on the Bering Sea broke early and on May 23, 1900, the *Jeanie*, an old whaler, reached Nome, the first of a large fleet to follow.

We were just three of an estimated 25,000 people who landed on the Nome beach that summer. The census taken in June, the month we arrived, showed only 12,488 people, but between 5 and 10 thousand more were believed scattered along the beaches for 25 miles.

The *Nome News*, the city's first newspaper, had bragged about the town in its first issue in 1899 and had helped to precipitate the rush: ''It is true it is built upon sand, but the sand is golden, and . . . it promises to be the greatest gold camp that has ever been known in the history of gold mining.'' The story of the golden sands caught the imagination of people all over the world.[2]

It was true that gold could be found on the beaches, although the creeks feeding the Snake River behind the city would eventually produce more gold than the beaches. But the lure was so strong that those lusting for the gold specks would endure anything to try to make their fortunes with a minimum of equipment and physical effort. All they needed was a wooden rocker box to sift the sand, a shovel, and a bucket. The gold was found mostly in the ruby-colored sand, anywhere from a foot to four feet below the surface. However, the richness of the sand varied from place to place. These shallow diggings along the beach were available to anyone by federal law and could not be staked out and claimed by any single individual. It was generally accepted that a person was entitled to hold his space on the beach—sometimes only the length of a shovel handle—as long as he worked it.

Nome had no safe harbor. Large ships had to anchor offshore and off-load their passengers and freight on barges and small lighters. Many people, boats, and cargo were lost during the violent storms that often roared toward the beaches.

The scene that greeted my young eyes as we landed was chaotic. Crowds of people stood around watching us disembark; freight was piled everywhere. Everything one could imagine was being hauled in on barges from the ships: machines, mining equipment, lumber, sewing machines, mirrors, bar fixtures, tents, liquor, hardware, tools, food, clothing, small boats, furniture, wagons, horses, dogs, and everything else needed to make life as easy and "civilized" as possible. The *Nome News* editorialized that there was a lot of rusting "jackass machinery" and rotten wood lying on the beach which would "tell the tale of overconfidence and misdirected energy and money."[3]

Along the beach as far as one could see were hundreds of people working almost shoulder to shoulder using the simplest hand tools, rocker boxes, and crude contraptions to look for those magic gold flecks among the sand grains. A few beach miners were able to take small fortunes. According to one historian, nearly two thousand men, women, and children were stripping the pay dirt that summer on the beach and took an estimated one to two million dollars in gold from the sand. Many averaged $20 to $100 a day, and it was not unusual for a beach miner to clear between $2,000 and $5,000 for that summer's labor, impressive sums in those days.

Of course, there were many who came to Nome with no desire to use a pick or a shovel. Hundreds arrived with literally no money in their pockets, hoping to get rich picking up gold nuggets off the beach.

Although there had been an attempt to plan the city layout properly, the streets were nothing but muddy trails winding around tents, cabins, and shacks that extended about two blocks wide and five miles long. Boardwalks were built in front of the stores and saloons to give the appearance of streets. Thousands of people slept outdoors in tents. Lumber was scarce, and all of it had to be brought in by ship or cut from driftwood logs that occasionally washed ashore. After all, the nearest tree was 100 miles to the east.

The only fuel was scrap lumber or coal, also hauled from the States. Sanitation presented serious problems. Sewage and garbage were dumped into the Snake River; typhoid fever, dysentery, and pneumonia were common. Along the Nome waterfront, public toilets were built on pilings; the toilets were washed clean each time the tide came in.

As the population increased, so did crime. Alaska during this period was a land without effective government. As a result, some citizens took the law into their own hands. Disputes were settled with guns, knives, or fists. At first, the armed ruffians of the western mining camps were relatively rare in Nome. There was only one murder during Nome's first winter of 1899–1900. However, the gold rush attracted not only optimistic adventurers, but also gamblers, thieves, confidence men, and prostitutes in droves.

The growth of Nome during the first 30 days of the summer of 1900 has never been equaled. The ships arriving daily carried knocked-down theaters, gambling halls, saloons, restaurants, and everything else needed to build an instant city. That summer, eight million board feet of lumber were off-loaded. Years later, when I witnessed the hundreds of vessels off-loading men and supplies for the invasion of Normandy, it reminded me of that scene at Nome.

One of the few recollections I have of that first summer was of the crowds along Front Street, the main thoroughfare. Because it was light all night long in the summer, there were often as many people on the streets at two o'clock in the morning as at two o'clock in the afternoon. I vaguely remember that new buildings were under construction everywhere and I assume my father was earning our living by carpentering, not mining. I learned later that there were 20 saloons in town, a brewery, and 4 wholesale liquor stores. Sixteen lawyers and 11 physicians had their shingles out; there were 12 general merchandise stores, 6 restaurants, 6 lodging houses, 4 drugstores, but only 1 bank.[4]

The Nome gold rush ended in the fall of 1900 as quickly as it had begun three months earlier. The onset of winter with its subhuman cold and long nights was too much for most gold seekers to contemplate. A U.S. revenue cutter gave a free ride south to numerous destitute men who did not have the price of a ticket and had no means of supporting themselves.

The population, estimated at more than 25,000 at its height, was reduced to about 5,000 in the following summers, probably 1,000 or less in the winters, and remained at those figures over the next decade. We were among those who stayed, at least for a time. Gold was still mined along the inland creeks by those with the stamina and the capital to remain. The peak years of gold production were said to be 1906 and 1907, when miners took out about $15 million.

One of the men who arrived in Nome in 1899 and stayed on to have an impact on the city's history was George Lewis "Tex" Rickard, a famous boxing promoter and one of the owners of the Northern Saloon. He was elected to the seven-man city council in 1901 and led the move for some drastic changes. The council outlawed the driving of dog teams within city limits, firing guns or firecrackers, prostitution, and gambling at cards. However, gambling on the outcome of sporting or other measurable events was permitted. Men would bet on anything, including what day the first ship would arrive offshore in the spring and when the last one would disappear from sight in the fall. Sports of all kinds were the favorites for the gamblers. They would bet on pool matches, foot races, dog races, basketball and baseball games, and especially boxing matches, which were often brutal affairs lasting 25 rounds.

Life in Nome wasn't as bad as many writers have made it out to be during the years after the 1900 stampede was over. We actually had electricity, and in the winter, when the days were dark, every house in town was lit up, and as one writer recalled, "the winter of 1901–02 at Nome was light-hearted, happy and gay."[5]

Shortly after we arrived, my aunt Sarah married Gus Borgenson, who changed his name to Borgen. They had a child named Emily, who was the first white girl born in Nome.

If my parents had any problems between them, I knew nothing about them. I have often thought that one of the reasons my father stayed in Alaska was that it was one of the few places in the world where a skilled carpenter could make a dollar an hour. The going rate in the 48 states then for a craftsman was not much more than about 25 cents an hour.

My father built us a fairly comfortable house at 301 Third Avenue, and perhaps, as an only child, I was spoiled. I told my father I wanted a sled for Christmas. He spent a great deal of time making a small Arctic sled like the Eskimo kids had and as the white man had improved it. He fitted it out with a handlebar and steel-lined runners; the wooden parts were all laced together with rawhide. It was a beautiful piece of work. At first I was quite pleased with it. Then a friend of mine showed me he had gotten a little "store-bought" one, which in those days cost about two dollars. I was terribly disappointed because mine was homemade, and I said so. I didn't understand at the time, but I understand very clearly now, and it hurts even today to recall my selfishness.

Christmas was a happy time for the kids of Nome. We had three churches in town—Methodist, Congregationalist, and Catholic—and they all had activities for us. The Methodists always had a Christmas tree, a rare sight. The Congregationalists gave away prizes, and the Catholics served ice cream. I went to all three.

My father was a gambler of sorts—with people, not money. He grubstaked a large number of men with the understanding that, as was common practice then, if somebody put up the money for equipment and supplies to mine a claim that made a profit, half of the profit belonged to the grubstaker. As far as I know he got little if anything back from the considerable amount of money he spent grubstaking others.

At about age five I had my first fight. An Eskimo lad and I were alone on the beach one day and we got into an argument. He pushed me and I pushed back. He started to flail at me with his fists and I returned his blows. One of my punches caught him on the nose and blood spurted all over his parka. It scared us both. He began to cry and ran home to his mother. He thought he was dying. I ran home to my mother, certain that I had killed an Eskimo.

The first school was built during the summer we arrived. I enrolled in first grade the following year at age five and immediately discovered that I was shorter than the other boys in my class. To them I was a *chechako*, an Eskimo word for a newcomer, tenderfoot, or greenhorn, which everyone pronounced "cheechocker." It was a derisive name and I didn't like it. Furthermore, I had long curls, which promptly classified me in their minds as a sissy. In my anguish I pleaded with my mother to cut them off. We had quite a discussion about it. Although she was fond of them and didn't want to do it, she did, and I went to school from the second day curlless and much happier.

I had to fight all the same. A few of the taller boys took delight in teasing and provoking the shorter boys, and since I was the shortest one around, they tried to give me a bad time. They shoved and I shoved back. They punched and I returned their punches. My defense was not skillful and it was obvious they weren't going to let up until I did something about it.

Since my size was against me, I decided my survival could be insured only by a speedy attack right from the start. I began to blast my opponents with a flurry of punches regardless of the consequences. The tactics worked. I found it was easy to draw blood if you were nimble on your feet, aimed at a fellow's nose, and got your licks in early. After several antagonists went home with bloody noses, I earned a certain measure of respect. I hurt my hands a number of times because I made fists by doubling my thumbs inside. It was a while before I learned how to hold them properly.

My reputation as a brawler spread and some of my classmates would urge older and taller fellows to provoke me into fighting. Each new kid in the grammar school had to try to whip me in order to be accepted by the gang. My friends enjoyed seeing me plow into my opponents with my brand of intensity; and I must admit I enjoyed winning those early bouts. Early on I found that there was an advantage in being small. You might say it's an incentive to tiny excellence. I still consider fistfighting a suitable way for young boys to settle their differences. It's certainly better than the knives and guns some school kids use today.

My winning ways with fists were certainly not paralleled by academic performance in school, nor was I a model of discipline. One day my teacher caught me drawing a cartoon of the principal and sentenced me to write 25 times on the blackboard, "Jimmy Doolittle is the smallest boy in the school." She didn't have to remind me, but maybe she helped me resolve that whatever happened to me in the future, I would overcome any size difference with my peers one way or another.

During those preteen years, I developed a keen interest in tools. I found I liked working with my hands, and my father encouraged me by showing me how to use them and letting me help him build houses and furniture. He gave me my own little tool kit. The need for a man with his talents was great and he could work all year, unlike some of our neighbors whose work was seasonal.

There were two kinds of heroes to the kids of Nome in those days—runners and dog team drivers. We had a large gymnasium and the older boys and men would run 100- and 200-mile marathon races indoors. They would go round and round, stopping periodically to have a cup of coffee or a sandwich or to go to the bathroom. They never slept. A race would sometimes take two days and there was no letup.

Almost every kid in town ran. I didn't have a team of sled dogs, so I ran too. I ran one time until I collapsed. I also liked acrobatics and practiced handstands and tumbling, and worked out on the parallel bars by the hour. Years later, I was told I had a heart murmur, which gave me a little trouble in physical exams for flying. Doctors told me it was probably from overexertion when very young.

Dog sled races were then and still are a popular winter sport in Nome. Races were run from Nome to the Solomon River and back for a fair division of a public purse and side bets. It was always a time for celebration when the dog teams left and when they returned.

My first hunting experience was in 1903 or 1904. I had been given a single-shot .22 rifle and was out hiking on the tundra north of Nome when I came to a little lake that wasn't much more than a puddle. Sitting in the middle was a pair of teal ducks. I "Indian crawled" up to the edge of the lake until I was in range, aimed carefully, and hit one of them right at the waterline. The other flew away. I waded out and retrieved my prize, and vividly remember parading up and down Front Street with this duck in one hand and the .22 rifle in the other. I don't remember anytime since being as proud of a trophy as I was of my first game.

One recollection still sends chills through me. We had many dogs running loose in town all the time and some of them were vicious, especially when they were hungry. There was a black lad in our school named Phillip Goodwin. He was older than I but we were good friends. One winter day when school let out and we were all running home, Phillip tripped and fell. In an instant, a half dozen or more malemute sled dogs jumped him. Many people came running but before the dogs could be pulled off, they killed him. It was my first loss of a close friend.

I remember my mother with great fondness during those days. She was a Spartan in every sense of the word, a typical outdoor person and excellent with a dog sled team. One day the two of us took a dog team about five miles out of town to get water from the river. On the return trip, the dogs bolted and she cracked three ribs on the handlebars of the dog sled. She had her ribs bound up and never complained of the pain.

My relationship with my father was often strained. He did not engage in long conversations and was mostly silent when we were together. We were never close, never pals, and I've always regretted it. I must have made many overtures but he didn't respond very much, although he was a good teacher when it came to instructing me in the use of hand tools. He was an excellent cabinetmaker, a competent artisan, but a loner in spirit, a true pioneer with all the individualistic traits generally attributed to frontiersmen.

One day my father whipped me for something I didn't do. A bunch of boys had vandalized a boat that had been pulled up on the beach, and the owner included me among the list of culprits. I was totally innocent and denied having any part in the incident. My father accused me of lying. I didn't lie then and don't lie now. I told him that when I was big enough, I was going to whip him.

Despite the strained relations between us, in the summer of 1904, my father took me on a trip to Seattle, San Francisco, and Los Angeles—"outside" as we called it. For reasons never explained to me, my mother stayed in Nome. We were gone about six weeks, but I never found out exactly why we went. Perhaps he was looking into job opportunities. If so, he never said that he found any.

The sights and sounds in the three big cities were strange and exciting to me at age seven, since I had forgotten everything of what I had seen before we went to Nome. I saw my first automobile, train, and trolley car. There were modern houses and stores with paint on them. My values changed right then and there. I saw everything in a new perspective and I wanted very much to be a part of the exciting life I saw all too briefly during that trip.

When we returned to Nome, everything suddenly seemed smaller to me. The streets seemed too narrow and crowded; the buildings were only two stories high; even the schoolrooms and hallways had seemed to shrink.

To make a little pocket money, I got a job selling the *Nome Nugget,* one of the town's several newspapers and the only one still being published there today. I also sold the *Seattle Post-Intelligencer* when the ships brought them in the spring.

There weren't any preliminary discussions about leaving Alaska that I recall but in the late summer of 1908, when I was 11, my mother and I boarded a boat for Los Angeles. Apparently, my mother had become quite disappointed and disillusioned and she didn't want me to go any further in school in Alaska where we were isolated from the advantages of modern living. We had some relatives in Los Angeles and I suppose she was ready to return to the warmth of southern California. We moved into a modest two-story frame house at 1235 Catalina Street in downtown Los Angeles. My father stayed in Nome and I assumed I would see him again soon. There was no tearful departure, so our leaving must have been something they had agreed was necessary.

I attended Borendo Elementary School for two years and then entered Los Angeles Manual Arts High School in 1910. I didn't have a fondness for school then except for the shop courses. My interests were more physical than academic. Three of my classmates were Lawrence Tibbets, who would make a name for himself as a great singer; Goodwin Knight, later governor of California; and Frank Capra, later an award-winning film director. Frank was slightly smaller than I and was top man in the school's pyramid team. He was rather heavy-footed and, in climbing to the top spot, would occasionally stomp our pyramid flat. Since I was interested in tumbling and acrobatics, we got along famously.

It was just after I turned 13 that aviation came into my life. In January 1910, the first aviation meet held in the United States west of the Mississippi took place at Dominguez Field outside of Los Angeles, near the present city of Compton. It was patterned after the first air meet ever held, which had been at Reims, France, the previous summer.

One pilot there whose name was to become famous was Glenn Curtiss. He set a new world's speed record with a passenger on board of 55 miles an hour in one of the machines he designed and built. Another star was Louis Paulhan, a Frenchman, who achieved instant fame for climbing his Farman to a record altitude of 4,165 feet. He also set a record by flying 75 miles in less than two hours and won $20,000 for his efforts.

There were two local airmen there: Roy Knabenshue and Lincoln Beachey. They raced each other in dirigibles, and Beachey won. The Wright brothers, already embroiled in controversy over patent claims about their flying machine, had sent Arch Hoxsey with one of their Wright B Flyers. Unfortunately, he was outshone by the others. What was interesting to me was to see the radical differences in the construction and design of the machines; yet, amazingly, they all could fly. However, the pilots demonstrated them only when the weather was clear and the wind not too high. I wondered why this was so.

It was two years later that I first tried my hand at flying. I had found an article in an old January–June 1909 issue of *Popular Mechanics* by Carl Bates, entitled "How to Make a Glider." Fancying myself now very handy with tools, I followed the plan drawings carefully and built a biwinged glider similar to what today we would call a hang glider. The pilot was supposed to stand in the middle and hold on to it with his hands; his legs and feet would serve as the landing gear.

My mother supported my efforts by giving me a little spare change for materials like muslin, wood, and piano wire, and I earned the rest by doing odd jobs in the neighborhood and selling newspapers. I did all the work except that my mother sewed the unbleached muslin for the wings.

Bates had made flying a glider sound very simple. He wrote:

> A gliding machine is a motorless aeroplane or flying-machine, propelled by gravity and designed to carry a passenger through the air from a high point to a lower point some distance away. Flying a glider is simply coasting downhill on air, and is the most interesting and exciting sport imaginable.

Proud of the finished job, I placed it on a wagon and towed it to a nearby bluff about 15 feet high. I carefully strapped it on and ran fast toward the edge, jumped off, and tried to glide down. Unfortunately, the tail of the glider hit the edge of the bluff and I came straight down. The glider fell on top of me in pieces and banged me up pretty badly. I dragged what was left home and assessed the damage as well as my ineptitude at getting it airborne. Obviously, I wasn't able to run fast enough. What was needed was more speed.

One of my friends had access to his father's car. So, after I made repairs, we got a rope and tied it to the bumper, and I donned the glider. He started off and I ran to keep up. I ran faster and faster and soon couldn't run any faster. I leaped into the air, put the tail down and planned to ease upward into full flight. But there was no lift and I was dragged quite a few feet while the glider splintered around me. This time there wasn't enough left to rebuild another biwinged glider.

Soon after, I read in another issue of *Popular Mechanics* about Alberto Santos-Dumont, the Brazilian air pioneer, who had designed a monoplane he called *Demoiselle*. I also saw pictures of Louis Blériot's monoplane that he flew across the English Channel. I looked at my wreckage and decided that there was enough left to make a monoplane, so I made some modifications and decided that the power problem could be solved by installing a motorcycle engine. I acquired two bicycle wheels and worked many hours trying to make something that looked like it would fly. Meanwhile, I started to save up enough money to buy the engine.

After I had begun repairs, a storm came up one night, snatched my "baby" and blew it over the back fence, scattering it in small bits over several neighboring yards. I was out of money, out of materials, and out of enthusiasm. It was quite clear that I was out of the airplane design, construction, and piloting business. The more I think about it, the more I realize how lucky I was that I didn't succeed.

Years later, I was invited to join the Early Birds, an organization of airmen who had flown before the First World War. I respectfully declined because not even by the most magnanimous stretch of the human imagination could I claim that I had ever achieved controlled flight in 1912.

It was at this time that boxing caught my fancy. We had an English teacher named Forest Bailey, who was also a boxing instructor. He saw me in a schoolyard scrap one day and said,

"Look, young man, I know a little about boxing and you're going to get hurt badly fighting the way you do. You get mad when you fight. If you lose your temper, you're eventually going to lose a fight because you let your emotions instead of your head rule your body. Think about that. If you really want to learn to box, I'll teach you."

I was eager to learn. Mr. Bailey didn't like my flailing style and introduced me to the finer points of feinting, balancing, targeting my blows, and anticipating what an opponent was going to do. He convinced me that with my short arms I had to punch so that my blows would arrive with more power. He taught me how to bob and weave and keep my right hand ready to strike the second the other fellow's guard was down. I learned how to set myself and not make wild roundhouse swings of my arms but hit all the way from my heels with my fist. In short, he taught me the difference between street fighting and scientific boxing.

I began winning bouts immediately. At age 15, I entered the Pacific Coast amateur boxing matches at the Los Angeles Athletic Club and won the West Coast Amateur Championship as a flyweight in November 1912 at 105 pounds, then later moved into the bantamweight class at 115 pounds. At about five feet four inches, I was as tall as I was going to get. (I've always told people I'm five-six. It sounds better.)

While competing as a bantamweight amateur in 1912, I boxed exhibitions with Eddie Campi, who was a runner-up for the professional U.S. bantamweight championship. During the next two years, I had a fairly good knockout rating, which wasn't easy to do with the eight-ounce gloves we used as amateurs. My notebook for 1912 shows that I fought 15 three-round bouts between June and December. In 1913, I fought 13 times and either won or fought all of them to a draw. The next year, I boxed in an exhibition match with Kid Williams, who was the world champion, and was able to hold my own with him without getting hurt.

My mother did not like the idea of boxing. My split lips, swollen eyes, and facial bruises couldn't be ignored. I'm sure she thought I would be hurt seriously, and she could see no future for me in the sports world when all I would get for the pain was a ribbon or a cheap trophy. To her, boxing was nothing but legalized brawling, and she tried to encourage me to take up other sports.

One Saturday night, four of us—two friends of mine and the sister of one (who happened to be the fiancée of the other), and I—got involved in a little altercation. The event was a party given by a local dairy and we thought it was an open house affair. However, sometime during the evening, a committee began moving among the guests collecting admission fees. This was a surprise to us and the price asked was rather steep. We objected. Physical reaction followed words and in the ensuing melee, the sister-fiancée was pushed down a flight of stairs.

My old street-fighting emotions got the better of me. I landed a solid punch on the man who had pushed her, a truck driver much older and larger than me. People rushed to stop us, and before it could turn into a brawl, someone suggested the two of us settle our differences outside. The crowd followed and formed a circle.

We squared off and I knew it wasn't exactly going to be a fight by the Marquis of Queensbury rules. The crowd was mostly made up of the other chap's friends. Whenever I got close to the ring of onlookers, someone would punch me hard in the back or side. It was easy to see that I had to stay in the middle of the ring or be kidney punched until I dropped my guard and my adversary would find my chin. Fists flew, girls screamed, and two policemen showed up. They introduced a modicum of fairness into the fracas by holding the crowd back. I was holding my own against the truck driver, but then the police sergeant arrived and the two policemen suddenly became zealous defenders of the law. Both of us were arrested and hauled off to jail.

We were charged with disturbing the peace, a petty offense, and fined a few dollars. The other fellow paid the fine and left. Since I was only 15, the sergeant notified my mother while I languished in a cell. When I asked what she said, he shrugged and replied, "She wants you to stay here until Monday morning. She'll drop by then and get you out in time for school."

Mother had obviously decided it was time I learned a lesson—and it was. Being incarcerated in a cold, unheated cell for two nights and being totally deprived of the right to leave was a shocking experience for me. The jailer issued me two blankets, but a prisoner in an adjoining cell complained of the cold, so I gave him one of mine. I found out later he then had three blankets while I shivered for two nights under one. I never mentioned that to my mother. She gave me a memorable lecture concerning my transgressions on the way to school. I vowed never again to let my emotions overcome reason. Freedom is something very precious. We really don't appreciate what freedom is until we've lost it.

To encourage me to quit boxing, Mother bought me a motorcycle. I complied with the spirit if not the letter of her request. From then on, I boxed professionally under the name of Jimmy Pierce instead of Jimmy Doolittle. The motorcycle proved to be an economical way to get to my boxing matches. I spent hours tinkering with it and enjoyed using it to explore the world beyond walking or bicycling distance. It was the first machine of any kind that I owned.

While I had been going through these teenage experiences, a pretty girl came into my life. Her name was Josephine Daniels. She had come to California from Louisiana with her parents and had retained the unhurried, calm demeanor that was characteristic of cultured families from the Old South.

She was a very good little girl. I was a very naughty little boy. She was a Memarian, which would be the equivalent of a Phi Beta Kappa in college. She got all A's; I had a hard time getting C's. She always had a happy disposition. Teachers loved her. I'm sure they only thought of me as "that Doolittle boy," a cocky kid who was always going around getting into fights. We were almost complete opposites. So, for the first three years of high school, we just didn't seem to travel in the same league. Then she began to tolerate me and slowly seemed to reciprocate my affections. I thought of her as "my girl" and was so smitten I told her in 1913 that after I got through school and had a job, I'd marry her. If she'd wait, I told her I'd take her on the most beautiful trip in the world—up the inside passage of Alaska. (I kept that promise. We had an enjoyable trip through the inside passage in 1973—sixty years later!)

Although her name was Josephine, she was known as "Joe," spelled with the "e," which she claimed was because she had a favorite uncle named Joe and the family called her "Little Joe." I always said it was because her father named her Joseph before she came into the world; in view of her equipment, they changed the name to Josephine but still called her "Joe" and spelled it that way.

Her mother considered, quite rightly, that I was no bargain. Even my mother, who was devoted to me, fell completely in love with Joe. When we began going steady and boldly considered marriage sometime in the future, my mother told her it would be wonderful to have her as a daughter-in-law but for her own good suggested that she shop around a little longer. She never did, although there were always rivals hovering around vying for her attention.

Joe was unimpressed with my boxing and my motorcycle. It seems she wanted me to be a gentleman, and gentlemen did not go around looking for fights. Only the "fast" crowd rode motorcycles, and certainly good girls did not ride on the backs of motorcycles.

There's no doubt that Joe changed my life. I began to comb my hair, wear a tie, look after my clothes, and watch my language around her. I wanted to take her out on dates, but my finances were always meager. However, when we did date, I always gave her carfare to get home because if anybody said anything nasty to her, I was going to punch them in the nose.

The best way for me to earn money was by boxing professionally under the name I had already adopted—Jimmy Pierce. Although I was only a junior in high school, by then I looked older than my contemporaries. Unknown to my mother, I motorcycled up and down the coast on weekends, entering bouts in the various boxing clubs that were so popular then. Being undersized compared with some of the pros I fought made me seem like the underdog, and fans rooted for me. I either won each bout entered or boxed to a draw, and made as much as $30 a bout.

Joe was not happy when she found out I was still boxing. She refused to see a bout and wouldn't even talk to me about it. It hurt me when I displeased her and one day during our high school senior year, I suddenly asked her if she would marry me.

"You must think I'm out of my mind," she replied indignantly. "I could never marry a man who wants to fight all the time."

"I'll give up fighting," I said. "As soon as school's out I'm going to Alaska and get a good job. As soon as I have some money, I'll send for you."

Joe seemed pleased but said, "My mother would never approve."

Her reply made me a little angry. "I'm going to marry you, not your mother," I retorted.

When I graduated from high school I thought I knew all I needed to know to make a good living. My father had written and asked me to visit him in Seward, Alaska, where he had relocated after leaving Nome. Perhaps he thought he could persuade me to live there permanently, but we had never talked about it. After completing high school in late spring of 1914, I withdrew the money I had saved and took the boat to Seward with visions of making a lot of money working there and living with him. He had bought two lots, and that summer we built a house on one of them—more like a shack. He paid me apprentice wages.

My relations with my father were still uneasy. Shortly after I arrived, he asked me if I remembered what I'd said when he had whipped me years before for something I didn't do.

"Sure," I said.

He asked, "Are you going to do it?"

Full of confidence from my boxing experience, I looked him in the eye and asked if he figured I could. Thoughtfully, he replied that he believed I could.

I have never been proud of this conversation. Perhaps he meant it as a compliment, that I had grown up and was now a man. But I think this exchange showed the distance between us, a distance that was never closed. I don't think that kind of dialogue between father and son should ever have to take place. He never said that he was sorry or that he was wrong in accusing me of lying. I just wish he had had more faith in me because I've never tolerated or engaged in lying. I have always thought lying is a form of cowardice.

Alaska was not the land of opportunity I thought it might be. I had saved enough money to get there, but there were no jobs available for a teenage kid, even one who had graduated from high school, a rarity among Alaskans in those days. World War I had started in Europe, and no foreign companies were investing in Alaskan enterprises.

I bought some provisions and left my father to search for gold. I ended up at Six-Mile Creek and lived in a tent and subsisted on salmon three times a day for about three weeks while I tried to pan for gold. Now, sure that there was no future for me in Alaska and being somewhat homesick to see Joe, I hiked back to Seward. To get back home, I got a job as a steward on a Seattle-bound ship, but couldn't afford the fare to get from there to Los Angeles. I stowed away aboard the SS *Yale* and arrived home in time to enroll at Los Angeles Junior College in 1915. It was a far wiser Jim Doolittle who entered college. I told Joe that we'd have to wait a while before we tied any knots. I wanted to get a college education. She seemed pleased at the thought.

When I was very small, I knew that there were two things I wanted to do in life: build things and see the world. To build things, one had to be an engineer. In those days, there were only two types of engineers who could see the world. One was the civil engineer who built bridges, harbors, and dams; the other was the mining engineer who went everywhere looking for different minerals. The latter seemed the most attractive.

The engineering courses in junior college were the same for all types of engineers the first two years—mostly mathematics and science. I found that I liked the challenge and surprised myself by getting fairly good grades. To carry out my career goal, I worked in the Comstock Lode in Virginia City, Nevada, in the summers between college semesters and, later, in the January Jones Mine, a cinnabar, or quicksilver, mine.

I really got into the nitty-gritty end of mining by pushing a tram car and digging with a pick and shovel. I learned to use a water liner, which is the drill used to drill holes in which to put the powder to blast the face off the rock. Despite the strenuous nature of the work, I enjoyed it.

After junior college, I entered the University of California's School of Mines at Berkeley and continued toward a degree in mining engineering. The university had a fine gymnasium and I began working out on the horizontal and parallel bars. I was now 19 and weighed about 130 pounds. I wanted to box again so I talked with Marcus Freed, the boxing coach, and asked to try out for the team. The lightweight and welterweight positions were filled, but they didn't yet have a good middleweight (165-pound class) team member. There were three contending for the slot. I offered to move up into that class if he'd let me try out.

Reluctantly, Mr. Freed let me go into the ring with one of them. My opponent outweighed me by 30 pounds. Several inches taller and with a longer reach, he eyed me rather like an older brother looks at a much younger sibling. As soon as we touched gloves, I let go with a few quick lefts and rights and he was down. Coach Freed put the gloves on the second contender and he went the way of the first.

Two days later, the third fellow and I went at it, and although it took me longer, I won the match and was designated the university's middleweight champion who would represent UC against Stanford, our arch rival. Coach Freed gave me some good tips about fighting opponents who would be taller, heavier, and always have a longer reach. I felt sure my speed and my right-from-the-heels punch would equalize the difference.

When I climbed into the ring with the Stanford boxer, he gave me what I interpreted as a condescending smile, and for some reason it made me angry. After we touched gloves and parried a few blows for about a minute, I rushed at him, ducked under his guard and planted a solid blow on his chin. He dropped to the canvas, out cold. My diary shows this match took place on March 26, 1917, and lasted 83 seconds.

When my opponent regained his composure, he got up, came over and introduced himself as Eric Pedley. I was no longer angry and was surprised to have him congratulate me. I replied weakly that it was a lucky punch. He disagreed. Said I had deserved to win the match. Eventually Eric Pedley became a noted polo player. I happened to attend one of his matches with my sons some years later and congratulated him on a fine game. He smiled that sportsmanlike smile again and shook my hand. "Yes, I remember you," he said. "We met some fifteen years ago rather quickly and informally."

Since I had now returned to boxing, in order to make extra money I began to box professionally again under the name of Jimmy Pierce. Mr. Freed set up some matches for me, one of which was with Willie Hoppe, a celebrated boxer from San Francisco. My diary shows that I boxed him in May 1917 and won by a knockout in the first round. It also noted that I knocked out a fellow named Oldrick that same month in five seconds of the first round.

As I might have expected, there was an end to my string of successes. I was matched one night against a ringwise veteran named "Spider" Reilly. Within a few seconds after we touched gloves, I knew he was good. As I went after him with my usual fast attack, he danced lightly away and I could land only a few light blows on him. He came back with some jolting right-hand blows that stung and rocked me back on my heels. Tried my best but lost the fight on a unanimous decision.

Thus I learned another lesson: no matter how good you think you are in a sport, eventually someone will come along who proves that he is better. I decided then that getting an education was more important than sports, so I began to apply myself seriously to my studies at UC's School of Mines. In April 1917, during my junior year, the United States declared war on Germany. Such a momentous event didn't seem to penetrate my thoughts too deeply at that time. I wanted to make a lot of money that summer, so when the semester ended, Bill Downs, my best friend, and I left on my motorcycle for Virginia City, Nevada, where the famous Comstock Lode was located. Although the rush had been over for several decades by then, a few mining companies were still operating.

I don't remember what town it was but we were stopped by a police officer for speeding. He took us before a judge who called us "wicked" for going 50 miles an hour and fined us $15. We had only $12 between us so the judge took that and asked the arresting policeman if there was anything attached to the motorcycle that would be worth $3. The officer replied that we had a carbide light worth about 50 cents but it was out of carbide.

The judge gave us a lecture and let us go after taking the $12. We were now flat broke. We had bedrolls and a rifle and planned to live off the land by "borrowing" corn, potatoes, or whatever else we could find at farms along the way. We would worry about gasoline when it ran out.

Fortune smiled on us. As we chugged along the desert roads, we came upon a stalled automobile with an old man seated inside. We stopped and asked if we could help. He said his son was the driver and had walked on ahead to get a tow truck. He said the engine had quit and wouldn't restart. Bill and I tinkered and got it started. Bill drove the auto and I followed on the motorcycle until we came upon the son, who had been walking for hours without seeing a single soul. The old man was so grateful, he gave us two dollars, which bought enough gas to get us to the mines.

We were hired by the Union Sierra Nevada Mining Co. Two memorable things happened to me during that summer at the mine. A cage—the elevator that took the men down to the 2,900-foot level in the mine—broke. The shift boss and one miner were in the cage when it plummeted to the bottom of the shaft. Since I was the only one who had first-aid training (it was part of the college course in mining engineering), I agreed to be lowered down the shaft on a rope to see if I could get them out. I got down to the 2,700-foot level without difficulty, but that last 200 feet seemed impossible. They began to spray some water down to try to get air circulation in the shaft because by that time the acetylene light on my miner's cap had gone down to where it was just barely burning. That was always a danger signal. The water put the light out.

I was lowered away in the dark to where I could get on top of the cage. There was a tremendous coil of cable on top of the cage that had unrolled off the winch. I picked blindly through the cable, dropped down into the escape hatch and felt the pulses and hearts of both men, but they were dead.

When I sent word back up that they were gone, another man was lowered. The two of us got the broken cable straightened out and hooked a new cable in its place. Then we got into the cage and were lifted up. We were quite worried because the cage had sprung and it came up in fits and jerks.

When we got to the top, I found that, instead of being just another college kid who was detested by the hard rock miners, I had suddenly become a fair-haired boy. One of them patted me on the back and made a remark, typical of the miners' back-handed expressions of praise in those days. It was one of the greatest compliments I've ever received. He said, "Kid, there's no shit in your neck!" It was his way of saying that there wasn't any yellow streak down my back.

I had the other memorable experience over the July Fourth holiday when the other miners had the day off. Since it meant overtime pay, I volunteered to remain with an old miner and mind the pump that was used to keep the hot water from the underground hot springs from seeping into the mine. Our job was to keep the water at a certain level so the pump wouldn't go dry. It was a boring chore and the droning of the pump was monotonous. The old man dozed off and so did I.

The pump suddenly stopped and I awakened with a start. The water level in the mine was rising. The old man awoke, too, and gave me some choice epithets, the mildest of which was to tell me I was one of those no-good, "damned college kids." He told me that since it was my fault the pump had stopped I had to get it started again.

This meant I had to wade into the nearly scalding water, reach down, and prime the pump with a hand lever. I did it but suffered scald burns for several days afterward. The only thing that eased the pain was that the old man seemed to have a little better respect for me from then on.

After these two incidents, I was treated entirely differently from other college students in the mine. I was considered "one of the boys" while the other kids still had to prove themselves.

All in all, it had been a worthwhile summer and I looked forward to my final year of college. Ever optimistic, I thought I would then get a good job and put my education and experience to work.

NOTES

1. *Klondike Nugget*, January 21, 1900.
2. *Nome News*, October 9, 1899.
3. *Nome News*, June 23, 1900.
4. One of the best books about the gold rush days in Nome is *Nome: City of the Golden Beaches*, by Terrence Cole, published by the Alaska Geographic Society in 1984. It was originally published in *Alaska Geographic*, volume 11, number 1, 1984.
5. See *Old Yukon*, by Judge James Wickersham, Washington, D.C.: Washington Law Book Co., 1938, pp. 409–411.

CHAPTER 3

Bill Downs and I had not been able to keep up with news from the outside world while we worked at the mines that summer of 1917. When we got back to the Berkeley campus to enroll for our senior year, everyone was talking about the war in Europe and the plans for the United States to send troops over to fight the Huns. Many of our classmates had already joined one of the services. Bill and I caught the fever and, without thinking very far ahead, decided we should join the crowd.

Bill joined the infantry, but I held out for what I thought would be a much better opportunity—to learn to fly with the Aviation Section of the Army's Signal Corps. The recruiters said that as many as 5,000 pilots would be trained immediately, so I expected to get into uniform within a day or two of signing up for the Signal Enlisted Reserve Corps. I didn't enroll at UC for my senior year.

Instead of going to flying school right away, I was told to wait for orders. Days went by without any notice to report and I ran out of funds. Since I was not enrolled, had no money left from my summer work, and had developed a continuing desire to nourish myself, I found a little restaurant where I could get a bowl of soup for 15 cents. They always placed two stacks of bread at each table, so I ate both stacks with my soup. I got away with this for two days and then the proprietor discovered why his bread was disappearing so fast. When he saw me come in the door on the third day, he quickly removed the bread. I had to take some definitive action to get a job.

I found a job in a tin can factory working the night shift and worked for a week, nearly starving while I waited for that first paycheck. When I went up to the window to get it, I was told the company always withheld the first week's check for all employees until they quit or were fired. I had to quit in order to eat.

Unemployed again, I found a job at the January Jones Mine near Eureka in Napa County, California. No one there seemed to care about my past experience in Nevada or my mining education. They put me to work pushing a hand car full of quicksilver ore and then operating a water liner. When the compressor broke down, I had to drill by hand.

My orders finally came in October, sending me to my alma mater, the University of California, for aviation ground school. I left the mine with a great deal of relief.

Unknown to me at the time, if I had just registered as a senior and then gone into uniform, the university, as an indication of appreciation for the patriotism of those near graduation, would have given seniors their degrees. Years later, through the efforts of two friends of mine, I finally was granted the degree because of the experience and education I gained in the service.

Now designated a "flying cadet," with pay of about $50 a month, I had eight crowded weeks of ground school ahead. It was relatively easy for me—at least, the courses in theory of flight, meteorology, map reading, engines, and structures were. I didn't like close order drill at all. Navigation was difficult but interesting, while Morse Code was almost impossible. More people seemed to wash out of ground school for failing the code tests than anything else. I guess there was a psychological handicap there, but I persisted and finally got through it.

During ground school I was tempted into entering the Pacific Coast Amateur Boxing Championship bouts as a lightweight. Unfortunately, I didn't have enough time to train and I wasn't in as good shape as I should have been. I was badly mauled for the first time in my life and, although not knocked out, lost by a decision.

After I started college, Joe had gone to work for the Pacific Mutual Life Insurance Co. in Los Angeles. She thought she would like to be a librarian and had taken some courses in library science in high school. By the time the war began, however, she had acquired considerable information and experience running the Holowitz, a filing system that was possibly a forerunner of some of today's computer concepts. She went to work in the shipyard and eventually had several hundred girls working for her.

When the Christmas vacation arrived, I persuaded Joe that we should get married even though I hadn't finished ground school. She consented, although her mother still considered me incorrigible. But we were both over 21 now and didn't need her permission. I always said Joe wouldn't marry me until I got a uniform on and then always had to leave the area because that remark made her furious.

I hitched a ride with a friend to Los Angeles and we went to City Hall on Christmas Eve in 1917. I didn't have a dime because we hadn't received our December pay yet, so Joe paid for the license with money her mother had given her for Christmas. We were married by the clerk of the court.

Joe had about $20 left, which was enough to get us on a train to San Diego and a brief honeymoon over the holidays. We spent most of the time at one of the cafeterias where servicemen and their girlfriends or wives were given free meals.

The start of 1918 saw Joe back at work in Los Angeles while I returned to ground school at Berkeley. I graduated a couple of weeks later and was sent to Rockwell Field on North Island, San Diego, for pilot training where two small fields had been operating in the area since 1912. Back in 1914, civilian flying instructors had been added to the staff because the Army officers were untrained and had no precedent to guide them in training others. An Army report noted that teaching men to fly was probably the most dangerous occupation in the world and that men who could do it were rare "and their services are cheap at almost any price."[1]

When my class arrived for primary training, there were only 14 civilian instructors available as a teaching force. My instructor was Charles Todd, a very calm individual. He gave me the first-day briefing and we climbed into the Curtiss JN-4 "Jenny" for my first flight. As we taxied out, we heard two trainers overhead and then the sickening sound of metal and wood impacting, followed by silence. Two Jennys had collided over the field and crashed a few yards in front of us.

We shut off the engine and both of us ran over to the nearest Jenny. There was one student in it who had been flying solo. He was dead. We rushed to the other plane and found a student and instructor badly injured. We helped them out of the wreckage and awaited the ambulance.

When the wreckage was cleared, Mr. Todd looked at me carefully and said we should get on with our business. I was shaken by what I had seen but nodded in agreement, and we went up for my first lesson. If there is such a thing as love at first sight, my love for flying began on that day during that hour.

I was eager to fly solo and, after about six hours of instruction, was terribly distressed that Mr. Todd wouldn't let me go. I felt quite confident and adept and wondered if he was ever going to let me go up alone. He must have sensed my impatience and said, "Now I want you to fly this plane just exactly three feet off the ground. I don't want you to fly at two feet or ten feet. Fly as far as you can exactly at that altitude."

This was called grass cutting, and to my amazement, I found that I couldn't do it. I was either bumping the ground or hopping up to about 20 feet—overcontrolling. For the first time I had a realization of my inadequacies. Just after I had completely lost my confidence, he climbed out of the airplane and said, "Now you fly it around."

Every pilot remembers his first solo and I remember mine vividly. I took off easily and flew around for a while, exhilarated at my mastery of the machine. When I got ready to land, I cut the power and everything seemed to be all right. But then I began to have doubts about whether I was too fast or too slow. It seemed that during the glide and just before landing there were many more things to remember than I had to when the instructor was along to take over if anything went wrong. But I got down all right and Mr. Todd seemed satisfied. My logbook shows that I soloed after seven hours and four minutes of dual instruction.

In the weeks following, we practiced cross-country navigation, aerobatics, and formation flying. There were a number of our classmates who "washed out" for one reason or another. They say that one out of four was eliminated in ground school for academic deficiencies; half of those remaining for the flying phase were eventually let go or quit for various reasons.

Crashes were frequent during that period and many were fatal. When you witnessed one, it was very desirable that you get up in the air as soon as possible to wipe out what you had just seen. It was hard because you knew everybody in your class. Crashes always bothered me but never changed my mind about wanting to learn to fly.

The basic reason for most crashes in the early days was because a student stalled the plane and got into a spin. At first, none of us knew why airplanes got into spins or what to do to get out of them. Later, we learned why they happened and how to recover from them. Stall and spin recoveries became a vital part of all flight curricula.

Graduation from flight school was March 5, 1918, and commissioning as a second lieutenant and rating as a reserve military aviator was six days later. I was eager to go overseas to get into the scrap. However, instead of getting orders to proceed to the port of embarkation on the East Coast, most of my classmates and I were ordered to Camp Dick, Texas, which was called "the concentration camp." At first we thought this was merely a place where they outfitted us before sending us on. Not so. There were no aircraft there, and there was nothing to do. We were housed in smelly barracks that had once been a livestock collecting point.

Two of my barracks mates there were to become lifelong friends—John S. "Jack" Allard, a Bostonian, and Bruce Johnson, from Binghamton, New York. Both were from families of means and we got along famously. After many days of doing nothing, we were sent to the port of debarkation at Hoboken, New Jersey, but since there wasn't enough equipment available for us to fly in France, and no ships available to take us there, we were sent to Dayton, Ohio, briefly, and then to Gerstner Field near Lake Charles, Louisiana, where we took advanced flying instruction in the Thomas-Morse S-4C Scout, a pursuit aircraft. The Scout was a nice step up from the Jenny and I liked it because it could get up to 100 miles per hour. Bruce called it "the most miserable piece of aircraft engineering ever foisted off on an unsuspecting pilot." Most were powered by a Gnome rotary engine; some had the Le Rhône engine. The engine rotating out front and its resultant centrifugal force made the Scout difficult to control.

We didn't wear parachutes in those days; they were used only by balloonists. However, we did have safety belts, which were invented by Major General Benjamin D. Foulois, the Army's sole pilot when he took the Army's Wright Flyer to San Antonio in 1910 and was told by the chief signal officer, "Teach yourself to fly." But safety belts have to be buckled. One of the student pilots at Gerstner, Major John P. Mitchel, a former mayor of New York City, was flying a Scout one day when he flipped the plane into a violent maneuver and literally threw himself out of the cockpit. He had forgotten to fasten his safety belt. Mitchel Field on New York's Long Island is named for him.

During this period, Joe was working at the Terminal Island shipyard in Los Angeles and received a phone call from a newspaper reporter who told her that I had been killed in a crash in Buffalo, New York. I'm sure Joe was shocked, but she answered calmly, "I don't believe it." She was reasonably sure I wasn't in Buffalo and said so.

She hung up the phone and wired the post commander at Gerstner. I immediately called her. There was a logical reason for the mixup. There was another James Doolittle stationed at Gerstner; however, his middle initial was "R." A veteran Lafayette Escadrille pilot who had been wounded and was then a civilian instructor, he had been on a training flight to Buffalo and had been killed. I guess it was only the first of many heart-stopping instances for Joe during my subsequent flying years.

Fortunately, the stay at Gerstner was short-lived. A hurricane whipped across the Gulf of Mexico and leveled everything on the field. About 300 planes were smashed into splinters and fabric remnants. There were no buildings left; several men were killed and many injured.

While the mess was being cleaned up, Jack, Bruce, and I were transferred back to Rockwell Field on San Diego's North Island. We thought we were going to get more advanced training, but to my great distress I spent the rest of World War I there and at Ream Field, located eight miles south of Rockwell Field on the oceanfront and adjacent to the Tiajuana River, as a combat and gunnery instructor. I was then 21 and it seemed to me a sad commentary on life that I should be sending other people out to combat instead of going myself. The only good thing about the assignment was that I was near Joe.

The requirements of a good pursuit and gunnery school were plenty of level ground, large expanses of water or unoccupied country for aerial gunnery, and still water for placing targets to be fired at from the air. These features were obtained at Rockwell, Ream, and Otay Mesa—the last was used for formation and aerobatic flying.

We had no special training to be instructors. They just took us up, showed us a maneuver, then said, "You've seen how to do it; now go teach your students how to do it." You didn't want to look foolish before your students, so being an instructor had its compensations: you learned how to fly with greater precision than you might otherwise. You did not want to embarrass yourself by announcing to a student that you were going to demonstrate a maneuver and then be unable to do it. I think I really perfected my flying skills during that period.

Despite my desire to have fun in an airplane, I took my instructional duties seriously and never did any stunts with students, who might be tempted to try to duplicate them when they didn't have the experience. Therefore, I stuck to the curriculum and didn't take kindly to any student trying to show off or get smart. I wanted them to emulate my seriousness about flying.

One day when I was on the final approach for a landing in a Jenny with a student, a solo student pilot in a Thomas-Morse Scout came across at right angles underneath our plane. Neither my student nor I saw him. His plane smashed into our underside and took our landing gear off, damaged our propeller, and weakened our lower wing. We belly landed without injury, but the fellow in the other plane was dead. His upper wing had collapsed and he had plummeted onto the flying field. Our propeller had taken his head off.

Immediately after the accident, I insisted on taking the same student back up in another plane for another lesson. One of the other instructors believed I was wrong to take a novice pilot up so soon after the tragedy and accused me of not caring about the other lad's death. But I did care and thought about it for a long time. I wondered if there was anything I might have done to prevent it, even though he wasn't my student. They say that if you fall off a horse, you should get back in the saddle as soon as possible or you may never ride again. That was my thinking in that instance.

When I returned and my student got out, I gestured to those waiting who had seen the accident and yelled, "Next!" If any one of them had refused to fly then, I would have eliminated him. I wanted to impress on them that flying is serious business and is unforgiving of carelessness, incapacity, or neglect.

Joe learned about this accident while riding a trolley car on the way back from a funeral. A passenger sitting in front of her had a newspaper with a headline that read "Flier Killed in Crash." The subhead began "Lt. Doolittle . . . ," and that was all she could see before the person turned the page. She was stunned and got off at the next stop to buy a paper. When she read the story, she found out that I was all right. It was a repeat of the false alarm she had received while I was at Gerstner Field, another one of many instances when she thought I might have met my maker.

In another instance, a student and I were taking off for a dual ride when a solo student drifted across our flight path slightly below us just as we were getting airborne. Our lower wing blanked him from our view. Our plane's propeller sliced off his plane's tail and he dived into the ground and burned. He could not escape.

Life wasn't all monotony and tragedy; there were lighter moments that could have been tragic. We flew the Hisso-powered Jenny on gunnery practice with a Lewis machine gun mounted on the top wing so it would fire over the propeller. After you fired all of your ammunition, you were supposed to clear your gun to make sure there were no bullets left in it. One chap remembered to do it belatedly as he was coming in to land. The gun still had bullets in the belt and they began to fire as he was directly in line with a bunch of latrines, all of which seemed to be occupied. As the bullets sprayed by the clapboard buildings, about six guys came dashing out with their pants at half mast. Fortunately, no one was hurt. From then on, there were new regulations about clearing your Lewis gun before returning to the field.

It was during my assignment at Rockwell and Ream that Lieutenant Colonel Harvey B. S. Burwell, the commander at Rockwell, came into my life. A strict disciplinarian, he was one of the youngest lieutenant colonels in the Regular Army, and was very bright—in fact, a genius. I made repeated formal requests through channels to go to France, but Colonel Burwell always turned me down. When the armistice was signed on November 11, 1918, I think he was grateful that he wouldn't have to sign those letters back to me anymore.

The end of the war meant a big decision had to be made. Should I return to college and get a mining degree or stay in uniform and take my chances that there was a career for me flying airplanes? I had found a great deal of pleasure in flying and I enjoyed the military life. The men who got out of the service and took up barnstorming lived a rather precarious existence, from the point of view of both eating and living. I was making about $140 a month and the money was there on payday without fail. The security of the military life was very appealing to me as hundreds of men were demobilized and had to look for jobs while the nation tried to rebuild a peacetime economy. But it was the flying that made up my mind.

During the war, most Army flying in the States was limited to the local area. Seldom did we fly far from our bases. But the armistice brought quick changes because funds were still available for the time being and the Air Service took it upon itself to arouse public interest in aviation. The official policy was that the Air Service should accept invitations to put on exhibitions and demonstrations. Any reasonable request to flying field commanders for air shows received prompt approval. We found that county fairs, patriotic parades, and other large public gatherings were excellent events to show off what we and our planes could do. The word came down from Washington that we could attempt to set or break records and make cross-country flights that were considered newsworthy and would project a favorable image of the Army Air Service.

One of the first approved postwar events that helped me decide to stay in the Army was a giant military air show at San Diego, including a large flyby of 212 planes, scheduled for November 25, 1918. The *Los Angeles Times*, in the gee-whiz writing style of the day, announced that "nothing on so massive a scale as this will be or has ever been attempted either in this country or in Europe. The flight will probably be the last of its kind held in this country or Europe for many years, according to Colonel Harvey Burwell, commander at North Island, as the large permanent aeronautical institutions will be reduced to peace strength within a short time."

After the event the *Times* reported:

> Promptly at 10 o'clock the comparatively slow-going Curtiss training planes left the ground at Rockwell Field and began to circle the island. Fifty of these got into the air and then an equal number of fast two-seaters rose and started to trail them. Then forty of the spidery Thomas-Morse Scouts took the air and the huge squadron moved over Point Loma, gradually

> working into the form of a huge V, which we all know stands for Victory.
>
> Meanwhile from East and Ream fields, the two subsidiary training plants, seventy more fast machines preceded by five strata-stunt artists climbed to get into the aerial swim. Soon the 210 fast planes were swarming over North Island like so many bees and being herded into formation by the fifteen leaders who conversed [by radio] quite as casually as you and I pass the time of day!
>
> By 11 o'clock the formation was complete, and with the quintet of daring acrobats the greatest fleet of airplanes ever assembled in this country proceeded to write victory in the sky while thousands of spectators in the streets and on housetops cheered themselves hoarse, their excited shrieks and yells completely drowned by the shattering roar of the mighty motors.
>
> So close to one another that they seemed almost to touch, they formed a ceiling over the sky that almost blotted out the struggling rays of the sun and with majestic solemnity they patrolled the air, magnificent in the perfection of their formation, and while they framed a perfect background at 5,000 feet, the five acrobats below swooped, dived, looped and spun in as perfect unison as though they had been operated by a single hand.

It was a fun exhibition, for we "five acrobats" executed "the side slip, the verille, the barrel roll, loop, reversement and many other stunts employed by pursuit pilots while engaged in deadly combat." According to the paper, "The five daring acrobats whose daring skill provided the chief thrill of the day were Lieutenants D. W. Watkins, H. H. Bass, J. H. Doolittle, W. S. Smith, and H. O. Williams, all from Ream Field, who won the right to form the stunt squad in open competition from a score of the pilots."

Extensive air circuses were also put on at Kelly Field, Texas; Hazelhurst Field, on Long Island; Bolling Field, Washington, D.C.; and Ellington Field, Texas, that received much front-page space in local newspapers. In April 1919, a Victory Loan Flying Circus was organized in three groups that traveled more than 19,000 miles making one-day stands in 88 cities in 45 states. Eighteen different aircraft were used, including French and British aircraft and Fokkers captured from the Germans.

The spirit of this newly found freedom to fly was contagious. After instructing students, I took an airplane up at every opportunity and practiced aerobatics. I tried to invent new stunts and realized there was a similarity between aerobatics in the air and acrobatics on the ground in that you mentally previewed a maneuver, then did it as you had planned. If you failed, you tried it again and again until you mastered it. And one principle that I learned in acrobatics carried over directly to aerobatics: never change your mind in the middle of a maneuver; you'll mess it up every time.

I admit to being a bit of a mischief maker and am guilty of having had a little fun in an airplane. One incident during this period reminds me of my stupidity. It happened while I was hedge hopping. I saw two soldiers walking along a road and decided to give them a little scare. I buzzed a few feet over their heads, thinking they would be completely surprised. However, they just waved at me. I was indignant and came around for another pass lower than before. I zoomed over them and felt my wheels hit a bump. I looked back and saw one of the soldiers lying prostrate on the ground.

I was so shocked at my miscalculation that I didn't look where I was going and caught a barbed wire fence in my landing gear, and as I pulled up, the fence came along. The extra weight caused the plane to stall and smash into the ground. I wasn't hurt and was consumed by the thought that I had killed someone because of my stupidity. I jumped out of the wreckage and rushed to the two boys, one of whom was rubbing his head. Amazingly, he wasn't hurt, but said he had a slight headache. One wheel had just grazed his head, and he had fallen flat on his face, which softened the blow. Instead of being angry at me, he said, "Gee, Lieutenant, I'm glad you weren't hurt."

I was greatly relieved because my foolishness could have killed him. But I had to face Colonel Burwell because I had wiped out a $10,000 government airplane. The colonel was a man who believed in going by the book. He didn't want to ground me because he needed every instructor he had, but he did confine me to the post for a month.

Although it meant I couldn't be with Joe off post on weekends, being able to continue flying enabled me to keep on having fun and doing mischief in the air. I had a friend named John

McCullough who would fly dual with me. When we were airborne, I would do some wingwalking, just as many exhibitionists were doing at country fairs—all out of sight of the colonel, of course. One day, feeling especially exuberant, unknown to McCullough, I made a five-dollar bet with some friends that I could sit on the axle between the wheels while he made a landing. We took off and I got out on the wing, climbed down on the gear, and then motioned to McCullough to land. He kept motioning me to come back inside the plane, but I refused. He was afraid of running out of fuel so he landed with me sitting there gripping the landing gear struts. I won the bet but McCullough was very angry.

I didn't know it but the famous movie director Cecil B. DeMille was making a film on the field, and the cameras were rolling when we landed with me sitting there with a silly grin on my face. It so happened that Mr. DeMille and Colonel Burwell were good friends. That night, the two of them were reviewing the rushes from that day's filming when the sequence of a man sitting between the wheels came on. It wasn't too clear a shot but the colonel was positive he knew who the culprit was. He jumped up, called his adjutant, and shouted, "Ground Doolittle for a month!" The adjutant later told me he asked the colonel how he knew it was me and Burwell replied, "It has to be Doolittle. No one else would be that crazy!"

Now I was not only confined and grounded but Burwell also made me officer-of-the-day for a month. This meant I had to be in proper uniform all day and couldn't work in the shops with the mechanics, as I often did on my time off, or participate in any kind of athletics. But there was one thing I could do: ride my motorcycle all over the post doing my duty as OD.

One day while I was racing around the perimeter road "inspecting" the field's boundary, I saw a Thomas-Morse Scout coming in for a landing. I steered the cycle directly in its path, knowing the pilot would go around. He did and came around for a second attempt. I ran in front of him again and the pilot, frustrated, finally landed on the other end of the field. My selection of this particular airplane couldn't have been worse. The pilot of the Scout was Colonel Burwell.

I was confined to the base for another month.

My records show that during the period of five months I was an instructor, I was confined to the post for three months and grounded for a month and a half.

Being free of spirit and a rebellious fighter pilot at heart, I conceived a scheme to get back at the colonel. I went to the post athletic officer, a fellow named Barrett, and suggested that he should organize some boxing bouts for the troops for evening entertainment. It would be good for morale, I argued, and their morale was low right then.

I had heard that Colonel Burwell had been on the boxing team at West Point and suggested that the men might enjoy an evening of boxing, especially if Colonel Burwell and I went a few rounds. He was only a little taller and heavier than I was, so it would be a fairly even match and the troops would love it. Barrett said it was a great idea.

The colonel was no dummy. He had heard about my professional boxing and told Barrett he would do it on one condition—that Barrett box him after our match was finished. Barrett lost his enthusiasm for the idea at that moment, to my great disappointment.

Sometime during this period, I gave Joe her first airplane flight. It had to be done on the sly, since we weren't allowed to carry civilian passengers in a military airplane. I borrowed a car and drove her to an orchard that was located between Ream Field and San Diego and let her off. Knowing that she would be hungry before I could get back, I gave her a half dozen bananas. I drove to the field and checked out an airplane. As soon as I could, I flew back, picked her up, and gave her a ride.

During the course of that ride, I had the opportunity to show Joe some stunting. But I had forgotten about those bananas. Joe became nauseated and got rid of them over the side of the cockpit during the exhibition of my prowess as an aerobat.

Adding insult to injury, consider that this was an airplane that used castor oil in its Hisso engine. The oil came out of the exhaust in tiny blobs. She had a helmet and goggles on and when she took them off, there were those two big white eyes surrounded by a black face up to where the helmet began.

I didn't think it was very wise to let her off where I had picked her up lest some suspicious person wonder why this military plane was giving rides to girls. So I let her out on the other side of the bay where there was a smelly potash plant with a pasture beside it big enough to land on. She got out and was nauseated all over again. She went to a phone at the plant, managed to call a cab, and then took a streetcar to get back to the Coronado Hotel where we were staying. As she walked through the long corridor we called Peacock Alley to the elevators, she noticed people staring at her and smiling. She smiled back, wondering how they knew her secret. When she got to her room and looked into the mirror, she burst out crying. She said she had never seen anyone as horrible as she with her castor oil–besplattered face and two big gogglelike eyes. She vowed she'd never fly again. (She later began to take flying lessons at DeMille Field in Hollywood until she decided it was too expensive for our budget.)

When I told a group of friends about her first flight and everybody laughed, she began to bawl. She said my sense of humor was warped. It was a long time before I mentioned that episode in her presence again.

Anxious to find relief from the boredom of life as flying instructors, we pilots were always trying to think of something that would put aviation in the news. Brigadier General William "Billy" Mitchell, who had become an outspoken advocate of aviation's potential after the war was over, was beginning to make waves nationwide. At our level, the bottom of the rank totem pole, we pilots liked what he said and were eager to do what we could to advance the case for Air Service appropriations in Washington. The battle of the budget then brewing would be the first of many between the Army and Navy.

Even before the war was over, the push had been to show what the airplane could do. One truly historic event took place on May 15, 1918, when a group of Army Air Service pilots under the leadership of Major Reuben Fleet inaugurated the first scheduled airmail service between Washington, D.C., Philadelphia, and New York. With a surprising flight completion rate of well over 90 percent, they did an excellent job showing how the airplane could speed up mail delivery. The Post Office Department took over with civilian pilots in August of that year.

Lieutenant John E. Davis made a widely publicized 4,000-mile flight from the Gulf of Mexico to the Great Lakes and back during October 1918. He made the flight without any mechanical difficulties, without knowing the route or the location of any landing places, and without a mechanic or landing lights for night flights. He covered the distance from Ellington Field to Mount Clemens, Michigan, and back in 64 flying hours over a period of nine days.

Other record-breaking flights were being attempted. On September 8, Lieutenant M. B. Kelleher took a de Havilland

DH-4 to 23,000 feet using a new oxygen breathing apparatus. Ten days later, Captain Rudolph W. "Shorty" Schroeder set an altitude record of 29,000 feet over Dayton, Ohio.

At Love Field, in Dallas, Texas, Lieutenant William T. Campbell looped his Jenny 102 times. Several men jumped out of planes to test the practical use of parachutes. Speed dashes became common. On July 31, 1918, Major C. K. Rhinehart and Captain Fred Harvey made a flight from New York to Washington in two hours, fifteen minutes. A few days later, a de Havilland was flown from Dayton to Washington in two hours, fifty minutes. Many other record-setting flights were made between major cities.

Other potential uses of aircraft were tested. For the first time in the country's history soldiers under orders for duty were transported by air, from Rantoul to Champaign, Illinois. Planes were used to spot fires and direct fire-fighting crews. The Navy got into the act when a three-engined seaplane took off with a record number of 50 men aboard.

Major Albert D. Smith, stationed at our field, led the first transcontinental flight of Army planes across the country from San Diego to Jacksonville, Florida, in December 1918, which gave me an idea. I suggested that a flight of three Jennys be authorized to fly from San Diego to Washington, D.C., to show how the airplane could link an Army post located at one of the most distant points in the United States with the nation's capital. It would prove how speedily important messages, people, and things could be transported across the country in an emergency.

Colonel Burwell promptly bought the idea with no questions, somewhat to my surprise. The word had come down to all field commanders to encourage and approve any worthwhile flights that would give the Air Service some favorable publicity. I prepared a flight plan and selected Lieutenants Walter "Sump" Smith and Charles Haynes as the other two pilots, along with three mechanics. It wasn't easy to find an air route across the country in 1919. The only maps we had were Army maps, which were unreliable or out-of-date in regard to mountain heights and important landmarks. Now that the war was over, Army landing fields were few and far between and we would have to land in pastures or on roads when we needed fuel. We would take what tools the mechanics could stash in the cockpit; I had a spare propeller strapped outside my plane.

In the spring of 1919, we left Rockwell Field and headed

northeast. We landed uneventfully at Indio, California—about 90 miles away. We gassed up and headed for Needles, near the Arizona border, 120 miles farther. This stretched the Jenny's range to the limit but I decided to risk it. Shouldn't have. When we arrived, the airfield we thought was there wasn't. The town was there, but we could see only desert with no clear stretch of rock-free area to land on. We couldn't go anywhere else, so I landed on the main road outside of town. Smith followed and had no difficulty, but Haynes ran out of gas in the main tank and didn't have time to switch to the emergency auxiliary tank. His engine died during the approach and he landed among a bunch of rocks. He was unhurt but his Jenny was mortally wounded and he, his mechanic, and the plane had to return by train to Rockwell.

Smith and I and our mechanics stayed in Needles overnight and were ready to go next morning. I took off down the highway and circled while Smith began his takeoff run. As he lifted off, a wingtip clipped a telephone pole. His plane spun around and stopped in a cloud of dust. I landed quickly and found the two of them were all right, but the plane was not flyable. Now two wrecks had to be shipped back to Rockwell.

Colonel Burwell was not happy when I telephoned him to report the mishaps. He called me a "damned Chinese ace"—a term developed from the reputation Chinese pilots had in those days for crashing more of their own planes than they shot down of the enemy's. He ordered me to return to Rockwell.

We were returning through the Imperial Valley on top of an overcast when we bucked into heavy headwinds that rocked the Jenny and caused the plane to lose or gain hundreds of feet. I didn't know what my ground speed was but a landing seemed appropriate, since we didn't seem to be going anywhere. I found a hole and dropped down through it to see farmland in a valley. I picked out a likely clear space and touched down.

My bad luck held. The field had been freshly plowed and was soft. When the full weight of the plane settled down, the front wheels caught and the Jenny flipped over on its back, leaving us hanging upside down. I unbuckled the safety belt and fell out into the mud. As I did, I ripped the seat of my pants wide open on the edge of the cockpit.

Some farmhands rushed out and helped us turn the plane over. Fortunately, not much damage had been done. The propeller had split but we put the spare on quickly and made a few minor repairs to the tail. The sudden stoppage of the propeller didn't seem to have harmed the engine, so I cranked it up and flew back to Rockwell.

When we landed, a mechanic told me to report to Colonel Burwell immediately. It sounded urgent so I went right to his office, covered with oil and dirt, and he gave me a bawling out to which I was fully entitled. His tirade did not require or invite a reply, so when he finished, I saluted smartly and about-faced to leave, leaving my bare posterior in full view. Apparently, he thought it was my way of having the last word, so he bawled me out again with great, new embellishments, saying something to the effect that I was so stupid that I couldn't even keep my ass in my pants.

Another flight shows the primitive conditions under which we operated in those days. I had to fly from San Diego to March Field near Riverside, California, which had just been built. Upon landing at March, I found I had no castor oil left in my engine. I had to go to all the drugstores in the Riverside–San Bernardino–Redlands area to find enough to fill the tank.

Flying fields were few and far between in those days, and consequently, when you had trouble, ran out of gas, or were forced down by weather, you landed wherever you could—on a road, a street, or any flat piece of country. If you landed on a farm and it wasn't planted, the farmer would usually be kindly disposed toward you. On the other hand, if you landed in a field and destroyed his young wheat—or particularly if people came to see your plane—the farmer would be especially annoyed. An airplane was so rare that people would come from miles around to see and touch it, and it was these people coming onto his land who usually stomped his crops flat and caused the farmer to be somewhat opposed to airplanes landing on his property.

During this period, my immediate superior officer at Ream Field was Lieutenant Robert Worthington. We were very close and he did his best to advise me how to stay out of Colonel Burwell's doghouse. He came up with the suggestion that it would be better for all concerned if Joe would give up her job in Los Angeles and move to San Diego. This wasn't an easy decision for us because she was making more money than I was, but we decided to do it. Bob Worthington helped us find a three-bedroom rental house with a three-car garage close to the field, and we moved in. But the rent was $55 a month, and we wondered how long we could last on the remaining $85 from my lieutenant's pay. Joe had the answer: rent out the two extra bedrooms and the garage, which we did.

Bob Worthington was about 12 years older than I and had a lovely wife named Louise. They helped us get settled and Louise discovered immediately that Joe did not know how to cook. Joe's mother had never taught her how to make anything more than fudge; apparently, she thought Joe would marry a rich man and wouldn't have to learn to cook. Louise helped her with simple recipes and Joe obtained a copy of Fannie Farmer's cookbook. She learned quickly, and cooking for her became an art form. She not only learned to prepare memorable meals but became adept at making home brew, which made our house a popular place for my imbibing pilot friends during the days of Prohibition.

There were many times in our lives when I tested Joe's patience and forbearance to the limit. I had many pilot friends who wanted to enjoy a few hours of home life. Since I was living off post, our house became sort of a pilot's lounge. I would bring them home at all hours of the day and night, and Joe would somehow manage to stretch whatever food and drink we had on hand without saying a word. She seemed to enjoy being a hostess and listening to their wild flyers' tales. Her tolerance was tested severely one time when I invited 25 friends to dinner and then couldn't get there myself. Somehow she managed to stretch whatever she had on hand. I never heard that anyone complained of going hungry.

Joe became my social conscience and my memory for names, dates, places, and events. Her excellent recall enabled me many times to look brilliant when, actually, I have always had a poor memory. She was a stabilizing force between my individualistic proclivities and the requisites of military life. A newspaper reporter asked me one time what was the most important thing I had ever done in my life. My response: "Got married to Joe."

While I was being domesticated, my urge to try different things in an airplane got stronger with each passing day. I tried all kinds of aerobatics to test the limits of the plane and my own limitations. I took pride in performing maneuvers no one else could do. However, I always practiced them thoroughly at a safe altitude before I performed them close to the ground.

One day, Bruce Johnson and I were up in a Jenny fooling

around over a mountainous area when we sighted a flock of ducks below us. In those days, going after ducks in a Jenny was great sport. The plane and the ducks were capable of about the same speed, but the ducks could dive away faster than we could when they tired. I dove down and flew among the mountain peaks and canyons in hot pursuit. The ducks eventually did tire and dodged away. I lost sight of them. To my very great embarrassment, the ducks had led me into a dead-end canyon where the walls were higher than the Jenny could negotiate. I couldn't turn in either direction so had no choice but to give it full throttle and pull back hard on the stick, hoping that I could urge the struggling Jenny over the top. The nose went over but the tail didn't make it. We went smashing into the brush and rocks on top of the peak.

Bruce and I were unhurt but the airplane was a mess. We both cussed our bad luck, and I was concerned about how I was going to explain this latest mishap to Colonel Burwell. A crowd gathered and, finding us unhurt, went away without offering any assistance. When another crowd gathered later, Bruce wanted some sympathy so he complained that he was hurt internally. He was promptly invited into town where he spent the night as the guest of a pretty widow who had an attractive maid.

One thing I remembered from previous Burwell lectures was that the pilot had to stay with the plane in the event of a forced landing or crash. Since I was the pilot, I had to spend the night in the wreckage huddled against the chill. Once again, when I returned to our base, I felt the wrath of the colonel as he reminded me that the taxpayers had to pay for my foolishness and that I had no right to wreck their airplanes. He was right, of course. I had no defense.

In spite of my crack-ups, I never had any thoughts about quitting. In those early days, airplanes were quite fragile and landed slowly. A crack-up was not always serious, particularly if you could hook your wingtip on a tree or on anything that would cause the plane to break up gradually. Going in headfirst or nose-first, of course, could be dangerous. But if you were able to break the initial impact, you could often walk away without a scratch. As a reminder of those days, I have two facial scars—a cut over an eye and one on my chin—acquired when I stuck my face into the instrument panel on one occasion. Perhaps my experience as a tumbler helped. A tumbler learns how to fall and not be hurt. I think some of the things I learned in tumbling became very useful in aerobatics and in the frequent crack-ups I had.

On one occasion, in my exuberance to prove what an airplane could do, I thought I should help one of our enlisted mechanics with an onerous chore. He had been given the extra duty of sweeping out a hangar on a Saturday afternoon as punishment for some "crime" he had committed during the week. I felt sorry for him and told him if he would open both big hangar doors, get my plane out, push the other planes back, and step out of the way, we could get the place cleaned out in record time. He helped me crank up the old de Havilland and I took off. After he cleared the hangar and gave me the all-clear signal, I aimed for the open doors and flew through one side and out the other. Most of the dirt and dust was propelled out the door in the opposite direction from which I had come. The mechanic seemed very grateful. We congratulated ourselves that we had discovered a new use for airplanes!

In 1918, the commanding officer of Rockwell Field, headquarters for the air training units, was Colonel Henry H. "Hap" Arnold, one of the nation's first pilots. Lieutenants Ira Eaker and Carl "Tooey" Spaatz were also assigned to Rockwell. We didn't think so then, but all four of us were to become lifelong friends, although we would have some honest differences in the future. Hap had learned about some of my escapades at Ream Field and on one occasion had passed the order to Burwell to ground me temporarily. He stated in his memoirs he thought it was for riding on the axle of a landing plane to win a five-dollar bet. Hap must have forgotten that Colonel Burwell had seen my escapade on Mr. DeMille's film and had already meted out my punishment.

After World War II, when his excellent autobiography *Global Mission* was published, Hap sent me an autographed copy. Inside the cover he wrote, "To Jimmy Doolittle: As a lieutenant you caused me worry but as time passed, your real qualities came out. Your skill as an airman, your ability as an aviation engineer and finally your all-around aviation knowledge brought admiration of all who came in contact with you." I value that inscription very highly. In my opinion, Hap deserves much more credit than he has been given for his farsighted direction of the Army Air Forces during World War II.

* * *

Ream Field closed early in 1919 and I was transferred to nearby Rockwell. In the latter part of that year, it was announced that the military budget for the following fiscal year would be cut and the number of students made available for flying training would be greatly reduced. The 1920 budget for Army aviation was so meager that Major General Charles T. Menoher, chief of the Air Service, announced, "Not a dollar is available for the purchase of new aircraft." The Army, which had numbered nearly four million men on Armistice Day, was to be reduced to about 19,500 officers and 254,000 enlisted men. The Army Air Service would have about 1,500 officers and 16,000 enlisted men.

There were to be only nine instructors left at Rockwell in the summer of 1919. Transfers elsewhere were inevitable. In July 1919, orders transferred Bruce Johnson and me to the 104th Aero Squadron at Kelly Field, in Texas. It didn't take me long to get in trouble there. My personnel file shows that I received a form letter from the commander of the Air Service Flying School with certain blanks filled in. It said Lieutenant Doolittle was "hereby restricted to the limits of the Post for 30 days beginning 12 noon, August 14, 1919, to 12 noon, September 13, 1919 for the reason of stunting de Havilland airplane." I don't remember what I did, but I'm sure I deserved the restriction.

One of the tasks assumed by the Air Service was to patrol the Mexican border from Brownsville, Texas, along the Rio Grande to El Paso and then westward all the way to San Diego. Airfields were established every 150 miles or so, usually at or near Army posts.

In October 1919, Bruce and I were transferred to the 90th Aero Squadron at Eagle Pass on the Rio Grande. We were under the administrative control of the 12th Cavalry, which was located at Camp Robert E. L. Michie, at Del Rio. Our patrol area extended from Las Caeves to Del Rio.

There had been trouble along the border since 1913. The 1st Aero Squadron, under the command of Captain (later Major General) Benjamin D. Foulois, had been ordered to take part in General John J. "Black Jack" Pershing's punitive expedition in pursuit of Mexican revolutionist Pancho Villa in 1916. During World War I, Mexican bandits raided American ranches to secure supplies, cattle, and horses, and U.S. Army troops would chase them back across the border. The biggest clash came in August 1918 when more than 800 American soldiers fought 600

Mexicans near Nogales, Arizona. In June 1919, Villa's men attacked Juárez across from El Paso and stray fire killed an American soldier and a civilian and wounded six other persons. American troops crossed the river and dispersed the bandits.

By no stretch of the imagination could the area where we were assigned be considered a garden spot, especially in the baking heat of the summer. However, it was a welcome change from instructing; my only regret was that I had to leave Joe behind in San Diego.

Living conditions were less than comfortable. We had to sleep in Army pup tents. We were given de Havilland DH-4s to fly, known as "flaming coffins," and Curtiss JN-4 "Jennys." Our job was never well defined. We were supposed to look for illegal border crossers, smugglers, horse thieves, and any unusual activity that looked suspicious. Many Americans remembered the days in 1916 when Pancho Villa raided Columbus, New Mexico, and knew that the Mexican government still had no control over what happened along the border.

Although our machine guns were loaded, we were instructed not to fire on the Mexicans, even if they fired on us first. If they did shoot at us, we were supposed to make notes of when and where and report it when we got back to Eagle Pass. Fortunately, they missed most of the time, but not always. Lieutenant Fonda Johnson, one of the pilots who had rented one of our bedrooms at San Diego, was struck in the head by a single bullet and died instantly.

Since we couldn't fire on the Mexicans legally, we devised a method of paying them back when we saw smoke from their rifles coming from clumps of brush where they usually hid when they heard us coming. They were no doubt there to run off some cattle, so we would fly around until we found a few, then fly low overhead and stampede them toward the Mexicans' hiding places. The Mexicans would flush out of the brush and jump into the river, shaking their fists and screaming at us.

The boredom on the ground was more than we could stand sometimes, so we tried to find new things to do in the air. Fifty miles west of Del Rio on the Pecos River near Comstock, there was a Southern Pacific Railroad bridge known as the Pecos River High Bridge, said to be the highest in the world when it was built before the turn of the century. It looked easy to fly under, so I did. But I had to bank the wings nearly vertical to get between the upright piers.

A few weeks later, I had a forced landing at Langtry. As

I stood around waiting for someone to arrive to help me repair the engine, the biggest, toughest Texan I have ever seen rode up on horseback and said, "I'm looking for the SOB who flew under the Pecos River High Bridge and tore down the telephone wires which were strung under it. I'm the lineman who had to swim the river and restring them."

I expressed sympathy at his inconvenience and advised that I would endeavor to get his complaint to the proper party when I returned to my base. Luckily, I was flying a plane other than the one I had been using when I flew under the bridge. Consequently, the cuts dug in the struts by the telephone wires were not there to indicate my culpability.

Bruce Johnson had a special knack for acquiring the necessities of life for us during those days: food, tequila, furniture, and other comforts of civilization that we so badly yearned for. He obtained rifles and shotguns for hunting and even managed to "liberate" a piano for off-duty partying.

Bringing tequila into the United States was supposed to be illegal, but there was no enforcement unless somebody provoked the border officials. On one trip across the river to Piedras Negras in a car they hired with a driver, Bruce and a friend of his, neither one of whom had a pass, tried to hide a case of tequila under their seats when they passed through the border checkpoints. They had no trouble at the Mexican side, but American border patrol officers spotted the tequila and arrested them. They were turned over to the Army and charged with smuggling and illegally crossing the border. They were sent to Fort Sam Houston in San Antonio to stand a general court-martial.

We couldn't let that happen to Brucie and his buddy because conviction meant dishonorable discharges, which we didn't think was fair. A bunch of us went to Fort Sam to appear as character witnesses. Fortunately, somewhere between the border and the court, the liquid evidence had mysteriously disappeared. The charge was dropped. Brucie, consumed with guilt, decided to resign his commission and go home.

Boredom and loneliness overtook all of us after about five months at Eagle Pass. I sent for Joe to join me, knowing full well that she might be unhappy with the accommodations. I found a house, more like a shack, which had no furniture. I hurriedly made a bed, table, and some chairs and acquired some odd pieces that made our collection what could only be called "early Army Air Service."

Joe had decided early in our marriage that she would bloom wherever she was planted, so she really got into the cooking and baking routine as soon as she arrived. She got tips from a Chinese cook on the post and made it a point to learn how to make Mexican food. Her sister Grace joined us, and the two of them played hostess to my flying buddies. Their presence made life a lot more bearable for everyone. Grace met Lieutenant L. S. "Andy" Andrews, one of my squadron mates, and they eventually married. Andy later became a pilot for American Airlines.

We stayed at Eagle Pass for almost a year, then briefly at Del Rio. On July 1, 1920, I was transferred back to Kelly Field and assigned to the Air Service Mechanics School. It was a memorable day for me because I was promoted to first lieutenant. I graduated from the Mechanics School the following September with a grade of 95 and a few days later was commissioned as a first lieutenant in the Air Service, Regular Army. The slight increase in pay of the promotion was welcome, but the appointment as a regular was especially appreciated because, with upcoming budget cuts, only the reserve officers would be let go, not the regulars. The assignment was also pleasing because it meant Joe and I would be moving onto a permanent Army post with better quarters and all the advantages of living near a relatively large city. Besides, Joe was pregnant and was due in the fall.

On October 2, 1920, our first son was born at Fort Sam Houston Hospital. As seemed to be the custom in those early postwar days with the firstborn male child, we named him James, Jr. I'm not sure we did him any favors.

Our second son, John, arrived at the same hospital on June 29, 1922. We gave him the middle name of Prescott after the military doctor who had delivered both of them.

There is a special delight when a man's wife bears him a son, and the feeling of elation is doubled when he has two. Our sons were active American boys with all the native abilities to bedevil, harass, and embarrass their parents. In other words, they were normal kids. Through the years of their growing up, Joe and I tried to guide their development carefully and did what we could to help them into adulthood with the best education we could afford for them. We believed we succeeded. It is difficult to describe how immensely proud we were when both boys were commissioned in the Air Force and received their wings. Both served their country with distinction in peace and war.

* * *

The assignment to Kelly Field was a most important one for me professionally, now that I was committed to make the Air Service my career. Although I had tinkered with engines, electrical systems, instruments, and all the other kinds of plane components in the shops at San Diego, Eagle Pass, and Del Rio for many hours, the tinkering had always been an unstructured learning experience. The chance to legitimately get my hands on airplanes and engines and be taught by men who knew what they were doing gave me a lift that I had not felt before. Besides, there were different types of aircraft to fly, including captured German planes.

I also attended the Parachute School. When you finished the course, it was optional whether or not you jumped in a 'chute you had packed. I chose to jump. That was my first. Of course, I had no way of knowing then that I would later owe my life to the hundreds of tiny silkworms that made the silk parachute canopies and that I would become a three-time member of the Caterpillar Club.

The opportunity to put to work what I was learning about airplanes came in April 1921 when Lieutenant Alexander Pearson attempted to make a solo cross-country flight from Douglas, Arizona, to Jacksonville, Florida, in a DH-4. He got lost and came down in the Big Bend country about 80 miles below the border, southwest of Del Rio. He was missing for nearly a week while making his way on foot to the Army camp at Sanderson, Texas.

The plane was badly damaged but, if repaired, could be flown out. It would take some doing. I volunteered to take a pack train with a new engine and spare parts, a couple of mechanics, and a detachment of cowboys. We took 20 carrier pigeons along to send messages back to Del Rio when we needed supplies. Planes from our base flew over frequently to keep an eye on us and dropped water, rations, and mail when weather permitted.

It took us nearly two weeks of hard work but we got the DH fixed up and I flew it out. I received a letter of commendation from Major General Joseph T. Dickman, commanding general of the VIII Corps Area, for "the energy, good judgment and courage displayed by you in the repair and recovery by air of the Pearson aeroplane during the trip into Mexico, April 28 to May 11, 1921, for that purpose."

I was pleased, of course, to be so recognized. It was the encouragement I needed. I could now see my future more clearly. Not only would flying still be my main interest, but I was determined to become as knowledgeable as possible about airplanes and everything attached to them. As an officer and a pilot, I thought I should know as much as the enlisted men who worked on them. This assignment would prove to be a milestone in my life.

Note

1. From a report by General George P. Scriven, as quoted in *The Army Air Service,* by Arthur Sweetser, New York: D. Appleton Co., 1919, p. 24.

Chapter 4

Two of my best friends—Jack Allard and Bruce Johnson—had left the service before I transferred to Kelly Field. Jack went to work for the Gillette Safety Razor Co. and Bruce went home to manage his family's farming property in New York State. I missed them both and kept in touch with them through the years. Both became extremely valuable to me during the war two decades later.

And if you believed Brigadier General Billy Mitchell, there was sure to be another war within a very few years. Mitchell had returned from France after World War I a self-proclaimed, outspoken advocate of air power. He was positive that the fate of the country in any future war would be decided by the airplane. The Army and Navy were disputing the future use of aircraft against enemy naval forces, although neither service knew if surface ships could survive attacks by aircraft.

Mitchell, however, advocated a separate air force, free of control by the Army and Navy hierarchy and equal with both services. Articulate, persuasive, and with great showmanship, Mitchell insisted that the airplane would be the dominant and decisive weapon in future warfare, and kept his superiors constantly aggravated. As assistant chief of the Air Service when he returned from France, he served under a nonpilot—Major General Charles T. Menoher—and then under Major General Mason M. Patrick, who eventually took pilot training when he was in his fifties. Mitchell felt strongly that only a pilot should command the Air Service and said so in many different ways.

Soon after joining General Menoher's staff in March 1919, Mitchell proposed a test of planes versus ships. He said that the days of the battleship were numbered and he wanted to prove it by actual tests. He told a congressional committee that a fleet composed of 20 aircraft carriers could always annihilate a fleet of 20 ordinary battleships.

Nothing was done over the next 18 months—which only encouraged Mitchell to become more and more vocal. He made many claims about the potential of aircraft, not only in national defense but for civil purposes as well. He appeared before congressional committees, made many speeches, gave numerous interviews to newspaper and magazine reporters, and wrote many articles expounding his views. He crossed swords with the Navy, especially Rear Admiral William A. Moffett, chief of the Navy's Bureau of Aeronautics.

Mitchell's chance came on July 13 when the target was a former World War I German destroyer anchored 50 miles offshore with no one on board. While Mitchell circled in a DH-4 and other planes photographed, a half dozen Army SE-5s simulated a strafing attack and then each dropped four 25-pound bombs from 200 feet. The SE-5s scored 25 hits in four passes. Next came 16 Martin MB-2s that dropped 300-pound demolition bombs and scored about 10 hits. The destroyer went to the bottom.

But it was on July 21, 1921, that history was made. The former German battleship *Ostfriesland* was the target. Many witnesses were transported by Navy ship to a point near the scene, including the secretary of War, the secretary of the Navy, Generals Pershing and Menoher, members of Congress, and a host of reporters. Josephus Daniels, former Navy secretary, stated publicly that he would be glad to stand bareheaded on the deck of any battleship while Mitchell tried to sink it from the air. He was just one of many pro-Navy enthusiasts who had ridiculed Mitchell for his views and were anxious to see him fail.

The Army led off with 1,100-pound bombs and scored several hits. These were followed by an attack with eight Martin bombers and three Handley-Page bombers armed with 2,000-pound bombs that had been specially prepared by the Ordnance Department. Under the rules, the Army was allowed a maximum of three bombs and two direct hits, with a pause after the first hit for an inspection by the Board of Observers. However, Mitchell did not want his pilots to make direct hits; he ordered them to try for near-misses, whereby the explosive force and water pressure would cave in the sides of the ship. One bomb hit the side of the *Ostfriesland*, glanced off and exploded about 15 feet away. Within a few minutes, the old German veteran turned turtle and disappeared.

Mitchell's success made him a national hero. He said the tests showed beyond doubt that ships of any kind, including the most modern of battleships, can be destroyed easily by bombs dropped from aircraft. He said they demonstrated beyond a doubt that an adequate air force would constitute a positive defense of our country against hostile invasion. He advocated that national defense policy should be revised at once, with the Army defending the land, the Navy operating on the high seas, and an air force established to defend the frontier and provide coastal defense against aircraft and ships extending 200 miles out into the oceans. He added, "Aviation can only be developed to its fullest extent under its own direction and control. An efficient solution of our defense needs will not exist until a Department of National Defense is organized."[1]

I was transferred on temporary duty to Langley Field, Virginia, on May 16, 1921, to join the Air Brigade as an engineering officer, flight leader, and night flying instructor "in connection with experiment in bombing naval vessels from aircraft," according to my orders. When the squadron commander wasn't there, I was in command. I served as an aide to General Mitchell for one day during this period and he almost wore me out. I've never moved so fast or worked so hard in my life. As Lieutenant Lester J. Maitland, one of the pilots assigned with me on the tests, said, "He [Mitchell] slept little, never rested, flew thousands of miles, and seemed to be everywhere at the same time."

We flew practice missions in DH-4Bs almost daily and had briefings every day on the progress of the project, which served to keep up our enthusiasm. I participated in one mission bombing the destroyer and another going after the submarine. Both were relatively small targets. We used 100-pound bombs against them, but I don't recall that we did much damage.

One incident does stand out in my mind, however, and I still wonder about it. We were ordered to do some night bombing practice using 100-pound bombs and magnesium flares. The target was located on a small uninhabited island where a fire was to be lit by a small party of men who would withdraw after they set it. We found the island; we found the fire; we bombed the fire. The next day, we found out that the people who were to go to the island and light the fire hadn't gone because they couldn't get their boat motor started. We tried to find out who was there and who we bombed. But we never heard that anyone had been hurt, nor did any alternative fire makers show up. So we were simply left to wonder how a fire could have been set exactly where it was supposed to be while the folks who were to set it never got there. That's always been a mystery to me.

In addition to the naval ship tests, Mitchell organized simulated bombing attacks on New York City, Philadelphia, Baltimore, and Annapolis. I flew a Martin MB-2. I also led a flight of DH-4Bs in September against the USS *Alabama* at night with mufflers on the engine exhaust stacks and lights covered, so we wouldn't be seen from the surface.

I was at Langley Field from the start to the finish of the bombing operations and returned to Kelly Field after the Air Brigade was disbanded. One of my duties was as an instructor in the Boeing GA-1, a twin-engine attack plane with two gunners, a 37-mm cannon in the nose, and eight .30-caliber guns in the fuselage. It was armored with protective plating and was intended for low-level strafing and bombing. Twenty had been ordered, but the plane was too heavy and slow, required too much space for takeoffs, and had a short range. The order was subsequently reduced to 10. An argument, which went on for a long time, was whether or not attack planes should be armored. It wasn't until much later that the consensus was that aircraft used for low-level attacks should be fast and maneuverable, with only light armor to protect the crews.

There was something bedeviling me during this time that had been stimulated by the continuing encouragement we received to make news by demonstrating the potential of airplanes. When Lieutenant Pearson was forced down in Mexico, he was flying as part of a plan to try to cut down on the time for deploying Army aircraft from one part of the country to another, just as I had hoped to do while stationed at Rockwell. On Washington's Birthday in 1921, Pearson was to proceed from Jacksonville, Florida, to San Diego, flying from east to west with stops at Houston and El Paso, Texas. It was while flying to Jacksonville to get in position that he had crashed south of the border. At the same time, Lieutenant William D. Coney was to fly in the opposite direction with just one stop at Dallas.

Coney departed Rockwell Field but had engine trouble in Texas, which delayed him, and it took him 2 days, 9 hours, and 22 minutes to cross the country. His actual flying time was 22 hours, 27 minutes.

Coney didn't give up. He thought he could make it coast to coast from east to west in less than 24 hours and was given permission to try again. This time he departed Jacksonville on March 25, 1921. He ran into fog somewhere over Mississippi and developed engine trouble. While making a forced landing, he hit a tree. He died in a Natchez hospital five days later.

I, too, thought it would be possible to fly coast to coast from east to west in less than 24 hours despite having to fly against the prevailing winds. My reasoning was that flying east to west would give me more daylight. If I took off at dusk from Florida and flew through the night, I should arrive the next day at Kelly and then at San Diego in daylight. I would have to navigate precisely and pick a day when the westerly winds were light.

The flight would be a challenge. Apparently, no one else had thought about it after Coney died, so I applied through channels to the chief of the Air Service in May 1922. I flew to Washington and personally asked General Mason M. Patrick, who had replaced General Menoher as chief of the Air Service, for his blessing. I had a very long presentation all lined up in my mind, but before I could get into it, the general agreed. However, no government per diem funds would be authorized for my living expenses. In those days, you didn't complicate your efforts to do something by asking for government funds, because if you did, you'd get a no before you got started.

I wanted to plan more carefully than Coney and Pearson had done and learn by their mistakes. I flew the route from Kelly to San Diego in a DH-4B in 12 hours and 30 minutes and kept a detailed diary of the performance of the plane and its Liberty engine. After returning to Kelly, I flew from there to Carlstrom Field, in Arcadia, Florida. In my request to Washington, I said that the purpose of this latter flight was to acquaint me with this stretch of country and to prepare for a one-day transcontinental flight from Jacksonville to San Diego. The practice flight and the transcontinental attempt were approved.

I also made a trip to McCook Field at Dayton, the Army's

main aviation test facility, to consult with engineers about gas tank modifications and obtain a new instrument being tested—a turn-and-bank indicator—that was to prove extremely valuable. I then set up some specifications for the ground crews at Kelly, which consisted most importantly of the installation of an additional 240-gallon fuel tank and a 24-gallon oil tank where the front seat was; a small lifting device was fitted onto the landing gear fairings to cut down a little on drag.

Since I was going to make only one stop, there was a personal problem I had to solve. As far as I know, I conceived the first little pilot dehydrator, a funnel and tube going out the bottom of the aircraft, facing aft. Unfortunately, occasionally the tube swiveled the wrong way so it blew instead of sucked. You can imagine what that did to the dignity of the pilot who wanted desperately to dehydrate in flight and couldn't turn that dehydrator around! We solved the problem later. A pilot's relief tube became standard equipment on all subsequent military aircraft.

On August 4, 1922, I flew from Kelly and arrived at Camp Johnson near Jacksonville nine hours later. The news had gotten out that I was going to make the attempt from Pablo Beach, Florida, on Sunday, August 6. A crowd had gathered to see me off. I had chosen Pablo Beach because I had heard that automobiles were often driven on the beach for speed checks, and a pilot named Robert Fowler who had flown across the country in 1912 or 1913 had landed there. It seemed like an ideal spot from which to depart for an ocean-to-ocean record attempt.

Joe was there and helped me refuel. When I was ready to go at 9:40 P.M., I waved to the crowd, pulled my goggles over my eyes, and started down the beach. Just when I was nearing flying speed, the left wheel caught in soft sand. The plane slewed to the left and headed toward the water. Before I could straighten it out, a wave came in and caught the wheels, and the airplane went over on its back.

When I hit, my helmet and goggles slipped down over my eyes and nose and I was sure I was in water over my head. I held my breath, unbuckled my safety belt, dropped out, grabbed the side of the fuselage, and began to climb up. I was shocked to find how heavy I was because I thought I would be more buoyant in the water. When I pushed the helmet and goggles off my eyes and put my feet down, I found I was standing in only about 10 inches of water!

The crowd, many of them laughing when they saw me

stand up unhurt but soaking wet, rushed over to help, and I was embarrassed as I had never been before. One lady asked me if I was hurt and I replied, "No, but my feelings are."

This was one more lesson learned. I vowed I'd never tell anyone of any future record attempts because there was always the risk of failure, which was bad publicity, not only for me, but for the Air Service, too. If permission was granted, I planned to try again as soon as possible because I was confident I could succeed.

The DH-4 definitely couldn't be flown. In a report I made later, I noted that the nose was crushed and the motor moved back four inches, tearing out its supports. The propeller, a wing strut, and the rudder were broken. The wings were apparently in good shape, but the upper panels had been underwater for a half hour so I considered them unsafe for further use until overhauled. The wreck was returned in an open boxcar to the San Antonio Intermediate Air Depot at Kelly Field for repairs.

Instead of being chastised as I expected, I received a telegram from General Patrick, head of the Air Service: REGRET UNFORTUNATE ACCIDENT PERIOD BETTER LUCK NEXT TIME PERIOD INSTRUCTIONS FOLLOW.

During the next few weeks, I supervised the installation of new wings, tail assembly, engine mounts, engine, and propeller and was determined to plan more carefully this time. Since I had lacked a clear and distinct straight line on the beach during the first takeoff attempt, I asked for a series of lanterns to be set up to help me avoid any tendency to go right or left and stay on the hard beach area. The newspaper reporters kept after me to discuss my plans, but I wouldn't tell them anything. Consequently, a story came out in a San Antonio paper headlined: "San Antonio Flyer Is Silent as to Plans for Trans-Continental Flight."

On September 2, just before Labor Day in 1922, I flew from Kelly Field to Camp Johnson at Jacksonville, and at 6 P.M. on September 4, went to nearby Pablo Beach. Two mechanics from Montgomery, Alabama, set up lanterns for me at 50-yard intervals and I made a fast taxi run down the beach to check for soft spots. Finding none, at 9:52 P.M. EST, I gave the Liberty engine full throttle. The tail came up nicely and I was airborne fairly quickly. Turning toward the Atlantic briefly, I banked westward and settled down for the long 1,050-mile night flight to San Antonio, which I thought would take about eleven hours.

A full moon greeted me for about two hours after the start.

I was then flying at an altitude of 3,500 feet and at a speed of 105 miles per hour. A favoring wind was on my quarter. A severe thunder and lightning storm then came up. Some of those lightning strikes were so close that I could smell the ozone. I realized the storm area was too extensive to dodge, and plunged directly into it, trusting my compass to steer a straight course. At each flash of lightning I peeked over the side of the cockpit, saw familiar landmarks, and, after consulting the Rand-McNally road maps spread out before me, knew that I was flying high and free and true. The turn-and-bank indicator that I had installed proved to be an excellent aid to keep me proceeding in the direction I wanted to go when there was no horizon. This extremely valuable instrument would prove to be a help to all pilots in night flying and flying through clouds.

Over New Orleans the rain, sweeping in gusts, stung my face. The rain continued until after I had passed New Iberia, on the Texas border. By veering a little to the northward I passed out of the storm area. From that time until I landed at Kelly Field, in San Antonio, I encountered nothing but pleasant weather. It was a wonderful sight to see dawn breaking over the Texas country and to feel the thrill of having successfully completed half of my journey through the long hours of darkness. There is an exhilaration in night flying that more than makes up for the solitude and the incessant purr of the motor.

I hadn't known what was going on at Kelly while I was en route, but the *Air Corps Newsletter*, an official journal for Army airmen, later reported in the somewhat flowery fashion of the day:

> Long before daylight, people began to assemble at Kelly Field to watch for the arrival of the "Lone Pilot" who was to make a new record for American aviation. They came from all parts of the surrounding country and in all sorts of cars. . . .
>
> As dawn broke and no sign appeared of Lieutenant Doolittle, his comrades began to be a bit anxious, and from time to time recalled the bad points along the route from New Orleans. Finally, this spirit could no longer be continued, and several ships took the air to look for him in the low clouds. Among the hundreds present, all the aviation activities in the district were represented—from the Air Office, Eighth Corps Area,

to his brother officers from neighboring fields. Finally, after two or three false alarms as ships that took the air to look for him returned, a lone ship glided into the field at 7:05 A.M., September 5, and a cheer went up that proclaimed to the world that the first leg of the greatest transcontinental "one-man trip" had been accomplished. As soon as the motor was cut a picked outfit of enlisted men hopped to work, and while Lieutenant Doolittle was getting a much-needed breakfast and a chance to stretch his legs, they gassed, oiled, and watered the plane. The ship was completely gone over, wires tightened, radiator leak repaired, motor examined, and when the Lieutenant took the stick 1 hour and 15 minutes later everything was in order.

At 8:20 A.M., September 5, the great ship once again took the air and slowly climbed toward the low ceiling. Everyone was confident that the trip would be made; for, in spite of the bad weather, Doolittle would be flying over country with which he was well acquainted, due to his border service, and would have daylight to help him in reading his maps. He was accompanied on his trip by planes from the field as far as Medina Lake, although one went along as far as El Paso.

What the article didn't mention was that when the mechanics took off the gasoline strainers to check them, one of them got cross-threaded, and it looked like the flight was going to end right there. But thanks to Lieutenant Delmar H. Dunton, the engineering officer, the problem was corrected very promptly and I got off with only a very slight delay.

I was concerned about the second leg of the flight because I knew that in my state of fatigue, the drone of the engine would tend to lull me to sleep. A few days before leaving San Antonio for Florida, I had written a letter to my friend Lieutenant John McCullough, then adjutant at Rockwell Field, and asked for his assistance: "Please send two pacemaking planes to meet me either at El Centro, California, or Yuma, Arizona. This will give me something to think about and help keep me awake. You see, I will have been in the air from 20 to 25 hours with only one 30-minute stop at Kelly for gas and oil, so I will be pretty tired."

From Kelly to the Arizona border, nothing happened to disturb the serenity of the voyage. The desolate appearance of the country and the constant throb of the Liberty engine began to lull me to sleep. Despite the fact that sleep meant death, my head began to nod. But good fortune perched on the cowl. A light rain began falling. The raindrops, whipped back by the propeller, began eddying over the windshield and running in a tiny stream down my back. This made me angry, but was the stimulant I needed. The rain refreshed me, woke me up, and I settled back feeling safe.

After the folks at Rockwell were notified that I had passed El Paso, Captain William Randolph and Lieutenant C. L. Webber were sent aloft to intercept me. They circled over Yuma and just when they thought they might have to land and refuel, my DH-4 appeared in the east. I was groggy and the sight of these two friends snapped me awake. They took formation positions on my left and right and we descended together for a landing at Rockwell. I had made it. Total flying time for the 2,163-mile coast-to-coast trip was 21 hours, 19 minutes. Total elapsed time was 22 hours, 30 minutes.

Shortly after landing, I was taken to the field hospital where they checked me over thoroughly to see the extent of my fatigue and what mental and physical changes might have taken place. What the doctors didn't know was that as I had stepped out of the plane, one of my friends had handed me a drink, saying, "How'd you like a little snort?" I took a fair-sized gulp of good whiskey, which went right to my head, and I felt no fatigue from then on. I'm quite sure that whatever the doctors were looking for was completely voided by that shot of whiskey.

The *Los Angeles Times* extravagantly praised the flight. I received a complimentary letter from General Patrick, but more important to me was a handwritten note from General Mitchell: I am very much pleased at your flight and congratulate you in every way possible. Achievements of this kind are what advances aviation."

To my pleasant surprise, I was awarded the Distinguished Flying Cross seven years later for this flight. The citation noted that it "demonstrated the possibility of moving Air Corps units to any portion of the United States in less than 24 hours."

One of the interesting immediate consequences of the flight occurred when Senator Park Trammell of Florida learned that I had financed the flight out of my own money. He wrote a letter in September 1922 to General R. C. Davis, adjutant general of the Army, suggesting that I be reimbursed, and he asked for an investigation.

General Davis responded that it was not possible to authorize payment of my expenses and that it was necessary for the individuals on similar "air voyages" to defray their own expenses. "This expense has usually been large," the general stated, "for the reason that flying personnel, owing to the location of landing places, have been required to secure means of transportation to and from such landing fields and to meet the usual large expense for board and lodging in cities and towns."

However, as a result of the senator's inquiry, the chief of the Air Service recommended to the War Department that legislation be introduced that would permit the payment of eight dollars a day for meals and lodging to pilots on cross-country flights. I never was reimbursed.

The flight did get national publicity, and the United States had been crossed in less than a day for the first time, but the flight simply showed that the airplane could do a job. In May 1923, Lieutenants Oakley G. Kelly and John A. Macready made a coast-to-coast nonstop flight in 26 hours and 50 minutes, a much more difficult flight that deservedly got very good news coverage.

When Kelly and Lieutenant Muir S. "Santy" Fairchild had proposed a nonstop flight in 1921, they had been ridiculed. The doubters said no plane could carry that much fuel and no human could stand the fatigue. Kelly and Fairchild studied a number of planes and settled on the Fokker F.IV, designated the T-2, then being produced under contract to the Air Service. About a month before my flight, General Patrick approved theirs. John Macready, one of McCook's outstanding test pilots, later replaced Fairchild, and he and Kelly finally succeeded after setting several prior endurance records.

I wanted to stay at San Diego for three or four days to rest up after my coast-to-coast dash, but orders had just arrived at Kelly transferring me to McCook Field, in Dayton, Ohio. I departed Rockwell in the DH on September 8 at 8 A.M. and arrived at Kelly at 7:40 P.M. When I landed, I found Colonel Howard, the commanding officer at Kelly Field, waiting at the head of the reception committee. Joe, her mother, and I were bundled into a car that led a parade of all the private automobiles at Kelly Field to the city hall, where the mayor and members of the city government and various civic organizations greeted us.

After a short address by the mayor and Colonel Howard, and a weak reply from me, we led a parade of automobiles through the principal streets of San Antonio.

After the flight, I made a full report with recommendations based on my aborted coast-to-coast flight and on the successful one. I praised the people at Jacksonville and San Antonio who had helped me prepare and the Liberty engine that could "be depended upon for much more than 12 hours continuous running if care is exercised." I noted that night flying in the light of the full moon "is but little more dangerous than flying in the daytime but the immediate proximity of lightning at night has a strong tendency toward retrospection, regret and reform."

It was nice to be honored by my peers and superiors, but the greater honor was to receive an assignment to the Air Service Engineering School at McCook Field. McCook was the Air Service's postwar aviation research center, and although its job was to further technical development of Air Service aircraft and equipment, its work also benefited the development of civil aviation. There were very few people in uniform then who had a technical education at the college level. It was thought to be more beneficial for the Air Service to educate pilot officers in its own facility so it would be less dependent on civilians for technical advice.

In those days, airplanes were unreliable and I thought they might become more so. I never flew without a pair of pliers, a screwdriver, and a crescent wrench in my pocket so I could fix things on the airplane. This was being a mechanic, not an engineer. I had applied for the Engineering School because I thought there should be a better rapport between the aeronautical engineer and the pilot. It seemed to me that the engineers felt pilots were all a little crazy or else they wouldn't be pilots. The pilots felt the engineers as a group were, if not incompetent, at least not thoroughly acquainted with the pilot's viewpoint—that all the engineers did was zip slide rules back and forth and come out with erroneous results and bad aircraft. I thought from a philosophical point of view that it would be good to have engineers and pilots understand one another better. It seemed desirable to marry these two capabilities in one person—and I wanted to be that person. With my mining engineering background and as a graduate of the Mechanics and Parachute schools, it seemed the next logical school for me was the Engineering School. I also felt that sooner or later I wouldn't be doing as much flying, and when that time came, it would be well if I knew something about aircraft design.

The Engineering School had been established for Air Service officers in 1919 as the Air School of Application. The one-year course covered mechanics, business administration, armament, materials, electricity, power plants, and theoretical aeronautics.

Much of the credit for the development of the philosophy behind the work at McCook was due to Colonel Thurman H. Bane, a pilot with an engineering background—a rare man in those days. I don't think he has ever received adequate credit for his many contributions to aeronautics in that early McCook Field era.

Colonel Bane was a fine administrator. He always gave new pilots a lecture when they arrived at McCook. One part of the lecture was devoted to encouraging us to develop a sense of order in everything we did. "If you don't do things in an orderly way," he said, "you tax your memory. For example, if you wear glasses, and when you take them off you always put them in one particular pocket, you can always find them—you don't have to think about where they are. On the other hand, if you lay them down, chances are you won't remember where you laid them, and every time you want your glasses again, you have to search for them."

One of the helpful hints that Colonel Bane gave us was something I adopted and have used ever since. He kept a small notebook—called a Mem-Index—in his shirt pocket: one side of it is chronological, and here you note things that have to be done and check off things done. It has enough pages for about three weeks, so you always have about three weeks' plans ahead in your pocket at all times. As you take the pages out, you can file them and you have a permanent record. The other side is alphabetical. Here you note things you want to remember—for example, the license plate number on your car, the names, addresses, and phone numbers of certain people with whom you come in contact, or facts you want to recall later for record purposes.

I was so impressed with that little notebook, which I first started using in 1922 that I am still using one—not the original because they only last two or three years in your pocket. Our son John also adopted the notebook; neither of us feels we can do without it.

* * *

McCook was piloting heaven to me because there were many different types of planes to fly and so much interesting experimental work was going on all the time. There were many questions to be answered about aeronautics, and I wanted to see what I could do to help answer them. If I saw a new plane, particularly if it was sleek and looked like it might have fine performance, I wanted to fly it right then. In the following months, I was given opportunities that someone else might not have had. My logbook shows that I flew the Bristol XB-1A, Lawrence-Sperry M-1 Messenger, Fokker TW-4, French Moraine-Saulnier 30 E.1 pursuit trainer, Fokker D.VIII, French Nieuport 27, Fokker CP4A observation plane, Junkers-Larsen JL-6 all-metal ground attack plane, and Lewis-Vought VE-t tandem trainer. As far as I was concerned, there was no better place in the world to be than McCook at that time. That assignment marked another important milestone in my life.

Colonel Bane laid down some rules to be followed by all test pilots that showed his concern for safety. They also reveal the unsophisticated beginning of test piloting as a profession. His Special Memorandum No. 27 said:

1. Test flights have priority over all other flying. All test flights will be under the direction of Major [R. W.] Schroeder. He will designate the pilot to fly the test, the time at which the test will be flown, and he will give all instructions covering the flying of the test. The Planes and Engines Maintenance Department will furnish the machine and the crew.

2. Pilot will inspect machine before taking it up.

3. Pilots will make sure that they thoroughly understand the operation of all controls, especially the motor controls, before taking off.

4. Be certain that the air pressure, the oil pressure, and the temperature are right before leaving the ground.

5. Taxi machines slowly, well away from the hangars before taking off in order not to blow a cloud of dust and dirt into the hangars.

6. Take full advantage of the wind and the size of the field in getting away.
7. Never leave the ground with a missing motor or if anything else is wrong.
8. Pilots will remain within gliding distance of McCook Field at all times. There is no excuse for a landing outside the field.
9. Whenever possible land into the wind.
10. No stunting will be done below 2,000 feet.
11. Report any trouble that may develop during flight or anything else that is wrong with motor or machine, no matter how slight, to the crew chief immediately upon landing.
12. Owing to the small number of machines available and the large number of officers desiring flights, no machines will be flown to Wilbur Wright Field or to other outside fields, except on important official business that cannot be handled otherwise. This rule will be strictly observed.
13. Certain parts of the field have recently been graded and seeded. These spots are soft in wet weather. In order not to cut up the field, avoid these spots when field is in a muddy condition.
14. Whenever the field is muddy and the wind is from the right direction, take off and land on the runway.
15. All flying, except important tests that cannot be delayed, will stop at 4:00 P.M. from Monday to Friday, and at 11:00 A.M. on Saturday, and all machines will be at the hangars by that time.
16. Except on test flights, flying will be limited to one hour per day.

I had many experiences at McCook that were memorable for one reason or another. One of them had to do with weather flying. Too often, a pilot got a good or bad reputation that wasn't entirely warranted. For instance, we were running a test on night lights between Dayton and Cleveland, a distance of about 160 miles. This was in support of the airmail because the lights we were experimenting with on the ground and on the airplanes were to be used on the airmail routes then being established across the country. We flew every night, regardless of weather.

I felt it was important to know just exactly what was on this route, so day in and day out, in my spare time, I would fly it at ground level. I got to know every silo, every barn, and every telephone line along that route. I don't believe any of the other pilots did that, so I was able to fly that trip when other pilots had difficulty in bad weather.

Then I extended this experiment to Middletown, and I could fly that route when other folks couldn't fly it—not because I was a better flyer but because I had flown it so much that I memorized everything and knew instantly where I was, even if I could see only a few feet ahead.

The point is that when you speak of people being daring or people being skillful flying in weather, their daring and their skill are to some considerable degree a result of the experience they have had. Yet Colonel Bane admonished me severely for doing this. He said, "You don't have enough sense to be a good airplane pilot because you have repeatedly flown in weather no one else would fly in." He never gave me the chance to explain to him how I could do it when others couldn't or wouldn't.

Another instance I recall happened shortly before John Macready took a Le Père with a supercharged Liberty engine up for a world's altitude record of 43,508 feet. Lieutenant Albert Stevens and I went up in the Le Père so he could take some aerial photographs. The objective was to fly over certain areas, the dimensions of which we knew precisely, measuring the altitude of the plane by taking photographs and, at the same time, reading the instruments in order to determine air density, pressure, and so on. The photographs were an additional check enabling one to make a better interpretation of the instrument readings. We were also to test a new liquid oxygen system and report on how it functioned.

We took off from McCook and flew west until we got to Richmond, Indiana, climbing steadily. At that point we hit what we had never experienced before—what we now call the jet stream. Although we were flying with full throttle, we backed up to Columbus, a distance of about 100 miles. We were both sucking on the oxygen and apparently I sucked a little harder than Steve did because at 38,000 feet—which was the highest we got—I noticed that Steve had slumped forward in his seat. The temperature was minus 60 degrees Fahrenheit. I reached over the fuselage to pat him on the back to see how he was. In reaching out to him, I passed out.

The airplane was very stable and it flew itself for about 30 minutes. The reason we knew this is that for a 30-minute period, Steve took no pictures and I made no notes on my notepad. The plane gradually drifted lower; we both came to and finished our mission. The photos Steve took that day were, at that time, the highest ever taken from an airplane.

During 1921 to 1923 at McCook, we were experimenting with all types of parachutes. Many of us still didn't wear them because it was considered "sissified" to put one on. Few of us wore them until Lieutenant Harold R. Harris, one of the top test pilots at McCook and head of the Flight Test Section, saved his life with one on October 20, 1922. He was assigned to stress test a Loening PW-2A equipped with experimental balanced ailerons. This type of test was usually done by dogfighting with another aircraft in order to put the stresses on a plane that might be expected in combat.

Manual 'chutes had been available for only about a year and many pilots erroneously thought that if they jumped in an emergency, they wouldn't have enough control of their arms to pull the ripcord. What was ironic was that Harris had almost been tempted to leave the 'chute on the ground because he had a new seat cushion fitted to it but the harness was then so tight that he couldn't buckle it easily. In disgust, he started to climb in the cockpit without it but then changed his mind and put it on.

After Harris had climbed to altitude, he rendezvoused with an MB-2 flown by Lieutenant Muir S. Fairchild, who had to test new elevators. They started to dogfight. After several minutes of trying to get on each other's tail, Harris suddenly felt the stick vibrate so uncontrollably he couldn't hold it. One of the new ailerons had failed because of excessive fluttering and was torn off. The wing fabric began to tear away. He unbuckled his safety belt, stood up, and was plucked out of the Loening like a cork out of a bottle. He had no trouble disentangling his arms and pulling the ripcord. He landed unhurt in a grape arbor in the backyard of a home on Troy Street in Dayton. He gathered his 'chute in his arms and hiked a half mile to the test pilot office. In his report he said:

> I knew it was impossible to regain control of the

airplane. There was only one thing to do to save my life. I had seen a good many airplane crashes. I had helped pick up a good many pilots who had been killed. In a collapse of the sort I was experiencing, if I stayed with the airplane, I would undoubtedly have been killed. The next thing for me to do was to leave the airplane and trust my parachute.

Harold Harris thus became the first man to save his life in an emergency jump through the use of a manually operated parachute. We all wore them from then on. A sign was posted in the pilots' room that read: DON'T FORGET YOUR PARACHUTE. IF YOU NEED IT AND HAVEN'T GOT IT, YOU'LL NEVER NEED IT AGAIN.

Many of my contemporaries called me a practical joker in those days and I guess they were right. We took advantage of every opportunity to "sell" aviation and accepted all invitations to put on a show at public functions. We always attempted to do something different from the usual that would be memorable. Major Ed Hoffman, our parachute test expert, used dummies filled with buckshot to simulate jumps from all types of aircraft. Lieutenant Lewis Meissner, a World War I ace, and I came up with an idea to shock the crowd at a picnic. We announced that there would be three live parachute jumps by men we called Hart, Schaffner, and Marx, which were really three of Hoffman's dummies.

We climbed to altitude and threw Hart out first. His 'chute, attached to a rope on the side of the plane, opened nicely and he floated serenely to earth while the crowd watched. We then threw Schaffner out and he also came down easily nearby. We then threw Marx out, but his 'chute didn't open and he came down like a brick. Buckshot splattered all over the ground.

Lieutenant (later Brigadier General) George W. Goddard, the "granddaddy" of aerial photography, recalled in his autobiography that "women fainted, strong men paled, and when they learned it was all a joke their anger soared and the two test pilots had to make themselves scarce." He was certainly right about that last part.

In order to keep my hand in, I flew as much as possible at air shows. I performed solo aerobatics and also did formation stunts. Lieutenant Alex Pearson and I flew aerobatics with our wings tied together; later, Lieutenant Wendell H. Brookley joined us for a three-plane formation. This was the "fun" part of being assigned to McCook. Stunting was our avocation; testing was our vocation.

On some test flights, we would send pilots up in pairs to conduct parallel tests. One day another pilot and I were designated to take two ships up to determine which was the faster diver. We climbed to 15,000 feet and simultaneously nosed over and dove vertically toward the field. I had what is called a flat pitch propeller—that is, the blades were set so the engine turned over faster. That of the other plane was set at a greater pitch. Naturally, he dove down much more rapidly than I did.

Whistling earthward, I heard a terrific crashing sound and realized something was wrong. It was as if the plane were breaking up at the nose; pieces flew past me. I tried to check my dive, only to find that the propeller had come off. The flying pieces ripping through the fabric of the wings were parts of the metal hub shield. Luckily, the field was directly below me and I made a landing without difficulty.

What was curious—and incredibly lucky—about this mishap was that one blade of the prop, four feet long and weighing 40 pounds, landed among three children playing on the sidewalk a mile and a half away. It actually smashed a hole in the concrete walk. Rebounding, it imbedded itself in a nearby porch. Not one of the children was touched!

The engineering course at McCook was not all flying. We had plenty of classroom instruction during which we were required to put our math to work solving aerodynamics problems. We were encouraged to seek ways to reduce drag, increase load-carrying capability, improve engine efficiency, and enhance airborne equipment. We worked in the shops with the civilian technicians and put our book knowledge to practical use by testing our solutions in the air. It was the beginning of what is today's sophisticated school for Air Force test pilots.

Around the time when I completed the Engineering School, word was passed down that the Air Service was going to attempt the first around-the-world flight, with four aircraft being built by the Douglas Aircraft Company. I wanted desperately to go but was turned down. John Macready and I then proposed to try for another aviation "first" that we thought was possible: a 2,408-mile hop from San Francisco to Honolulu, Hawaii. We planned to use a sister ship to the Fokker monoplane in which John and Oakley G. Kelly had flown nonstop from New York to San Diego in 1923. If the flight to Hawaii in the Fokker was disapproved, we were going to ask for a plane similar to the Douglas World Cruisers that were being outfitted for the around-the-world flight then scheduled for the spring and summer of 1924.

We planned to equip whichever plane we selected with pontoons and estimated that we could make the flight in 21 hours. If John couldn't go for some reason, I proposed to make the flight alone.

In May 1923, we applied to the War Department for approval. We were turned down. Later, John and I asked for permission to make a flight from Point Barrow, Alaska, across the North Pole to Spitzbergen. Our purpose, we said, was "to explore uncharted sections of polar areas." We sought backing from Henry Ford, who indicated he would lend us a Ford Trimotor if the War Department expressed any interest. Again, we were turned down.

Meanwhile, two of my friends—Captain Eddie Aldrin* and Lieutenant Samuel P. Mills—persuaded me to apply for one of six Army vacancies to attend the Massachusetts Institute of Technology to pursue a master's degree in aeronautical engineering. One of the requirements for entrance was a degree from a recognized university. If I had taken the 15 minutes to sign up for that final year at the University of California and then gone into uniform, the university would have granted me the degree as it had other seniors during the frantic days after the United States entered World War I.

Fortunately for me, Eddie and Sam felt I had the aptitude, interest, and background. On their own they contacted the University of California and persuaded the authorities to grant me the bachelor of arts degree based on my previous studies there and my grades at McCook. I have always been grateful for their initiative and encouragement. I kept the December 1922 telegram from the university that stated I had been awarded the bachelor's degree. I was promptly accepted at MIT to pursue the course toward a master's degree, was placed on detached service from McCook Field for a period of two years, and enrolled for the fall session of 1923.

---

*Ed Aldrin's son, "Buzz" Aldrin, became an astronaut and was the second man to step on the moon.

* * *

In September 1923, Joe, young Jim, John, and I packed up and moved to Massachusetts. Joe found an apartment in a three-family house in Dorchester close to Cambridge. Monthly rent was $65; my pay was $160 a month. I was still assigned to McCook Field to get my flying time. This gave me access to all the aircraft there for any test work I wanted to do in connection with my studies for the master's degree. It was an unprecedented opportunity and I intended to take full advantage of it.

While Joe and the boys settled in, I buckled down to an unaccustomed regimen of sitting in class for hours on end, doing lab work, and trying to sort out the significance and possible application of what I was learning. I was impatient and always felt pressed for time because I wanted to complete all the master's degree requirements, including the thesis, in two semesters.

Joe became my "secretary." After I put in a day of note taking in class, she would type my notes neatly on a special typewriter she had rented that had mathematical symbols. She mastered this quickly and became as familiar with the course materials as I was. We would often study together far into the night. She would ask me questions, and her technique served to refresh my memory and reinforce what I had heard that day. She often put into words the thoughts I was trying to express. She seemed to know how I wanted to say something when the words wouldn't come.

I will not admit to any academic brilliance. Although I passed all the courses, the grades I received were largely due to Joe's flawless typing of my notes and papers and her suggestions as we discussed the theories and lectures I had endured in class. How she also managed with two very small, high-spirited boys to herd around all day, I'll never know.

In addition to heavy courses in mathematics and science, a thesis was required. One of the mysteries of flight in those days was how much stress an airplane could take before it fell apart. Structural research became all-important as aircraft progressed from wooden structures to metal and from biplane to monoplane designs. Unfortunately, we didn't know exactly what the failure limits of each military aircraft were when it was subjected to in-flight maneuvering accelerations.

Previously, all measurements of how much an aircraft could take before it self-destructed had been done on the ground by placing sandbags on the wings and horizontal stabilizers until they broke from the weight. When aircraft were manufactured, a safety factor number was designated, based on the weight of the aircraft and the weights placed on the wings. For example, if an airplane had a safety factor of eight, it meant that it would take weights eight times the weight of the aircraft before failure would occur. I didn't think that was necessarily true.

The many in-flight breakups, such as the one that Harold Harris had experienced, made the basic question seem like an ideal subject for my master's thesis. It was approved and I set about working out a test program with McCook for aircraft like the Fokker PW-7 fighter, DH-4, and JNS-1 that were made available to me for test purposes. Primary focus would be on the PW-7. It had a broad-span upper wing and a smaller lower one, both internally braced, with a steel tube, fabric-covered fuselage. Powered by a Curtiss D-12 liquid-cooled, in-line engine, it was longitudinally unstable and very slow.

What was needed was a good recording accelerometer to measure changes in velocity, and one was sent to me by E. H. Norton of the National Advisory Committee for Aeronautics (NACA). I tested this first in the DH-4 and a JN-4. After conferring with technicians at McCook, I came up with a test program for the PW-7 that included loops at various airspeeds, single and multiple barrel rolls, snap rolls, half rolls, spins, tight spirals, Immelmann turns, chandelles, inverted flight, dive pullouts at various speeds and weights, and flying in rough air.

I began the test program in March 1924. It was a test not only of the plane's ability to withstand the punishment I was going to give it but a test of my own ability to withstand the g-forces I intended to produce. I had flown a Fokker monoplane on one occasion and the download on the tail and the lower longerons caused the tail to break apart. Although I got it on the ground and didn't have to jump, I felt sure the download on that airplane hadn't been enough to make the tail come off.

From this experience, I thought I knew when an airplane would break up and when it wouldn't. So what I was trying to do for the thesis was impose increasing loads on the PW-7 to see what would happen. I carried an accelerometer in the cockpit so I would know exactly what acceleration there was. If there was an acceleration of four times gravity and the aircraft weighed 20,000 pounds, I was putting a load of 80,000 pounds on it.

My logbook shows just under 100 hours flying time running

through my test program. What made the whole effort worthwhile was that I found out exactly what the Fokker could withstand because it nearly came apart during a dive at 200 miles per hour when the accelerometer registered a 7.8 g-load, or nearly eight times the weight of the aircraft. The design value given by the manufacturer was 8.5 g's. The rear wooden structure of the upper wing cracked—thus refuting the commonly held belief that the leading edges of the wings would fail and shear backward toward the tail. The wing had actually broken at the connecting points at the fuselage. When the load was taken off by throttling back, it settled back into its normal position. Many pilots used to tighten the bracing wires running from the leading edges of the wings. I concluded that this practice actually encouraged wing failure.

After landing, I found that the upper wing, which was veneer covered and internally braced, had started to fail. The veneer had pulled apart from the trailing edge to the rear spar on the bottom of the wing, and from the trailing edge to a point just in back of the rear spar on top. This failure was in direct tension and was caused by the wing tips moving forward because of antidrag.

I was glad I wore my parachute that day. I almost needed it.

When the tests were completed, I wrote my thesis, "Wing Loads as Determined by the Accelerometer." From that I developed a paper for NACA entitled "Report No. 203—Accelerations in Flight," which was translated into a dozen other languages for circulation abroad. No one considered it significant in the United States, but in Italy, Germany, France, and England it was regarded as worthwhile. I had a deluge of mail from all over the world asking for more information.

While they seem very elementary today, my conclusions at the time appeared to be a contribution to aeronautical knowledge:

> The accelerations in suddenly pulling out of a dive are greater than those due to any maneuver started at the same speed.
>
> The accelerations obtained in suddenly pulling out of a dive with a modern high-speed pursuit airplane equipped with well-balanced elevators are shown to

> be within 3 or 4 percent of the theoretically possible accelerations. . . .
>
> Accelerations due to flying the airplane in average "rough air" do not exceed 2.5 g.
>
> The maximum acceleration which a pilot can withstand depends upon the length of time the acceleration is continued. It is shown that the pilot experiences no difficulty under instantaneous accelerations as high as 7.8 g, but that under accelerations in excess of 4.5 g, continued for several seconds, the pilot quickly loses his faculties. While this is disconcerting to the pilot, it is not necessarily dangerous for one in good physical condition unless continued for a period of 10 to 12 seconds.

The last finding was particularly interesting to pilots because we didn't know much about "blackout" in those days. For the benefit of other pilots, I wrote the following:

> From the results of these tests it is apparent that serious physical disorders do not result from extremely high accelerations of very short duration, but that accelerations of 4.5 g, continued for any length of time, result in a complete loss of faculties. This loss of faculties is due to the fact that the blood is driven from the head, thus depriving the brain tissues of the necessary oxygen. To the pilot it seemed sight was the only faculty that was lost. The flight surgeons at McCook Field are of the opinion that sight is the last faculty to be lost under these conditions, even though the pilot may be under the impression that he retains all others.
>
> This opinion is based on the observations of men undergoing the rebreather test. The acceleration which an individual can withstand for any length of time depends upon his blood pressure, the person with the higher blood pressure being able to withstand the higher acceleration. Upon the condition of the heart depends the ability of the individual to recover quickly from the effect of prolonged acceleration. If the heart is in good condition, there is no danger in undergoing

> such a strain unless the acceleration is continued for a period in excess of 10 or 12 seconds, after which death will result. The same is true of the rebreather test; unconsciousness will result from the deprivation of oxygen and death will result if this is continued for the same length of time.*

Despite the seriousness of my studies, it wasn't all work at MIT. I relieved the academic tension by flying whenever I could find the time. An old friend from earlier days, Captain Bob Brown, was commanding officer of an Air Service reserve unit at Boston Airport. The airport had been built on reclaimed land that juts into Boston Harbor.

Bob let me fly any type of aircraft he had available, but they were mostly DHs and Jennys used by the reservists to maintain their flying proficiency. Jack Allard, my buddy from Rockwell days, had gone back to the civilian world but had retained his reserve status and often went flying with me in another plane.

We liked to play follow-the-leader and would take turns leading. If Jack was leading and flew under a bridge, I followed. If I led and decided to do some low-level aerobatics down the main street of some small town, he would follow. Jack was leading one day in a Jenny and when we broke off for a landing on the Boston Airport runway approaching from the bay, he decided he would just skim the water, pull back at the last second to raise up to the runway level, and touch down on the end of the runway. I was following closely and was going to land beside him. Just before reaching the lip of the runway, he pulled back, but the Jenny didn't respond promptly enough. His wheels hit the edge of the runway and sheared off. The Jenny skidded on its nose and came to rest with an ear-shattering crunch down the runway. I had been concentrating on copying what he was doing and did exactly the same thing. I veered off slightly, my gear hit the lip, the wheels were wrenched off, and

---

*In 1929, again belatedly, I received a second Distinguished Flying Cross for this work, accomplished five years before. It was unexpected and I do not know who prompted either of these awards. The citation for the 1924 tests noted that I had performed a series of acceleration tests, described the tests I had conducted, and noted that "through them scientific data of great and permanent importance to the Air Corps was obtained."

I went skidding down the runway and stopped beside Jack. The two Jennys sat side by side on their bellies with their props in splinters, a pitiful sight indeed.

Neither of us was hurt. I jumped out and rushed to Jack, who sat in the cockpit dumbfounded. He couldn't believe our two planes were sitting there in exactly the same sorrowful condition. I knew he hadn't planned it that way so I kidded him unmercifully. "Didn't think I'd follow you, did you, Jack?" I said.

Jack was beside himself. "I didn't mean to do this," he said over and over. "How are we going to explain this to Bob Brown?"

Just then, Bob roared up in his staff car. We dreaded the thought of having to make out a long report explaining why two of Uncle Sam's venerable Jennys were damaged beyond repair. Both of us were prepared to apologize profusely and withstand the tongue-lashing we deserved, but it wasn't forthcoming. Instead of acting as a commanding officer should and giving us verbal hell, Bob asked if we were all right and then broke out into a big smile.

"You two have done me a great favor," he said, to our surprise. "I've been trying to get rid of these old clunkers for months, but the Army wouldn't replace them with newer planes until these were unflyable. I'd say you two have made them definitely unflyable."

My logbook shows that in the summer of 1924 I made a 6,765-mile flight in a Liberty-powered DH-4 from Dayton to San Diego with a number of stops before returning to the life of an academician. I don't recall what the purpose of the flight was, but it could have been that I wanted to take a long break from studying.

By the time my master's program was nearing completion I had begun to like the academic atmosphere. It gave me a sense of personal accomplishment, especially when I received some kudos for the thesis. Since I had been given official permission to attend MIT for two years and had finished the master's program in one, I wanted to strive for a doctorate and continue trying to make some lasting contribution to aeronautics through research for the required dissertation. I had been ordered to McCook on temporary duty "in connection with studies to be pursued coming year at MIT" and used the time to formulate a plan for the dissertation. The application was approved and the Doolittles remained in Dorchester for a second year.

Joe was relieved not to have to pack up and move to whatever job at whatever post the Army might have planned for me if I had not been given approval to go after the doctorate. To her eternal credit she never complained about the hardship of her multiple roles as mother, wife, advisor, counselor, cook, hostess, house cleaner, laundress, and typist. But I knew that the extra duties she assumed because of my academic requirements were a strain that would have been difficult enough without two lively siblings demanding their rights all day. I couldn't have gone on to satisfy the scholarly demands of a doctorate without her continuing support.

The most stressful and often defeating requirement for any candidate for a doctorate is the dissertation, which is always supposed to be an original contribution to knowledge. This meant that I had to choose a unique question and come up with an acceptable answer based on scholarly investigation.

For my research topic, I chose to investigate the wind velocity gradient and its effect on flying characteristics. There was a belief among pilots in those days that they could sense the direction of the wind, even when they couldn't see the ground at night or were on top of an overcast or in the clouds. This belief was associated with the general belief that good pilots could always fly "by the seat of their pants."

There had also long been an uncertainty in the minds of pilots regarding the effect of the wind on the flying qualities of an airplane. Some pilots claimed that it is much easier to turn into the wind than fly with it. This group thought they could tell wind direction by the feel of the ship in a turn, even in a dense cloud that precluded obtaining their relative motion from a stationary object.

Other pilots maintained that, regardless of the wind velocity or the proximity of the ground, there is no difference in the feel of the plane when turning into the wind and when turning with it. They claimed that any apparent difference was wholly due to the psychological effect on the pilot, resulting from the difference in ground speed in the two cases. If there was any difference in the ship's performance, from a time or altitude standpoint, it was because the pilot handled the controls differently. In other words, if the pilot was blindfolded he could not tell the wind direction when turning—a turn into the wind would be identical with a turn made with the wind.

This disagreement among experienced pilots seemed like a worthwhile subject for research. I suggested as a topic for the dissertation "The Effect of the Wind Velocity Gradient on Airplane Performance." It was approved.

I began the research by formally querying seven of the most experienced pilots I could find: Captain Lowell Smith; Lieutenants Leigh Wade, Erik Nelson, John Macready, Harold R. Harris, and Russell Maughan; and along with this military group, Art Smith, a civilian airmail pilot flying for the Post Office Department. The first three named had been on the 1924 around-the-world flight. Their answers to my questionnaire confirmed my contention that highly experienced pilots could not agree on the effect of wind on their aircraft. None of them agreed completely on any of the answers to my questions.

To carry out a study of the wind velocity gradient at various altitudes and the effect of the wind on aircraft at sea or at ground level, I borrowed a TS-1 pontoon plane from the Navy. The tests I conducted were not as precise as I wanted because I had nothing better than my eyes to gauge how high I was above the water surface when I put a heavy load on the plane. That was a basic weakness in my research. I could tell when I was very close to the water because every so often I would touch it. I could tell the difference between six inches and a foot and a half, but at 5 to 10 feet, I could never be sure whether I was at 5, 8, or 12 feet.

In addition to the TS-1 seaplane tests, I made test flights in Curtiss JN-6H, de Havilland DH-4, and TG-4 aircraft. I flew a total of 178 flying hours on 292 separate flights.

When the test results were analyzed, I concluded as follows:

> Both theory and experiment indicate that neither wind velocity nor wind velocity gradient exert an influence on airplane performance in straight level flight. In spite of this, numerous cases may be cited where planes have been known to settle when flying with a strong wind and to climb when flying into it. A possible explanation is that when a pilot is flying with a strong tail wind, his ground speed is increased by the amount of the wind velocity; his angle of climb, with respect to the ground, decreased. The natural tendency is to pull the nose up to increase the climb. This ten-

dency is even greater if there is an obstacle to clear and when altitude must be obtained in as short a time as possible.

If the plane is lightly loaded, no trouble is experienced, but if heavily loaded and already flying near its most efficient climbing angle, the increase in angle of attack causes a decreased rate of climb and, if the rate was already low, causes settling. Instead of nosing over and picking up some speed, the average pilot, experiencing a panicky feeling, continues to pull up and hope. An inexperienced pilot often spins into the ground at this point. If the plane can be brought around into the wind, the apparent increase in the rate of climb resulting from the lower ground speed makes the plane appear to be climbing much better.

I submitted a draft of the dissertation to my advisors and it was rejected. At first they said it wasn't erudite enough. This was disappointing and when I pressed for more information, was told that it needed more mathematical calculations to fit the actual flight results. I reworked the draft with plenty of mathematical formulas to satisfy the professors but was unhappy with the outcome. I wanted the paper to be read and understood by the average pilot, not by an aeronautical engineer. I personally profited by the information and the experience in later test work, but received only one letter after the dissertation was finished and released to the academic community. The fellow who read it offered no criticism or comments. He condemned it by what he didn't say, and since that time I have never heard one word about it.

As far as I'm concerned, the master's thesis was far more significant. I felt at the time that they wanted a doctoral dissertation to be so abstract that few people could understand it. That's a condemnation of the system, which is not a fair statement, but that's what I thought at the time.

Regardless of my personal feelings, I was awarded the doctor of science degree in aeronautical sciences in June 1925, one of the first such degrees to be awarded in the United States. I have always felt they should have awarded the degree to Joe for having to type, retype, and put up with my frustrations as I struggled to master the secrets of abstract writing.

Much relieved that Joe and I had been able finally to satisfy my mentors, we packed up our household goods, corraled the boys, and returned to Dayton. It was now time to put my newly won knowledge to practical use.

NOTE

1. From "Report of the Operation of the First Provisional Air Brigade in Naval Ordnance Tests," August 29, 1921.

Chapter 5

By 1925, aviation in America was very much on the public mind. The number of air races held in the good flying months proliferated; racing pilots became role models for the kids of America. For a pilot, there was a strong desire to participate, to compete, to set any kind of record or establish an aviation "first."

I was no exception, and when Joe, the boys, and I settled down again at McCook Field, I wanted to see if my aeronautical education could be put to use to help solve some problems that plagued aviation and threatened to stymie its growth. That may sound idealistic, but it's the way I felt deep down. Of course, being competitive by nature, I thoroughly enjoyed stunting, racing, and trying to outdo my contemporaries in the air. Winning and excelling was always my goal.

But there were problems for the military pilot. The military establishment was very small. It was difficult to get government funds to improve aircraft, although racing did have the effect of providing an incentive, a stimulus, to the development of aircraft and engines. The competition between the Army and Navy for funds was intense, as was resistance to increasing military expenditures in the postwar era. On the other hand, public interest in aviation was strong, and the services were encouraged to allow their pilots to compete in all kinds of newsworthy air racing events.

One of the first Air Service competitors in open competition air races immediately after World War I was Major Rudolph W. "Shorty" Schroeder, a test pilot at McCook until he resigned in late 1920. He represented the Air Service at the Gordon Bennett Airplane Race in France in September 1920, but lost out when the Packard engine of his Verville VCP-R overheated. On Thanksgiving Day, 1920, Lieutenant Corliss C. Moseley flew the same plane with a larger engine in the first Pulitzer Race held at Mitchel Field, in New York. He won at a relatively low speed of 156.54 miles per hour. He had wanted to break the world speed record, which was then 192 miles per hour.

There was no money in the military aviation kitty to fund an entry in the second Pulitzer Race, held in Omaha in 1921; however, Lieutenant John Macready was permitted to fly a Thomas-Morse MB-6 in the race because it had not yet been accepted by the Army and no government funds were used for maintenance or fuel. He placed third.

Although money was still scarce for racing in 1922, Army and Navy pilots and planes entered the National Air Races, which were held at Selfridge Field, in Michigan, that year. Beginning at that time, Army pilots were permitted to accept cash prizes, certainly a welcome incentive to compete, considering the low military pay scales of that era.

One of the races was restricted to Navy and Marine pilots competing for the Curtiss Marine Flying Trophy. Another race awarded the Detroit News Aerial Mail Trophy to "inspire performance in the postal service." Lieutenant Erik H. Nelson, later to become one of the around-the-world flyers, won $1,200 flying a Martin transport in that one. Lieutenant Harold R. Harris won the Aviation Country Club Trophy flying a DH-4; Lieutenant Bob Worthington, my old buddy from Ream Field days, placed second in a Fokker T-2; and Lieutenant Theodore J. Koenig won the Liberty Engine Builders' Trophy in a Le Père. But the Pulitzer was the main event. The Navy had asked various aircraft manufacturers to design new pursuit planes, and four were entered. The Army entered ten aircraft of various descriptions. The Army's Curtiss R-6 racers came in first and second: Lieutenant Russell L. Maughan won with a speed of 205.8 miles per hour, and Lieutenant Lester J. Maitland was second with a speed of 198.8 miles per hour. The Navy took third and fourth places; the Army came in fifth and sixth.

Encouraged by these results, Army and Navy pilots were

caught up in the racing frenzy. In 1923, Navy pilots captured the first four places in the Pulitzer; the Army entered older planes and again placed fifth and sixth.

There was no Schneider Marine Cup race held in 1924 because the Italian, French, and English entries had to withdraw for various reasons. Instead, the Flying Club of Baltimore, the sponsors, arranged a sort of aerial regatta with only Navy pilots participating. A number of closed-course speed records were set by Navy lieutenants George T. Cuddihy and Ralph A. Ofstie.

The Navy did not compete in the Pulitzer Race held in Dayton in 1924. This left only Army pilots to compete against each other. General Mason M. Patrick, chief of the Air Service, wanted to spread the glory around and directed that other pilots be given the opportunity to race. The Pulitzer was won by Lieutenant Harry H. Mills flying a Verville-Sperry R-3; Lieutenant Wendell H. Brookley was second in a Curtiss R-6; Lieutenant Rex K. Stoner placed third in a Curtiss PW-8A. Lieutenant Alex Pearson, flying a Curtiss R-8 borrowed from the Navy, was killed that day when the wings peeled off during a steep dive to gain speed for the start. He was the chap whose plane I had flown out of Mexico in 1921 after he had gotten lost while trying to get in position for a coast-to-coast record attempt.

Perhaps the death of Pearson had an effect on General Patrick. In March 1925 he appointed a committee, headed by Dexter S. Kimball, dean of Cornell University's College of Engineering, to study the Engineering Division at McCook, and one of their recommendations was that the Air Service should give up racing. The consensus of the committee was that although racing had been good for attracting public attention to aeronautics, the Air Service could now "stand on its own real worth and dignity." No longer should government funds be used for racing because the work of the Engineering Division could be upset by the preparations necessary for the various events each year.

But the report was too late to stop the preparations for the 1925 Pulitzer and Schneider Cup races. Army and Navy pilots wanted to recapture the world speed record of 278.8 miles per hour, held by Florentin Bonnet of France. The previous world record of 266 miles per hour had been set by Navy lieutenant Alford J. "Al" Williams a month after winning the 1923 Pulitzer Race.

In an unusual cooperative arrangement during those days of intense competition for funds between the Army and Navy, the two services were permitted to expend $250,000 each to purchase four R3C-1 racing planes from Curtiss. That doesn't sound like much money today, but that half million dollars bought four brand-new racing planes and all of the design and engineering that was required to bring them into being. They were very clean biplanes with "I" struts and wing skin radiators and were designed to fly on wheels or pontoons. They had Curtiss 12-cylinder V-type engines that developed over 400 horsepower, and Reed aluminum propellers. They flew well and were comfortably stable and easily controllable.

Of the four, one of them was tested to destruction in static tests. Of the other three, two were given to the Navy and one to the Army. Fortunately, the Army got the fastest one of the three. Each service entered one aircraft in the last Pulitzer Race, which was held at Mitchel Field in early October 1925.

The Pulitzer was held in conjunction with the New York Air Races organization, and we Army pilots were encouraged to make the public aware that the races were scheduled. We did our best. We performed aerobatics all over downtown New York City. It was a rare thrill to fly down the city streets and look up at the tall buildings. It was also interesting to do it inverted. We also "fought" balloons and did low aerobatics wherever there was enough of a crowd to be impressed. If there was anyone in the city or its environs who didn't know there was going to be an air show at Mitchel Field, he or she had to be deaf and blind.

The races were to be followed by "a giant aerial maneuver," as the papers called it, in which the Air Service was "to repel an enemy fleet approaching the Atlantic Coast, on the supposition that the Navy has been bottled up on the Pacific Coast by the blowing up of the Panama Canal."

All of this, of course, was to keep public attention focused on aviation and what the airplane could do in time of war, which, as Billy Mitchell was preaching so vociferously, was bound to come.

I was designated to be the Army's alternate pilot for the 1925 Pulitzer Race; Lieutenant Cyrus Bettis was the principal pilot for the Army's lone R3C, fitted with wheels and powered by the 600-horsepower Curtiss V-1400 engine. In accordance with our orders we traveled from McCook to Mitchel Field "to witness certain phases of the construction work [on these airplanes] and for necessary training and test flights."

The race was held on October 12, 1925. Cy won it easily.

His speed was officially set at 248.975 miles per hour. Al Williams placed second in his R3C with a speed of 241.695 miles per hour; and Army lieutenant Leo H. Dawson, flying a Curtiss P-1 Hawk, was third at 169.9 miles per hour.

I watched carefully as they rounded the pylons and thought they could be shaved closer and with sharper banks. I didn't tell anyone, but I intended to try out my theory during the Schneider competition.

The Schneider Cup race, to be held at Baltimore two weeks after the Pulitzer, was reserved for seaplanes only. The race had been first run in 1913 and was sponsored by Jacques P. Schneider, pilot son of a wealthy French industrialist. It was considered the most important international air race at the time and received much press coverage in the flying nations of the world.

Since I had been the alternate pilot for the Pulitzer, I was to be the principal pilot for the Schneider competition. Cy was then the substitute for me if I couldn't fly for any reason. I had never flown a seaplane before; it behooved me to learn how.

I had previously reported in August to Anacostia Naval Air Station, in Washington, D.C., for training for the Schneider, which was scheduled for October 26, 1925. Its rules were unusual in that two preliminary tests had to be passed to "establish the seaworthiness of the machine." First was the "navigability" test, followed by the "watertightness" test, described in the official rules as follows:

> Each machine must complete a course of from 5 to 10 nautical miles over the sea, or in a creek, gulf, estuary, or bay, as decided by the Test Committee.
>
> For this test, the pilot must taxi over the starting line, then rise and continue the course, during which he must taxi the machine over two distances of one-half a nautical mile at a minimum speed of 12 knots, the limits of each of these distances being indicated by two buoys.
>
> The remainder of the course will be covered in flight.
>
> The pilot must, however, alight again before completing the course and taxi over the finishing line.
>
> After having taxied over the finishing line, the machine must be moored immediately to a buoy allot-

> ted beforehand, where it must remain afloat for six hours without anyone on board. Any machine leaving its moorings during this period will be disqualified.

What this meant was that I had to prove I could taxi, take off, land, and moor a seaplane, an exercise I had never performed before. It was no problem for the Navy pilots, since they had that kind of training before they won their wings. As it turned out, it wasn't difficult to learn; it just took a little practice.

There were two Italian and three British entries in the Schneider, plus the two Navy and one Army R3Cs. The British brought two impressive-looking Gloster-Napier III biplane racers and a Supermarine S.4 midwing monoplane. The Italians had two heavy Macchi M.33 flying boats, which were powered by Curtiss D-12 engines.

During the qualification tests before the speed runs, British pilot Henry C. Biard, flying the Supermarine S.4, had wing flutter problems and crashed into Chesapeake Bay. Biard suffered a broken wrist and was rescued from the icy water by speedboats. The S.4 was a washout.

The British lost one of the Gloster-Napiers when one of the struts bent and the pontoon structure collapsed so that it couldn't pass the navigability and watertightness tests. This left the second Gloster-Napier as the lone British entry.

The first of the two Macchis had engine trouble and was eliminated because the rules stated that all engines had to be sealed at the time of the navigability trials and no repairs or adjustments could be made. This left Giovanni de Briganti, one of the Italians; two U.S. Navy pilots—Lieutenants Cuddihy and Ofstie; and me.

The race committee had laid out a triangular course that was 31.07 miles in length, with pylons at three positions in Chesapeake Bay off Bay Shore Park, Maryland. Each plane had to fly around the course seven times for a total of about 217.5 miles, or 350 kilometers, to satisfy the race rules. An article in *Aviation* magazine described the scene:

> The weather was ideal for the race. The surface of the water off Bay Shore when the starting gun was fired at 2:30 P.M. was choppy. The sun shone brightly and glistened on the shining planes.

> A squadron of Navy planes flew in formation over the heads of the spectators. Lt. Frank H. Conant, alternate pilot for the Schneider Cup Race, thrilled the thousands with spectacular stunts in the pursuit plane used in the trip to Baltimore by Lt. Cyrus Bettis, winner of the Pulitzer Air Race at Mitchel Field a few weeks ago. The TC-5, a United States Army airship from Aberdeen, soared over Bay Shore like a majestic silver fish. . . .
>
> Lt. Cyrus Bettis roamed through the crowd. He was in flying clothes, ready at the instant to replace Lt. Doolittle in an emergency. In fact, for several days Bettis had practically played the part of mechanic to Doolittle. It was remarked by many of the visitors that these two lone Air Service representatives surrounded by Navy pilots, mechanics and ground crews, were more observed by their businesslike modest bearing than any of the other flyers.

There were many VIPs in the audience at Bay Shore Park. Generals, admirals, and army and navy attachés from all over the world were there; aircraft and engine manufacturers attended to see what information and tips they could pick up that would help improve their products. Orville Wright was also in the audience, and, much to my liking, Joe had been able to have the boys taken care of at McCook and had arrived by train.

I was first in line for takeoff over the speed course. The water was just choppy enough to enable the pontoons to break the surface tension, yet not so choppy as to throw excessive spray and slow down the takeoff. The wind came from the right direction and I was airborne. My technique was simple: climb slowly under full power before approaching the pylon, make a tight diving turn, and then level out until approaching the next pylon. It was in the steeply banked diving turns where I thought I could gain a critical speed advantage. Other pilots hadn't done this at the Pulitzer and, as far as I know, didn't do it during this race.

British captain Hubert Broad was next off, followed by Lieutenants Cuddihy and Ofstie. De Briganti trailed in the Macchi. I had no trouble staying in the lead, and it quickly became a U.S. Navy versus U.S. Army contest. Cuddihy crept up on me briefly, but Ofstie and the other two were never a threat.

Ofstie developed engine trouble during the sixth lap and dropped out; then Cuddihy's engine ran out of oil and burst into flames on the final lap. He managed to land not far from Ofstie and put the fire out with a hand extinguisher. My time over the course was fastest and set a new record for seaplanes of 232.573 miles per hour. Captain Broad was second at 199.169 miles per hour; and de Briganti came in third at 168.444 miles per hour. De Briganti, however, was not through flying. After he crossed the finish line, he continued out into the bay to look for Ofstie and Cuddihy, whom he had seen down in the water. However, both pilots had already been taken in tow; de Briganti then ran out of gas and had to be towed himself. His act of courtesy and concern for his brother pilots earned him an ovation when he returned to shore.

Naturally, I was very pleased to win that race for the Army. It wasn't easy for the Navy to accept the fact that an Army pilot, inexperienced in water flying, had his name on that prestigious trophy. They weren't very elated, especially when they saw a *New York Times* editorial the next day:

> The insatiate United States Army won the race for the world's premier seaplane trophy, the Schneider Marine Cup, on Chesapeake Bay Monday, in spite of rooting by Father Neptune for the naval entries. As the Army holds nearly all the world records for flying in the *Aircraft Year Book,* it must have been a grievous sight to sailors when Lieutenant James H. Doolittle, U.S.A., putting pontoons on his landplane, romped away with the cup which Lieutenant David Rittenhouse of the Navy brought over from England two years ago. But that was not the worst of it. The naval Lieutenants Cuddihy and Ofstie had engine trouble, dropped out of the race and were "towed to safety." The Army men never seem to take tows in Neptune's realm.

Much as I enjoyed the ribbing the Navy was getting in the press, I wasn't completely satisfied with the speed I had coaxed out of the R3C. It had not yet fully demonstrated what it could do as far as I was concerned. I asked for observers from the National Aeronautics Association and the Fédération Aéronautique Internationale to be present for a world record attempt the next day. Their sanction was required in order to claim any national or world aviation record. I flew the required three-kilometer course and was able to squeeze 245.713 miles per hour out of the R3C, for a new world seaplane record.

There wasn't any big secret to getting more speed out of the R3C. Anyone else could have done it. Before the record flight, I changed the pitch of the propeller slightly to give it a higher number of revolutions per minute at full throttle. We didn't have controllable pitch props yet, and it seemed to me the propeller was always set for an average cruising speed, not full-throttle speed. It seemed to work. My speculation was based on something that Lieutenant Muir S. "Santy" Fairchild had ventured several years before. He tried to devise a way to reverse the blade angles on a propeller so it could act as a brake and thus reduce landing distance. Unfortunately, the blades reversed on takeoff and he ended up in the river at McCook. That stopped experimentation with reversible propellers for a long time.

There was an interesting aftermath to the 1925 Schneider race. Within hours after the race, Secretary of War Dwight F. Davis sent me a telegram:

> YOUR SPLENDID ACCOMPLISHMENT IN WINNING THE JACQUES SCHNEIDER ONCE MORE PROVES AMERICA'S POSITION AMONG THE NATIONS OF THE WORLD. THE VICTORY WAS WON THROUGH YOUR SUPERIOR KNOWLEDGE OF AERONAUTICS. IT IS ESPECIALLY PLEASING BECAUSE OF THE WORTH OF YOUR COMPETITORS. THE WAR DEPARTMENT IS PROUD OF YOU. I AM CERTAIN THE ENTIRE PERSONNEL OF THE AMERICAN ARMY DESIRES TO ADD ITS CONGRATULATIONS.

General Mason M. Patrick, the top Air Service general, had been present at Bay Shore Park and sent a letter of commendation. He said:

> The great speed which your entry displayed in contrast to sister airplanes was ample proof of the careful preparation and painstaking effort displayed in preparing it for the race, and the efficient manner in which it was handled. This was one of the most able demonstrations I have ever witnessed, one of which I am extremely proud.

> I was also particularly pleased with the conscientious manner in which you applied yourself to preparing for the Pulitzer and Jacques Schneider contests, and of the assistance which you rendered Lt. Bettis.

I was grateful for these expressions of appreciation and the favorable coverage of the race in the country's newspapers. I am still a little surprised that winning the race engendered so much national attention. It just shows how high the public interest in aviation was during those years we now refer to as the golden age of aviation.

When Joe and I returned to McCook Field, we were given a memorable reception by townspeople and our friends on the base. Shortly after our arrival John Macready and Roy Barksdale advised that they had a lifeboat mounted on a truck bed and an admiral's uniform, complete with fore and aft hat. They further advised that all arrangements had been completed; I was to be the seafaring man, and the landgoing boat was outside the door. I demurred. They broke out several short lengths of rope and advised me that I could go gracefully and graciously—or else. Knowing that this group of thugs wouldn't hesitate to tie me up, I thereupon made the best of a bad situation. I was driven through the city sitting in the boat. On each side was a large sign that read: Admiral James H. Doolittle.

That year, while a good one for Army aviation, was not so good for General Billy Mitchell. After the 1921 tests against the naval vessels, he had become more zealous and outspoken. He remained as assistant chief of the Air Service when General Charles T. Menoher was replaced by General Patrick in late 1921. I'm sure he expected to get the top job, but he had made too many people angry. Patrick gave Billy a number of assignments that seemed designed to keep him away from Washington and, hopefully, out of the news for long periods.

In 1923, Mitchell was put in charge of more bombing tests of obsolete warships, and the press saw this as a reopening of the controversy between the Army and Navy. As a result of the Washington Conference, on the limitation of naval armaments, held in 1921, a number of warships were to be scrapped. The appropriations for fiscal year 1924 permitted the expenditure of funds for the Air Service to carry out tests against the battleships

USS *New Jersey* and USS *Virginia,* similar to the ones Mitchell had conducted in 1921. Both ships were badly damaged and sunk.

"There can be no doubt that those who saw the *Virginia* and *New Jersey* sent to the bottom of the sea so quickly after vital hits were scored," *The New York Times* said, "are deeply impressed with the necessity for command of the air in modern naval engagements." Mitchell proclaimed the tests a complete success and told the press, "The problem of the destruction of seacraft by Air Forces has been solved and is finished."

He promptly went on an extended honeymoon and inspection trip with his second wife to Hawaii, the Philippines, and the Far East.

When he returned from Japan in 1924, Mitchell wrote an extensive report of his observations and declared that a war between the United States and Japan was inevitable. His theory was that the military strength of the United States was so great, in Japanese eyes, that Japan could win a war only by using the most advanced methods possible. Those methods would include the extensive use of aircraft.

General Mitchell, during the period 1922–1924, had made a number of contributions to Air Service doctrine. He had prepared a "bombardment manual" and expanded on his concept of how the attack by the Japanese would be launched against America and its island possessions. General Patrick put some of Mitchell's defensive ideas into effect without fanfare.

When Billy had solidified his thinking, he began a vigorous campaign to gain public acceptance of his views about air power. He wanted to reach the politicians and went public with his writings and preachings. He became a zealot and, like all zealots, eventually lost sight of the objective.

Mitchell raised enough national interest so that he was invited to testify before Congress and thereby managed to antagonize President Calvin Coolidge, Secretary of War John W. Weeks, the Army General Staff, and the top admirals of the Navy. Although General Patrick supported Mitchell in the beginning, political pressure was such that even he eventually had to give up. In March 1925, Secretary Weeks refused to recommend reappointment of Mitchell as assistant chief of the Air Service when his four-year tour was up the following month. Mitchell reverted to his permanent rank of colonel from temporary brigadier general and was transferred from Washington to Fort Sam

Houston, in San Antonio, Texas, as air officer for the VIII Corps Area.

The transfer and loss of rank did not prevent Mitchell from continuing his crusade. He published a book entitled *Winged Defense*, which was a collection of his previously published articles. When a Navy plane was lost on a flight between San Francisco and Hawaii in August 1925, and the Navy dirigible *Shenandoah* crashed in Ohio in September, Mitchell's reaction was immediate. From his post of "exile," he charged that both accidents were "the direct result of the incompetency, criminal negligence and almost treasonable administration of the national defense by the Navy and War Departments." These two accidents and others that had occurred over the previous three or four years were unpardonable as far as he was concerned. He said the actions of the service in regard to aviation had been "so disgusting in the last few years as to make any self-respecting person ashamed of the cloth he wears."

To make the accusations more stinging, he added that "all aviation policies, schemes and systems are dictated by the non-flying officers of the Army and Navy, who know practically nothing about it. The lives of the airmen are being used merely as pawns in their hands."

President Coolidge, not noted as an aviation enthusiast, appointed a board of military men and civilians in March 1925, headed by Dwight W. Morrow, a New York banker, to study a national policy for aviation. Mitchell was called to testify. He did so mostly by reading from *Winged Defense*, which did not help his case at all. He advocated a complete reorganization of the country's defense structure, calling for a separate Air Force, equal with the Army and Navy, under a Department of National Defense.

Shortly thereafter, when Mitchell continued to insist on being heard and got more vitriolic in his public statements, President Coolidge himself preferred court-martial charges against Mitchell under the 96th Article of War. The judges, all Army generals, were to determine whether or not Mitchell was guilty of conduct prejudicial to "good order and military discipline [and] . . . conduct of a nature to bring discredit upon the military service."

On October 26, two days after I flew in the Schneider race, Mitchell's trial began. It ended on December 17 with a verdict of guilty. His sentence: five years' suspension from active duty without pay or allowances. President Coolidge, in reviewing the sentence, changed it to five years' suspension at half pay. After thinking it over, Mitchell resigned on February 1, 1926.

The Morrow Board, meanwhile, concluded that the Army and Navy should retain control over their own aviation branches; that a Department of National Defense was unnecessary and too costly; and that a separate service could not be justified.

Those of us at the bottom of the rank totem pole did not hear much about the Morrow Board's recommendations. We were saddened to learn of the outcome of Mitchell's court-martial, but understood why it was necessary. Although many of the young pilots agreed with his concepts of air power, most of us thought he had gone overboard in his criticisms. Like all zealots, he was intolerant of any view other than his own. I think he would have been successful if he had been more flexible in the application of his ideas.

The Chinese have two woodcuts that express my thinking about Billy Mitchell. One is of a stand of bamboo. A strong breeze comes by and the bamboo is blown flat. When the wind dies down, the bamboo comes back up. The other woodcut is of an oak tree. A strong wind comes by and the oak is uprooted and lost.

I am inclined to think that if there had been a little more bamboo and a little less oak in Billy Mitchell, he would have been more effective. Mitchell died in 1936 still preaching the gospel of air power. He would be completely vindicated five years later. A surprise attack on Hawaii would come about precisely as he had said it would—by air on a quiet Sunday morning. Eleven years after his death, there would be an autonomous Air Force equal with the Army and Navy under a Department of Defense.

After I went back to work at McCook, I was made chief of the Flight Test Section—one of the finest jobs in the Air Service as far as I was concerned. I not only was supervisor of all flight test work but could choose the tests I wanted to fly. It was the opportunity I had hoped for—the chance to be both pilot and engineer. I could alternate between drawing board and cockpit, recommend innovations, draw them up, and then try them out.

One of those innovations was a new type of rudder trim tab that could be controlled from the cockpit. Billy Mitchell had seen one in Europe and suggested we try out the idea on our aircraft. In those days, a plane would often get out of trim—wouldn't fly hands off for even a few seconds without skidding into a turn. It was like driving a car with the front wheels out of alignment. The only way to correct a rudder out of trim was for the pilot to get on the ground, bend a small piece of metal on the rudder a bit, then try it again in flight. If this trim tab could be controlled from the cockpit, an out-of-trim condition could be corrected immediately.

I test flew a trim tab we worked out in the shops because it was a new idea and deserved a fair evaluation. Would it work or would it tear the rudder off at high speeds when the tab was moved to extreme positions?

One day, Lieutenant James T. Hutchinson and I were trying out the new tab with a planned series of tests, flying aircraft at varying speeds and maneuvers. I performed stalls, spins, inverted flight, Immelmanns, and everything else I could think of, followed by steep dives and pullouts. During a dive at high speed, the rudder vibrated uncontrollably and the rudder attachment wires snapped. I had no control over the rudder; it just flapped in the breeze. I throttled back and did a few stalls. At slow speeds, the plane was controllable to a certain extent. Flying without control of a rudder wasn't difficult at altitude but I didn't know if I could land safely. The plane could be turned with the ailerons alone by putting one wing down and the other up but it made for sloppy and imprecise maneuvering at low speeds. I asked Hutch if he wanted to jump.

"What about you, Jim?" he yelled back.

I told him I thought I could bring it down, but wanted to give him the option.

"Then I'll stay with you," he said.

I got it down all right and this in-flight emergency answered a question I had puzzled about for some time. Now I knew that it was possible to bring a plane in without much rudder control provided the vertical stabilizer was intact; you didn't have to bail out. An aviation myth had been shattered. This incident was typical of the kinds of things test pilots encountered in those trial-and-error days.

Early in 1926, I was given an unprecedented opportunity. Curtiss Aeroplane Exporting Co. president Clarence W. Webster and Curtiss-Wright president C. M. Keyes asked the Army to put me on extended leave and allow me to go to South America to demonstrate their pride and joy: the Curtiss P-1 Hawk fighter with the Curtiss D-12 engine. The plane was one of my all-time favorites. They wanted to sell it to foreign governments and they wanted me to be their flying salesman. My job would be to demonstrate its capabilities in flight and prove that it was the finest pursuit airplane in the world. I spoke a little Spanish and my name had gotten into the news frequently, so they thought I could help the Curtiss cause. I would be gone about five months; Joe would stay at McCook with the youngsters. I didn't relish that long an absence from the family, but I thought it might be good experience for whatever might follow careerwise. Joe agreed.

They didn't have to ask me twice. It was a dream assignment. I would get paid for stunting and there would be no rules about how low I could get or what maneuvers I could perform.

The Army had no objection and put me on extended leave without pay. I left for Santiago, Chile, in late April 1926 with Boyd Sherman, an outstanding Curtiss mechanic. We left New York with the crated P-1 in the hold, sailed leisurely through the Panama Canal, made several stops in Peru, and disembarked at Valparaiso, Chile. The P-1 was shipped to El Bosque, the military airport outside of Santiago, the capital, where Boyd and I would assemble it.

When we arrived at Santiago, we discovered that we weren't going to have the skies to ourselves. The British, Italians, and Germans were there, too, all trying to show that their products, not ours, should be purchased for the Chilean military inventory. I looked the planes over but wasn't worried about the Italian or British models. It was the German Dornier flown by Karl A. von Schoenebeck that was the greatest threat. Von Schoenebeck had flown with the famous Richthofen Squadron during World War I and was said to have been an ace. Demonstrations were scheduled for late June at El Bosque.

On May 23, 1926, the Chilean pilots held a cocktail party in the officers' club in Santiago. I was introduced to a delightful, powerful drink called a pisco sour, a specialty of the fun-loving Chileans. During the course of the evening, the name of actor Douglas Fairbanks came up. Silent motion pictures had come to South America, and his legendary balcony-leaping, sword-playing, swashbuckling motion picture roles had captured the imaginations of the Latins. Fairbanks was a common topic of cocktail party conversation, especially when Americans were present.

I'm not exactly conversant in South American Spanish but I quickly sensed the admiration they had for the actor. Feeling devilish, I said that Mr. Fairbanks wasn't so unusual. All American kids could do those things. When my poor Spanish was finally understood, my Chilean pilot friends raised their eyebrows in doubt and wanted proof.

With the utmost confidence, inspired by the pisco sours, I upended into a handstand and "walked" a few paces. The pilots clapped and yelled "Bravo!" and "Olé!" I did a couple of flips to more applause. This was encouraging. One of them said that he had seen Fairbanks do a handstand on a window ledge. That seemed reasonable, so I went to an open window, crawled out onto a two-foot ledge, and did a two-hand stand first, then a one-hand stand. The applause was stimulating, so I tried one more stunt. Grasping the inside of the ledge with one hand, I extended my legs and body parallel with the courtyard one story below. This isn't difficult. Just requires a little practice and knowledge of body leverage.

As I held there for a few seconds, I felt the sandstone ledge crumble and pull away. With practically all of my body hanging in midair it was inevitable: the law of gravity took over. I plunged about 15 feet into the courtyard. I landed on my feet and felt sharp pains in both ankles. I knew I was in trouble.

My hosts were concerned and whisked me to a hospital where the doctors confirmed from X rays that I had cracks in both ankles. One was a simple fracture; the other was a complicated series of small breaks and more serious than the other. In reading the X rays, they got them reversed. They put the casts on the wrong ankles; the fractures were therefore being improperly set. Of course, I didn't know this.

I was in considerable discomfort, so a few days later they put on new casts—one up to just below the knee and the other about a half foot above. They told me to stay in bed for several days and said I would have to stay off my feet for about six weeks.

Embarrassed at my stupidity, I thought about what my buddies at McCook Field and elsewhere would say when they heard what I had done. I'm sure many were jealous and wished they had been invited to demonstrate airplanes in a foreign country. I would be laughed at wherever I showed my face.

Joe would have done what she usually did when I was a bad boy—pick up a spoon, put it to one eye as if viewing me under a microscope, and stare at me without saying a word. This gesture was always effective to remind me she didn't approve of some action I had undertaken.

And I was doubly embarrassed when I thought about what the folks at Curtiss would say when they learned their "salesman" had become totally incapacitated and there was no one else present who could demonstrate their prize product.

Embarrassment overcame pain. There was no way I was going to stay in that hospital while my competitors were touting their wares at El Bosque. On the morning of the ninth day of incarceration, I had Boyd come to the hospital with a hacksaw blade and cut off the long cast to below the knee. I told him I was going to fly the demonstration, casts or no casts, and to get the P-1 ready for some practice aerobatics. He made clips and attached them to my flying boots so my feet wouldn't slip off the rudder pedals. The boots fitted nicely over the casts.

On June 24, 1926, I was driven to the airport, hobbled on crutches to the plane, and had to be lifted into the cockpit. I took off and intended to go through a practice stunt routine to see if I would have any difficulty. Snap rolls require more-than-normal rudder pressure, so I decided that if I could do them, I could do any other stunt. I did a series of snap rolls to the right, which required the right leg, strongest of the two, to do the work. The cast on my right foot cracked from the strain. I didn't get it replaced. The next day I practiced again, this time doing all my practice stunts to the left. Then the cast on the left foot split. After I landed, I was so uncomfortable that I couldn't even hobble around on the crutches.

I told Boyd that both casts had to be reengineered and strengthened around the ankles. He took me to the hospital, but the doctors refused to have anything further to do with the "crazy Yankee" and wouldn't let me back in.

Boyd helped me get the casts off and found an old German who made prostheses. He fashioned new heavier plaster casts with something you can't find today—corset stays. These were flexible metal pieces about a foot long, 3/8 inch wide, and 1/36 inch thick that were put in women's corsets in those days to give them an hourglass shape. They proved to be quite satisfactory. However, I couldn't get around on the ground without crutches.

On the day of the official demonstrations, I was taken to the field and lifted into the cockpit. The president of Chile was there, along with his cabinet and a large contingent of Chilean army and navy officers. Von Schoenebeck was already putting the Dornier through his aerobatic routine and got much applause from the crowd. It was clear to me that he needed some competition, so I took off and climbed to meet him. I did a few stunts and then made a pursuit pass at him, which he sensed immediately was a challenge. He tried to get on my tail and get me off his but was unsuccessful. The Dornier with its 260-horsepower engine was no match for my Hawk with its 400 horses. The Hawk was obviously more maneuverable and much faster. I made some close passes at him, zoomed overhead to show the superior speed of the Hawk, and then got in position for another pass.

Von Schoenebeck suddenly broke off the contest and landed. As I watched him descend I noticed the fabric was tearing loose from the Dornier's upper wing. I went through the rest of my aerobatic routine and then made a low pass over the field inverted. That seemed to please the audience; they applauded vigorously when they saw me being lifted out of the cockpit with my casts.

A group of Chilean pilots gathered around von Schoenebeck's Dornier and some thought I had deliberately brushed my wheels against the Dornier's upper wing during one of my close passes. Not so. I convinced them that I wouldn't deliberately damage another aircraft in a peacetime demonstration. On close inspection it was plainly evident that the fabric had failed, not a good selling point for a military aircraft designed for combat.

There wasn't any doubt in the minds of the Chilean pilots about which plane was better. We sold several Hawks that day.

I made more demonstration flights in Chile, then flew the Hawk to Bolivia on August 18–19, 1926, according to our planned itinerary. The Hawk had an extra gas tank installed, which gave it about seven hours' range. With my crutches stowed in the machine-gun mounts, I set a record of 11 hours, 25 minutes flight time between Santiago and La Paz, with one stop for fuel at Antofagasta, Chile. I landed at the world's highest airport (13,000 feet), overlooking La Paz, the capital. I stayed in the Strangers Club there, but was not received very cordially. A group of about a thousand demonstrators shouting anti-American and anti-Chilean slogans gathered outside shortly after I arrived: "Down with the gringos! Down with Chile! Long live Bolivia!"

Landlocked, tin-rich Bolivia was having a border dispute

with Chile. Apparently, they suspected me of being a spy for Chile, and I was told later that I was soundly denounced in the Bolivian parliament. The mob apparently wanted to hang me and I wondered how fast I could run on crutches.

Bolivian soldiers were called in to disperse them, and the mob went on down the street and smashed up the Chilean legation. I did make one demonstration flight but the Bolivians weren't buying, possibly fearing an uprising if they should acquire the same type of plane that the Chileans had just committed themselves to purchase. The Bolivian secretary of war quietly ventured to me that if he were an American pilot on crutches and couldn't move very fast and had a fast airplane waiting at the airport, he would get in it and fly it back to where it came from. I took his suggestion and departed on August 22. I must have been in a hurry because I made the return trip in 9 hours, 55 minutes flying time, with fuel stops at Oruro, Bolivia, and again at Antofagasta, thus beating my own record time between the two capitals.

Next stop was Argentina, which required flying over the Andes and coaxing the Hawk up to 18,000 feet. My logbook shows I made a 6-hour, 45-minute, one-stop flight from Santiago to Buenos Aires on September 3, 1926. This was said to be a record. The Andes had been flown before, but several pilots had died trying. I didn't wear a parachute because I had my boots clipped to the rudder pedals and there was no way I could unclip them in time, slip the casts out of the boots, and bail out if I had a problem. Besides, I didn't relish landing in a parachute with two broken ankles. I would have to ride the Hawk down and hope for the best. After landing I was told that I was the first North American to fly an aircraft of any type across the Andes. As far as I know, I am the only man ever to fly over them with two broken ankles, a rather dubious honor.

The Argentinians liked the Hawk and bought several for their air force. I left the airplane there, sailed for New York, and immediately checked into McCook and requested sick leave. My ankles were not healing properly and continued to give me much discomfort, so I was transferred to Walter Reed General Hospital in Washington, D.C., on October 5, 1926. The doctors were shocked at what they saw on the X rays. It had been more than four months since I had my fall and the ankles were healing abnormally. However, because the healing process was so far along, they decided not to refracture the bones. They put on new casts and I was sentenced to spend the next few months relatively immobile.

When Joe learned that I was going to remain in Washington for a while, she and the boys moved to an apartment near the hospital. I spent the first month in bed, then another month hobbling around on crutches and taking leg therapy. I had to wear corrective shoes for a while. This torment went on until I was finally released on April 5, 1927.

Although my body was inactive, my mind wasn't. During a discussion with other pilots at the hospital one day, the subject of outside loops came up. The inside loop, with the pilot sitting on the inside of the circle, can be performed easily in almost any airplane. Centrifugal force holds the pilot in his seat. There is usually no danger of blackout unless the pilot pulls up sharply enough to put excessive g's on himself.

But an outside loop would put the pilot on the outside and thus place great strain on the pilot as well as the plane. Would the centrifugal force send the blood to his head and damage his brain? Would the blood vessels burst? Would a pilot's internal organs be so scrambled up that it might kill him? Would he "red out" and lose consciousness from the excessive pressure in his head as he tried to push the plane around on the last half of the loop? Would the airplane hold up under the strain? When I got back on flying status I intended to find answers to these questions.

I returned to McCook after a leave of absence and secretly set about practicing the first half of an outside loop in a P-1 Hawk. Pushing down at high speed, then around and under, was difficult at first, but I gradually got used to the unpleasant sensation, which reminded me of being upside down for prolonged periods on a horizontal bar during gymnastic exercises. It was the second half of the loop that was difficult because you needed sufficient speed left at the bottom of the loop to push the plane on around and come out on top. You also needed sufficient presence of mind to keep on pushing the stick forward to keep the nose going on around. I tried a number of times and finally did it or thought I did. The Hawk held up and Doolittle held up without any lasting discomfort. I wanted to be sure I wasn't kidding myself that I had flown a true outside loop.

One day, I asked Lieutenant James T. Hutchinson, a friend of mine, to watch a patch of sky as I climbed to about 10,000 feet. I pushed over and around successfully and when I landed, the chap was beside himself. "You did an outside loop, Jim!" he said excitedly. He wanted to spread the word but I shushed him up. It was a sloppy loop and I thought I could do better.

On May 25, 1927, four days after Charles A. "Slim" Lindbergh made his widely acclaimed flight across the Atlantic, I passed the word to six of my brother test pilots that I wanted them to witness something. They did and confirmed to all who would listen that I had indeed performed an outside loop. They were so happy for me that they passed the word to the newspapers. I was once more on the front pages, as "the first man in history to perform an outside loop." When a reporter asked me how I had done it, I replied, facetiously, "Don't know. Just thought of it on the spur of the moment." I guess that wisecrack helped propagate my growing public reputation as a daredevil pilot who would try anything.

The newspapers reported that my eyes were bloodshot and that I had suffered a lung hemorrhage. My eyes *were* bloodshot, but I suffered no other ill effects. It was most uncomfortable, but as far as I was concerned, what had been proven was that the development of military aircraft had reached the point where the pilot could rely on the strength of his plane to perform such a high-stress maneuver.

I did perform outside loops at air shows for a while, but in a few weeks, the word came down from General Patrick in Washington that Army pilots were prohibited from doing outside loops because most Army aircraft weren't stressed for such a maneuver and they were considered dangerous to both plane and pilot. The restriction didn't say anything about not doing the first half of an outside loop, so I continued to do that with a half roll at the bottom to level flight—sort of an inverted Immelmann. If I had enough altitude, I would continue inverted and do a half inside loop, which amounted to a large S in the sky. No one ever said I couldn't do that.

Army and Navy pilots continued to participate in air races around the country and I got to know my rivals fairly well. Lieutenant Al Williams was the Navy's outstanding racing and aerobatic pilot, and Lieutenant Lawson H. "Sandy" Sanderson competed for the honor of the Marine Corps. We frequently gave stunting exhibitions at the same place. We always tried to do the best we could, each hoping he could outdo the other two. We always did the routine stunts and then tried to think up some new ones that nobody else had done. You always got a little extra accolade if you could do all of the routine stunts and then do something that was unusual or was flown for the first time.

One experience that I remember as rather embarrassing took place after the 1927 Spokane Air Races where Sanderson and I put on our usual show. We were then invited a few days later to Portland, Oregon, to perform there. When we arrived, the papers had played up our rivalry as if it were a battle between us to see who could do the most hair-raising stunts.

When we were preparing to put on our respective shows, the ceiling was only about 1,000 feet, which is too low for aerobatics. So Sandy and I got together and agreed, "Let's both put on our best show but not make it a competition because we don't want to jeopardize our own lives or the lives of anyone on the ground." We thought we made this clear to the show sponsors and the reporters before we took off. However, when the papers came out that afternoon, it was reported that in the competition between Sanderson and Doolittle, Doolittle had won. I was very, very embarrassed because of our agreement. I guess this made a better story, but that didn't lessen the embarrassment I felt. Reporting like that has always made me a little wary of the press. When truth goes out the window, we all lose something.

In January 1928, the Curtiss-Wright Corporation asked the Army to let me make a second tour of South America. Permission was granted, and on this trip, I was accompanied by Clarence W. Webster, president of the Curtiss Aeroplane Exporting Co., and two mechanics, named Van Wagner and Todhunter. We were joined at Lima, Peru, by a civilian company pilot, William H. McMullen. We took two aircraft—the faithful P-1 Hawk and a larger, two-place Curtiss O-1 observation plane. Although the O-1 was to be demonstrated for possible sale, we also used it to take up important people for sight-seeing rides as a public relations gesture.

When I left Joe at McCook, she said, "Be careful, Doolittle." I replied that I always took care of myself in airplanes. She responded, "Oh, I don't mean in airplanes. I mean in officers' clubs where they serve pisco sours."

After we arrived at Lima, our first debarkation point, I had another one of my unforgettable embarrassing moments. Shortly after we got the planes uncrated, we met two very unhappy lady tourists who had missed their ship. The ship's next stop was at a port about 300 miles north. In a weak moment, I offered to fly them there if they didn't mind being crowded into the backseat of the O-1. They didn't, so I did. I landed on the beach as near to the port as I could. As I was helping them out of the plane, a large yellow mongrel dog ran up to me snarling, grabbed my pant leg, and bit me. It hurt. He then relieved himself against my leg. Satisfied, he turned on his heels and left. I wondered if I was going to get the same kind of reception during the rest of the tour.

Bolivia was our next stop, and much to my surprise, I was welcomed grandly this time and did not have to flee the scene as a suspected spy. Curtiss offered both the P-1 and O-1 on pontoons as options this time, hoping to make sales to the naval air arms of the Latin American countries. Although Bolivia has no opening to the sea, they do have Lake Titicaca, the highest large lake in the world. The Curtiss people thought the Bolivians might like to buy planes that could operate from it, even if they didn't have a navy. I took the P-1 to the lake where it was put on floats and taxied out for takeoff. The water was glass-smooth and there was no wind. I tried to get the Hawk unstuck from the lake's surface friction but couldn't raise it off the water. I taxied around in circles to make waves, rocked the plane back and forth, and tried lifting one pontoon off at a time as I attempted a takeoff run. Then I gave up. You can't demonstrate a plane that doesn't fly. As far as I know, Bolivia still doesn't have an airplane for its Lake Titicaca navy.

During our stay in Bolivia, we met an American named Charles Wallen, manager of a gold mine about a hundred miles away at a place called Tipuani. It had taken him nine days to journey to La Paz, mostly by burro, to get medical supplies for some native workers who had been playing a game they called *probando la suerte* ("trying your luck") when things got dull. They were called the "bad Indians" because they had a nasty habit of permanently eliminating tax collectors who occasionally ventured into their territory to collect for the government.

Wallen explained the game this way: about forty men would stand around in a circle, arms outstretched with hands barely touching. One of them would take a quarter stick of dynamite, attach a long fuse, light it, and pass it quickly to the next man. It would be passed from hand to hand until the inevitable happened. The last man to handle it was considered *sin suerte* ("without luck"). Wallen said the mine's doctor was keeping about a dozen of the Indians alive from the last game solely on native whiskey and quinine. He had to get medical supplies back as soon as possible.

I volunteered to fly him there, knowing there was no place to land at Tipuani. Wallen and the medicines were loaded in the O-1 and we flew about 75 miles to the site. We located a clearing near the mine and as I dove the plane at the open space to be sure the supplies would land in it, Wallen dropped the bundles over the side. Within an hour we were back in La Paz. Wallen was so impressed that I learned later he had a strip cut out of the jungle and acquired a plane of his own to fly back and forth with supplies. A one-hour round trip was a lot better than eighteen days. Several years after that, he bought a fleet of small planes and started his own regional airline.

Before we left Bolivia, I made several trips from La Paz over the Andes to the headwaters of the Amazon. These, as far as I know, were the first such flights ever made. On one occasion, I volunteered to fly supplies to a mountain mine and was assured that a field would be prepared for my landing—that Indians were already at work on it. When I arrived I found they had spiked the entire field with rows of trees in the belief that these would be needed to catch and stop the plane! I had to throw the supplies over the side without landing.

For this and various other short flights, I received the National Order of the Condor of the Andes from the Bolivian president on March 22, 1928, the highest honor they could bestow on a foreigner. According to U.S. law, I had to send the medal and the certificate to the Department of State. However, the honor was much appreciated. What a difference from my first visit!

Chile was our next stop, and when we arrived we met some British officers, some of whom were pilots. They watched as McMullen and I put the P-1 and O-1 through their paces on wheels and then on floats, the latter for the Chilean navy. One of them, Commander Bruce Jones, expressed interest in the O-1 on floats. He said he had flown one before and asked if he could have "a go" at it again.

For all I knew, maybe Jones had influence back home and would like it well enough to recommend Britain buy a few for the Royal Air Force. It would be a nice coup if I could sell the British on a Curtiss airplane while in Chile!

I took Jones at his word and he settled into the front seat. I got in back in the observer's seat, which had no controls. He turned the engine over and started to taxi out into the bay. Although he had a little difficulty, I attributed it to the choppy water. However, when he thought he was lined up for takeoff and gave it full throttle, I knew we were in trouble. He overcontrolled with the rudders and we sashayed back and forth sickeningly until I thought I was going to throw up in the rear seat. As we neared flying speed, still rocking back and forth, the wing floats nosed into the waves. Each time they dug in, we slowed perceptibly. In the rear seat without controls, I was helpless. I knew a crash was coming and braced for it. The left wing float caught a wave, the plane swerved, and the left wing and pontoon dug into the water. The plane plunged with throttle wide open nose-first into the bay and cartwheeled onto its back.

Jones was catapulted headfirst out of his seat and landed clear of the plane. He had not fastened his safety belt. Upside down, I unbuckled mine and swam clear to look for Jones. He came up a few feet away but seemed dazed. His fellow officers onshore dispatched a boat as soon as they saw the crash, but it didn't look like it was going to get there in time. Neither one of us had life preservers. I swam to Jones, held his head out of the water, and pulled him to a pontoon that had been ripped off and was floating nearby. Jones was a big man and wasn't helping himself. Since both of us had our flying clothes on, I had a hard time hanging on to the float. The float had been punctured and started to sink. Just as I thought I couldn't hold on to him any longer, the boat arrived and picked us up. The O-1 was never seen again.

Jones was properly grateful for my saving his hide, but I was furious at myself for letting him talk me into allowing him to take the controls when I had no proof he had any previous experience with seaplanes. Once again, I had embarrassed myself badly, but this time also lost an airplane through my stupidity. I was not happy to tell Mr. Webster what had happened. I was sure this was the last demo trip he would ever ask me to take.

Despite this setback, I put on many subsequent demo flights with the P-1, and then it was time to take it to Buenos Aires again. I made one stop at Mackenna, Argentina, but still flew the distance of 750 miles in 5 hours, 45 minutes, to break the previous record by almost half an hour. I demonstrated the P-1 for the Argentine army at El Palomar and then for the navy at Bahía Blanca, 500 miles south, in May 1928. I made a side trip to Montevideo, Uruguay, to put on a show for their army and navy. On all of these trips, I took passengers up in a borrowed plane for publicity purposes.

On the over-jungle flights, it appeared the only way out of the jungle if I had a forced landing was to follow a stream, so I carried a machete and rope to make a raft. I also carried a set of mechanic's tools to make minor repairs.

My schedule called for me to fly demos at Buenos Aires and at Asunción, Paraguay. The flight from Buenos Aires to Asunción was made on July 1, 1928, followed by a 4-hour, 30-minute trip next day to Rio de Janeiro. The route took me over the Mato Grosso area of Brazil and I found out later that I was the first to pilot a plane over that vast expanse of solid, uncharted jungle. It would have been a rough place to try to land a plane, with trees probably about 200 feet high. Even if you got down uninjured, it would be almost impossible to claw your way to civilization. The only signs of life I saw were flocks of bright green parrots. I crossed many rivers that weren't on the primitive maps I had. All I could do was fly a compass course and hope for the best.

I finally saw a railroad and, as pilots have done before and since, dropped down to look at the sign on the side of a station to tell me where I was. The sign read "Mictorio." I climbed back up but couldn't find any such town on the map. I followed the railroad to another station, dropped down again, and saw a sign that said the same thing: "Mictorio." Puzzled that two towns would have the same name, I ignored the railroad and continued on my planned compass course until I eventually found Rio. Later I found out that *mictorio* was the Portuguese word for "public urinal."

Much to my surprise, no one at Rio was expecting me. My wire announcing my arrival that afternoon was not delivered until two days after I landed there.

I returned to the States on the *Western World* and arrived in New York on August 15, 1928. I was now 31 years old and still a first lieutenant. A captaincy was too far off to contemplate in what was now called the Army Air Corps. During the trip on the boat, I had a long time to think about what I was going to do with the rest of my life. The chance to fly more demonstrations for Curtiss had been a welcome respite and another interesting experience, but I wondered about the future. The boys were growing fast, and now Joe and I had to support our mothers. That was quite a financial burden, even for a first lieutenant on flying pay.

Should I get out of uniform? If I did, what would I do? Who would want me? If I got a nonflying civilian job, would I miss flying and regret my decision to resign my regular commission? What kind of flying jobs were available where I could meld my flying experience and academic credentials and make a better living for us?

I returned to Joe, the boys, and McCook Field with these questions uppermost in my mind. While Joe and I were wrestling with the answers, the opportunity of a lifetime came my way. I was contacted by Harry F. Guggenheim, son of a multimillionaire, whose father had provided $2.5 million for an organization he called the Daniel Guggenheim Fund for the Promotion of Aeronautics. Harry asked if I would be interested in participating in experiments in fog flying. What happened next turned out to be one of the most important developments in the history of aviation.

CHAPTER 6

Aviation had come a long way by 1928. The world speed record was now 249.342 miles per hour; the altitude record was 38,474 feet; the aircraft endurance record was 51 hours, 11 minutes. There had been many improvements in engines, propellers, aircraft structures, radios, fuels, and instrumentation. Flying was becoming safer because the military services and the aircraft industry realized that, in order for the potential of the airplane to be fulfilled, the risks had to be reduced. The Air Commerce Act of 1928 became the law of the land for aviation and helped make safety the watchword for commercial aviation. Pilot licenses were required, and I was issued transport license number 18.

Post Office Department airmail pilots had pioneered the airways that now crisscrossed the country. They had been replaced by commercial airlines that carried the mail on schedule and had begun to carry passengers. And they did it day and night when the weather was satisfactory.

That was the catch: "when the weather was satisfactory." Most flying in the early 1920s was "contact" flying. When a pilot was unable to see the ground and therefore had no horizon, he often became disoriented. His senses were unreliable and contradicted what his instruments told him. He felt he was turning in one direction when he was actually turning the opposite way. He was confused and tended to believe his senses rather than the instruments. Many accidents where weather was a factor were dismissed simply as "pilot error," without further explanation. This was true, but the error was too often the pilots' refusal to believe their instruments instead of their senses. They suffered from vertigo, which Malcolm W. Cagle, a veteran naval pilot, said was "a flight hazard since the first aviator flew into a cloud, happily discovered that he didn't get wet, and then stalled and spun out the bottom." Weather was aviation's worst enemy.

When I was an instructor at Rockwell, I remember telling our students not to rely on the instruments. We believed then that they had to get the "feel" of the ships they flew—whatever that meant. As a result, aviation could not progress unless planes could fly safely day or night in almost any kind of weather.

There had been some progress in solving the problem of what we called "flying blind." The turn-and-bank indicator had been invented by Elmer A. Sperry, Sr., during World War I, which told us when we were turning right or left. If we entered clouds, we could tell in an elementary way that we were flying straight and level by referring to this instrument and our airspeed indicator.

On a test flight in 1921, Army lieutenant J. Parker van Zandt flew a de Havilland DH-4B equipped with a turn-and-bank indicator through heavy fog and clouds from Moundsville, West Virginia, to Washington, D.C. It took him an hour and a half, but he made it. Two Martin bombers that were escorting had to turn back; neither had the indicator.

For the 1922 cross-country flight from Pablo Beach to San Diego, I had a turn-and-bank indicator installed. It proved itself to me on the first leg when I ran into solid overcast and then severe thunderstorms. For a while the lightning flashes were almost constant and, in the otherwise black night, so intense as to light up the ground clearly for a considerable area. Some flashes were so close that their familiar ozone odor could be detected, but although it seemed that one could reach out and touch them, none struck the plane.

The air was extremely turbulent and the airplane, despite its excellent stability characteristics, was violently thrown about its axis as well as up and down. I held it on a relatively even keel only with great concentration and effort. After the lightning died away, the turbulence appeared to intensify, and there was about an hour in the jet-black darkness when no ground reference point could be seen. It would have been quite impossible to maintain proper attitude and course without the blessed turn-and-bank indicator. Although I had been flying almost five years "by the seat of my pants" and considered that I had achieved some skill at it, this particular flight made me a firm believer in proper instrumentation for bad-weather flying. I'm not sure I could have made the night portion of the flight without it.

Slim Lindbergh told of his first experience with instruments in his classic book *The Spirit of St. Louis*. He was caught in a snowstorm while flying the mail one night, and his description vividly explains what this veteran mail pilot was thinking at the time:

> Instrument flying was new. I'd never flown blind, except for a few minutes at a time in high clouds. Could I keep my plane under control? If I turned to the instruments, how could I make contact with the ground again? Night had closed in behind me as well as ahead, and there was a low ceiling over both Springfield and St. Louis. Besides, even if I found a hole in the clouds, even if I saw the lights of a village farther on, how could I tell where I was, how could I locate the Chicago airfield—unless the ceiling there is much higher? "A good pilot doesn't depend on his instruments." I was taught that when I learned to fly. . . .
>
> Suddenly, the vague blur of treetops rushing past at 80 miles an hour, a hundred feet below, jumped up in a higher mass—a hillside? I didn't wait to find out. I pulled the stick back, gave up the ground, and turned to my instruments—untrusted needles, rising, falling, leaning right and left.
>
> At a thousand feet, my DH was out of control—skidding, and losing altitude. . . . Finally I got the DH headed straight and the wings leveled out. I thought I was getting my plane in hand. The altimeter went up to 1,500 feet. But then—she whipped! Loose controls—laboring engine—trembling wings—the final snap as the nose dropped. I shoved the stick forward, but it was too late. While I was concentrating on turn and bank, I'd let my airspeed get too low, and the wings stalled.

> . . . By then I'd learned that above all else it was essential to keep the turn indicator centered and the airspeed needle high. But in recovering I pulled the stick back too far and held it back too long. The DH whipped again, this time at only 1,200 feet. But I made my recovery a little quicker. I'd decided to jump the moment the wings trembled in the stall, if my plane started to whip a third time. But I regained control after the second whip, and climbed slowly, and taught myself to fly by instruments that night.[1]

Slim was lucky. Thousands of aircraft accidents before and since have occurred because pilots either couldn't fly by instruments or didn't believe them. No human can fly for long without visual reference either to the ground or to instruments.

By the end of the 1920s, flying was still an unreliable means of transportation because of this human deficiency. Too many pilots had contempt for the weather and thought it was a blight on their reputations if they refused to make an attempt to reach their destination. Too often, pilots would fly into steadily worsening conditions and encounter situations where they couldn't turn back and had only two choices left: bail out (if they wore a parachute) or try to luck it through. Those who didn't bail out, more often than not, ended their careers in a pile of wreckage because their "seat of the pants" instincts were not good enough to overcome the fact that they could not possibly tell when they were in straight and level flight with no outside reference to guide them.

Some pilots said the problem could never be solved—that flying would depend on men with the skill of flying by instinct. Others said that planes were not meant to fly on schedule and that if people wanted to meet schedules, they should take a train. Besides, planes were getting to be so fast that they could almost always overcome the time differential by waiting out the weather and then racing the distance to the next stop when the weather cleared.

I thought these views were foolish. Progress was being made in the design of aircraft flight and navigation instruments and in radio communication. If these sciences could be merged, I thought flying in weather could be mastered.

In the early and middle 1920s, the Jones-Barany revolving

chair test was given to all military pilots as part of their periodic physical examination for flying. Normally, this test was given with the pilot's eyes open, and the flight surgeon looked for variations in the timing and amount of the rhythmic side-to-side movement of the eyes called nystagmus.

In early 1926, Captain (later Colonel) David A. Myers, an outstanding Army Air Corps flight surgeon, decided to augment the routine physical examination by giving an additional test consisting of several rotations of the chair with the pilot's eyes closed. The testing produced some astonishing results. After the rate of rotation became steady, a normal pilot, with eyes closed, could not tell which way he was turning. If the rate of rotation was slowed down and stabilized at a somewhat lower speed, the pilot thought the rotation had been stopped. When the rotation actually was stopped, he thought he was turning in the opposite direction.

The explanation is that people normally maintain their equilibrium by sight, touch, hearing, muscle, and vestibular sense. Touch and hearing are not important in flight orientation. By using the three remaining senses a pilot can ascertain and maintain his position, accurately sense the rate and direction of his motion, and generally orient himself in relation to the earth.

Sight is by far the most reliable of these three senses, and when sight is lost we must get our sense of balance and motion from our muscles and from the fluid movement sensors in the vestibular canals. If an individual is merely displaced, the fluid motions return to zero very rapidly. But if one is rotated, it may take from 5 to 25 seconds for the fluid motions to stop. During this period an individual can experience the false sense of motion we call vertigo. This, of course, explains why early pilots became completely confused and occasionally spun in and crashed.

Captain (later Colonel) William C. Ocker, an early and extremely competent Air Corps pilot and flight researcher, had long been interested in instrument flying and, in 1918, had tested the then new turn-and-bank indicator. When he took Captain Myers's new "blindfold test" in 1926, his first reaction was that the doctor had played a trick on him or, if not, that his senses had failed him. After further consideration, he decided that here was proof positive that no normal pilot could consistently fly "blind" without reference to instruments.

Ocker had considerable experience flying with the turn-and-bank indicator by that time. He frequently carried a quickly attachable unit complete with venturi in his flight baggage and believed this instrument could correct the pilots' faulty senses. He designed a light-proof "black box" that contained a turn-and-bank indicator and a magnetic compass. This box was mounted on the front of the Jones-Barany chair. The pilot sealed his face against the opening in the box and observed the turn-and-bank indicator and compass. With this piece of equipment he could correctly identify the direction and rate of his rotation. After the rotation stopped and the compass settled down, he could then determine his heading.

Myers and Ocker continued their experiments, and the arrangement of the black box and revolving chair were patented and subsequently used in the training of pilots. Later, some pilots learned to fly by instruments alone before they learned to fly under normal visual conditions.

In the late 1920s and early 1930s, Captain Ocker and Lieutenant (later Colonel) Carl J. Crane collaborated in the study of instrument flying techniques and developed, among other things, a unitary arrangement of instruments that could give the pilot a maximum of useful flight information with a minimum of effort and fatigue. They called this a "flight integrator."

The development of instrument flight owes much to Daniel Guggenheim, one of the great industrialists, philanthropists, and citizens of the twentieth century. He was interested in everything that could lead to a fuller life and a better world. One of his great contributions was the Daniel Guggenheim Fund for the Promotion of Aeronautics, which was established for the purpose of advancing the art, science, and business of aviation. It proved to be very effective in the accomplishment of that goal. The basic concept of the fund was "to maintain a simple, inexpensive directing organization depending on established outside agencies, whenever possible, to carry out the aims of the fund." It was to be a primer—a spark plug—to stimulate and promote action.

The fund was established in January 1926 with a grant of $2.5 million. It was to be administered by a board of trustees composed of men of "eminence and competence" in cooperation with the federal government. Harry Guggenheim, gifted son of Daniel and a World War I naval aviator, was chosen the fund's president.

Rear Admiral H. I. Cone, an outstanding naval officer, was the initial vice president of the fund; he was succeeded by Captain (later Vice Admiral) Emory S. ''Jerry'' Land of the Construction Corps of the Navy, who served until the fund's work was completed. The strength of character, sound judgment, organizational ability, understanding, and capacity for cooperation of Harry Guggenheim and Jerry Land were, in large part, the cement that held the fund together.

The Guggenheims wanted to do several things. One was to have a competition for the development of a ''safe'' airplane. In those days, many people were killed after getting an airplane into a spin and not knowing how to get out. Harry Guggenheim offered a first prize of $100,000 for the development of an airplane that wouldn't spin no matter what you did. Additional prizes of $10,000 each were awarded for the first five aircraft to meet the minimum flying requirements.

The Guggenheim-sponsored International Safe Aircraft Competition was held in October 1929 at Mitchel Field, on Long Island, and was won by the Curtiss Tanager. The Handley-Page Company also had an airplane in that competition and claimed patent infringement. It had unique wing slats installed that helped prevent spins.

Harry Guggenheim also recommended to the trustees that the fund ''encourage perfection of control in a fog'' and ''finance a study of and solution to fog flying.'' From the first, it was understood that flight safety and reliability were important considerations and that one phase of the fund's work would be to study means of assuring safe and reliable flight despite weather conditions. With this in mind, a special committee of experts was organized to define the problem. A directive was prepared that authorized a study to include the following: dissipation of fog; development of some means whereby flying fields might be located from the air regardless of fog; development of instruments to show accurately the height of airplanes above the ground, to replace barometric instruments, which show height above sea level; improvement and perfection of instruments allowing airplanes to fly properly in fog; and the penetration of fog by light rays.

To carry out the program, the Full Flight Laboratory was established in 1928 at Mitchel Field and furnished with all the necessary facilities and equipment. When Jerry Land was asked who was the best chap to run the blind flight laboratory, he endeared himself to the Army and earned the Navy's enmity by naming me. He was roundly criticized by his Navy contemporaries for "going outside the circle" and choosing me instead of a Navy test pilot. When asked why, he said, "This chap has the advantage over any of our Navy people of not only a lifetime of flying, but a technical education that has given him a distinct advantage in the development of new equipment." I didn't know him before but came to know him very well. He was a wonderful man.

Although I had been offered a well-paying job as a test pilot by Curtiss, I felt that the potential benefits of the experiments to aviation made the flight laboratory job the chance of a lifetime. I turned the Curtiss job down and was officially borrowed from the Air Corps for a one-year period of "detached service" to head the laboratory. I was ably assisted by Professor William G. Brown of the Aeronautics Department of MIT; Lieutenant Benjamin S. Kelsey was assigned as my flight assistant and safety pilot. I asked for Corporal (later Sergeant) Jack Dalton to be assigned as our mechanic.

Joe, the boys, and I moved from McCook to Mitchel in the fall of 1928. We were assigned to a long-vacant, termite-ridden wooden building that had been built during World War I. We devoted part of it to an office. As usual, Joe found herself being hostess to all kinds of people, from scientists and professors to mechanics and radio and instrument specialists, coming and going day and night. Her beer-making skills made our new home an oasis for all and sundry. Almost every friend who cared to imbibe learned to fetch some hops so she could stay in production. It was here that Joe took some more flying lessons. I took her along on some short flights; she especially enjoyed seeing New York at night.

Young Jim was now eight and John six. My responsibilities to them were growing and I realized that now that they were of school age, uprooting them too frequently was probably not in their best interests. It was another reason to think seriously about whether or not I should stay in the service. But that decision could be delayed. I was committed to the job at hand.

This was a most interesting period in my life. The Good Book says, "No man can serve two masters for . . . he will hold to one and despise the other." I had three: an Army boss, Lieutenant Colonel (later Major General) Conger Pratt, commanding officer at Mitchel Field; Captain Jerry Land, a naval officer; and Mr. Guggenheim, a civilian. They were such fine, understanding, and cooperative people that my existence, instead of being complex, was uncomplicated and extremely pleasant.

Our first activity was to study the work previously done on blind landing in fog. We conducted experiments with tethered balloons strung along a landing area and had very limited success, in still air and when the fog was not thick. We abandoned this concept because experience had indicated that a fog layer might be very thick, and still air could not be depended upon at all times when visibility was restricted, as, for example, in a blizzard.

In both England and France, the lead-in cable idea was tried out. In this system, an electrified cable circled the field and led the pilot into a landing. It required very sensitive sensing equipment in the airplane and it was necessary to make a precision turn into the field at low altitude. This turn was extremely difficult to make. Lieutenant LeRoy Wolf of the Army Air Corps also experimented with the electrified cable concept at Wright Field. The Navy had some limited success with an electromagnetic cable guide at Lakehurst Naval Air Station.

The low-frequency radio range had been developed by the Bureau of Standards and the Army and was in limited use for aerial navigation. An adaptation of this radio range in the form of a homing beacon seemed to offer the greatest promise for our use. It could also readily be tied in with the radio receiver and other conventional airborne equipment.

Actual blind landings had been attempted with dragging weights and with long tail skids in order to determine height above the ground before touchdown. These either gave an indication upon touching the ground or were rigged to actuate the aircraft controls. Neither idea was satisfactory.

The first important expenditures authorized for the Full Flight Laboratory were for two modern airplanes, at a total cost of $26,000. One, a Consolidated NY-2 Husky two-seat training plane (a Navy version of the Army's PT-1 primary trainer) with a Wright Whirlwind J-5 engine, was to be used in the instrument landing experiments and to test instruments, equipment, or devices that might be helpful in overcoming fog flying problems. It had large wings and was used by the Navy for pontoon seaplane training. In place of the pontoons, we had a specially reinforced landing gear installed with long oleo strut action to absorb excessive shock. As a training plane, it had a very high factor of safety and was extremely rugged and inherently stable about all three axes. We made it into a blind-flying test vehicle by installing a special canvas hood that could isolate the pilot from any view outside the aircraft. I accepted the aircraft from the Consolidated factory near Buffalo, New York, on November 3, 1928. When I returned to Mitchel Field, my logbook shows I made 25 flights with passengers in it on November 18, 1928, including Joe, young Jim, and John.

The second plane was a two-seat Navy Vought Corsair O2U-1, which was accepted on November 21, 1928. Harry Guggenheim was its first passenger. It was to be used for cross-country practice flying and was an excellent airplane for this purpose. It was a fast, good-flying airplane, but not as rugged as the NY-2. I also took up many passengers in this plane, including Mr. and Mrs. Igor Sikorsky and Jack Allard. I made many short trips in it testing the equipment with Joe as my navigator.

Though I liked both planes, the NY-2, at 98 miles per hour, was too slow. I wrote to Major Reuben Fleet, president of Consolidated, and asked him to consider installing an NACA cowling in order to give the aircraft more speed. I said: "In flying from Mitchel to College Park, Md., it took me four hours and ten minutes actual flying time, two stops being made for gasoline. On one occasion, while we were flying low over a road and into a head wind, a green automobile overtook and passed us. Hurt my pride no end." I asked him about the possibility of installing larger wing tanks. Shortly after I brought the NY-2 to Mitchel, I flew it to Boonton, New Jersey, where a voice radio system was installed by the Radio Frequency Laboratory.

When flights under the hood were made, it was essential, for safety reasons, to have Lieutenant Ben Kelsey in the airplane to look out for other planes and also to make sure that I didn't get into trouble due to instrument or equipment failure. Ben's piloting help, criticism of tests carried out, sound technical counsel, and ever-pleasant personality contributed greatly to the results achieved. And I couldn't praise Corporal Jack Dalton enough for his competence and devotion in keeping the two planes in flying condition.

As the preliminary practice flights progressed, it soon became apparent that even with the very stable and sturdy NY-2, the available instruments were not adequate. For determining heading when maneuvering and when landing, the compass, because of the northerly turning error, was entirely unsatisfactory. The turn-and-bank indicator, though excellent for its purpose, was more a qualitative than a quantitative measuring instrument. It told the pilot that he was making a turn or was skidding. Also, at the moment of touchdown in a blind landing, it was imperative that the wings be level with the ground. This was not easy to assure with the turn-and-bank indicator, particularly when the wind was gusty. What was needed was an accurate, reliable, and easy-to-read instrument showing the exact direction of heading and precise attitude of the aircraft, particularly for the initial and final stages of blind landings.

Two German artificial-horizon instruments—the Anschutz and the Gyrorector—were studied but were deemed not entirely satisfactory. They were too large and had a tendency to "tumble" and become inoperative. I sketched a rough picture of the dial for an instrument that I thought would do the job and showed it to Elmer A. Sperry, Sr., a great engineer and inventor who headed the Sperry Gyroscope Company. It had the face of a directional gyro superimposed on an artificial horizon.

Sperry advised that a single gyroscopic instrument could be built, but recommended, for simplicity of construction, two separate instruments. I agreed, so Sperry assigned his ingenious son, Elmer, Jr., to work with us and be responsible for their design and fabrication. Elmer soon became a member of the team and spent as much time at the hangar and at the evening discussion sessions in our quarters at Mitchel Field as the rest of us. These evening sessions were frequent and long. The wives joined their husbands and helped in the work. Out of this effort came the Sperry artificial horizon and the directional gyroscope from which today's improved, space age, electronic instruments have descended.

The artificial horizon (also called the attitude indicator) is the instrument that serves as a direct substitute for the natural horizon and shows a pilot whether the aircraft is flying straight and level, diving, or banking. It exactly duplicates the orientation of the natural horizon seen through the windshield.

The directional gyro is a heading reference instrument. It is not magnetic but is aligned to the heading of the magnetic compass or any other directional reference. It depends upon the gyroscopic property of rigidity in space.

I made a number of test flights with Elmer, Jr., to test the directional gyro. I would pick out a section of railroad track near Mitchel Field, check the compass heading, and set the directional gyro. I would then fly around over the countryside for a few minutes and return to that same section of track to see if the gyro setting remained the same. At first, it drifted off course because of bearing friction, but we kept refining the mechanism until the gyro would remain set for a fairly long period of time.

As time progressed, I made literally hundreds of blind and simulated blind landings. To make a landing, the plane was put into a glide at 60 miles per hour, with some power on, and flown directly into the ground. Although this was about 15 miles per hour above stalling speed, the NY-2's landing gear absorbed the shock of landing, and if the angle of glide was just right, the airplane didn't even bounce. Actually, after a while, it was possible to make consistently perfect landings by this method. To assure just the right amount of engine power in the glide, a mark was placed at the proper place on the throttle quadrant.

We received excellent cooperation from the companies and people we worked with during this period. Among them were the Pioneer Instrument Company, the Taylor Instrument Company, Radio Corporation of America, and the Radio Frequency Laboratory at Boonton, New Jersey. Bell Telephone Laboratories installed the radio transmitter and provided miniature earphones with molded plugs.

Very valuable help was also received from the U.S. Bureau of Standards, which designed and installed most of the ground and airborne radio navigation equipment. The low-frequency radio range was in limited use by the Army at that time for air navigation; an adaptation of this radio range in the form of a homing beacon seemed to offer the greatest promise for our use. Bureau personnel, working with the Airways and Radio Division of the Department of Commerce, designed a semiportable two-leg radio range and a fan-type marker beacon. This system could be readily tied in with the radio receiver and other conventional airplane equipment of that period.

The homing range was installed on the west side of Mitchel Field. The marker beacon sat along the leg of the homing range and was located on the east side of the field.

It was during the radio phase of our tests that we concluded that while aural signals were satisfactory for rough aerial navigation, it would be much better if we had a visual indicator in the cockpit for the precise directional control needed during the final phase of blind landings. We installed a visual indicator in the

NY-2 consisting of a pair of vibrating reeds that were connected to the radio set. If the pilot was to the right of the radio beam, the left reed vibrated more vigorously. If the pilot was on course, both reeds vibrated through the same arc. As the plane approached the radio station, the amplitude of vibration increased. A single reed started to vibrate as the fan marker beacon was approached. It reached maximum amplitude, then quickly dropped to zero when the plane was directly over the station, rapidly built up to maximum again, and then tapered down as the plane pulled away. The homing range indicator also had a distinct null (period of silence) in the headset when the plane was directly over the range station.

As the tests progressed, the instrumentation and equipment were continually improved. Toward the end of 1929, during the final stages of the flight tests, we had 11 instruments installed in addition to the normal engine instruments. These were a magnetic compass, an earth inductor compass, a turn-and-bank indicator, a directional gyro, an artificial horizon, an airspeed indicator, an altimeter, a rate-of-climb indicator, an outside air thermometer, a vibrating reed homing range indicator, and a vibrating reed marker beacon indicator.

We gave considerable thought to the location and arrangement of the instruments in order to facilitate reading and reduce pilot fatigue. Fatigue led to errors, and pilot errors could not be tolerated in instrument landings. The airplane, in addition to its flight instruments, carried a Radio Frequency Laboratory radio receiver, a Bell Telephone Laboratories radio transmitter, two six-inch Pyle-National landing lights, and a parachute flare.

Small instruments were preferred over the conventional larger ones because, even though they were somewhat harder to read individually, the small instruments permitted a more compact and logical arrangement and were easier to read and interpret en masse. It was soon determined that small instruments could be made easier to read by use of broader hands with white or radium paint applied to the outer half of their length. We found that over a long period the instruments could be read more quickly and with less fatigue if the arrangement of the instruments and the position and direction of motion of the indicating hands were "natural." For example, the hands of all directional indicators formed a straight vertical line when flying straight and level. The hands of all indicators affected by fore-and-aft inclination formed a horizontal line when in normal fore-and-aft attitude. Any abnormality or improper indication could be detected automatically by a quick glance at the instrument panel. This did not solve all the problems of instrument flight, but it did simplify it for the pilot.

A larger than customary Leece-Neville generator was installed on the engine to assure an adequate and continuous electrical supply. The mast-type receiving antenna, which was used to minimize directional effect, required considerable development before a tendency to vibrate under certain flight conditions could be corrected. A trailing wire antenna was used for transmission in normal flight. This was reeled in and a fixed wire antenna was used for transmitting when landing.

The specialized ground equipment consisted of a radio receiver and transmitter that provided voice communications with the aircraft and a Kollsman sensitive altimeter with which the altimeter in the airplane was synchronized by radio. In addition, there was the visual homing range and the visual fan-type marker beacon previously mentioned. The standard Mitchel Field Army-type aural beacon was available to lead an aircraft to the general vicinity of the airfield.

Other problems very much on the minds of the fund directors during this period were collisions of aircraft in the air and the formation of ice on the wings, structure, and propeller, and in the carburetor of aircraft when atmospheric conditions were conducive to icing. W. C. Greer and Merrit Scott at Cornell University carried out work, under fund sponsorship, on the underlying causes of ice formation on aircraft. The fund also sponsored the work done by John P. Kilgore, of New Haven, Connecticut, on an electrically heated wing blanket for deicing on the ground. The Full Flight Laboratory did no development work on deicing equipment, but many test flights were made under icing conditions to determine effects and limitations.

The NY-2 was frequently out of commission during the installation of new instruments or equipment. These were convenient periods for cross-country flying practice under unfavorable weather conditions in the O2U-1. This airplane had all the necessary flight instruments but no blind landing equipment.

During this period, while flying the O2U-1, I experienced an extreme example of a cross-country bad weather flight. I took off from Buffalo, New York, on March 15, 1929, and headed for Mitchel Field. It was night and the weather was fair and improving at Buffalo, but marginal to the south and west. This was to be a difficult flight but possible—just the sort of thing required to establish flight "limitations." In a pinch, I thought I could return to Buffalo at any time up to the point where nearly half of the gas supply was used up.

It is a truism that the most important thing in flying is to learn your limitations and stay within them. I knew the wisdom of this from a previous night flight while flying "contact" from Cleveland to New York. On that occasion the weather was gummy and I had been checking each revolving beacon as I passed it. When I came to the hills west of Elizabeth, New Jersey, a beacon failed to show up. As a consequence I almost ran into the low hills. I threw out a landing flare and landed. A farmer came out and asked why I'd landed. I explained that I'd been unable to check on the beacon. He advised that it had been out for about six weeks—and that the mail plane had just passed over. This was the first time I'd ever been "flown over." The tendency to take off and push on was strong. I reasoned that the mail pilot knew the beacon was out and knew the terrain better than I. He was flying within his limitations when he flew on. I'd be flying beyond mine if I followed.

I stayed on the ground until morning and thereafter was a better pilot. I had realized that the pilot who flew within his limitations would probably live to a ripe old age, whereas the pilot who flew beyond them would not. I also knew that different pilots had different limitations. This had been pointed up a few years before at McCook when we had few facilities and little ground equipment to do environmental testing on new airborne devices. It was therefore necessary to test them out in flight, and the test pilots spent many hours flying around the airfield to see how a new device held up under the accelerations, vibrations, and changes in temperature and pressure experienced in flight. Lieutenant Alex Pearson always spent these hours practicing precision flying; for instance, holding constant speed and altitude. As a result, he became extremely proficient and could fly a better speed course and do a smoother sawtooth climb than any of the rest of us.

I spent the hours flying low in the vicinity of McCook Field and on the main air routes in and out, memorizing the terrain. I knew every high building, tree, silo, windmill, radio tower, and high tension line in the area. I could therefore fly in—or under—adverse weather safely when other equally experienced pilots did not fly. This was not because I was a better or more daring pilot than my colleagues; constant practice had simply expanded my limitations. The trick was to learn your limitations, gradually expand them, but never go beyond them.

These thoughts went through my mind as I proceeded toward Mitchel while the weather deteriorated. I had planned to fly "contact" all the way and avoid any weather. In order to avoid the mountains I took the route from Buffalo by way of Rochester, Syracuse, Utica, Schenectady, and Albany and then down the Hudson River. There was no problem getting to Albany, but from there on the ceiling and visibility became marginal. I soon passed the point of no return and no longer had enough gas to return to Buffalo.

At one point as I flew lower and lower, I found it expedient to slow down and hover with the left wing of the plane over a brightly lit, southbound passenger train traveling along the east side of the Hudson. Presently it went through a cut and wiped me off. This procedure was too hazardous, so I left the train behind and followed the riverbank. I thought about landing on the parade ground at West Point, but adandoned the idea because the weather remained flyable—barely.

When I reached the area of New York City, the ceiling and visibility improved slightly. I flew south to the Battery, hoping to reach Mitchel Field from there, but the East River and the area to the south were socked in, so I could not go on. I tried to get to Governor's Island and land on the drill field, but it, too, was completely covered by fog.

I then turned back up the Hudson, intending to land on the Yonkers golf course, which I knew well, but the fog was below the riverbank. Turning back, I then thought of crash landing in Battery Park. Just as I was about to set the plane down, a chap ran out into the middle of the park and waved me off. He apparently thought I mistook it for a flying field.

It is interesting to note that the George Washington Bridge across the Hudson was under construction at that time. There were as yet no suspension cables or other horizontal structures. Only the great vertical piers on each side of the river had been completed. I had passed the east pier three times without seeing it.

About this time it appeared that a crash landing in the river might be necessary, so I removed my parachute in order to be able to swim ashore. The water, on closer inspection, looked uninviting, so I decided on a final try—this time for Newark

Airport—and headed across the Hudson. As soon as I crossed and the lights of Jersey City appeared, I knew this last chance wasn't practical.

I pulled up into the fog and climbed through it. It was only about a thousand feet thick and crystal clear above. My new plan was to fly west until past the populated part of the metropolitan area and then jump. I didn't know how much time was left, but the gas gauge had been fluttering around zero for some time. I noted about this time that my parachute harness was off and promptly put it on. It would have been a terminal embarrassment to jump without it.

Somewhere near Kenilworth, New Jersey, I saw a revolving beacon through a hole in the fog and a flat-looking area adjacent to it with no lights. Hoping it might be an emergency field or at least an open area, although realizing that it might be a woods or a lake, I turned the landing lights on and dove through the hole to scout the area. The bottom of the fog was still very low and I tore the left lower wing badly on a treetop. The airplane still flew, although almost completely out of gasoline, so I returned to the most likely spot and crash-landed.

I took the impact by wrapping the left wing around a tree trunk near the ground. The O2U-1 was completely washed out, but I was not even scratched or bruised.

The moral of the story is that if I had been flying the NY-2 with its blind flying equipment and if the laboratory radio station had been alerted at Mitchel, it would have been a routine cross-country flight.

The flight pointed up to me the importance of constant radio communications between an aircraft and the ground and the need for frequent and accurate weather reports by radio during flight. It also showed the desirability of marking emergency fields for night landings. Later, green lights were used on the opposite side of the flashing beacons to indicate a landing field.

This flight also brought home the fact that weather flying was a function of airplane characteristics, ground facilities, airborne equipment and instruments, procedures, the pilot's skill, and his knowledge of the local aids to air navigation, the terrain, and the weather conditions to be expected in a landing area.

At this stage of aviation development, it was important that a better altimeter be developed so a pilot would have a precise measure of altitude when approaching for a landing. The conventional barometric altimeters of the day measured, at best, to the nearest fifty or one hundred feet. They also lagged and often gave a misleading indication of height. We considered them undependable for altitudes less than 100 feet. It would be handy if an altimeter were available that, near the ground, would measure to ten or even five feet.

Paul Kollsman, a scientist formerly with the Pioneer Instrument Company, had formed the Kollsman Instrument Company and developed such an instrument. A perfectionist, he had contacted Swiss watchmakers who made extremely precise gears to provide a mechanism for the needles. He developed a much-improved diaphragm for the altimeter that had very little lag in its spring. The combination was exactly what was needed.

I was very pleased on August 30, 1929, to take Kollsman and his new instrument up on its first test flight in the second O2U, an improved version that was purchased after the crash of the first. Kollsman held the sensitive altimeter in his lap during the flight and it performed perfectly. It responded immediately to any changes in air pressure without lagging. We promptly installed it in the NY-2.

What made this instrument so valuable then was that it had two hands and a multiplication factor of twenty between them. The fast-moving hand made one complete revolution for each 1,000-foot change in altitude, which meant a movement of about 5/32 of an inch for each 20 feet of altitude. This was an order of magnitude more accurate than earlier altimeters.

Although the Kollsman altimeter provided a very considerable advance in instrumentation, it still measured the barometric altitude, or height above sea level. An instrument that could measure the height above the ground regardless of changes in barometric pressure would be of even greater value.

With this in mind, several companies were encouraged to work on a sonic altimeter. One built by Sperry was tested in the NY-2. A note on a frequency of about 950 cycles was directed at the ground from a megaphone on the bottom of the airplane; the elapsed time interval was measured, as in a marine fathometer, and the altitude above the ground thus determined.

The concept was theoretically sound, but in its initial form the equipment caused considerable drag on the outside of the aircraft. It was unduly large, heavy, difficult to install, and complicated. It appeared that a radio altimeter measuring the phase difference of radio waves reflected back from the ground offered more promise. Several radio altimeters were under development with fund encouragement. The sonic altimeter experiments were abandoned.

Although the Full Flight Laboratory gave major emphasis to flight tests designed to permit flying safely and reliably despite fog, the fund and the laboratory were also interested in experiments on the penetration of fog by light rays and on the dispersal of fog.

Studies of fog penetration were made by S. Herbert Anderson of the University of Washington and James Barnes of Bryn Mawr College under fund sponsorship, and by Julius A. Stratton of MIT. The visual, infrared, and ultraviolet portions of the spectrum were carefully explored.

It was concluded that though there was some difference in penetration depending on wavelength, there was little likelihood of finding any visible light that would penetrate thick, dense fog. Stratton's further investigations gave some promise that at very short wavelengths—below one centimeter—there was a possibility that fog might be penetrated by dispersing it. In addition to the scientific studies carried out, various inventors presented ideas for seeing through fog, all of which received careful consideration.

Four basic methods of fog dispersal were originally considered:

1. Dispersal by mechanical means. Here the concept was to have a large propeller or series of propellers churn up the fog and literally blow it away.

2. Dispersal by chemical means. Experiments carried out by Harry G. Houghton, Jr., of MIT, using hygroscopic materials, showed some promise both in the laboratory and in full-scale tests that were conducted in South Dartmouth, Massachusetts.

3. Dispersal by electrical means. From the early 1920s, a Dr. Warren of Hartford, Connecticut, in collaboration with the Army Air Service, had been experimenting with cloud and fog dispersal by dropping electrified sand particles from an aircraft. He was occasionally successful in dispersing small clouds. A man named Flowers experimented with fog dispersal through the use of electrified water particles and achieved some interesting results.

4. Dispersal by heat. Experimentation on, and the actual accomplishment of, fog dispersal by heat was carried on from the 1920s until the 1950s. Called FIDO (for "fog, intense dispersal of"), it was effectively used during World War II on 3 of the long emergency fields and 10 main landing fields in England. It consisted of powerful heat sources at intervals along the runways that heated the air to a temperature above the dew point, thereby dispersing the nearby fog. Approximately 2,500 bombers and fighters returning from missions and finding their home bases (and much of England) covered in pea-soup fog were directed to the cleared "tunnels" in the fog over these FIDO fields and were able to land safely.

The Full Flight Laboratory's first experience with FIDO occurred in 1929. Harry Reader, of Cleveland, who operated a gravel pit and used a large blowtorch type of heater to dry the gravel and sand, observed that if there was an intense fog when he turned the heater on, the fog in the immediate area dispersed. Learning of the Guggenheim fog-flying experiments, he wrote to tell us of his experience and said he was interested in helping solve the fog problem. We invited him to install his equipment at Mitchel to await a foggy day.

For several months thereafter we waited in vain for a dense fog. Finally, on the morning of September 24, 1929, the conditions seemed perfect for such a trial. I was awakened about six A.M. by Jack Dalton, our mechanic, and our gang was quickly called together. We immediately notified Reader, who arrived shortly thereafter. Harry Guggenheim was also notified, but he had to come from Port Washington and didn't arrive until later. Captain Land and the rest of our associates were hurriedly called to witness the demonstration. My wife, Joe, realizing the significance of what we were trying to do, came by to watch.

Reader fired up his equipment, but the fog did not disperse except in the immediate vicinity of the blowtorch. The experiment was a disappointing failure. In retrospect it appears that FIDO is a successful way to cope with dense fog only when the air is comparatively still. When there is any considerable movement of the air and fog—the cleared air mass moves on and new fog comes in faster than it can be dispersed.

Though we were all disappointed, we were there and the fog was there, so I decided to make a real fog flight. The NY-2 was pushed out of the hangar and warmed up. The ground radios were manned and the radio beacons turned on. I taxied out, took off, came through the fog at about 500 feet, and made a wide swing coming around into landing position. By the time I landed ten minutes after takeoff the fog had started to lift.

About this time, Guggenheim arrived along with several other people, so we decided to do an "official" under-the-hood flight. Since I had just made a real flight in the fog, I wanted to go alone, but Guggenheim insisted that Ben Kelsey go along as safety pilot. The fog had lifted considerably by this time and he was afraid there might be other aircraft in the vicinity.

We both got into the plane, and the hood over my cockpit was tightly closed. I taxied out and took off toward the west in a gradual climb. At about 1,000 feet, I leveled off and made a 180-degree turn to the left, flew several miles, then made another left turn. The airplane was now properly lined up on the west leg of the Mitchel range, so I started a gradual descent. I leveled off at 200 feet and flew level until I passed the fan marker on the east side of the field. From this point, I flew the plane down to the ground using the instrument landing procedure we had developed. However, despite all my previous practice, the approach and landing were sloppy.

All during the flight, Ben Kelsey rested his hands on the upper wing of the aircraft or held them aloft so everyone could plainly see that he was not manipulating the controls.

The whole flight lasted only 15 minutes. So far as I know, this was the first time an airplane had been taken off, flown over a set course, and landed by instruments alone. This was just 10 months and 3 weeks after the original test flight of the NY-2.

The night of September 24, 1929, was a special one for all of us associated with the blind flying work. We had quite a party and it was here that Joe inaugurated a Doolittle family custom. All who worked on the blind-flying project autographed Joe's large white damask tablecloth; Jerry Land was the first to sign it. Afterward, Joe embroidered the signatures in black thread to preserve them. Over the years, everyone who broke bread at our table was asked to do the same. In time, Joe painstakingly stitched over 500 signatures on the tablecloth during trips with me or at home when she felt the urge. When she ran out of space on the tablecloth, she started getting signatures on a dozen napkins, then on portable screens. We had an interesting collection of signatures of people from all walks of life. Of course, many pilot friends, their wives, and their offspring autographed their names or nicknames, but we also had movie stars, singers, comedians, neighbors, scientists, politicians, and everyone else who visited. Only one signed who had not actually been our dinner guest: Orville Wright. John Macready took the tablecloth to Dayton to get Wright's signature for us.

Joe was very proud of this hobby, as she had a right to be. The tablecloth was one of her most prized possessions. When we moved from Santa Monica to Carmel, California, many years later, we donated the tablecloth to the National Air and Space Museum in Washington.

After our flight, *The New York Times* ran an optimistic story under the headline: "Blind Plane Flies 15 Miles and Lands; Fog Peril Overcome."

Harry Guggenheim was so enthusiastic that he dashed off a note to Orville Wright, saying: "It is significant that the achievement is realized through the aid of only three instruments which are not already the standard equipment of an airplane."

Although I had been able to make this flight successfully, more experimentation was needed. Much work remained for commercial and military organizations to prepare facilities, manufacture radio equipment and instruments, and train pilots before the *Times*'s headline "Fog Peril Overcome" would be realized. The tests indicated at the time, among other things, that before all-weather flying would be practical, there was a need for several improvements: better coordination between the long-range aural beam and the short-range visual landing beam; accurate measurement of distance along the landing beam; and a slant glide beam at right angles to the vertical landing beam that might be curved to become tangent to the earth rather than intersecting it in a straight line. An automatic volume control would be helpful, as would an automatic pilot to assist the pilot and prevent fatigue. This could be, and later was, tied in with the instrument landing systems. In addition, much more work was needed on ignition system shielding, not only to reduce noise but to permit flight in heavy rain.

Although more work was needed, we had made an initial contribution to instrument flight, so at the end of 1929 the Guggenheim Fund trustees felt that further development could be carried out better by other organizations and disbanded the fund. The equipment was moved to Wright Field for further use in instrument landing experimentation, and the Full Flight Laboratory went out of existence.

The NY-2 was flown back to the Consolidated plant in Buffalo for minor modifications and inspection. On October 3, 1929, a Buffalo streetcar collided with the flatbed truck on which the NY-2 was being transported from the airfield to the factory. Only the cockpit and the plane's outer wing panels survived. The rest of the plane had to be rebuilt. After the lawsuits that developed had been settled, the plane was eventually sold to the Air Corps for one dollar and ferried to Wright Field where it was later operated by the Ohio National Guard.

Lieutenant Albert F. Hegenberger and the Materiel Division's Fog Flying Unit took up where the fund left off. Al made the first official solo blind flight on May 9, 1932 (my first flight alone was unofficial), and received the Collier Trophy in 1934 for his work. Over a period of years he and his colleagues greatly improved the equipment previously used and developed additional equipment. He devised blind-landing procedures that became standard military practice for many years. This system was put into actual use in 1934.

The Bureau of Standards and the Bureau of Air Commerce of the Department of Commerce also continued their work, and on March 20, 1933, James L. Kinney, with William La Violette as mechanic and Harry Diamond as passenger, flew a Bellanca airplane by instruments from College Park, Maryland, to Newark Airport, a distance of about 200 miles. He landed blind, using the recently developed bent landing beam.

Flying by instruments soon outgrew the early experimental phase. It became a practical reality, and aviation entered a new era. I was grateful for the opportunity to participate in the initial experiments. This work was, I believe, my most significant contribution to aviation.

During 1929, the Full Flight Laboratory experiments did not take up all my time. I had applied for permission to take a Curtiss P-1C Hawk to South America, again for demonstration purposes, using up my accrued leave. I intended to visit eight countries: Cuba, Panama, Colombia, Ecuador, Peru, Chile, Bolivia, and Argentina. Harry Guggenheim approved the request and it was approved all the way to the top of the Army. However, Assistant Secretary of War F. Trubee Davison wrote me a letter saying I did not have enough accrued leave to make the trip and disapproved it.

However, all this became moot. I wrecked the P-1, and the Curtiss people decided to postpone the flight until January 1930.

At that time I intended to go back to South America after I had completed my work with the Full Flight Laboratory. Curtiss was going to replace the P-1's D12 engine with a V1570, which would have given the Hawk much more speed.

During the Cleveland Air Races in late August 1929, a Mr. Logan of the National Air Races committee asked me if I would come to the races on September 1, 1929, and put on a stunting exhibition. He said a new Curtiss Hawk would be available for me and that Lieutenant Al Williams, my old racing competitor, would be exhibiting his wares. I refused, pleading that I had too much work to do at Mitchel and that I couldn't leave without Harry Guggenheim's permission. I don't know what political power or persuasive argument Logan used, but Guggenheim gave his reluctant permission and Major General James E. Fechet, then the chief of the Air Corps, issued the necessary travel orders.

I flew the O2U to Cleveland and upon arriving was embarrassed by immediately being taken to the grandstand and introduced to the race crowd. I was informed that the Prestone-cooled P-1 that I was to use was at the National Guard hangar on the other side of the field. I looked at the Hawk and found the radiator cowling was cracked and the radiator leaking. I had a plate riveted on the cracked cowling and flight-tested the plane. The engine overheated, so I landed and inquired of the mechanic if he was sure there was sufficient Prestone in the radiator. He put in another half gallon to be sure. The mechanic stated the radiator was too small for this plane and always ran hot. I took off again and flew to a spot about seven miles from the field in order to practice a few stunts without being observed and where I would not interfere with the flying around the field. Since I had been flying the slow-flying NY-2 mostly during the previous months, I wanted to get the feel of the P-1 and practice my act at a safe altitude.

Remembering that General Patrick had ordained that we were not to perform outside loops, I decided that I would do the first half of one at the show. I climbed to 4,000 feet and, with the throttle set about three-quarters advanced, slowly pushed over into a dive. When I was about 30 degrees past vertical at about 2,000 feet, there was a sharp pop and the wings broke but did not separate completely from the fuselage. The airplane slowed down and began to tumble. I throttled back, unbuckled my safety belt and was literally thrown out of the cockpit.

I have no definite recollection of what happened except for hearing that pop, which sounded like the snapping of a wire. When I was clear of the plane, I pulled the parachute rip cord but the 'chute did not open immediately. That gave me something to think about. I jerked the rip cord again and the 'chute came open at about 1,000 feet.

I came down in a field about 20 feet off a road near Olmsted Falls, west of Cleveland. I gathered up the parachute and was soon picked up and driven back to the field. When I arrived at the Air Corps headquarters, a friend of mine looked up, startled, saw my parachute, and asked what happened. I said, "The airplane broke up."

He said, "Did you get out all right?"

It wasn't an intelligent question, but I assured him I had and asked for another Hawk. I took it up for more practice (and to see if the wings would stay on this one). Last on the program, I flew my routine, which included the half outside loop. Meanwhile, Al Williams had put on an excellent exhibition in a specially equipped Curtiss pursuit plane with a Pratt & Whitney Wasp engine. The fuel and oil system had been so altered that the engine ran equally well erect or inverted and could fly indefinitely in the inverted position. Al's most spectacular stunt was to fly around the traffic pattern and glide into the field on his back, turn over, side slip, and land.

A newspaper, under the headline "Two Old Air Dogs Thrill Race Fans," reported that Al also did a stunt I wish I had thought of. The article stated:

> Those who follow aviation had read that Williams flew upside down and had even turned around pylons in this position, but they gasped in amazement this afternoon when they saw him roll his ship smoothly and easily onto its back following his usual repertoire of tricks and fly it accurately all the way around a triangular course such as the regular right-side-up flyers follow in the closed course races.

The only thing I didn't like about the article, which didn't play up my near demise, was its referring to Al and me as "old dogs." However, since we were survivors and many of our contemporaries in the stunting business had passed on at early ages, perhaps that reporter was right.

Slim Lindbergh took off after our demonstrations, leading two Navy flyers, and the three of them put on a beautiful exhibition of formation flying and aerobatics in formation. By comparison I had put on a lousy exhibition. I was very angry about the whole episode and promptly returned to Mitchel.

Since the Irvin Parachute Company had come up with the idea of the Caterpillar Club, I thought it appropriate to drop the company a brief note of thanks, saying: "Airplane failed. Parachute worked." I didn't think I had to say anything more.

A few days after the event, the War Department put out a much-overblown press release that typifies how the Doolittle image was developing in the public mind and how much the Air Corps was trying to stay in the news:

> Lieutenant Doolittle, who joined the Caterpillar Club September 1 by reason of the fact that he was forced to make a parachute jump when his plane disintegrated in the air while practicing aerobatics for an exhibition before a crowd of 150,000 people at the National Air Races at Cleveland, is the 150th airman in this country to join this mythical organization. . . .
>
> Army officials at the Air Races had been anxiously waiting his return in order to service his plane for the exhibition flight when he walked into Army headquarters with his parachute under his arm and said, "Gentlemen, I guess I'll have to borrow another plane." This was the first intimation received of his jump.
>
> Within the prescribed thirty minutes Lieutenant Doolittle taxied his borrowed plane to the starting line, took off at the wave of the flag, and staged as beautiful a demonstration of aerobatic flying as had ever been witnessed. . . . In submitting an official report on an emergency jump, the person making the jump is required to answer in detail eleven questions covering place, date, and time of the jump; the type of aircraft used; whether the plane was under control; description of the method of leaving the aircraft; complete and accurate account of the feelings and reactions during and immediately after the jump; weather conditions at the time; and what ill effects or injury was sustained.
>
> Lieutenant Doolittle used just thirty-eight words

> in his report. Under the question, "Cause for the emergency jump," he states: "Wings broke." No answer was given under the question, "Feeling and reaction of the jump." Describing his method of leaving the aircraft, he just states: "Thrown out."

Although I tried to put on a happy face, the incident was not humorous to me. The Army news release didn't tell the full story of what went on from my viewpoint, but I was not about to tell the press what I really thought. As soon as I returned to Mitchel, Major W. O. Ryan, then the field's commanding officer, requested that I write a complete report on the loss of the Hawk. I was convinced that getting me to Cleveland was purely an advertising scheme, to get me to exhibit with Williams and Lindbergh and thus get larger crowds on the final two days of the races.

I recommended that if the Army were to participate in competitive exhibitions the airplanes should be specially prepared for that purpose. I said that when flying is to be done before an audience as large and important as the one in Cleveland, Army pilots should have the best possible equipment and training, not only to permit the Army pilots to show to better advantage, but for greater safety.

I also wrote a note to Captain St. Clair Streett, head of the Materiel Division at Wright Field, the organization that had furnished the airplane. I explained what had happened and that I had performed the half outside loop previously without any problems. "The point I am bringing out," I wrote, "not in apology nor as an alibi, but in the interest of science, is that at this particular time, although I may have been punishing the ship too much, it was in no way near the extent that I have punished them in the past." Without saying it, I was implying poor maintenance on the aircraft. I never received a reply.

Despite my unhappiness with the incident at Cleveland, all was not so serious in other aspects of my flying life. On November 15, 1929, my old pal Jack Allard, some other convivial souls, and I were on our way to a New York pier for the purpose of putting Leigh Wade on a midnight boat and wishing him bon voyage on his way to South America. Leigh, one of the 1924 around-the-world pilots, had dropped out of the Army and was going to South America on behalf of an aviation manufacturing company.

As was (and is) customary in aviation circles, we managed

to dilly-dally considerably on the way to the boat, and when we were halfway there, I suddenly remembered I had to catch a train for Buffalo where I was to pick up a plane the next morning and fly it back to New York.

I tried to break away, making apologies to Leigh, but before I could tear loose, Jack Allard had a countersuggestion: If I'd stick around until Leigh's boat sailed, he would be the pilot to Buffalo that night in a plane we had available. That way, I'd be there before I could make it by train and he would fly the other plane back to New York. It sounded like a good idea. I called my faithful mechanic Jack Dalton and asked him to have the plane ready at Mitchel.

It was well into November 16 and I had forgotten to tell Dalton that a passenger was going along with me. When we got to Mitchel, Dalton had my winter flying suit ready, but nothing for Jack Allard to wear. It was a beautifully clear night, but bitterly cold. Jack was a big man and my flying clothes wouldn't fit him, so we tried all the clothes lockers to find something that would fit, but all were locked. We hunted and scraped and finally located an oversize pair of canvas coveralls and an extra helmet and goggles for Jack.

The coveralls did more harm than good, I'm afraid, because I'm sure they cut off the circulation in several vital spots. But there we were, more or less set to go, so we climbed into the ship with its two open cockpits and took off. I climbed up until we were across the Hudson River and then pointed in the direction of Buffalo. Jack was acutely miserable with the cold by that time, and I felt that if he flew the ship it would at least keep his mind occupied and might even keep him a little warmer through the slight exercise required in flying.

Jack had no maps, no compass, nothing. All he had to go by was the direction in which I'd pointed the ship when I handed it over to him.

Very shortly after I'd relinquished the controls to Jack, I settled down into my nice, warm winter flying suit and dropped off to sleep. That's not hard to do when you're warm and comfortable, with the air smooth and the engine droning out a steady, rhythmic sound.

It must have been three hours later when I was rudely awakened by Jack shaking the stick to get my attention. In the cold, gray dawn of a brand-new morning I saw a large body of water off to our left. Jack throttled back and asked the customary question: "Where are we?"

I had no idea and neither did he. He not only had no maps, compass, or instruments in his cockpit, he had never flown to Buffalo before. I sat up, looked around, and pointing directly downward, shouted, "Go ahead and land." We were exactly over Reuben Fleet's Consolidated Company airport! I don't mean one mile one side of it or one mile the other side of it. We were exactly over the center of it.

Jack was not exactly frozen or even frost nipped, although he was so cold all the way through that it required some hours before he regained possession of all his physical faculties. Afterward, I always told him he was the world's greatest navigator, who needed nothing more than to have someone point in a general direction and he would arrive precisely at the destination. I never told him I had slept the whole way.

During this period, I received a letter from the Army's adjutant general informing me that I had been awarded the Distinguished Flying Cross twice, in recognition of my 1922 cross-country flight and "in recognition of the acceleration tests made by you during March 1924 at McCook Field." The DFC had been authorized by a 1926 act of Congress. I received the awards at Governor's Island from the commanding general of the II Corps Area.

In August 1929, I was notified by the chief of the Air Corps that I had received the Mackay Trophy for the year 1925 for having won the Schneider Cup race that year. Clarence H. Mackay had established the trophy in 1912 for competitions by military aviators. If there was no annual contest, the trophy could be awarded by the War Department to the officer or officers who made the most meritorious flight of the year.

I was grateful but never did find out why those who decide such things waited until 1929 to tell the Army I had won it. It's one of the mysteries of my life.

The question of whether or not to stay in uniform was still eating away at me as the Guggenheim Fund's equipment was being crated at Mitchel. The test pilot job at Curtiss had been filled, so I contacted people at the Shell Petroleum Company in St. Louis to see if they might be interested in my services in some capacity as a pilot and engineer. They were. I was invited to St. Louis to discuss the establishment of an aeronautical branch for Shell. But since I still wasn't sure I really wanted to resign my regular commission and didn't want to burn any bridges if

I decided not to resign, I applied to the chief of the Air Corps on December 20, 1929, for permission to take 29 days of accrued leave that was due me and go to St. Louis to start an aeronautical branch for Shell. In my letter I said: "In case the work is satisfactory and the Shell people are satisfied with me, I intend to resign from the Service at the expiration of said leave. If I do not resign, I hope to be ordered to Dayton where I may be permitted to carry on fog flying experiments started by the Guggenheim Fund."

While I waited for a reply, I received orders on December 21 to make a cross-country flight to the West Coast starting the day after Christmas, "to familiarize yourself by first-hand observation as to the present regulation, control and development of airports in California and at other points en route." A report was required after the flight was completed.

I picked up a four-passenger Cessna monoplane at Columbus, Ohio, and visited 21 airports in 12 states before returning to Columbus on January 7. I also made a stop at Aguascalientes, Mexico. I reported that I had had no difficulties with engine, airplane, or weather, and all the fields I visited were generally in excellent condition, prompt and courteous service was obtained, and excellent mechanics were found on hand.

I added a couple of paragraphs that reflected my recent experience with the blind flying experiments and my erroneous thinking then in regard to airport runway operations. Obviously, I did not envision the precise instrument landing systems in worldwide use today. In hindsight, it shows how far aviation has come since those days:

> The one outstanding and unfortunate feature was the strong tendency towards "runway" fields. Even at the present time runway fields are not entirely satisfactory, especially where there is a large amount of air traffic. In the future this defect will become increasingly noticeable. A runway field cannot be used in connection with blind landings, and it is inevitable that in the future air transportation will be carried on regardless of weather conditions and landings made by instruments alone.
>
> The only condition under which runway fields should be tolerated is where the rest of the field is

> level and even with the runways and is usable at all times except after extremely heavy rains or when melting snow has made the use of the runway imperative.

I sent the report to the adjutant general of the Army, who had it placed in my personnel file. I don't know what value this trip was to the Army. It might have been assigned just to keep me busy. The experience, however, would come in handy later when I would head a presidential commission to study airport problems in the 1950s.

When I returned to Mitchel Field, there was good news awaiting me. I had been selected to receive the Harmon Trophy, Ligue des Aviateurs for my instrument work with the Guggenheim Fund. I also found that Shell's offer of salary to head their aviation department would be three times my military pay. With Joe, the boys, and both our mothers to support, it was an offer I couldn't refuse.

NOTE

1. Lindbergh, Charles A., *The Spirit of St. Louis*. New York: Charles Scribner's Sons, 1953, pp. 325–326.

CHAPTER 7

The decision to resign from the service was not an easy one because I knew I would miss the opportunity of flying and testing every type of aircraft the Army had or anyone wanted to sell to it. As chief test pilot at McCook I was privileged to know all the aircraft manufacturers on a first-name basis. The aviation fraternity was quite small at that time and everyone knew everyone else. They were all people of substance, people of ideas, some of them geniuses. Some were good business people, most were not. The creative genius is not always the chap who is best able to make a buck and run an airplane factory efficiently.

But the offer from the Shell company was one that I literally couldn't afford to pass up. Three times the military salary of about $200 a month meant a better life for the Doolittles. Joe's mother and my mother were both ill at the time. So my decision was purely economic.

My resignation from the Army took effect on February 15, 1930. One of my friends advised me to apply for a commission as a major in the Specialist-Reserve and I received that commission effective March 5, 1930, thus skipping the rank of captain. This was to cause me some difficulty later with my contemporaries who remained in the service because I outranked them when I went on my annual two-week tours of reserve duty. They said I had left the service to "feather my nest" and didn't deserve a two-step promotion, even if it was in the reserves.

The night before my resignation was effective, Joe and I were given a dinner party in New York City by the many friends we had made over the previous decade, including newspaper reporters, industrialists, businessmen, and civilian neighbors. We were overwhelmed that so many people would turn out to wish us well in our new life. I was asked to say a few words and I said as few as I thought I could without insulting our hosts. I said I was getting out of uniform because of my advanced age.

I didn't want to criticize the Army's low pay scales publicly, but I had been a first lieutenant for almost ten years and no promotion seemed to be in sight for perhaps another ten. It seems to me that the military pay scales have always lagged behind those of industry, especially for those who engage in hazardous duties such as test flying.

What Shell had in mind for me sounded almost too good to be true. The company had conceived the idea that there was a future for aviation as a means of mass transportation, and decided to get into the business of providing aviation fuel and lubricants in America as it had been doing in Europe. All of the "name" oil companies were hiring well-known pilots at that time to represent their products at air races, by setting records and otherwise getting their respective companies in the news in a favorable way. Among them was Jimmy Mattern at Pure Oil; Frank Hawkes at Texaco; Eddie Aldrin at Standard Oil; Billy Parker at Phillips; Al Williams at Gulf; and Roscoe Turner at Gilmore Oil Company.

At that time Shell Union had three oil companies—Shell Oil in San Francisco, Shell Petroleum in St. Louis, and Shell Eastern in New York. Shell had hired John Macready in 1929 to set up an aviation department in California, and John recommended me for a similar job in St. Louis.

Part of the arrangement I had with Shell included the company's purchase of a Lockheed Vega for $25,000. The slick, barrel-shaped fuselage with its 425-horsepower Pratt & Whitney Wasp engine enabled the plane to flash along at better than 200 miles per hour. I took delivery of the Vega at the Lockheed factory in Burbank and flew it to Mitchel. The company said I could fly Joe and the boys and some of our belongings to St. Louis, so we planned to leave early on February 16, the day after my resignation was effective.

It had snowed the night before and was very cold and windy. At daylight we loaded our things into the Vega and said our good-byes to a number of folks who had come to see us off, and I taxied out to the takeoff area. Previous rains had softened up the field and there were deep ruts, now frozen and snow covered, which had been made by aircraft wheels before the ground froze. I lined up and gave it full throttle. The takeoff roll seemed sluggish and I should have sensed something was wrong. After going a few yards, the wheels caught crosswise in a snowdrift. The door between me and the cabin where Joe and the boys were strapped in flew open and I fell backward. I thought Joe had opened it, which she had not done. I hurriedly righted myself and continued the takeoff. The left wheel hit another snowdrift, and the sudden drag on the left side was more than the plane could take. The gear gave way and the Vega plowed into the frozen ground, careened sideways, ground-looped, and nosed up in the snow, causing damage to the left wing and propeller.

Luckily, although the fuel tank was ruptured, there was no fire. I say luckily because the cabin door was jammed by the snow and we couldn't have gotten out quickly if there had been one. People came running and we extricated ourselves from the mess of suitcases and boxes. It seemed obvious that we had ended the flight this way because the Vega was overloaded.

Those who witnessed this scene say that the unique, unprintable language I used against myself and my stupidity was something they never expected to hear again. It is also said that Captain John McCullough, a good friend of ours, wisely led young Jim and John away so they wouldn't hear such invective from a parent. One of them is reported to have told McCullough, "You should have heard what my father said to my mother—and it wasn't her fault he cracked up the plane!"

I'm sure the story is true because I did blame Joe at first for opening the door behind the pilot's seat when it was actually the latch that had failed, or I hadn't closed it tightly. The real cause of the accident was overloading, something I could have controlled but didn't. I called the Shell people in St. Louis to tell them what had happened and that I would be late reporting for work.

Of all the embarrassments any brand-new employee could have, mine cost Shell, my first real employer, about $10,000 to repair the Vega. Worse than that for a pilot who had been so glamorized in the press, I had to take the family to St. Louis by train. Not a very auspicious way to begin a new job and a new life as a civilian. To add insult to injury, *The New York Times* ran a story headlined, "Doolittle's First Civilian Hop in 12 Years Fails; Ex-Army Pilot Crashes in Snow Before Start."

Much to my relief, no one at Shell ever criticized me for the accident. They didn't have to. I reported to work a very humble individual.

Soon after I was hired, I was given the job of coordinating the activities of the aviation departments at all three Shell locations. This was a matter of some delicacy, since Macready, who had gotten me my job, was now to some degree responsible to me. So was R. G. "Gil" Ervin, who held the aviation job at Shell Eastern. Both he and Macready had been senior to me in the military. Fortunately, both kept their sense of humor and we had no disagreements. There could have been problems by my having to report to three presidents, too. But these gentlemen were such wonderful characters that I had no trouble working for them.

After I felt comfortable in the job, I received a call from Jack Allard. By 1930, he had become president of the Curtiss-Wright Export Company. He wanted to know if I would be interested in going to Europe to represent Curtiss as I had done twice in South America. He was sure Shell would be interested in having their logo and name exposed to the Europeans, and he was right. Jack outlined an 8,000-mile, three-month itinerary. William F. Goulding, vice president of Curtiss-Wright Export, went along to demonstrate the Curtiss Robin, a small single-engine cabin plane. The Army loaned us Captain John K. "Joe" Cannon, who flew the Curtiss Fledgling, and Lieutenant James E. Parker, who flew the Falcon. I was to "do my thing" with the Curtiss P-6 Hawk. Major Melvin Hall and two mechanics rounded out the Curtiss-Wright–Shell team. None of our wives accompanied us.

We left in April 1930 and our first demonstrations were on May 1 in Athens, Greece. For the next 10 weeks we toured through Europe via Turkey, Bulgaria, Yugoslavia, Hungary, Poland, France, Germany, the Netherlands, Austria, Norway, and Sweden. The tour gave me an opportunity not only to see how these countries had recovered from the war, but also to observe their progress in aviation. The Germans were building good-looking Dorniers; the French had an impressive Farman; and Fokker was, as usual, putting innovations into its new aircraft.

There were two minor incidents on this trip. On a flight from Munich to Bern, Switzerland, I ran into fog and, without visual reference and radio aids, was unable to ascertain my most probable position. In other words, I was lost. When I found a hole, I thought it prudent to land in a pasture to find out where I was.

I landed in a section of muddy pasture and immediately got stuck. I knew right away I wouldn't be able to blast out without some help. I saw a man standing on the other side of the pasture and walked over to him. Knowing that most Swiss speak two or more languages, I tried my Spanish, then a little French, then a little German, but nothing got a response. At that point, the man asked in very plain English, "Mister, just what are you trying to say?" He was a Boy Scout leader from Spokane, Washington, who was escorting some Scouts through Europe. He rounded up his boys and we got the plane onto solid ground. The boys had maps and told me where I was. When the fog lifted, I took off for Bern.

On another occasion, in Budapest, Hungary, we were given a reception by Admiral Miklós Horthy, the country's dictator. The American ambassador, J. Butler Wright, reciprocated with a dinner where we met Horthy's 20-year-old son. Afterward, young Horthy wanted to show us the Budapest night spots. En route, when we were driving alongside the Danube with its many low bridges, young Horthy asked if I could fly under one of them. I took one look, estimated that I could, and volunteered to show him. We immediately drove to the airport where I warmed up the Hawk. They returned to the bridge and waited. I gave them the spectacle they expected, although I admit the squeeze underneath for the Hawk seemed a little tight, especially in the dark.

I didn't think much about this afterward until I heard that the British minister had written to Ambassador Wright, criticizing me for the escapade, which had apparently become the talk of the town. He said it would have been an awful affront to international relations if I had killed myself. I don't know how that was so, but his opening line in the very formal note was a jewel. He said, "I would do little to belittle Doolittle but . . ."

In fact, I did have a belittling experience on that trip, in Sweden. I departed Oslo for Stockholm and decided to give my welcoming committee a buzz job upon my arrival—inverted. I dove down and turned over. As soon as I did, I was drenched in gasoline and inhaled and swallowed a lot before I could turn back over. Obviously, the filler cap on the gas tank had either not been replaced by a mechanic at Oslo after refueling or had come loose. I landed quickly, shut the engine down, climbed out, and walked toward the welcoming committee. I stuck out my hand and as I did, my queasy stomach had all it could take. I regurgitated right there in front of everybody.

Next day, I thought I owed it to everyone who had witnessed my sickening arrival to put on a good show, so I gave it everything.

We returned to the States in mid-July, but there was bad news awaiting me. During my absence, my mother, who had been ill for some time, had gotten much worse. She passed away two months later, on September 22, 1930.

Since I had been hired by Shell to "show the flag" for the company wherever and whenever it seemed appropriate, my interest was always in the air races. One ship that captured my attention was the Beech Travel Air "R." In 1929, Douglas Davis had won the free-for-all race in it for the Thompson Cup (not the Charles E. Thompson Trophy, which was first awarded the following year). He had defeated Lieutenant R. G. Breene, who had been flying a Curtiss P-3A; it was the first time that a civilian plane had outflown a military aircraft. The press dubbed the plane the "Mystery Ship" because as soon as Doug arrived at Cleveland, it was put under wraps and he refused to let anyone see it until race time. He easily won the race with a speed of 194.9 miles per hour for the 50-mile course, but that was misleading. He had missed a pylon on his second lap, so he had turned back to get around it and then passed everybody again. His speed might have been clocked at nearly 240 miles per hour otherwise. During the air races that year, Frank Hawkes flew a Travel Air "R" coast to coast in 12 hours, 25 minutes, for a new record.

About this time, Jimmy Haizlip, a racing pilot with many air race victories and speed records to his credit, was hired by Shell. The Haizlips became our next-door neighbors in St. Louis. I persuaded Shell to purchase a Travel Air so that Jimmy and I could do our part to keep the Shell name in the papers with speed runs and racing. Jim Wheeler, another Shell pilot, flew a Howard that the company had purchased to round out our fleet. The company sponsored a number of different trophies for various classes of aircraft, which also kept the Shell name visible.

Although I flew the Mystery Ship several times at the 1930 National Air Races held at the Curtiss-Wright-Reynolds Airport in Chicago, I did not enter any races. Jimmy Haizlip did and placed second in the first of the Thompson Trophy races with the Mystery Ship. He also won the Transport Race flying the Vega. By this time, the National Air Races had grown to 44 events plus 5 air derbies, 2 of which were for women pilots. Five of the 44 events were only for the military services—Army, Navy, Marine Corps, and National Guard.

I flew the Mystery Ship several times at other air shows, putting on 20-minute aerobatic shows each time. Later, I had a midair collision with Lieutenant John R. Cross, who was flying a PT-3 trainer, over Kansas City Airport during an exhibition. I don't know who was at fault. He bailed out successfully. I landed without difficulty and with only minor damage to the plane.

At another exhibition at Akron flying the Mystery, I made a dead stick landing in a pasture. I made another at Georgetown, Indiana, when the engine bolts broke.

A while later, when Haizlip was flying the Travel Air, he had a crash landing because of engine failure and fairly well washed the airplane out. Shell didn't want to spend any money fixing it up, but I thought it could be repaired and, in so doing, could possibly be made the world's fastest aircraft with a few modifications I had in mind. It took all of the Doolittle family savings but I bought the wreckage and began to rebuild it. I didn't want Shell to take any unreasonable financial risk, so I never asked for help from the company.

In addition to installing a more powerful Pratt & Whitney engine, I redesigned the wings and fuselage slightly, streamlined some exposed parts, such as the wing struts, and put "pants" over the wheels. While the modifications were being made, I flew the Vega on a number of trips to keep the Shell name in the papers.

The rebuilt Travel Air was ready for a test hop on June 23, 1931, at the Curtiss-Steinberg Airport, near St. Louis. I named it the *Doolittle 400*. The announcement that I was going to fly it spread around the field, but I didn't mind an audience because I was convinced the airplane was ready. I took off and gradually put the ship through its aerobatic paces. It flew beautifully. Exhilarated, I dove for the field, came over at about 100 feet, and was pleased to see that the airspeed needle was almost reaching 300 miles per hour. As I pulled up to about 500 feet, I heard the ominous sound of cracking metal. The wings had begun to break; the ailerons snapped off and my control was gone.

The sequence of events was so sudden that I'm not sure what I did, but a motion picture crew photographed the disintegration of the plane and my departure from it. The pictures show that I pulled the rip cord immediately, the 'chute opened, and I hit the ground almost as quickly as I can describe the incident. The plane hit the ground simultaneously a half mile or so away. No need to say that it was demolished beyond repair. I wrote in my logbook: "Lost ailerons, ship crashed. God passenger."

I used two safety belts in those days and I remember being almost sorry I had put on that second belt because I think I spent a few seconds trying to find the latch for it.

Jimmy Haizlip and I walked over the path of the flight and picked up pieces that showed that the entire right aileron and part of the left had failed under the stress of the pull-up.

For the second time, I had joined the Caterpillar Club, that group of pilots who had saved their lives thanks to a group of silkworms who had spun the silk for their parachutes. I know how lucky I was because it was said to be one of the lowest unplanned parachute jumps in history.

Joe was not happy when she heard the news that our savings were now represented by a heap of metal, fabric, and wire. And I was not happy because it was my redesign that was the probable cause. I had installed new ailerons and reworked the aileron torque tubes by bending them. The ailerons must have been overbalanced at high speed and weakened the torque tubes. I had no one to blame but myself.

This incident did not lessen my desire to compete in the upcoming 1931 races. I called E. M. "Matty" Laird at his plant in Wichita, Kansas. I knew he had built the plane that won the 1930 Thompson Trophy. It had been flown by Charles "Speed" Holman, who was clocked at an average speed of 201.9 miles per hour. Matty had called Speed's plane the Laird Solution, and a new one was going to be named Super Solution. I thought it would be ideal to fly in the 1931 Bendix cross-country race. Matty was delighted that I was interested and gave his okay. I checked it out, liked it, and flew it to California.

The Bendix cross-country race was sponsored by Vincent Bendix, an industrialist, whose Bendix Aviation Corporation held 5,500 patents for automotive products. He had been persuaded by Clifford W. Henderson, the originator and promoter of the National Air Races, to put up $15,000, which was matched by the Cleveland Air Race committee for prize money for the first Transcontinental Free-for-All Speed Dash for the Bendix Trophy, to be flown from United Airport at Burbank, California, to Cleveland. The winner would receive $7,500.

The race was scheduled to begin right after midnight on September 4, 1931. Entrants had to cross the finish line at Cleveland before 7 P.M. eastern time that day. Bendix also posted a special award of $2,500 to induce the transcontinental pilots to continue to New York in an effort to break the west-east speed record of 12 hours, 25 minutes, held by Captain Frank Hawkes.

I planned to make refueling stops at Albuquerque and Kansas City. Shell refueling teams would be at both fields; they had worked out a fast method of servicing the plane with 140 gallons of fuel in under 10 minutes. If I landed at Cleveland in sufficient time to gas up so that the record could be broken, I was determined to try. The race officials promised that special refueling provisions would be made at Cleveland for those continuing to the New York area. With luck, it looked like an hour might be shaved off Frank's time.

I had seven competitors at the start. Six were flying Lockheeds and one, Walter Hunter, was flying a Travel Air Mystery S. The other participants were Art Goebel, an ex-Hollywood stunt pilot, who had won the Dole Race from Oakland to Honolulu in 1927; Beeler Blevins, a barnstormer from Atlanta; Harold S. Johnson, a Chicago-based airline pilot, first to loop a Ford Tri-motor; Captain Ira C. Eaker, flying a modified civilian Lockheed Altair; Lou Reichers, pilot for magazine publisher Bernarr MacFadden; and James G. Hall, a wealthy stockbroker, who had achieved the dubious distinction of having been catapulted out of a plane after crashing into a house and whose life had been saved when his 'chute opened and landed him safely in a churchyard a half block away.

A crowd had assembled to see us off at Burbank even though it was after midnight. First off was Reichers in his Altair, followed by Hunter in the Mystery S, and Eaker in another Altair. Johnson was next, and then Blevins, both in Orions. I was next off, at 1:40 A.M. Pacific time, followed by Goebel in a Vega and Hall in another Altair.

Each of us had 2,046 miles to go; each chose his own route of flight, altitude, and fuel stops. Weather reports were not reliable in those days, and we fully expected to run into some submarginal conditions at some altitude when flying that distance. Some of us were experienced in instrument flying, others were not. Ira Eaker had already established an aviation "first," flying coast to coast on instruments while under the hood.

Two hours, 52 minutes out of Burbank, I landed at Albuquerque, where my Shell crew gassed the Super Solution and handed me a glass of milk. I was off for Kansas City, not knowing where my competitors were.

As it turned out, Hunter landed at Winslow, Arizona, and at Fort Riley, Kansas. Near Terre Haute, his engine quit and caught on fire. He had a broken fuel line and was burned slightly as he landed at Terre Haute's Dresser Airport.

Lou Reichers also failed to finish. Without much, if any, experience flying on instruments, he had tried to follow a railroad and must have followed the wrong track at a switch. Lost and out of fuel, he landed at Beatrice, Nebraska. Meanwhile, Goebel, Hall, Blevins, Johnson, and Eaker were en route, each hoping they were in the lead.

My speed average looked good to me: I figured I was making about 228 miles per hour. I landed at Kansas City three hours, five minutes after leaving Albuquerque. If the winds held up and I had no problems, I would gas up at Cleveland, no matter what the outcome, and continue eastward to Newark and the $2,500 prize, even if I didn't win the Bendix.

The fairly good weather and a favoring tailwind held and I landed at Cleveland 9 hours, 10 minutes, 21 seconds after leaving Burbank. I wasn't sure I had won, because others might still beat my elapsed time, but Ephraim W. "Pop" Cleveland, chairman of the Bendix Contest Committee, said I was first in and had probably won the $7,500 prize.

It was drizzling at Cleveland when I landed, and there wasn't much of a crowd there. Joe and the boys were there, however, and I told them I intended to push on for the transcontinental record. I took off quickly and headed into steadily deteriorating weather. A squall line lay ahead, so I hunkered down in the cockpit and rode out the rain and rough turbulence on instruments. Once I cleared the Allegheny Mountains, the weather lightened up, and I dove at high speed over Newark Airport for a landing a little before five P.M. eastern time.

The press had gotten the word of my intentions, and my

coast-to-coast flying time from Burbank to Newark was verified at 11 hours, 11 minutes, more than an hour better than Frank Hawks's transcontinental record. I now had the honor of being first to fly coast to coast in less than a day and in less than half a day. I had to pay my own expenses on the first trip, but I won $2,500 for the second one. Both flights had begun on the same date—September 4, an unplanned coincidence.

I learned after arrival at Newark that my average speed for the Bendix was 223.058 miles per hour. Second was Harold Johnson, who came in at Cleveland an hour after I did, for the $4,500 prize, followed by Blevins, who received the final prize of $3,000. Eaker, Goebel, and Hall followed in that order. With my $10,000 winnings, it had been a worthwhile day's work.

Pilots who continued to Newark were requested by the race officials to return to Cleveland at their earliest convenience, although it didn't have to be the same day. Since there were still some hours left in the day, I waved good-bye to the crowd and returned to Cleveland, where Joe and the boys were still waiting. As soon as I landed, I called St. Louis and found the office force there was jubilant. Vice President Alexander Fraser said he was hosting a big celebration party and wanted me to be there. It sounded like an order to me, so Jimmy Haizlip and I took off in the company Vega and arrived about 10 P.M. Next morning, Fraser and I returned to Cleveland to watch the rest of the races and accept the prize money. I didn't receive the Bendix Trophy until later, since it wasn't ready yet.

The Super Solution was all right for straight-and-level flight, but not necessarily for racing around pylons. It had a 21-foot wingspan and 108 square feet of wing area, carried about 112 gallons of gas, and weighed 1,580 pounds light and about 2,500 pounds fully loaded. Matty hoped the plane's high speed would be about 300 miles per hour. The airplane was stable longitudinally and laterally, but extremely unstable directionally. This directional instability increased with speed, and the airplane was barely manageable at a speed of 200 miles per hour. The problem seemed to be the wheel pants and fairing, so they were removed; nine inches were added to the tail fin and rudder height. When these changes were made, the plane became directionally stable, but not as stable laterally as before.

The Super Solution was extremely temperamental. It seemed impossible to "rig," or adjust, the landing and flying wires evenly so that the plane would not be wing heavy on one side of the ship. It would fly perfectly for a while and then gradually become left-wing heavy.

Finally, in desperation during a test flight, I slapped the stick over hard to the right, but after leveling off, wing heaviness was greatly increased. This gave me an idea. The right wing was depressed and the stick moved sharply to the left. The airplane was then only slightly left-wing heavy. The maneuver was repeated and the airplane balanced perfectly. I repeated the process again, and actual right-wing heaviness resulted. Here was an airplane that could actually be rigged in flight!

The difficulty was that it wouldn't hold its rig. This fault became continually and rapidly more apparent and annoying. In one flight in very rough air, the rigging became so flabby that an actual lateral motion of the trailing edge of the upper wing could be seen when the ailerons were moved and when a bump hit one wing more severely than the other.

Before the flight was completed, I found it impossible to get the airplane out of the left bank at cruising speed without throttling back; so I made all turns, even around the landing field, to the right.

In addition to this problem we had another. The original engine had been a direct-drive type; we installed a geared engine in its place, which gave us about an eight-mile-per-hour increase in speed. Now there was a very strong tendency to roll to the left. The airplane was then rigged very right-wing heavy in order to correct this tendency at full throttle, but it was doubtful if it could be handled safely in a race.

I practiced flying the course for a few laps at 240 miles per hour, then opened the throttle wide. A teammate on the ground was instructed to watch until I rocked my wings and then to time the next lap, as it would be the only one at full throttle.

Coming down the home stretch, I rocked the stick laterally, but the rolling motion of the airplane was so slight that I was afraid my ground observer would not see it. The 10-mile course in 1931 was an irregular pentagon. The first two pylons were executed successfully, but at the third, where the angle was sharper, the left wing would not come up and I was unable to recover from the bank until I rolled completely over. I rolled into a steep right bank to get back on the course and had difficulty getting back out of the right bank.

I banked to the left of the fourth pylon and the bank increased, even with the controls reversed, so I had to throttle back to regain control of the airplane. Obviously, the geared engine could not be used in the Thompson race, not because of any torque difficulties but because wing warping at high speeds induced the aileron reversal. This condition became critical at about 260 miles per hour.

In order to check the speed of the airplane with geared versus direct-drive engine, I made an attempt to fly the three-kilometer course. On the first run, the airplane gradually rolled to the left until it was out of control. I throttled back and tried again. This time I entered the course with the right wing down about 30 degrees. After about one kilometer, the airplane was level, and at the two-kilometer mark, the left wing was down some 30 degrees and depressing rapidly. I throttled back and landed, unable to make even one run across the three-kilometer course.

The Thompson race was scheduled for the next day, and we were convinced that the geared engine had to be replaced with the direct drive. The engines were changed overnight and we spent the morning before race time rigging the airplane.

The difficulty I had in the test flights and in the race itself indicated something was loosening up and that the wing warping tendencies were rapidly becoming worse. We finally rigged the plane very right-wing heavy to facilitate getting out of left banks and I entered the Thompson Trophy race on September 7. My competitors, in addition to Ira Eaker, were Lowell Bayles flying a Granville Brothers Gee-Bee Z, a stubby-winged racer in which Bayles had been clocked at 286 miles per hour; Jimmy Wedell in a Wedell-Williams; Dale Jackson in a Laird Solution; Bob Hall with a Gee-Bee Y; Benny Howard in his self-designed Little Pete; and Bill Ong in a Laird Speedwing.

I didn't fare too badly until the seventh lap when the engine overheated and a piston failed. I had to call it quits and drop out.

Bayles won the race with the Gee-Bee Z with an average speed of 236.239 miles per hour. He was killed in this aircraft the following December near Detroit when his plane, very close to the ground, suddenly flipped, crashed, and burned.

In the weeks following the 1931 races, at the behest of the Shell public relations folks, I began to establish a series of city-to-city records as an advertisement for the company's fuels and lubricants. One of these flights that received some notice would link the capitals of Canada, the United States, and Mexico in a single day. I flew the Super Solution to Ottawa, where I was handed messages from Premier Richard B. Bennett to the two presidents.

I landed in Washington after flying through bad weather in 2 hours, 20 minutes. I wanted to get off quickly, but the officials there dragged out the ceremony and it was a half hour or more before I got off the ground. I landed at Birmingham and Corpus Christi, where my faithful Shell teams fueled me in seven minutes and sixteen minutes respectively.

Things were going smoothly and as planned, but en route to Mexico City at about 18,000 feet over the most jagged part of the Sierra Madre Mountains, I began to feel faint and nauseated. At first, I thought it was because of lack of oxygen or maybe lack of sleep. I began to ask myself some elementary questions, such as, "What year did Columbus discover America?" and "When was the Declaration of Independence signed?" I gave myself some simple math problems, like, "What is 13 times 13" and "Subtract 164 from 321," but the faintness and goofy feeling continued. I told myself that when I couldn't answer a simple question, I'd jump. That would be better than passing out and crashing unconscious.

After what seemed a very long time, I started the letdown to Mexico City and hoped the lower altitude would make me feel better. It didn't. Something was wrong with me, but I couldn't figure out what it was.

Instead of making the expected Doolittle speed run across the airport, I made a conservative approach and taxied up to the terminal. As soon as I set the brakes, cut the engine, and got out, I regurgitated in front of the welcoming party, just as I had done in Stockholm, only more so. It was another of my most embarrassing moments.

The flight had been made in 11 hours, 40 minutes flying time, as advertised, thankfully. But I was worried. What was the matter with me? I felt slightly better the next day and went out to the airport to see if I could figure out what had happened. Could it be exhaust fumes from the engine leaking into the cockpit? No leaks were found.

I checked the cockpit, and behind my seat was the solution to the mystery. I always carried a small can of tetraethyl lead on my flights. The Super Solution's engine required a higher-octane fuel than that available at most airports, so I carried the lead to pour into the gas tank to prevent knocking. One of the cans had burst, probably because of the altitude, and the highly toxic fumes had filled the cockpit. I felt ill for several days. Had I not been in excellent shape, I would have had serious trouble. Another valuable lesson learned.

I stayed in Mexico City for about a week and told the Mexicans I was going to set a record from Mexico City to St. Louis. I did. I returned to St. Louis, with stops in Brownsville and Shreveport, in 6 hours, 35 minutes of flying time.

When 1932 began, we came up with a new idea to help sell air travel and prove it was safe. Joe, two other passengers, and I left St. Louis in the Vega early one morning and landed at Jacksonville, Florida, for breakfast. We then flew to Havana, Cuba, for lunch, where I put on a demonstration for Cuban officials. We then flew to Miami for supper. The flight made news, not because of the speed I made between each stop but because we deliberately made it look casual. Writers predicted that businessmen would be able to save valuable time with company-owned planes, which is what we hoped they would say.

Another venture the Shell public relations folks planned for me was a flight to commemorate the bicentennial year of George Washington's birth by flying over all the routes covered by our first president during his lifetime and do it in a single day. Prior to that time, anyone affixing an airmail stamp to a letter would drop the letter in a mailbox with the same feeling with which a sailor on board a ship might toss a sealed bottle containing a letter into the ocean. The real purpose of the flight was to make Americans conscious of the fact that the burgeoning commercial airlines could be trusted to deliver letters anywhere in the country. It was also to convince Congress that appropriations for the airmail service were not being tossed into some speculative, boondoggling operation.

The flight would also commemorate the one hundred fifty-seventh anniversary of the founding of postal service for the united colonies with Benjamin Franklin as its first director. The flight would cover 14 states—from Maine to North Carolina and west to Ohio. Commemorative mail would be carried and dropped along the 2,600-mile route at points of particular significance either in Washington's travels or in his career as a military or political leader. Anne Madison Washington, an attractive, middle-aged great-grandniece of our first president, would go along, plus Alphius F. Maple, editor of Shell's magazine, who represented the Aeronautical Chamber of Commerce.

Shell did a good job of publicizing the flight beforehand. I figured out the flight plan and said we would drop the mailbags on a preannounced schedule with two stops for fuel: Washington and Pittsburgh. The bags would be dropped at landing strips, if there were any, or at the closest vacant lot to the post office. We would circle certain other towns without dropping any mail and proceed on our preset course.

On the morning of July 24, 1932, I took off from Washington, D.C., in a bright yellow Lockheed Orion 9C Special that Shell had purchased, named *Shellightning*, with Miss Washington aboard. I landed at Newark where Maple got aboard. We then flew to Boston where we stayed overnight. At 4:35 A.M. on July 25, we picked up 30 bags of mail and flew to Kittery, Maine, the official starting point for the flight.

We flew low over Kittery, which had no airport, so the mailbag was thrown out the door. We swung south and repeated the mailbag drops at Providence, Rhode Island; New Haven, Connecticut; Brooklyn, New York; and Philadelphia. We circled and dropped letters to certain townspeople at Morristown, Trenton, and Camden, New Jersey, and at Valley Forge and Philadelphia, Pennsylvania, all places with special significance in Washington's life.

I landed at 9:15 A.M. at Washington, D.C., for gas, then headed for Mount Vernon, Wakefield, and Yorktown, Virginia, more towns with special meaning to the first president. The next mail was dropped at Sunbury, North Carolina. Turning north again, we flew over Christiansburg and Winchester, Virginia, then turned northwest to Fort Necessity and Pittsburgh, Pennsylvania, where we stopped for refueling.

Leaving Pittsburgh, we flew to Point Pleasant and Pomeroy, Ohio, the point farthest west to which Washington ever traveled. Heading northeast, we went to Fort Le Boeuf, near Waterford, Pennsylvania, then to Rome, New York, for a dusk mail drop. From there we went to Crown Point, Ticonderoga, and Albany, and made a final mail drop at West Point on the U.S. Military Academy grounds. We landed, exhausted, at Newark at 9:17 P.M., 15 hours, 40 minutes after dropping the bags at Kittery. As advertised, we had dropped mail or circled every town on our itinerary and completed the entire run on the schedule we had announced prior to the flight. Shell had prepared many postcards and covers with special cachets which were addressed to politicians and customers on our mailing list and mailed at the various drop points. Those might be very valuable today; however, I understand that very few ended up in the hands of philatelists.

In addition to being a nice advertisement for Shell, the flight was another plug for aviation. We had shown it was possible for a pilot to navigate to a number of towns, drop mail at any of them, and do it on a reliable schedule. And it could be done with passengers aboard.

While a number of other publicity flights were accomplished during that time period, I wanted to enter the 1932 Bendix race and then the Thompson Trophy race. We all felt sure a modified version of the Super Solution could be designed that would be much faster. Over the next few months, Laird and his people made a number of changes on the original, including a larger engine, new engine cowling, stronger wing trussing, increased gas capacity, and installation of a controllable pitch propeller and retractable landing gear. I figured these changes, especially the retractable gear, would allow me to get from 50 to 60 miles per hour more out of it. We also raised the pilot's seat 10 inches so I could see over the upper wing. A slide door was arranged in the cockpit covering so I could stick my head and shoulders out to see ahead when landing.

It seemed we had corrected all the faults in the original design by August 1932. The first test flight of the redesigned plane on August 23 at Wichita tended to prove our belief correct until time came to land. Then a new problem arose. The landing gear, in ground tests, dropped all the way out and then was spread and locked into place. In actual flight, however, the air loads and the rotation of the slipstream spread the gear before it could drop out and lock. I spent almost two hours trying to jar the gear loose and finally managed to crank one wheel partly down, but that was all.

I wrote a note about the difficulty and dropped it to the ground crew: "Something wrong landing gear. Can get three and one-half turns both ways. If you have suggestions, write them on side of plane and come up. Otherwise, will use up gas and belly in."

After a hurried consultation among the mechanics, one of them wrote on the side of a plane that flew alongside me: "Zoom right. Zoom left. Power dive." I acknowledged by waving, but had already tried these things and nothing worked. I had to land belly up on the grass at the Wichita Airport. There was no damage to me, but the damage to the Laird was so extensive that trying to repair the racer in time for the Bendix race was out of the question.

My misfortune made the papers nationwide and I received a number of offers from racing plane manufacturers who wanted me to fly their planes. The race was scheduled for August 27 and there wasn't time for me to test fly their planes, choose one, and then go to Burbank for the start.

One of those who called was Zantford D. Granville, oldest of the five Granville brothers, who had been making a line of racers they called Gee-Bee Sportsters in Springfield, Massachusetts. Their shop was located in an abandoned dance hall near the city dump. They had obtained financing through the Springfield Air Racing Association and were intent upon producing the world's fastest planes, all hand built. They had built the Model Z Super Sportster with which Lowell Bayles had won the 1931 Goodyear and Thompson trophies. Unfortunately, he was killed in it in December 1931 when a gas cap apparently came loose, shot through the thin canopy, and hit Bayles on the head. The plane then crashed and burned.

The Granvilles had just completed two new models powered by new Pratt & Whitney 750-horsepower Wasp engines, which they designated the R-1 and R-2. Lee Gehlbach was going to fly the R-2 in the 1932 Bendix race, so I was asked if I wanted to fly the R-1 in the Thompson.

I immediately flew to Bowles Airport near Springfield to check the R-1 out. It had been flown only once, by Russell Boardman, but he had aborted the flight because the plane was too dangerous. The vertical fin was so small it was virtually nonexistent. There is no doubt the R-1 was a very directionally unstable airplane, despite the fact that the Granvilles had hurriedly added two square feet to the vertical fin and rudder. Boardman was to fly it in the Thompson but had crashed a few days earlier in another Gee-Bee and was still in the hospital.

The red-and-white plane with the 7-11 dice painted on the side was fascinating to look at. Only 18 feet long from prop to tail, it seemed like it was all engine with a minuscule set of wings and a bomblike fuselage. The extremely small cockpit sat far back and was faired into the fuselage just in front of the vertical stabilizer. This was no doubt to counterbalance the weight of the heavy engine. The airplane would be difficult to taxi because the cockpit position provided no straight-ahead visibility, and with such a small tail area, the wing would also blank out rudder action until the tail was well up on takeoff. On landing, blanking from the wing would probably mean loss of rudder control at a relatively high speed.

Recognizing that this airplane would be extremely hot to handle, I knew I had to fly it delicately. I walked around it several times to try to predict what it would do in flight. I climbed in, had the hatch closed from the outside, and warmed up the engine. The engine was obviously extremely powerful and ready to go, so I blasted off and headed for Cleveland. I didn't even make a turn around the field. I could tell from the first moment that it was a touchy and probably unpredictable airplane.

I made a conservative approach and landed at Cleveland without difficulty, but I didn't trust this little monster. It was fast, but flying it was like balancing a pencil or an ice cream cone on the tip of your finger. You couldn't let your hand off the stick for an instant, and I didn't know how much angle of bank would be safe when making pylon turns. The other pilots would be cutting close to the pylons, but the speed of the Gee-Bee seemed to be so great that it would be prudent to stay outside of the rest of them, climb between pylons, dive before each turn, but remain outside.

My prudence was justified when I took the R-1 up for a test hop before the race. I climbed to 5,000 feet, and it's a good thing I did. It did two snap rolls before I could get it under control. If I hadn't had some altitude, I would have been dead. There was no doubt that I had to fly this thing every second I was in the air.

The Thompson race officials required qualification tests, and on September 1, 1932, I was clocked at 293.19 miles per hour, which would have been a new world's speed record except for one thing: there was no barograph installed to measure altitude, which was required by the National Aeronautic Association before a record flight could be considered official. The reason for the barograph was that a plane was not allowed to get above 1,300 feet while making its speed runs. I bitterly told the press that I thought such details were handled by the race officials in case someone did set a record. I said, "That's their business, not mine. A pilot has all he can do to fly his ship."

While that was disappointing, several things had happened

during the flight that concerned me. The engine cowling had begun to pull forward because some fastenings had split. This was compounded by propeller vibrations, and a vibrating prop is an invitation to a quick disaster.

Some repairs were made and I tried for the speed record again, this time with a barograph installed, but I couldn't exceed the world record of 278.48 miles per hour established by a Frenchman, Florentin Bonnet, in December 1924 by the required 4.97 miles per hour. However, the Doolittle family exchequer was richer by $1,575 for my having made the fastest qualifying time.

On September 3, we were required to make speed dashes in excess of 200 miles per hour that year in order to qualify for the Thompson. Although I had already qualified, I wanted another shot at the record. I had the barograph installed and made the four required runs, which were clocked at an average of 296.287 miles per hour. One run had been timed at 309.040 miles per hour. The Gee-Bee was now officially the world's fastest airplane.

There was tragedy later that day when Al Wilson, flying a 1910 Curtiss Pusher, was killed in a collision with an autogyro flown by John Miller. The two planes were to have a "dogfight" as one of the many events during the 10-day extravaganza. Miller and a passenger were unhurt.

A near tragedy occurred during a closed-course race for sportsmen pilots when a Lambert-powered Monocoupe flown by Paul S. Bloom collided with a Davis monoplane piloted by William A. Warrick, Jr., as the two rounded a pylon at the start of the second lap. Both were injured but survived.

The Thompson Trophy race was usually the final event in the Cleveland Air Races. My competition was impressive. In the order they qualified, they were: Jimmy Wedell, Roscoe Turner, Jimmy Haizlip, Bob Hall, Ray Moore, Bill Ong, Les Bowen, and Lee Gehlbach. Although I had the fastest qualifying time, everyone there knew by this time that anything could happen to a Gee-Bee or its pilot. The day was almost spoiled for the two Gee-Bees when Lee Gehlbach was taxiing the R-2. (He had placed fourth in the Bendix; Jimmy Haizlip won it flying a Wedell-Williams racer in 8 hours, 47 minutes.) While taxiing near my ship, he nearly rammed it because he couldn't see it. Only frantic arm-waving by a mechanic saved both aircraft from being wrecked.

Something else almost happened that could have ruined my day. I was starting up the R-1's engine when the carburetor backfired; flames suddenly engulfed the cowling and started to spread to the rear. I leaped out and a mechanic and I extinguished the fire. Fortunately, no damage was done. I started it up again and taxied out to the starting line.

Takeoffs were at 10-second intervals. Bob Hall was first off in his Hall Bulldog and I followed. Moore, Wedell, Haizlip, Gehlbach, Turner, and Ong got off in that order, but Moore soon had to drop out. Bowen never got off the ground.

I passed Hall quickly to take the lead and never lost it. I completed the 100-mile triangular course at the winning speed of 252.686 miles per hour, which was a new record for the Thompson race. Wedell was second, Turner third, and Haizlip fourth. Lee Gehlbach in the R-2 Gee-Bee came in fifth.

I breathed a very deep sigh of relief when they opened the canopy. My eyes were watering and blinking because of the hay fever that has plagued me all my life. Hundreds of people crowded around, and newspaper and radio reporters pushed and shoved trying to get to Mr. and Mrs. Thompson and me for some words of wisdom. I didn't have any, but I was happy. I had won the Thompson Trophy, considered by many to be the most prestigious racing prize, which had been my goal. The prize: $4,500. I also won the Clifford W. Henderson Trophy for winning the Thompson and having the fastest qualifying time. This award was won on points based on winning or placing in any events entered. In addition, I was awarded the Lowell R. Bayles Trophy for setting the world's speed record.

I flew the Gee-Bee back to Springfield the next day. I landed it, taxied up to the line, gratefully got out, and thanked the Granvilles. That airplane was the most dangerous airplane I have ever flown. I was asked many years later why I flew it if it was so dangerous, and the only answer I could think of was, "Because it was the fastest airplane in the world at the time."

The R-1 and R-2 later proved just how dangerous they were. During a takeoff from Indianapolis in the R-1 on the last leg to Cleveland during the next year's Bendix race, Russell Boardman died when the plane snap-rolled and crashed on takeoff. That same year, Jimmy Haizlip wrecked the R-2 during a landing at Springfield, but, fortunately, wasn't injured. The airplane was salvaged and rebuilt. In 1934, Zantford Granville, the real genius of the Granville brothers, was killed while landing at Spartanburg, South Carolina. Again, enough pieces were salvaged to rebuild the plane, but it was run into a ditch and wrecked by Roy Minor later that year. The R-2 was rebuilt a final time and met its end, along with Cecil Allen, after a takeoff from Burbank for the 1935 Bendix race.

Flying the Gee-Bee in that race had a profound effect on my thinking, especially when I learned that a bunch of newspaper photographers had crowded around Joe and the boys waiting to take pictures of the expressions on their faces if I crashed. Now that aviation had reached a threshold of maturity, I felt the time had clearly arrived to examine the role of the air races. They had served a useful purpose by arousing public interest in aviation. They had also become the inspiration and proving ground for new concepts in aircraft design and construction. Cockpit venting, retractable gear, and bold new wing and fuselage designs were born in the competition for the various trophies. But the price in planes and pilots had been high. I thought aviation should now begin to serve world commerce rather than be considered mostly a sport.

I surprised many people when I announced shortly after the 1932 races that I was retiring from air racing. What many had forgotten was that I had mentioned this the previous year after I made my bailout. At that time, I said I was quitting because of my advanced age of 34. Joe had told me how she felt about my racing and said she would like it better if I cut back on the more spectacular flying in favor of my engineering duties. She told reporters that she thought I had done my share of speed flying, but she left the decision up to me and never mentioned it again.

I told the press that we had learned a lot about engines and airplanes through racing, but at great cost in lives and equipment. The racing planes were the guinea pigs of aviation—the machines in which we had done years of experimenting. I thought the time had come to give attention to safety and reliability so that commercial aviation could develop for the common good.

My much-publicized views were not liked by the folks running the National Air Races. Here's what they said in a post-races news release:

> The value of air racing as a means of developing faster, more efficient and safer aircraft was clearly

> demonstrated at the 1932 [races] which were brought to a close at Cleveland on Labor Day.
>
> Some still will shout that the races are but a "Roman holiday," staged for the entertainment of the blood-thirsty. The records, however, disprove such statements. There were two serious accidents, one of them fatal, yet neither involved especially-designed racing planes.

My personal retirement from air racing didn't change anything. Racing continued until the outbreak of World War II, and a few closed course races are still held today; however, current federal regulations and race rules are much more strongly in favor of good maintenance and safe flying.

The mid-1930s were difficult economic times for the nation and especially for aviation. The Great Depression was devastating for most Americans, and President Franklin D. Roosevelt initiated various public programs to get us out of it. Shell, like all companies, was struggling against its competition here in the United States, but not many people were driving cars in those days, and flying commercially, although appealing, was certainly not commonplace.

It was different for commercial aviation in Europe. In May 1920, KLM, the Royal Dutch Airlines, had begun its first scheduled airline service between Amsterdam and London. Four months later, KLM inaugurated an Amsterdam-Hamburg-Copenhagen schedule. In 1924, it began regular service to Batavia, Java.

We were not progressing that fast in the United States. The U.S. Army Air Service had begun airmail service between Washington, Philadelphia, and New York on May 15, 1918. After proving it was possible to fly the mail on schedule, airmail flying was turned over to civilian pilots flying for the Post Office Department. Late in 1925, the Post Office awarded its first general airmail contracts to five airlines: Varney Air Lines (later merged with others to form United Airlines); Robinson Air Lines (the contract was later transferred to American Airlines); Western Air Transport (later Western Airlines); National Air Transport (also merged later into United); and Colonial Air Transport (a predecessor of American Airlines).

Shell actually had a long history of selling gasoline for aircraft use overseas, beginning in 1909 when Shell gas had fueled Louis Blériot's cross-channel flight. Shell companies on the Continent had become active sellers of aviation gasoline soon after. In 1920, Shell had set up a department in London to handle aviation fuel sales to such airline customers as KLM.

By 1929, Shell was becoming active in the aviation fuel business in the States. That's when they hired John Macready from General Motors' Frigidaire Division to head up their operation in San Francisco. His department started officially on January 1, 1930. My official hiring date was January 15, 1930, although I was not officially released from the Army until February 15; Gil Ervin was hired away from Curtiss Flying Service in March for the Shell Eastern aviation department.

At the end of 1929, two years after Lindbergh's flight to Paris, Shell was selling 20.5 million gallons of aviation gasoline annually to private fliers and unscheduled operators; less than a third of this production (about 6.25 million gallons) was sold to the scheduled airlines. During this period, hundreds of Americans bought and were learning to fly their own airplanes, just as their fathers had bought and learned to drive automobiles a quarter of a century before. Many people thought that the airplane was now about to displace the automobile, just as the auto had displaced the horse. But with the coming of the Depression, private flying proved far more dispensable than the automobile.

In 1930, sales of aviation gasoline to the burgeoning airlines equaled private plane consumption. Sales to airlines took the lead in 1931 and continued to account for an increasingly large percentage of the total, until by 1935 airlines were using a full two thirds of the aviation gasoline sold.

It was in 1935 that a single airplane—the Douglas DC-2—began to lead the way for the maturation of the airline industry. Radically different from its predecessors, with retractable gear, variable-pitch propellers, 14-passenger capacity, and other innovations, the DC-2 was followed two years later by the DC-3, which could carry 21 passengers. Substantial cuts in airline fares meant increased public interest in flying, which in turn meant more flights and, consequently, more sales of aviation gasoline.

Our three Shell aviation departments went after our share of the increased airline business. We captured accounts at Northwest Airlines, Chicago and Southern, and American.

* * *

Despite the success in selling gas to the airlines, I was concerned that we were falling behind other nations in military aeronautics and thought we should be looking forward to the development of more powerful engines for war planes so that heavier loads could be carried faster. While the airlines were struggling to become profitable by hauling passengers in addition to the mail, the nation's air arms were woefully inadequate because of meager appropriations. The Army Air Corps was not even a third-rate air force, compared with the air forces of other nations.

More powerful engines would demand better aviation fuels. Even back in the early 1920s we had begun to realize that there was a difference in the gasolines we used in our military aircraft. Harold R. Harris, chief test pilot at McCook in those days—he preceded John Macready—was always able to win races when other people were having trouble. The reason he won was that he installed higher-compression pistons in his engine. Others soon did the same thing, but Harris's pistons never burned out, while other people's pistons did. Long after, I found out what he knew that others didn't. He knew that some gasolines tended to cause detonation which decreased an engine's power; other gasolines tended to inhibit detonation.

He also knew that the Pennsylvania gasolines, which were high in paraffin content, had an excellent capacity for making lube oil, but had a very low knock grading and would burn out pistons rapidly. And he knew that California gasoline, high in aromatics, had a high knock rating. He found that out, probably, just by accident or by experiment, but he would always import California gasoline and use it in his racers, and he always won.

Out of this came the first notion that great differences in gasolines and their proper use in aircraft engines resulted from the crude from which they were made. In those days we understood a little bit about knock ratings, but not much—and the term "octane rating" hadn't even been invented. And this was before there were unique manufacturing processes.

Much work was being done here and in England on getting more power out of aircraft and automobile engines. A chap named Sam Heron at Wright Field, along with a British counterpart, did some fine work in determining those attributes of a fuel that would be most suitable for aviation use. They learned what caused detonation and how to avoid it. They had a profound effect on the development of gasolines and their improved knock grading. There were others at Wright Field who carried on these experiments and were working enthusiastically with the Ethyl Corporation and General Motors.

Meanwhile, those of us who were flying during the 1920s knew that if we wanted to try for a record flight, we'd better have the gasoline shipped in all the way from California to Ohio, rather than get it from Pennsylvania, right next door. It became obvious very shortly in our test work that if we had better fuels we could get substantially more power out of an aircraft engine by going to higher compression ratios. But then we came up against a chicken-and-egg situation: the engine manufacturers weren't interested in building an engine of superior quality when they couldn't get fuel for it; and the fuel manufacturers could see no point in developing an improved fuel for which no engine requirement existed.

That was when tetraethyl lead was introduced and made the gasoline better. However, if you put too much in, you would get spark plug fouling. The trick was to blend in the right mixture.

Eddie Aldrin, then at Standard Oil of New Jersey; Billy Parker at Phillips; and I at Shell were all pushing our companies to develop a superior fuel. In the thirties, most airline aircraft were using 87-octane fuel. If larger, more powerful engines were to be built, they would need fuel with a higher octane rating for smoother burning and decreased detonation. Other users were ordering 18 different leaded and unleaded aviation fuels that ranged in octane rating from 65, for Army trainers, to 95, requested by the Wright Corporation for special test work. It was clearly time to standardize and reduce the number of fuel specifications.

I also felt strongly that Shell should begin to make 100-octane fuel; in my campaign within Shell for its development, I based my argument on the "super planes" being proposed at Wright Field. I was in the know about them because I made frequent trips there and kept my Army contacts active. The bombers and fighters they had on the drawing boards or were flying experimentally would never see full production without engines that were not yet in existence.

Shell officials had to be convinced first. Since I worked there, I could lobby from the inside. Although Shell had an aviation gasoline division, fuel for aircraft was not its chief moneymaker. We were making 87-octane fuel for airline aircraft because the demand was there. But I argued that the demand was sure to increase for a higher-octane fuel, and no one else was doing anything about it. Shell should be ready to meet that demand when it came. We'd be ahead of the game, I argued, if we would just put some dollars into research.

In the ensuing years, I got more credit than was due me for persuading the company to take the risk. I think it was because Doolittle is kind of a weird name, and I seemed to get my name before the public when other people who did more didn't get as much recognition. I've always considered that the name Doolittle, in a strange way, has its advantages.

There was also considerable advantage to an advanced degree. I had to deal first with two Dutch scientists, Dr. Tydeman and Dr. Tymstra. I am sure that Jimmy Doolittle the stunt pilot and Jimmy Doolittle the racing pilot would not have been able to influence them. But I went to them as Dr. Doolittle, with an earned doctorate from MIT, and they listened patiently to my discourse.

I think there are two great benefits of an advanced degree: one is the increased knowledge and greater capability that you have, and the other is the prestige it gives you with your associates, particularly those who also have advanced degrees, so I took a calculated risk in pushing vigorously for what I believed was not only good for Shell but good for the military as well. I believed in 100-octane fuel, but I would not have been able to sell the idea had I not had the educational background that the Army had given me.

Of course, there was also an economic side to the decision that the company had to take into account. It was the middle of the Depression, and understandably, there was great reluctance to invest in expensive research and new facilities to manufacture iso-octane, the basis for 100-octane gasoline. Finally, the company's top management agreed to take the risk and invest several millions in the project, even though there was no market at the time. Of course, the profit motive was there, but we felt that we were competing for technical prestige and excellence, even though it meant doing temporary damage to the company's bottom line. Many in the company often and publicly called the effort "Doolittle's folly" and "Doolittle's million-dollar blunder."

In 1934, Shell made the first delivery of 1,000 gallons of iso-octane to the Air Corps for test purposes. The 100-octane rating was obtained from a blend of 40 percent iso-octane, 50 percent high-quality, straight-run gasoline, 10 percent iso-pentane, and three cubic centimeters of tetraethyl lead per gallon. But getting to the point of selling even that small quantity to the Army hadn't been easy. There was great opposition to the idea among the top nonflying leaders in the Army's general staff in Washington. In their wisdom, they had adopted a theoretically perfect but practically absurd idea: design all engines from motorcycles to bombers so they would use a single fuel and thus simplify supply problems in wartime.

In the tests at Wright Field using 100 octane, even with existing engines, increases of power output of from 15 to 30 percent were obtained over the power obtainable with the regular fuels. I did have strong support from people in the Air Corps who believed wholeheartedly in a superior fuel. But they were, unfortunately, all technical people without much clout. It was up to them and a few of us in the oil industry to persuade what, in essence, was the senior management of the Army Air Corps.

To their credit, certain brave souls at Wright Field in the spring of 1935 leaked the data on the tests to the public. This had an immediate effect on the aircraft engine industry. Wright Aeronautical Company began to develop an eight-to-one compression ratio engine that would use 100 octane. In 1936, test results showed that not only did the Wright engine make substantial increases in power possible, but fuel savings of up to 15 percent were also reported. An Army committee was appointed and held hearings at Wright Field in November 1936. The committee, after long study, finally recommended the adoption of 100-octane gas for combat aircraft. The Army subsequently issued an order that all Air Corps aircraft engines (except those for training planes) would be designed for 100-octane fuel after January 1, 1938.

So we eventually succeeded, but only after assuring the military that we could get the cost way down. We were selling regular 87-octane gasoline to the airlines for 15 cents a gallon. It cost $2.50 a gallon to make that first batch of 100 octane for the Army, and we sold it for 50 cents a gallon to develop the market; we dropped the price to 20 cents per gallon within a year.

By 1938, the Air Corps requirements had built up to 15 million gallons per year, and the FOB refinery price had dropped to about 17.5 cents per gallon. Standard Oil of New Jersey and Phillips Petroleum made small quantities and also sold theirs at a loss initially. In due time it became possible to reduce the cost of production and at the same time sell enough to make a reasonable profit.

Shell had taken a big commercial gamble. But there are various types of gambles. I don't think any commercial gamble can be as great as a gamble with your life, and I don't believe that any gamble with your life can be as great as a gamble with your good name. A commercial gamble is the least of all gambles. As time told, the venture paid off handsomely when the company was later asked to supply 20 million gallons of 100-octane fuel to the military services *daily*.

While Shell had been considering the 100-octane question initially at the highest corporate level, Curtiss-Wright invited Joe and me to take a round-the-world trip in 1933. My job was, of course, to demonstrate their P-6 Hawk and show the flag for Shell, as I had done before, with the two companies sharing expenses. We traveled by boat from San Francisco to the Far East. Joe took her portable typewriter along and acted as secretary for our party.

There was a little Italian steward on board the ship who took a shine to Joe—he must have thought she was a queen or something. On the first day out, he asked her if she liked partridge or pheasant. She said she liked them both. From that time onward, he served her double portions of everything—twice as much as the rest of us at breakfast, dinner, and supper. Joe put on some pounds. In fact, she gained a pound a day, and the voyage lasted 17 days.

Joe was concerned and thought she'd better do something about it. She tried exercise, walking around the deck several times each morning. Every time she was out on deck, the little Italian steward would approach her with a tray of sweet rolls, butter, and coffee. Next, she tried working out in the gym, but the steward would be waiting for her when she came out. By the time the trip was over, she was well on her way to being the fat lady of the circus.

When we docked, I tried to give the steward the customary tip. He refused it, saying his feelings would be hurt if I insisted on offering him any money. All he would like to have, he said, was the flowers in our room. He never told us why—another mystery in our lives.

Joe soon lost her excess poundage. The Far East, with its food, nourished by human fertilizer, took care of that.

...okohama, en route to ...he States, the State ...pan because the ... The second ...be the occupa- ...ted with selling ... was likely to be

... aboard at Yokohama ...y saw mine, one of them ...do in Japan?"

...round the world. "Oh, go to ...knew that's where the boat was ...length among themselves, but left ...ore.

... under suspicion, but Joe and I wanted ...ent ashore later, trying to be as inconspic- ...sians could in the Orient. We visited some ...ch at the Imperial Hotel, and made a trip to ...ever thought I would later see Japan from a far ...spective. If I'd had any inkling that we would be at ...he Japanese, or if the Army had asked me to, I would ...ken a better look at landmarks and potential military ...s. However, during the entire trip I made notes about air- ...d locations, airport drainage, weather, distance of airports from towns, aircraft servicing, and communications. This information was turned over to Shell and the War Department when I returned.

We arrived in Shanghai after a short stop at Kobe. We had the plane unloaded and I put on aerobatic demonstrations there. The night before each demonstration I would map out several sets of flights—one for each type of weather condition. I included a wet-weather scenario because I was determined that if hundreds of Chinese were going to come to watch me in the rain, they were going to see a demonstration.

Each day, I noticed a group of Japanese on the far side of the field taking pictures of my plane on the ground and in the air with telephoto lenses. Obviously, they were photographing military equipment.

On one of the flights, the cowling around the Hawk's engine slid forward into the propeller, damaging the cowling and the prop. I had to make a forced landing. We looked it over

and found that someone had loosened the
cowling in place. Sabotage, as far as I wa

At a Chinese flying school during anot
put the Hawk into a dive, but when I pul
quit. Another forced landing. I took a look
fuel pump drive shaft had been hammered in
the pump would fail in flight. It was another c

From that time on, I put a guard on the plan
Americans on whom I could depend. We never to
about either incident because it would have seemed
making excuses for the aircraft's poor performance

We put on a demonstration at a polo field outsi
where we were told that the largest crowd ever asse
waiting for "Doo-rittle" to fly. The grandstand was j
and there were hundreds more on the roof. Joe was
cerned because the stand appeared to be a very flimsy s
With me putting on a low-altitude show and this structur
ingly about to collapse, she was badly bothered. Nothin
pened, although I know why she was disturbed abou
grandstand. Anyone who has been to Hong Kong or to Ch
cities and seen the rickety bamboo scaffolding used during
construction of large buildings will understand.

On a trip to Peiping, I was "privileged" to fly as copi
on a China National Airways Corporation aircraft. It was th
first time in my life that I had been a copilot. The weather was bad and forced us far off course over country where the people had never seen a plane before. The pilot asked me to take the controls, since he had heard I had done some instrument flying. I had no idea where we were, but eventually we made a landing at a small airport where we were refueled by coolies lifting five-gallon cans. We took off and were forced to land at an emergency airport—really a wheat field knee-deep in water—near Tsingtao. We finally made it to our destination; it was typical of the rather uncertain plane trips we made during our stay in China.

One side trip was without Joe. Major General Fred Wong, chief of the South China air force; Brigadier General Arthur Lim; the Curtiss representative Joe Lum; and one other man, from the Chinese Purchasing Agency, invited me to a restaurant. I was the only Westerner there. It was a very interesting place. There were bunks along the wall where men were smoking opium. We sat at a table in the center. Behind each of us was a young Chinese waitress called a sing-song girl. We men played the Chinese "finger game" where each of us held up from zero to five fingers. Each was to guess the total. The losers would then take a sip of rice wine.

After a while, with enough sips of the wine, one had a tendency to hold up five fingers and guess four or less. Meanwhile, the girl behind me seemed to be intelligent enough for me to teach her how to speak English. I spoke slowly to see if she would understand: "Where . . . are . . . you . . . from?" She promptly answered in a plain Midwestern American accent: "I'm from Chicago and wish to Christ I was back there now!" I learned she had been born in Chicago of Chinese parents; her father had become prosperous and returned with his family to China. He lost everything in bad business ventures and the daughter had to work as a hostess. I never learned what happened to her.

At this time, the Japanese invasion of China had already begun. Manchuria was completely under Japanese control and Japan dominated a number of Chinese coastal areas. Colonel Jack Jouett, then in charge of flying instruction for the Chinese army, and I flew over the Chinese coastline together to see firsthand what the Chinese were doing in the way of airfield construction and defenses.

Our next stop was in the Philippines, where I made several observation flights. At each subsequent stop on our tour, I visited commercial and military facilities and performed my aerobatics, some of which had never been seen before in that part of the world. I had left the Hawk in China, so I had to borrow an aircraft to put on my show. This was almost my undoing at a field located at a high altitude in the Dutch East Indies.

I borrowed a Hawk from the Dutch air force and went through my aerial routine. To conclude my act, I put the airplane into a power dive, intending to pull out as close to the ground as possible. When I started to pull out, the airplane didn't respond in the thin air as I had expected. It began to "mush," and the ground came up too fast. I managed to pull out, but only after my wheels hit the ground rather hard, though without damaging the Hawk. I had not calculated that the Hawk wouldn't perform in thin air as it would have at a lower altitude.

Several Dutch pilots who had seen the near accident congratulated me. The commander of the group said it was "the most delicate piece of flying" he had ever seen. But I thought it was stupid flying and said so. He smiled and said, "We knew; we wondered if you would lie about it."

We left the Dutch East Indies and flew on KLM to Burma, India, Iraq, Egypt, and Europe. We arrived in England in late August and took the boat home.

We had thoroughly enjoyed the trip, which not only had been educational, but had enabled me to meet and chat with military and political leaders and get an unusual insight into their thinking and planning. I was disturbed by some of the things I saw. Some of the Far East countries, considered backward by our standards, were building air forces with substantial numbers of planes and pilots. In Japan and Germany, although they seemed outwardly to be putting great emphasis on civilian airline expansion and pilot training, this capability could be quickly exploited if those nations decided to switch to military operations.

After my return to the States, I decided that the time had come to speak out about what I had seen and heard. My theme was simple: The United States was falling behind in aeronautics, especially in military aviation. Since my name was fairly well known, it was not difficult to get an audience, but I felt that I wanted to be a responsible spokesman, not one who would embellish the facts, make an emotional appeal, or seek news coverage by making shocking statements. In February 1934, when President Roosevelt canceled all contracts with civilian airlines and ordered the Air Corps to fly the mail, the sad state of military aviation became painfully obvious.

The problem had its beginning in 1925, when Congress passed a law "to encourage commercial aviation and to authorize the Postmaster General to contract for airmail service." In the years between 1918 and 1925, after the Air Service had shown initially that mail could be flown on schedule, during a three-month period in the summer of 1918, the Post Office Department had operated the nation's airmail. The 1925 law, called the Kelly Act, gradually took the government out of the airmail business and authorized the carrying of mail by air on a contract basis by privately owned companies. This marked the real beginning of the commercial airlines in this country.

Only mail was transported at first. Pilots considered passengers a nuisance and only occasionally would carry them sitting on top of the mailbags. However, as passenger requests grew, it was obvious that they could be a source of revenue. The airlines started to install seats and charge for the privilege of flying. Later, by altering the basis of payment from weight alone to the volume of space available for mail, Congress encouraged the airlines to buy larger planes that could carry both mail and passengers.

When the airmail contracts expired, the Postmaster General continually favored those companies for renewal that had the strongest financial backing. The smaller lines that refused to merge with larger ones and could not survive without the mail contracts became doomed to extinction. The resentment of the small entrepreneurs and allegations of scandal among the large airlines led to a congressional investigation, which in turn caused President Roosevelt to cancel all airmail contracts.

In order to continue airmail service, the Army Air Corps was asked to carry on. In the "can do" spirit that had become a tradition with the fledgling Air Corps by that time, Major General Benjamin D. Foulois, chief of the Air Corps, accepted the assignment. However, he knew that the pilots and the obsolescent pursuit planes, bombers, trainers, and observation planes of the Air Corps were poorly equipped to fly scheduled runs in all kinds of weather, especially in the middle of the winter. Only a few Army test aircraft had blind flying instruments installed, and only about a dozen military pilots had any real experience in weather flying.

General Foulois was aware that he was taking on a difficult responsibility, and weaknesses were quickly discovered. In the ensuing weeks there were several crashes as Army pilots tried valiantly to push the mail through despite the severest weather in several years. Four fatalities occurred on airmail flights; six other Air Corps pilots died on training or aircraft ferrying flights.

The public uproar that resulted from the deaths caused the President to authorize new commercial contracts. The Air Corps settled back into its former status as the Army's stepchild, with antiquated aircraft and inadequate funds for the training of pilots and ground personnel. But to satisfy public concern, a 12-member board was appointed to investigate the Air Corps. It was headed by Newton D. Baker, who had been secretary of war during World War I. The board (known as the Baker Board) was charged to study all phases of military air operations, including technical flying equipment and training.

In addition to several nonflying Army officers, four active

pilots were asked to serve: General Foulois and three civilians—Clarence Chamberlain, Slim Lindbergh, and me. Lindbergh declined the invitation. Then a consultant for Transcontinental and Western Airlines (later TWA), he had come down hard against President Roosevelt when the airmail contracts were so arbitrarily canceled.

I saw the invitation as an opportunity to contribute my thoughts on the future of military aviation in a public forum. During 25 days of listening to statements that took up 4,300 pages of transcribed testimony, we heard 105 witnesses, including generals, admirals, airline pilots, and specialists in engines, instruments, blind flying, and meteorology.

The final report reflected the thinking of those on the board who refused to admit or could not understand the potential of the airplane as a military weapon. The report declared that the idea that aviation could produce decisive results in a war was "visionary," as was the idea that an independent air force was necessary to defend the country.

The report added that "the fear that has been cultivated in this country by various zealots that American aviation is inferior to that of the rest of the world is, as a whole, unfounded."

The air officers who sought a separate budget, separate promotion list, and freedom from the bias of the Army general staff were censured in the report. They were accused of "continuing agitation" and disturbing "harmonious development and improvement."

The report was concurred in by all the board's members except me. I was one of those accused of disturbing "harmonious development and improvement." Even General Foulois had given in and signed the report, but later acknowledged that it was a compromise. He said that it contained some concessions that meant a step forward for the Air Corps, and that was better than no step at all.

I insisted on submitting a minority statement. After reading it, General Foulois told me he wished he had joined me in signing it. The statement said:

> I believe in aviation—both civil and military. I believe that the future security of our Nation is dependent upon an adequate air force. This is true at the present time and will become increasingly impor-

> tant as the science of aviation advances and the airplane lends itself more and more to the art of warfare.
>
> I am convinced that the required air force can be more rapidly organized, equipped, and trained if it is completely separated from the Army and developed as an entirely separate arm. If complete separation is not the desire of the committee, I recommend an air force as a part of the Army, but with a separate budget, a separate promotion list, and removed from the control of the General Staff.

I was disgusted at the board's conclusions. When asked by a reporter what I thought, I replied, "The country will someday pay for the stupidities of those who were in the majority on this commission. They know as much about the future of aviation as they do about the sign writing of the Aztecs."

Like many such government efforts, the Baker Board report was shelved after getting some press coverage, but it did have a favorable impact on future Army Air Corps planning. The board had recommended a minimum of 2,320 aircraft for peacetime operations; pilots should average 300 hours per year and receive more training in night, instrument, and cross-country flying. The recommendations also stated the Air Corps should develop better aircraft equipment, communications, and armament, and urged improvements affecting personnel in such matters as promotion stagnations, rank commensurate with responsibility, and the shortage of officers. These were pluses that tended to offset the minuses in the Baker Board's findings. Progress in implementing the Baker Board's recommendations, however, came very slowly.

On Labor Day, 1934, at the National Air Races in Cleveland, Douglas Davis, an experienced racing pilot, was killed during the Thompson Trophy race. A speech at the National Safety Congress in Chicago gave me an opportunity to speak out once more about the dangers inherent in racing. I said that air racing, especially closed-course racing, had outlived its usefulness. I traced the development of five principal advancements that racing had stimulated: new engine cowling, wing flaps, controllable-pitch propellers, retractable landing gear, and streamlined construction. However, I felt that the value received was not commensurate with the personal risk involved.

Although I had begun actively campaigning against racing around the pylons because of the reduced margin of safety introduced by increased speeds, I was not opposed to racing point to point against the clock in passenger and cargo planes. American Airlines had bought an eight-passenger single-engine Vultee and asked me to make a speed flight in it from Burbank to Floyd Bennett Field, in New York. The purpose: to try to better Captain Eddie Rickenbacker's coast-to-coast mark in an Eastern Airlines DC-2 of 12 hours, 3 minutes, set in December 1934. Breaking Eastern's record would be a public relations coup for American.

I tested the Vultee but didn't do myself any favors. I thought I could coax a few more miles per hour out of it by slicing off a few inches of the engine's exhaust pipes at the cowling. Unfortunately, I sliced about three miles per hour off my airspeed instead. I should have known better, but I also gave myself another problem when flying at night because the engine's fiery exhaust cut down on my forward vision. It was a distraction that would bother me when flying on instruments.

I invited Joe to go along as a passenger, and we were joined by Robert Adamson, a Shell publicist. I planned a direct, nonstop flight and chose mid-January as the time for the attempt because the prevalent high-altitude west-to-east tail winds of more than 100 miles per hour would help us along, just as they had Rickenbacker a month before. The Vultee had two-way radio and oxygen equipment, the latter because I intended to fly at 15,000 feet.

At that time, Irving Krick, a meteorologist on the faculty of the California Institute of Technology, had achieved some distinction at weather prediction through his study of air masses and their movement. An enthusiastic, self-assured individual, he said he could predict the weather accurately as much as a month in advance. I contacted him and asked him to tell me when I might have the best clear weather across the country. He studied his data and finally said, "Plan on the night of January 14, 1935. You'll have a typical California overcast at takeoff time, but once on top you'll have clear skies and tail winds all the way to New York."

Trusting his prediction, we departed Burbank that evening. The weather was overcast on takeoff, but I didn't break out on top as he predicted. I flew on instruments, following a direct course for New York. Krick had said I would run into completely clear air over Arizona. He was wrong. The overcast was solid. The plane began to load up with ice, and our airspeed fell off. The plane almost stalled out three times. The radio went dead because of ice buildup. I headed south of my planned course into warmer air, which melted the ice, but I still did not run out of the clouds. I climbed on top to about 16,500 feet. Joe and Bob passed out from lack of sufficient oxygen and I felt goofy, so I let back down into the clouds.

We flew the rest of the night in the soup, but I held the compass course that I thought would put us back on track. I had no way of knowing that the wind had shifted strongly to the northwest and we were being blown far south of my intended course.

When daylight came, the cloud cover broke up and I could see the ground. Suddenly, I saw some landmarks I recognized. "Richmond!" I shouted to Joe and Bob as I quickly turned northeast. We were actually between Richmond and Langley Field, Virginia, about 250 miles southwest of our destination.

I calculated that we might still make it under the Rickenbacker mark if I pushed the 750-horsepower Wright Cyclone engine a little harder. The weather cleared and I set the Vultee down at Floyd Bennett Field after 11 hours, 59 minutes—seconds short of beating the record by the five minutes required to set an official point-to-point record. I was not pleased with my performance and told the press that I had gotten off course and should have been there an hour and a half sooner.

I didn't mention Krick's totally erroneous forecast. I would not have guessed that Krick and I would be at odds many years later, during World War II, because of his overconfident forecasting. When I met him a few months after the flight and told him that his forecast had been 100 percent wrong except for the takeoff conditions, he quickly replied, "If you had stayed on course and hadn't gotten lost, you would have found my forecast was 100 percent accurate!" Here was a scientist whose predictions exceeded his technical capabilities. Even now, with all of our meteorological knowledge and weather satellites, I still find it difficult to be confident of precise weather predictions made very far in the future for any particular location, certainly not a month in advance.

Despite my unhappiness with Krick, I did achieve an aviation first—barely. Our flight was the first time anyone had flown coast-to-coast in a plane with passengers in less than 12 hours.

The point was made and the press picked up on it. If a single-engine passenger plane could make a nonstop transcontinental trip in less than half a day without any difficulty with the aircraft, civilian aviation had come a long way. It was a far different story for military aviation.

CHAPTER 8

The years after the 1935 trans continental flight were busy ones for the Doolittles and for Shell. I gave many talks on aviation subjects and volunteered my knowledge and experience to aircraft manufacturers and the military services. Shell engineers, meanwhile, were going ahead with the construction of facilities to produce 100-octane gasoline. I stayed active in the Air Corps Reserve and served my annual two-week tours of active duty as a major. My exposure to all kinds of problems and advancements in aviation gave me a privileged insight into the state of aeronautics in America. I became a member of the Institute of Aeronautical Sciences (and subsequently president), which enabled me to make even more industrial, scientific, and academic contacts.

My records show that I was not an exemplary pilot in those days, however. At least the Civil Aeronautics Authority (CAA) under the Department of Commerce didn't think I was. I was fined $500 and had my license suspended for 45 days in 1937 for ''navigating an aircraft at an altitude below 1,000 feet over a congested area'' and had another $500 fine for landing at a closed field in Miami during an air show. Apparently, I had caused a formation of Marine aircraft to go around. I appealed and got that fine reduced to $50, but the suspension remained. I did, however, get the starting date of the suspension changed by pleading that I had a series of fuel tests scheduled that were important for national defense. I also had minor mishaps during that period, which I reported as required at Burbank and St. Louis in 1936, at Long Beach in 1937, and at South Washington, Virginia, in 1938. There were no injuries, and I can't recall what happened, but one of the mishaps netted me a $25 fine for a "landing incident."

I was not entirely beyond redemption. My files show that in January 1935, James A. McKinney, a Civil Aeronautics Authority inspector, gave me a grade of 100 for an instrument check and noted in my file, "That's the highest grade I've ever given."

Since I was able to observe what was happening in military aviation on a frequent basis, I was privy to some foreign intelligence reports indicating we were woefully short in aircraft research and development, compared with the European countries. Adolf Hitler, a corporal during World War I, had risen to German chancellor, führer, and supreme commander of the army by 1933. A bloody civil war started in Spain in 1936; Russia and Germany sent pilots and planes to fight on opposing sides. Spain was being used as a testing ground for war planes and equipment. Both sides were learning valuable lessons about the employment of air power.

Many changes took place in Germany under Hitler. When I passed through in 1930, when the republic was declining, the Germans were a discouraged, dejected, disappointed people. When I returned in 1933 at the beginning of the Nazi regime, there seemed to be a rising spirit, an optimistic feeling that Hitler would restore their national strength and pride. In March 1935, Hitler repudiated the terms of the Treaty of Versailles, signed in June 1919, which were intended to end military aviation in Germany and to preclude a resurrection of the German Flying Corps. Under the supervision of the Allied Control Commission, Germany was obliged, in 1920, to demobilize the entire Flying Corps and surrender all aeronautical material to the governments of the Allied and associated powers. At the end of World War I, Germany had possessed approximately 20,000 military aircraft, of which some 2,400 were bombers, fighters, and reconnaissance aircraft. In accordance with the treaty, over 15,000 aircraft and 27,000 aircraft engines had been surrendered.

It is generally believed that the birth of the German air force was a result of the aggressiveness of Hitler and Hermann

Goering, his top air officer, between 1933 and 1935. However, historians have found this is not true. As early as 1920, a small group of Flying Corps officers had begun secret preparations to revive the air force. Meanwhile, various German aircraft manufacturers—Hugo Junkers, Ernst Heinkel, Claude Dornier, Heinrich Focke, and George Wulf—were permitted to build civil aircraft, since they were not restricted from doing so by the treaty. By 1926, Germany was already the most air-minded country in Europe. The nucleus for a new air force was therefore in place by the time Hitler came to power in January 1933.

Hermann Goering had commanded a squadron of fighters during World War I and met Hitler in 1922. He was the first leader of Hitler's storm troopers and played a prominent part in Hitler's futile putsch of 1923. In 1933, Hitler appointed him air minister.

By March 1935, Hitler was sufficiently confident of his strength that he appointed Goering commander in chief of the new air arm and authorized him to announce to the world the existence of the Luftwaffe. In March 1936, Hitler's forces occupied the Rhineland, an industrial area of Germany that had been demilitarized as a buffer zone to protect France and Belgium. According to historians, the Luftwaffe then consisted of nearly 2,000 aircraft; the production rate has been estimated at 300 per month.

In the late summer of 1937, I returned to Europe on Shell business. When I arrived in Germany, I saw uniformed kids marching happily down the streets like overeager Boy Scouts, drilling as soldiers, and singing Nazi war songs.

One of the men I wanted to see again was Ernst Udet, the famous World War I German ace credited with 62 victories over Allied planes, second only to the great Manfred von Richthofen (the Red Baron), who had 80 victories. Udet had acted in German motion pictures after World War I and had tried to get started in aircraft manufacturing, but his carefree, untroubled nature prevented him from being successful. I had met him during my first trip to Germany in 1930 and in 1931 and 1933 at the Cleveland Air Races, where he put on quite an aerobatic show in a 100-horsepower Flamingo during the international pilot performances. Since the Flamingo was very slow compared with the American planes, he put on what he called his "ground-floor aerobatics." He flew upside down close to the ground and dragged his wing across the ground, raising a cloud of dust. He would perform "loopings," as he called them, with the engine shut off and would recover just a few feet off the ground in front of the grandstand. The performance would end with a stalled landing on the exact spot from which he took off.

Another of Udet's favorite crowd-thrilling stunts was to snare a handkerchief off the ground with one wingtip. He would skim slowly across the field, dip one wing at the precise moment, and pick it up. Such a maneuver would probably have been disastrous in one of our faster military ships of the period.

During a visit to America in 1933, Udet purchased two Curtiss-Wright Hawks for his government for $11,500 each. He demonstrated one of them at the Luftwaffe's test center the following December to impress the high command. He put it into a steep dive aiming at a ground target and pulled it out dangerously close to the ground to show how it might be used as a dive bomber. Apparently, no one but Udet was impressed. The following summer, he pulled the tail off one of the Hawks while stunting over Berlin's Tempelhof Airport and had to bail out. It occurred to me much later that this purchase of two planes was part of the Nazi master plan to procure our best pursuit planes and have them analyzed by their engineers. It is said that the famous Stuka dive bomber design was developed from ideas derived from the Hawk.

Fearless and impetuous, Udet had been called by his squadron mates *der Wespe* ("the wasp") during World War I because of his habit of flying alone, dropping down on a group of Allied planes, singling one out, shooting it down, and then letting the others chase him. However, as a civilian, he was known in the German press as *die Floh* ("the flea") because of his habit of hopping gaily all over Europe. In 1935, he had been commissioned in the Luftwaffe as a colonel with the title of "inspector of fighters and dive bombers." Udet and I got along famously. Born the same year, we were about the same size and build, and both of us had a proclivity for having fun in airplanes and flying them to the edge of their performance limits. When I met him again in 1937, he was still the fun-loving, good-humored, dashing pilot who had a great disdain for politics and discipline.

As head of Luftwaffe technical developments in the late 1930s, Udet presided over German military aviation advances. Although he was too busy to stay with me during the day, we spent our evenings in Berlin together. He gave me a military aide and made his personal plane available for me to use as I wanted.

The aide and I flew to the Junkers plant, where I was impressed by the quality of the engines and airframes being turned out at an alarming rate. There I saw the Ju.88 Stuka dive bomber that had been tested extensively in Spain.

Udet's aide took me through the Mercedes-Benz factory, where they made the engines used in the Messerschmitt Me-109 and Me-110 fighters. Udet also arranged for me to see other German aircraft designs and manufacturing processes. It was perfectly obvious the Germans were not observing any of the limitations placed on their military aircraft production in accordance with the Versailles peace treaty. The types of fighter planes and bombers being produced in the plants I visited were top of the line from what I could see. I wish I could have flown them.

Udet detested Hitler and his aviation boss, Goering. In the privacy of his apartment he liked to imitate Hitler. He would take a small black comb, put it under his nose and do a Nazi stiff-armed salute with hilarious, unprintable comments.

One evening, after I had returned his hospitality with a dinner in the city, he invited me to his apartment to meet his mistress and test some champagne that members of a French mission had given him. A multitalented and infinitely clever man, Udet could recite poetry from memory, could sing well, loved music, and was an excellent conversationalist, with a fluency in English that was rare in Germany. He was also an excellent cartoonist and had drawn caricatures of both of us that had appeared in a Cleveland newspaper during the 1931 races. It was said he was also an excellent marksman with any kind of weapon.

As we consumed the excellent French champagne, Udet suddenly said, "Let's have some pistol practice."

"Where?" I asked.

"Right here," he said, and pulled out a steel box filled with sand. He placed it on the fireplace mantel atop a large sheaf of papers. The box had a curved back that would deflect bullets downward into the sand. He covered it with a paper target and we took places against the opposite wall. Udet pulled out an unusually powerful air pistol that shot lead pellets. Between us, we did some very good shooting, which we were sure improved the more champagne we consumed.

Since we were getting to be very expert, Udet then pulled out a large .455-caliber pistol that was much heavier and more powerful than our Army .45 automatics. He handed the gun to me. I took aim, but the gun was so heavy that I shot low. The bullet blasted into the papers, which were technical documents Udet had brought home to study. The papers flew everywhere, but my host didn't seem to mind.

"Here, let me show you how to do it," he said, as he took the gun away from me. He took careful aim, but yanked the gun upward just as he fired. He completely missed the target and blasted a hole through the apartment's plaster wall. The frightened folks in the next apartment could look right through at us but never said a word. And neither did Udet, who calmly took another shot, which went into the box through the bull's-eye.

The next time I saw Udet was in midsummer 1939, when I was again sent on a Shell visit to Frankfurt. He had been appointed director of the Technical Department of the German Air Ministry and later became director general of air force equipment.

By this time, Hitler had announced his plans for *Lebensraum,* annexed Austria, marched into the Sudetenland, and destroyed Czechoslovakia, and was negotiating an economic agreement with Russia. The turmoil that was going on behind the scenes was manifested in the hundreds of uniformed men with swastika arm bands and civilians with unsmiling faces on the streets and in the shops. The atmosphere in the country had changed; there was an ominous air of impending catastrophe. I felt very uncomfortable, stayed only three days, and did not go to Berlin.

Now a major general, Udet had also changed. He had difficulty recalling English words and seemed much subdued. The old ebullience, the ever-present grin and laugh, were gone. Apparently, he had had little if any contact with English-speaking people during the previous two years. In public, he appeared embarrassed to have me around, although he did take me to an air meet in Frankfurt, where I may have been the only American there. The show was heavy with modern military aircraft, and the precision of a regimented, highly disciplined air force was plainly evident.

Udet did not provide me an escort on this trip, nor was I given an opportunity to see German aviation activities behind the scenes, as I had been before. On the streets, uniforms were everywhere; people went about their daily business with a grimness that was distressing.

I did meet a few German pilots and some civilian engineers

briefly. The pilots were always in uniform and their conversations with me were consistently one-way. Those who spoke English asked me questions about American aircraft production with an impudence bordering on rudeness, but never answered my questions. They talked openly of war in Europe as being inevitable and wanted to know what America would do about it when it came. Their arrogance was irritating. I learned later that the Luftwaffe's strength consisted of 3,750 first-line combat aircraft, of which 1,300 were twin-engine bombers, mostly Heinkel He.111s and Dornier Do.17s, and a few new Junkers Ju.88s. In addition, there were about 25 percent more combat aircraft being held in reserve. There were also about 3,000 trainer aircraft and 500 operational types used for transition training in the inventory and more of all types being built in increasing numbers.

Udet told me he was going to take a 10-day vacation in Munich and invited me to go along. I wanted to go, but something told me it was not the right thing to do. If war were coming, it did not seem wise for a U.S. Army Air Corps reserve officer to be vacationing with the top technical man in the Luftwaffe. Besides, my accompanying him might make it difficult for him to explain to Goering and Hitler why he was fraternizing with an American flyer who was probably a spy.*

I returned to the States via London, where I stopped at the American embassy to report what I had seen to Major Martin "Mike" Scanlon, the American air attaché. To my surprise, Scanlon seemed completely uninterested. He said, disdainfully, "You know 'Hap' Arnold. Go back and tell him what you saw. There's nothing I can do about it." By contrast, the naval attaché was very interested and encouraged me to tell him about my observations.

I knew Hap Arnold very well. He had been my commanding officer at Rockwell Field just after World War I. One of the Army's first pilots, he was well liked by enlisted men and officers alike. He had survived the early anti–Air Corps years and was now a major general and chief of the Air Corps. I had kept in touch with him through the years. He was the ideal man for the job in the critical years that seemed to lie ahead.

I left London by ship in mid-August 1939. As soon as I

---

*Udet is alleged to have committed suicide on November 17, 1941. Some have said he had fallen out of grace with both Hitler and Goering and had been given a choice of suicide or the firing squad. The actual circumstances of his death remain a mystery.

arrived in the States, I went to Hap's office at the War Department and told him what I had seen. Although my observations coincided with what Slim Lindbergh had seen on his four visits to Germany between 1937 and 1939, my reactions were different. Slim advocated isolationism for America and believed that a war in Europe would be a catastrophe for Western civilization. If there were a war, he hoped it would be between Germany and Russia. He thought that France, Great Britain, and the United States should remain neutral.

Slim had written to Hap in 1938 urging him to visit Germany as soon as possible to see for himself the state of German aviation, but Hap had been advised not to go for diplomatic reasons. Slim wrote again, emphasizing the need for the development of high-speed aircraft that could fly at high altitudes. Thanks to intelligence sources and the surveys Slim had made in his visits to Germany, Hap knew the location of most of the German aircraft manufacturing facilities and airfields. My visit to his office gave him more information and further proof that a rapidly expanding Luftwaffe was readying for war.

I told Hap that I was totally convinced that war was inevitable, that the United States would be involved in hostilities, and that we would be unable to remain aloof from whatever happened in Europe. I was so sure of it, in fact, that I told him I was willing to give up my job with Shell and serve full time or part time, in uniform or out, in any way he thought would be useful.

Hap seemed pleased. He knew I'd be taking a large reduction in pay. With my military flying background and 10 years in the aviation industry, I thought I could be of assistance in getting the country geared up for war production. Hap said he couldn't order me to active duty immediately because I was a reserve major and no reservists above the grade of captain could be recalled until the start of the next fiscal year—July 1, 1940. I told him my offer would be good whenever it was possible.

In January 1940, I was named president of the Institute of Aeronautical Sciences, an honor I valued greatly. The organization consisted of about 3,000 members who represented the whole spectrum of aeronautical interests, from aircraft component manufacturers to airline executives. I felt that one of my duties was to encourage young engineering students in the country's colleges to consider a career in aeronautics. It was still a relatively young science and I felt that there would be very little progress for aviation in this country unless we developed an interest in it among college students. If there were a war in our future, and I was convinced there would be one, we would need our best minds working on aeronautical problems. I made many trips during the spring of 1940 telling students about my personal experiences in aviation, hoping that I could stir their interest in aeronautical careers. It would be interesting today to know if I succeeded in persuading any of those young people to enter aeronautical engineering.

On September 1, 1939, two weeks after I had returned to the States, Nazi troops marched into Poland and 1,400 Luftwaffe planes bombed and strafed a stunned populace. With contemptuous ease, the blitzkrieg rolled on until 36,000 square miles of Poland were annexed to Germany. World War II had begun. On September 3, Great Britain declared war on Germany, and France reluctantly followed suit.

A week later, President Roosevelt declared a state of national emergency and announced that the United States would become the "arsenal of democracy." At that time, the United States began to build its airpower in earnest by providing orders that enabled the aviation industry to expand factories and tool up for mass production.

On May 16, 1940, President Roosevelt appeared before Congress to make a significant speech. Six days before, the Netherlands, Belgium, and France had been "blitzed" and the Allies faced grave danger of annihilation. "These are ominous days," he said, "days whose swift and shocking developments force every neutral nation to look at its defenses."

Commenting on "the amazing progress in the design of planes and engines," he called for a program that would eventually produce "at least 50,000 planes a year."

On June 4, 1940, Ira Eaker, then executive officer for General Arnold, wrote to me: "Would you be interested in coming on active duty on July 1st for station at the Allison plant [at Indianapolis] as Army Air Corps representative? This is one proposition which the General has been considering, and another is for duty here in the office, on extended active duty."

I promptly accepted the recall to active duty and asked that I be given "such duty or duties as will best take advantage of my particular experience, associations and abilities." I suggested that "it might be sound for me to headquarter in Washington and work out of there, taking on the Indianapolis job as a first detail and returning to Washington when and if the production problems there were straightened out."

I mentioned that I was a member of the NACA subcommittee on aircraft fuels and lubricants of the committee on power plants for aircraft. Our task was to study the availability of and draw up specifications for 100-octane fuel and suitable lubricating oil for an expanded air force. I asked that I be permitted to remain a member. I added that I had 7,209 hours of flying time, of which 67 hours had been flown the previous month in the company's P-35 and Stinson aircraft.

France surrendered to the Nazis on June 22, 1940. Now Great Britain stood alone in the war against Germany.

Shell graciously gave me an indefinite leave of absence for the duration of the emergency. On July 1, 1940, I reported to the Allison Engine Company, Indianapolis, as assistant district supervisor for the Central Air Corps Procurement District. My boss, Lieutenant Colonel Alonzo M. Drake, was located at Wright Field, in Ohio.

Soon after I checked in at the plant, I realized that I would need an aircraft available to do my job so I could travel at my pace and convenience. Frequent flights between Indianapolis, Dayton, and Washington were essential to accomplish my duties on a man-to-man basis, which I found to be the most effective way to cut red tape and get things done expeditiously. I went to General Arnold and asked for a P-40 for my personal use—one that no one else would be permitted to fly. He said, "Very well."

I had prepared a justification lecture, so I went right on telling him why I needed this airplane. He listened patiently, then interrupted. "Jimmy, are you trying to talk yourself out of this P-40?"

I said, "No, sir. Thank you very much."

An early-model Curtiss P-40 was placed at my disposal, but I had a problem the first time I wanted to fly somewhere when the weather was below minimums for fighter aircraft. P-40 pilots were having considerable trouble spinning in during bad weather, so a regulation was put out that prohibited fighter planes from taking off under instrument conditions. A young second lieutenant, an operations duty officer, refused to sign my instrument clearance. He was well within the regulations to do so and wouldn't acquiesce despite my claim that I had extensive experience in weather flying and had important business to conduct in Dayton. I didn't go that day.

Instead, I called Hap Arnold and asked for special dispensation to go when and where I wanted to, regardless of regulations. He promptly sent me the following letter, which I had photographically reduced to wallet size and carried with me for the next several years:

> 1. Existing regulations and instructions prohibit intentional flight under instrument conditions in pursuit-type aircraft.
>
> 2. In your particular case these restrictions are waived, and this letter will serve as authority for you to obtain instrument clearances at your discretion in pursuit-type aircraft.
>
> 3. This authority is granted in recognition of your exceptional qualifications and to enable the Air Corps to obtain valuable information on the behavior and flying characteristics of modern pursuit-type airplanes under instrument flying conditions.

Again I went to Hap and said, "I would like to get a little special equipment on this airplane—navigational equipment—to see if I can help solve the fighter problem." He agreed. I recommended training of fighter pilots be improved by giving them additional instrument instruction in training planes to enable them to cope with bad weather conditions. In due course, these changes were made and fighters were again turned loose to fly in bad weather.

In November 1940, I was transferred to Detroit as assistant district supervisor and designated Air Corps factory representative at the Ford plant. I was also to be the liaison officer between the Air Corps and the Automotive Committee for Air Defense. Before leaving Allison, however, I wrote a detailed, critical nine-page report of observations at Allison directly to General Arnold, as he had requested. The same criticisms were reiterated in a letter to Fred Kraeger, general manager of Allison. I cited the history of Allison and my previous associations with it:

> General Motors purchased Allison in 1929 on the

> basis of its patents on lead-bronze, steel-backed bearings. It was also thought the organization would be a suitable nucleus for aircraft engine development should General Motors desire to enter this field. My first dealings with an Allison product go back to the early 1920s when I flight-tested their air-cooled, inverted, converted Liberty. Immediately after the initial takeoff, it cut out and dropped me into a baseball diamond just east of old McCook Field. No damage was done, but the airplane had to be disassembled and hauled back to the field.

I reviewed the difficulties Allison engines were having, varying from crankshaft and bearing failures to coolant pump and Prestone leaks. I noted that the Allison liquid-cooled engines would not take the punishment and overloads that could be imposed on older air-cooled engines. I recommended that until their "temperamentality" could be corrected, pilots should be cautioned to operate the Allison engines within strict limitations.

The problems with Allison were largely managerial. I commented on the many personnel changes that had taken place and how certain top managers were more interested in quantity than quality. I gave credit to C. E. Hunt for straightening out the mess that I had found upon arrival and stated that the progress toward turning out reliable engines was due to "his knowledge, skill, patience, honesty, and never-failing cooperation." I also cited the cool judgment of Jack Hedwell, chief Air Corps inspector, and the excellent advice of Captain (later General) C. E. Irvine.

The most disturbing single production problem, as I saw it, could be summarized in a four-letter word: dirt. Failures prior to assembly and during engine run-ins were due to sand from castings, metal chips from machine operations, emery dust, magnaflux powder, dirt from new construction, and dirt introduced during engine run-ups.

I was not bashful about calling deficiencies to the attention of management. I made some individuals very unhappy but felt strongly that we could never get any fighters with Allison engines in the air unless attitudes were changed among the foremen and supervisors. Corrections caused much delay but were finally, albeit reluctantly, accomplished.

Other delays were caused because the company made too few engines available for testing. "Whenever a failure occurred," I wrote, "the whole program was held up. With more engines, the program could have gone forward more rapidly." On the plus side of the ledger, I noted that future engines, if redesigned as planned, should develop 1,500 horsepower, but would entail a substantial increase in weight and alteration of the cylinder head, induction system, and exhaust system to increase strength and volumetric efficiency. I felt, however, that any new engines should fit in the same space and on the same engine mount. A four-row, 24-cylinder V-3420 engine, then under development, "should be capable of development into a 3,000 h.p. model."

I summarized the report this way:

> a. No organization, unaccustomed to making aeronautical equipment, can produce a satisfactory product until they acquire the "aviation viewpoint" and start working to aeronautical instead of commercial standards.
>
> b. The bigger and more successful an organization is, the harder it is for them to realize this.

Coming back on active duty from an active business life presented some difficulties in dealing with my contemporaries who had remained in uniform. Many who had opted for a service life were captains and resented my return as a major. In their eyes, I appeared to be a favorite of Hap's and enjoyed special privileges. Thus, I came back to a hostile environment, which often became noticeable in meetings and one-on-one encounters when I presented my ideas for change or improvement. But I persisted because I believed I had learned some things about management in the business world that they had missed in the military, especially when it came to dealing directly with industry, as I was now required to do. I'm sure I was accused of impatience and brusqueness, but I felt someone had to be the "bad guy" to get things moving.

The job as I saw it was to effect a shotgun marriage between the aircraft industry and the automotive industry. Neither one wanted to get married, but it was necessary in order to meet President Roosevelt's requirement of 50,000 planes a year. Mass production methods for aircraft had to be found and new perspectives adopted. I spent many frustrating hours in conferences and negotiating sessions while we tried to hammer out answers to many questions: Could autos continue to be manufactured? What about new facilities? How would subcontracting be handled? How could patents and company secrets be protected? How many planes and what kinds could be produced if the country went on a wartime footing?

The aircraft industry thought that if they gave all their know-how to the automotive industry, then when the war ended, they would have developed a new and stronger competitor. The automotive industry felt that in building airplanes they would be doing something that they didn't know how to do, didn't want to do, and therefore preferred not to do.

However, in time, both industries operated in good faith, and there were some considerable improvements in manufacturing methods that the aircraft industry derived from its association with the automobile industry. In retrospect, the automobile industry eventually did a splendid job building aircraft as well as guns, tanks, and other munitions of war.

In August 1941, I asked Hap to send me to England to study what the British were doing under wartime conditions. My orders stated that I would be a military observer "in connection with aviation training and the production, maintenance and supply of aviation materiel." I was authorized "to proceed to any additional countries, including belligerent countries, that may be deemed necessary in connection with the performance of [my] duties." I left on September 7 and returned on October 13, 1941. It was thought at first I might go to Africa, where the British were fighting tank wars in the desert, but that didn't eventuate. I might have gone to Russia, but Lieutenants Hubert Zemke and Johnny Alison, who had also been sent to England as observers, went instead. Good men, they both became aces later in the war; Johnny became a major general.

I wrote to Joe shortly after my arrival and noted, "Have never been as busy—factories, conferences, and report writing. I've written reams. Haven't been able to pinch in a half hour for a haircut (on the sides) and look like one of the kids at their worst."

Colonel "Pop" Powers and I spent six weeks visiting some of the British aircraft and engine manufacturing plants to see what we could learn from them. In addition, I was to see how the British were handling the American aircraft they were getting from us. While there, I flew the Lockheed Hudson, de Havilland 89A, Typhoon, and Flamingo. We got some very good ideas from the British engineers and production people, brought them back, and tried to spread them around. We also found some unsatisfactory practices that we did not want to duplicate. I wrote a detailed 48-page report with 132 observations on what we had seen, probably the longest report I ever wrote. Here are some highlights:

- The most serious problem was the almost complete absence of spare parts for our planes, engines, propellers, and accessories. Most of the parts received could not be located when required. The supply system was unduly complicated, and the difference between British and American designations caused confusion.
- The British wrote off 30 percent of their planes every six months. Half of the losses were due to crashes, not combat.
- British planes were built with the idea that disassembly and movement or repair must be readily accomplishable. I thought we should consider this feature in future designs.
- All engines, no matter how badly wrecked or burned, were completely disassembled and invariably yielded some usable parts. School engines are assembled from parts that are not repairable.
- Repair was carried on to what we would consider a dangerous extreme on airplanes, engines, and propellers. During the Battle of Britain, anything that was "airworthy" was flown. Aircraft were repaired if time allowed and flown without repair wherever the chance of a plane's accomplishing its mission was greater than its chance of falling out of the sky.
- Underground manufacturing and repair facilities were being built. One expert said he believed that if a site was properly selected, it should cost no more to put in depot or manufacturing facilities underground than it would to build them above ground. I was favorably impressed with the underground plant of the Bristol Aeroplane Co. I commented extensively on the dispersal of the British aircraft industry,

camouflage, training of workers, tool making, and how quickly a plant could resume operation after a severe bombing. This latter observation came in handy in regard to strategic planning and operations, as will be discussed in a later chapter.

- American aircraft required extensive alterations after arrival in the UK to make them operational. "Due to the rapidly changing tactical picture and the necessity for incorporating changes found desirable through service use, it will probably always be necessary to make some changes on this side, but it is axiomatic that all possible work should be done in the States."

- The pilots of a bombardment squadron, made up largely of enlisted men, ordinarily flew 200 hours, which averaged about 35 trips, and then went to a training center. Theoretically, this training center work was supposed to be a rest, but they were obliged to work harder there than with the squadron. As a consequence, most of the squadron's pilots preferred to remain with an operating unit, even after their time was up. In one case, a pilot requested that no further record be kept of his flying time in order that he might continue to fly combat.

- The relative merits of liquid-cooled and air-cooled engines and of sleeve valves and poppet valves were discussed with pilots and mechanics. Our technical people in England subsequently followed the British research closely on this and forwarded results to the States.

- The British were sold on the 20-mm cannon and not enthusiastic about the .50-caliber machine gun and our 37-mm cannon. "Their preference for the .30 or .303 over the .50 is probably due to lack of experience with the .50. Their thinking is that the .50 will not pierce the new German armor and is only useful, therefore, like the ..303 for cutting tubing, controls, wires and generally disabling miscellaneous equipment. For this reason they feel that one shell is as good as another so they prefer the greater number of .303s available for a given weight."

- I noted the extensive use of women in industrial jobs for which they were previously thought untrainable. "They are good workers and have proved entirely satisfactory on any job that does not require heavy lifting, skilled setup or a definite mechanical turn of mind. On small parts inspection and any monotonous, repetitive work they are far better than men. They make good welders, and are particularly good on light riveting. They tire more easily than men and should not be worked more than eight hours. Their attitude and responsibility was uniformly better than men of the same age."

- I was surprised at the number of boys 12 to 14 years old I saw operating various types of simple machinery and doing handwork. When I queried the value of these youngsters, I was advised that they were all right if enough supervision was exercised over them and they were kept on the job. The use of these boys, other than as apprentices, is obviously a necessary and unsatisfactory expedient.

- "As on our side, the greatest use of the automotive industry, from an aviation viewpoint, has been to furnish management for and operate government-built airplane and engine 'shadow' factories. . . . The problems encountered are the same as our automobile people are now experiencing. The cooperation between the aircraft industry and the automobile industry was not always the closest. Drawings received from the aircraft people were always inadequate and frequently inaccurate. The airplane people, on their side, feel that the automobile group desired to tool up too extensively for the numbers involved and that the proper flexibility and the ability to make changes and incorporate improvements is lost if a mass production line is established. This all has a familiar ring and a compromise is indicated."

- Of all the skills required in the aircraft industry, I found that carpenters picked up airplane work the quickest. "This is of interest if we put our furniture industry to work making wooden aircraft."

- "The most interesting wooden airplane being built in England is the de Havilland Mosquito. The original conception of the Mosquito was as a high-speed bomber carrying a moderate bomb load at a speed so fast that pursuit could neither intercept nor overtake it. It has no armament, carries four 500-pound bombs, has a range of 1,800 miles, and carries a crew of two—pilot and bombardier. . . . It is our thinking that this airplane is worthy of serious consideration should it be desired to put the furniture industry to work on the manufacture of aircraft in the U.S."

- Gun flash was particularly troubling to pilots at night. The British felt that the flash from the two .50-caliber guns in the nose of the P-39 was so bad that these guns should not be used. They considered wing guns better than nose guns, and guns under the nose, as in the BeauFighter, best of all.

- The amount of armor placed in all combat planes was steadily increasing. Single-seat fighters had 500 pounds; the Blenheim bomber had 1,100 pounds.

- As the fight went to higher altitudes, the British became sold on engine turbo-superchargers. Direct fuel injection and fuels 20 percent higher octane than 100 octane were being considered. Much experimentation was being conducted on engines, fuels, lubricants, and engine accessories at this time.

- "Every possible effort is being made to simplify the pilot's job. The constant-speed propeller and constant manifold pressure have assisted in the project. In addition, they are now working on a single throttle control which will operate both propeller and manifold. A study of optimum performance curves indicates that economical as well as simple operation is possible with such an arrangement."

- "The control forces on British planes are uniformly less than those on American planes. This is very apparent in the Spitfire, Hurricane and Tornado. They argue that a plane must be violently tossed about during combat, and at high altitude, it is desirable that this be accomplished with a maximum of speed and a minimum of physical exertion."

- Pilots who flew the Lancaster, Halifax, and B-24 Liberator were unanimous that the Lancaster had the best flying characteristics, Halifax next, and Liberator last. This was because of the high control forces required on the Liberator.

- "We have heard a great deal about German mass production and part interchangeability, but great difficulty has been experienced here in building up complete airplanes from wrecked ones. We were told that in the case of two supposedly identical Messerschmitt 110s, a slot taken from one did not fit the other by some half inch, and the better part of three weeks was required to make the installation."

- I made an extensive report on the Typhoon after flying it. I also commented on a new fighter being manufactured by the Martin-Baker Co., calling it "by far the neatest and cleanest thing I have seen in England. The design speed at critical altitude is 430 miles per hour. Should it prove successful and be half as good as it presently appears, it will be a truly outstanding effort."

One of my concluding observations is interesting to look at 50 years later:

> "There seems to be a feeling of optimism on the part of many British officials that the war will be over in 1942 and that, while they are anxious to get all the equipment they can from us, they are merely taking out insurance, as the American equipment will probably not be required by the time we reach maximum production. The main hope, of a majority of the British, is that we will probably join them through a declaration of war on the Axis powers. They feel that the favorable psychological effect here, the unfavorable effect in Germany, and the increased production through greater effort will more than balance the tendency to send less materiel out of the country after we become actively involved."

After Hap read my report, he said, "I don't see how you were able to cover so much ground in such a short time." We couldn't have if our British contacts hadn't made it easy for us to get around.

Fortunately, the Air Corps had already started to expand. In a message to Congress in January 1939, President Roosevelt had stated that American air strength was "so utterly inadequate that [it] must be immediately strengthened." Three hundred million dollars in new funds were made available to procure new planes to a maximum number of 6,000.

By the time I was called to active duty in July 1940, President Roosevelt had authorized a much-expanded Air Corps with

10,000 planes and 16,000 more pilots and crewmen. Although new bombers—such as the B-17, B-25, and B-26—were in limited production, there were not enough fighters and light attack aircraft coming along. My transfer to Detroit gave me an additional appreciation of how difficult it was for the civilian sector to translate peacetime production into making machines of war. Those of us in uniform thought time was too short to dally and argue. In the waning months of 1941, United States involvement in the war was foreordained. The rest of the world seemed to be on fire. It would take only a tiny spark to involve us.

Our sons, Jim, Jr., and John, were caught up in the excitement of the war in Europe and talked with Joe and me about what they should do. In late 1941, young Jim was 21 and John was 19. Both wanted to be pilots, and Jim had already taken some flying lessons under the Civilian Pilot Training program at Purdue University. Both were now taller than me—the men on Joe's side of the family were all big fellows. I had boxed with the boys frequently all during their growing-up years. When they were small, I would box with them by getting down on my knees. After I was back in uniform, they had grown so tall that it looked like they should get down on their knees to box with me.

The only person ever to knock me down, hitting me so hard that I had to be helped to my feet, was young Jim when he was 19. John, while on vacation from Culver Military Academy, knocked out one of my front teeth. When he returned to Culver, he told the school doctor that his nose hurt. The doctor took a look and said, "There's nothing in the world wrong with you except that your nose is broken." John won the bout; I was the true loser because I had to pay for both injuries.

By December 1941, young Jim had two years of mechanical engineering at Purdue University and John had finished up his high school years at Culver. Both boys wanted to become Army pilots as soon as they qualified with two years of college, but I hoped they would get their baccalaureate degrees first.

The December 7, 1941, disaster at Pearl Harbor was a shock that kept everyone glued to their radios that infamous Sunday afternoon to hear Lowell Thomas and others report on the bad news. In the 1 hour, 45 minutes that the Japanese attack lasted, they nearly destroyed the U.S. Navy's strength in the Pacific. A total of 18 American ships, including 7 battleships, were sunk or seriously damaged. Naval installations were severely crippled. Of 169 U.S. naval planes in Hawaii, 92 were destroyed and 39 badly damaged. Three Army installations had been blasted. Ninety-six of the 231 planes assigned to the Hawaiian air force were completely destroyed. Only 79 could subsequently be used for combat. During the attack, 2,403 American civilian and military personnel were killed.

It was later disclosed that only during the last half hour of the attack could any resistance be mounted. About 30 Army Air Corps fighters were able to get airborne. Eleven Japanese planes were claimed shot down. Two P-40 pilots were credited with seven enemy planes shot down between them.

I didn't sleep well that night. Next day, the news got progressively worse as the extent of the damage was gradually disseminated. On December 8, I wrote to Hap Arnold through channels as military protocol required, asking that I be relieved of my duties and reassigned to a tactical unit. I said I then had 7,730 hours of flying time, most of which was in pursuit-type aircraft. I added that the reason for making the request was a sincere belief that, because of recent developments, production problems would be simplified and operations problems aggravated. Consequently, I felt that my training and experience would be of greater value in operations than production and concluded by noting that my organization had been carefully trained and was entirely competent to operate without me.

I hand-carried the letter to Colonel Alonzo Drake, my immediate boss stationed at Wright Field. He endorsed it, and I then took the letter to his superior at Wright Field, Brigadier General George C. Kenney, and asked him to approve it.

"The answer is no," Kenney said flatly. However, he didn't want to buck General Arnold so bluntly in writing in case I went over his head to Hap, so he invited me to see his superior, Major General Oliver P. Echols, chief of the Materiel Division.

"I've been expecting you," General Echols said. "General Kenney just called. His answer was no. My answer is no." However, being just as cautious as General Kenney, he wrote a single noncommittal word in his endorsement: "Forwarded."

I didn't want to call General Arnold personally to ask for the transfer, although I would have done so if I were still a civilian. I flew back to Detroit, frustrated and disgruntled.

I had planned to fly to California the day before Christmas to be with Joe and the boys, who had gone there for the holidays, but a message arrived from Hap ordering me to Washington. There I was told I was being transferred to the Air Staff, located in the Munitions Building. The Pentagon was under construction, but hadn't been completed. My title would be director of operational requirements.

I was very, very disappointed. I had missed combat in the first war. Now it looked like I was going to be chained to a desk shuffling paper for this one. The only good thing about it was that, unknown to me, General Kenney had nominated me the previous October for promotion to lieutenant colonel. The nomination had been seconded immediately by General Echols, who had recommended that I remain in Detroit and had added, "An increase in rank will enable him to perform his duties more effectively."

In those days, you didn't mention promotion recommendations like this to subordinates because the recommendations might not be approved higher up in the chain of command. I wish I had known then that they both thought I deserved a promotion, although it wouldn't have changed my desire to get into a tactical unit. My dissatisfied attitude may have spilled over in my work. I was embarrassed at my disgruntlement when I saw the letter in my military files many years later. When the recommendation reached Hap's desk, he approved the promotion to take effect on January 2, 1942, when I reported to Washington.

By this time, young Jim was scheduled to enter Army Air Force flight training in March. He had completed more than two years at Purdue University with a major in mechanical engineering.

John had indicated during his two years of high school at Culver Military Academy that he wanted to go to the U.S. Military Academy at West Point. He attended Millard West Point Preparatory School in Washington, D.C., in 1940, but broke his leg in an automobile accident after receiving an appointment. He attended the University of Michigan the next year and subsequently received an appointment from Senator Prentiss M. Brown of Missouri and was scheduled to begin his plebe year at West Point in July 1942.*

---

*John, whom we called "Peanut," qualified for the boxing team during his plebe year; during his West Point career, he scored 62 wins in 63 fights; 54 wins were by knockout or technical knockout.

With the boys gone from the nest, Joe and I put most of our household goods in storage and moved to an apartment at 2500 Q Street in northwest Washington, D.C. The nation's capital was on a wartime seven-day-a-week schedule when we arrived. The military forces were expanding so rapidly that we couldn't get clerical help. Joe volunteered her services and for a time was my unpaid secretary.

As soon as I reported to Hap's office in the Munitions Building, he gave me my first assignment. The Martin B-26 Marauder, a fast, highly streamlined medium bomber, had turned out to be an unforgiving airplane. It was killing pilots in training because it never gave them a chance to make mistakes. Young pilots went from primary trainers to basic trainers to advanced trainers before receiving their wings and then, after graduation from flying school, were sent directly to B-26 transition schools. This was a difficult jump, especially for pilots who had graduated from single-engine advanced training and had never flown multiengine aircraft. Those who had gone to twin-engine advanced training had less trouble; even so, no trainers in those days had nose wheels, so the B-26 was a step up in difficulty for all new pilots.

Hap asked me to check into the problem and recommend whether or not the B-26 should continue to be built. I checked out in it at the Martin factory near Baltimore and liked it. There wasn't anything about its flying characteristics that good piloting skill couldn't overcome. I traveled to several flying training schools and B-26 transition units, gathered the student pilots together, and asked them what they had heard about the B-26 airplane. Almost all said they had heard it wouldn't fly on one engine, you couldn't make a turn into a dead engine, and landing it safely on one engine was just about impossible.

To prove them wrong, I lined up on the runway, feathered the left engine during the takeoff roll, and made a steep turn into the dead engine, flew around the pattern, and landed with the engine still inoperative. I did it again in the other direction with the right engine feathered. And I did this without a copilot, which made a further impression. This convinced the doubters that all of these "impossible" maneuvers were not only possible, but easy, if you paid close attention to what you were doing. I had no trouble getting volunteers after each demonstration.

I recommended that the B-26 continue to be built. It was. The transition training had to be improved and lengthened. It was. Although the Marauder remained a dangerous airplane in the hands of the unskilled, it had an excellent record later when properly trained pilots took it into combat. Pilots nicknamed the original model the "Martin Prostitute" because it had relatively short wings and thus had "no visible means of support." Subsequent models had the wings lengthened, which increased its safety margin.

When this project was completed, Hap called me into his office in late January and asked, "Jim, what airplane do we have that can take off in 500 feet, carry a 2,000-pound bomb load, and fly 2,000 miles with a full crew?"

I thought a moment before answering. Certainly, it would have to be a medium bomber, because fully loaded Boeing B-17 and Consolidated B-24 heavy bombers could never get off in 500 feet. We had four medium bombers in the inventory then that might qualify—the Douglas B-18 and B-23, the North American B-25, and the Martin B-26. The first three might do the job if the fuel tanks were modified to carry more fuel, but all would have difficulty getting off in 500 feet. The B-26, with its fast landing and takeoff speeds, would never get off safely in that short a distance with a 2,000-pound load.

"General, give me a little time and I'll give you an answer," I said.

I looked up the performance figures on all four aircraft and told Hap the next day that the B-23 and the B-25 would meet his specifications, but only if additional fuel tanks were installed.

"One thing I should have added," Hap said. "The plane must be able to take off in a narrow space not over 75 feet wide."

"Then there's only one plane that can do it within that space restriction," I told him. "The B-23's 92-foot wingspan is similar to the DC-3's and therefore rules it out. The B-25 is the answer to your question. It has a wingspan of 67 ½ feet."

Hap nodded his thanks and I left, wondering why he had asked. I had no idea what had caused him to pose the question or what he was going to do with my answer. He called me back next day and I was off on the most important military assignment of my life thus far.

CHAPTER 9

Hap's questions were rooted in circumstances that I didn't know about at the time. It was many years before I learned the full story and how I eventually fitted into the picture.

Two weeks after the December 7, 1941, attack on Pearl Harbor, President Franklin D. Roosevelt held a meeting in his White House office. Those attending were General George C. Marshall, Army chief of staff; General Henry H. "Hap" Arnold, now designated chief of staff of the Army Air Forces; and Admiral Ernest J. King, chief of naval operations. Also present were Harry Hopkins, Roosevelt's special advisor; Admiral Harold R. Stark; Secretary of War Henry Stimson; and Secretary of the Navy Frank Knox.

The generals and admirals briefed the President on global war developments in Africa and Europe, and then discussion focused on the Far East. The President said he wanted to strike back at the Japanese at the earliest possible moment and asked everyone present to consider ways and means to take the war to the Land of the Rising Sun.

Roosevelt emphasized that he wanted a bombing raid on the home islands of Japan as soon as possible to bolster the morale of America and her allies. This request, repeated over and over again in the weeks following, was transmitted to the respective staffs of Marshall, King, and Arnold each time they returned to their offices. Hap dictated notes of the first meeting to his secretary, which resulted in a memorandum to the War Plans Division of the Air Staff directing that plans be drafted for retaliatory air strikes against Japan.

Meanwhile, almost immediately after Pearl Harbor, Prime Minister Winston Churchill had asked for a meeting with the President along with each of their military advisors to hammer out a united grand strategy for the conduct of the war. This first meeting of the heads of government and the combined chiefs of staff, known as the Arcadia Conference, took place in Washington on December 22, 1941, through January 14, 1942. The group met almost daily with the President and followed up with meetings of "working committees" to develop long-range plans to defeat Germany, Italy, and Japan, the three Axis powers.

One of the principal subjects at a January 4, 1942, meeting was the unsettled French situation in North Africa. While the British battled the Germans and Italians in the Middle East, French forces in northwest Africa were aligned with the pro-Axis Vichy government of France. The Axis powers, by the terms of the armistice with France, had left the Vichy French with North African ground and air forces that were large enough to control any internal revolt and could discourage an Allied invasion.

The decision was made to invade the area and neutralize any resistance by unfriendly French forces. Admiral King suggested that three U.S. Navy aircraft carriers should be used to transport the needed aircraft. He recommended that one carrier should carry about 75 to 80 Navy fighters and one should carry about 80 to 100 Army fighters. The third would be used to transport Army bombers and cargo planes, gas, bombs, and ammunition.

Arnold did not discuss the logistical difficulties involved in King's suggestion during the meeting. That night he transcribed his notes of the meeting and wrote:

> By transporting these Army bombers on a carrier, it will be necessary for us to take them off from the carrier, which brings up a question of what kind of plane—B-18 bomber and DC-3 for cargo?

in extremely short distances. The pilots selected would have to practice on land with varying bomb loads until they could take off in the short distance of a carrier's deck. A Navy flying instructor should be assigned to teach them.

Modifications to the B-25s would be required to give them extra gas capacity. Every extra mile the B-25s could add to their range would mean one less mile that the task force had to venture into Japanese waters. But added fuel meant added weight, which increased the takeoff distance required and would probably lessen the bomb load that could be carried. To be sure of his computations, Duncan thought it advisable to experiment and see if B-25s could be launched from the *Hornet*.

At the end of the fifth day, Duncan and Low met with Admiral King. Duncan briefed him, was thoughtful for a moment, then said, "Go see General Arnold about it, and if he agrees with you, ask him to get in touch with me. And don't you two mention this to another soul!"

As they turned to leave, King told Duncan, "If this plan gets the green light from General Arnold, I want you to handle the Navy end of it." Duncan and Low immediately made an appointment to see Hap on January 17, 1942.

When Low and Duncan talked with Hap, he was "most enthusiastic," but did not tell them his staff were already working on the possibility of taking Army aircraft off a carrier. Instead, he called Admiral King, and the two of them decided on the division of responsibility between them. Duncan would be the Navy coordinator for all their arrangements; whoever Arnold selected as his representative would be "tasked" with the job of overseeing modification of the planes and training of the crews.

It was then that Hap called me in and asked me those questions that had me puzzled. When he briefed me on the concept, I went to my office and studied the basic question about which of our medium bombers would be used. Not knowing what Captain Duncan had calculated, I decided independently the B-25 was the plane to be used, provided it was properly modified.

When I reported to Hap, he said, "Jim, I need someone to take this job over . . ."

I interrupted and said, "And I know where you can get someone."

"Okay, it's your baby," Hap said. "You'll have first prior-

> We will have to try bomber takeoffs from carriers. It has never been done before but we must try out and check on how long it takes.[1]

Officers in Arnold's War Plans Division studied this unusual memo from their chief and began checking the aircraft technical data to see if his idea for a North African invasion was feasible. Plans that might be followed to attack the Japanese home islands were also being studied in both Army and Navy staffs to attempt to come up with a workable plan to carry out the President's request in that part of the world.

Meanwhile, in the Pacific since the "day of infamy" at Pearl Harbor, one Japanese victory had followed another with discouraging rapidity. American forces in the Philippines were retreating to the Bataan Peninsula. British army forces, having surrendered their base at Penang, Malaya, were retreating everywhere, and the Japanese were able to continue their advance upon Singapore with only token resistance. In the Dutch East Indies, enemy forces had landed on Borneo, Timor, Celebes, and New Guinea.

The sinking of the British battleships *Prince of Wales* and *Repulse* in the Gulf of Siam on December 10 added to the bad news. The fall of Wake Island on December 23 confirmed the American public's worst fears that the situation was desperate and that the U.S. Navy had indeed been made impotent by the raid on Pearl Harbor.

As the year ended, organized resistance in the Philippines seemed at an end. On December 20, President Manuel Quezon and Vice President Sergio Osmeña were sworn in at the entrance to Malinta Tunnel on Corregidor. The Filipino and American forces were to try to hold out for six months to await reinforcements from America. These reinforcements did not exist, but the 15,000 Americans and 65,000 Filipinos on Bataan and Corregidor did not know it. All they could do was fight, try to stay alive, and hope.

On December 18, Amon G. Carter, publisher of the *Fort Worth Star Telegram,* wrote to his friend Major General Edwin M. "Pa" Watson, military secretary to the President. Carter suggested that 500 long-range bombers, manned by airline pilots, should bomb Tokyo. Watson forwarded Carter's letter to General Arnold on December 30. On January 7, knowing that the War Plans Division was considering all possible ways to bomb Japan, Arnold replied to Watson that "the fundamental idea is sound but the problem of execution is something more than that expressed by Mr. Carter. However, we will have a solution in the near future which we hope will get the results desired."[2]

On the evening of January 10, Admiral King went to the Washington Navy Yard and boarded the *Vixen*, a former German yacht, which served as his flagship and second office, where he could work undisturbed. Earlier that day, the President had reiterated his desire to strike Japan as soon as possible, but no one had yet advanced a plan to carry out his wishes.

After dinner, Captain Francis S. Low, a submariner and operations officer on King's staff, asked to speak with King privately. King, unsmiling and tired, asked what was on his mind.

"Well, sir, I've got an idea for bombing Japan that I'd like to talk with you about. I flew down to Norfolk today to check on the *Hornet*, our new carrier, and saw something that started me thinking.

"The enemy knows that the radius of action for our carrier planes is about 300 miles. Today, as we were taking off from Norfolk, I saw the outline of a carrier deck painted on an airfield where pilots are trained in carrier takeoffs and landings."

"I don't see what you're getting at, Low," King said, impatiently.

"Well, sir, I saw some Army twin-engine planes making bombing passes at this simulated carrier deck. I thought if the Army has some twin-engine bombers with a range greater than our fighters, it seems to me a few of them could be loaded on a carrier and used to bomb Japan."

King leaned back and said nothing for a minute. Low was not a pilot and fully expected to be rebuffed. Instead, King said, "You may have something there, Low. Talk to Duncan about it in the morning. And don't tell anyone else about this."

Low immediately phoned Captain Donald B. "Wu" Duncan, a 1917 Naval Academy graduate and veteran pilot, who was King's air operations officer. Early on the morning of January 11 Low cautiously presented his idea to Duncan. "As I see it," Low said, "there are two big questions that have to be answered

first: Can an Army medium bomber land aboard a carrier? (
a land-based bomber loaded down with bombs, gas, and c
take off from a carrier deck?"

Duncan listened thoughtfully, then said, "The answe
your first question is a definite negative. A carrier deck is
short to land an Army bomber safely. Even if one could
stopped in time, it wouldn't fit on an elevator to be sto
below so the next one could land. Even if you could land t
on a carrier, the tails of Army bombers aren't designed to
the shock of sudden stops with our arresting gear."

"And my second question?"

"I'll have to get back to you on that," Duncan said.

Duncan went to work immediately. He consulted
technical manuals for performance capabilities of Army m
bombers, checked Navy files for carrier deck space, and c
historical records to determine if the Navy had any exp
with launching heavily loaded land-based planes. Five da
beginning his study, Duncan completed a 30-page han
copy of his analysis, which he did not entrust to a t
perfectionist and brilliant staff officer who later rose to
rank, he concluded that the North American B-25 was
plane that could carry out a mission such as Low env

This would be a very high-risk mission for the N
task force taking bombers to a launching point in th
Pacific would be a prime target for marauding Japa
forces. Duncan cautioned that absolute secrecy wou
be observed and few, if any, records kept of arrang
cause the lives of 10,000 men would be at risk, a
large task force of ships, which were in extremely s
after Pearl Harbor. The one vital element to such
would make such an operation worthwhile would b

The *Hornet* would be the ideal carrier to t
launch B-25s, Duncan thought. Commissioned in O
she was due to sail from Norfolk for the Pacific
Her decks were wide enough to accommodate som
she could steam at a maximum of about 25 kn
screening force of another carrier, cruisers, destroy
ers for protection, the *Hornet* could be brought t
500 miles of the Japanese coast for the bomber lau
the B-25s couldn't be retrieved by the carrier
would need the range to proceed to friendly fiel

Duncan knew that Army pilots were not tra

ity on anything you need to get the job done. Get in touch with me directly if anybody gets in your way.''

Hap and Admiral King decided on a tentative departure date of April 1 for the *Hornet* from the West Coast. This would give the Navy time to permit some experimental B-25 takeoffs from the *Hornet* and get the carrier there via the Panama Canal. Meanwhile, Captain Duncan would go to Hawaii to work out the Navy's task force details. I knew what I had to do.

Since so many men would be involved and the entire operation's success rested on the element of surprise, it was obvious that the biggest problem would be maintaining secrecy. If we could not achieve surprise, the Japanese would be lying in wait with their numerically superior naval and air forces.

By mid-January, the Air War Plans Division had already advanced plans to establish a major fighting air command—the 10th Air Force—in Burma to support the Allied effort against the ever-encroaching Japanese on the Chinese mainland. Operation Aquila was to be launched to establish an advanced detachment that would be the nucleus for the eventual buildup of American air power in China. There were to be five separate but related projects in this initial buildup:

1. The flight of B-25s to be dispatched from a carrier was to provide the first medium bombardment aircraft for use in China. Pilots and crews were to be absorbed into the 10th Air Force after their mission.
2. Thirty-five DC-3 transports were to be provided to form the aerial lifeline of supply.
3. A group of 33 A-20 attack planes under the command of Colonel Leo H. Dawson were to be ferried from the factory to the Chinese air force under the lend-lease agreement; the pilots were to be assigned to the 10th Air Force.
4. Twenty-three B-24 heavy bombers under the command of Colonel Harry A. Halverson were to be the first long-range bombers assigned to the 10th. It was this unit, known as the Halpro Group, that was to open up long-range strategic attacks on Japan from Chinese bases.
5. Fifty-one P-40Es were to be assembled at Takoradi, in West Africa, and ferried to China for the use of Chennault's Amer-

ican Volunteer group, whether or not it was to be later absorbed into the U.S. air forces.

These five separate projects, when approved, were assigned to the various leaders to carry out. The last four projects were to be carried out independently and given secret status. The first one was assigned to me and given a top-secret label because the B-25s were now going to bomb Japan en route to the China-Burma-India theater. At this point, only five of us knew what was being planned: King, Arnold, Duncan, Low, and me. And that's the way I wanted to keep it until whoever the Navy selected to lead the task force was given the details.

At two P.M. on January 28, 1942, General Arnold again met with the President, the secretary of war, Admiral King, General Marshall, and a few top-level staff members. Discussion of strategy centered on the depressing situation in the Pacific and the Far East. President Roosevelt asked once more about the progress being made on plans for bombing Japan. My project was under way, but not all those present at the meeting knew about it, so Hap talked only about bombing Japan from China and Russia. The President reiterated that from a psychological viewpoint, both of Japan and of the United States, it was important to bomb Japan as soon as possible.[3]

While all of this was going on at the highest level, I had my verbal marching orders from Hap and his authority to get the job done. That was all I needed. I called the assignment "Special Aviation Project No. 1" and took off in my P-40 for Wright Field to lay the groundwork for the job ahead.

On January 31, Captain Duncan flew to Norfolk, Virginia, and made arrangements with Captain Marc A. Mitscher, skipper of the *Hornet*, to prepare to have three B-25 Mitchell medium bombers hoisted aboard next day for trial takeoffs. Mitscher did not press Duncan for details.

Lieutenant John F. Fitzgerald, who had won his wings in 1940, was in charge of the three two-man Mitchell crews. During the previous week they had practiced about 30 short-field takeoffs from the simulated carrier deck on an auxiliary field near Norfolk. One of the B-25s had an engine failure and did not participate further.

On the afternoon of February 1, the two B-25s were loaded.

Duncan reported to Mitscher to discuss the details of the experiment without giving him any reasons why the trials were to be conducted. Mitscher, a veteran naval pilot, knew there were risks involved. Next day, the B-25s were hoisted aboard and the *Hornet* steamed out of sight of land. That afternoon, Fitzgerald, Lieutenant James F. McCarthy, and their copilots were given the signal to man their planes.

While Duncan and Mitscher watched from the carrier's island, Fitzgerald revved up his engines to the maximum and, at the signal from the launching officer, roared down the deck and was off. His takeoff was not without its moments of excitement.

Fitzgerald recalled years later that when they spotted the planes for takeoff he was surprised to see that he had about 500 feet of usable deck and that the plane's airspeed indicator showed about 45 miles per hour sitting there. This meant he had to accelerate only about 23 miles per hour.

When he got the "go" signal and let the brakes off, he was almost immediately airborne—well ahead of his estimate. The wings of the B-25 rose so rapidly that he thought the plane was going to strike the island that projected out over the flight deck. He pushed the control column forward and the wing just barely passed underneath.

Lieutenant McCarthy also got off quickly and the two Mitchells returned to Norfolk. None of the pilots knew why the experimental takeoffs had been requested. They were unaware of the significance of their flights until many months later when the information about our mission was finally released. They deserve much credit for their willingness to take part in the trial takeoffs—something that had never been attempted before.

Both planes had been lightly loaded with fuel; neither had bombs or equivalent weight to lift. The wind had been about 20 knots and the *Hornet* was making only a little over 20 knots during the takeoffs. However, Duncan was satisfied that a fully loaded B-25 with a full five-man crew could be safely dispatched from the *Hornet*.

I concurred with Duncan's figures provided the carrier was making 20 knots or more and there was a strong wind straight down the deck. However, I wondered how much space would be available for takeoff for the first few planes when we crowded a bunch of B-25s on the deck.

While Duncan was preparing the Navy's plans for the operation, I made hurried trips to Wright Field to have engineers make drawings for the installation of additional B-25 fuel tanks and asked the procurement people to determine the best contractor to do the work. On January 22, I prepared a memo requesting that 18 B-25Bs be sent to Mid-Continent Airlines at Minneapolis, Minnesota, for modification to my specifications.

On January 23, I met with Brigadier General George C. Kenney at Wright Field to tell him what else I needed for "the B-25B Special Project." Although he was naturally curious, I didn't tell him why. He called in his top people and we went over my specifications for the modifications. Not only was special plumbing for the extra gas tanks needed, but new bomb shackles and other unique equipment were required. I wanted several planes to have electrically operated 16-mm motion picture cameras installed that would take 60 pictures at half-second intervals, starting automatically when the first bomb was dropped. Landing flares normally carried on the B-25s were to be relocated forward of the rear armored bulkhead to protect them better against enemy fire.

I knew the toughest part of the job would be the installation of the auxiliary gas tanks. First, a steel tank of about 265-gallon capacity was manufactured by the McQuay Co. This tank was later removed and replaced by a 225-gallon leak-proof tank manufactured by the United States Rubber Co. of Mishawaka, Indiana. We had difficulty with this tank because of leaks in the connections. After one satisfactory tank was made, the outer case was reduced in size in order to facilitate installation, but without reducing the size of the inner rubber container; consequently, wrinkles developed that reduced tank capacity and increased the tendency to fail and leak. However, we put the tank under air pressure, which increased the capacity by 10 to 15 gallons, and new outer covers alleviated the trouble. There wasn't time for the manufacturer to provide new covers for all the tanks before we were obliged to fly the aircraft away. In order for the tank to be fitted into the top of the bomb bay, special extension shackles for the four 500-pound bombs were also built by the McQuay Co.

A second collapsible 160-gallon rubber tank was manufactured by the United States Rubber Co. and installed in the crawlway above the bomb bay. It could be squeezed flat after it was emptied so that the crawlway could be cleared for the engineer-gunner to come forward if needed. In addition, collapsing the tank, sucking out the vapor through a vent, and pushing the tank to one side minimized the fire hazard. Unfortunately, we had much difficulty with this tank because of leaks in the seams. The trouble was reduced somewhat through the use of a heavier material and more careful handling of the tank.

The third tank was a 60-gallon leak-proof tank installed in the space from which the lower turret was removed. This tank would be refilled by the rear gunner from 10 five-gallon cans to be carried in the rear compartment. After the cans were emptied, they were to be punctured so they would sink when thrown overboard.

With these additional fuel tanks, there would be a total of 1,141 gallons of fuel on board, of which some 1,100 gallons would be available.

Once I had this part of the project started, I asked Hap to have Brigadier General Carl "Tooey" Spaatz, his deputy for intelligence, prepare target folders to include the best industrial targets in Japan without divulging why they were wanted or who had requested them. His staff prepared a list of industrial targets located in Tokyo, Yokohama, Kobe, Nagoya, and six other cities. Iron, steel, magnesium, and aluminum industries were included, along with aircraft manufacturing plants, petroleum refineries, and shipbuilding facilities. Beside each target suggestion was listed the reason for its selection.

Meanwhile, the other projects were in the final planning stages. The Halpro Group project, to locate a heavy bomb group in China, was begun with the activation of a headquarters and headquarters squadron on January 26.

At this time, as I learned later, President Roosevelt was growing increasingly impatient about the prospect of operating heavy bombers against Japan from Mongolia. He wanted to know when something could be worked out, but Hap replied that there was no way at that time that heavy bombers could be operated from Mongolia without the cooperation of the Soviet government. He pointed out that the Chinese government had had no effective control of Outer Mongolia for the past several years, and there was no likelihood that it would try to invade the area.

For this reason, Hap noted in a memo to the President, he felt that the plan for carrying out an attack upon the Japanese enemy's center of gravity from China was the logical and most effective plan. He did not mention the mission I was planning.

When some of my logistics requirements were put in motion, I felt I had to straighten out in my mind what had been done and what needed to be done to get trained crews and combat-ready airplanes to the debarkation port by April 1. As I had done before and many times since, I closed my office door and wrote a memo to clarify my thinking and make sure I hadn't forgotten anything (see Appendix 1). This has always been a very useful mental exercise for me. I recommend it for anyone confronted with a complicated project that has many important details to be worked out.

My memo was comprehensive, but I knew there was much more to be done and that there would probably be changes made along the way. It had been my experience in industry that plans that included new methods or devices and involved other people must always be followed up, because, as the saying goes, "There's always someone who doesn't get the message." In this case, there would probably be people who didn't appreciate the urgency of what I wanted done, and I wouldn't be able to tell them the why of it all.

Most worrisome of the logistical arrangements was the construction and installation of the auxiliary gas tanks. Fuel tank capacity and fuel consumption would be vitally important to complete the mission. Just as important over the target would be the B-25's defensive guns.

Shortly after writing the memo, I asked to have the number of aircraft to be modified at Mid-Continent increased from 18 to 24. This would assure that at least 18 would be in top shape for the mission. I also inquired about what flying units were operational with the B-25 and were available for assignment to my project. The answer came back that the 34th, 37th, and 95th squadrons of the 17th Bombardment Group, commanded by Lieutenant Colonel William C. Mills, and its associated 89th Reconnaissance Squadron, under Major John A. "Jack" Hilger, all stationed at Pendleton, Oregon, could be released most easily. Most of the pilots were qualified in the B-25, and some crews already had experience patrolling for enemy submarines off the Oregon-Washington coast.

On February 3, orders were teletyped to Pendleton to transfer without delay all planes and personnel to the Columbia Army Air Base, in Columbia, North Carolina. Mills and Hilger were instructed to pass the word among their men that volunteers would be needed for an extremely hazardous mission. En route to Columbia, the planes would have the fuel tanks installed.

At the same time, I asked for assignment of an air base where the selected crews could train in relative seclusion. Ideally, the base should be near water so that the navigators could practice overwater navigation. There should be facilities for gunnery training and an auxiliary field available where the pilots could practice short-field takeoffs. Eglin Field, Florida, was assigned; it met all my specifications.

Since I intended to make arrangements at Minneapolis, Wright Field, Edgewood Arsenal, and Washington personally, I wanted an experienced deputy to take over during my absences from Eglin. I asked Colonel Mills for a recommendation and he suggested Jack Hilger, a no-nonsense perfectionist. Hilger's job was to get the men and planes assembled at Eglin and set up training operations there as far away from curious eyes as possible. The remainder of the 17th Bomb Group would remain at Columbia and await further orders.

Colonel Mills delegated the selection of crews for 24 aircraft to the 17th's three squadron commanders—Captains Edward J. "Ski" York, Al Rutherford, and Karl Baumeister. They were to come up with the names of volunteers for the mission. All three squadron commanders had volunteered, but Mills would allow only York to go. Since almost every officer and enlisted man in the four squadrons volunteered, the three squadron commanders made up lists of an approximately equal number of men each to make up 24 crews. Mechanics, armorers, radio operators, and other ground personnel were also designated and ordered to proceed to Eglin as fast as planes could be made available to transport them.

My Form 5, the Air Force pilot's individual flight record, shows that I checked out in the B-25B on March 1, 1942. I didn't want to give up my P-40 for traveling back and forth, but I did not want to be responsible for any flying unit unless I was proficient in the same types of planes my men were assigned to fly.

Hilger and the major part of the contingent arrived at Eglin between February 27 and March 3. I had confided to Hilger the elements of the mission we were going to perform so that he could transfer the urgency and necessity to the men for what we were going to do, but without telling them the reasons. Hilger suggested that it would probably be a good idea for the Navy to assign an instructor for a short time to teach the pilots about carrier takeoffs, something Army Air Forces (the new name for the Army Air Corps) pilots had never practiced. Very seldom in peacetime would a bomber pilot be required to take off a heavily loaded aircraft in an extremely short distance. Duncan had already earmarked a young Navy pilot instructor to join us at Eglin, Lieutenant (later Rear Admiral) Henry L. "Hank" Miller. We would value his expertise.

While the men were settling down at Eglin, Hank arrived from Pensacola where he had been instructing naval cadets. He had been told why he was being sent, but Captains York, David M. Jones, and C. Ross Greening, the senior captains assigned, didn't know yet what their training was going to be like there. They were surprised when Hank told them he was to teach them carrier takeoffs. They were even more surprised when they learned he had not only never flown a B-25, but never even seen one before he arrived.

Hank checked the performance data on the B-25 and the pilot's handbook and then proceeded to an auxiliary field that had been set aside for the group and made two practice takeoffs. He acted as copilot for Davey Jones and Ski York while Ross Greening observed. He gave them instructions that they followed to the letter. On the first takeoff, the indicated airspeed was 50 miles an hour. Jones, York, and Greening were skeptical and would not believe that we could take that plane off with a gross weight of 27,000 pounds at 50 miles an hour. They agreed that the airspeed indicator must be off. They didn't realize it then, but before long they would be able to take off within 350 feet in a 40-knot wind with the plane loaded to 31,000 pounds—2,000 pounds over its designed maximum load.

I landed at Eglin Field on March 3, called all the men together, and told them that they would be training for an exceptionally dangerous mission. I wanted only volunteers; anyone could drop out for whatever reason and nothing would ever be said about it. One young pilot raised his hand and asked if I would give them more information. I told them they might guess why they were doing certain things, but the entire operation was top secret and they were not even to discuss their guesses among themselves. I stressed the importance of secrecy repeatedly and said that any violations could mean that the lives of hundreds of people would be at risk. I cautioned them about spreading rumors and said that if anyone got particularly nosey about why we were at Eglin or what we were doing, they should give me his name and the FBI would take it from there.

I stressed the necessity for teamwork in getting the planes in shape and told the pilots that their job was to learn how to take their B-25s off in the shortest possible distance with heavy loads. I said we had about three weeks, maybe less, to get ready.

The organization was set up along normal squadron lines. Jack Hilger was my executive officer; Major Harry Johnson was adjutant; Ski York was operations officer; Davey Jones was navigation and intelligence officer; Ross Greening was gunnery and bombing officer; First Lieutenant William M. Bower was engineering officer; First Lieutenant Travis Hoover was supply officer; and Second Lieutenant J. Royden Stork was photographic officer.

During the first days at Eglin, I took Hilger, York, Jones, and Greening aside and told them the general nature of the mission, with as few particulars as possible. I explained why the B-25 had been selected, the main objective of the raid, and how the planes were to be carried within range of their targets, although I did not tell them what the targets would be. They would learn these later after we were aboard the carrier. I felt telling them this much would help them transfer the urgency of the training to the rest of the men. Secrecy was stressed every time I talked with any of them; it was uppermost in my mind and was the reason why I kept no written records and kept the purpose of my frequent trips to Washington and elsewhere to myself.

I knew it wasn't easy for the pilots to practice minimum-speed takeoffs. Throughout their training, they had always been taught to have plenty of airspeed before attempting to lift a plane off the ground. They were used to operating from mile-long runways; yanking a B-25 off the ground at near stalling speed took some courage and was very much against their natural instincts.

I took Hank Miller's course because I was determined to go on the mission. However, if I couldn't pass the course or wasn't as good as the younger pilots, I was going to go as a copilot.

While the pilots were training at an auxiliary field, modifications were continuing on the B-25s at Eglin. I wanted each crew to get about 50 hours of flying time in the planes, to be divided up into day and night navigation, gunnery, bombing, and formation flying. However, because of maintenance problems with the gas tanks and gun turrets, I don't think anyone got that much practice.

A major problem we encountered concerned the electrically powered gun turrets. The early B-25s had a top and lower turret with twin .50-caliber machine guns. The bombardier had a single .30-caliber machine gun in the nose that he could poke through a gun port and operate if attacked. There were no guns installed in the tail section, which made those early models of the B-25 very vulnerable to fighter attacks.

Much credit must go to Ross Greening for solving our armament problems. He suggested that we install two broomsticks in the tail and paint them black to simulate a tail gun position, which would, hopefully, deter attacks from the rear. I approved. Since we were to bomb at a low altitude, he thought we did not need the top secret Norden bombsight and risk having it fall into enemy hands. I agreed. He designed a simple "Mark Twain" bombsight to replace it, consisting of only two pieces of aluminum, which cost about 20 cents to make in the Eglin metal shop. The bombardiers found that it worked far better than the Norden at low altitudes. And since the lower turrets gave us nothing but headaches and were very complicated to operate, Greening suggested removing them. Again, I approved. I thought a man could learn to play the violin well enough for Carnegie Hall before he could learn to fire that thing. I felt very strongly that only equipment that is natural to use should be installed on any airplane.

We quickly found that many of the gunners had never fired a .50-caliber machine gun or operated a power turret before. I wanted them to get as much practice as time would allow, but guns and ammunition were in short supply and so much work had to be done on the turrets that few, if any, got the practice they needed in the air. When a few guns were finally made available, we soon found they would not operate properly; some didn't fire at all, and the best of them would fire only short bursts before jamming. The gunners had to get familiar with the .50s by ground-firing them on the firing range; none of them ever fired on a moving target from the B-25 in flight before we left Eglin.

The machine guns had been made by Delco according to government specifications, but they wouldn't work. The longest burst we could get was about five rounds. One old sergeant told me the problem was they hadn't been finished. He was right. W. C. Olson, an armaments expert from Wright Field, was largely responsible for overcoming the difficulties we had by supervising the replacement of faulty parts, smoothing down others, adjusting clearances, and training the gun maintenance crews. When we left Eglin, all the guns, but not the turrets, were operating satisfactorily.

Since I had put in a request for special incendiary bombs to be manufactured, I contacted Colonel Max F. Schneider, an ordnance expert at Edgewood Arsenal, Maryland, a few miles north of Washington. He immediately understood what I wanted, and his people made up 500-pound clusters that had a reasonable scatter when dropped from a low altitude. He and his people came through magnificently and on time. Max saw the benefits of these for future bombing operations, and the ones he made for us were the basis for incendiary bombs used throughout the rest of the war.

Once the bombs were available, we found the bomb racks wouldn't release the bombs. This problem was also eventually solved, but was typical of the difficulties we ran into during our brief stay at Eglin.

While the crews were wrestling with their problems, I continued to fly back and forth to Washington, Dayton, and elsewhere to iron out details on a personal basis, always conscious of the need for secrecy, never telling my contacts why I needed this or that now. Whenever I had resistance from someone and my using General Arnold's name didn't get something done fast enough, I called or saw Hap personally and the path was suddenly cleared. Word of such authority soon got around and I had less and less difficulty when I asked for information or action. Without Hap's personal interest in the project and unquestioning approval of whatever I wanted to do, we would never have been able to make our deadline.

One of the other officers who played a vital role in our forthcoming mission was Dr. (First Lieutenant) Thomas R. White, a physician attached to the 89th Reconnaissance Squadron as flight surgeon. As soon as "Doc" White heard of the call for volunteers for a special mission while he was en route to Columbia, South Carolina, he wired Major Hilger and asked to be "squeezed in somewhere." A physician on our mission would be an asset, but Hilger told him the only way he could go would be as a gunner, and Doc wasn't qualified. Doc assured Hilger he could qualify, and to his great credit, he did. He scored second highest of all the gunners on the firing range with the twin .50s and thus earned his way onto a crew.

Doc had other duties. He was responsible for seeing that every crew member received appropriate immunizations. This required each man to be inoculated against pneumonia, typhus, bubonic plague, yellow fever, and smallpox. Doc was not very popular with those who found that they had to have as many as 11 shots over a three-week period.

On one of my trips to Washington in mid-March, I dropped in to see Hap and report on the progress we were making. Toward the end of our conversation, I said, "General, it occurred to me that I'm the one guy on this project who knows more about it than anyone else. You asked me to get the planes modified and the crews trained and this is being done. They're the finest bunch of boys I've ever worked with. I'd like your authorization to lead this mission myself."

Hap stared at me and his ever-present smile disappeared. He knew I had missed combat in World War I just as he had and understood from my previous request when I was in Detroit that I didn't want to miss this war. He shook his head and said, "I'm sorry, Jim. I need you right here on my staff. I can't afford to let you go on every mission you might help to plan."

I thought he was going to say that and launched into a rapid-fire sales pitch I had mentally prepared beforehand. Finally, Hap gave in. He shrugged and said, "All right, Jim. It's all right with me provided it's all right with Miff Harmon." Miff was Brigadier General Millard F. Harmon, Jr., Hap's chief of staff.

I smelled a rat so I saluted, about-faced, and ran down the corridor to Miff's office. I knocked and opened his door.

"Miff," I said breathlessly, "I've just been to see Hap about that project I've been working on and said I wanted to lead the mission. Hap said it was okay with him if it's okay with you."

Miff was caught flat-footed, which was what I had intended. He replied, "Well, whatever is all right with Hap is certainly all right with me."

I thanked him and closed the door. Just as I did, I heard Hap's voice on Miff's squawk box. Miff said, plaintively, "But Hap, I told him he could go."

I didn't wait to hear any more. I beat it back to Bolling Field, got into my B-25, and headed for Eglin.

The training of the crews, difficult as it was with so many maintenance problems, was going ahead as best it could. Since

I now had an okay from Hap, tentative as it was, I completed my course of short-field takeoffs. Captain Vernon L. Stinzi, one of the pilots, had become ill and it was expedient to declare myself his replacement. The copilot was Lieutenant Richard E. Cole; Lieutenant Henry A. Potter was the navigator; Sergeant Fred A. Braemer, the bombardier; and Sergeant Paul J. Leonard, the engineer-gunner.

I hadn't known any of these men before, but I liked the way they worked together. Paul was one of the hardest- working, most dedicated mechanics I had ever been associated with; I was satisfied they all knew their jobs.

While we were straining against time to get ready for the flight west, the *Hornet* was making its way through the Panama Canal, headed for San Francisco, with a brief stop at San Diego. Captain Wu Duncan was at Pearl Harbor working with Admiral Chester Nimitz's staff ironing out the logistics for their part of the project. During the third week in March, Wu wired Admiral King's office in Washington: TELL JIMMY TO GET ON HIS HORSE.

King relayed the message to Hap, and Hap called me at Eglin. That seven-word message was our signal to send the planes and crews to the air depot at Sacramento where we were scheduled to have last-minute checks on each plane, pick up some equipment, and then proceed to the naval air station at Alameda, California. En route, the pilots were to get some low-level navigation experience, which they thoroughly enjoyed because legal hedgehopping was a rare experience.

On the morning of March 23, I called all the crews together and told them to get ready to move out. Those who were going knew who they were. The others were to return to Columbia. I repeated what I had been saying time and time again: "Don't tell anyone what you were doing here at Eglin—not your families, wives, anybody. The lives of your buddies and a lot of other people depend on you keeping everything you saw and did here a secret."

I dismissed everyone but the crews of 22 planes and told them our destination: the air depot at McClellan Army Air Field, in Sacramento, California. The crews of two planes that had been damaged during the takeoff practice would not go with us.

* * *

While we had been preparing for our mission, the war news in the Far East had gone from bad to worse. The situation in the Philippines was hopeless. Manila had been declared an open city the day after Christmas, and American and Filipino forces were fighting delaying actions as they backed down the Bataan Peninsula toward the island of Corregidor. On February 22, President Roosevelt ordered General Douglas MacArthur to leave Luzon and go to Australia, where he was to assume command of Allied forces when—and if—those forces ever came into being. He finally left a month later and upon arrival in Darwin announced: "The President of the United States ordered me to break through the Japanese lines and proceed from Corregidor to Australia for the purpose, as I understand it, of organizing the American offensive against Japan, a primary purpose of which is the relief of the Philippines. I came through and I shall return."

While the battles in the Philippines were going on, Hong Kong, Singapore, and other areas of Allied influence in the Far East had fallen under the fierce advances of the Japanese war machine. Burma became a new objective and Rangoon fell on March 7. Sumatra was captured and Java was shut off two days later. The 96,000 troops in the Dutch East Indies surrendered.

Next on the Japanese master strategic schedule was the invasion of Australia. The naval base at Port Darwin was attacked by the Japanese in February; in the weeks following, New Britain, New Ireland, part of New Guinea, the Admiralty Islands, and the Gilberts were occupied. Within four months after Pearl Harbor, the enemy had made extraordinary conquests and had acquired control over three million square miles of land rich in natural resources. The entire Pacific Ocean generally west of a line drawn from Alaska to Hawaii to Australia was now dominated by powerful Japanese military forces.

The fall of the Philippines, Malaya, Burma, and the Dutch East Indies had allowed the Japanese to push westward as well as southward. The master strategy now appeared to be a linkup with Axis forces in India.

By the time our planes arrived in Sacramento at the beginning of the last week in March, Admiral Nimitz had been briefed on the plan and had his staff working to form a task force under Admiral William F. Halsey to get us to the launch point. Halsey, an aggressive, feisty leader itching for combat, was delighted to have a part in the effort. American forces had already launched two raids in the Pacific—one on Wake Island and the other on Marcus Island—in an attempt to lure the Japanese back from the south and release the pressure on the Philippines.

I arrived at McClellan on March 26 and met with Colonel John M. Clark, commander of the depot, and his top engineering and maintenance personnel to discuss the inspections I wanted on the B-25s. I insisted that no one was to tamper with or remove anything from any aircraft. The planes were to be inspected. Period. I explained that a number of modifications had already been made that were nonstandard. I wanted new propellers installed; 60-gallon gas tanks not already installed were to be fitted in where the lower turrets had been removed; and hydraulic valves for the gun turrets were to be replaced. Back-type parachutes were to be substituted for the seat types we had been issued at Eglin. In addition, new covers for the leak-proof bomb bay tanks had to be replaced because the original ones had been made too small, causing wrinkles that, in turn, caused leaks. The 230-pound liaison radios were to be removed and new glass navigation windows installed in place of the Plexiglas type. I emphasized that under no circumstances were the carburetors on the engines to be touched, because they had been especially tuned at Eglin and were adjusted just as we wanted them.

I was told that some of the work could not be accomplished as I described because all of the materials had not been received at the depot yet. Once more I could see the resistance building up, as I had experienced previously at Wright Field and in Washington until Hap interceded. The attitude of a few of the supervisors also reminded me of the days at Indianapolis and Detroit dealing with the engine and automobile industry people when I tried to convince them that they should "get with the program." The sense of urgency had not filtered down from Washington with the supply requests and instructions, and I couldn't tell them the why of my requests for action.

Despite my pleading at this meeting, the civilian maintenance crews went about their assignments at a leisurely pace. This naturally made me very angry. I told my crews to stay with their planes and watch the work being done. They were to report anything they didn't like to me or Ski York. It wasn't long until the complaints started. Ted W. Lawson, in his excellent book *Thirty Seconds over Tokyo*, recounted his experience, which unfortunately was typical:

> . . . I had to stand by and watch one of the mechanics rev up my engines so fast that the new blades picked up dirt which pockmarked their tips. I caught another one trying to sandpaper the imperfections away and yelled at him until he got some oil and rubbed it on the places which he had sandpapered. I knew that salt air would make those prop tips pulpy when they had been scraped.
>
> The way they revved our motors made us wince. All of us were so afraid that they'd hurt the ships, the way they were handling them, yet we couldn't tell them why we wanted them to be so careful. I guess we must have acted like the biggest bunch of soreheads those mechanics ever saw, but we kept beefing until Doolittle got on the long-distance phone, called Washington and had the work done the way we wanted it done.[4]

I did indeed call Washington and refused to speak to anyone but Hap. "Things are going too slowly out here," I told him. "I'd appreciate it very much if you would personally build a fire under these people. They're treating this job as 'routine' and that won't get the job done in time."

I don't know what Hap did or said, but it seemed like only minutes before our work order became the most important mission at McClellan. We suddenly became the focus of interest for a lot of folks who wondered what was going on that was suddenly so important. As I think about it now, those B-25s and the work that had to be done on them must have seemed very strange: broomsticks in the tail cone; no liaison radios; new propellers; a strange, cheap-looking contraption where the bombsight should go; rubber gas tanks; no bottom gun turrets; special camera installations in the tips of the tails between the broomsticks. Whenever the civilians would ask questions, my crews watching over them would tell them to mind their own business and get on with what they were supposed to do.

One incident was typical of several that happened. I was standing in base operations talking with a couple of pilots when I noticed a civilian worker trying to start one of our B-25s. He churned and churned the prop, but couldn't get the engine started. Then there was a loud bang and backfiring with black smoke and flames pouring out of the exhaust stacks. I ran out to the plane and shouted to the mechanic to shut the engine down, but he kept on turning the engine over and paid no attention to my arm waving. I crawled up into the cockpit and yelled in his ear to stop. I'm afraid I used some expletives I hadn't used before and probably haven't since.

The man turned to me indignantly and said he was running up the engines as he was required to do whenever carburetors had been changed or adjusted. I was very, very angry. I had specifically told the supervisors that no one was to touch the carburetors because they had all been bench-checked at Eglin and were adjusted just the way we wanted them. He said he was only doing his job as he had been instructed. Obviously, the word had not filtered down from the supervisors to those who would do the work.

I conveyed my unhappiness to the engineering officer and Colonel Clark, the base commander, and called Hap again. Hap called Colonel K. B. Wolfe, Wright Field's commander, with whom I had worked to get the work begun in the first place. K.B. was responsible for the depot at McClellan and demanded a written report from Clark. When I was preparing my clearance for the flight to Alameda, I was handed a form to fill out that asked for my opinion of the work that had been performed on our aircraft. I took a look at it and wrote diagonally one word in large letters: "LOUSY."

As the planes were being readied, I noticed that several had objectionable, anti-Japanese slogans painted on their sides. I had them quickly removed because if any crews were captured, any words that would seem offensive to the enemy would be an additional reason or excuse to cause them harm. Besides, if the B-25 crews that had painted them on had guessed right about where we were going, those slogans would jeopardize the security of the mission.

One by one, the B-25s were released, even though all the work had not been completed, and the crews flew them to Alameda. Jack Hilger got into some heated discussions with the civilians in charge when he told them we were taking the airplanes no matter what. I left first because I wanted to meet the crews when they arrived at Alameda. I asked them all to give their planes a good test hop and get at least an hour's flying time before landing at the naval base. When they arrived at the naval air station,

Ski York and I greeted each crew and asked if their aircraft had any malfunctions. If the pilots or engineers admitted to anything wrong, we directed them to a parking area instead of toward a ramp near the wharf. I told the crews that every B-25 crew member was to board the carrier, whether or not his aircraft was loaded. They would go as spare crew members if anyone dropped out. I didn't want anyone who had gone that far with us to be left at dockside. The word about what we had done or speculation about what we were about to do couldn't leak out if everyone was at sea.

Although I had originally thought 18 B-25s could be loaded, it was decided that only 15 could be handled safely. But knowing some of the crews were apprehensive about taking off when they saw that short deck space, I asked Captain Mitscher if we could have a sixteenth B-25 loaded. After we were about 100 miles at sea, I thought two of the pilots, with Hank Miller aboard, could take off to show the rest of the crews that it was possible. That plane could then return to the unit's home base at Columbia, South Carolina.

Mitscher shrugged and said, "All right with me, Jim. It's your show."

As the 16 "good" B-25s had their engines shut down, Navy handlers drained gas from the tanks and hooked up nose-wheel tow bars. They were towed to the side of the *Hornet* and hoisted aboard; the crews walked silently behind. Each crew member then carried his bags up the gangplank where Hank Miller was waiting. As far as I know, not a single one of them had ever been aboard a carrier before. Neither had I.

"I was proud of those fellows that day," Hank said later. "As each man came aboard, he saluted the national ensign and then the officer of the deck and said, 'Sergeant or Lieutenant or Captain so-and-so reporting for duty, sir.' They were a smart-looking outfit and I was mighty proud of the way they responded to my teaching. They looked smarter in all respects than the Navy personnel that were going to and fro."[5]

We were all impressed by the efficiency of the *Hornet*'s crew as they maneuvered the B-25s on the deck, chocked the wheels, and tied them down. It was so nicely done that you would have thought they handled Army bombers every day.

Hank Miller met several officers he had known at the Naval Academy or at Pensacola and they wanted to know what the activity was all about. Hank refused to comment. He knew he was supposed to be a passenger in that sixteenth B-25. By the time it departed, they would all be at sea and would then be told where they were going. Since his friends knew he had been born in Alaska, they speculated that they were probably heading that way. Perhaps some thought our B-25s were going to be flown off the carrier to fields in Alaska; there were probably many on board who remembered the takeoffs of the two B-25s the previous February off the East Coast.

During my duty at Eglin, Joe had gone from Washington to Los Angeles to visit her father, who was very ill. When I got to McClellan, I called her and asked her to come to San Francisco where I would meet her in a downtown hotel.

On the night of March 30, I drove from Alameda to San Francisco. I had received a classified message from Hap earlier that Admiral Halsey, Wu Duncan, Miles Browning (Halsey's chief of staff), and I were to meet at the Fairmont Hotel. We met first at the hotel bar, but Halsey thought I had too many friends who might see me there, so we eventually moved to his room, where we wouldn't be interrupted.

Halsey and Duncan explained the details of the Navy's plan and we discussed it from every point of view during the next three hours. We tried to think of every contingency that might arise and have an answer for it. One of the things we talked about in detail was what we would do if the Japanese located us before we got to our planned takeoff point. It was agreed that if we were within range of Japan, we would go ahead and bomb our targets, fly out to sea, and hope, rather futilely, that we would be picked up by one of the two submarines that were in the area. If we were within range of the Hawaiian Islands or Midway, we would immediately take off and proceed to the closest of the two.

On the other hand, if we weren't within range of anyplace, we would push our aircraft overboard so the *Hornet*'s deck could be cleared and its own planes brought up from below to help protect the task force. This was understandable and I accepted this possibility. After all, if the two carriers, the cruisers, and the destroyers were lost, it would mean the end of American naval strength in the Pacific for a long time. The Navy was, therefore, taking an extraordinary risk in our attempt to bring the war to the Japanese homeland.

The *Hornet*, accompanied by the cruisers *Nashville* and *Vincennes*, the destroyers *Gwin, Meredith, Monssen,* and *Grayson*, and the oiler *Cimarron* would be designated Task Force 16.2 and leave Alameda on April 2 with Captain Marc Mitscher as task force commander. In addition, two submarines—the *Trout* and the *Thresher*—were to be secretly dispatched to certain patrol stations and report any information about enemy naval forces they might encounter in their assigned areas.

Halsey was to return to Hawaii and depart April 7 on his flagship, the carrier *Enterprise*. His task force, designated 16.1, would sail from Pearl Harbor and include the cruisers *Northampton* and *Salt Lake City*, the destroyers *Balch, Benham, Ellet,* and *Fanning*, and the oiler *Sabine*. The two forces were to rendezvous on Sunday, April 12, at latitude 38°00′ N, longitude 180°00′. Then to be designated Task Force 16, the 16 ships would steam westward and refuel from the two oilers about 800 miles off the Japanese coast. The oilers would then detach themselves, and the rest of the force would continue westward and get as close as possible to a launching point about 400–500 miles off Japan.

On the afternoon of April 1, the *Hornet* was maneuvered carefully into the middle of San Francisco Bay to berth number nine. I called my boys together and, to their surprise and delight, let them go into town for a last fling. I gave them one final lecture about secrecy.

I went to the hotel where Joe was staying. As I was going up in the elevator, the operator took one look at my uniform and said, knowingly, "Understand you're moving out tomorrow." I was shocked, but said nothing. His remark proved to me that it is extremely difficult to keep military movements secret, but to this day I wonder how much he really knew. However, as anyone could plainly see, the *Hornet* was sitting in the middle of San Francisco Bay with 16 Army Air Forces B-25s aboard, obviously ready to go someplace.

Next morning, I had an early breakfast with Joe and packed my B-4 bag. I told her, "I'll be out of the country for a while. I'll be in touch as soon as I can."

She knew nothing about what I had been doing over the past few weeks at Eglin and McClellan. When I was working in industry I always kept her informed of my itinerary during my many trips. But when I put the uniform on, she always believed that a military man's wife, family, and friends have "no right or need to know" official secrets. We never discussed it, but she knew that if I could tell her anything, I would, because we shared everything in our lives that was of mutual interest. I always appreciated her attitude about that, but know how difficult it is for any wife to accept not knowing where her husband is going or when he'll be back.

We had had many separations before in our lives together, but I had the feeling she knew this departure was different. I kissed her tenderly. She held back her tears, but I'm sure she thought it was going to be a long time before she saw me again. I wondered if we would ever see each other again.

NOTES

1. Arnold, Henry H., memorandum of White House meeting, January 4, 1942. General Henry H. Arnold files, Library of Congress.
2. Arnold, Henry H., memorandum to Major General Edwin M. Watson, January 7, 1942. General Henry H. Arnold files, Library of Congress.
3. Arnold, Henry H., memorandum of White House meeting (undated). General Henry H. Arnold files, Library of Congress, p. 289.
4. Lawson, Ted W., and Bob Considine, *Thirty Seconds over Tokyo*. New York: Random House, 1943, p. 32.
5. Glines, Carroll V., *Doolittle's Tokyo Raiders*. Princeton, N.J.: Van Nostrand Reinhold, 1964, p. 70.

CHAPTER 10

On one of my flights to Washington before we left Florida, I had a talk with Hap about the arrangements being made in China to receive the B-25s after the mission. It would be much easier if the Soviets would let us land and refuel in their territory, but we knew we couldn't count on it. Any information we sent to China had to be carefully worded because it was common knowledge that strict secrecy was extremely difficult to maintain in any dealings with Generalissimo Chiang Kai-shek's staff in Chungking.

Hap decided not to tell anyone in Chungking about our mission, although General Joseph E. "Vinegar Joe" Stilwell had been told a few bare details of the project before he left the States in February to take over the China-Burma-India command. The need for preparation of airfields to receive the "First Special Aviation Project" was discussed, but Stilwell was not told from where the planes were to come.

By the middle of March, we had had no word from Stilwell on what progress was being made on airfield preparation and on bomb and gasoline supplies. Hap sent an urgent message: REFERENCE SPECIAL AIR PROJECT DISCUSSED WITH YOU BEFORE DEPARTURE, TIME FOR SPOTTING GAS AT AGREED POINTS GETTING SHORT.

On March 22, Stilwell replied that the Standard Oil Company of Calcutta had 500 gallons of 100-octane gasoline on hand. He asked why it was needed and requested authority to have it transported to China. Stilwell's lack of a sense of urgency about our project was understandable. He was not a pilot, and Hap's inability to communicate openly with him was a severe limitation.

By March 25, Hap was getting more concerned that arrangements for our arrival were not proceeding in China. He sent another message to Stilwell specifying the amounts of 100-octane gasoline and oil needed, the airports where the stocks were to be located, and the arrangements required for the B-25s. Stilwell advised Hap that according to the Chinese, Kweilin and Chuchow were the only fields safe for heavy bomber operations. Chiang had disapproved the use of three other fields unless an inspection was made by an American officer.

As soon as this latest information about the airfields was received, Hap asked Admiral King to relay it to me for planning purposes. I was not too worried about the apparent misunderstandings in China. I thought any problems would be worked out by the time we left the carrier. Meanwhile, Hap sent a telegram to Stilwell: SPECIAL PROJECT WILL ARRIVE DESTINATION ON APRIL TWENTIETH. SHOULD A CHANGE IN ARRIVAL DATE ARISE AN ATTEMPT WILL BE MADE TO NOTIFY YOU. YOU MUST HOWEVER BE PREPARED FOR VARIATION WITHOUT NOTICE.

When I returned to the *Hornet* on the morning of April 2, I went directly to Captain Mitscher's cabin. It was a suite of rooms below the flight deck. There was one large room used for conferences and briefings, a head, and a small but comfortable bedroom. Mitscher had graciously turned over his cabin to me as my quarters: "You'll be holding meetings with your people and it will be more convenient for you to have a place where you can do that. My quarters makes that possible. Besides, it's the only place on the ship large enough for private meetings." Whereupon, he moved into a small room off the bridge.

The planes were being loaded in plain daylight, so we had put out the story that they were being taken to Hawaii and would be flown off the carrier in order to deliver them as quickly as possible. Mitscher and I discussed the carrier's departure plans and agreed that all hands should be informed of our true destination after we were a day out of port.

We were interrupted by an officer who handed me several messages. One of them told me that arrangements I had requested were now being made in China for gas, oil, and airport markings. Other messages were good luck wishes from Generals Marshall and Arnold.

I was handed a handwritten memo from Admiral King that said: "When I learned that you were to lead the Army air contingent of the *Hornet* expedition, I knew that the degree of success had been greatly increased.

"To you, your officers and men I extend heartfelt wishes for success in your job—and 'happy landings' and 'good hunting.' "

One by one, the other seven ships in the task force got under way and sailed under the Golden Gate Bridge in broad daylight. Thousands of people going to work that bright April morning could see the *Hornet* loaded down with Army bombers waiting to follow. All of us wondered why the Navy did this, and it was not until much later that we learned the reason. Captain Frederick L. Riefkohl, skipper of the *Vincennes*, commented in a postwar interview that he was uneasy about his crew at the time, because about 50 percent of them were recruits. No skipper wanted to take the risk of trying a night departure with a green crew.

While my boys and I watched the departures of the other ships from the *Hornet*, I received a call to report ashore in the captain's gig immediately to take an urgent phone call. My heart sank. I was sure it would be Hap telling me I couldn't go. When I got to a phone onshore, the caller was General Marshall. If it had been Hap trying to cancel me out of the mission, I would have argued with him, but not with General Marshall.

"Doolittle?" he said, sternly.

"Yes, sir," I answered, expecting the bad news to follow.

"I just called to personally wish you the best of luck," he said. "Our thoughts and our prayers will be with you. Good-bye, good luck, and come home safely."

All I could think of to say was, "Thank you, sir. Thank you."

It was a nice feeling to know that the top general in the Army had taken the time to make such a personal call to a lieutenant colonel, especially after he had sent a personal note and a message. With all the things he had on his mind, his personal interest showed how important our mission was to him and the war effort. Best of all, I wasn't ordered to stay home. I went back to the *Hornet* feeling much better.

Just before noon, the *Hornet* sailed into the Pacific. Captain Mitscher's orders were to take a meandering course westward to the rendezvous point with Admiral Halsey's force on April 12. What we didn't know was that Admiral Halsey had difficulty getting back to Hawaii. He had expected to be back at Pearl Harbor on April 2, but their Pan Am Clipper had been delayed several days because of strong westerly winds. On April 6, with a bad case of the flu, he finally arrived in Honolulu. Meanwhile, he had radioed Mitscher that the rendezvous with his task force would be delayed one day, until April 13.

As we slipped out of sight of land, Captain Mitscher decided to inform Task Force 16.2 where they were going. He told his chief signal officer to notify the rest of the ships by semaphore that "this force is bound for Tokyo." He personally made the announcement over the *Hornet*'s loudspeaker. Cheers could be heard all over the ship.

I had already told our crews the elements of the plan. I told them what five cities we were to bomb and said they'd be getting all the information they needed in the days ahead. One more time, I told them that I wanted only volunteers; anyone could still drop out, no questions asked. Again, no one did. Some members of the spare crews tried to persuade some of the assigned crew members to trade places, but got no takers. As far as I can recall, only one crew member was replaced. That was because Sergeant Edwin W. "Ed" Horton, the man who took the other's place, was an excellent armament specialist and we knew we would need his expertise because of the trouble we had had with the turrets and guns.

There was relief among the assigned crews now that they knew where we were going. The training at Eglin and all the things we had done to the planes now made sense to them. There was now a clear purpose to what each man was to do, and I noticed each crew had a greater concern about the condition of their plane and its equipment.

Just before noon on April 3, Lieutenant Richard O. "Dick" Joyce, pilot of the sixteenth plane, was talking with Hank Miller about his planned takeoff to show the rest of the crews that it could be done. I asked Hank to get up into the cockpit with me. "Hank, that deck looks mighty short to me," I told him, implying that I wondered if Joyce could get off safely.

"Don't worry about it, Colonel," he said. "You see that

toolbox way up there on the deck ahead? That's where I used to take off in fighters.'' His confidence was encouraging. He was not only willing but eager to ride in the B-25 that would prove how easy a takeoff would be.

''What do they call 'baloney' in the Navy?'' I said, facetiously. I went to the bridge to see Captain Mitscher and told him I wanted to take that sixteenth bomber with us.

A few minutes later, Hank was called to the bridge. Mitscher said, ''We've got a light wind. You probably can't get 40 knots down the deck, Miller. Still want to try it?''

Hank assured him that he did and that they could get off in less space than the 450 feet available with the *Hornet* at top speed.

''Do you have any of your clothes aboard?'' Mitscher asked Hank.

''Yes, sir. I do because we're going to take that B-25 all the way back to Columbia, South Carolina. Why do you ask, sir?''

''Well, if you think it'll be so easy, we'll take that sixteenth bomber with us.''

Joyce was elated because he would now participate in the mission. Hank was concerned. He had no official orders even to be on board the *Hornet*. He had only the authority of a phone call to come this far and thought he'd be demoted to ensign for being at sea without proper written authorization. Mitscher assured him he wouldn't be. Those who doubted that a B-25 could take off from a carrier would have to take Hank's word that it could be done easily and be comforted by the fact that the *Hornet* had already launched two of them two months before.

Shortly after this, a Navy blimp, the L-8, hovered over the carrier and slowly lowered some boxes of spare parts and the glass navigators' windows we had ordered but which hadn't arrived before we left McClellan. Air coverage was provided by PBY patrol planes from the Navy's Western Sea Frontier until we were out of range.

After the crews had settled in below decks, I called them all together again and gave them the targeting information they had been waiting for. The pilots were to choose primary targets and alternates if conditions made it impossible to bomb their primaries. I would precede everybody by about three hours. The remaining 15 planes would be divided into five flights of three planes each. Each flight was assigned a course, and then each plane had specific targets within the flight's general area. We planned to spread the mission over a 50-mile front in order to create the impression that a larger number of planes took part in the raid than were actually used, and to dilute enemy air and ground fire. This also negated the possibility of more than one plane passing over any given point on the ground and assured an element of surprise.

The five flights were assigned as follows: the first, led by Lieutenant Travis Hoover, was to cover the northern part of Tokyo; the second, led by Captain Davey Jones, was to cover southern Tokyo; the third, led by Captain Ski York, was to cover the southern part of Tokyo and the north-central part of the Tokyo Bay area; the fourth, led by Captain Ross Greening, was to cover the southern part of Kanagawa, the city of Yokohama, and the Yokosuka navy yard; the fifth, led by Jack Hilger, was to go around southern Tokyo, proceed to Nagoya, and break up—one plane bombing Nagoya, one Osaka, and one Kobe.

In these briefings it was emphasized that once the mission took off, everyone was on his own and no one was expected to fly in formation. I wanted everyone to know what to do; I had no doubts that everyone could and would do what was expected of him if humanly possible. There was to be no radio communication of any kind, in order to ensure complete surprise and our personal safety.

Commander Apollo Soucek and Lieutenant Commander Stephen Jurika were introduced. Soucek was air officer for the *Hornet* and gave us instructions on carrier operations. Jurika was the ship's intelligence officer and gave us much information on Japanese industry and the layout of the various cities. It was soon obvious why he had been assigned to the *Hornet* to brief us. He had been assigned to Japan in 1939 as an assistant naval attaché and naval attaché for air at the American embassy in Tokyo. One of his principal tasks was to locate and pinpoint industrial areas and specific industries for possible future use. Jurika told us that one of his greatest sources of information was the Soviet naval attaché, who had been collecting data on the Japanese for a long time.

Jurika gave us frequent lectures on the geography of Japan that were very helpful. After studying the target information we had brought and what Jurika had on board, I allowed the crews to pick the target city they wanted to bomb. After much discussion, each crew finally agreed on their choices, and target folders were passed out. We studied our maps very carefully in order to be able to identify the targets at low altitude. It is much easier to identify a target from high altitude where you can see the various landmarks and navigate accurately to the target area. Not so when you're flying on the deck and then have to pull up near the target so your bombs will get a proper distribution and not endanger your own plane with their fragments. Gaining altitude was especially necessary so the incendiary clusters would disperse properly.

I met with the crews every day and we always ate together in the wardroom. On one occasion, I heard a couple of the boys talking about bombing the emperor's palace—the "Temple of Heaven." I promptly jumped into their conversation.

"You are to bomb military targets only," I told them. "There is nothing that would unite the Japanese nation more than to bomb the emperor's home. It is not a military target! And you are to avoid hospitals, schools, and other nonmilitary targets."

I told them about my visit to Britain in 1940 when the German Luftwaffe had bombed Buckingham Palace, a useless attack that only served to bring the British even more closely together. Attacking the Temple of Heaven, the home of Japan's venerated spiritual leader, would unite the Japanese people just as much, if not more so. The emperor's home was of historic as well as religious value to the Japanese; therefore, before leaving the States, even though I could have designated it a specific target, I unilaterally made the decision that we would not bomb it. I consider this admonition one of the most serious I ever made to bombardment crews throughout the war.

The crews were told about the types of bombs and kinds of bomb loads we would be carrying. Some aircraft carried demolition bombs, some carried incendiary bombs, and some carried a mixed load, where it was felt the demolition bombs would make the targets more vulnerable to the incendiary bombs.

"You will drop the demolition bombs in the shortest space of time," I said, "preferably in a straight line, where they will do the most damage. The incendiary clusters should be dropped as near to the others as possible in an area that looks like it will burn. If you can start a fire in a Japanese city, their buildings are so inflammable they'll have great difficulty putting it out. Avoid hitting stone, concrete, and steel targets because you can't do enough damage to them."

One pilot asked me if they should deliberately head for residential areas to drop their incendiaries. I said, "Definitely not! You are to look for and aim at military targets only, such as war industries, shipbuilding facilities, power plants, and the like. There is absolutely nothing to be gained by attacking residential areas."

Several times during the next few days, I reiterated my warning about bombing the imperial palace because I heard a rumor that a couple of pilots had been cutting cards to see who would get the emperor. "It's not worth a plane factory, a shipyard, or an oil refinery, so leave it alone," I remonstrated again. Apparently, my previous cautions about this had not had the desired effect, which made me very angry.

Unknown to us while we were en route westward, Japanese forces began a series of air raids against the five fields that we were to head for in China. Fortunately, damage was slight, but it was related to a drive southeastward of strong occupying forces and it would not be long before the area surrounding the five fields would be lost. Generalissimo Chiang Kai-shek had finally been given a few details about our mission and had given his reluctant consent to our landing there. However, he was still very apprehensive about their use because of the threat of retaliation by the enemy.

The details of the mission had also been kept from Colonel Claire L. Chennault, commander of the Flying Tigers. Even though he was given a short briefing at the same time Chiang was informed, he was not told that the B-25s were to be coming in from the east after bombing Japan. He had built an efficient aircraft warning net that would have been invaluable to us. It would have been very demoralizing to us if we had known that he had not been informed about the specifics and why the requests for assistance had been made. If he had, the outcome might have been very much different.

Also unknown to us was the difficulty being experienced by American pilots in trying to get radio homing beacons located at the destination airfields. On April 2, Hap Arnold wired Chungking requesting that transmitter frequencies between 200 and 1600 kilocycles be made available for us. However, no one in China yet knew why the requests were made or why they had to be complied with before the night of April 19.

On April 5, Chungking reported to Arnold that four of the

fields could provide adequate radio facilities for homing. Arnold responded that the numbers "57" should be used for identification. However, something else we didn't know was that a C-39 transport plane that had been sent to survey the fields had crashed and the survey had never been made. The homing beacons were never installed.

On April 12, Colonel Clayton Bissell, Stilwell's air officer, sent out two American pilots in Chinese Curtiss Hawk fighters to check the fields. However, weather conditions were so poor that after a number of hazardous and unsuccessful attempts, they were forced to postpone the effort. Both planes were wrecked on landing.

Sometime between April 3 and 6, Chiang began to have serious misgivings about supporting our project. He still didn't know that we would be coming in from the east after a carrier takeoff and bombing Japan. He told Colonel Bissell to wire General Marshall that he wanted the project delayed until the end of May so his ground forces could prevent the Japanese occupation of Chuchow, one of our destinations. Chuchow was in a vital area that he wanted to retain if at all possible.

General Marshall replied that the project could not be recalled and affirmed that the planes would pass into Stilwell's control after one landing for fuel. On April 13, Hap wired Chungking and reaffirmed General Marshall's message that the project could not be stopped. He added, "We are depending upon your assistance as regards flares for landing and guidance and supplies for refueling."

On April 14, Bissell, obviously caught in the middle, wired Arnold that "special project requiring only one landing the Generalissimo wants delayed." Bissell added that "details on mission cannot be given to Generalissimo since they are not known here." Marshall immediately replied on April 15 and directed Stilwell to explain the timing and reasons for our mission to the Generalissimo. Hap followed up this message the next day, stating that "no changes in plans or additional discussion of information feasible re project at this late date."

As we were approaching the Japanese coast, General Marshall sent a final message to Chungking directing that an "atmosphere of total mystery will surround special project. Stilwell to deny any connection with project, re public information. No publicity desired for project. Desire Generalissimo to observe same policy. Report any information on results of project immediately to War Department."

This lack of information and understanding would have been disturbing if I had known about it. We received little news aboard the carrier, and while all this had been going on, we had to delay the rendezvous with Halsey's force because of foul weather. We knew it was coming because we were able to get excellent weather data from Navy lieutenant Arthur A. Cumberledge, who got his input from Pearl Harbor, Alaska, and the West Coast. Our task force ran into fierce storms with high winds, heavy seas, rain squalls, and poor visibility. The winds loosened the ropes holding our planes down. Two seamen were thrown overboard from the *Cimarron* but, fortunately, were rescued.

We finally joined with Admiral Halsey's force of eight ships on April 13. As the next few days dragged by, our crews were having difficulties with the planes. There were generator failures; spark plug changes were required; gas tanks leaked; and hydraulic troubles plagued almost every plane. The *Hornet*'s maintenance men did an excellent job of helping our mechanics solve their problems. We were all impressed with their know-how, their innovative solutions to mechanical difficulties, and their complete willingness to help us out.

Time hung heavily on our hands during the long days of relative inactivity for us. Since our gunners were concerned about their inexperience with the turrets and the twin .50s, they practiced shooting at kites flown from the ship. The navigators practiced taking celestial shots and followed our course and position with the *Hornet*'s navigator. Doc White gave us lectures on first aid and sanitation and we had classes on meteorology by Lieutenant Cumberledge. Our pilots talked shop with the Navy pilots, who were chafing at not being able to fly. We had religious services on the way, but there was no specific service just before the takeoff, except that the Catholic chaplain made himself available to the boys who wished to see him before we left.

The days were not all filled with serious thoughts. There were many card games far into the night. Not being a gambler, I didn't take part. The odds in favor of winning any game of chance never seemed right to me.

While the 16 ships were sailing due west, we learned that the American garrison on Bataan had fought its last battle and surrendered to an overwhelming Japanese force on April 9. General Jonathan Wainwright and 35,000 of his men escaped to Corregidor for a last-ditch stand. On April 10, thousands of captured American and Filipino soldiers began a forced march that historians have since called the Bataan death march. There was never a darker period in American history.

To keep occupied as much as possible, we had many bull sessions talking about what we thought lay ahead. We discussed our targets frequently and what damage we thought we could inflict with our bomb loads. One of the pilots asked me what I would do if my plane was badly damaged and would have to be abandoned. I replied, "Each pilot must decide for himself what he will do and what he'll tell his crew to do if that happens. I know what I'm going to do."

There was silence and the same chap asked me what that was.

"I don't intend to be taken prisoner," I replied. "I'm 45 years old and have lived a full life. If my plane is crippled beyond any possibility of fighting or escape, I'm going to have my crew bail out and then I'm going to dive my B-25 into the best military target I can find. You fellows are all younger and have a long life ahead of you. I don't expect any of the rest of you to do what I intend to do."

We didn't know it at the time, of course, but by April 10, before the two task forces merged, the Japanese were aware of our presence in the western Pacific. They apparently deduced from various exchanges of intercepted radio messages that we were in a task force that included two or three carriers. If that were confirmed, they estimated the force would be close enough for an attack by carrier-based planes by April 14. Also unknown to us, they had a line of small picket boats equipped with high-powered radios patrolling about 650 miles offshore. If a large American task force were approaching, it would be spotted long before its carrier planes could be launched to attack targets on the home islands.

On April 15, Halsey ordered the two large tankers to refuel the heavy ships for the run to our launching point, hopefully about 450 miles off the coast of Japan. During the refueling, the weather was getting increasingly foul and it seemed like a ticklish operation. It was interesting for us landlubbers to watch the process, which was carried off with great precision despite the rough seas.

That day, an English-language radio news report was picked

up from Tokyo which called "laughable" a Reuter's report that "three American bombers had dropped bombs on Tokyo." Radio Tokyo told its listeners, ". . . it is absolutely impossible for enemy bombers to get within 500 miles of Tokyo. Instead of worrying about such foolish things, the Japanese people are enjoying the fine spring sunshine and the fragrance of cherry blossoms."

We could feel the tension increasing on the *Hornet* on the sixteenth as we plowed onward. The weather continued to deteriorate to the point that the seas became too rough for the eight destroyers to proceed at the speed of the two carriers and four cruisers. The destroyers were left behind with the tankers. This would have been a very serious handicap had there been a naval engagement before we left the carrier.

The *Enterprise* sent up fighter and scout bomber patrols for the dash into the launch point, but made no contacts. On the seventeenth, the B-25s were spotted on the deck for takeoff. My aircraft was parked 467 feet from the forward end of the deck. The tail of the sixteenth aircraft was hanging out over the stern. Two white lines had been painted on the deck—one for the left wheel and one for the nose wheel. If we kept our wheels on these lines, we would miss the island on the right by about six feet. There should be no crosswind because the *Hornet* would be heading into the wind when we launched.

Captain Mitscher called me to the bridge, and the tension there was evident. "Jim, we're in the enemy's backyard now," he said. "Anything could happen from here on in. I think it's time for that little ceremony we talked about."

Some medals had been forwarded from Secretary of the Navy Frank Knox, which had been sent to him by three former Navy enlisted men. The medals commemorated a visit by the U.S. battle fleet that had visited Japan in 1908. The men had asked Secretary Knox to attach them "to a bomb and return [them] to Japan in that manner." We called the crews to the flight deck to comply. When Lieutenant Jurika learned what was happening, he added a medal he had received from the Japanese in 1940.

We all gathered around a bomb that had been brought on deck and a Navy photographer took pictures. Mitscher made a short speech and read the messages from King, Marshall, and Arnold. I attached the medals to the bomb. The group was in a lighthearted mood and several wrote slogans on the bomb, such as "You'll get a BANG out of this!" and "I don't want to set the world on fire, just Tokyo."

I told the gang to get their equipment packed and make final inspections of their planes. Dog tags were checked and Doc White gave last-minute inoculations to those who had escaped his needle previously.

We were well equipped with survival gear. Each of us had a Navy gas mask, a .45 automatic, clips of ammunition, a hunting knife, a flashlight, emergency rations, a first-aid kit, a canteen, a compass, and a life jacket. There was a five-man rubber life raft aboard each plane. In addition to their clothes, some of the fellows took extras like candy bars, chewing gum, cigarettes, and razor blades. Lieutenant Jacob E. "Shorty" Manch, six-foot, six-inch copilot, planned to take along his phonograph and records. Lieutenant Horace E. "Sally" Crouch, bombardier-navigator, mindful of Doc White's lectures about the lack of sanitation in China, jammed rolls of toilet paper in his bag.

On deck, the planes were giving us last-minute problems. Gun turrets did not function properly, hydraulic lines leaked, spark plugs fouled, and gas tanks dripped. An engine on one plane cracked its blower while it was being run up. Navy carpenters rigged up a platform so mechanics could remove it to take it below decks for repair.

I called the crews together for a final briefing and told them to be ready to go at any time. Although we were originally to take off on April 19, it looked like it would be the eighteenth instead. "If all goes well," I said, "I'll take off so as to arrive over Tokyo at dusk. The rest of you will take off two or three hours later and can use my fires as a homing beacon."

I reminded the gunners who would be in the rear of each plane to remember to puncture holes in the five-gallon gas cans after they were emptied and drop them overboard all at once so as not to leave a trail back to the *Hornet*. I admonished the pilots and bombardiers once more that under no circumstances were they to bomb the emperor's palace. I told them to get rid of all film, identification, orders, letters, diaries, and anything else that would link them with the *Hornet*, their units in the States, or the places where we trained. The Navy would mail anything we left behind to our homes. I offered everyone a last opportunity to drop out. No one did.

As a final gesture, I made the boys a promise. "When we

get to Chungking,'' I said, ''I'm going to give you all a party that you won't forget.'' I never make promises lightly, and I always try to keep them, no matter at what personal cost or inconvenience. It was to be a long time before I could keep this one.

By dusk on the seventeenth, ammunition and bombs had been loaded, gas tanks topped, and last-minute engine runups made. Deck crews moved the aircraft back as far as possible in order to make maximum deck space available for takeoff. Crew survival equipment was placed in each plane. Doc White passed out 80 pints of rye whiskey that he had thoughtfully acquired from the Navy ''for medicinal purposes'' before we left Alameda. He cautioned everyone to take care of all cuts and abrasions because of the likelihood of infection.

As usual, the poker games resumed that night. At 3:00 A.M., the *Hornet* received a message flashed from the *Enterprise*: TWO ENEMY SURFACE CRAFT REPORTED.

The ''*Big E*'' 's radar had spotted two enemy ships off the port bow 21,000 yards away. Two minutes later, lookouts saw a light on the horizon. General quarters was sounded; an order was flashed to all ships to change course to avoid detection. When the radar blips faded, the all-clear was sounded and the westerly course was resumed. At dawn the *Enterprise* sent up fighters and patrol bombers. The weather, which had been marginal all night, worsened. Frequent rain squalls swept over the task force; low ceilings hung overhead; the sea rose into 30-foot crests. Gusty winds blew spray across the decks, drenching the deck crews.

At 6:00 A.M., a Navy lieutenant piloting a scout bomber sighted a small fishing craft. He quickly turned back to the *Enterprise* and jotted down a message on his plotting board: ENEMY SURFACE SHIP—LATITUDE 36-04N, LONG. 153-10E, BEARING 276 DEGREES TRUE—42 MILES. BELIEVED SEEN BY ENEMY.

When he arrived over the carrier, he handed the message to the rear gunner who put it in a bean bag container. As the plane passed over the carrier, the gunner threw it down on the deck where it was scooped up on the run by a deckhand and delivered to Halsey on the bridge.

Halsey ordered all ships to alter course. The question uppermost in everyone's mind was whether the scout bomber had been seen. Shortly afterward, another small vessel was sighted from the *Hornet* about 20,000 yards away. It was now daylight and if we could see it, there was every reason to believe its crew could see us. This seemed certain when the *Hornet*'s radio operator intercepted a Japanese radio message that had originated from close by. It was definitely confirmed when a Navy pilot sighted a small vessel only 12,000 yards away. Halsey ordered the *Nashville* to sink it.

It was decision time. Halsey quickly flashed a message to the *Hornet*: LAUNCH PLANES X TO COL DOOLITTLE AND GALLANT COMMAND GOOD LUCK AND GOD BLESS YOU.

It was 8:00 A.M. I had been on the bridge during the excitement and when it was positive that we had to go, I shook hands with Mitscher, ran to the cabin, grabbed my bag, and dashed to the plane. I yelled at everyone I saw to load up pronto. The ear-shattering klaxon horn sounded and Mitscher's voice blared over the loudspeaker: "Army pilots, man your planes!"

In retrospect, I'm not sure all the crews were conscious of what was going on around us at the time. There was a mad scramble as some hurriedly jammed their belongings and equipment into their bags. Navy deck handlers helped our men remove engine covers and unfasten the restraining ropes. A Navy "donkey" pushed and pulled the B-25s into position. Gas tanks were topped off and the planes rocked back and forth to get air bubbles out so more fuel could be added. Sailors passed the gas cans up into the rear hatches.

Hank Miller shouted to each crew to remember to put down flaps, place trim tabs in neutral, and watch his blackboard for any last-minute instructions. "Look at me before you let your brakes off!" he yelled.

Our airplane was maneuvered into position. My crew was in place. Ran both engines up, tested them and gave the thumbs-up signal to the officer holding the checkered signal flag. We were ready. I glanced at my watch. It was 8:20 A.M. ship time.

As I recounted in the opening chapter, we bombed our target in Tokyo and escaped over the preplanned route toward the Chinese mainland. When we headed out over the China Sea, we ran into headwinds that cut down on our ground speed. There was a strong possibility that we would have to ditch the aircraft. Providentially, the headwinds turned into tailwinds. However, as we reached the coast, the weather and darkness cut down on the forward visibility. If the ground radio beacon didn't work or we couldn't receive a homing signal, it would be impossible to locate our destination airfield. The only alternative was to bail out or crash-land, which we all did successfully, with one exception: the crew that landed in the Soviet Union.

Sitting on the side of that Chinese mountain with the wreckage of our B-25 all around me, I realized there was nothing I could do to reverse anything that had happened. Now that my own crew was safe, I had to find out what had happened to the others.

Paul Leonard and I returned to the headquarters of the Chinese major who had found me; as I had requested, search parties were already out looking for other crews. While we waited for news, Paul told me of his experience the night before. When I gave him the word that we were going to have to bail out, he knew that it was important to get the motion picture film, so he went to the back of the plane in the dark and removed one of the cameras. He put it inside the front of his coveralls. Unfortunately, when his 'chute popped open with a severe jolt, the camera tore the front out of his coveralls and he lost it. At daylight, he walked about six miles trying to find the rest of us. When he didn't, he returned to his starting point. He reported later what happened:

> Returning to where I landed, I encountered four Chinese men armed with rifles. One motioned to me to raise my hands while the other three proceeded to cock their rifles. One took aim. At the same moment, I pulled out my .45. The one who was aiming fired, so I fired twice. All four of them turned tail and ran, so I turned and climbed to the mountaintop where I could see men gathering around below. All had rifles. I hid myself as best I could and they left. I then figured out a course to travel at night.
>
> After about an hour and a half, I saw a crowd of people returning back down the valley. In front I could see Lieutenant Potter and Sergeant Braemer. I reloaded my clip because I figured they were captured. I started yelling and ran down the mountain but found they were in good company.

According to Potter and Braemer, however, they had not been

in good friendly company when they landed. They had been discovered by a band of guerrillas, robbed, tied up, and marched off. Fortunately, they came across an English-speaking boy who led the guerrillas and their captives to his house and spread the word. Soon the guerrilla chieftain arrived and they were given back their belongings. They had then set off and were looking for Leonard when he found them.

When Paul and I arrived at the governor's house, we were relieved to learn that four other crews had been found. As soon as I could arrange it, I sent a wire to Hap Arnold in Washington through the American embassy in Chungking: TOKYO SUCCESSFULLY BOMBED. DUE BAD WEATHER ON CHINA COAST BELIEVE ALL AIRPLANES WRECKED. FIVE CREWS FOUND SAFE IN CHINA SO FAR.

What about the other 11 crews? I soon learned through Chinese channels that some had been taken prisoner, but we didn't know if by the Japanese or some renegade Chinese guerrilla band. Before I left the States, I had obtained $2,000 in Chinese money, which I offered as ransom. I tried to persuade a local commander to send troops out to rescue them. Their efforts were to no avail.

Our job now was to get from Tien Mu Shen, the headquarters of the local Chinese guerrillas (about 50 or more miles southwest of Hangchow) to Chuchow (Chuhsien)* the best way we could. We boarded a riverboat to transport us to a point downriver to the juncture of another river, then up the second river out of Japanese-held territory. As we moved out, we could see the searchlights of the enemy patrol boats. Fortunately, we were not intercepted. However, one incident occurred that was to have an interesting aftermath.

While we were hiding in the cabin of the boat, a Caucasian man in civilian clothes came aboard. He had been told there were Americans inside. Suspicious, he hesitated, but finally banged on the door. He called out in a strong southern drawl, "Are there any Americans in there?"

We tensed and stayed quiet. The question was repeated. The voice was convincingly American, so Paul Leonard finally said, "Hell, no Japanese can talk American like that," and opened the door.

---

*"Chuchow" and "Chuhsien" are used interchangeably by the Chinese. Our narratives and reports reflected this.

Outside was a tall, gaunt white man with a several-days' growth of beard. He told us his name was John M. Birch, age 27, an American missionary based in Hangchow. After December 7, when the Japanese began to round up all Caucasians, he had fled to Shangjao, 250 miles to the southwest. He was returning on foot to Shangjao from a trip downriver when he stopped at a small Chinese inn and met a man who told him to go to the dock. There the man pointed to the riverboat and said, "Americans."

Birch was as delighted to see us as we were to see him. He obviously knew his way around and could speak the language. I briefed him on our predicament and he agreed to join us, translate for us, and help us get on our way to Chuchow. He said he would accompany us to Lanchi on the Chientang River, halfway between Hangchow and Shangjao.

En route, Birch told me he had been living off the cuff and was having a rough go of it. Having seen what the occupying Japanese were doing to his beloved Chinese, he wanted to join the American forces in some capacity, preferably as a chaplain. I promised to put in a good word for him and get in touch if we needed him to help round up my men.

Birch left us, and over the next several days friendly Chinese led us to Chuchow by rail, bus, rickshaw, and boat around areas where the Japanese were searching. We heard reports that the Japanese were enraged at what we had done and were taking out their fury on innocent Chinese. Our crew made it safely to Chuchow, and I tried to do everything possible to find out what had happened to my boys. On April 27, I sent a message to Birch asking him to come to Chuchow and await instructions from the American miltary mission in China. He came immediately but arrived after we had left for Chungking. Birch met Davey Jones and other crew members at Chuchow and acted as their interpreter. It was there we learned that Corporal Leland D. Faktor, a gunner, had died bailing out.

Birch was given the $2,000 in Chinese money I had left for ransom and was asked to buy a burial plot, bury Faktor, obtain as much information as possible about the others still missing, and then proceed with the last group to Chungking. Birch arranged with the Chinese air force for a burial plot for Faktor and obtained hearsay information on the fate of the other crews. Birch's information was not wholly accurate, but his report reflected his ability to obtain information from Chinese sources, which would make him extremely valuable to our forces in China (see Appendix 2).

When I arrived in Chungking, I told Colonel (later Lieutenant General) Claire Chennault, leader of the Flying Tigers, about Birch and how he had helped us. I recommended Birch be commissioned as a chaplain. Chennault already had one but said he could use an American for intelligence duties who could speak Chinese and knew the country well. I never saw this fine young man again but learned later that Chennault commissioned him as a first lieutenant on July 4, 1942, the official birthday of Chennault's 14th Air Force.

Although Birch served as an intelligence officer, he was still a chaplain at heart. Wherever he was on Sundays, he conducted religious services for Chinese Christians, often at the risk of his life behind Japanese lines. He was later promoted to captain. Chennault, fearful that Birch would crack under the strain of continual clandestine activities, tried to persuade him to take a leave of absence in the States. He thanked Chennault but refused, saying, "I'll leave China only when the last Jap is gone."

Birch was killed on August 25, 1945, by Chinese communists—10 days after World War II was officially over. He had no way of knowing that the John Birch Society, a highly vocal postwar anticommunist organization, would be named after him because its founders believed him to be the "first casualty of World War III." I feel sure he would not have approved.

When the crews began to arrive in Chungking, we learned what had happened to most of them. Colonel Merion C. Cooper, a former Hollywood writer and producer, was the air intelligence officer and had the men write out reports of their experience.*

The tally on our crews was not good. One had died bailing out; two had drowned after ditching; four were seriously injured and under the care of Doc White at a hospital dangerously close to searching Japanese units; one crew had landed in Soviet territory; eight men were prisoners of the Japanese. All planes were

*A summary of what happened to each crew appears in Appendix 3.

lost to the American cause. It wasn't a happy summary. However, from the accounts that reached us, we had apparently accomplished the first half of our mission; all aircraft except one had bombed their targets and escaped.

Unfortunately, we were unable to get any motion picture footage of the mission. The aircraft that landed at Vladivostok was confiscated, along with all its equipment, and we were never able to find out what happened to it.

We had hoped someone would have saved one of the motion picture cameras that were installed in a few of the planes, but none did. Apparently, Paul Leonard on our crew was the only one who had tried to save one. However, Lieutenant Richard A. "Knobby" Knobloch, copilot on crew 13, had a small pocket camera with which he and his navigator, Lieutenant Clayton J. Campbell, took a few snapshots. These were the only photos that survived the raid.

In time, we learned that the psychological effect we had hoped to have on the Japanese had been even greater than anticipated. Our intrusion into Japanese airspace over their home island had frightened and embarrassed the Japanese war leaders as nothing else could have at that point. Their morale was badly shaken as they tried to defend their actions. The Japanese propaganda machine tried to make light of our raid, but the damage was there and was difficult to refute. However, we didn't learn how much damage was done until later. It was minimal, of course, compared with damage inflicted later in the war by our B-29s.

We also learned later that our surprise bombing of Tokyo was everything President Roosevelt had wished for and what we hoped we could deliver for him. American morale soared. It showed that our country, faced with the greatest adversity we had ever experienced, had fought back. The news sped around the world, but security dictated that the details of the raid should not be divulged at that time, especially any information related to our departure from a carrier. The President told the press that we had come from "Shangri-La," that mythical, timeless kingdom featured by James Hilton in his novel *Lost Horizon*. This air of mystery confounded the Japanese and delighted our allies. Unfortunately, it was nearly fatal to the eight boys who had been captured. Unknown to us, they were being tortured and starved in an effort to wrest from them the details of our mission. They were flown to Tokyo where experts at extracting "confessions" from prisoners of war were waiting. I will tell what happened to them in a later chapter.

In Chungking, none of us was yet fully aware of the impact the raid had had in the States or among our allies. However, on April 28, while at Chuchow, I learned that the first of Paul Leonard's predictions had come true. Hap had promoted me from lieutenant colonel to brigadier general, skipping the rank of colonel, a complete surprise. It was rare for anyone to skip a rank, even in wartime. I was pleased, of course, but wondered what my contemporaries would say among themselves when they learned that Doolittle was now a one-star general. They would probably think there was no better proof that Doolittle was Hap Arnold's fair-haired boy. Not only had he skipped the rank of captain, now Hap had seen to it that he would never even wear the eagles of a full colonel.

I didn't have any stars to wear, so Colonel Clayton Bissell, Chennault's air operations officer, promoted to brigadier general on the same orders, gave me a set. He offered me a swig from his high-priced Scotch whiskey in celebration and I took a large gulp, which he didn't appreciate. He estimated my gulp was worth about $80.

Since I had been promoted, I tried to see to it that every man on the raid was also promoted. It took some doing in a couple of cases because of Army red tape, but was eventually accomplished.

There was another surprise in Chungking. On April 30, our gang was invited by the Nationalist Chinese leader, Generalissimo Chiang Kai-shek, and Madame Chiang to their palace to be decorated. All those crew members present at the time were decorated, and my second in command, Jack Hilger, received the highest Chinese decoration. Then when I walked in, Chiang and his wife looked at each other and realized that something had gone wrong with the presentation ceremony—they didn't have a decoration to give me.

Chiang looked toward one of his highly decorated generals, approached him, and removed a beautiful decoration from around his neck. He then hung it on me.

It is said that the Chinese are emotionless, but that general sure showed emotion when stripped of his medal by the Generalissimo!

Since the Generalissimo didn't speak English, Madame

Chiang read our citations. We were honored but not exactly dressed for such an occasion. We wore a varied assortment of coveralls, leather jackets, and khaki uniforms spattered with mud and grease.

Although grateful for the gesture, there was only one thing on my mind. I still didn't know what had happened to all my crews. After the brief ceremony, perhaps a little brusquely, I asked Madame Chiang what was being done about rescuing the two crews that had been captured. She assured me that they were doing everything they could, but as we know now, nothing could be done at that time.

Perhaps she didn't want to tell me that the Japanese, in their fury at our violation of their empire, were deliberately attacking Chinese villages along our escape path and murdering people by the hundreds. We learned later that an estimated 53 Japanese battalions slashed their way through Chekiang province, where most of us had parachuted. On April 30, the Japanese army expeditionary forces were given orders to "thwart the enemy's plans to carry out air raids on the homeland of Japan." This was interpreted to mean they should annihilate any Chinese forces in the area and destroy their principal air bases. This they did with great intensity.

Chiang was seething about the enemy onslaught and sent a cable to the U.S. State Department:

> After they had been caught unawares by the falling of American bombs on Tokyo, Japanese troops attacked the coastal areas of China where many of the American flyers had landed. These Japanese troops slaughtered every man, woman, and child in these areas—let me repeat—these Japanese troops slaughtered every man, woman and child in these areas, reproducing on a wholesale scale the horrors which the world had seen [carried out by the Germans] at Lidice [Czechoslovakia], but about which the people have been uninformed in these instances.

Chiang was not exaggerating. General Chennault, in his memoirs, recalled that the Japanese drove 200 miles inland from the coastal areas to seek revenge. Twenty thousand square miles of Chinese territory were searched; landing fields were plowed up;

hundreds of villagers who were even remotely suspected of having aided us were murdered. He noted in his memoirs that "one sizable city was razed for no other reason than the sentiment displayed by its citizens in filling up Jap bomb craters on the nearby airfield. . . . A quarter million Chinese soldiers and civilians were killed in the three-month campaign."

Contrary to what some historians have reported, we all expected to return to the States after we delivered our B-25s to Chungking. However, orders came through for only a few of us. I was ordered home first and assumed that all the rest would follow, especially since they had no planes to fly. My orders stated I was to return to Washington "by any means possible" and without any publicity.

The "any means possible" in my orders to return to the States included passage on a China National Airways Corporation (CNAC) 21-passenger Douglas DC-3 piloted by Captain Moon Chin, a native of Baltimore, Maryland. He was a veteran of 10 years' flying for Pan American Airways, which was then under contract to fly CNAC routes. I boarded the DC-3 on May 5 with a few other passengers at Chungking, destined for Myitkyina, Burma, not knowing that our destination was under attack from Japanese fighter planes. Halfway there, Chin received a radio message about the attack and landed at an isolated emergency field. We waited there about an hour, then resumed the flight.

When we arrived at Myitkyina, the place was in chaos. The airport was jammed with refugees fleeing from the rampaging Japanese. Hundreds surrounded the plane wanting to get aboard. While the DC-3 was being refueled, Chin supervised the loading of additional passengers; soon there were 30 of us in the passenger cabin. He didn't stop. He let 40 get on, then 50. I couldn't watch without saying something. "I sure hope you know what you're doing," I said, not believing what I was seeing. Fortunately, they were almost all small people; many were women and children, including babes in arms. They had no baggage, just carry-on bundles.

Moon Chin was not at all bothered by the number, as if he hauled this many passengers every day. "We're fighting a war over here," he said when he saw how perturbed I was. "You do lots of things here you wouldn't do at home," he said calmly.

When the sixtieth person crammed his way into the cabin, Chin shut the door and picked his way among the human cargo to the cockpit. Despite the load, that faithful Douglas "Gooney Bird" was airborne before we ran out of runway and I breathed a sigh of relief.

Being jammed in with so many desperate people didn't make for a comfortable ride. We were supposed to go to Dinjan, but Chin decided to go directly to Calcutta, where we arrived after a four-hour flight. As we debarked, however, I got another surprise. Out of the rear compartment, usually reserved for baggage, tumbled eight more disheveled Chinese. I'm sure this must have been a record passenger load for the famous Douglas DC-3.

I waited in Calcutta for four days and was joined by several of my boys. When authorization came for me to continue, they gave me a sendoff party. Bill Bower and the others presented me with a chamber pot "in fond remembrance of our most serious difficulties—'the screamers.' " We had all contracted that uncomfortable malady in some degree after our arrival in China. The pot was a fitting souvenir of our mutual discomforting experience.

While in Calcutta, I tried to get a decent uniform to replace my mud-stained khakis, but nothing was available. I had to settle for a native tailor whom I called January Jones to make me an English bush jacket and shorts; these were supplemented by knee-length stockings and a pith helmet. I wouldn't have passed any U.S. Army inspection and was anxious to get home before someone called my attention to the fact that I not only looked ridiculous but was out of uniform. Joe would have gotten the laugh of her life if she had seen me in the English shorts and helmet.

The next leg of the trip home was on a British Overseas Airways Company (BOAC) flying boat—a laborious flight with eight stops in India, Iran, and Egypt, where I arrived on May 11. I left Cairo on May 13 on an Army Air Forces plane with a TWA crew for Khartoum, in the Sudan, then to Dakar, Senegal, and over the South Atlantic to Natal, Brazil. I made an overnight stop in Puerto Rico and arrived in Washington on May 18, 1942, two weeks after I left Chungking. I was met by a staff car sent by Hap's office.

The driver had instructions to take me up a back stairs directly to Hap's office in the Pentagon. Hap greeted me warmly. He didn't say anything, but he must have been amused when he saw me in the weird getup. We had a long chat as I related the details of the mission and expressed my concern for my boys, especially those who had been captured. I told him I felt I had only partially succeeded in the mission he had assigned me. He assured me no one would ever blame me for our not delivering the aircraft, the second half of the assignment.

After we chatted, Hap and I met with General Marshall, who was in a rare jovial mood. He greeted me with a big smile that he rarely exhibited, and I gave him the highlights of the mission. Hap suggested with his usual grin that I should go to the uniform store to get properly attired, as befits a new general. I was then told to go to our apartment at 2500 Q Street in northwest Washington and remain there out of sight and incommunicado until he called. I wanted to call Joe on the West Coast where she had decided to remain until she found out where I was, but I didn't dare use the phone.

While I was en route home, Hap had received reports from Chungking and Honolulu and sent a summarizing memo to the President to explain what had happened:

> On the 18th of April when the *Hornet* was 668 nautical miles east of Tokyo, the naval task force ran into a Japanese patrol ship. This ship was sunk by the *Nashville*, but not before it had had an opportunity to send a message stating that it was being attacked by hostile enemy ships. It is to be noted that at this point the task force was some 150 to 400 miles farther away from Tokyo than General Doolittle had planned his takeoff. . . .
>
> At 1:30 P.M., in the midst of an English propaganda broadcast from Japan in which a woman (presumably "Tokyo Rose") was telling how safe Japan was from bombing, the broadcast was cut off and another broadcast made giving information that fast, low-flying bombers were at that time bombing Japan. A later broadcast told of fires and requested people to pray for rain. It was not until 48 hours later, however, that a broadcast was made stating that the fire was under control. Still later, another broadcast was made which stated casualties amounted to three or four thousand. . . .

Completely unknown to me, Hap had called Joe when I arrived in the States and asked her to come to Washington, without telling her why. He arranged a reservation for her on a commercial airliner and she left promptly that afternoon. She flew all night. The only woman passenger, she had been unable to get into the lavatory, which seemed to be continually occupied. When she arrived in Pittsburgh, she thought her chance had come, but as soon as she landed, an Army officer whisked her off the airliner and onto a military plane. It had no suitable lavatory facilities for women passengers and she was becoming slightly desperate. She looked forward with great anticipation to having a few minutes in the washroom at the airport in Washington, but this was not to be. A young officer from Hap's staff met her at planeside with a staff car, put her bags in the rear, and told her that they'd have to hurry.

Joe's problem was getting more critical by the minute. She didn't think anything could be so important that they couldn't divert somewhere so she could take care of her necessary business. But the young officer would not be deterred from his mission. He finally told her, "Mrs. Doolittle, I'm sorry but we are due at the White House in ten minutes."

Joe said she looked like a "carpetbagger" and wouldn't have gone anywhere, especially to the White House, rumpled as she was after the long flight from California.

Joe was ushered into an anteroom of the Oval Office, still not knowing why she was there. She revealed her distress to a secretary and was excused to take care of it.

Meanwhile, I had received a telephone call from Hap at our apartment. He told me he would drop by in a few minutes to pick me up, but didn't say where we were going. When his staff car arrived, Hap was sitting in the rear to the left of General Marshall. Surprised, I saluted them and climbed in the front seat beside the driver.

There was silence as we drove off. Finally, I asked where we were going. "Jim, we're going to the White House," Hap replied.

I thought about this for a minute, then said, "Well, I'm not a very smart fellow and I don't want to embarrass anyone. What are we going to do there?"

General Marshall answered, "The President is going to give you the Medal of Honor."

I was shocked and quickly said, "General, that award should be reserved for those who risk their lives trying to save someone else. Every man on our mission took the same risk I did. I don't think I'm entitled to the Medal of Honor."

Hap flushed and I could see he was angry. General Marshall, obviously displeased at my remark, scowled and said, "I happen to think you do."

There was no further discussion. In all our later association, this was the only time Hap ever got mad at me and General Marshall ever spoke sternly to me. The highest-ranking man in Army uniform had made his decision. It was neither the time nor the place for me to argue.

We arrived at the White House and were ushered into the anteroom where Joe was waiting. We were both startled and immensely pleased. Hap beamed happily as the two of us embraced; General Marshall managed a smile. I wanted desperately to hear about Jim, Jr., and John and catch up on what she had been doing, but we were quickly led into the Oval Office where a beaming President greeted us warmly. He was in a jovial mood and shook my hand long and hard. He said our raid on Japan had had the precise favorable effect on American morale that he had hoped for.

General Marshall read the citation for the award and handed it to Joe. Nervous at her sudden appearance in the office of our country's leader, a place she never imagined she would ever visit in her entire life, she began twisting the citation scroll. Marshall told her later he was tempted to take it away from her before she ruined it.

The President pinned the medal on my shirt and asked me to tell him about the raid, which I did. I thanked him for the award and we were ushered out. On the way through the door, Hap congratulated me. I couldn't resist telling him that while I was grateful, I would spend the rest of my life trying to earn it. I felt then and always will that I accepted the award on behalf of all the boys who were with me on the raid. I have always felt that the Medal of Honor should be reserved for men who risk their lives in combat to save others, not for individual feats like shooting down a number of enemy planes or bombing enemy targets.

NOTE

1. Arnold, Henry H., memorandum for the President, May 10, 1942. General Henry H. Arnold files, Library of Congress.

CHAPTER 11

The mission against Japan was over, but the aftermath was just beginning for me and would last past the end of the war. I still didn't know what had happened to all my boys and I intended to find out. The ones who had made it to Chungking were still scattered all over, and I learned that some had been retained in the theater to serve the balance of a combat tour. On May 24, I wrote a memo to Hap: "I feel it would be a good project to bring the rest of the gang home as soon as they can be spared from where they are. Understand they haven't enough planes so I'd like to have them with me again."

I also wrote a letter to the next of kin of every man on the raid, telling them as much as I knew about their welfare. To the relatives of those captured, I did the best I could to give some hope for their eventual release. Meanwhile, I kept after the International Red Cross to determine their status, hoping they would be treated humanely as military prisoners of war.

The exact status of the five men in the Soviet Union was still unknown but we did learn that Ski York had been promoted to major and Robert G. "Bob" Emmens to first lieutenant on May 25. They had accepted the promotions via a message from our air attaché in Moscow. The five were being kept together, but were virtual prisoners; however, they were far better off than the eight men captured by the Japanese, as we learned later.

At this time, the Treasury Department received the first of a series of monthly bills from the Soviet embassy, each for 30,000 rubles for the upkeep of the five men. Secretary of the Treasury Henry Morgenthau, Jr., became very upset about these bills and personally called me a number of times complaining about them. The Soviets kept and used the airplane; that should have compensated them for lodging and meals for five men for a lot longer than the 14 months they were there.

A few days after the White House ceremony, Hap asked me to take a B-25 on a tour of the war plants to speak to the employees for morale-building purposes. I was happy to do so because these people were making the tools of war. It gave me a special pleasure to tell those who had made our B-25s and its components how grateful we were for their handiwork and dedication. The B-25 was a superior airplane; all they had to do was make more of them.

When I took off in the B-25 for the first flight of my speaking tour, it occurred to me that all three of Paul Leonard's predictions had come true. I'd been promoted to brigadier general, had received the "big medal" as he called it, and now had another airplane. I had made him a promise on that Chinese hillside that if I ever got another airplane he could be its crew chief. When I returned to Washington, I asked the personnel people to transfer "T/Sgt Paul Leonard to 4th Bomber Wing (8th Air Force) which is being established at Bolling Field, where he will again be responsible for my airplane." The request was quickly approved.

Hap assigned Lieutenant Max Boyd, a former wire service reporter, to assist me with the paperwork that resulted from the raid and with the handling of public relations matters. I have always insisted that all correspondence be answered as promptly as possible and do so to this day. There were many telegrams and letters of congratulation on hand; some letters included war bonds made out to me; a few had money enclosed. The gestures were appreciated, but the bonds and money were promptly returned with the request that the senders invest in war bonds for themselves or donate to the Air Force Aid Society, which was then being organized.

One of the letters that finally found me after my return was marked "Personal and Secret." It was dated April 24 and had been written at sea by Admiral Halsey. I value it highly:

> Dear Doolittle:
>
> The hats of Task Force Sixteen are on high to you. Superb!
>
> The takeoff was splendid. The conditions were trying for our trained carrier pilots, and for men who had never taken off from a carrier deck before, is little short of marvelous. I wish you would accept and extend my congratulations to your gallant command.
>
> We dodged one patrol vessel at 0310 in the morning, and were busy dodging the second one, when we were picked up by a third. The ocean where we were was studded with them. I hated to dump you off at that distance, but because of discovery there was nothing else to do. I believe we covered this pretty thoroughly at San Francisco.
>
> I stated to my staff that on landing you should have had two stars pinned on each shoulder and the Medal of Honor put around your neck. I am delighted to see that you got at least half the stars.
>
> I am highly honored in having had you, and the very gallant and brave lads with you, serve under my command for a short period of time. It is something I shall always remember. I do not know of any more gallant deed in history than that performed by your squadron, and that it was successful is entirely due to the splendid leadership on your part. It was a pleasure to meet you in San Francisco, and my immediate reaction was that I had met a real man. Events proved me right. You have struck the hardest blow of the war directly at the enemy's heart. You have made history.
>
> God knows when or where this will reach you, but if and when it does, I would appreciate hearing of your experience. This, of course, at your leisure. Again, my most hearty congratulations. Keep on knocking over those yellow bastards.

Another message that was in the pile was a telegram from Roscoe Turner, whom I had known from our racing days as one of my competitors. A flamboyant showman who always amused me with his attention-getting gimmicks, Roscoe sent a telegram which was typically Roscoe:

> CONGRATULATIONS, YOU DOG! WHY DIDN'T YOU TAKE ME WITH YOU? I COULD HAVE BEEN YOUR CO-PILOT. GUESS YOU HAVE SHOWN THE WORLD WE OLD BOYS CAN STILL BE OF SERVICE AS COMBAT PILOTS. I MADE THE STATEMENT MORE THAN A YEAR AGO I WOULD LIKE TO HAVE A GROUP OF 100 B-17S OR SOMETHING SIMILAR, WITH PILOTS FROM THE FIRST WORLD WAR AT THE CONTROLS, AND WE COULD RAISE A LITTLE H——. HOW ABOUT MAKING ME YOUR AIDE NOW, SINCE YOU ARE A GENERAL? PHONE ME TONIGHT IF POSSIBLE. ROSCOE.

I called Roscoe, and as soon as he recognized my voice, he shouted: "Jimmy! You son of a bitch!" He reminded me that when he had made the statement about a bunch of old men flying combat missions just after Pearl Harbor, I had told him we were too old to fight in the war. Wars were for young men, I had said, not old fogeys like us. He never forgave me after he found out I had led the raid.

By June 27, 1942, a number of my gang had returned to the States, so Hap arranged to have the troops assembled at Bolling Field, in Washington, D.C., for an award ceremony. Hap presented them all with the Distinguished Flying Cross. I later went to Walter Reed Hospital where Lieutenants Harold F. "Doc" Watson, Charles L. "Mac" McClure, and Ted Lawson received their medals. Secretary of the Treasury Henry Morgenthau, Jr., represented the President.

With the recent experiences still in my mind, I wrote to all the raiders whose addresses we had asking for the names and background information on the Chinese who helped us escape the Japanese. I told them that Congress had just passed a law that everyone could wear the medal or ribbon of the award that the Chinese had presented us in Chungking and intended all raiders to have.

During this period, I was flattered to learn how much the American people appreciated the raid on Japan and was pleased to

…elligence sources that the Japanese were …its from their front lines to defend their …ad hoped. It was also during the two …at our code breakers learned the Japanese …surprise attack on Midway Island. They feared …attacks like ours on Japan and wanted to push their …line to Midway. If they could do so, they could then be in position to attack Hawaii again and eventually push our front line back to the mainland.

The Battle of Midway, on June 4–6, 1942, was disastrous for the Japanese. Four of their carriers and a heavy cruiser were sunk, 5 other large ships badly damaged, 322 aircraft destroyed, and 2,500 men killed, including many of their most experienced pilots. Historians now agree that the battle took place because our raid induced the Japanese to extend their forces beyond their capability.

…le I was doing my bit making speeches, I made it a point to check out new airplanes I hadn't flown before, such as the Spitfire, P-51, P-38, and P-47, as well as trainers such as the Piper Cub, AT-7, and AT-9, and the Sikorsky helicopter. I didn't know what Hap had in mind for me next, but I wanted to be useful. He had made me a general officer and I was anxious to prove he had made the right decision.

Unknown to me, events were happening at the highest level behind closed doors that were to eventually involve me. While we were on the high seas en route to Japan, there had been a conference in London attended by Prime Minister Winston Churchill, Harry Hopkins, and General Marshall. The British reluctantly accepted an American plan, code-named Bolero, to build up American forces in the UK in preparation for an invasion of Nazi Europe in 1942 (Operation Sledgehammer) or 1943 (Operation Roundup). In June 1942, Prime Minister Churchill, President Roosevelt, and their respective staffs met in Washington. They abandoned the idea of Sledgehammer and decided on an invasion of French North Africa instead, under the code name of Operation Torch. However, they affirmed the concept of Roundup but not the date.

This agreement filtered down from General Marshall to Hap and their respective staffs. The planners on the staff—men like Laurence S. Kuter, Haywood S. Hansell, Harold L. George, and Kenneth N. Walker—all of whom later became generals, were members of the Air War Plans Division (AWPD) who viously prepared an unprecedented plan for the war th ahead. It had been submitted in August 1941; it outlined a tained air offensive against Germany, if war should come.

The plan specified four principal air tasks: air operations defend the Western Hemisphere; an air offensive against Ger- many and any countries occupied by German forces; supporting air operations for a land invasion and subsequent campaigns on the European continent; and air operations for strategic defense in the Pacific. The plan, labeled "AWPD-1," was based on doctrine developed at the Air Corps Tactical School during the 1930s by Lieutenant Colonel (later Lieutenant General) Harold L. George and his colleagues. Its main thrust was to blueprint the way for air power to undermine the capacity and the will of our enemies to wage war. They believed that the basic functions of American airpower fell into five categories:

1. Strategic offensive air warfare, principally to disrupt enemy's capability and will to wage war, and destroy the enemy air forces if they constituted a threat to our own nation, to our military forces, or to the success of our air offensive.

2. Air support of friendly ground forces in the attainment of their immediate goals.

3. Air support of sea forces.

4. National air defense against enemy air forces threatening our own sources of national power.

5. Air operations against surface invasions threatening our shores.

This basic concept of the employment of aircraft in warfare made sense to me, although I had not attended the Air Corps Tactical School and had never engaged in any extensive discussions with my contemporaries about the principles they expressed and were about to test. Those early thinkers and planners were brilliant. Their thinking at that time was purely theoretical, but was proved out on every point during the course of the war, and the country owes much to their collective foresight and intellect. Although I didn't realize it at the time, it was going to be the role of fellows like me to turn those principles into action and make them work.

After Britain went to war in 1939, Brigadier Generals Carl A. "Tooey" Spaatz and George C. Kenney visited England as air observers, and substantive Anglo-American planning was begun. If we were to enter the war, priority target systems would include electric power, transportation, petroleum, and synthetic oil, with neutralization of the German air force a priority intermediate objective.

After we entered the war, there was little doubt among Army Air Force planners that the first priority must be the defeat of Germany and not Japan. As Hap said, "The strength of Japan is relative, the strength of Germany is absolute." He felt the way to go about defeating Germany was by precision daylight bombing of that country's internal economic structure.

In early 1942, the Soviet Union applied strong pressure on the Anglo-American leaders to open a second front in western Europe to divert German attention from their hard-pressed forces. The landings in North Africa were scheduled not only to relieve the pressure on the Soviet Union but to attack German field marshal Erwin Rommel, who was sweeping across the western desert of Africa, determined to drive the British out.

Meanwhile, the 8th Air Force was brought into being on January 28, 1942, at Savannah, Georgia. A small group of officers, headed by Brigadier General Asa N. Duncan, began the task of forming what was to become the most formidable war-making air organization in history. In May, Tooey Spaatz, now a major general, and Brigadier General Ira Eaker, his deputy, arrived in England with 39 officers and 384 enlisted men, the first contingent of U.S. Army troops to do so under American command.

During this period, Tooey and Ira discouraged any publicity. In June 1942, Ira was asked to speak at a ball given by the lord mayor of High Wycombe, where the 8th Air Force headquarters was located. His speech is remembered for its brevity: "We won't do much talking until we've done more fighting. We hope that when we leave you'll be glad we came. Thank you."

Tooey and Ira worked hard to get some 8th Air Force planes into the air. They finally did on August 17, 1942. A few B-17s struck at a rail target in France. It was a beginning.

Soon after I went back to work on Hap's staff, he called me into the office one day and said that General MacArthur was in need of an airman to replace General George H. Brett as head of his air effort in the South Pacific. MacArthur was not satisfied with Brett's performance and wanted an immediate replacement.

Hap said, "I have recommended George Kenney and you. I expect that he will select one of you, and I just wanted you both to know that you have been recommended."

MacArthur didn't want me. He chose Major General George C. Kenney, one of the capable old hands who had remained in the service through the rough formative years. It is probable that my public image as a so-called daredevil racing pilot got in the way. I was a reserve officer, and many of the old regulars didn't believe reservists could handle the big jobs.

George might have had his problems with MacArthur's autocratic ways, except that he nipped them in the bud in their first meeting. MacArthur reportedly liked to pontificate before his subordinates and when he started to lecture about loyalty, George got mad. He said, "General, I didn't ask to come out here. You asked for me. I think it's one of the smartest things you ever did, because I'm the best goddamn air force commander in the world today." George then told MacArthur that his men would be loyal to MacArthur because "they're always loyal to me, and through me they'll be loyal to you. You be loyal to me and my gang and make this thing fifty-fifty, or I'll be calling you from San Francisco and telling you that I've quit."

MacArthur was taken aback and was silent a moment. He walked over, put his arms around Kenney, and said, "You know, George, you and I are going to get along just fine." And apparently, they did. I think Hap made a wise decision to approve MacArthur's request for George rather than me.[1]

Note

1. This story is told in *Makers of the United States Air Force* by John L. Frisbee, Washington, D.C.: Office of Air Force History, 1987.

CHAPTER 12

In midsummer 1942, Hap called me in and told me about the invasion of North Africa and the basic plans for Torch. It was originally planned to be a small, all-American effort, but it grew into a joint British-American operation, using ground, naval, and air forces. A separate air unit, to be designated the 12th Air Force, was to be formed for the invasion and subsequent air actions against the Italians and Germans until they were driven out of North Africa. Hap said, "General George Patton will be in charge as the ground commander. They're looking for an air commander. Would you like to do it?"

I said I would.

"Then go and talk with Patton."

Patton and I had a good talk and hit it off very well from the moment we met. He had the responsibility for preparing one of the first American ground units to go into offensive action against the Germans, and he had established himself as a potential war leader of unusual dimensions. As a cavalryman in the twenties, he had been known as "Horse George" because of his antics in polo and riding. In 1941, he had been given the challenge of changing ordinary, peaceful civilians into disciplined, aggressive fighting men. He insisted that the training conditions of the men should simulate the conditions of actual combat. To prepare them for fighting in the African desert, he took them to a tract of scorched and lifeless desert near Indio, California, where the daytime summer temperature averaged 120 degrees. Inside the tanks it averaged 145 degrees.

Patton drove his men hard and they grumbled. At the end of a day's training, when everyone was hot, tired, and hungry, he made the officers run a mile while he would run a mile and a quarter. No matter how hard the men were driven, Patton drove himself harder—and he made sure the men knew it.

His reputation had preceded him. After we talked at length, we reported to General Arnold that we'd like to work together. He took us to General Marshall, who had no objection.

"Now you've got to go over to London and see Major General Dwight Eisenhower," Hap said. "He'll be in charge of the invasion of North Africa. He has to approve your assignments."

"Georgie," as Patton liked us to call him, returned to his unit in the desert to get them ready for transfer overseas. I learned later that he called his men together to talk to them. His talk was typical of many he would give later on the battlefield:

> Well, they've given us a job to do. A tough job, a mansize job. We can go down on our bended knees, every one of us, and thank God the chance has been given to us to serve our country. I can't tell you where we're going, but it will be where we can do the most good. And where we can do the most good is where we can fight those damn Germans or the yellow-bellied Eyetalians. And when we do, by God, we're going to go right in and kill the dirty bastards. We won't just shoot the sonsabitches. We're going to cut out their living guts—and use them to grease the treads of our tanks. We're going to murder those lousy Hun bastards by the bushel.

Patton talked in a high-pitched, almost feminine-sounding voice that penetrated his listeners' psyches and demanded their undivided attention. His enthusiasm for combat was contagious. He was a born showman who could turn his act on or off as he chose; obscenities and his two ivory-handled revolvers were his trademarks. He was a unique individual. We saw eye-to-eye. I knew we could work together in whatever lay ahead.

Georgie and I left for London on August 5. Two days later, we, along with Tooey Spaatz and Colonel Haywood "Possum" Hansell, met with General Dwight "Ike" Eisenhower. From the first moment I sensed that Ike had taken an immediate dislike to me. Once again, I had the uncomfortable feeling of being an illegitimate offspring at a family reunion. Ike knew of my reputation as a racing pilot through the press and had probably translated that to mean that I would be too reckless to command an air force. He knew from my military record that I had never commanded a unit larger than the Tokyo raid gang. He probably also knew that MacArthur had turned me down.

With a minimum of formality we sat down and immediately began discussing Torch. George led off with a briefing on his intentions and his plans "to drive the bastards into the sea." Ike seemed satisfied with that and turned to me. He said, "Our first job will be to acquire airfields in North Africa. As soon as they're acquired, we've got to be able to operate."

He was right, of course. However, instead of saying, "Yes, sir, that's exactly what we'll do," I very stupidly said, "General Eisenhower, the fields will be of no value to us until the ground troops have cleared and occupied the air bases, have brought in fuel, supplies, ammunition, bombs, food, and spare parts. Then we'll be able to operate."

I saw his face change, and I knew that I had blown it. It was a dumb thing to tell a general with as much logistics experience and military service as Eisenhower. Here was a one-star reserve officer implying that a two-star general who had spent his entire adult life in the service didn't know what he was talking about.

I realized I had made a horrible mistake, but it was too late to recover from it. His face froze and I fumbled for words. I never got to tell him much about our plans for the 12th.

I was mighty discouraged about my performance after that meeting and Ike's apparent opposition to my presence. After we left, I learned he immediately wired Hap Arnold saying that he was pleased with Patton as his ground commander but "for an airman I would like to have Spaatz [Major General Walter H.], Frank or Eaker, in that order."

Marshall and Arnold replied jointly that he could have anyone he wanted for his airman, "but we still recommend Doolittle."

He might have ignored Hap's opinion, but with that reply

also coming from Marshall, Ike accepted me reluctantly. When I was notified I was staying, I realized I was in a bad spot. In subsequent briefings in London, Ike was always stiff and formal with me, and I was very sensitive to his antagonistic, hostile attitude. He had to accept me, but he didn't have to like me. If he had refused me, and whoever he chose for the job hadn't performed, he knew he would then be asked why he hadn't accepted Doolittle.

It wasn't a comfortable way to start off in a difficult assignment. I returned to the States resolved that someday he would change his mind, that I would work overtime and do anything and everything to prove him wrong.

After getting the wheels in motion in Washington with the units that would eventually serve under me in North Africa, I told Joe I was leaving again and didn't intend to come home voluntarily until the job was done. We didn't realize it then, but we wouldn't see each other for three very long years.

From the moment that the invasion of North Africa was firmly decided, it was clear that a special air force would be required as part of the invading force. That force was designated the 12th Air Force and was activated on August 20, 1942, at Bolling Field.

The date of the invasion was set originally for early October 1942, but was changed later to early November, still not much time to put together a combined land, sea, and air force. Meanwhile, I returned to England in September with a small planning staff. We were known locally as "8th Air Force Junior," or simply "Junior." We were concerned not only with planning the air part of the African invasion, but also with the transfer of units from the 8th Air Force into the 12th, and the training of those units for the task ahead.

As soon as I sat down for our first planning meeting I realized that we were going to have to fight both the Germans and our own people who were fighting the Japanese in the Pacific. General MacArthur and Admiral Nimitz in the Pacific were demanding more of everything. If they got everything they asked for, the forces in the European theater would never be able to carry out their mission against Germany. I had to protect the interests of the command I was about to be given. One of those whose support I needed was George Patton; I hoped his loud, strident voice would have some effect in Washington with the big decision makers. My plea was for an understanding of the role of air power versus the traditional ground-bound thinking of wars past. I felt sure Georgie was someone who would be listened to, so I wrote him a letter explaining my problem and asked for his support:

> Unless we want our task forces overwhelmed by superior German forces, we must make our requirements known, and continue to urge them in the most emphatic terms by official messages to the War Department.
>
> I know, after having talked to you, that you have a great appreciation of the vital role that air forces must play in the forthcoming operation. But many others do not have that appreciation, nor do they understand that the requirements as submitted by you and General Eisenhower are minimum ones and reflect your knowledge of our overall shortages.
>
> Another point . . . is the fact that the operations for North Africa, the Middle East, and the bombing offensive against Germany from the United Kingdom are inseparable and are therefore basically complementary. It is not generally realized that the best insurance for our particular operation is an intensive bombing offensive against the backs of forces operating against us. The fact that the backs are at the same time the heart of the enemy's strength makes it doubly vital that the effort be in such force as to pay dividends. That force in the United Kingdom can be no more than a token unless these diversions are stopped. Token forces do not impress the Germans.
>
> Let me impress upon you, that all these facts are preached here by our air officers, but without the expression of beliefs and demands by responsible field commanders like yourself to confirm them, it is almost a "voice in the wilderness". . . .
>
> It would help greatly if you and General Eisenhower, individually and together, would clarify the points I have raised, and that by frequent reference you do not allow these points to be forgotten. Otherwise we are in danger of having our ultimate requirements pushed aside because of more vocal and oft-repeated demands.
>
> Please consider this as a matter of urgency. Steps

> are already being taken to divert a heavy group prior to September 10, 1942.

George was on my side and pushed the air-power message as fervently as I hoped he would. He was a very vocal asset, even though he had not yet been tested in battle with air support.

It was a time of confusion. The 12th had two headquarters—one in England and one in the States. In England we dealt with operational training; the other headquarters had to get the subordinate units—the 12th Fighter Command, 12th Air Force Service Command, 12th Air Support Command, and 12th Bomber Command—activated and ready to move from the States to the North African theater. The fighter unit was activated at Drew Field and the service unit at MacDill Air Force Base, both in Florida. The support command was activated at Birmingham, Alabama. The bomber command was created in England at High Wycombe on September 2, and personnel were transferred to it from the 8th. The 4th Bomb Wing was organized at Bolling Field for shipment to England, but was under the control of the 8th.

I assumed command of the 12th Air Force officially on September 23 and assembled the staff, with Colonel (later General and Air Force chief of staff) Hoyt S. Vandenberg as my chief of staff, and Colonel (later General) Lauris Norstad as deputy for operations. Both were superior individuals. My old friend Jack Allard had been recalled to active duty as a lieutenant colonel, and I put him in charge of personnel. Lieutenant Colonel John F. Turner was our intelligence officer, and Colonel Robert T. Lane was our supply officer.

On July 29, Hap Arnold wrote a letter to General Marshall in which the air-power message came through loud and clear. His main concern was that planes and personnel were being dispersed too widely. He stated that the principle of employment under which he wanted all the air units in the European theater to operate was to exert direct pressure against Germany, because that would be our only hope for a second front for many months.

"Successful air operations depend upon the continuous application of massed air power against critical objectives," Hap wrote. "Germany remains our primary objective and I feel strongly that the Air Force operating directly against her, which is permitted only from bases in the United Kingdom, must be maintained at sufficient strength to permit strict adherence to this principle."

In August, Hap again voiced his unhappiness to General Marshall about the dilution and dispersion of the air forces and the comparatively small number of planes assigned for the North African operations. Hap pointed out that the Germans could provide overwhelming air superiority to the tune of 1,500 to 2,000 planes in the North African invasion, while we would have only about 900 planes available during the landing phase.

During the convoy and seizure of airfields phase, Hap said, there would be only 166 carrier-borne aircraft of all types available, which would clearly be inadequate:

> The entire operation will surely fail unless the task forces are given effective fighter protection against superior German capabilities prior to the seizure of local airfields.
>
> . . . Unless air force units are withdrawn from other theaters, the U.S. Army strength can only be secured by taking all available planes out of England and using the trained units as fast as we can get them from O.T.U.'s [operational training units] in the United States.

Against our forces, Hap said, the Germans could employ 494 bombers during the move to the landing points, 623 bombers after the first day's operations, and considerable fighter and reconnaissance strength in addition to the bombers. "Any of the above can be accomplished without weakening their operations in Russia or Egypt and after taking only 50 percent of those available in other theaters. . . ."

Since this was our first major effort in the war, Hap insisted it was of the utmost importance that everything possible be done to ensure its success and said the present plan to disperse our forces should be overhauled:

> Our policy at the present time contemplates building up aerial superiority in Alaska, Hawaii, Southwest Pacific, Australia, India, Near East, and in the future in North Africa. At the same time we plan to maintain a fairly large force in the Caribbean. In carrying out

> such a policy, we achieve overwhelming superiority in no theater, while we vainly endeavor to secure a decided superiority in all theaters, in none of which even successful action would be decisive.
>
> . . . I urge that, since many considerations have led to the acceptance of the great risk involved in the North African operation, it be accepted as an offensive operation in fact, and that it be undertaken with the full power available to us. This must include the assignment of maximum offensive forces to the combined North African–European theaters, both to ensure tactical success and to permit decisive strategic operations.[1]

Tooey Spaatz wrote a personal note to Hap in which he expressed his concern about spreading out the worldwide air effort too thinly:

> I hope the idea can be put across that the war must be won against Germany or it is lost. The defeat of Japan, as soul-satisfying as it may be, leaves us no better off than we were on December 7.
>
> The war can be lost and very easily if there is a continuation of our dispersion. It can be won and very expeditiously if our air effort is massed here and combines its strength with the RAF.[2]

Hap's plea to Marshall for concentration of forces in the European theater was taken to heart, and many important decisions were made in the following weeks. Units began to arrive in England to get ready for the invasion of North Africa while our plans underwent continual revision and refinement. November 8, 1942, was selected as North African D-Day.

The days and nights blended together as I spun from one organizational problem to another and from planning sessions to strategy discussions. It would not have been so time-consuming and complicated if only our forces had been involved, but the operation had now grown in size and effort. All our meetings had to include our British counterparts. Under Torch, British and American units were to land in Algeria to seize the port of Algiers, and British forces would then advance on Tunis. American units would land in western Algeria and Morocco to seize Oran and Casablanca–Port Lyautey. Once that was accomplished, American forces would move eastward and assist the British in Tunisia.

The purpose of all this was to force the Germans and Italians to defend a North African front and thus take troops away from other battle fronts. The Torch forces would advance from the west while British forces would advance from Egypt in the east.

Two commands would be responsible for air support. The British Eastern Air Command would support the ground forces advancing from Egypt toward Algiers and Tunis. The Royal Air Force would then protect the port and convoy routes as those areas were liberated on the march westward. The 12th Air Force would support the landings at Oran and Casablanca and put up fighters to defend the convoy routes and ports on the push eastward.

The one complication was the possibility of resistance by French forces loyal to the Vichy government who were siding with the Germans. No one knew how much fight they had in them. If, after we overcame French resistance, the Spanish entered the conflict from Morocco or German forces moved through Spain to intervene, 12th Air Force B-17 units would operate against them from captured North African fields. Our ground forces would be assisted by naval aircraft, mostly British, operating from carriers.

Tooey Spaatz was relieved from assignment as commander of the 8th Air Force and assumed command of all American air forces in the European theater and thus became my immediate boss. Ira Eaker took Tooey's place as the 8th's commander. The overall boss of all American ground and air units in the theater was General Eisenhower. For the North African invasion, he would operate from Gibraltar and move to North Africa afterward.

Day by day, we gathered resources into the 12th from the 8th, much to Eaker's dismay. We took 14 units of fighters, bombers, and transports, more than half of the 8th's strength. This continual drawdown of his fighting strength caused a bit of friction between Ira and me, which kept surfacing over the next two years.

Throughout the war, I always tried to write to Joe at least once a week. She kept every one of my letters. I couldn't keep any of hers. Of course, I couldn't tell her what I was doing in any detail, but would mention any old friends who passed through. Jack Allard and I and several of our staff were staying at the Claridge Hotel in London, and everyone we ever knew would get in touch. Their brief visits would lighten our day. In one letter to Joe, I wrote: "Haven't got my flying time in yet this month. This is the first time in almost 25 years of flying where ships [planes] have been around and still wondered about getting my four hours in. Another of the penalties of command."

A few days later, I wrote: "Flew a Spitfire three hours and some minutes yesterday. Fired the [gunnery] course or as much of it as I had time for. Was busy on both the ground targets and tow target but at that got higher scores than the boys who were with me. As a matter of fact got higher scores both on the ground strafing and sleeve than their combined scores. Not that I was good—they were lousier. Got to keep my hand in. Can't have some punk shooting down the 'old master.' "

I was concerned about both our sons. Young Jim was flying combat in the South Pacific and couldn't write much. John was in his plebe year at West Point and the upperclassmen were harassing him no end by making him "bomb Tokyo" by running around the cadet area with his hands outstretched, making noises like an airplane engine and dive-bombing imaginary targets. That was the penalty he had to pay for what I had done a few months before. While the value of demeaning first-year cadets is debatable, I was sure "Peanut" could survive whatever they dreamed up. He did and made his own mark as one of the first plebes to make the West Point boxing team. It is quite possible that he got some revenge against the upperclassmen by bombing them—in the ring.

All during the war, Hap encouraged all of his top generals to write him directly. We all took full advantage of the invitation. My letter to him of October 21, 1942, conveyed what was going on in my area of responsibility, what we had been doing to get ready for the landings in North Africa, and the itineraries of my staff:

> I have the best staff, the best commands and the smoothest-running organization in the Air Force. We

> are short as everyone else is, on experienced secondary personnel, but our key people are really tops.
>
> The morale of our operating units is excellent and the average experience level acceptable. It varies from the superior heavy bombardment groups to the newly arriving groups who have had no combat experience and will have to complete their training in the theater. We had hoped to be able to operate these new units here for about six weeks prior to taking them into the new theater, but it now appears, due to difficulties and delays experienced in getting them across the northern route, together with equipment shortages and inoperability of hastily made installations there, that these units may actually be somewhat delayed in getting into the theater.

I told Hap that our principal worries were the unhealthy concentration of aircraft at points where they couldn't be dispersed or adequately protected, and the considerable distances and unfavorable weather through which our other fighters must be flown into the theater. Our problems resulted from the short time allowed to organize, plan, and train; the shortage of experienced personnel; the unavailability of essential equipment, especially communications; the shortage of suitable airports in the theater; the unfortunate necessity of marrying ground and air units that had not had previous training together in the field; and the shortage of transport aircraft. I wrote:

> We mention the above problems, not because we are awed by them but merely to indicate that we are aware of them. We plan to overcome them by careful planning, preparing for eventualities, and Yankee ingenuity.
>
> Conditions in air warfare are changing so rapidly that our very inexperience is often an asset—we have little to forget.
>
> We have a job—a hard job—to do. We are looking forward with pleasant anticipation to the altogether successful accomplishment of it. In this we hope to justify your confidence and your policies and even re-

flect a little on the justifiable pride we intend to enable you to indulge in.

The move to Gibraltar was planned with the utmost secrecy. The success of the invasion depended on the element of surprise, since no one knew what the French would do. There could be no period of softening up the area with lengthy bombardment first.

General Eisenhower was to direct the overall operation; Brigadier General Mark Clark was his deputy. A false press release was put out in London to the effect that General Eisenhower was returning to Washington for consultation. Ike and his staff secretly moved one night from their headquarters in Norfolk House in London to a small cottage in the suburbs.

Meanwhile, six B-17s of the 97th Bomb Group at Hurn Airdrome on England's south Channel coast were earmarked to take us to "Gib." Ground crews removed all excess equipment from them, including the waist guns and their ammunition, in order to have seating and baggage room for passengers. Only the nose gun, radio compartment, and top and ball turret guns remained. No gunners would be among the crew.

Early on the morning of November 5, 1942, Ike, Brigadier General Mark Clark, Brigadier General Lyman Lemnitzer (temporary chief of staff for the invasion, and later Army chief of staff), Colonel T. J. Davis (Ike's adjutant general), and a number of other American and British officers, including me, boarded the six waiting B-17 Flying Fortresses for the 1,200-mile, eight-hour flight. Ike's plane was piloted by Major Paul W. Tibbets, an excellent officer and bomber pilot, who would later go down in history as the pilot of the *Enola Gay* when it dropped the first atomic bomb on Japan. He had already flown a number of B-17 missions against enemy targets in France and was one of those officers I mentally earmarked to be a future general.

The rest of us passengers were spread among the B-17s. My plane was piloted by Lieutenant John C. Summers; copilot was Lieutenant Thomas F. Lohr. Also on board were General Lemnitzer; Colonel Davis; Major Joe Phillips, former editor of *Newsweek* and public relations officer for the Allied Force Headquarters; W. H. B. Mack, of the British Foreign Office and head of political warfare associated with the invasion; and Freeman Matthews, political advisor to Ike.

We were the last of the six to taxi out for takeoff. As Summers tried to swing around beside the others to run up the Fort's engines, he found he had no brakes. "We've lost hydraulic pressure," he yelled to Lohr. "Hit the wobble pump!"

Lohr began pumping the emergency hydraulic pump furiously to get some fluid into the system as our B-17 slowly coasted toward the B-17s in front of us. If we crashed into them, loaded with gasoline as we were, there would surely be an explosion and fire. Ike and the other top leaders of the invasion effort were innocently sitting in them, unaware of what was happening. The other planes were lined up like birds on a wire, not knowing we were having trouble. Just as it seemed a collision was inevitable, Summers hit the left brake hard and yelled to Lohr to "Pump! Pump!"

The left brake grabbed and the B-17 spun around, narrowly missing the B-17 beside us. It was close; the invasion effort might have been stymied right there in one giant fireball if Summers hadn't been able to get a little hydraulic pressure in that left brake. We ended up in the mud beside the run-up strip.

The other planes took off in marginal weather, and it was frustrating to see them go. We would follow as soon as possible. We learned that one of the B-17s never reached Gibraltar. One of the passengers was Major General Asa Duncan, who was supposed to play a major logistics role in the upcoming operation. To this day no one knows what happened to the plane.

It took all day for the mechanics to repair and test the hydraulic system. We left the next morning, November 6, and had no trouble getting off.

We headed southwest over the Atlantic well away from land to avoid patrolling German fighters. Unknown to us, four German Junker Ju.88s, stationed at a field near Biarritz, France, took off for an ocean patrol to search for shipping west of the Bay of Biscay. They flew for about five hours and were about to return to base when they sighted us. We were then about midway to our destination.

Summers was the first to see the Germans from our plane. Without the normal complement of guns, we were not helpless but sadly undergunned, especially with no trained gunners on board. The Ju.88s were equipped with 20-mm cannons and 7.9-mm machine guns, enough to knock us down quickly. At first, the four planes just flew formation a respectful distance away, two on each side, to take a look at our defenses. I tried to see them from where I was in the radio bay, but the window was too small. I went to the waist gun position where I could get a better view and wished we had guns poking out of those openings.

Lemnitzer began to fiddle with the gun in the radio compartment and started firing. The Ju.88s were too far away. When they saw his tracers looping at them, they pulled off and lined up to attack. Apparently, they thought we were fully armed and decided not to attack from the rear. Summers dove toward the water, hoping to outrun them and give them no chance to fire from below.

The German pilots were probably sure they would score a kill that day by making off-angled, head-on passes. As they dove, Summers kicked the plane into a skid, which threw off their aim. We got no hits. We were now level over the ocean and Summers had the throttles firewalled.

The Ju.88s lined up for another head-on pass and Summers turned into them until a collision seemed inevitable. It was close and I thought they had missed again. They didn't. This time a .303 tracer bullet ripped into the cockpit and threw glass all over Summers and Lohr. The number-three propeller began to run away, a possible prelude to its breaking off and slicing into the fuselage like a giant power saw. If it did, it could cut the airplane in half.

Up front, Summers was nearly blinded but kept control of the plane as we roared along only a few feet above the waves. Lohr, however, had been hit in the arm and fell against the control wheel. Blood soaked his clothing. The bullet had struck the instrument panel, bounced around the cockpit, and burned a scarf Lohr had in his lap. Dazed, he got out of his seat and stood by the throttle quadrant.

Summers shouted for me and I came forward as Lohr stumbled toward me. I helped him to a seat; Lemnitzer was still firing the gun, but stopped to help Lohr when he saw how badly he had been hit. I took Lohr's place in the copilot's seat and realized we were in real trouble with that number-three prop. Summers wrestled with the controls to keep us out of the water while I tried to feather it. I had never flown a B-17 before and was glad Summers seemed to be all right.

Fortunately, the propeller slowed down somewhat, but held at a high rpm. This meant the governor had not failed completely, but our speed was cut down. Our troubles weren't over.

The Ju.88s were still there making head-on passes, and Lemnitzer returned to firing his gun from the radio compartment. We think he damaged one of them.

Suddenly, the four enemy planes, one of them smoking, broke away from us and headed toward land. After the war we learned that the only reason they broke off the attack was that they were low on gas and almost didn't make it back to their base.

Four hours after takeoff from Hurn, we landed at Gibraltar. It was my first combat mission as commander of the 12th Air Force. I logged two hours of B-17 copilot combat time in my logbook. Lohr was sent to the hospital and joined his unit a few weeks later at Biskra.

NOTES

1. Arnold, Henry H., memorandum for the Chief of Staff. Subject: North African Operations. August 19, 1942.
2. Spaatz, Carl, personal letter to General Henry H. Arnold, signed "Tooey," dated August 27, 1942.

CHAPTER 13

The invasion of North Africa was now imminent. Previously, on October 24, 1942, 700 ships had sailed out of British ports and New York Harbor almost simultaneously. They carried 22 million pounds of food, 38 million pounds of clothing, 10 million gallons of gasoline, and guns, tanks, bulldozers, and trucks by the hundreds.

Before dawn on November 8, the 700 ships in small contingents were turning toward shore off the North African coast. Aircraft were already in the air from aircraft carriers and battered airstrips on Malta. Landing craft were approaching shore along 1,000 miles of coastline between southwestern Morocco and Algiers.

The big question was still not answered: How much resistance would the French put up against us? President Roosevelt had gone on the air speaking in French. He asked for all loyal Frenchmen to join the liberators who were at that moment about to land on their beaches. He ended the brief message with, "Vive la France éternelle!"

Admiral Jean François Darlan, commander of all Vichy French army and naval forces in Africa, had his headquarters in Algiers. His first clue that there was an invasion occurred when British warships began to shell the city. By 7:00 P.M., Admiral Darlan and General Alphonse Juin surrendered the city.

The capitulation was not so easy at other landing places.

Our troops encountered heavy fire along the Moroccan beaches, and the defenders of Casablanca held out for an extended time. Two French cruisers were able to get out of the harbor and battled briefly before they were silenced. But there was obviously no cohesion among the defending forces. It seemed that any resistance was directly related to the fighting personalities of the individual leaders of the French defending units. Some units gave up as soon as they realized what was going on. Others fought savagely. Our forces took some heavy losses.

Admiral Darlan was captured and agreed to call off the resistance. He sent word to his commanders to cease and desist and to cooperate with our forces. On the morning of the third day, the French tricolor was raised over his headquarters with the American flag on one side, the British on the other. His acquiescence saved many lives.

By the fourth day, all resistance had ceased, and American ground forces formed up for the push eastward toward Tunisia. The few planes of the 12th that had managed to get to French fields covered the advance. At the same time, Field Marshal Bernard L. "Monty" Montgomery and his 8th Army were pushing Rommel's 10,000-man panzer units westward out of Egypt.

I had flown across from Gibraltar as planned and tried to get things in some sort of order. On November 19, 1942, I wrote a letter to Hap explaining what had happened up to that time. My letter and his reply show the rapport we enjoyed and how Hap was able to receive news and recommendations from his commanders without having the information delayed by having to go through any middle channels. In turn, his letters, always written directly to his commanders, brought them up to date on what he was thinking and planning. My letter was as follows:

> The American carrier-borne Navy aviation at Casablanca and the British 1st Air Arm at Oran did the major part of the air fighting. By the time airports were secured they had destroyed either in the air or on the ground the majority of French aviation.
>
> Joe Cannon, at Casablanca, has done an outstanding job. His 33rd Fighter Group gave air support and the necessary reconnaissance to General Patton's forces. We had no actual air fighting and lost only one

pilot; he in an airplane accident. Nick Craw, while going forward under a flag of truce in a jeep, was most unfortunately shot through the head by a sniper and killed instantly. Cannon unloaded some 72 aircraft from the *Chenango* at Port Lyautey. The principal runway had been bombed and was not usable. The field was soft and seven of the aircraft sustained minor damage in landing. Part of these aircraft were later removed to the Casablanca airport and some 35 more were shot off the *Archer*. Joe now has, in addition to these, a half dozen B-25s from the 310th Group and more are now coming in steadily. He also has such transport as he requires of the 62nd Group.

In addition to Port Lyautey, there are some good fields at Sale, Rabat, and Casablanca. The field at Casablanca is large but has no prepared runways, and there are some spots which will not hold a B-17. I proved this the other day by landing there and bogging down. Apparently the small footprint and high unit loading was more than the sod would stand, and it required four tanks to pull the B-17 out so that we could take off again. Joe Cannon and George Patton have the western situation well in hand and get along together beautifully.

The first airport was secured at Oran on noon of D-Day. Twenty-four Spitfires of the 31st Group, with Shorty Hawkins in command, hopped over from Gibraltar. Four aircraft, which the boys took to be British Hurricanes, were doing lazy eights high overhead. As the squadron was landing, they peeled off and attacked. One of the Spitfires, which had lowered its landing gear and flaps, was shot down and the pilot was killed. Three ships which had not landed immediately attacked the four aircraft, which turned out to be [French] Dewoitine 520s, and shot down three. The fourth got away. The Dewoitine 520 is apparently no match for our modern fighters.

[Before daylight on] the following morning a French bomber flew over the field and dropped a single bomb, damaging one of our transports. We had a flight in the air, but it was so dark that they could not pick up the bomber, which was flying at a very low altitude.

The ground radio equipment had not yet come in, so the people on the ground, who could see the bomber and fighters, were unable to direct them to the enemy.

The fighter units did a splendid job, taking out tanks, batteries, lorries, and foot columns, and even attacking a concrete gun emplacement in order to drive the crew away from the guns and permit the ground forces to capture it. The French capitulated at Oran shortly after this battery was silenced. The buildup of the first airport secured, which was Tafaraoui, was continued with additional units from the 31st and the 52nd, the latter under Dick Allison. These ships were flown in from Gibraltar.

I neglected to mention an instance in connection with our fighters: Six French artillery batteries were put in place on a hill about two and one half miles from Tafaraoui. They shelled the airport. Two flights of the 31st group strafed this emplacement, and in a matter of minutes the batteries were silenced and six vertical columns of smoke arose from their previous position. Some 14 tanks were observed to be approaching in the distance and as the airplanes were about out of ammunition they permitted the honor of destroying the tanks to go to our tank force, which immediately took them out.

I cannot speak too highly of the work done by these groups. They twice stopped mechanized columns that were attacking the airport at Tafaraoui from the south. The ground units had moved forward to take La Senia airport, which is closer to Oran. Had it not been for the prompt and efficient action of the Spitfires, Tafaraoui and our air units would have been lost and the war at Oran lengthened and made much more bloody. One column taken out and routed was the French Foreign Legion moving in from its headquarters at Sidi-Del-Abbes. Our fighters destroyed five tanks and routed the foot soldiers.

La Senia airport was secured, lost, and secured again. During the process it was bombed by our own people and shelled by the French. We have finally moved into La Senia, in addition to Tafaraoui, and are rehabilitating it.

The necessity of marrying ground and air forces on the field of battle precluded the training and study in recognition necessary to assure perfect collaboration. In spite of this the cooperation was of the highest order. In only two instances were mistakes made. On one occasion we were directed to attack an enemy column east of La Macta on Arzew Bay. By the time the message got to us, it read west of La Macta. Two airplanes flew over the column to the west, which was actually ours. The ground forces, being light on the trigger, shot at the airplanes. The pilots, thinking that these must be French troops, started to strafe them. Fortunately, our tanks are not as vulnerable as the French, and no damage was done to our ground troops, but two of our planes were shot down by our own people. After this, General Oliver gave his troops instruction in aircraft recognition; we got pieces of all of our mechanized equipment on the airport and permitted pilots to study them both from the ground and the air.

The other incident occurred almost at the same time, when some tanks stuck their noses up over a hill and our mobile artillery started shooting at them. The tanks withdrew over the brow of the hill, and the artillery requested that we attack them, which we did. In this case I personally asked the artillery officer who had requested the strafing if he was positive these were French tanks and he assured me they were. Our ships went out and took one pass at the tanks, which promptly displayed a white and an American flag.

We lost a total of six fighters shot down. Three were shot down by enemy ground troops—two on low reconnaissance flights just after Oran had capitulated.

[Colonel] Larry Norstad went to Oran on the command ship and was in charge of all 12th Air Force operations until I arrived. He did an excellent job. He proved himself to be not only a fine planner but an outstanding operator. I intend to recommend Larry and P. L. Williams for promotion [to Brigadier General] as soon as the final action is taken on the recommendations for Van [Vandenberg], Tommy Blackburn, and Claude Duncan. Jack Allard and Bob Zane carried the brunt of the personnel and supply situation and also showed up most favorably. . . . An operation of this kind promptly separates the sheep from the goats and I am happy to report that all of our people showed up well and most of them were superior.

The one project that did not come off as well as we had hoped was the initial paratroop operation. The drop was to be made on the Oran airport at H-Hour. Upon assurance from political advisors that the French would be friendly, it was decided to arrive after daybreak and if possible land the airplanes without dropping the parachutists in order to have them available to proceed immediately to the eastward, where they would be more urgently needed.

With the assurance of the politicos that the French would not fire on them, the boys sailed blithely in and four of them were shot down long before they even arrived over the airport. Most of the rest landed on a dry lake bed some 30 miles to the westward. One plane got lost and landed in Gibraltar, one landed in the water, and at least two in Spanish Morocco. The only mollifying thought is that the paratroopers stuck machine guns out of the windows and shot down two of the De 50s which attacked them.

. . . I personally feel that the initial plan of the paratroop operation was sound. The fact that the operation was not entirely successful was due to three factors: first, the misinformation received from political advisors; second, unfavorable weather en route; and third, inadequate communications. In connection with the last I want to say that our principal difficulty has been the establishment of satisfactory radio communication. This has been true in both the air forces and the ground forces. It is imperative that in any future operation of this kind we have special aircraft that can fly in complete ground radio equipment. These aircraft must be able to protect themselves and go in with the advance element. An airplane like the B-26 but with considerably increased wing area to permit operation from small airports would be ideal for this purpose. The large fuselage would permit the installation of reliable VHF, RDF, HF, and DF equipment. The armor and armament would permit it to fight its way in. A transport could carry the equipment necessary but would be too vulnerable.

Two of my principal worries were the concentration of aircraft on Gibraltar and the long flight down from the UK in the season of bad weather. Gibraltar is now pretty well cleaned out, and to date far less difficulty than I anticipated has been experienced in connection with flying the aircraft down. In addition to the paratroop plane that landed in the water, we had another that landed a few miles from Gibraltar due to bad weather there. The crew was promptly picked up. Two P-38s landed in Portugal. One took off under a ruse and the other is interned. Day before yesterday when one of the B-17s was about an hour and one half out of the UK, number three engine caught fire and burned so furiously that it fell out. The ship crashed in the sea but was immediately enveloped in flames due to the gasoline spreading on the water and burning all around the ship. Two of the other B-17s went back and saw several people in the water but no sign of life. . . .

When I was last at Casablanca there were about 4,000 air people ashore. Yesterday at Oran we had 14,000 men and about 1,000 officers. These are all stationed at Tafaraoui and La Senia at the moment, but as these fields were built to accommodate only about 300 officers and 3,000 men we are dispersing them on adjacent fields as rapidly as the latter can be prepared. Operations to date have been primitive due to difficulty of getting organizational equipment from the boats to the airports. The boys lived mostly on B, C, and K rations. It is unsafe to use the water, so water has been brought in and rationed. As a matter of fact, the local water system was plugged and the engineers had to clean it out before we could get even enough for normal sanitation. The sewer system was blown up and had to be repaired. In the meantime, it is necessary to utilize very homely facilities. These conditions are being corrected and we expect to be fairly permanently established in the near future.

The fight has moved to the eastward. In order to get the Hun out of Tunisia and occupy this area before he can, we have made available to the RAF and to General Anderson's army, who are charged with this chore, as many of our [air] units as they can use. The arrangement under which these airplanes are made available is for the British to assign the missions but we operate. For the first few days, before we had an organization at Algiers, they operated our aircraft, but that unsatisfactory condition was corrected almost immediately. They now have the services of one squadron of the 14th group, two squadrons of the 97th heavy group, one squadron of the 27th light group, and a varying number of transports here in Algiers. . . . We expect to move the rest of the 14th, 27th, and 97th groups from Oran as soon as facilities here and to the eastward can support them. Additional units will not be moved to the eastward until we have the principal part of our striking force set up in eastern Algeria and Tunisia.

We must prepare and maintain adequate bases in the Casablanca and Oran areas in case the Hun decides to invade through Spain, in which case we will establish a holding force here and to the eastward and operate from the western bases. Oran will be our major training and maintenance center. The 12th Air Service Command and regional weather organization will be established there. Initially, we can stage, consolidate, and perfect our teamwork there while extending to the eastward. We must be prepared to combat periodic nuisance raids, which may become frequent if the concentration warrants. We must keep the Straits of Gibraltar open and provide fighter cover and later submarine protection for convoys along the west and north coasts of Africa.

With all of the above in mind we have decided to break this entire area up into districts; one at Casablanca, one at Oran, one here [Algiers], and one to the eastward, probably at a convenient point south of Bône. Each one of these districts will have a composite organization that will be in substance a small air force.

For convenience we have, temporarily, left the 12th Air Support Command at Casablanca with such bombardment and pursuit attached as are required. The

12th Air Support Command proper will eventually move to Oran and will have assigned to it such bombardment, transport and so forth as is required.

The 12th Bombardment Command will be established east of here and again will have its requirements of fighters and transports assigned. The commands are utilized only in the interest of simplicity; because they already contain trained organizations that permit them to function as composite units; and because each one has an extremely competent commander.

The 12th Air Force headquarters is now established at Algiers, and the three previously noted units will be directly responsible to this headquarters.

The whole of this operation is so clear in my own mind that it is possible I have not made it entirely clear to you. I can only say that a single air force built up on the old lines cannot operate satisfactorily over this large an area with the required degree of flexibility. For this reason we are breaking it up into individual composite commands, each responsible to this headquarters.

I have discussed this with General Eisenhower, General Clark, and General Spaatz, and they are all in complete agreement. As a matter of fact, General Spaatz had already, for convenience, decided to break his bomber command into districts, and we are going only a step further in the formation of composite commands.

Hap replied on December 21:

Your interesting and informative letter of the action between November 8 and November 19 gave me the first authentic account of the actions during that important period. In some ways you made it appear too simple, but I can visualize the difficulties which had to be overcome and the hardships which were suffered before the airdromes were captured and your forces were in operation. . . .

The help which your air force rendered the ground forces was evidently the deciding factor in the early success of your mission. When this can be done without adequate communications, it should be much easier when all the equipment and specially trained air support troops are available. If we can make such troops available to you, your fighters and bombers can then be released for their primary missions.

We are having some trouble here in opening up the ferry route to forward replacements to your theater. The utilization of the South Atlantic ferry route was based primarily upon the belief that all aircraft, other than fighters, could be flown nonstop from either Bathhurst or someplace in the vicinity of Kano. I am now informed that the prevailing north winds make it a very dangerous gamble for B-26s to attempt either one of these flights. Strenuous efforts are being made to obtain intermediate fields and to stock them with the necessary supplies. I have sent General C. R. Smith of the Air Transport Command to Dakar to negotiate with the French for the early opening of such fields, and he is very hopeful that, within a short time, we will be able to use them. The shipping situation is still serious, and replacements of fighters as well as personnel are dependent upon convoys.

You have already been informed by cable of the location of succeeding groups and replacements for your groups which have been in action. There has been some difficulty, due to misunderstanding in cables, in separating replacements for the 12th Air Force from those intended for the United Kingdom. This matter has now been straightened out, and you should be kept informed fully and thoroughly of what you are going to get and when you are going to get it.

I have been engaged for the past several weeks in negotiations with the British on the allocations of the 1943 aircraft production. The papers are finally signed and, although we believe we have given the British more than they asked for, they still believe they didn't get as much as they wanted.

I have started the Air Staff working on your suggestions as to what is needed in future operations of this kind. The provision of the flying communication station, completely self-contained with all types of radio equipment, is dependent on our ability to obtain the required airplanes and to incorporate the changes in them.

Your organizing into districts and small composite commands to meet your particular needs looks all right to me as long as you can do it with the troops made available to you for your headquarters. It will not be possible for me to continue to pyramid large headquarters and to furnish any excess in overhead or service troops. The shipping situation will continue critical for a long time. Every man and every piece of equipment must be maintained; therefore, every unnecessary increase in personnel overseas must be ruthlessly eliminated, remembering at the same time that the necessary needs must be supplied. The Air Staff is now working on a study to determine the maximum number of troops which can be maintained in each theater, and balancing this against the number of groups set up. As soon as this is determined, you and other Air Force commanders will be notified of just what you can expect.

I am delighted with what you have done. Keep on slugging 'em—for the sooner you can get the German out of North Africa, the sooner we can proceed to our main business of pounding him down in his homeland.

I am writing this just before Christmas. I hope that you can help in giving the Nation and me what would be a wonderful Christmas present—Tunisia.

Unfortunately, we couldn't deliver Tunisia to Hap for Christmas. We were plagued by poor communications between our units and my command post. However, when Tooey Spaatz arrived from England, he established what he called his "red line service," which was a direct communications system between his headquarters and all his major commanders.

Another problem was intelligence information. This deficiency surfaced quickly as I found out that we had no reliable intelligence service whatsoever in the early days of the campaign. We were dependent on the British for information about the enemy. We had little knowledge of what the enemy's intentions and capabilities were, and this seriously penalized us. I learned that when you have to depend on someone else for communications and your intelligence, they are inclined to exercise command. It took a long time to remedy this situation.

Looking back, I must admit now that when we started in North Africa, we didn't know our job as well as we should have—especially me. From the commanding general on down, we had to learn how to identify and solve our logistics problems. I made some mistakes, but I had a magnificent staff that often put me on the right track when I strayed. And I can't say enough for the group commanders, who were the backbone of the fighter and bomber units—and the sergeants, who were largely responsible for maintaining the aircraft during that period while we were getting our feet on the ground.

One of our basic mistakes in the beginning was that we were more oriented toward the fighters and bombers than we were toward ground support. And that's where our poor communications penalized us most. We had to learn on the job because no one in our whole military establishment had had much experience with ground support. Even in England, where we had the 8th Air Force doing medium and heavy bombing, we had no experience giving air support to ground troops.

There were some incidents that reflected our deficiencies. When the French Foreign Legion troops started toward our two airfields at Oran, we sent our fighters out to shoot up their column. Shortly after the mission was launched, we got word that the French were now coming in in truckloads to surrender. Their leader said, "We could not give in immediately; we had to preserve French honor. The French honor has now been preserved; we surrender completely."

We had a very hectic time, because of poor communications, trying to get in touch with our fighters before they attacked the columns. I don't know if those Legionnaires ever realized how close they came to being annihilated.

As a result of the French surrender, I had a joint French-British-American command. We gave a group of P-40s to the French to keep their pilots gainfully employed. They immediately stole all the stove lids they could find to put under their seats because there was no armor to protect the P-40s from below. Thus, they were further anxious to preserve the honor and property of the French.

Our own ground troops gave me some problems during

those initial days by requesting ground support when I knew it shouldn't be provided. In December 1942, I had a ground commander ask me to give fighter cover to a Jeep that was going out to repair a broken telephone line. I refused. The plane that would have wasted its time on this mission shot down two German Me-109s. If each ground commander had his own "air umbrella" overhead to use defensively, there would have been little or none to use offensively. I had to defend myself often to ground commanders, even down to company commanders, who insisted that they have air cover at all times. We wanted to keep American losses to a minimum, of course, but the ultimate objective was to win the war and that could not be done by employing defensive tactics. Air power must be allowed to operate offensively.

Georgie Patton was one ground commander who understood this philosophy. He didn't want to lose any men, but he was willing to release his air cover for offensive purposes. His feeling was that a soldier's duty was not to keep from being killed, but to advance, kill enemy soldiers, and win the war.

Probably my most unsettling personal experience during those opening days in North Africa happened shortly after we arrived. I always insisted on flying all aircraft assigned to my commands. When we received the first improved model of a new British fighter, a Spitfire IX, I took it up for a local test hop and found it flew very well. It had a supercharged engine that gave it high-altitude capabilities—an excellent airplane. Once I was in the air I looked for German or Italian playmates but couldn't find any.

While I was flying, General Eisenhower, who was still on "Gib," sent word that he wanted me over there "right now!" He was told I was flying a Spitfire. Our communications were still so poor that they couldn't reach me in the air, so when I landed and found out he wanted me, I fueled up immediately and headed for Gibraltar. On the way over, I saw two cruisers, one British and the other Italian, lobbing shells at each other. I flew over to get a better view and both turned their antiaircraft weapons on me, so I hastily withdrew and proceeded to Gib.

As soon as I reported to Ike, I could see he was very upset. He wanted to know why I was flying instead of being on the ground commanding my units. I told him that I felt it was my duty to test-fly any new aircraft assigned to my command—that it was a clear responsibility for every air force commander. Flying the airplanes assigned would enable them to do a better job of supervising other people who flew airplanes.

That rationale didn't go over with Ike. His face reddened and he said, "I want my airmen available when I want them. Doolittle, you have a choice. You can either be a major and fly Spitfires or you can be a major general and be my senior air officer down here."

The choice couldn't have been put more clearly. I assured him I chose the latter. As I flew back to Oran, I realized for the first time that Ike had implied he had recommended me for promotion to major general. I found out later that he had already replied to a query from General Marshall, with Tooey's approval. Ike had written:

> Promotion of Doolittle is fully justified and I recommend it be accomplished at once. Apparently my fault that Doolittle has not been recommended since November 8, but it was my impression that you had already planned his promotion to take effect shortly after initiation of [Operation] Torch. It is appropriate to announce his promotion as a result of leadership in actual battle command as well as in organization of 12th Air Force.

I was promoted to major general on November 20, 1942.

Ike must have still had reservations about me. He wrote to Hap that he thought Doolittle was "stronger as a field commander than he is as an organizer." In a letter to Lieutenant General Frank M. Andrews, Ike said he thought Doolittle had "established himself as a commander and, although he had to learn the hard way, he has learned something of the responsibilities of high command."

He was certainly right about learning the hard way. I was learning something new and useful every day. I intended to keep on learning.

The period between November 8, 1942, and February 18, 1943, was a time of experimentation while we began flying missions against the enemy. The very extent of the territory that fell to our forces in a matter of days after the initial landings created monumental problems. Many units had previously been split into small parallel units or separate entities located in England and the United States. Now those echelons were redivided. Some units were split into as many as five separate echelons divided between the States, England, North Africa, and the high seas. Within North Africa, these various echelons remained separate entities for weeks while we tried to get them transportation to join their parent units. In some cases it took six months to make a whole unit out of its various parts.

The main ports of entry for 12th Air Force units in the early days were Casablanca for units arriving from the States and Oran for units coming from the United Kingdom. At the same time, other units were moving closer to the enemy. As early as November 30, 1942, the advance echelon of my headquarters was moving from Tafaraoui to Algiers. A week later, fighter groups were moving to Youks-les-Bains and Bône.

What this meant from a command point of view was that I had some ground and rear echelons well over a thousand miles from the rest of their units. To join up they had to rely on the small, slow French railways, insufficient motor transport, and transport aircraft that were continually hampered by bad weather and fields in poor condition.

Despite the fact that no group could function as it was supposed to, with a full complement of men and equipment, air defense of the harbors was established, airfields were built, air support was given to the Army, and we were able to send out bombing missions. All this was possible only because of the excellent planning that had taken place before the invasion. I was blessed with a staff of career Army Air Forces officers with superior intellect and drive. I relied on them and let them have their heads, and they came through magnificently.

One of those close to me who was not a career officer was Bruce Johnson, an old friend from Mexican border days. He had been commissioned a captain and had talked his way by military aircraft all the way to North Africa. His ticket: a packet of letters addressed to me from Washington. He showed up one day in Algiers, much to my pleasant surprise. He said, "Sir, Captain Johnson reporting for duty. I am instructed to give you this packet. I must have your signed receipt."

I was glad to see Bruce but didn't know what to do with him, so I turned him over to Jack Allard to find a suitable job that would take advantage of Bruce's unusual ability to acquire life's necessities and make our war as comfortable as possible, as he had done on the Mexican border years before. We were quartered in the Shell Oil Company building in Algiers, so Jack made him the headquarters commandant. It was an ideal job for Brucie. He saw to local security for the headquarters, acquisition of office space, handling of food service facilities for us, and making sure we always had ground transportation available. He did such a good job right away that I promoted him to major about six weeks after he arrived.

In typical Johnson form, he wrote into his own headquarters regulations the statement: "In exercising the allotted function, the Headquarters Commandant is authorized to issue in the name of the Commanding General such instructions as become necessary." I didn't mind because I was sure he would never do anything for his personal gain but only for the benefit of all of us in the headquarters. I just didn't want to know the details of whatever it was he did.

Bruce's job was also to mollify and cooperate with the British as much as he could to get the job done as he saw it. He noted in his memoirs:

> Getting along with the British was almost as hard as winning the war. I did business with them almost daily in supplies, but the American troops and officers in my command did not see eye-to-eye with their allies. They treated us like step-children, unwelcome ones at that, and more than once a group of Britishers would force one of our soldiers into the street from the sidewalk. These situations developed into head-on collisions and I had to keep an iron hand to prevent all-out combat.[1]

The guiding light in all we did in the 12th in those initial days was Major General Tooey Spaatz. He made sound decisions and never lost sight of the objective. It was announced on December 5, 1942, that he was acting deputy commander in chief for air, Allied Force, in addition to his other duties. This was a good idea because the men who had planned and organized the 12th could continue in the same relation to it.

It was the coordination of the British and American air effort that gave us headaches. It was decided that a complete and separate higher headquarters should be established to prevent misunderstandings and botched missions. On January 5, 1943, a new headquarters was activated, called the Allied Air Forces, with Tooey Spaatz in charge. Thus, the 12th Air Force, Eastern Air Command (RAF), and some French air units were brought together under one commander. However, the commanders of the 12th and the Eastern Air Command were each given clear and distinct operational responsibilities. I would support the U.S. ground forces under General Patton; the commander of the British Eastern Air Command, whoever was to be appointed, would support their 1st Army. If the situation warranted, we could switch operational control back and forth with Tooey's approval.

Serving within this basic organization were all the fighter, bomber, transport, and support wings and groups, who had to be indoctrinated and learn what was expected of them. I saw it as my job to visit every unit I was responsible for, find out what their problems were, and seek solutions. To do this, I flew a B-26 mostly, but occasionally took a P-38 or Spitfire because of their increased speed. I flew on B-26, B-25, and B-17 missions as copilot or observer. I would drop into a field and announce that I was going to fly with them that day, climb aboard one of their planes, and go. I was convinced that nothing gives your men the confidence in you and in themselves that having you go with them does. I have often heard some lads say about their commanders, "Must be an easy one today, the old man is going." So I picked only the tough ones. I selected aircraft that would be flying in different spots in a formation so I would know firsthand what difficulties they had joining up, flying formation, approaching the target, dropping their bombs, evading flak, and returning to base. I also wanted to see firsthand the tactics of enemy fighters. There was no better way to get that kind of information.

I had some "interesting" experiences, but my luck held. Got shot up by enemy flak and fighters quite a few times, but was never shot down. The aircraft I occupied were never damaged severely and no one was wounded. In North Africa, as in Europe, the greatest difficulties were posed not by the enemy but by the weather.

I learned a lot on each mission I flew and passed my information on to other units I visited. I never wanted anyone in my command to think the "old man" wouldn't fly the rough ones. I never wanted any pilot or crew member in any units I commanded to say I didn't know what I was talking about when it came to bombing tactics, flak and fighter evasion, and formation flying.

Probably the most valuable thing I learned was that American lads wanted to know only three things: that the job they were given to do was worthwhile, that the sacrifices they made were appreciated, and that they had a fair chance of survival.

One of the capabilities we needed badly in the early days in North Africa was photo reconnaissance, so we could assess the results of our attacks and determine future targets. The first photo mission flown was made by Lieutenant Colonel James Anderson in a modified B-17. A unit of camera-equipped British Spitfires had been transferred from England to help us, but their airfield at Maison-Blanche was bombed day and night by the Luftwaffe after the Allied landings. Within a few days the Spitfires were only piles of wreckage.

Anderson's flight of November 19, 1942, was one to remember. He headed for the Kasserine Pass, where the Germans were massing their forces. He stayed above the flak level until he reached the pass, then dove the Fortress down to about 6,000 feet to photograph the activity below. He then flew to Gabes and made three photo runs over the city before returning to Algiers. He logged seven and a half hours flying time that day. When he returned, we had his film developed quickly. Since we had no photo interpreters assigned, the two of us analyzed the pictures ourselves and saw what targets had to be hit as soon as possible. They were.

One of those responsible for getting us excellent photos during this campaign was Elliott Roosevelt, son of the president. He was not a pilot but flew on many missions as an observer. I wrote to Joe that I had the pleasure of decorating him "to get even with his old man for decorating me."

During those beginning weeks, we were having a very high rate of training accidents in the B-26 Marauder. The word was out that it was a "killer," and I suspect that many crew members were convinced they could never survive the war in that airplane, not because of the enemy but because they would meet their maker in a noncombat accident.

Having tested the airplane thoroughly before many of the combat crews had ever seen one, I knew it was my job to show them it was an airplane to be respected but not feared. Paul Leonard, my faithful crew chief on the Tokyo raid, was still with me, and I took him along as my copilot to the various B-26 units to show that it could easily be flown as a one-pilot airplane, although regulations required two pilots on every flight. When they saw Paul in his mechanic's coveralls refuel and care for the plane and found there was no one else aboard, they had their first lesson in B-26 management—it could be flown as easily with one pilot as with two. Proper training and confidence in the equipment was the answer, and I stressed this to the group commanders and the pilots. I then put on a show for them to prove that single-engine operation was as easy as flying with both engines operating.

On one occasion, I took Major Paul W. Tibbets up for a ride. Paul was one of the pilots who had flown General Eisenhower down to Gibraltar and was partial to the B-17 because he felt the role of the B-26 as a medium bomber would be limited. He wanted to fly the big ones, but I wanted him to see what the Marauder could do. Paul tells what we did in his memoirs:

> I should have suspected that Doolittle knew more about the B-26 than he admitted when he said, "It's just another airplane. Let's start it up and play with it."
>
> That is exactly what we did. We got in the air and circled to 6,000 feet, remaining close enough to the field to reach the runway if we had trouble. But everything went smoothly.
>
> Doolittle then shut down one of the engines and feathered the propeller. He got the plane trimmed and we did some flying on one engine, turning in both directions, climbing, making steep banks. The Marauder was a tame bird with Doolittle at the controls.
>
> Suddenly he put the plane into a dive, built up excess speed, and put it into a perfect loop—all with one engine dead. As we came to the bottom of the loop, he took the dead propeller out of feather and it started windmilling. When it was turning fast enough, he flipped on the magnetos and restarted the engine as we made a low pass over the airfield. We came around in a normal manner, dropped the gear and the flaps, and set the B-26 down smoothly on the runway.
>
> The pilots and operations people who had been watching us were impressed. The flight was an important start toward convincing them that the B-26 was just another airplane.[2]

There was one B-26 trip that Paul Leonard, my crew chief, and

I took to Youks-les-Bains, Algeria, that I have tried to forget but can't. I had to go into town to attend to some business with the ground commanders there. I left Paul to take care of the airplane. About midnight that night the Germans came over and bombed the airfield. I tried to get out there to see if our plane had been damaged but couldn't because an ammunition dump had been hit along the road and ammunition was exploding all over the place.

The next morning I found the airplane. Paul had moved it to the other side of the field. The plane was there but not Paul. I found that he had manned the top turret machine gun in the plane as long as the batteries held out and had shot back at the German planes that were bombing and strafing the field. Empty .50-caliber shells were all over the place beneath the plane.

Finally, I found a bomb crater nearby. It was part of an older one and I pieced together what had happened. Paul had fought the attackers as long as he could and then leaped into the crater for protection. But another bomb, aimed at the plane, had missed its mark and had hit the old bomb crater instead.

I found what was left of Paul. It was his left hand off at the wrist, with a wristwatch still in place. This was all that remained of the wonderful boy who had tried to cheer me up in China in my saddest moment. I had to write to his widow to tell her the bad news. I said, "The softening point of this tragedy is that he never knew that it was coming and never knew that it hit him. If he had to go it was the way he would have preferred, quick, clean and painless."

Paul's loss was my greatest personal tragedy of the war.

In January 1943, President Roosevelt and Prime Minister Winston Churchill met with the Combined Chiefs of Staff in Casablanca. Four of the seven basic decisions they reached affected what we were trying to do in North Africa. Our job was to continue the assault against Germany, knock Italy out of the war, and draw enemy attention away from Russia. After we completed the Tunisian campaign, we were to invade Sicily in June or July. A high priority was to be given to a combined bomber offensive against Germany and German-occupied Europe from the United Kingdom. Hostilities would be terminated only upon the unconditional surrender of the enemy.

These decisions may seem elementary in hindsight, but they gave guidelines for future actions to those of us at the lower echelons. It was our road map. It was the job of people like me to follow the map and carry out the strategy worked out at the highest levels of our governments. The military forces of the allied nations wanted to achieve these objectives. However, combining these forces in a harmonious way when they were spread out over great distances proved extremely difficult.

The victory over Tunisia we had hoped we could achieve was not possible in December 1942. Heavy rains had kept us on the ground and stalled the advance of our ground troops. The day after the Casablanca Conference ended, I sent a confidential memo to my commanders and their subordinates:

> You and I know that the 12th Air Force was faced with tremendous problems when it arrived in North Africa. Expected equipment did not arrive, was incomplete, or wouldn't work. Officers and men alike lacked training and experience in the type of warfare with which we were faced. . . . We arrived in the rainy season, and the mud made airports impossible and living conditions unpleasant. The move to the eastward was more rapid than had been planned and the 12th was obliged to move forward, fighting, far ahead of schedule and under the most difficult conditions.
>
> In order to meet a threatening situation, you have been obliged to fly long missions over highly defended territory, under extremely difficult operating conditions. To the best of my knowledge and belief, you have flown more missions under such conditions than were ever accomplished before. In the past two months you have dropped thousands of tons of bombs, shot down or destroyed hundreds of enemy aircraft, and damaged many more. We have had losses, too, but the enemy has paid a price of more than two to one for every airplane we have lost. This record against an experienced enemy, operating from established bases, is better than good—it is damned good.

While we were trying hard to organize the air effort to bring pressure on General Rommel and drive the Axis forces out of Africa, the ground forces didn't find the going as easy as they might have first believed it would be. The Germans had forced the Allies out of Tebourba, Tunisia, but Monty Montgomery had forced Rommel to retreat from El Agheila. The situation stabilized in north and central Tunisia by the end of December 1942. But in the middle of February, Rommel forced a showdown and American forces were pushed back at the Kasserine Pass after a 10-day battle.

By May 3, however, the British had recovered and began a final offensive in Tunisia; Bizerte and Tunis were taken on May 7. On the thirteenth the last Axis forces surrendered. Altogether 250,000 troops were captured in the final days, half of them German.

The trials and tribulations we weathered in North Africa were great learning experiences for all of us. Unfortunately, during the first three months we had not yet been able to conduct strategic operations against targets in Sardinia, Sicily, and Italy to the extent we had originally intended, although we did let the enemy know we were coming by staging raids as often as we could to Palermo, Sicily, an important shipping point between Italy and Tunisia. Our attention had to be devoted to attacks against enemy aircraft on airports, bridges, communications facilities, and supply lines that connected the Axis forces with Europe. On February 7, however, our bombers were so effective against torpedo bomber installations on Sardinia that not a single enemy torpedo bomber was able to attack a British convoy progressing from Algiers eastward along the coast of Africa. Tooey Spaatz, in one of his frequent personal letters to Hap Arnold, gave his assessment of the situation as of the middle of February. He reported favorable results against bridges, railheads, and shipping, and noted that medium bombers were successful with area bombing targets at medium and low altitudes, but were not doing well with precision bombing. However, low-level attacks against surface vessels using skip bombing tactics were very profitable. He predicted that results were certain to improve tremendously with development of intelligence and communications, with the arrival of P-38 aircraft, and with the arrival of the 86th Dive Bombardment Group. Tooey wrote:

> Of all our fighter aircraft, the P-38 deserves special mention. As reports indicate, P-38s have been shot down but the enemy refuses to attack unless he has

> superior numbers and altitude advantage. In spite of these unbalanced encounters, the P-38 has accounted for 127 German aircraft of all kinds while losing only 74 to enemy aircraft (as of February 5, 1943). This ratio might well be higher except that escort missions necesarily limit freedom of action.
>
> As escort for the bombers, P-38s have contributed largely to successful bombing by actively denying enemy attacks on bombers (especially over the target), by boosting the morale of bomber crews and by furnishing cover for straggling crippled bombers. On January 12 a section of 12 P-38s successfully defended a badly damaged B-17 from persistent enemy fighter attacks while returning from Tripoli more than two hours overdue.
>
> As a low altitude ground support aircraft, the P-38 has established itself as a dual purpose weapon. The ship has high speed for surprise and the necessary heavy fire power. Its distinctive appearance assists the pilot materially in that he may operate at very low altitude without hesitation or fear of friendly ground fire, thereby permitting more complete concentration on the job at hand.

Tooey commented on the use of the Spitfires, P-39s, and P-40s as escorts and against ground targets. The "ever dependable" C-47 was praised for the air movement of supplies and equipment, and the B-17 for its ability to score against a variety of targets. He reported that 125 enemy aircraft had been destroyed, with the loss of only seven B-17s.

Two days later, Tooey wrote to Hap again to explain how he was reorganizing his forces based on a decision by the American and British chiefs of staff at the Casablanca Conference. The Eastern Air Command and the 12th Air Force were to be formed into a single air force to be known as the Northwest African Air Force (NAAF). The staffs would be made up of a mixture of British and American officers.

I was to be relieved of command of the 12th and take on a new job. I wasn't happy about it. In my final staff meeting as commander of the 12th, held on February 22, I explained the situation as I saw it. I said there were two schools of thought about the administrative setup of the new organization. One school of thought believed that the highest levels of the new command should be composed of British and Americans, while lower echelons should be segregated because of differences in arms, in temperament, in training and operations, in equipment, in supplies, and so on.

The other school of thought was consolidation, which felt that throughout all echelons, from the highest to the lowest, British and American people should be thoroughly intermingled. Their belief was that through this, the real or imaginary differences could be overcome by close association. The differences were settled in Casablanca, when the President and the Prime Minister decided that consolidation was the answer. There would be one head of the air forces in the Mediterranean area. There would be one head for all air units in the northwest African area. Air Chief Marshal Sir Arthur Tedder would be the overall chief of all air units. General Spaatz would be head of the NAAF. They decided also that the NAAF was to be broken into four units: the Tactical Unit, Strategic Unit, Coastal Unit, and Service Unit. NAAF General Order No. 1 explained:

> . . . The Twelfth Air Force is to remain nominally in existence until such time as outstanding problems, particularly courts-martial, can be brought to conclusion. Then its skeleton, which will consist of the name only because all units will have been absorbed, will either have to return to the U.S. and be reformed or it will have to be abandoned through War Department orders. Then if the Twelfth Air Force is desired in the future it will have to be reactivated.

To show how rapidly plans changed during those trial-and-error days, the 12th Air Force was not deactivated. Tooey wrote to General Eisenhower several days later recommending that the 12th should continue "for an indeterminable length of time." Ike approved. Tooey assumed command of the 12th on March 1, 1943. Under the new arrangement, names were changed and a fifth unit added. I would command the Strategic Air Force; Air Marshal Arthur Coningham, the Tactical Air Force; Brigadier General John K. "Joe" Cannon, the Training Command;

Brigadier General Delmar H. Dunton, the Service Command; and Air Vice Marshal Hugh Lloyd, the Coastal Air Force.

It was the task of the Strategic Air Force to attack the ports at both ends of the Axis supply route across the Mediterranean and go after airfields that the enemy used for air resupply and as bases for their fighters and bombers used to attack our ports and sea traffic. I had six types of bombers assigned to me: B-17s, B-24s, B-25s, B-26s, A-20s, and two squadrons of RAF Wellingtons.

I was not happy about the organizational changes. I thought things were working out properly under the original organization as I had constituted it. It seemed like a demotion to me. I wrote to Joe in longhand saying that I was enclosing a typed letter that I called "a short report of my downfall," which is the way I saw it then. In the typed letter, I explained what was taking place and implied that I was being downgraded in responsibility with much-reduced control over operations. I wrote:

> I feel no resentment over the change, only a very keen disappointment that I have failed my gang. I had the administrative, technical, and even the tactical side in hand. The latter through competent staff and command personnel. On advertising and politics I was weak. I have found many times in the past that one can't simply do a job and rest on results. There are "angles" and in a job as big as mine was here, where conflicting desires between services and nations exist, there are more angles than a diamond has facets.
>
> In retrospection I see many mistakes. Places of weakness where immediate ruthless remedial action should have been taken. Accomplishments should have been pointed out—advertised. Above all, I should have fought for my job—thrown what little weight I had around in an effort to direct policy and overcome adverse politics. Politics! I have always sneered at the word "politics." Whenever anyone has failed he has never said, "I couldn't have cut her." Always, "Politics booted me out." Now I at least appreciate the power of politics, realize that it must be molded in one's favor, and understand that in some instances, nothing can be done about it by the individual concerned.

> I have advised Tooey that I will be glad to accept any job that he feels will take advantage of my training, experience, and ability and am now much smarter, ready, willing, and anxious to start over again.

I didn't know whether or not Joe really understood what I was trying to express, but my letters to her gave me an opportunity to have a catharsis and examine my own thoughts. Several days later, I wrote this to Joe:

> Have been on a half dozen missions recently and thoroughly enjoyed them. Got a bang out of watching our fine American boys in action. They are tops. On one occasion with flak bursting on all sides, we were taking violent evasive action. One burst went off right in front of the bombardier in the nose of the plane, a B-26. I was in the copilot's seat and watched him throw up his hands and fall back. Thought he was hit but it was only a close miss. He promptly glued his eye to the bombsight and said, calmly, "Hold her steady now, sir."
>
> Every indication was to call for further evasive action, but he had a job to do so requested straight and level flight. It was the most intense and accurate flak I or any of the rest of the gang had ever seen. We lost two ships to enemy fighters and one was badly shot up with flak. The latter got home and with only one badly wounded crew member.
>
> On another occasion, we were attacked from below by fighters. One boy said, "Shall I cut down on them?" Another said, "Don't shoot yet. You'll scare them away. Wait until they get closer." No worry about what the fighters might do to him, only wanted to be sure that they got close enough so he could knock them off. The enemy fighters must have had a premonition as they did not press the attack and finally went their way. This was a long-range mission in B-17s and we did not have fighter escort.
>
> Have a lot of stories and experiences to tell you. Guess I've gotten to the point where "every flight is an adventure." Have flown with each one of our bomber groups, sometimes as observer and sometimes as co-

pilot. They are all exceptionally good considering the fact that many of them had absolutely no combat experience when they arrived. They had to learn their jobs while fighting.

Notes

1. Johnson, Bruce, *The Man with 2 Hats*. New York: Carlton Press, 1967, p. 113.
2. Tibbets, Paul W., with Clair Stebbins and Harry Franken, *The Tibbets Story*. New York: Stein and Day, 1978, p. 123.

CHAPTER 14

After we began operations under the new command setup, I mellowed and wrote Joe in March that my job was "far smaller but equally interesting. As a matter of fact, except for injured pride, I like it far better as I have more time with the fighting men and very little 'diplomatic' work."

In April, I wrote, "Am doing my best and working the old shell 24 hours a day. One problem, originally, was that I argued with my superiors and, according to Army standards, wasn't severe enough with my subordinates. Have improved quite a bit. Now avoid inviting attention to the stupidity of my superiors but haven't yet mastered the art of bawling out my subordinates to cover up my own stupidity."

On April 4, 1943, I wrote: "Just heard a roar and went to the window. It was my heavies coming home. Guess I'm soft. Tears came to my eyes as I saw them lumbering along on the last leg of their trip home. Think we made history today, so remember the date. Imagine you will see the dope in the morning papers. Had intended to go along but got tied up in a conference and couldn't make it."

What was happening then was that we were making extensive attacks on German convoys trying to resupply Tunisia. We also mounted heavy B-17 raids on Sicily. What made our job easier was that our code experts had broken the German high command code and we were able to read most of their messages. The system was known as "Ultra" and access to it was reserved for only top commanders. Those of us who knew about Ultra were not supposed to fly missions. If any of us were captured, we might be drugged or tortured and let the enemy know we had broken their code. I disagreed with this policy and continued to fly missions. I felt the effect on morale of my being up there with my boys far outweighed the theoretical possibility of revealing intelligence information.

In early April we learned that preparations were under way by the Germans to mass about 500 airplanes—mostly Ju.52, Ju.87, and Me-323 transports—to shuttle troops and supplies from Italy to Tunisia. They would be escorted by Me-109 and Fw 190 fighters. Our attacking fighters subsequently shot down or destroyed on the ground nearly 100 cargo and troop transports trying to beef up the desperate enemy forces. We were getting less and less opposition in the air, thus enabling our ground forces to operate more freely. In short, we were proving our theories about air power by first getting control of the air.

The reporters covering the war in North Africa at this time reminded me about the raid on Japan on its first anniversary—April 18, 1943. Several of my Tokyo Raiders were flying B-25s and B-26s in 12th Air Force units then, and we were photographed having a mini-reunion in an Arab's old barn. We toasted those who couldn't be with us because of other assignments and those who would never be with us. We had no hard spirits to drink the toast with, but someone had liberated several bottles of champagne so we could fulfill that tradition. It was not what I had in mind when I promised them I would give them a party when we all got to Chungking. That same day, the War Department disclosed most of the details of the raid and revealed the fact that "Shangri-La," our departure point, had been the carrier *Hornet,* which the Japanese had sunk at the Battle of Santa Cruz in October 1942. President Roosevelt also announced the sad news that several of the captured raiders had been executed. He said, "It is with a feeling of deepest horror, which I know will be shared by all civilized peoples, that I have to announce the barbarous execution by the Japanese government of some of the members of this country's armed forces."

Concurrently, Hap Arnold prepared a message to all personnel of the Army Air Forces: "In violation of every rule of military procedure and of every concept of human decency, the Japanese have executed several of your brave comrades who took part in the first Tokyo raid. These men died as heroes. . . ."

As if in answer to Hap's message, we learned that Admiral Isoroku Yamamoto, the commander in chief of the Japanese navy, who had planned and carried out the attack on Pearl Harbor, had been shot down over Bougainville in the Solomon Islands on the first anniversary of our raid on Japan—April 18, 1943. His plane had been intercepted by Army Air Forces P-38s on the longest fighter intercept mission in history. It was a welcome announcement that helped to compensate for our sadness about those of our gang who had been executed.

The identities of those executed were not revealed. All we knew was which eight men had been captured. A few weeks later, reports of Japanese atrocities against the Chinese were released. They had been obtained from missionaries who had traveled through the provinces where most of us had bailed out. These were the Chinese who had helped us escape through the enemy lines or through whose villages we had traveled to get to Chungking.

When the North African campaign ended with the Axis surrender on May 13, 1943, the Northwest African Air Forces and the 12th Air Force had made three significant contributions to the victory: we had established complete air superiority over the African mainland; we had successfully interdicted the Axis supply lines by bombing their ports, sinking their ships, and shooting down their air transports; and we had given ever-increasing support to ground troops, which enabled them to conclude their land battles successfully.

When the score was added up, we had dropped 11,708 tons of bombs, shot down 1,304 enemy aircraft, and sunk 76 Axis ships. What made it all worthwhile was a "Dear Jimmy" note from General Eisenhower. He said, "President Roosevelt has asked that I convey his thanks for the superb job you have done in the Tunisian campaign. I am profoundly grateful to you and all portions of your command for having carried out their assigned tasks so magnificently as to earn this commendation from the President."

My elation at receiving this accolade was short-lived. Drew Pearson, the nationally syndicated columnist noted for his muck-raking and sensationalized reporting, wrote a column under the title "Headlines for Doolittle, but Not Planes; He's Restless and Unhappy." It said:

> While Jimmy Doolittle has been getting the headlines here, things haven't gone so well with him in North Africa. This is no fault of Jimmy's, just Army politics. Actually, it began long before the raid on Tokyo, when Doolittle, a flier in the last war, wanted to get in again. Jimmy held only temporary rank in the first war and was a Major in the Reserve Corps before this war started. So despite the fact that he had won the Schneider Trophy, the Bendix, Thompson and Mackay trophies, also had set the world's speed record, Army bureaucrats at first wanted to reinstate him as a Captain. They were overruled, however, and he came in as a Colonel, later climbing swiftly up the promotion ladder with the raid on Tokyo. In North Africa, however, Doolittle has chafed at inactivity. Here he was given a "strategic" command, not a "tactical" command. A "strategic" command means bombing fixed objectives; a "tactical" command gets into active battle with the enemy. Doolittle found that there wasn't much strategic bombing to be done in North Africa. Also he found that his bombers gradually melted away. He could get few replacements. Finally he was left with only a baker's dozen. Restless, chafing, he finally staged his bombing of Palermo, which electrified the world. Jimmy will never complain and probably will deny this, but he still is not too happy. An active, racing pilot all his life, he wants to be in the thick of things. But Regular Army Air Force commanders, always favoring Regular Army, don't give him planes.

This "publicity" made me very angry. As soon as I saw it, I immediately wrote to Tooey:

> Am sorry the attached article by Drew Pearson

> was printed. It is wholly incorrect. Am afraid my superiors will feel that I, directly or indirectly, instigated it. This is also incorrect. I have the best job in the Air Force. Strategic bombing is the Air Force. It represents Air Power.
>
> As a matter of personal pride, I should like some day, if it is ever unravelled, to resume command of the Twelfth Air Force. In the meantime, I am thoroughly happy and can think of no one I would care to trade places with.

Tooey immediately responded, saying that he knew I had nothing to do with it, and added, "I would not trade you for anyone else to be in command of the Northwest African Strategic Air Force."

I have been victimized by the press many times in my life, and this instance was not the last. I guess it is one of the penalties for being in the public eye. What has always grieved me is that some men and women journalists who would not steal, rob a bank, or physically mistreat anyone, will injure someone by making false statements in print without checking the facts with the person most directly concerned. Some will lie or misrepresent in order to get a story and, under the pressure of deadlines, will proceed with their writing undeterred by the truth. In wartime, an unscrupulous few will also refuse to honor security or respect what the military is trying to do to deny information to the enemy. I had many friends who were journalists—Lowell Thomas, Quentin Reynolds, Edward R. Murrow, Howard K. Smith, and Walter Cronkite, to name a few. They were honorable, ethical men who played by the rules and put country before self-interest.

Another "name" journalist who gave me a problem was Margaret Bourke-White, the famous and very charming woman photographer, who visited our units in North Africa in 1943. She arrived in Algiers from a boat that had been torpedoed, almost destitute except for a camera or two that she had hung on to through it all. I gave her handkerchiefs, towels, soap, and, grudgingly, my fancy green silk pajamas.

She then charmed her way onto one of our bases and took an infinite number of photos of two wounded German bomber crew members who had been shot down. She got to them before our own official prisoner interrogation officer did. He got there just as she was leaving, and the wounded men were so jumpy after her interrogation and photography that the intelligence officer was unable to get anything out of them. This was unfortunate because at this stage of the battle it was most important to get some information on the enemy's air effort. As a matter of fact, the Hun at that time had such air superiority that he was actually patrolling our forward airdromes.

On May 12, 1943, President Roosevelt, Prime Minister Churchill, and the Combined Chiefs of Staff met in Washington to discuss the next steps to be taken toward victory. They agreed that a cross-Channel invasion of Europe, code-named Operation Overlord, would begin on May 1, 1944. This was to be preceded by an intensified air offensive from the United Kingdom. Operations following the conquest of Sicily were to knock Italy out of the war; concurrently, the Ploesti oil fields in Romania were to be attacked from Mediterranean bases. Consequently, the Northwest African Air Forces were to develop and carry out plans to accomplish these objectives.

One of the missions I flew after the surrender at Tunisia was as copilot on a B-17. It was the most unsuccessful mission I ever participated in. We had learned that three Italian warships—two heavy cruisers and the battleship *Roma*—were in the harbor at La Spezia. It was desirable that they be kept bottled up there—even more desirable that they be sunk. My staff and I decided to devote three B-17 groups to the effort—one group to each ship—about 100 planes total. We loaded them with 2,000-pound demolition bombs and 1,600-pound armor-piercing bombs. We scheduled the mission for June 5, 1943.

We had no opposition en route to the target area. There was light, ineffective flak overhead, and the ships were in plain sight. All three groups dropped their eggs and we could see all kinds of geysers blossoming up around the ships below. We couldn't have missed, we thought, and headed home satisfied we had accomplished our task.

A day or so later, reconnaissance photos revealed that we had missed one of the cruisers completely and only a gun turret was damaged on the other; the *Roma* was sitting peacefully in its berth. One bomb had gone through its deck and came out the bottom without exploding. We had accomplished nothing. This was a disturbing revelation. What made it worse was that weeks later, after Italy had joined the Allies, the *Roma* left the harbor to be turned over to the British at Malta. Near southern Italy, a single German dive bomber dropped two radio-controlled bombs and sank it. Another one of Doolittle's embarrassing episodes.

I had a nice surprise in the summer of 1943 when Ike presented me with the Distinguished Service Medal. He sent me a "Dear Jimmy" letter, saying, "When you joined me last year in London, you had much of what it takes to exercise high command; but I am not exaggerating in any sense when I tell you that in my opinion you have shown the greatest degree of improvement of any of the senior United States officers in my command. You have become a soldier in every sense of the word and you are, every day, rendering services of inestimable value to our country and to the United Nations."

I still chuckle when I read this. It meant that I must have really had a long way to go in his estimation. I didn't mind the backhanded compliment. I had worked hard to gain his confidence and was glad he appreciated what I was doing.

Mail was a problem for all of us in the war zones. We were fortunate if we could get letters in less than two to four weeks after they were mailed in the States. I realized early the importance of letters from home. It worried me when I didn't hear from Joe for a while. When she did write, she would sometimes mention that she was busy on her projects, but didn't explain what the projects were. With me in North Africa, Jim, Jr., in the Pacific, and John at West Point, she had time on her hands, which was difficult for her to accept. She wanted to do her part for the war effort while the men in her life were each doing their share. When I eventually learned what she was doing, I was very proud of her but concerned that she was taking on too much.

Shell Oil Company officials were among the first to take advantage of Joe's help. She toured the Shell facilities in Texas, California, and elsewhere and gave talks to the employees. She was especially interested in chatting with the many women who were working in the war industries, to bolster their morale. She wrote an interesting syndicated column for wives of servicemen, which gave not only hope but advice. Here's an excerpt from one:

Recently I returned from a trip that took me from coast to coast and back again. In spite of the many signs I saw posted, warning against careless talk, there was an amazing amount of it in public places. I'm appealing to you to help stop the dangerous chatter.

First, when your husband receives his orders, don't ask where or when he is going. Military orders are military secrets and should remain so.

Almost two years ago my husband returned to active duty. To date I've found my first line of defense a full-time job in our home . . . that is, when we've been able to maintain a home. When he's away there have been many places for me to work. As a matter of fact, there is no day long enough for me to do the things I would like to do. Choose your particular place and work . . . work hard!

Guard yourself against the feeling of depression . . . it will try to overtake you. When it does, change your stance. Change horses in the middle of the stream if you have to. There again it will depend on you as an individual. Choose the thing that offers you the most.

If it's possible, write him . . . tell him you miss him . . . but don't fill your letters with petty grievances and woe. Write interestingly and amusingly. If you have a joke on yourself, repeat it.

If you have courage, strengthen it . . . if you have none, develop it. We'll need it all through this conflict and afterward. Develop a sense of humor and see that it helps you carry on. Tolerance, too, is essential . . . eliminate petty greed and jealousy . . . start today. Think nationally rather than selfishly . . . let's join together . . . do our bit and help our men win this war!

Joe kept a file of letters received and scrapbooks of news clippings as a result of her wartime efforts, which I didn't know about until afterward. She gave innumerable speeches and wrote many articles to sell war bonds, bolster morale at war plants, encourage participation in volunteer activities, and spread hope that the war would eventually conclude with victory.

As her visits increased and her availability became known, the Owens-Illinois Glass Company invited her to give "Uncle Sam's message to women" on their regular *Broadway Matinee* radio program, which she did for 14 months. She built up a corps of listeners who were inspired by her sincere, concerned messages. One of the themes for which she received wide publicity was telling her listeners not to insist on knowing what their husbands and sweethearts were doing and where they were going. "We don't have a need to know about military matters," she said. "Neither do we have a right to know."

The huge file of Joe's fan mail shows how greatly her efforts were appreciated. The large number of requests she received also show the pressure she was under as her fame spread.

Joe was an inveterate letter writer and kept accurate records. One year she listed over 600 letters written to friends in response to theirs or because she heard they were ill or she thought they needed a morale boost.

During the war, she refused to accept any income from her appearances, only expenses. In some cases, she paid her own way because the sponsors had no funds for guest travel and accommodations. When she received an honorarium of $2,000 from Owens-Illinois, she created the Doolittle Fund within the Air Force Aid Society, which had been organized to provide financial aid to families and widows of fliers who had been wounded or killed in action. She also received $5,000 checks from the Boeing Company, Consolidated Vultee, and North American Aviation, and numerous donations from other large corporations.

In 1944, she received more than $30,000 for her speaking and writing and always asked that all fees offered to her should be made out to that fund; she didn't want a single penny for her work. The fund was carefully controlled and was run by Bea Arnold, Hap Arnold's wife.

Joe attended many ceremonies such as tank and airplane christenings and campaigns for war bonds. On one occasion, she led the pledge of allegiance for 2,000 new U.S. citizens at a swearing-in ceremony in Baltimore. One ceremony that pleased me very much was the 1944 christening of the USS *Shangri-La* (CV38), a new Navy carrier named after the mythical place from which President Roosevelt said we had departed for the Tokyo Raid. In the invitation to Joe from Secretary of the Navy Frank

Knox, he wrote, "Prospective sponsors are advised that the Department has no funds out of which to defray the transportation expenses of the sponsor to and from the place of launching. Because of war restrictions it is requested that any information concerning the proposed launching date of this vessel be kept confidential."

Joe received many kudos and awards for her war efforts. One of them was during the *Carnation Bouquet* program, broadcast over 50 U.S. stations. The announcer said it all:

> To Josephine Doolittle . . . wife of Major General Jimmy Doolittle, who led the first bombing raid on the enemy capital of Tokyo . . . .
>
> For her constant encouragement of her husband's long and successful flying career . . .
>
> For hiding any worry over her husband's daring flights, behind her quiet pride in his achievements . . .
>
> For raising two fine sons, who are following in their father's "flying" footsteps . . .
>
> For her calm, inspiring faith in the Divinity that protects those who fly the skies to make them free . . .
>
> We present the Carnation Bouquet of Honor—to Josephine Doolittle . . . our tribute to her outstanding gallantry in daily living.

One of Joe's favorite wartime activities was her association with the rehabilitation center at Pawling, New York, which the Air Force had established to get our men back on their feet after being wounded or injured in line of duty. Joe soon found that not only did the patients need rehabilitation, but their wives and families needed counseling and information about long-term care for their men. She established courses for the wives that ranged from nursing to arts and crafts. She didn't reveal these things to me until long after the war, when we had a chance to go through her scrapbooks and photo albums. No man could ever be more proud than I was of her unselfish service to her country.

While we were preparing for the invasion of Italy, I grew concerned about our manpower resources. The nation was doing a good job turning out airplanes and everything that goes into or

> We will have to try bomber takeoffs from carriers. It has never been done before but we must try out and check on how long it takes.[1]

Officers in Arnold's War Plans Division studied this unusual memo from their chief and began checking the aircraft technical data to see if his idea for a North African invasion was feasible. Plans that might be followed to attack the Japanese home islands were also being studied in both Army and Navy staffs to attempt to come up with a workable plan to carry out the President's request in that part of the world.

Meanwhile, in the Pacific since the "day of infamy" at Pearl Harbor, one Japanese victory had followed another with discouraging rapidity. American forces in the Philippines were retreating to the Bataan Peninsula. British army forces, having surrendered their base at Penang, Malaya, were retreating everywhere, and the Japanese were able to continue their advance upon Singapore with only token resistance. In the Dutch East Indies, enemy forces had landed on Borneo, Timor, Celebes, and New Guinea.

The sinking of the British battleships *Prince of Wales* and *Repulse* in the Gulf of Siam on December 10 added to the bad news. The fall of Wake Island on December 23 confirmed the American public's worst fears that the situation was desperate and that the U.S. Navy had indeed been made impotent by the raid on Pearl Harbor.

As the year ended, organized resistance in the Philippines seemed at an end. On December 20, President Manuel Quezon and Vice President Sergio Osmeña were sworn in at the entrance to Malinta Tunnel on Corregidor. The Filipino and American forces were to try to hold out for six months to await reinforcements from America. These reinforcements did not exist, but the 15,000 Americans and 65,000 Filipinos on Bataan and Corregidor did not know it. All they could do was fight, try to stay alive, and hope.

On December 18, Amon G. Carter, publisher of the *Fort Worth Star Telegram,* wrote to his friend Major General Edwin M. "Pa" Watson, military secretary to the President. Carter suggested that 500 long-range bombers, manned by airline pilots, should bomb Tokyo. Watson forwarded Carter's letter to General Arnold on December 30. On January 7, knowing that the War Plans Division was considering all possible ways to bomb Japan, Arnold replied to Watson that "the fundamental idea is sound but the problem of execution is something more than that expressed by Mr. Carter. However, we will have a solution in the near future which we hope will get the results desired."[2]

On the evening of January 10, Admiral King went to the Washington Navy Yard and boarded the *Vixen*, a former German yacht, which served as his flagship and second office, where he could work undisturbed. Earlier that day, the President had reiterated his desire to strike Japan as soon as possible, but no one had yet advanced a plan to carry out his wishes.

After dinner, Captain Francis S. Low, a submariner and operations officer on King's staff, asked to speak with King privately. King, unsmiling and tired, asked what was on his mind.

"Well, sir, I've got an idea for bombing Japan that I'd like to talk with you about. I flew down to Norfolk today to check on the *Hornet*, our new carrier, and saw something that started me thinking.

"The enemy knows that the radius of action for our carrier planes is about 300 miles. Today, as we were taking off from Norfolk, I saw the outline of a carrier deck painted on an airfield where pilots are trained in carrier takeoffs and landings."

"I don't see what you're getting at, Low," King said, impatiently.

"Well, sir, I saw some Army twin-engine planes making bombing passes at this simulated carrier deck. I thought if the Army has some twin-engine bombers with a range greater than our fighters, it seems to me a few of them could be loaded on a carrier and used to bomb Japan."

King leaned back and said nothing for a minute. Low was not a pilot and fully expected to be rebuffed. Instead, King said, "You may have something there, Low. Talk to Duncan about it in the morning. And don't tell anyone else about this."

Low immediately phoned Captain Donald B. "Wu" Duncan, a 1917 Naval Academy graduate and veteran pilot, who was King's air operations officer. Early on the morning of January 11 Low cautiously presented his idea to Duncan. "As I see it," Low said, "there are two big questions that have to be answered with them, but crew training was lagging. In late May 1943, I wrote a letter to Major General Barney Giles, in charge of Air Force personnel in the Pentagon:

> I think we might as well face this problem now, and base our airplane production not on the maximum amount of aircraft we can build, but on the maximum number of crews that can be developed to most efficiently utilize them. We can either continue with the present airplanes and develop the inevitable surplus, some of which may be utilized in the OTUs [operational training units] and some of which may be given to any of those Allies who may develop crews to manage and man them or, alternatively, we may divert part of our production to the tooling up and manufacture of new and superior aircraft and thus automatically reduce the quantity and increase the quality of those aircraft we are producing.

I don't know that this letter ever did any good, but I had to get it off my chest. My feelings were the result of my command experience as of that time.

Once the Tunisian campaign was over, we began to fly more strategic missions against the Germans and Italians on the other side of the Mediterranean. The next large objective was Sicily, which we intended to soften up with continuous bombardment well ahead of landing ground forces. D-Day was set for July 10. This was Operation Husky. Concurrently, we planned to take Pantelleria, an island 53 air miles from Cap Bon, Tunisia, and 63 miles from Cape Granitola, Sicily. We also planned to take three small islands of the Pelagie group—Lampedusa, Lampione, and Linosa, which stood between Tunisia and Pantelleria. The plan to take Pantelleria was code-named Operation Corkscrew.

What was significant about Corkscrew was that it was to be the first attempt to conquer enemy territory with air power. The Strategic Air Force was committed to the action, and I had assigned four groups of B-17s, two of B-25s, three of B-26s, three of P-38s, and one of P-40s, plus three wings of Wellingtons. South African air force and British units were also assigned to me for this operation—making a total of 2,374 combat planes, of which 1,276 were serviceable. Our opposition was composed of 1,385 German and Italian planes, of which 698 were serviceable. Of their total, only about 900 planes were located within range of Pantelleria. We had a numerical advantage that we intended to exploit.

I sent out B-17s on June 1 to bomb the Pantelleria harbors and airdromes, and the rest of my inventory of planes to neutralize coastal batteries and gun emplacements. We continued the attacks for several days, always followed by photo reconnaissance to find out how well we had done. On D-Day, we offered the island a chance to surrender unconditionally by dropping leaflets and messages. We got no response.

According to plan, ships loaded with troops left North Africa and Malta and prepared to go ashore on the night of June 10-11. Meanwhile, we kept up our bombing attacks and began to furnish air cover for the ships. British cruisers opened fire on the island, and the first assault landing craft began the run to the beaches. There was no opposition. Our reconnaissance photos showed a large white cross on a runway at their principal airport. As a British committee that studied the operation reported, "Active resistance on Pantelleria had ceased when the amphibious forces arrived."

As far as we know, the only casualty was a British soldier who was nipped by a local jackass. There was no further need for my force to lay down any more bombs or for the Tactical Air Force to back up our ground forces with close air support. Contrary to some accounts, we did not fly in, land, and accept the surrender.

Between May 8 and the capitulation of Pantelleria, our bombers and fighters had flown 5,285 sorties and dropped 6,200 tons of bombs. We lost four planes shot down, 10 missing, and 16 damaged over the island. Tooey Spaatz sent me a letter of commendation in which he said the surrender of the island was almost entirely due to the precision and weight of our air attacks.

Despite our success, valuable lessons were learned from Corkscrew. We needed improvements in communications and coordination of intelligence, better control of our fighters, and some system of canceling attacks to prevent hitting our own troops. An analysis was quickly made to determine the effects of our effort. The official history of the Air Force comments:

> The evidence showed how extremely difficult it was to obtain direct hits on an object as small as a gun emplacement even when there was little or no enemy interference. Examination of 80 guns which had been attacked from the air showed that . . . only two batteries had received direct hits. Inconclusive evidence indicated that in attacks on batteries the effective radius of the U.S. 1,000-lb. bomb was only one and a half times that of the 500-lb. bomb; hence it was better to use the smaller bomb against pinpoint objectives because of the larger number of bombs which could be employed.[1]

As far as I was concerned, air power had been the major reason the island surrendered. Problem was, I told reporters that I thought so. Apparently, I had implied that strategic bombardment would decide the outcome of the war and that the surrender of Pantelleria had proven this doctrine. The statistics were in my favor: my Strategic Air Force had dropped 80 percent of the bombs; Air Vice Marshal Arthur Coningham's Tactical Air Force, 18 percent; and naval forces, the remaining 2 percent.

When Ike read an article quoting me about these statistics, I found myself once more crosswise with him. He prepared a memo for Tooey Spaatz referring to what the press reported and said my statement had "escaped proper action by the censors." He concluded: "It is highly unwise, therefore, to issue statements that generalize and develop a doctrine of war from incidents that happen in our theater." Ike never sent the memo to Tooey. Instead, Ike read it to him, and I found myself once more having to prove myself to the theater commander.

Later, to appease my critics, I revised my statement to conclude that it was a "combined naval and air victory." In view of the statistics, I wish now I hadn't given in and said that.

After the fall of Pantelleria on June 11, we used the island as a base so that we could now concentrate on Sicily—Operation Husky. Our combined air forces put increased pressure on enemy airfields and ports while at the same time bombing major strategic targets in Italy and Sardinia. As we sent out our combined air forces day after day, the enemy's air opposition got stronger; our main objective was to knock out those intercepting planes either in the air or on the ground. By D-Day on July 10, about half of the island's planes had been driven to the mainland. We counted about 1,000 enemy aircraft destroyed or abandoned on the ground in Sicily. Only 139 enemy planes were downed in combat as we wore down the numbers that got airborne.

Husky came off as scheduled with assault forces and paratroops taking over their land objectives, but not without strong resistance. The main Allied landings by George Patton's 7th Army and Montgomery's 8th were followed by 38 days of hard fighting as they raced each other to be first to take Messina, the city nearest the "toe" of Italy. Georgie won. Meanwhile, NAAF planes battered the island day and night; the 16 hours of daylight were a big help. The going was not easy for the airborne glider troops and paratroopers being ferried to the drop zones. The fire from the ground was intense from the time the planes were on their approach and over the island. Sixty percent of the paratroopers were dropped far from their intended drop zones. According to one historian, on one of four airborne troop missions, 124 C-47 transport planes were dispatched with British troops aboard; of these, 11 were shot down by friendly fire, 50 were damaged, and 27 returned to base with full or partial loads undropped. On other missions, a total of 23 C-47s was lost, the 2,000 paratroopers who were dropped suffered heavy casualties, and half of the planes that returned to Tunisia were heavily damaged.

It was certainly not a successful operation as far as airborne operations were concerned. Tooey Spaatz wrote to Hap Arnold that parachute and glider operations could be conducted without excessive losses only if surprise were obtained. He believed that airborne troops could not be dropped into an organized battle position without incurring heavy losses.

General Eisenhower appointed a board of officers to study what had happened and it was concluded that the decision to carry out or terminate an operation must rest with the air commander in charge, since every feature of the mission—such as fighter protection and routing—was an air matter until after the drop was made. Planning had to be centralized in one headquarters under the air commander. In addition, missions that would take place over water had to be made known to any naval forces involved; concurrently, air force commanders had to realize that surface vessels are sensitive to air attack and could not afford to tolerate aircraft in their vicinity unless the planes were positively identified as friendly. All of these lessons were valuable for the operations to come later in the invasions of Italy and Normandy.

After Sicily had been captured, I reported my assessment of what we did:

> A part of Strategic's contribution to this operation was the careful herding of a large part of the Axis air force into a small area of eastern Sicily and then destroying it there. The method was simplicity itself. There were a limited number of airfields in Sicily. We started on those in the west, destroyed as many planes as possible on the ground (the concentration was high and dispersal poor) with fragmentation bombs, then "post holed" the fields with demolition bombs until they were no longer usable. The remaining enemy planes were forced to move eastward, securing operational fields in the Gerbini area. An all-out air offensive then destroyed many of these planes and drove most of the rest out of Sicily. The almost complete freedom from air opposition experienced by our ground troops spoke highly for this operation and for the effective cover furnished by the Tactical Air Force.

While we were supporting the Sicilian effort, we could not ignore targets in Italy. Once we had Sicily we could use it as a staging base, but that would take some time, so we continued attacks on strategic targets in the major Italian cities. One of the most important and potentially vulnerable was the pair of railroad marshaling yards at San Lorenzo and Littorio and the airports, all located a short distance from the central part of Rome. While we knew they should be knocked out, we were confronted with our first real moral problem. Rome was the world center of Catholicism and contained priceless art treasures and architecture, not to mention the Vatican. If they were destroyed, the Allies would probably go down in history as ruthless, barbaric hordes worse than those of Genghis Khan.

While we agonized, the Germans were using the marshaling

yards to distribute hundreds of troops into Italy to fight our forces in the coming Allied invasion. More airplanes were being massed on the airfields. If we went after these targets, it would be a challenge for precision bombing. We decided to try.

We prepared target folders that clearly marked the areas we did not want to hit: Vatican City, Santa Maria Maggiore, St. John Lateran, and St. Paolo Basilica. We had these marked in large letters: MUST ON NO ACCOUNT BE DAMAGED.

To signal our coming, we preceded the raid by dropping leaflets warning the populace of our intentions. This also served notice to the German and Italian military. We knew by then that the latter were wavering in their desire to continue on the side of Hitler, and we thought attacks on their capital city might hasten their disaffection.

We were concerned about the Catholic boys in our bomb groups who might have severe misgivings when they learned what the target areas were. We gave any Catholic crew member the opportunity to withdraw on religious grounds. I never heard how many, if any, dropped out.

Experience was essential, so we had to select the best of our bomber groups. I chose the 97th Bomb Group, led by Colonel Leroy Rainey, and I interposed myself into the copilot's seat on his airplane. We flew in the last plane—"Tail End Charlie." It was the most vulnerable position in any formation, but I wanted to see the results. We scheduled 500 aircraft for the initial mission—158 B-17s from my Strategic Air Force and about 110 B-24s from the 9th Air Force, as well as several groups of B-25s and B-26s, and P-38s as escorts. It would be the largest aggregation of bombing planes ever assembled up to that time.

The mission was launched on July 19, 1943. My B-17 formation attacked the San Lorenzo yards; the B-24s, the Littorio. We did major damage to the yards, but, unfortunately, a few stray bombs fell near the basilica at San Lorenzo, noted for its priceless frescoes. It was not hit, but suffered some blast damage. We followed up that day with B-25 and B-26 attacks on airfields near Ciampino and the Littorio. Much to our surprise, active enemy fighter opposition was light; only about 25 or 30 got airborne and made token attacks on our formations. The only planes lost that day were a B-25 and a B-26; none of the heavy bombers went down.

We knew that the German propaganda machine would go

into action and claim that we had deliberately bombed religious shrines, so we ordered reconnaissance planes to take aerial photos as soon as the smoke cleared. Ironically, it was the American and British press that gave us the most difficult time. We were accused of bombing indiscriminately exactly as the Germans had done against Britain in 1940.

Just as with the raid on Tokyo, the raid on Rome had a significant psychological effect on the Italian people. Taking their losses in North Africa and the islands leading to the mainland into account, they now doubted Mussolini's ability to protect them and lead them to victory. The alliance with Hitler soured and they no longer enjoyed having the Germans dominate their land. On July 25, 1943, shortly after our raid, Mussolini resigned.

In mid-August, President Roosevelt and Prime Minister Churchill and their staffs met in Quebec, and more decisions were made that affected our theater. The defeat of Germany was to remain a primary objective; an intensified combined bomber offensive was to be conducted, followed by the invasion of France (Operation Overlord), still scheduled for May 1, 1944. The invasion of Italy was to be speeded up now that Mussolini and his government had fallen.

The Italians capitulated on September 3, but meanwhile, the Germans had declared martial law in Italy, and it was clear that our invasion forces were going to have a very rough time. The German fighters became more aggressive, which meant they were probably transferring some of their best pilots from their eastern and western fronts. To divert the Germans' attention, I ordered a 180-plane bomber attack on airports in southern France at Istres–Le Tube and Salon, where reconnaissance indicated they had concentrated about 140 twin-engine bombers. They were probably there to divert our attention from Italy. Our bombers destroyed and damaged 94 planes on the ground and 23 in the air.

Between August 17 and September 6, NAAF planes raked Italy from the toe of the boot to the Brenner Pass in the Alps. Nearly 150 of the 12th Air Force's P-38s flew the first mass, long-range, low-level strafing mission of the war, against several airdromes around Foggia. Photos from the area showed that the Germans had gathered 230 planes there, which would pose a serious threat to the forthcoming landings by our forces. The P-38s destroyed or damaged 143 of them while losing only two.

The day the Italians put down their arms, I wrote to Brigadier General Hoyt Vandenberg, my former chief of staff, who had been transferred to Washington to become deputy chief of staff to Hap Arnold:

> The air battle is becoming interesting. The Hun realizes that if we are successful invading Italy, we can establish air bases and attack vital military manufacturing facilities in southern Germany. Apparently fearing this, he is fighting desperately. His fighters are far more aggressive than we have previously found them. He is using aerial bombing and rockets extensively. Yesterday, a half dozen rocket planes got through the fighter escort and attacked the bombers which had finished their bombing and were down on the deck. The enemy fighters raised their noses and lobbed a half dozen rockets in—without damage—before our fighters closed in and dispersed them. Sixty to 70 enemy fighters attacked the escort—they always attack now—and shot down six. Three more are missing. The P-38s shot down 23 enemy fighters.
>
> Every day brings its air battle, and while we are more than breaking even, the Hun has the advantage of initiative (against escort fighters), fighting over his own territory, and the inherent advantages in a short-range fighter over a long-range fighter. Our losses will increase until the Hun is knocked out.
>
> Our crying need now is for escort fighters. . . . I appreciate Eaker's need for escort fighters, but I feel that our need is equally great. . . . We will soon require escort fighters with the same range as our heavy bombers, so we might just as well start facing that difficult prospect.

Meanwhile, B-24s of the 9th Air Force struck oil refineries at Ploiesti, and a substantial part of Ploiesti's refining capability was destroyed. However, 54 B-24s and 532 men were lost. Attacks were made on Regensburg and Schweinfurt in which

U.S. forces operating from the United Kingdom lost 120 bombers and hundreds of crewmen. During one week, Eaker's 8th Air Force had lost 148 planes and had to cancel further deep raids into Germany. He pleaded for long-range escort fighters—P-51s with auxiliary drop tanks—which were then on the production lines.

The first landing of Allied troops on the Italian mainland took place on September 3, 1943. Other landings followed on subsequent days. All had heavy casualties. As the Allied forces plodded forward, the German resistance stiffened. However, by October 1, Naples and Foggia were secured.

As I look back on our campaign against Sicily, I am reminded of the trouble Georgie Patton, now a lieutenant general, was involved in because of the infamous "slapping incidents" that received wide, unfavorable coverage in the press. Georgie had been touring a hospital in Palermo, Sicily, giving out Purple Hearts when he came upon a young soldier who had no visible wounds. When Georgie asked him what his problem was, the soldier replied, "I guess I just can't take it." He was suffering from what the medics called "psychoneurosis anxiety state, moderately severe." Patton reacted by slapping the boy with his gloves, grabbing him by the scruff of the neck, and kicking him out of the hospital tent. Later tests on the lad showed that he also had malaria.

Several days later, Georgie visited another hospital and saw a boy who was sitting on his bed huddled up and shivering. Georgie asked what his trouble was and the boy replied, "It's my nerves. I can't stand the shelling anymore." Once more Georgie reacted imprudently. He accused the boy of being a coward and slapped him—hard. He shouted an order to send the lad back into the front lines.

When news of the incident reached General Sir Harold Alexander, Patton's superior, it was decided to keep the affair within the military family. Ike agreed but ordered Patton to apologize to the boy himself and to all those who witnessed the second incident. Patton did. It was Drew Pearson who blew the whistle on Patton in a radio broadcast in late November; the incidents had occurred in August. Although many newsmen covering the war knew about them, they had agreed to keep the story quiet in the national interest.

The Stateside press and thousands of Americans at home bombarded Washington with demands to have Georgie court-martialed and thrown out of the Army. Ike had to take some action. He reprimanded Patton severely and sent a detailed report to General Marshall and Secretary of War Stimson, both of whom supported Georgie. The end result was that Patton was withdrawn from consideration to lead American troops in the invasion of Italy. He was exiled to remain in Sicily at Palermo as sort of a military governor.

One day while I was flying from Italy back to my base in North Africa, I decided to call on Georgie because I knew he must be depressed. As I approached the field, I called the tower, identified myself, and said I would like to land and pay my respects to General Patton if that was agreeable and convenient. I was cleared to land. When I parked, there was Georgie in his famous Jeep with the three-star flags flying, his helmet reflecting the sun gloriously and his ivory-handled revolvers at his side. He rushed forward, threw his arms around me, and with great tears streaming down his face, said, "Jimmy, I'm glad to see you. I didn't think anyone would ever call on a mean old son of a bitch like me."

Georgie was fortunate that Ike didn't send him home, but Ike knew he would be needing him for the battles ahead on the Continent. There were no other battlefield generals who could inspire his men as well and accomplish what Georgie could with such total dedication. To Ike, Patton was one of those rare, indispensable leaders who won wars; unfortunately, men like Georgie were too often unfit for peacetime assignments. I have often thought Ike used Georgie as one would use a pit bulldog. When there was a fight, he would tell Georgie to "sic 'em." But when the fight was won, he would have to put him in isolation somewhere until the next scrap. However, no matter how Ike felt toward officers who were his longtime friends, he never let friendship interfere with his judgment in regard to the objective at hand. As an example, a certain major general whom Ike had known at West Point became very talkative at an English pub about the date and some aspects of the Normandy invasion, even though he had not been briefed and knew none of the details. When Ike learned about it from counterintelligence sleuths, he promptly demoted him and sent him back to the States as a colonel.

One of the big missions we set up was a coordinated bomber

offensive whereby aircraft from the RAF and the 8th in the United Kingdom and our air forces in North Africa would attack German targets from two directions. On October 1, 1943, we sent out four B-17 groups to attack aircraft factories in Augsburg, Germany. Simultaneously, five B-24 groups went after the Messerschmitt factory at Wiener Neustadt, in Austria. The B-24 groups found their target easily, but the B-17s couldn't see theirs because of a thick overcast; one group dropped their bombs by dead reckoning; the others had to bomb their secondary targets in Germany and Italy. We didn't expect the stiff defense we got from fighters and heavy flak. The groups were met by nearly 120 enemy fighters. We lost 14 B-24 Liberators and only downed about eight of their fighters. These attacks showed us what heavy opposition we were going to get when we continued to bomb the Fatherland.

The 8th Air Force and RAF bombardment units in the United Kingdom suffered very heavy losses, culminating in the "black week" of October 8–14, 1943. The losses and extremely bad weather forced a slowdown in daylight strategic operations from England. Full-scale operations could not be resumed until the new year.

During all the weeks of fighting the paperwork, sand, weather, and logistical problems in North Africa, I always tried to write to Joe so she would know she still had a live husband. I didn't get much mail from the boys; Joe would try to keep me informed about their doings, but they both apparently gave vague answers to her inquiries, so I seldom got any enlightenment. I always wrote what I could to her without divulging anything of military importance. Looking back over those letters now reminds me what I was thinking about then. Here are some excerpts from letters written in the fall of 1943:

> Must be getting cranky again. My aide suggested an inspection trip. That is his subtle way of indicating that I'm getting too grumpy to get along with and should therefore get out of the office for a day.
>
> Inspected two groups today and decorated almost two hundred officers and men. It was the biggest job of decorating that I've had yet. I've pinned on about everything but a Medal of Honor to date. Think the

biggest bang I got was pinning the Silver Star on Jack Allard. Have been obliged to do a few jobs in hospitals. Tough sometimes to decorate a boy who is shot to pieces—in pain—and getting the medal for one last thrill before passing on. Such a small payment for such a large service.

There is a bare possibility that I may remain in the Air Force—particularly if it becomes a separate service—after the war is over. Don't want any publicity about this. As you probably know, the only way I could be recalled would be to be made a permanent brigadier of the line. Talked this over with Tooey, who suggested it, and he intends to take it up with Hap. This is very hush-hush, naturally.

My spies tell me you christened the new carrier *Shangri-La*. Know you don't care for bubbly but it still seems a shame to waste it.

[We] can use all the good men we can get. Frankly, I prefer younger men as a rule because so many of the old-timers have slowed down. Many of the officers of our vintage who were red hot when we knew them in the Army are now unable to keep up with the tempo of this war and are actually a drag rather than a help.

Think I told you that Bob Hope and his troupe had been here entertaining the troops. We had them to supper the day they arrived and again the day before they left. They have been most generous with their remarkable talent and have brought a lot of happiness to my little flock.

I've just been advised that the King of England has made me a "C.B." A C.B. is a Companion of the Order of the Bath and is different from an S.O.B. Have heard that Ira was to be made a Knight of the British Empire but was not authorized by our government to accept the honor. If it hadn't been that our top people feel that it is undemocratic it would have been Sir Ira and Lady Eaker. Frankly, I'm very pleased that the British have seen fit to honor me, as I've tried to be eminently fair in commanding a combined RAF and AAF organization, and the award, to me, indicates that they appreciate it.

Got a note from Lowell [Thomas] mentioning Representative So-and-So's suggestion of "Doolittle for Secretary" [of War].

Think I am gradually selling myself to General Eisenhower but have a long way to go yet before he will be willing to admit that his original estimate was wrong.

Had a nice trip over Rome yesterday. Am very anxious to see Berlin from the air. Would sort of round out my cross-country.

Have finally come to realize what a good thing the plebe year at West Point is. The principle is that a man must learn to accept discipline before he can dish it out. I have never been properly disciplined. Would have gotten along better with my superiors if I had.

Haven't written to Jim or John for some time. It's hard to write of things I'd like to tell them and that they would be interested in, but when I delete those things that regulations forbid, there isn't much of interest to a kid left.

Sometime during December 1943, I received the news that some kind people in Los Angeles wanted to change the name of Los Angeles International Airport to "Doolittle Airport." The mayor fought this suggestion and wrote to me to ask for my support to leave the name as it was. I had always heard that airports were named for people only after they had passed on. I replied that I wasn't yet willing to make that sacrifice.

As we continued our strategic bombing attacks from North Africa, it was decided to supplement the combined bomber offensive against Germany by splitting the 12th Air Force into two air forces. The 12th would become a tactical air force and support the army advancing northward in Italy and the planned landings in southern France. The new air force, the 15th, would be the new strategic air force and would concentrate on bombing industrial targets in southern Germany that could not be reached easily from England. The 15th would be based on fields near Foggia. I was designated its commander.

The birth of the 15th took place on November 1, 1943, at Tunis, Tunisia. My orders read that I was to move my headquarters to Italy by December 1. Major General John K. Cannon replaced me as commander of the 12th.

Moving a large headquarters is no easy task, and I asked Bruce Johnson to do it in one day so we wouldn't lose any momentum with our operations. Bruce gulped and went to work. He flew to Foggia and found that "there wasn't one damn thing left in Foggia that wasn't blown to hell or too small." However, he found a huge building at Bari, a seaside resort that was unscarred by bombs. The building was the former headquarters of the Italian air force, which the British had control over. It was large and plush and was ideal for our purposes. The British gave Bruce a hard time, but I pulled rank on them and we took it over. Bruce met with the Italian general who occupied it and tells what happened:

> The Italian general was a pleasant-faced man, rather corpulent and voluble once he became friendly. I told him of the high regard my general held for his air force and then listened to his tales of how they shot down this and that for the better part of an hour. During a lull, I suggested how nice it would be if he and General Doolittle could have offices next to each other. He swelled like a peacock and took me on a guided tour of the place.
>
> Just before the day of the move, the Italians started raising hell over at their former headquarters. Some of them started ripping up furniture until I had guards posted. Then, a few of the lesser generals and colonels began trying to take this and that with them as they left. I finally got tired of the whole operation and had them kicked out bodily. I never did see my commanding Italian general. He just faded away, no longer dreaming of sharing office space with Doolittle.
>
> I was responsible for moving over 200 officers,

> 52 civilian technicians, and enlisted personnel whose ranks had been swelled to several hundred by a steady influx of new men. Just to give you an idea what makes a headquarters tick, stop to consider that I had to fit together a giant jigsaw puzzle—the Commanding General, his Chief of Staff, Personnel, Operations, Intelligence, Materiel and Maintenance, War Plans, Adjutant General, Air Inspector, Ordnance, Public Relations, Provost Marshal, Weather, Chaplain, Engineering, Communications, Quartermaster, Special Services, Medical, Signal and many others. I goddam near went nuts![2]

Bruce, true to his reputation, got us moved efficiently, and we kept on with our missions into Germany without missing a beat. But the Germans weren't pleased with our arrival. On the night of December 2, about 30 Luftwaffe bombers dropped parachute mines and bombs on the city and the harbor. As luck would have it, rather than skill at precision bombing, they hit two ammunition ships in the Bari harbor. The resulting explosions caused fires in adjacent ships, and the whole harbor was set ablaze. The explosions blew out windows in our new quarters. When we assessed the damage next day, 17 ships had been destroyed by fire and about 1,000 men had been killed or injured. I wrote to Joe next day that some unkind people had taken out our windows and I was writing to her with my overcoat on.

The raid should not have been that successful, but was the result of poor communications and coordination of our defenses. An important radar station was not operating that night, our night fighters were caught on the ground, and our antiaircraft batteries must have been asleep. Needless to say, my anger was transferred to where I thought it would do some good.

When the 15th was activated, 11 groups, consisting of 930 operational bombers and fighters, were transferred to it from the 12th. We had more than 3,600 officers and 16,900 enlisted men assigned. More aircraft and men were on their way from their planned assignment to the 8th in England. The goal was to build up the bomber force to 21 groups by March 15, 1944.

This diversion made Ira Eaker unhappy, but I had no say in the matter. It made good sense to me because, theoretically, we would have better weather and thus could launch more aircraft than Ira could from England, especially in the winter. It was the second time my air force had taken resources away from him. Ira was very annoyed and I couldn't blame him.

My assignment as commander of the 15th was spelled out as having four main objectives:

1. To destroy the German air force in the air and on the ground, wherever it might be located within range of our aircraft.
2. To participate in Operation Pointblank, the combined bomber offensive against aircraft plants, ball-bearing manufacturing sites, oil refineries, munitions factories, submarine pens, and airports.
3. To support the ground battle and attack communications facilities on the Italian mainland, along the route through the Brenner Pass, and in Austria.
4. To weaken the German position in the Balkans.

In addition to these goals, we were to choose targets that would pave the way for the invasion of southern France.

We started off the history of the 15th with a mission from Tunis to La Spezia on its first day. The next day, our B-17s and B-24s hit the Messerschmitt factory at Wiener Neustadt, a 1,600-mile mission that netted excellent results. That facility was turning out about 250 fighters a month. We estimated we put it out of action for at least two months.

Our bombers were met by about 150 German fighters that attacked them before, during, and after the bomb runs; they even flew through their own flak. Our fighters and gunners claimed 56 fighters destroyed, 27 probably destroyed, and 8 damaged. The price we paid was six B-17s and five B-24s.

We continued attacks like this, but the weather soured over the European targets in late November and December and we were able to mount only six similar attacks the rest of the year. We necessarily concentrated on communications, railroad marshaling yards, and airfields where the weather remained favorable.

On November 22, 1943, another strategy meeting of President Roosevelt and Prime Minister Churchill was held in Cairo. It lasted a week. Then they traveled to Teheran for a three-day meeting that included the Soviets, and returned to Cairo for another week's meeting.

At Teheran, it was agreed that, in compliance with Soviet requests, the Western Allies would give priority to Operation Overlord (the Normandy invasion) and Operation Anvil (the invasion of southern France). Stalin agreed on a major Soviet offensive in coordination with Overlord.

In addition to important decisions affecting the Far East, they decided at Cairo to establish a unified command in the Mediterranean under General Sir Henry Maitland Wilson. Ike would become supreme commander of the Allied Expeditionary Force on January 1, 1944, and take over total command of the all-out effort against the Germans planned for the next year. His deputy would be Air Chief Marshal Sir Arthur Tedder. Tooey Spaatz would move to England and head up the Strategic Air Forces, which would put him over the 15th and 8th Air Force commanders and thus coordinate our strategic bombardment efforts against Europe.

On December 9, Hap Arnold flew to Foggia where he met with Tooey, Cannon, and me to discuss what the conference decisions meant to us. As a result of our talks and unknown to me, Tooey returned to Washington and recommended that Ira Eaker be transferred to the Mediterranean to be commander in chief of the Mediterranean Allied Air Forces; I was to take his place as head of the 8th Air Force. Major General Nathan F. Twining would replace me as head of the 15th.

Ira was very upset when he found out about the decisions and felt that he had been fired. He sent an "eyes only" message to Spaatz, saying:

> Believe war interest best served by my retention command 8th Air Force. Otherwise experience this theater for nearly two years wasted. If I am to be allowed my personal preference having started with the 8th and seen it organized for major task in this theater, it would be heartbreaking to leave just before climax. If my service satisfactory to seniors, request I be allowed to retain command 8th Air Force. Reference your proposed slate, if I leave 8th Air Force recommend [Idwal H.] Edwards assume command of it. Also recommend Doolittle retain 15th. To do otherwise

> loses value of prior training and experience for their tasks in their respective theaters and at the most critical time.

Tooey replied that in view of the importance of having an American in command of Mediterranean Allied Air Forces and of establishing a U.S. Strategic Command in the United Kingdom, he thought the best interests in the conduct of the war would be served by assigning him as air commander in the African theater.

Ira also pleaded with Hap Arnold not to be transferred. Hap responded that "the broader view of the worldwide war effort indicates the necessity for a change." He thanked Ira for his "splendid cooperation and loyalty," but could not "see my way clear to make any change in decisions already reached."

General Marshall did not agree with the transfer of Eaker out of England. Neither did Ike at first, but then agreed that to have Spaatz and Eaker both in England did not spread out the talent sufficiently. Marshall did not overrule him. Like the good soldier that he was, Ira prepared to leave England without further argument. When his orders arrived, he replied to Ike on Christmas Eve: "Orders received will be executed promptly January one. Am in communication Spaatz discussing staffs and matters of mutual necessity." That same day, he ordered a mission that involved 700 bombers. It was a magnificent swan song that did him proud.

The New York Times editorialized that Eaker had demonstrated that mass air attacks could be made in daylight against heavily defended enemy territory after the Germans and the British had given up the attempt as hopeless. The editorial noted that Ira's transfer was a well-deserved promotion and that he would be missed in Britain, "not only by the officers and men of his command but by the British with whom he worked so smoothly."

Ira was given a very nice sendoff with a huge dinner in a hall at Bushy Park by his British and American staffs, in whom he had instilled a deep loyalty. It wouldn't be easy for me to fill his shoes. I was pleased that I had finally sold myself to Ike, but was sensitive about Ira's feelings. He had done a magnificent job of getting the 8th started, and I didn't want anyone to forget that. I hoped I could do as well.

I turned the 15th Air Force over to Nate Twining officially on January 3, 1944. I left for England accompanied by Brigadier General Earle E. "Pat" Partridge, whom I had selected to be my chief of staff.

NOTES

1. Craven, W. F., and J. L. Cate, *The Army Air Forces in World War II*, volume 2. Chicago: University of Chicago Press, 1949, p. 433.
2. Johnson, Bruce, *The Man with 2 Hats*. New York: Carlton Press, 1967, pp. 127–129.

CHAPTER 15

On January 5, 1944, I flew from North Africa to England. The next day was the birthdate of a "final" reorganization of our air effort to proceed with Operation Pointblank and get ready for the invasion of Europe. General Eisenhower set up Supreme Headquarters, Allied Expeditionary Forces (SHAEF), in London; the U.S. Strategic Air Forces in Europe was formed with Tooey Spaatz in command. I took command of the 8th Air Force effective that date and received promotion to lieutenant general two months later—the first air reserve officer ever to hold three-star rank. I wrote to Joe, "The confidence expressed by General Spaatz and General Eisenhower means far more to me, however, than the promotion."

Two days later, I moved my office from London to Wycombe Abbey, a women's college at High Wycombe, in Buckinghamshire, with the staff of the disbanded 8th Bomber Command as a nucleus for the organization. As soon as I had a staff assembled, I wrote to Hap Arnold thanking him for giving me the opportunity to head up the "mighty" 8th.

I soon found that letter writing was a large part of the new job. One of the first letters I received as commander of the 8th was a typical one from Georgie Patton, who wrote a note from North Africa: "Why the hell didn't you tell me you were going to England when I saw you the other day, so that I could congratulate you? In any case—in spite of your low nature, it gives me great pleasure to now congratulate you, and it may eventuate that our material desire to kill Germans in intimate association will be fulfilled."

I responded:

> Don't know whether or not congratulations are in order. I have a bigger and more interesting job, but at the same time it is infinitely more difficult than the one I had down below. Down there the problem was to make something out of nothing. Up here it requires an equal or greater amount of ingenuity to effectively utilize the almost unlimited resources at one's disposal. Down there, where you were not "under the guns," any modest success was apparently appreciated. Up here miracles are confidently anticipated. Have been a little slow in getting my Miracle Department organized but hope for the best.

I had addressed my reply to "Dear General Patton" and received a prompt two-sentence answer that was typical of the man and our friendship: "Why the goddam hell do you get so formal as to address me as General Patton? It would seem to me that two men of our low mental and moral characteristics should be more informal."

I inherited the 8th Air Force at a natural turning point in its history. Ira had left me a "going concern" that he had practically built from scratch. On August 17, 1942, Ira had personally accompanied the first independent American mission, led by Frank Armstrong, against Rouen in enemy-occupied France with only 12 B-17s while six others flew a diversionary mission. Seventeen tons of bombs had been dropped on enemy runways; all the bombers returned.

Due to the small number of aircraft and crews made available to him, Ira was never able to overwhelm the enemy's defensive force. Short on bombers and without long-range fighter escort, he had been forced in 1943 to absorb prohibitive losses of upwards of 20 percent on missions against such targets as Regensburg and Schweinfurt. Rarely was he able to send out more than 200 to 300 bombers at one time.

Hap Arnold was the decision maker, and he had not been able to give Ira the crews and planes he needed in time; although theoretically, the European theater of operations (ETO) held first priority in the overall war planning. Eaker had come heartbreakingly close to his goal when I took over.

The story of the 8th might be said to be the story of an experiment—to determine if the economic fabric of an enemy nation could be destroyed by daylight precision bombing. It was undertaken and successfully completed despite the experiences of the Royal Air Force and the German air force, both of which were convinced that losses of aircraft would be prohibitive in daylight bombing.

The British had tried daylight bombing when the war started, but they didn't have enough long-range fighters for deep penetration into enemy territory and their bombers weren't sufficiently heavily armed to make daylight bombing reasonably safe for the crews. The British fighters were chiefly for defense of their home island. So they adopted night bombing, and when Sir Arthur Harris, air chief marshal of the Royal Air Force, took over, his objective was to achieve maximum destruction, in the sincere belief that this was the best way to break the German will to resist.

Our outlook was somewhat different. Our bombers were much more heavily defended—they had many more machine guns. We couldn't carry as big a bomb load because our armament and armor took up space and weight that would ordinarily have given us greater weight-carrying capacity for bombs. At first, we didn't have enough long-range fighters either, but they were coming off our production lines and would be available later. So it was a tradeoff of risks. Our bombers were able to protect themselves better, but the British bombers could carry more bombs. Therefore, we committed ourselves to precision daylight bombing while the RAF specialized in area bombing at night.

After Tooey Spaatz arrived in England to take over as the first commanding general of the 8th back in the spring of 1942, he held an off-the-record press conference in which he said that the 8th was "interested" in the possibilities of daylight bombing. This shocked the British and American correspondents in attendance, but not anyone who had been following aviation news in the several years preceding our entry into the war. The

B-17 Flying Fortresses and B-24 Liberators were designed from the beginning for high-altitude, daytime, precision bombing. And this was done with the full knowledge that the RAF and German Luftwaffe had converted their strategic bombing operations from day to night because of their heavy losses during day operations over Europe.

When it became known that the 8th was committed to bomb by day, there was much official and unofficial criticism. A leading British aviation writer stated that while the B-17 and B-24 had done much useful work in antisubmarine and shipping patrols, they were not suited for combat over the Continent. He said it was a great pity that the U.S. Army Air Forces and the entire American aircraft industry had committed its vast potential to turning out bombers for daytime operations. Instead, in his opinion, we could have provided the British with a war-winning flood of four-engine Lancasters for night bombardment, which had been very successful. To their credit, Tooey Spaatz and Ira Eaker never gave in to the criticism that persisted throughout Ira's tenure as head of the 8th; the policy still had its doubters when I arrived.

The conflict boiled down to this: we believed that we could destroy the enemy's ability and will to wage war by hitting specified targets with precision, rather than by bombing large areas of cities in which thousands of civilians lived and worked. To us, it was the most ethical way to go. However, when the German aircraft industry went underground, we were forced to bomb the areas in which these factories were located. So the two philosophies made little practical difference.

After Ira took command of the 8th from Tooey on December 1, 1942, the number of bombers available to him slowly began to increase, although my requirements in North Africa had priority. In the beginning, British Spitfires were the only escort protection the 8th's bombers had available, and they could escort the bombers only 175 miles from their bases—about as far as Paris. In May 1943, Republic P-47 Thunderbolts arrived. At first, their range wasn't much better than the Spits'. However, 70-gallon belly tanks were added, and by July 1943 the P-47s could escort up to 340 miles. Then 108-gallon drop tanks were approved, giving the fighters 375 miles of range, or about as far as Hamburg.

By the time I arrived in England, 150-gallon tanks were available and we were able to hang two of them on a P-47, so they had a tactical radius of 425 miles. The Lockheed P-38 Lightning and the North American P-51 Mustang had greater range than the P-47s; they began to arrive in the theater in November 1943. These were given even more range with the addition of drop tanks, so that eventually the escorts could fly a very welcome 850 miles from their bases. This steadily increased range of the escort fighters was an inheritance from which I benefited as commander of the 8th; their genesis began long before I took over. It was my job to use this increased capability to best advantage.

One of my first protocol duties after taking command was to pay my respects to those I would be working with and for. I decided that I should ask for an appointment with King George VI, so I sent a letter to Buckingham Palace.

Of course, I was there at the appointed hour and when the king entered the room, I stood up. Without saying a word, he motioned for me to be seated. I said nothing because I had been told that any conversation should be initiated by the king. He was silent for what seemed like several minutes.

Feeling uneasy, I finally broke the silence by saying that I was very pleased to be in England, that my relations with the British were very satisfactory, and that one of my jobs was to see that the excellent relationship between the men and women of both nations serving in my command would continue.

He looked at me and said, slowly, "We're certainly sorry to lose Eaker!"

I was more than somewhat nonplussed. I said a few pleasantries and took my leave as soon as I politely could. His remark gave me a clue that I would have to work very hard to take Ira's place in the minds of the top-level British.

Another incident took place when I wanted to call on Air Chief Marshal Sir Arthur Harris of the RAF's Bomber Command—my counterpart. I was told I had to make an appointment, which I did. I entered his office, gave him a smart salute, and announced that I was reporting for duty. Sitting at his desk, he nodded and went back to shuffling some papers. After a minute or two, he finally motioned me to sit down and we exchanged brief comments. I left after a few minutes, but not without saying that he would always be welcome to see me in my office at any time—without an appointment.

The British, probably since the Middle Ages, have been

suspicious of outsiders until they prove themselves loyal to the Crown. I learned from a member of the press who was a good friend that their supersleuths had assigned a British intelligence officer to my headquarters who was to report anything I did that seemed worthy of inserting in a dossier they had started on me. Knowing this, I made a statement in front of this gentleman one day that was a little farfetched and inaccurate. Meanwhile, I put one of my counterintelligence men on my case and asked that he find the dossier and report what it said. Sure enough, my fallacious statement had been duly recorded.

There was also an entry attributed to Harris that was interesting. He noted that "Doolittle is entirely dependable but is more difficult to deal with than Eaker." Despite this air of suspicion in the beginning, "Bomber" Harris and I got along very well as we worked closely during the following months, and I benefited immensely from his wisdom and vast knowledge. I discovered that he liked garlic salt, so I asked Joe to send some shakers periodically to please his palate. No doubt it helped our relationship.

As quickly as I could after taking over, I visited every wing and group for which I was responsible and held meetings with their commanders and planning staffs to determine what missions had been planned before I arrived and what they recommended for the future. I received some good ideas and insight from those who had been flying the missions, and brought these thoughts back to my staff for discussion.

One of the ideas was to "shuttle bomb" by flying missions deep into Germany and continuing to western Soviet airfields for refueling and rearming. I proposed the idea to Tooey that, if the Soviets would agree, landing and refueling in the western USSR would break the long flight, tend to confuse the enemy fighter control, which would be alerted on the eastbound flight, and permit a surprise westerly return flight. If permission were obtained to use Soviet airfields, I suggested, then full information on aircraft recognition procedures and communications facilities between Soviet front-line bases, the United Kingdom, and Mediterranean air bases should be made available. I also requested that all interested Soviet agencies be notified when the aircraft were coming to avoid any possibility of our aircraft being inadvertently shot down. The seed was thus planted for a new way to get at targets deep inside Germany, but I knew it would be some time before it could be worked out with the Soviets.

Meanwhile, I got involved in operations and proposed some changes in bomber formations, changes that we had worked out in the 12th and 15th for better protection of the bombers. By this time, German fighter tactics had improved; new enemy armament outranged our .50-caliber machine guns. Rocket mortars, mounted on twin-engine fighters, were lethal beyond the range of our guns. An increasing number of improved P-47 Thunderbolt and P-51 Mustang long-range fighter escort aircraft, long planned, were due soon. With the addition of these long-range fighters, the bomber formations had to be reorganized so they could be readily escorted all the way to the target areas. The bombers had to be broken down differently in order to give a better bomb pattern and permit the passage of a number of units so rapidly over an area of heavy flak that the antiaircraft guns could fire on only a few of the units.

The mission of the escorts was unequivocal at that time: protect the bombers and not leave them. This policy concerned me because fighter aircraft are designed to go after enemy fighters. Fighter pilots are usually pugnacious individuals by nature and are trained to be aggressive in the air. Their machines are specifically designed for offensive action. I thought our fighter forces should intercept the enemy fighters before they reached the bombers. The "don't leave the bombers" escort philosophy came to a halt when I visited Major General William E. "Bill" Kepner's 8th Fighter Command. On the wall in his office was a sign: THE FIRST DUTY OF THE EIGHTH AIR FORCE FIGHTERS IS TO BRING THE BOMBERS BACK ALIVE.

I took one look at the sign and asked, "Bill, who dreamed that up?"

"The sign was here when we arrived," he answered.

"That statement is no longer in effect," I told him. "Take that sign down. Put up another one that says: THE FIRST DUTY OF THE EIGHTH AIR FORCE FIGHTERS IS TO DESTROY GERMAN FIGHTERS."

"You mean you're authorizing me to take the offensive?" he asked.

"I'm directing you to," I said.

Tears came to Bill's eyes. He had been urging Ira and Tooey for months to give him permission to go after the enemy fighters and had been turned down repeatedly. As a fighter pilot myself, I knew how he felt.

We discussed how he would unleash his fighters under my

new directive, and I liked his enthusiasm for my "escort the bombers but pursue and destroy the enemy" philosophy. I told him he would still assign fighters for escort duty, but the bulk of them would go hunting for Jerries. "Flush them out in the air and beat them up on the ground on the way home," I said. "Your first priority is to take the offensive."

As we shook hands and I turned to leave, I looked at that sign again. "Bill, take that damned thing down," I said as I went out the door. I heard him tear it off the wall.

Bill confirmed later that he was "overjoyed" at my decision and said he could now use his fighters as he knew he should. After he spread the word to his fighter boys, he told me they greeted the news with wild cheers. Not so with the bomber crews. As soon as my decision was announced to the bomb groups, their commanders descended on me individually and in bunches to tell me, in polite terms of course, that I was a "killer" and "murderer." I had taken away their "little friends" and they were sure their bomber formations would now be picked off wholesale. There was no compromise as far as I was concerned, and many bomber crews remained very unhappy. Some still are.

My decision was based on the fact that when I took over the 8th, we had greater numbers of long-range fighters and bombers assigned and en route to the theater than when the escort policy was originally established. The long-range P-51s that Eaker had pleaded for were now available; the P-47s and P-38s had long-range drop tanks added. All of them could now go as far as Berlin.

We used to call our fighters "pursuit" planes between wars, and that was what they were supposed to do—pursue the enemy. Fighter group commanders could now exercise their own judgment in leaving the bombers to search for the enemy, under the doctrine that such offensive tactics accelerated destruction of the German air force. If the German fighters didn't come up to the bomber formations to give battle, I wanted our fighters to go after them, picking out airfields, transportation, and other ground targets to strafe and bomb. In short, the doctrine was now one of "ultimate pursuit."

As far as I'm concerned, this was the most important and far-reaching military decision I made during the war. It was also the most controversial. Had we continued to operate our fighters defensively, however, the German air force would have grown until our losses became prohibitive. By initiating offensive action we took greater immediate losses; however, by neutralizing the Luftwaffe, we not only eventually reduced our own losses from six percent to six-tenths of one percent, but had the Germans out of the sky for the invasion.

The organization I had inherited was formidable. There were 25 heavy bomber groups assigned to me on arrival, plus 15 fighter groups. Also, the 9th Air Force, organized largely for tactical operations in support of ground forces, but independent of the 8th, gave us an additional 18 fighter groups if we needed them for bomber escort missions. That meant more than 5,000 combat aircraft were in the theater.

As I observed the planning, briefing, and dispatch of aircraft on missions, I found it necessary soon after my arrival to recall large bomber formations twice while they were en route to their targets, on January 11 and 24. On the eleventh, we sent out 633 B-17s and B-24s in three large formations, which were to be accompanied by several groups of P-38s, P-47s, P-51s, and Spitfires. The weather was poor, which caused difficulty in forming up the units over their bases; however, the weather was forecast to be satisfactory for visual bombing over the targets, which were fighter production plants at Oschersleben, Halberstadt, and Brunswick. I was assured their bases would be clear upon their return.

As the formations approached their objectives, I learned that the weather was closing in over the target areas. At the same time, the weather at our bomber fields was also going down. When the first division of bombers was about 50 miles from its target, I ordered them all home. All complied except one wing of B-17s, whose commander thought they might as well fly the remaining few miles and do what damage they could even if their bombardiers couldn't see the areas clearly. The other bombers were to drop their loads on secondary targets or targets of opportunity in western Germany on their way home. Of the original 633 bombers dispatched, 238 dropped their bombs on their assigned targets with satisfactory results.

Unfortunately, the Luftwaffe hit the bomber formations with great numbers of rocket-firing Me-109s and Fw 190s. Only one group of P-51s had been able to accompany the bombers all the way to the target areas and give them protection. We lost 60 bombers but no fighters that day; 39 German fighters were shot down. The weather closed in for the next several days and no missions could be dispatched.

The weather cleared sufficiently for another large mission on January 24, and I recalled the entire force for the second time. Once more the weather over the targets was not as forecast, and it was getting dangerously low at our home bases. When bad weather reached the coast of England, it might speed up, it might stand still, or it might slow down. Unfortunately for me, the bad weather approaching the coast slowed down and our bases remained open.

As soon as Tooey learned of my decision and saw that the bases were clear, he called me in and let me know in very specific terms that he thought I was wrong. He really struck me where I was tender when he said, "I wonder if you've got the guts to lead a big air force. If you haven't, I'll get someone else who has."

I tried to explain that I didn't want to gamble the lives of my men on an uncalculated risk. I pointed out that if the airfields had closed down we could have lost, on one mission, a major part of the force that we had so laboriously built up. It would have been a needless waste of lives and planes. Although he didn't answer, it was obvious that he didn't agree. Despite our long friendship, he dismissed me with a curt, "That'll be all."

As I turned to go, he handed me a letter that stated that in the future the doctrine would be that no recall should be issued by my headquarters after the aircraft crossed the enemy's coast. He advised that the commander in the air should be kept aware of changing weather conditions at the base and of conditions wherein he could not receive the fighter cover promised him. The decision was to be left up to the air commander as to what course of action he should take.

"We probably could get away with recalls as they occurred on the eleventh and twenty-fourth in most cases," he wrote. "However, the Germans are going to use every stratagem to turn us from doing our job, and one of those will be false recalls to our formations."

It was a mild written rebuke compared with what Tooey had verbalized. I admit I had difficulty holding my temper, but I accepted Tooey's right as my boss and Ike's chief air strategist to disagree with my decisions. He wanted Operation Pointblank to proceed as rapidly as possible. Pointblank was the operation designed to eliminate the German Luftwaffe and aircraft industry so that the Normandy invasion could begin on schedule (now the first week of June) without Luftwaffe interference.

I responded by letter that I agreed that recalling of missions should be avoided. However, I said we could not leave the recall up to the air commanders involved because the fighter commander handles fighter cover for the three air divisions, and any withdrawal or recall had to be coordinated through my headquarters in order to assure that no outfit was left without fighter cover.

In retrospect, I believe a part of the blame for the recalls should be shared by Colonel Irving Krick, who had given me an entirely wrong forecast about the weather on the 1934 record-seeking, coast-to-coast flight I had made with Joe aboard. He had promised excellent weather for the last half of our transcontinental flight, which did not eventuate. Now the top weatherman in our theater of operations, he had predicted that the two missions I had recalled would have no difficulty due to weather in finding their targets or returning to their bases. I'm sure he was an excellent meteorologist, but he probably thought his forecasting was more of a science than the art it really was in those days.

A few days after the second recall, Tooey invited me to go with him on *Boots*, his personal B-17, to inspect several of my units. His pilot was Lieutenant Colonel Bob Kimmel, who had a lot of heavy bomber experience. After visiting several bases, we remained overnight at one of them. The next morning we checked with the weather forecaster and were assured the weather was okay for more visits. We walked outside into a heavy drizzle with minimum visibility. Always suspicious of weathermen, I wanted to head for home before we got weathered in somewhere, but Tooey wanted to visit three more bases first. We did get to two of them, but searching for the third proved impossible because of ever-lowering overcast and decreasing visibility. Kimmel chose to stay under the clouds and hedgehop over the countryside, hoping to locate himself visually and find someplace to land. Hedgehopping in bad weather has killed hundreds of pilots before and since, and I had lost many friends who had chosen to stay in visual contact with the ground. I was more than somewhat concerned. I'm sure Tooey was, too, but he didn't say anything.

Kimmel finally found a pasture that seemed long enough for a B-17 and free of obstructions; he managed to sideslip the four-engine bomber in for a bumpy landing—heading right toward a stone fence. He jammed on the brakes and we stopped only a few feet from it.

As we got out of the plane, Tooey was a little shaken. He put his arm around me and said, "You were right, Jim. I see what you mean about uncalculated risks."

He didn't say any more. He didn't have to. It was a close call. He knew our kids flying the heavy bombers didn't have the experience of pilots like Kimmel. In those days, pilots were not getting enough instrument training in flying school. Their chances of surviving were greatly reduced whenever they had to descend through a thick overcast and attempt to find their bases under conditions of low ceilings and poor visibility.

My distrust of long-range weather forecasting surfaced many times during the succeeding weeks, and it came to a head again when I was giving a briefing for Tooey and Ike one day at High Wycombe. I was telling about a mission then in progress and explained that the bombers were proceeding to their secondary target. Tooey immediately interrupted to ask why. I said it was because the primary target was socked in.

"But Colonel Krick assured me the primary would be clear," Tooey said.

Before I could stop myself, I countered, "Colonel Krick is full of crap."

Tooey was shocked and there was an awful silence for a moment as Ike looked back and forth at the two of us. Tooey asked me why I would make such a derogatory statement. Colonel Krick was, after all, one of the top meteorologists in the United States, if not the world.

"Because we have a fighter pilot over the primary target who told us it was closed in," I replied.

It was true. Colonel Budd J. Peaslee, commander of the 348th Bomb Group, to his everlasting credit, had conceived the idea of sending out a fighter with one wingman ahead of the bombers to proceed to the target areas and report the weather. This was especially valuable as we moved deeper into Germany with our raids. Budd had been frustrated too many times on missions when his force was broken up and diverted because of inaccurate weather forecasts. It was a waste of effort and an unnecessary risk of lives.

As a result of Budd's suggestion, I approved the formation of the 1st Scouting Force, equipped with P-51s. They were piloted by bomber pilots who volunteered to serve a second tour for the privilege of flying fighters. This scheme enabled us to make best use of some of our veteran bomber leaders. They knew the limitations of the bombers and could make on-the-spot judgments. We were careful, however, to have the scouts fly to several potential targets, so as to avoid tipping our hand on what the actual target would be. It was an excellent idea that paid dividends in the form of fewer bombing missions canceled, lower accident rates, and lives saved.

Another idea we tried was the "flying bomb." This experiment was assigned to General "Pat" Partridge's 3rd Air Division. The idea was to take old war-weary B-17s, install radio-control equipment, and load them with 20,000 pounds of explosive or jellied gasoline. They would be flown off the ground by a pilot who would put the aircraft on automatic pilot and then bail out over England. A second B-17 would guide the "Weary Willie" by radio control and steer it into an assigned target. We called this project "Aphrodite." These "guided missiles" were not available in time to be used against V-bomb launching sites, but were used against a few targets in France. We eventually abandoned the idea as too dangerous when several blew up in flight with the pilot still aboard.

The exchange of letters I had with Tooey about the recall of the bombers presaged what I suspected would happen as I got more deeply involved in command of the 8th. I immediately had a mountain of correspondence to read and deal with daily that consumed much of my time. Maybe I was too concerned about it, but I have always thought, and still do, that all letters should be acknowledged.

One of those letters was from Hap in March 1944 that expressed his concern about the return of combat crews to the States after completing an "arbitrary" number of missions. Excerpts are worth repeating here for the record:

> When the opposition was much stronger than now it might have been all right to establish local policies such as returning of combat personnel after an arbitrary time period, without regard to the adequacy of replacements, the importance of the operation, and above all, the actual capacity of the individuals in question for

> continued combat. However, conditions will change once the German and Japanese air forces pass their peak. The life expectancy of our crews will improve with the increase in strength in our Air Forces and the decrease in strength of our enemies.
>
> If you have made any policies or understandings that combat personnel will be returned to the United States after fulfilling such arbitrary conditions as I have just described, those policies will be rescinded at once. Our combat personnel must understand that we plan to use combat crews in accord with war demands.

Hap wanted his theater commanders to know that the idea that combat crews could not be returned to a war zone for another tour was "beyond reason" and must be "unmistakably corrected."

At that time combat crew members were sent home after completing 25 missions and reassigned to Stateside units. It was generally believed by most returnees that they would not have to return to combat if they didn't want to. Most looked forward to completing their 25 missions and getting their war over with. During the early days of the war, when losses were high, 25 missions was an arbitrary but acceptable limit. However, by the time I arrived, which was coincident with the arrival of increased numbers of fighters and bombers, our losses were going down. The chances of any individual surviving a full tour were now greatly increased. It had been my observation that bomber crews did not reach an acceptable level of skill until they had about 10 missions in, and had reached the peak of their efficiency just when they were being allowed to go home. It seemed wasteful to me when we were trying so hard to build up an effective force. The same was true of fighter and reconnaissance pilots when they had about 100 hours of combat flying. I thought it was time for a change.

I pondered Hap's directive and conferred with my staff. I decided that combat heavy-bomber crews would be eligible for relief from combat duty after completing 30 sorties instead of 25; fighter and photo reconnaissance pilots, after completing 200 flying hours.

In my response to Hap's letter, I stated that henceforth, in the 8th Air Force, crews would not necessarily be relieved after the completion of a period of combat, but if the command is at a high rate of effectiveness, losses are as predicted, and the anticipated rate of replacements is satisfactory, crews may be removed from active participation in combat operations at the discretion of their commanders. I suggested that, if possible, combat crews should be sent home on leave by ship and return to their units after a period of rest as passengers or crew members of aircraft being ferried. This would keep the experience level high, and the number of replacements required would be reduced.

As expected, my decision was greeted with a great lack of enthusiasm, especially by the bomber crews. It took a while to prove, but the survival rate improved in direct proportion to bombing accuracy as we pursued the goals of Operation Pointblank. Later, I increased the bomber crew sortie requirement to 35.

One of the bright spots in the first four months of my duty with the 8th was the arrival of Bruce Johnson. He had been pestering Jack Allard for a transfer to the 8th from Italy, where he was still with the 15th. Jack, now recovered from a serious attack of phlebitis, had joined me in England after recuperating in the States. Bruce showed up one day with a 25-gallon jug of Italian wine and a crate of oranges, both of which were, as Bruce said, "as rare as platinum in England."

I immediately made Bruce our headquarters commandant and gave him the job of finding a set of quarters for my staff and me within 15 minutes of our offices. He found a very nice unoccupied place with about 10 rooms and five baths. It was owned by an American married to an Englishwoman. The man was willing to rent it to us, but his wife was not. After three visits, Bruce had to give up.

True to form, Bruce wouldn't be defeated. He persuaded a gracious British lady to move out and rent us her beautiful estate. It had 15 bedrooms, 7 baths, several well-kept outbuildings, and a caretaker's cottage, all overlooking the Thames. The house could accommodate my senior staff and leave us a guest room or two for visitors. A couple of gardeners went with the place, so we spent the rest of the European war like country gentlemen when the workday was over.

In the ensuing months, Brucie performed outstanding service as headquarters commandant. He described his duties in his memoirs this way:

> As headquarters commandant, I was many things to many people. I was asked to find a visitor a date. I had to round up a special holster for a .45. If your furniture needed repairing—call Bruce. Want another hot plate for your office—call Bruce. Then, from time to time, I had to keep the peace and hand out discipline.
>
> There was a dance held one evening in one of the buildings. During the course of the dance, a dog found his way on to the dance floor and bit the leg of a young lieutenant heavily under the influence of some of that good English gin. Not to be outdone, the lieutenant flung himself on the dog and just bit hell out of him, drawing blood and shrieks of anguish from the hound. The owner of the dog preferred charges and I had to call them both in, raise eight kinds of hell for such a bunch of nonsense and threw the complaint in the waste basket.
>
> A waste basket was a grand argument settler. Take the time that a full colonel chased a comely WAF up the broad cement steps of her building, this while driving a jeep. I did get the WAF commandant calmed down, but it took a bit of doing.[1]

Just as he had in North Africa and Italy, Bruce accomplished the impossible daily, no doubt by using my name as his authority. I had promoted Jack Allard to brigadier general; it was the least I could do to promote Brucie to colonel. Every commander should have a Bruce Johnson on his staff.

At the end of a busy day at my headquarters, I received a phone call from a Captain Doolittle, who said he'd like to see me. There was a Captain Doolittle on my staff, but I hadn't met him yet and intended to at the first opportunity. Thinking he had beaten me to the punch, I asked what I could do for him. He said, "I'd like to see you." I told him that since we shared the same last name, I'd like to meet him and he should make an appointment through my aide. I thought it would be interesting to see if we had any common ancestors.

Just as I was about to hang up, a plaintive voice on the other end said, "Gee, Dad. It's me. Don't you recognize my voice? Do I really have to make an appointment to see you? I've got a package for you from Mom."

It was Jim, Jr., now a B-26 pilot assigned to the 9th Air

Force. I had not expected to see him for several months. It was a happy time for both of us—the first time we had seen each other in two years. We saw each other frequently during the rest of our tours. Later, I had the pleasure of pinning the Distinguished Flying Cross on him for missions he had flown in the South Pacific. I was proud. He had left his unit in the Pacific before the medal and citation could be presented to him. I flew over to his field in a P-38. He looked longingly at it, so I let him take it up for a hop. On a subsequent visit, we boxed a little and I complained in a letter to Joe that "as a result of being both gaseous and slow, I am a bit black and blue. Isn't there some law against company grade officers beating up on generals?"

Jim, Jr.'s presence in the theater made me think about the future for Joe and me. Both boys wanted to remain in the service after the war, which meant we wouldn't see much of them. John was taking flight training while a cadet at West Point and would also be going to peacetime military assignments on a worldwide basis, just as Jim, Jr., would.

I wrote Joe that I thought I might like to stay in uniform until normal retirement if I were offered a commission as a permanent brigadier general. If so, I said, I would like to take an active part in the inevitable reorganizaton of our defense establishment and the Air Force after the war:

> After a very few years all of the "oldsters" should be kicked out and the new Air Force turned over to aggressive, progressive younger men. If we are financially independent at that time or are drawing retirement pay, I'd like to take a hand in government—if it can be separated from the less desirable aspect of politics. I know I'd never make a politician and doubt if I'd ever develop the ability to be a statesman, but I'd like to strive toward the latter if the former can be avoided.
>
> If we leave the Army immediately after the war or if we don't get retirement pay, we will have to get back into industry. Probably Shell, if they still desire my services. In any case, I hope when we retire from active military or commercial life that we may so order our declining years that we may both continue to be

useful forces for good in the world. Again, government and an attempt to improve government seems to be indicated. You are a big girl now and I realize cannot be bossed around any more, but I hope that whatever it is we do that it may be in the interest of a better world and that we may continue to do it together.

I liked to be present when my boys came back from some tough bomber and fighter missions. I often waited for hours until the last plane was either on the ground or it was confirmed that it had gone down somewhere. One day, after a particularly tough mission, a number of B-17s were landing with all kinds of damage and many wounded men aboard. I went with the ambulance crew to one of them as the crew members were getting out. A couple of them were bleeding from flak hits. The tail gun turret had been blown apart, and the tail gunner crawled out suprisingly unhurt. I couldn't believe it. I asked, "Were you in that turret when it was blasted?"

The lad looked at my three stars and replied, politely, "Yes, sir." He didn't elaborate.

As I walked away, the gunner said to a buddy of his standing nearby, "Where in the hell did that bald-headed bastard think I was—out buying a ham sandwich?"

His buddy tried to shush him up and said, "My God, man, not so loud. He'll hear you. Don't you know who that was?"

"Sure, I've seen his pictures," the gunner replied. "But I don't give a damn. That was a stupid question."

He was right.

On a visit to another unit that had been having bad luck and many losses, Tooey Spaatz and I went to the officers' club to try to buck them up a little. When we were about to leave, one of the young pilots, having imbibed a little too much, approached us and said, "I know why you're here. You think our morale is shot because we've been taking it on the nose. Well, I can tell you our morale is all right. There's only one thing that hurts our morale—that's when generals come around to see what's the matter with it."

Maybe he was right, too.

At another time, I scheduled a visit to northern England, but the weather was sour and the copilot on the crew suggested that the trip be canceled. I was waiting nearby and might have agreed if I'd been asked, but the young pilot making out the clearance shook his head and said we would go. I heard him say, "We'll have to go. From what I've heard the bastard doesn't give a damn about the weather."

He turned around and his face turned all shades of red when he saw me standing practically next to him. I never said a word. I would have if he had used the word "old" in front of "bastard."

In March 1944, a personnel problem surfaced that Hap Arnold called to our attention. In the Pacific, General George C. Kenney had lost two of his top pilots to Japanese fighters—Colonel Neel E. Kearby and Lieutenant Colonel Thomas J. Lynch. Kearby had shot down 22 Japanese planes, and Lynch, 20. Their fame as "Jap killers" and their ultimate demise received widespread publicity in the States. Hap was concerned that there was too much emphasis being placed on the number of kills a pilot could rack up in the hopes of being the top ace. He said he found it difficult to go along with the continuation of such active competition among the experienced pilots.

Hap told Kenney he wanted him to weigh very carefully the potential value of his heroes and consider taking them off flying when "their brilliance may dull the chance of the rest of the men—or when their loss may become a national calamity." He concluded by saying, "We are getting a rash of aces elsewhere and we are losing them in many cases because the individual score means more than the squadron score."

I asked Bill Kepner to give me his thoughts and he respectfully disagreed with Hap, saying:

> Apparently within the Army Air Force Headquarters there seems to be an impression that we take an individual high scorer and continually push him up front as you would a race horse or some other champion, then glamorize him and push him out so that he may become further outstanding with a higher score. If this be true, then such an impression in higher headquarters should be corrected at once, because it is 180 degrees wrong so far as our attitude in this matter.

Bill Kepner attached a separate note to me that he didn't want to be included in his official reply: "A dead hero is of infinitely more value for inspirational purposes than a live average man. A live hero is even better, but in order to achieve the hero status the distinct possibility of the corpse status must be accepted.''

In my reply to Hap, I said that the first job of the 8th Fighter Command was to whip the German fighters. In doing so, we hoped to inflict the maximum number of losses on the enemy while suffering the minimum losses among our own units. I wrote:

> Inevitably, some heroes develop, for in a large number of officers there are always a few whose capabilities and accomplishments make them outstanding. Our aim, however, is to conserve, insofar as practicable, those individuals whose skill and leadership would normally make them heroes, and meanwhile, use them to improve teamwork and to raise the effectiveness of all the fighter pilots. In spite of this, a combat leader must lead to maintain the excellence of his unit and the respect of his subordinates. Some leaders will therefore inevitably be killed.

Never heard about the matter again.

In the beginning of February 1944, in support of the objective of attacking the German single- and twin-engine airframe and component and ball-bearing production facilities, we planned what newspaper reporters and historians have since called the ''big week.'' It came about because of a message from Hap Arnold to Tooey Spaatz in which Hap had pleaded, ''Can't we someday and not too far distant, send out a big number—and I mean a big number—of bombers to hit something in the nature of an aircraft factory and lay it flat?'' We certainly wanted to comply.

The forecasters said we would have about seven consecutive days of visual bombing weather over Germany during the period February 19–25. As a result, we planned to launch a maximum-effort assault, code-named Operation Argument, lasting three successive days against the German fighter factories, beginning on February 20. Our aircraft would be assisted by fighters from the 9th Air Force. The RAF would precede with attacks on Berlin and Leipzig on the night of the nineteenth.

I was skeptical as always about long-range weather forecasts, but did not object strenuously. February is not noted for fine weather over Europe, but the need to proceed with our program was overriding.

On February 19, the skies were solid over England and the icing conditions were severe. We sent up weather planes during the night, and there was no improvement. Takeoffs would have to begin before dawn because the hours of daylight are so short during February at that latitude. The heavily loaded bombers and their escorting fighters would have to take off, go on instruments immediately for the climb through the overcast, and assemble on top in the dark. Not exactly a no-risk situation.

Major General Frederick L. Anderson, deputy for operations to Tooey Spaatz, although deeply concerned, strongly supported launching the attack. He urged me to make a firm decision to go. However, with such a risk to two of his air forces and the British, only Tooey could make that decision, and he did. He quietly and firmly issued the order to launch.

As they had been doing for many months, the RAF Bomber Command did strike at Leipzig on the night of the nineteenth, near where our bombers would penetrate the German defenses. On the twentieth, despite the lousy weather, we sent out 16 combat wings of over 1,000 heavy bombers and 17 groups of about 900 fighters to strike German aircraft factories, two of which were as far away as Posen, Poland. Bombing was good and losses were light.

That night the RAF sent out 600 bombers against Stuttgart, a city with several aircraft manufacturing facilities. Next day we sent out another force, but cloud cover over the targets reduced the bombing accuracy. On the twenty-second, we made another maximum effort, but again bad weather intervened. Two divisions had to abandon their primary targets, and the third found its targets partially obscured. We lost 41 bombers and 11 fighters; our escort fighters claimed 60 German aircraft.

The weather was so poor on the twenty-third that our entire force was grounded. On the twenty-fourth, the weather over Germany opened up and we launched another effort. The intensity of the resistance is reflected in the number of enemy aircraft claimed shot down by the bombers: 108. The escort fighters claimed an additional 37. We lost 33 B-24s out of 239 and 11 B-17s of 238.

The twenty-fifth brought more favorable weather, and the

8th went after aircraft factories in southern Germany while the 15th, operating from Italy, sent out 400 bombers. The two air forces lost a total of 64 bombers that day.

When the week ended, we assessed the results. The 8th and the 15th had launched 3,800 sorties against combined bomber offensive targets with a loss of 226 bombers and 28 escorting fighters. Our bomber loss rate was 3.5 percent, compared with 9.2 percent in October 1943—still high when you consider the number of men aboard those planes. Of course, many bailed out successfully and became prisoners of war.

Was it worth the effort?

Initially, I thought it was. We saw immediately that the Luftwaffe did not rise against us in the numbers that it had previously. The U.S. Strategic Bombing Survey reported after the war that those operations against the German aircraft industrial system damaged 75 percent of the buildings that produced 90 percent of Germany's aircraft. Historians tell us that we broke the back of the Luftwaffe that "big week" of February 1944, and it never again equaled its prior performance. Even so, our later experience showed that, although we slowed them down, the Germans never did run out of airplanes and were still able to turn them out in underground factories until the end of the war. Some factories were again in full production by the end of June. We learned much later that in spite of our repeated attacks on aircraft factories, the Germans reportedly produced an estimated 25,000 fighters during 1944, the highest number of any year of the war.

What hurt the Germans the most was the deterioration in the experience level of their pilots. The Germans lost an estimated 434 pilots during the "big week," out of a total strength of about 2,200. According to General Adolf Galland, head of their fighter force, they lost about 1,000 pilots between January and April.

Throughout the spring of 1944 we continued to attack aircraft assembly plants, ball-bearing factories, and enemy fighters, both in the air and on the ground. The main target areas were central Germany, from Hanover to Berlin and south to Leipzig; the Baltic coast of Germany westward from Stettin; the Hamm-Münster area north of the Ruhr; the Munich area; and the flying-bomb sites in the Pas de Calais.

The German high command withdrew the bulk of its fighter defenses to the great industrial centers inside Germany, leaving only a modest number of fighters in the probable invasion areas. To force the Luftwaffe out of the skies, we deliberately tried to goad their fighters into combat in a fight to the finish.

Concurrently, to prepare for the invasion, our target priorities were enlarged to include strategic rail centers, particularly those with servicing and repair facilities used to maintain the rail system in northern France, the Low Countries, and western Germany; coastal defense batteries; selected naval installations; and all airfields in a 130-mile arc from Caen to Normandy.

One of the personal frustrations I had after joining the 8th was that I was forbidden to fly any missions over the Continent while the enemy held it, for two reasons: I had been briefed on and given access to Ultra, the code-breaking system that permitted us to listen in on top-secret German military messages. Anyone let in on Ultra could not risk being captured. In addition, I had been briefed on the invasion plans.

Ira Eaker had refused a briefing on Ultra, saying he would rely on his intelligence officers to tell him what it produced, but he didn't want to know how it worked. Wish I had had the presence of mind to do that.

To get my flying time in, I was supposed to fly only in the British Isles or over friendly territory after the invasion. I may have deviated a little from the latter. As a result of the restriction, the poor flying weather, and the greater confinement to a desk, for the first time in over 25 years, I could not fly the one-hour-a-day average I had enjoyed. Although a certain amount of prestige went with the high rank, I thought that a lot of my flying ability and flying confidence was sacrificed. In the first four months with the 8th I flew as pilot less than 20 hours.

After the "big week," when the weather broke, we scheduled missions to Berlin to begin on March 4. I wanted to be in on this first effort and have the honor of being the first air commander to lead a raid over all three Axis capitals. I planned to fly a P-51 with one wingman ahead of the bomber stream over the capital city. To prepare for this, I sharpened up my fighter skills in the P-51 and then approached Tooey to get his permission. I thought I might be able to persuade him to let me go, just as I had talked Hap Arnold into letting me lead the Tokyo Raid. As before, I had my argument all prepared mentally and launched into it with gusto. Tooey finally gave in and reluctantly said I could go. However, just a day or so before departure, Tooey changed his mind and said he couldn't afford to risk the capture of a senior officer who had knowledge of invasion plans. I have always suspected that when Ike heard about it, it was he who canceled the idea with his customary, quick, no-nonsense response, although Tooey never said he did. So, contrary to what some have claimed for me, I did not participate in any bombing raids on Berlin. I admit, however, that I really wanted that honor.

The first raid on Berlin did not go as planned. The weather deteriorated and most bombers either turned back or bombed their secondary targets. Only 29 bombers got through with their P-51 escorts. Two days later, 660 planes got to the target area and met fierce resistance from an all-out effort by the Luftwaffe. We lost 69 bombers and 11 fighters. We learned after the war that Hermann Goering said he knew the air war was lost when he saw the bombers over the capital with their P-51 escorts.

Despite my personal disappointment at not leading the first Berlin mission, I tried to make the best of my background and experience by flying every new model of aircraft that came into our theater. We never had enough technical representatives to solve aircraft problems, so I was able to form my own conclusions by flying new aircraft myself, as I had done in my McCook Field test-piloting days.

My former testing experience did come in handy during a crisis period with the P-38 Lightning. For some reason the twin-engine P-38s were catching fire in flight, one of a pilot's worst flying nightmares. At the first opportunity, I drove out to a nearby depot and arranged to fly one. After I was briefed on the problem, I thought I might be able to induce a fire by backfiring the engine in flight, so I taxied out and took off. Almost as soon as I got the gear up, one engine backfired all by itself and started to burn briskly. Although the weather was quite bad, I was able to keep the field in sight while I made the turns around the traffic pattern. However, I couldn't see far enough ahead in case of a forced landing to be sure I didn't crash into a house or building.

I managed to get the Lightning on the ground and was met by the fire trucks. Fortunately, the fire was doused without too much damage to the plane. It was ironic. I was going to see if I could cause a fire by backfiring it, and it backfired all by itself. The problem was quickly resolved by our engine specialists.

It is generally conceded that the war in the air against Germany was won during the phase of our operations between the beginning of February 1944 and D-Day. The rate of attrition of the Luftwaffe's pilots exceeded Germany's rate of replacement. Also, the several months of reduced aircraft production during a crucial period created a temporary shortage of reserve aircraft that was difficult to overcome. Thus, Germany was low in two essentials at a critical point: aircraft and pilots.

Another of the many bombing innovations experimented with in the 8th during 1943 and 1944 was the use of fighters for high-altitude bombing. On November 25, 1943, a group of P-47 fighters following a B-24 dropped nearly 11 tons of bombs on an airdrome at St.-Omer in the Pas de Calais. Then another group dove from 14,000 feet and released 3.5 tons at 8,000 feet on the same target. Although this was successful, the effort couldn't be continued at the time because of the need to escort the bombers. However, we later modified some P-38s to carry a bombardier and his Norden bombsight in the nose. These aircraft were called "Droop Snoots."

Heavy flak was the most dangerous enemy threat to this type of fighter bombing, but with practice a loose formation could be flown to the start of the bomb run, then tightened up for 30 seconds until all aircraft dropped on the "Droop Snoot." Because of the close formation on the bomb run, a tight bomb pattern resulted.

Skip bombing was also tried, using bombs or partially filled wing tanks that were dropped and then set on fire by incendiary bullets from succeeding planes. Success varied. Losses from fighter bombing were proportionately more severe than those suffered on regular escort missions. Enemy flak, automatic weapons, and small arms fire shot down valuable pilots previously unscathed in aerial combat. When we looked at the results, we decided to abandon fighter bombing except in rare instances.

No one will dispute that weather was the most serious limiting factor the 8th Air Force had to cope with. In the early days, we were grounded an average of about four out of five days because visual bombing conditions were lacking. A way had to be found to overcome this. It was, in the form of an extremely valuable British invention: radar.

Radar is based on the time differential between transmission of a radio signal and its reflection by an object, and on the ability of such a reflection to illuminate the face of a calibrated cathode ray tube, or oscilloscope. The British had experimented with radar to locate targets through clouds with limited success. Their device was called H2S, an airborne radar, and with it bodies of water could be distinguished from land. Cities could be seen fairly easily, but pinpoint targets were almost impossible to locate.

The 8th also experimented with H2S, and an improvement was produced in the States that we labeled H2X. However, it was still incapable of distinguishing very small targets such as individual buildings, although it could locate enough area targets through the overcast that our bombing accuracy and capability was increased significantly. On visual days, it also proved useful in navigating over clouded areas before getting to the target areas.

In addition, our photo reconnaissance group, under Colonel Elliott Roosevelt, developed the capability to take radar photos, which was particularly useful when the target areas were clouded over. If we saw a target being built up, we didn't want to bomb it until the enemy had spent considerable time in the construction phase, then we would take it out. The reconnaissance flights and their resultant radar photos permitted us to select targets, determine the best time to attack, and, afterward, determine how much damage had been done. This photo capability was greatly enhanced as the resolution on our radar screens improved.

Elliott did a splendid job for us in North Africa and continued to show his leadership qualities in England. My only worry about him was that he was absolutely fearless and flew on some very difficult missions. I was greatly concerned that he would be killed and I would have to explain to the President why I let him do some of the things he did. I almost broke his heart when I took him off flying.

We were also able to adapt another British device used for navigation, called the "Gee-H." Its scope was activated by two ground-station transmitters. Depending on the distance from the ground stations, an aircraft could determine its own location and the location of a target area with fair accuracy.

Another instrument, called the "Micro-H," was devised shortly after along similar lines and was more accurate than the Gee-H. The accuracy of the Gee-H and Micro-H continued to improve as crews became better trained and more experienced. Unfortunately, the supply of these devices was limited, but the technique of bombing-on-the-leader gave us the capability to bomb through the overcast, a decided advantage in the war in

Europe. It cannot be said categorically that the Gee-H and Micro-H ever gave us the accuracy of visual bombing, but overcast bombing using these instruments made additional bombing missions possible, since the forces would go out prepared to bomb either way should the target be cloud covered.

As the date neared for the invasion of Normandy, the 8th Air Force, along with the 9th, 12th, and 15th, was committed to a broad program to ensure the successful establishment of the beachhead. Our job in the 8th was fourfold:

1. Continue to attack the Luftwaffe by bombing enemy airframe and engine factories, assembly plants, and aircraft on the ground.
2. Bomb strategic rail centers, particularly those with servicing and repair facilities in northern France, the Low Countries, and western Germany.
3. Bomb coastal defense batteries, V-bomb sites, and selected naval installations.
4. Interdict all airfields in a 130-mile arc from Caen to Normandy.

To do all this simultaneously meant we had to keep up a maximum effort. Because the tempo of our attacks increased, the Luftwaffe was well aware that an invasion was imminent. To prevent the enemy from knowing where it would take place, we did not focus on any single target system within the invasion arc. In the 15 days prior to D-Day, the 8th attacked 52 airfields, 45 marshaling yards, and 14 bridges. In addition, six attacks were made on coastal fortifications and four on gun positions.

Our fighters made sweeps against transportation targets, and the attacks on railroads were especially successful. Many locomotives and rolling stock were destroyed. Highway transportation was also seriously interrupted as bridges were destroyed across the Seine.

As we pressed on, the Luftwaffe was forced to withdraw to airfields farther and farther from the coast. Although some airfields could be repaired quickly, most of them could not. Enemy air resistance in the forward area became weaker and weaker.

At dawn on D-Day, June 6, 1944, six B-17s from the 422nd Bomb Squadron flew unescorted over the invasion coast, fanned out singly, and flew over towns and villages dropping pamphlets warning the French people to seek safety in open fields and stay away from highways and railroads. It was their first notice that the day they had prayed for was at hand.

Meanwhile, we dispatched 1,350 bombers divided into 225 squadrons of six bombers each. They made a predawn assembly and followed a route that gave them a right-angle attack on the beach targets. This gave the H2X overcast bombing equipment a clearly defined line at the beach, minimizing the risk of bombing our own troops. Because of the overcast weather, extra distance was added as an additional safety factor.

Two thirds of the 8th's fighters were sent up during the bombing missions, and the other one third during intervals between the bombing attacks. Fighter-bomber attacks were made against 17 railroad bridges, 10 marshaling yards, 4 railroad junctions, and many miscellaneous targets. Meanwhile, the 9th Air Force sent up 171 squadrons of fighters. In all, both air forces sent 3,000 planes on 8,700 sorties, while the RAF flew 5,700 missions.

I was up before dawn that momentous day and decided to fly a P-38 over the beaches. The twin-tailed Lightning was chosen because of its distinctive profile, which I hoped would be easily identified by ground gunners and our own aircraft. Pat Partridge joined me in another P-38 and we climbed up above the overcast to check on the bombing formations on top that were using radar on their bomb runs. Since the bombardiers had a very definite bomb line and didn't want to undershoot for fear of hitting our men, I suspect they added a "fudge factor" to their aiming points. As a result, many bombers did not drop as effectively as they could have.

Just as we hoped, enemy interception was almost nil, and Pat and I saw none. What few enemy aircraft did appear were promptly engaged and the skies were swept clear. Twenty-eight enemy fighters were destroyed and eight damaged. We lost five fighters. We did lose a few bombers on later missions that day because of enemy ground defenses, and two of them from a midair collision in a low-visibility condition.

On the way back to our base with Pat on my wing, I spied a hole in the clouds and decided to take a look underneath. Just at that instant, Pat must have had his head in the cockpit changing gas tanks. When he looked up, I had disappeared. He flew around in circles for a few minutes and then went home.

Meanwhile, I came in under the clouds over the English Channel and turned toward the invasion beaches. The scene below was the most impressive and unforgettable I could have possibly imagined. In the largest amphibious assault force ever assembled, more than 176,000 troops and 5,000 ships participated in the invasion. What was most personally satisfying was that the hundreds of ships and barges could unload thousands of troops without worrying about enemy aircraft. We had achieved what we had planned and hoped for: complete air supremacy over the beaches.

Adolf Galland, the Luftwaffe's fighter commander, noted in his postwar memoirs:

> Wherever our fighters appeared, the Americans hurled themselves at them. They went over to low-level attacks on our airfields. Nowhere were we safe from them; we had to skulk on our own bases. During takeoff, assembling, climbing, approaching the bombers, once in contact with the bombers, on our way back, during landing, and ever after that the American fighters attacked with overwhelming superiority.

I logged two and a half hours on the flight over the beaches. After I landed, I hurried over to Ike's headquarters to give him a verbal eyewitness report at his commanders' meeting that morning. Of course, I proudly emphasized the fact that the Luftwaffe had not been able to interfere. The impression I had was that everything was going smoothly everyplace except at Omaha Beach, where I saw many landing craft blow up beneath me. My firsthand, eyewitness account of the amphibious operations was the first that he received. My report beat his official intelligence report by several hours. I felt good about that.

Because of the softening up of the invasion area, Operation Overlord went as planned. By the morning of June 7, several beachheads had been consolidated and advances up to 10 miles inland had been made in some areas. Winston Churchill announced in Parliament that General Eisenhower had achieved "tactical surprise."

We had told General Eisenhower that the only aircraft our ground and sea forces would see over the beaches would be ours, and he passed this on to the troops. We didn't think of it as boasting, only a statement of fact.

Several weeks after D-Day, I had a confrontation with Lieutenant General Walter Bedell "Beetle" Smith, Ike's chief of staff, about a bombing mission. We had briefed our bombers to carry out a saturation attack to soften up an area ahead of our ground troops as they pushed inland. The wind, forecast to hold from one direction, had reversed and blown from the opposite direction. Unfortunately, the crews were already in the air and we didn't know about the wind reversal until later. Instead of blowing the smoke and debris away from the exploding bombs toward the enemy lines, it blew back over ours. As a result, the bombardiers were dropping visually and lost their aiming points. Succeeding bombers thought the target was under the smoke and dropped on that. Sixteen American soldiers were killed and 70 wounded.

The following day, we sent out a force of 2,500 bombers and a similar tragedy occurred as some bombs fell among the leading echelons of advancing U.S. troops. This time more than 100 were killed and 500 wounded. The most notable casualty was Army lieutenant general Lesley J. McNair.

When the news reached SHAEF headquarters, I was immediately summoned to Smith's office and blamed for the tragic and costly mistake. I accepted the responsibility but was very angry because I didn't think we should have been given such a job. About 60 bombers had dropped their loads short.

I told him that 2,500 bombers could not drop thousands of bombs accurately, especially when the target area is covered with smoke from previous bombs. I tried to explain that bombing in close support of ground troops was not the mission of the 8th and my men were not trained for it. They were trained for high-altitude bombing; close air support of ground troops was not a feasible mission for the 8th. I said I had accepted the mission even though I knew the risk we were taking.

Smith was not an airman and had little patience for anything that sounded like an excuse. "You were directed to carry out the mission and you didn't!"

I protested, but I could see it had no effect. He dismissed me curtly and I was certain he was going to tell Ike and recommend he fire me. I rushed out of his office and went straight to

Tooey Spaatz to tell him what had happened. "Please explain it to Ike before Beetle does or I'll be unemployed," I pleaded.

I don't know what Tooey said, but he prevented my demise as the 8th's commander. I never heard any further repercussions. However, that didn't help my conscience any about what had happened. American lives had been lost and it is impossible to deny that fact. How does anyone ever explain to their families that mistakes were made—that American fliers snuffed out the lives of American soldiers who had no way to defend themselves or even to know they were being bombed until it happened.

Tooey reported to Hap: "It had been previously explained to [General Omar] Bradley that in a large-scale operation of this kind, placing a heavy concentration in a small area in the proximity of our front lines would inevitably result in some casualties. The casualties were higher than I had hoped, but not so great as anticipated under conditions prevailing." Hap did his best to explain to Ike that we should not send large formations of long-range bombers over our troops to prepare the way for them.

Ike disagreed; consequently, there were more episodes in which the 8th Air Force bombed American troops. In late July, our ground army bogged down at St.-Lô. Eisenhower requested an all-out bombing effort in front of our troops in order to soften up the enemy and break the stalemate. My logbook shows that on July 25, I flew a P-38 from Bovingdon, England, to St.-Lô to observe the bombing requested by the Army. During the night, the ground troops had moved back from the front line, leaving us a cleared area between the original front lines and their new position in order to provide an added safety measure against bombing our own troops. Actually, an almost straight road indicated where a front line had been and gave the bombardiers a good bomb line.

Unfortunately, the wind shifted. After the bombing started, the wind blew back smoke and dust toward our troops and the obvious happened again. I was overhead watching this and was powerless to do anything about it. It was one of those harrowing moments that you sometimes dream about, but in dreams you are relieved to awaken and find it is not real.

The next day, I flew to a strip in France to explain the horrible mistake to General Bradley. It was a very unpleasant task. The only compensation was that General Bradley and his commanders praised our efforts and reported that what we had done made possible their breakout at St.-Lô and subsequent advances.

On August 2, to my surprise, I received a letter from General Eisenhower:

> I know how badly you and your command have felt because of the accidental bombing of some of our own troops. . . . Naturally, all of us have shared your acute distress that this should have happened. Nevertheless, it is quite important that you do not give the incident an exaggerated place either in your mind or in your future planning.
>
> All the reports show that the great mass of the bombs from your tremendous force fell squarely on the assigned target, and I want you and your command to know that the advantages resulting from the bombardment were of inestimable value. I am perfectly certain, also, that when the ground forces again have to call on you for help you will not only be as ready as ever to cooperate, but will in the meantime have worked out some method so as to eliminate unfortunate results from the occasional gross error on the part of a single pilot or a single group.
>
> The work of the 8th Air Force over many months in this theater has been far too valuable to allow the morale of the organization to be dampened by this incident.

I promptly replied that I appreciated his confidence in the 8th and explained why the accident had happened. To assure an absolute minimum of errors would occur when supporting ground troops, I listed some ways they could be reduced: through indoctrination, training, careful briefing, and, if possible, a practice mission beforehand to simulate the actual mission that would be flown. I assured him that "the high morale of the 8th Air Force is unimpaired and we are anxious to vindicate ourselves with a perfect job next time."

Because of the original accidental bombing, I had already given my staff the task of finding a solution for the problem. Having proved that a bomb line on the ground, no matter how clearly delineated, was undependable, we then worked out a plan, in collaboration with our antiaircraft people, to make a definite bomb line in the air. The idea was to mark the bomb line in the air with colored smoke. An antiaircraft battery would fire simultaneous, carefully directed and timed bursts that would indicate a straight line in the air just below the height at which the aircraft were flying. After passing this line, bombs could be dropped with safety. Using this method, however, it was necessary to fly over our own troops and away from them into enemy territory, where our aircraft would be more vulnerable to ground fire.

On August 13, I made a flight to Aberporth to watch antiaircraft marking practice. It was not satisfactory. The next day I flew to Dover and this time it was. We had learned from the previous day's mistakes.

In addition to the air-marked bomb line, we developed an electronic bomb line indicator. It consisted of an instrument landing system (ILS) mounted on a jeep with its beam pointed vertically instead of at an angle. The beam indicated to the bombers that they passed over the last of our troops and it was safe to bomb. This proved to be extremely effective.

Unfortunately, before developing these two systems, we were again asked to do a bombing job for the Army. On August 8, 1944, I flew a P-51 Mustang to France to observe this attempt. In this case we were to help soften up the enemy in front of Field Marshal Bernard Montgomery's troops at Caen. I arranged to have three separate crystals put in my VHF radio set so that I could talk to each of the three division commanders and actually control this operation from the air. The division commanders could talk to their wing commanders, who in turn could communicate with their group commanders and they to their individual aircraft. Timing demanded that the operation go forward without sufficient practice with the equipment. As a result, I found that my radio link with the division commanders didn't work. I was, therefore, unable to command and control the operation.

On this occasion, as an added precaution, we had the bombers fly parallel to the front lines—over on the enemy side. This meant that our losses due to enemy flak would be much higher because the bombers would be flying over the heavily defended enemy front lines; however, we would not be over our own troops, so we wouldn't inadvertently bomb them.

Another unavoidable tragedy occurred. One of our planes

was struck by enemy flak and I watched it break away from its formation and turn toward our lines. It lost altitude rapidly. The pilot and copilot had obviously been killed, and the plane was out of control. I followed it down but didn't see any parachutes come out.

With the irony of fate and the greatest of misfortune, the B-17 crashed into a British ammunition dump. The plane's bombs went off and these blew up the ammunition. Looking back overhead, I saw a distant formation turning toward the resulting smoke, thinking it was a new target. I climbed the P-51 toward the bombers and flew back and forth in front of the formation to try to convey my message not to bomb. This is a very risky thing to do because bomber gunners were notoriously light on the trigger when any fighters, even ours, acted suspiciously around them. Fortunately, I managed to turn this formation away so that no further damage was done. The ground commanders in all these inadvertent bombing instances were understandably bitter. Despite our best efforts, there were still more to come.

The shuttle bombing missions to the USSR that I had proposed earlier were finally authorized, and preparations were made for Operation Frantic, a combined operation with the 15th Air Force operating from Italy. On June 2, 130 bombers and 70 fighters from the 15th, with Ira Eaker in command, departed Italian bases and bombed Debrecen, Hungary, en route to Soviet bases at Poltava, Mirgorod, and Piryatin. No enemy fighters appeared and there was no flak over the target area. One B-17 unaccountably exploded in flight; otherwise there were no losses.

While in the USSR, one bombing mission was made against an airfield at Galatz, Romania, on June 6 while D-Day forces were storming ashore at Normandy. En route back to Italy later, they bombed another airfield in northeastern Romania. In all, only one B-17 was lost and two Mustangs; eight enemy fighters were claimed.

The first shuttle mission for the 8th departed England on June 21, 1944. Colonel Archie J. Old, Jr., the task force commander, led three 21-airplane groups in the lead combat wing. Two similar wings trailed the lead wing as closely as possible, for a total of 114 B-17s and 70 P-51s. En route to the Soviet bases, they bombed a synthetic oil plant at Ruhland, south of Berlin, in perfect weather. Unknown to our forces, a German

He.177 trailed the task force to Poltava. Shortly after midnight, a group of 75 German bombers dropped flares and photographic bombs to illuminate our B-17s and unloaded 110 tons of bombs of all types. To compound the surprise, a few German fighters then strafed the field and dropped antipersonnel bombs.

Archie Old reported, "There was hardly a square yard of ground in the task force dispersal area that was not hit with some type of bomb." On the next afternoon, there was a hard rain shower and, he went on:

> At least a hundred or so butterfly [antipersonnel] bombs were exploded by the rainfall. It sounded like a young war for a few minutes.
>
> The Russian sappers had a unique way of destroying anti-personnel bombs. One system was to pick the bomb up and throw it as far as possible and either fall flat on their faces or else run like hell. It worked, but also kept the medical section and coffin builders busy. Considerably more than a hundred Russian men and women were killed and wounded during the raid and the three days following. By the end of the third day, Russian sappers had cleared approximately 9,500 bombs.

The raid was successful as far as the Germans were concerned. Forty-three B-17s were destroyed and 26 damaged, some beyond economical repair. Fifteen Mustangs and numerous Soviet aircraft were lost. An ammunition dump blew up and 450,000 gallons of gasoline were ignited. One American pilot was killed and one copilot wounded. Not a single German aircraft was brought down. After the German surrender, Ira told Hermann Goering that this surprise attack was the best the Luftwaffe ever made against the American air forces. Goering's reply: "Those were wonderful times."

Our surviving fighters and bombers left the USSR for Italy on June 26. En route they bombed a synthetic oil plant at Drohobycz, Poland. One fighter was lost. They flew one joint mission with the 15th against targets in southern France and then returned to England on July 5.

Several more 8th Air Force shuttle missions were carried out; the last one with bombs aboard took place on September 12. By this time, autumn was setting in, and the shuttle bases were so far to the east of Soviet lines that they were of dubious value in attacking targets in Germany.

We scheduled one more shuttle mission that was different from the rest. A patriot force of Poles had been battling the Germans in Warsaw during August and September 1944 and were badly in need of supplies. The rebellious Poles, surrounded by powerful German troops, fought on with typical bravery. On August 15, General Eisenhower received a message from Washington urging him to dispatch a supply-dropping mission to the beleaguered city. Our heavy bombers couldn't make the trip from England to Warsaw and return, so another Operation Frantic mission to Soviet bases seemed to be the only answer.

While the Poles were fighting for their lives inside Warsaw against the Germans on the west, Soviet forces remained in positions 10 kilometers away to the east and refused to budge. Although the Soviets finally were persuaded to drop some supplies in a token effort on September 13, it wasn't enough and the situation was desperate.

On September 18, we dispatched 107 B-17s loaded with 1,284 containers of pistols, ammunition, machine-gun parts, explosives, food, and medical supplies. While we thought the mission was a success at first, it wasn't. Somewhere between 130 and 280 containers fell into Polish hands. The Germans got the rest.

Another supply mission was ordered by President Roosevelt himself, who was reacting to pleas from other nations. However, the second supply operation was never cleared by the Soviets, and the Germans put down the insurrection; 250,000 Poles were killed fighting for their freedom. The Soviets did not take Warsaw until the following January.

Operation Frantic was not a success as far as I'm concerned. While the concept made sense, there was an almost complete lack of cooperation from the Soviets who didn't seem to believe in strategic bombing or realize how they could benefit from what we were trying to do. We were convinced that the Soviet authorities wanted the Army Air Forces to pull out of the Soviet Union altogether. In late August 1944, the Soviets indicated they needed the three air bases we had been using.

My experience with the Soviets was limited, but this and other incidents that came to my attention convinced me that we were going to have great difficulty dealing with them after the war.

After the landings on Normandy, the air war turned into

what was designated "phase five." We didn't know it at the time, but it was to be 11 months after D-Day before hostilities would cease. On June 11, the first V-1 bombs began to fall on London. The Germans had other surprises in store for us in the months ahead. One of them was a new type of aircraft with a propulsion system that would have a lasting influence on the future of world aviation.

Note

1. Johnson, Bruce, *The Man with 2 Hats*. New York: Carlton Press, 1967, pp. 140–141.

CHAPTER 16

Air Force historical analysts have divided the efforts of the 8th Air Force during World War II into five phases. The first lasted from August 17, 1942, to December 11, 1942, when German fighter strength greatly exceeded the number of Spitfires and Hurricanes that the RAF could send up to escort the American bombers. The depth of penetration by the 8th's bombers was sharply limited, not by their own range, but by the range of the escort fighters. So the first phase was a period of trying out equipment, developing techniques, and gaining battle experience.

The areas of attack during this period were, generally, the Pas de Calais coastline in northern France, extending inland as far as Lille; the Atlantic coast of France from Brest southward; and German installations in the vicinity of Rotterdam. It was during this phase that the campaign in North Africa was launched.

In the second phase, from December 12, 1942, to July 24, 1943, Ira Eaker was able to extend the depth of his bomb missions. Major target areas were northwest Germany around Bremen and Kiel, the river Seine as far up as Paris, and the French coast southward from Brest. The principal new areas under attack were the submarine facilities on the northwest German coast and in the vicinity of Antwerp, and the enemy factories in or near Paris. However, approximately half of the bomb missions were still within the first area of penetration.

England-based bombing came of age during this period. The 8th was increasing in size and frequency of operations. Concurrently, the RAF was beginning its massive night area-bombing attacks on the metropolitan centers of Germany.

Phase three extended from July 25, 1943, to February 19, 1944, during which I succeeded Ira as commander of the 8th. This was when the first belly tanks were added to the P-47 Thunderbolts, which gave them the extended range to go farther with the bombers. It was on July 25 that attacks on Rostok proved that the 8th could penetrate into the enemy's heartland.

The maximum depth of direct penetration and withdrawal for this phase was reached during a B-17 attack on Schweinfurt, about 350 miles inland from the French coast, on August 17, 1943. On the same day, another force of Flying Forts, equipped with what we called "Tokyo tanks," bombed the Messerschmitt factory at Regensburg, deep in southwest Germany, and then flew on to North Africa. This was actually the first shuttle bombing mission.

My arrival in January 1944 coincided with a major extension of the fighter range, when P-51s and P-38s were integrated into the force. The principal target areas during this phase were the northwest German ports; the vicinity of Hamm and Münster, north of the Ruhr; Hanover-Brunswick; Frankfurt-Schweinfurt; and Paris.

The fourth phase, described in the previous chapter, covers the period February 20, 1944, to June 20, 1944, when I authorized our fighters to protect the bombers and pursue and destroy the enemy fighters. Our major assignment was to render the Luftwaffe impotent by a series of knockout blows to their fighters wherever they could be found, and to prepare for the invasion. Historians agree that the war in the air was won during this phase.

Although at the time we were all confident that we were eventually going to win, there was still a long way to go. Germany had not yet been defeated; the Wehrmacht was proving how strong it was on the ground. It was our job to do what we could to support the Allied troops by attacking the enemy's ground forces and denying them supplies and reinforcements.

The 8th first directly supported the Allied ground forces on D-Day. General Eisenhower had at his disposal 13,195 aircraft of all types, including those of the 15th Air Force in Italy and the RAF Bomber Command.

The invasion was accomplished under the most difficult weather conditions and was one of the most satisfying jobs the 8th ever performed. This was largely due to the fact that we had several weeks to plan, to prepare reconnaissance aids such as H2X radar photos of the coastline and enemy defenses, and to train our people.

But a new enemy threat had been developing for months. During a visit to the 8th by Secretary of War for Air Robert P. Patterson, I briefed him extensively on our operations and expressed my concerns about the German Messerschmitt Me-262 jet and Me-163 rocket fighters, which had made their appearance. The speed differential between our fighters and bombers and these aircraft was striking. If they were produced in great numbers, there was no doubt in my mind that they would become a serious threat. Their appearance would eventually require a similar counterweapon, such as our own Bell P-59 jet fighter, which was still in the experimental stage.

Another worrisome threat was the introduction by the enemy of radio-controlled rockets. Secretary Patterson and his staff took copious notes, and a transcript of our meeting was given to Hap Arnold when Patterson returned to Washington. Apparently misunderstanding what I had said to the secretary, Hap immediately wrote me a "Dear Jimmy" letter in which he said my concerns about the German jet fighters "perturb me very much." He said he wasn't perturbed so much because of these new enemy developments, "but because the comments don't sound like the old Jimmy Doolittle I know so well." He asked me to respond with tactical and engineering recommendations about these new weapons.

If Hap was perturbed, I was more so when I received his letter. It was quite a jab in the ribs. Again, I had to defend myself, so I sent a lengthy reply. I assured him that we were not afraid of the new German developments but were concerned because we were convinced that they planned to manufacture these fast new aircraft in great numbers; they were superior to our fighters, and our bombers would suffer. I was convinced that conventional Luftwaffe fighters were being deliberately conserved for use together with the new aircraft. I felt that the new high-speed fighters would intercept our fighter escorts, who would be forced to drop their wing tanks in order to fight, thereby reducing their range. The unescorted bombers would then be vulnerable to attack from conventional enemy fighters.

I told Hap that we were not awed by these new aircraft and would continue to try to decimate the German force, reduce production, delay the development of new equipment, and devise plans to successfully combat the new threat if and when it eventuated. I wrote:

> Our plan to meet their rocket and jet planes is by head-on attack and by superior turning. This plan has already been successfully put into effect. We are carefully watching the airfields from which he intends to operate his nonconventional aircraft and intend to strike as soon as he moves abroad. Attack will be by bomber or low-strafing fighter (probably fighter), depending upon dispersal and defenses. We want to catch and stop them before they can assemble units large enough to develop effective counteroffensive tactics.

I asked Hap for new gyro sights for our fighters because they would have to do more deflection shooting against the jets and rocket-powered planes. I also said we wanted larger-caliber, higher-velocity (flatter trajectory) guns with better computing sights for our bombers, preferably fitting into existing turrets, as soon as they could be made available.

Our intelligence people had been watching the progress the Germans were making with their jets and were able to obtain some capability information. The Me-262 was fast, well beyond the speed of our fighters, and its endurance at very high altitude was estimated at more than two hours. Its maneuverability was good, considering its speed, and its firepower, consisting largely of 30-mm cannon, was lethal against our bombers but no match for our .50-caliber machine guns in fighter-versus-fighter combat. Our weapons had higher muzzle velocity, rate of fire, and volume of ammunition. Their 30-mm cannon was designed primarily to attack bombers.

We felt the premature commitment of the Me-262 resulted in frequent accidents in training, with the loss of highly skilled pilots, which the Luftwaffe, at that time, could ill afford. When some of these aircraft were diverted to strafing and dive bombing, this further reduced the effectiveness of this new weapon against our bombers.

The rocket-propelled Me-163 was a failure as far as we could see. Although it demonstrated remarkable speed at full power, endurance was limited to 10 to 12 minutes of full-power flight. It lacked maneuverability under power, but could glide for great distances from altitude. If the pilot used a long glide after a short burst of power, it was believed, the aircraft could be flown a little over an hour.

Still, the Luftwaffe was a threat to the bombing missions of the 8th. In October 1944, there were about 780 German fighters that, by flying double sorties, could fly about 1,000 sorties against one of our deep penetration missions. My fighters were being pulled off escort duty to perform tactical missions, and I was concerned that the bombers were going to suffer heavier losses.

I put my thoughts on record with a letter to Tooey, which I hand-delivered to him. I forecast that we might easily lose 100 bombers destroyed, especially if the enemy could continue to produce their high-performance jets.

At this time, the Luftwaffe had developed a "line abreast" method of attack against our bombers. They would form in a line perpendicular to the bomber stream; this concentrated their fire and greatly reduced the effectiveness of the defensive fire of the bombers. The method proved so effective that the Luftwaffe were using it almost to the exclusion of other forms of attack.

Once a line-abreast attack was launched, we found it was nearly impossible to break up unless our fighters were in a position between the bombers and the attacking enemy. However, split-second timing was necessary, and we didn't have enough fighters to give close cover to all of our bombers. Our problem was made more difficult because the German local radar had improved and the defenders knew where we were, but we didn't know where the enemy was.

I pointed out that our ratio of fighters to bombers was lower than it had been since October 1943 and that we were courting disaster by reducing the number of fighters available for escort duty. I felt strongly that the Strategic Air Forces could render more effective aid to the war effort by denying the enemy the facilities he required than by giving direct support to our ground forces. Tooey agreed with me but was continually faced with having to deal with the ground war situation and the demands of the ground generals, who appealed their needs through General Eisenhower. I had to live with what Tooey was able to let me assign to our bombing missions.

Still concerned, I wrote a follow-up letter a few days later and asked Tooey for 9th Air Force fighters to be assigned to the 8th for missions as I needed them. I recommended ways by which the coordination between the units could be simplified and how the 9th's aircraft should be equipped for high-altitude, formation flying over long distances. It took some persuasion, but I finally won my point. Many joint missions with the 9th were flown, for which I was very grateful, as were hundreds of bomber crews whose morale, and hence effectiveness, was greatly improved.

Morale is always a factor to be considered in war planning, so when German pilots were captured and interrogated we spent much effort trying to determine how they felt about the war. In 1942, the morale of the German fighter pilots was very high. They were the elite of the German armed forces. Successful aces were highly publicized and the Luftwaffe was lavish with decorations.

From the beginning of the war, the Luftwaffe had been victorious for a long time—until they ran up against the RAF during the Battle of Britain. That defeat puzzled the Luftwaffe because they had been told that the British had only a handful of fighters. Yet, when the Germans sent air raids over England, the RAF was always there. The German pilots didn't realize that this was because of the superior British radar, the effectiveness of the controllers who directed the fighters, and the grim determination of the fighter pilots that kept them going back up again and again.

The Battle of Britain rattled the enemy's high command because of the high number of German losses; and their pilot morale suffered a shock at first, but was later restored. The pilots felt that, should the air battle be fought over German territory, they would be invincible. Thus, when 8th Air Force bombing missions began, German pilots were supremely confident.

Many other factors acted to keep German pilot morale at a high level. Their food and off-duty entertainment were good compared with the other German military services and the civilian populace. Unfavorable and unpleasant news was kept from them. Units moved from one front to another as the ground battles ebbed and flowed, and the pilots often did not realize the true situation in the air war. Some became more vicious and fanatical, however, when they learned their homes were being destroyed.

It was our assessment that the leading factor that kept the Luftwaffe's morale high was Hitler's promise of superweapons to come. The pilots knew of the jet and rocket planes and had uncommon faith in the Führer's ability to give them these and other new weapons in time to avoid defeat.

With all these pluses in favor of high morale, there were some negative factors. The German pilot had no fixed tour of duty after which he could go somewhere out of the war zone and relax. Every pilot had to fly and fight as long as he was capable. They could not help but observe firsthand how we continued to send our aircraft over day after day with declining losses. One by one, the Luftwaffe's high-scoring aces were killed or disabled. This had to have some effect on the units from which these men came.

By the fall of 1944, George Patton was wearing three stars as head of the 3rd Army, and units of the 8th were flying support missions for his fast-moving tank forces heading inexorably eastward. These missions put the two of us in touch by letter and radio message frequently.

In September 1944, Georgie wrote a letter addressed to "My Dear General Doolittle." He said he had just had the pleasure of decorating nine of my B-17 airmen from the 92nd Bomb Group with the Bronze Star. This crew, while flying a B-17 mission over Germany, had lost one engine but continued on the mission. However, the propeller could not be feathered and the aircraft developed a bad vibration. A second engine was then shot out, so they could no longer stay in formation. Just before they turned for home, they sought out a secondary target and dropped their bombs. On the way back toward England, they lost the third engine and all had to bail out. They landed behind Patton's front line at the Moselle river. Georgie concluded: "In my opinion, and in the opinion of the air officers at this headquarters, they did a very sporting job and showed great courage."

In the same classified envelope was a "Dear Jimmy" letter. It was a typical Patton-to-Doolittle communiqué and shows the nature and character of this unique American warrior:

> Don't get stuck up because I wrote you in an official manner. I don't think any more of you than I ever did, but I thought perhaps the first letter might be necessary for the record.
>
> I really was awfully pleased and want to compliment you on the fine spirit of the men of your command, and also to thank you for the great help you and all the other air people have been to this Army.

Shortly after, I received another "Dear Jimmy" letter from Georgie:

> This is to inform you that those low bastards, the Germans, gave me my first bloody nose when they compelled me to abandon our attack on Fort Driant in the Metz area.
>
> I have requested a revenge bombardment from the air to teach those sons of bitches that they cannot fool with Americans. I believe that this request will eventually get to you, and I am therefore asking that you see that the Patton-Doolittle combination is not shamed in the eyes of the world, and that you provide large bombs of the nastiest type, and as many as you can spare, to blow up this damn fort so that it becomes nothing but a hole.

I replied that it would be difficult to properly crack the thick cement emplacements at the fort. Instead of using the largest bombs we had available, we might have to use deep-penetration projectiles or fire bombs. "In any case," I said, "you may be sure that we refuse to allow the nasal proboscis of our favorite field commander to be sanguinated by these, as you so subtly put it, 'improper offspring of a long line of illegitimates.' " However, the fort proved to be too difficult to put out of action; it was simply bypassed.

In December 1944, one of our P-47s inadvertently strafed

Georgie Patton's troops. Since both the 8th and the 9th air forces had P-47s, Tooey Spaatz, Hoyt Vandenberg, then commander of the 9th, and I flew over to Patton's headquarters in two small Beech C-45 twin-engine transports to apologize. We spent New Year's Eve, 1945, with Georgie. On the way home, I had Tooey with me and planned to drop in to visit two 8th Air Force fighter groups that were located on the Continent. Shortly after takeoff, tracers began going by our planes—very, very close. Knowing that the Germans had been unusually active earlier that morning I thought it was a German fighter on my tail and immediately took violent evasive action.

Out of the corner of my eye I saw that Van, who had been flying formation with me, was also streaking for the deck. We were barreling along at full throttle close to the ground when I realized that it was our own flak that had chased us. We had been flying at about 1,500 feet and the ground troops (who had not seen many German aircraft for a long time) had been rigorously strafed that morning and were more than a little trigger-happy. They worked us over good before they realized that we were friendly.

Spaatz, sitting in the rear, wanted to know what was going on. I told him I thought at first that a German fighter was on our tail, but it turned out to be flak from Georgie's ground batteries. Tooey got madder than I had ever seen him. He was not particularly angry at Georgie's troops for shooting at us; he was mad because if we had waited just one more day, Georgie would have had to apologize to him instead of the other way around.

Tooey wanted to go back immediately, but I insisted on going to one of our fields where he could call Georgie and get his apology by phone.

When we approached for a landing at the fighter field, we saw a bunch of German fighter planes lying all around the area. The field group commander, a very eager chap, was to have flown a group patrol mission at 10 A.M. However, he decided to send up and lead an early dawn patrol and had just become airborne when the German planes came over intent upon destroying his planes on the ground. They were easy meat for our boys, who destroyed a couple of dozen then and there. It was a reward for a group commander who was an eager beaver. I was extremely proud of this gang.

Inadvertent bombing of our own troops was not the only

problem of this type I had. In November 1944, I received a letter from Air Commodore H. V. Rowley who complained, politely, that he was getting reports about bombs being dropped in his area of responsibility by Allied planes on practice bombing missions, and "I am afraid that the majority of the bombs are American."

My investigation showed that three B-24s had malfunctioning equipment and had dropped their practice bombs short. I invited him to my headquarters to partake of some refreshment to discuss any ideas he might have on the subject. Unfortunately, we were never able to eliminate having bomb hang-ups, malfunctioning releases, or just plain bad aiming.

As commander of the largest air force ever assembled, my responsibilities included much more than operational considerations. People problems and their solutions often took priority and a lot of my time. Our flight surgeons had to ground a high number of crew members because of sinusitis and respiratory diseases. There were far more cases in the 8th Air Force than we had experienced in the 12th and 15th in the Mediterranean. Although the groundings in these cases were usually temporary, it showed how environmental factors can affect war planning.

Frostbite was another common problem, which we tried to solve by installing windows to eliminate much of the wind blast in the bomber gun positions, procuring new face masks, and issuing electrically heated goggles.

Besides the occasional administrative foul-ups of orders and assignment of people to jobs for which they weren't trained, supply deficiencies sometimes became critical. Lack of electrically heated flying suits and other outer garments, oxygen masks, and even of winter underwear was enough to have an impact on mission scheduling at one time or another.

Food, a subject that armies have complained about for centuries, was often an item needing corrective action. One problem was the distribution of fresh meat. Another was the adoption of suitable rations for crews flying high-altitude missions. Some foods caused gas in the intestinal tract to expand, putting aircrews out of action from the pain if they couldn't get rid of it.

As if people problems like these weren't enough to give one a king-sized headache, there were others that have also probably plagued commanders throughout history. They had to do with matters concerning the civilian populace—particularly matters involving the heart and the physical cravings of males.

In one incident, an attractive Englishwoman and her equally attractive teenage daughter were brought into my office. The daughter was the spokesperson for both, and she inquired about a certain sergeant whom they had not seen for quite a while. I inquired immediately of my personnel officer while they waited, and was told that he had completed his missions and returned to the States.

"We were wondering why we hadn't seen him," the daughter said. "I work in the daytime and my mother works at night. To keep us from being lonely, he very kindly spent time with both of us between his missions. We live several miles outside of town and we loaned him our bicycle to go back and forth. We are both pregnant by him and we were curious why he had stopped seeing us."

I didn't know what to say and was about to send for the legal officer to explain their rights to them when the daughter interrupted. "Oh, no, please don't misunderstand," she said. "We don't want to cause him any trouble. We'd like to know if you can get our bicycle back."

By the end of 1944 we had refined our 8th Air Force operations, which represented more than two years of hard-won experience by Tooey, Ira, and me trying to knock out the German war industries and the Luftwaffe. As we encountered less and less enemy opposition and launched missions with ever-greater intensity, the 8th became a smooth team that worked together like the movement in a Swiss watch.

Every mission by the 8th was preceded by an operational staff conference in our underground war room at headquarters. Staff specialists would look at the "damage book," which contained graphic representations and reconnaissance photos of damage we had already inflicted on the strategic targets Tooey wanted us to concentrate on. The bomber specialists would estimate how much more effort was needed to destroy what had not been taken out. Aiming points for the bombardiers, routes in and out, assembly points, and rendezvous instructions would be determined. The fighter experts would estimate how many aircraft would be needed for escort and how many for strafing. The positions of the enemy's antiaircraft guns and fighter fields would be plotted to show what resistance could be expected.

The intelligence officer would give us the latest on German capabilities, defensive and offensive trends, and our success, or lack of it, in previous raids. The extent of the ground war was presented so we had an indication of how far the Allied troops had advanced. The intelligence officer would also give us the latest information obtained from debriefings of our own crews as well as from captured pilots and aircrews. Gun-camera film from the fighters and target photos of significance were often shown to prove a point or indicate where we needed to change our tactics. The operations statisticians would be available to summarize past operations and trends; the supply, maintenance, and communications staff members alerted us to any problems that might affect future operations. The chief flight surgeon would provide information that might affect our personnel. In short, our planning was based on past experience and accomplishments, as well as on our failures, and on what we thought the enemy was doing or might do to counter our plans.

I also held a daily meeting with my staff to discuss the next day's missions. One of the constant variables, especially in winter, was the weather. The staff weather officer would begin with a forecast for the target areas, the routes to them, and the expected weather at our bases between takeoff and return. There was a large map on the wall with red lights indicating fields that were closed in, green lights for those open. These indications gave me an instant clue as to which groups of bombers and fighters and how many of each would probably be available.

A briefing officer would describe the mission in general terms and explain, for example, that we would be dispatching 2,000 bombers, supported by 1,000 fighters. They were to attack a number of airfields, communications, manufacturing, or petroleum-refining targets in certain areas. The bomber controller would then state the time of takeoff, the time over target, and the bomber routes. The fighter controller would describe the planned operations for the fighters, which might include sweeps over the targets as well as escort. I would ask questions to ensure nothing had been overlooked and would make any decisions necessary.

There were always problems, changes, and alternatives to

be discussed. Nearly 200,000 men were involved in every day's missions; whatever we decided affected all of them in some way.

When the missions began, all of us would follow their progress. If the weather changed, it might mean that the commanders would have to bomb alternate targets. I would be apprised of that and, perhaps, have to make a command decision to divert or, if the weather was bad at any of their bases before their scheduled return, order them to withdraw and come home. In any event, changes from the original plan could mean replanning subsequent missions.

When the units returned, the crews would be debriefed and their reports analyzed by the intelligence and operations people. The medics would take care of the wounded; the chaplains would minister to them and the dead. The photographic people would rush the combat film to their labs for developing. Maintenance and repair personnel would assess the damage or malfunctions of equipment. The information at group, wing, and division level would be synthesized as it rose up the chain of command. I would then be briefed on the overall results and given information on any heroic acts noted, poor decisions made, or evidence of incompetence for which I should consider some disciplinary action or relief from command.

Lest any reader think we had no breaks from the daily grind of the air war, I should note that we had occasional headquarters parties, athletic competitions, dances, and other kinds of relaxation. Ira Eaker had done a superb job before I took over the 8th in providing relief from the long duty hours and getting the English people to accept Americans. One of the things he did was to have a group of people who had been in the theater business put on a show called *Skirts*. This was a burlesque in which there were no women—only men dressed as girls. By the time I arrived, it had become sort of a tradition in the command and I didn't want to stop it.

Shortly after I took over, I received a call from a member of the Queen Mother's staff in Bath. She said she had heard the Americans were going to put on a burlesque show and the Queen Mother wanted to know if she could see it. We couldn't refuse, so Jack Allard, my chief of staff, and the cast of *Skirts* went to Bath where a barn was prepared with a stage and a few dozen seats for the Queen Mother and her staff so they could see the show.

We put the Queen Mother between Jack and me so we could carefully gauge her reaction. The first part of the show was just a little risqué and we had arranged with the stage manager that he was to stick his head around the corner to look at me. If I gave him a thumbs-up, he was to go on with the show as planned. However, if I gave him a thumbs-down, he was to expurgate the risqué things out of the rest of the show.

After the curtain rang down on the first part, the Queen Mother bent over laughing hysterically, so as the manager stuck his head out he got my thumbs-up sign.

If I had had to make the decision about putting on the show in the first place, I have to admit that I wouldn't have done it. But seeing the Queen Mother's reaction and the way the troops liked it, I realized Ira was right. As a result, I encouraged more shows and we had a continuous flow of entertainers, many of them big names in the movie business. Clark Gable was on the public relations staff and was no doubt instrumental in getting many of them to contribute their time. Of course, Bob Hope was one of them. We first met in North Africa, where his show was always a crowd pleaser. Bob deserves the plaudits of all Americans for what he has done to bolster the morale of American fighting men in war zones then and many times since.

One day, a young, sandy-haired major came to my office and gave me a very superior report on his public relations activities. I was impressed and said, "Young man, are you in the regular establishment?"

"No, sir," he replied. "I'm a reservist."

"What do you do in civil life?"

"General, I'm an actor in motion pictures and a damn good one."

It was Van Heflin, a fine actor who had graduated from the University of Oklahoma.

Jimmy Stewart was the only motion picture celebrity to go all the way through pilot training, as far as I know. He put his promising acting career behind him and became a combat pilot and a flight and squadron leader. He then became a group operations officer and group executive officer. If the war had gone on another month Jimmy would have become a group commander, which was the most important job in the Air Force, in my opinion, much like a regimental commander in the Army or a ship's captain in the Navy. A group commander is the chap who knows everybody in his command. After that, the command gets too big and things become abstract.

Jimmy maintained his commission in the reserves, became a general, and retired as the law required at age 60. I have always thought him a very special individual for his continued support of the Air Force and his help in getting the Air Force Association started and running after the war was over.

Thanks to Bruce Johnson's special talents for acquiring items in short supply, we always had a little "tea" of various vintages and origins available for visiting dignitaries. The variety and quality of champagnes, cognac, and wines increased after the invasion of Normandy as Bruce commandeered space on supply planes that otherwise would be returning to England empty. After he dropped hints to visiting dignitaries, we always received various morsels of culinary delight from the States, brought over by government VIPs or Washington staff members on inspection trips.

I had the pleasure of pinning the Legion of Merit on Bruce, which he had earned serving under Ira and me in North Africa and Italy. The citation gave him credit for procuring buildings, building laundries and kitchens, supervising officers' messes, billets, a theater, amusement clubs, rest homes, recreational centers, and motor pools. His close liaison work with the British, French, and Italian military agencies and civilian authorities had been so expertly and diplomatically handled that the spirit of goodwill, unity, and friendship he created improved our relations immeasurably.

Our distinguished visitor list during 1944 included King George VI and Queen Elizabeth, and Bruce had total responsibility to plan for the occasion. I should mention here that Bruce stuttered when he was flustered, and this upcoming visit certainly flustered him. I tried to be as gentle as I could when I told Bruce I didn't want him to talk with the king. Since both stuttered, I thought it might upset our guest.

The royal party arrived on schedule. They inspected my home guard and then took a tour of the installation. I waited for the party at the headquarters building. Bruce thought he should place the queen where everyone could see her plainly. When she alighted from her car, he offered her his left arm, thus placing her on his left. Following Bruce's lead, I stayed on the right side of the king. It was not until later that I was told that we had committed a serious faux pas. No one is ever supposed to walk on the right side of royalty.

The next morning the front page of a London newspaper had a large picture displaying our crime to the world. The British reporters were kind to us in the story, however, never mentioning that we had committed a social sin.

I don't think our dual faux pas did any harm to our relations with our British allies. Before leaving Wycombe, we had a reception in the officers' club and the king invested me with the insignia of an honorary knight commander of the Most Honourable Order of the Bath. I wrote to Joe that since I was now a lord, she was a lady. Typically, she wrote back saying that it would take more than me being made a lord for her to become a lady.

I have always meant to look up the origin of the honor, but assume that it has nothing to do with the state of my personal cleanliness. In any event, I was very pleased and accepted it with as much aplomb as I could muster.

After General Eisenhower and Tooey went to France, leaving me as the senior American officer in Britain, I met with Prime Minister Winston Churchill many times at No. 10 Downing Street and at Chequers, his country estate. He was extremely knowledgeable about all aspects of the war, including aviation, and I thoroughly enjoyed the privilege of being able to talk with him alone. He was one of the most brilliant men I have ever known.

My first visit to Chequers was an experience about which I wish I could recall more. We had a few drinks and supper and then he ordered up a movie. Afterward we discussed the air war and how I was getting along with my British counterparts. As we talked, I tried to match his frequent refills of brandy. It wasn't long before I remembered that short fighter pilots have lesser resistance to its effects than larger people. I realized that I was a guest in the Prime Minister's home and was getting too gabby. However, before I lapsed into silence and listened to this great man discourse on events, I thought I should say something brilliant. After saying something brilliant, I planned to say nothing more, drink some black coffee, and reachieve sobriety.

When the opportunity came for me to speak, I made a very, very erudite statement. At least Churchill must have thought it so. He said, "Splendid, Jimmy, just splendid! I shall use that tomorrow in my debate in the House of Commons. It's just what I need to make a very important point!"

To this day, I haven't the foggiest idea what I said.

Perhaps I needed a rest about that time. At least, Tooey Spaatz thought so and said Hap had asked. I didn't think it was expedient with so much going on. I confided in a letter to Joe that I might be home for a short visit, provided there was a sufficiently important official reason. I thought Hap was interested in looking me over to see if I was holding up well enough in my present job and perhaps make a decision as to what job he might want me for after the war.

"I think he wants to find out if I have mellowed enough to get along with people, particularly in high places," I wrote. "I feel that I have, although the mellowing is not yet completed. I still have the unfortunate habit of expressing whatever is on my mind, which in many cases, even though it happens to be so, had better not be expressed. This old habit of talking when I should be listening is being gradually corrected. I still slip occasionally, but constant effort is producing results."

A few weeks later, I wrote that Tooey and I were going to take a short rest trip to the Riviera in the south of France in lieu of coming home where I knew I wouldn't get any rest. If I went home, I envisioned talks before the Staff College, press conferences, tea parties, and meetings, "all of which give me severe rectal pains and none of which is conducive to rest." The only reason I wanted to go home at that time would be to see Joe, John, and Jim III, our first grandchild, born in September 1944.

The trip to the warmer climate was a welcome relief from the daily grind of war, but after three days on the Riviera, we visited bases in Italy. As a result, I had to get back to England so I could rest up from the rest trip.

By November 1944, Allied air units could roam at will all over Germany. Control of the planes for supporting ground troops had been given over weeks before to General Eisenhower to parcel out as he saw fit to satisfy his ground generals. Priority had been given to tactical bombing and strafing. Strategic bombing took second place. Two thirds of my aircraft were assigned to assist ground forces.

On one of the days that month, 400 of the 8th's fighters made a bombing and strafing round trip of over 1,100 miles. They destroyed 27 German aircraft in the air, including one Me-262. Sixty-four enemy planes were destroyed on the ground. That day's mission summary showed 131 locomotives, 24 railroad cars, and 42 petroleum cars destroyed. They hit factories, warehouses, and plane hangars—anything that looked like it was contributing to the enemy's war effort. Our loss: eight fighters. The day's results reflected the success we had long planned for and were achieving. However, we could not rest on our laurels. The Germans had proven many times before that when we thought we had them licked, they rebounded with new ideas and weapons and found another way to give us a hard time.

As if to prove that the 1944 Christmas holidays should not be a time for the Allies to celebrate, German ground forces had started an offensive on December 18 and it intensified during a period of dense fog. The fog covered not only the entire battlefront but also our own airfields, and it settled down to stay, day after day.

We had also been carrying out a tactical offensive beginning on December 19 and continuing for several days thereafter, in weather that hitherto had been considered nonoperational. Some of our formations encountered clouds up to 32,000 feet. Bombing had to be accomplished by instruments.

We got our big break on December 24. There was poor visibility over England, but the forecast called for excellent weather over Germany. We dispatched more than 2,000 B-17s and B-24s with an escort of almost 1,000 fighters. Eleven airfields and 14 communications centers were hit with 5,000 tons of bombs.

Most of those 3,000 planes returned, one way or another. For those who got back it was a curious Christmas Eve. While they were airborne, the weather over England had grown worse. At some of our bases the weather had grown so thick that they could not land at their home bases. They came down on any airfield they could find open, and wherever they landed the officers and men who belonged to those fields took the visiting crews in and shared their Christmas with them—cigarettes or chocolate or talk of home or whatever else they had. The mechanics and other ground crewmen at these stations took over the repair and servicing of the visiting planes as willingly as they tackled their own—even though it meant double the work and no sleep that night. The next day, Christmas morning, the planes were ready to go again.

On another day during that period, when the bombers were able to get into the air, every fighter station was fogged in. Visibility was less than 100 yards. Realizing the urgency of the situation, many of the fighter group commanders asked for volunteers. At some stations, every fighter pilot volunteered, and one group put more planes into the air that day than it ever had before.

The statistics for December 18, 1944, to January 12, 1945, tell the story. We dispatched bombers 16,312 times against tactical targets during the period. They dropped approximately 40,000 tons of bombs on 19 German airfields, 64 railway marshaling yards, and 54 road and rail junctions and other communications targets, most of them between the Rhine and the battle line. Our fighters destroyed 403 enemy planes in aerial combat and 7 on the ground, while our bombers destroyed an additional 58. Our contribution was only part of the picture. The RAF and the Tactical Air Forces also deployed their forces in great strength.

Success was measured in other ways. We learned from intelligence sources that parts of a German division covered the 40 miles from their bivouac on the Rhine to the front on bicycles. Detraining points were forced back 50 to 60 miles, increasing the distance that German trucks had to haul supplies. Some of the German troops were without food for several days in the extremely cold and bitter weather. A considerable quantity of self-propelled guns and armored vehicles were captured intact and in perfect condition except for one thing: their gas tanks were empty. The crippling of communication lines contributed to the abandonment of equipment.

Unfortunately, these apparent victories were short-lived. We thought we had decimated the Luftwaffe's pilot ranks and had nearly stopped the manufacture of new aircraft, but we hadn't. We found that the production of petroleum products had increased, as had production of ball bearings, rockets, and missiles.

At Leuna, west of Leipzig, the enemy's largest synthetic oil plant was attacked 18 times by the 8th and 3 times by the RAF. It was the single most heavily defended industrial plant in Germany. The area was surrounded by 437 88-mm and larger rapid-fire heavy antiaircraft and artillery cannon. We halted all production there five times, but each time the Germans used thousands of repairmen to put the plant back into partial production. Obviously, we hadn't finished the strategic job, and as the new year began, it seemed like it might be another year before we could defeat the enemy and go home.

On February 3, 1945, I dispatched 1,000 B-17s to bomb transportation targets in and around Berlin. It was the first time we had bombed the capital city in two months. About 400 B-24s attacked oil refineries in the Magdeburg area; all were escorted by P-51s authorized to come down from altitude and strafe railway installations. The object was to interrupt troop movements and, concurrently, lower German morale. We made similar raids on February 13–14 against the transportation centers at Berlin, Leipzig, and Dresden, all three densely populated. The raid on the latter, targeted at the request of the Soviets, resulted in thousands of civilian casualties, for which we were severely criticized in some of the world's press for our "terror bombing" of innocent civilians.

On February 22 and 23, 1945, the 8th, in concert with the 15th operating from Italy, made raids all over Germany, mainly against transportation targets. Out of a total of 1,193 bombers dispatched, only 2 of the 8th's were lost.

The criticism we received caused me to analyze what we had done. I wrote a report in which I compared our efforts in 1945 with the missions of 1944 against three industrial cities, also heavily populated. The first two cities attacked were illustrative of the collaboration in which American heavy bombers destroyed the major industries on the fringes of the city and the RAF destroyed the city proper with the substantial number of factories situated in the urban center. In Magdeburg, the 8th hit the top-priority synthetic gasoline plant at Rothensee; the Krupp plant at Buchau making tanks, shells, guns, and other weapons; the ordnance depot at Friedrichstadt, where these weapons were collected for distribution to enemy units in combat on the Western and Eastern fronts; and the Junkers factory turning out the newest engine powering the Fw 190.

The RAF followed this by the destruction of the urban area. The final phase not only destroyed the houses of the factory workers and interrupted vital military industrial transport, but also destroyed a very large part of the remaining factories in this highly developed industrial center. In an armaments city of this kind, most of the industries were interdependent, using common sources of power, raw materials, and transport, with many smaller plants making parts for final assembly of war materiel in the larger ones.

Kassel was another example of the same coordination, with the difference that the RAF, in a night area attack, also destroyed a factory on our priority list of precision targets, the Focke-Wulf assembly plant at Kassel-Bettenhausen.

In the preceding months, RAF Bomber Command and the 8th had been attacking identical targets. The RAF, having reduced the production of the synthetic oil plants in the Ruhr to minor proportions by attacks during the summer and autumn of 1944, began in December to help us with the campaign that we had started the previous spring against the major synthetic plants lying much deeper in Germany. Zeitz was a good example of this. We knocked it out in late May 1944 and kept it from any substantial production until November 1944. Then in January, the RAF put it out for another three months.

The 8th and the RAF also engaged in a joint assault on the vital rail and water communications of western Germany. The RAF blocked the Dortmund-Ems canal and the western part of the Mittelland canal, while the 8th twice breached the aqueduct at Minden. These waterways were used for bulk transport, including coal from the Ruhr and prefabricated U-boat parts too large for shipment by rail. On the railways, we worked on major marshaling yards, bridges, and viaducts.

This program, which was too ambitious for either air force to tackle alone, made systematic operation of the railroads impossible. The economic traffic from and within the Ruhr, which was doubly important to the Germans because of the loss of Silesia to the Soviets, was curtailed. Enemy military movements east of the Rhine became slower and more hazardous every day.

It is a fact in the grim business of strategic warfare that the results of such bombing efforts do not show up immediately on the battlefront. It is also a fact that when strategic targets are attacked, noncombatants will be killed. There is no way to hit factory buildings, railroad yards, and other such things without killing or maiming the civilians who are making the enemy's war materials.

During March 1945, we put up heavy bombers on 26 days and flew 30,358 sorties—a record—and dropped the greatest tonnage of bombs of any month of the war. During the last week of the month, 67,365 tons were dropped, exceeding the previous record, established during the whole month of August 1944. We found that the Germans were so good at repairing damage that we had to go back time after time to keep some targets from getting back into operation. We experimented with Disney bombs, made to penetrate the heavily concreted submarine pens at IJmuiden. These were large bombs with rocket motors in their tails. At 5,000 feet, the rocket motors would start so that upon impact, the missile would be traveling at 2,400 feet per second and would pierce 20 feet of solid concrete before exploding.

While enemy opposition to our raids seemed to be dwindling, the numbers of Luftwaffe jets began to increase, especially on missions to Berlin. Their four 30-mm nose guns were deadly against our bombers, and their speed gave them an advantage we couldn't match with our fighters. We lost 24 B-17s in March to the Me-262s. Approximately a dozen of the jets were claimed as having been shot down.

Now getting desperate, the Luftwaffe put out the call for volunteers for "special and dangerous" operations, and 300 pilots showed up at Stendal for training. Half of these were chosen and formed the Sonderkommando Elbe. It was the German equivalent of the Japanese kamikaze squadrons. Flying Me-109s, they were instructed to attack a bomber by firing at extreme range and keep on firing until they rammed it, preferably in the fuselage aft of the wing. The pilots would then bail out. About eight of our bombers were brought down by being rammed.

By the beginning of April 1945, we were running out of targets. Victory was in the air as the armies of the Allies moved rapidly and pushed back the German defenders. As the official Air Force history notes: "Most of Germany was not enemy territory any longer."

We still sent out bomber armadas with heavy escorts against old targets that seemed to be able to respond as part of the Nazis' last-ditch defenses. Again, we found that we could still suffer losses. On April 10 about 50 jets brought down 10 of our bombers, the largest loss of the war to jets in a single mission.

By mid-April the German factories were not turning out war materiel; there were no more oil refineries; the submarine pens were no longer a menace to the Allied navies. Only tactical bombings remained. We were now ready to call a halt to the strategic air war.

On April 16, 1945, Tooey Spaatz, then at his headquarters at Rheims, sent out messages to me and Nate Twining at the 15th in Italy, announcing that the strategic air war was over and that we would henceforth operate with our tactical air forces in close cooperation with the ground forces.

As the Allied ground forces rushed to join up with the Soviets, we began to analyze what we had accomplished. Our assaults on the plants and refineries producing oil, fuel, and lubricants were, as the official history states, "the brightest phase of the triumphs." Despite the Germans' best attempts to disperse and repair damaged facilities, they had failed. As a consequence, their aircraft, tanks, and trucks were immobilized; they could not provide the minimums needed for their war effort or for their economy.

Although we were unable to stop completely their aircraft production, they had reached the bottom of their manpower pool, gasoline supply, and protected airfields. We had taken the Luftwaffe out of the sky and thereby made all other successes possible. Their transportation system of roads, bridges, and railroads had been destroyed; their communications system was in complete disarray.

I had our statisticians compile what the 8th had done in three years of war, and the figures are impressive: 701,300 tons of bombs dropped, including 531,771 tons on Germany; 18,512 enemy aircraft destroyed. On the other side of the ledger, we listed 43,742 American fighter pilots and bomber crewmen as killed or missing in action. We lost 4,456 bombers in combat.

On April 30, 1945, we learned that Hitler and Eva Braun, whom he had just married, had committed suicide. However, a few diehard Germans apparently thought there was still hope. Some sporadic ground fighting continued briefly.

Hermann Goering had been shunted aside as an heir apparent before Hitler's death, and Grand Admiral Karl Doenitz inherited what was left of the Third Reich. On Monday, May 7, the Allied commanders, including Tooey Spaatz, gathered in a war room in Rheims and witnessed the signing of the unconditional surrender documents by Colonel General Alfred Jodl. General

Walter ''Beetle'' Smith signed for the Allies. President Harry S Truman, who had succeeded to the presidency when President Roosevelt died the month before, and Prime Minister Churchill proclaimed May 8, 1945, as V-E Day.

There was still work to be done. The 8th flew many mercy missions and dropped food parcels to the famished population of the Netherlands. There were thousands of prisoners of war being released and all kinds of planes were mustered to bring them to evacuation centers. As a tribute to our men, I authorized 30,000 8th Air Force ground personnel to make aerial tours of Germany to see with their own eyes what they had helped to bring about.

CHAPTER 17

While the action was winding down, Hap contacted me in April to say that he wanted me to return to the States to take over the job held by Lieutenant General William S. Knudsen, who as head of the Air Technical Service Command was in charge of the Army Air Forces' air development, supply, and maintenance functions. He wanted me to return immediately because Knudsen was scheduled to go back to civilian life within a month. I didn't want to leave England until the job was finished, and then I wanted to go to the Pacific. However, I told Tooey that I might be tempted to accept Knudsen's job if I would be made a permanent brigadier general so I could deal more equally with those who would be senior to me in Regular Army rank and military experience.

By early May, Hap's plans for me had changed. I was to stay on as commander of the 8th and the mission of my command was to begin redeployment to the Pacific. Nine B-17 and three P-51 groups would become part of the occupation forces in Germany. The remainder of my command would return to the States, where selected units would train for further service in the Pacific. The bomb groups were to be flown back across the Atlantic; ground personnel would return by ship. The first B-24 left on May 19, 1945, followed by 2,118 heavy bombers over the next two months.

Meanwhile, as head of the 8th, I was to return home first and then set up my headquarters at Kadena Air Base, on Okinawa. Instead of flying B-17s and B-24s, we would be equipped with B-29 Superfortresses. Some of the 8th's B-24 units that had returned to the States in 1944 were already transitioning into B-29s and would have eventually gone to Okinawa. A preliminary organization, the 20th Bomber Command, had been activated at Salina, Kansas, in November 1943. Originally, the 20th Bomber Command, under Major General Curtis E. LeMay, was to operate principally from India and China, and missions began against targets in Bangkok on May 27, 1944. The last mission from there was against Singapore in March 1945. The first attack against Japan was made from China on June 15, 1944.

Meanwhile, the 21st Bomber Command was activated on Guam with Major General Haywood S. "Possum" Hansell, Jr., in command. Hap wasn't pleased with the results of the B-29 effort in the Pacific, so Possum was relieved, and Curt LeMay took his place.

The 20th Air Force, under which the two bomber commands would operate, was activated in April 1944. There had been quite a hassle in the Pacific between General Douglas MacArthur and Admiral Chester Nimitz; both wanted overall control of all Air Force operations in the coming all-out assault against Japan, but Hap refused to relinquish control of a major air force to either one. The 20th was to be operated as a global air force under the supervision of the Joint Chiefs of Staff. Tooey Spaatz would exercise command over the 720 B-29s of the 20th Air Force operating from the Marianas and the 8th Air Force's 720 Superforts in the Ryukyus, just as he had command over the strategic air forces in Europe. His Strategic Air Command headquarters was established on Guam.

When the B-29s started arriving in the Pacific in October 1944, bases were established on Guam, Saipan, and Tinian. The first attack on Tokyo from the Pacific took place on November 24, 1944. It was the first time American planes had appeared over the Japanese capital since our raid in April 1942. By June, the 20th had 700 B-29s in the Pacific; the daily number of sorties increased from 68 in June 1944 to nearly 6,000 a year later.

Hap was convinced that Japan could be driven to surrender without an invasion and was determined to make the bomber offensive decisive. If so, this would be used as evidence that the Air Force should be established after the war as an independent service—something all of us felt was absolutely essential to maintain the peace in the postwar world.

I was ordered home from England along with Pat Partridge on May 10. I turned over command of the 8th to Major General Bill Kepner, but my exodus was made under a cloud. A news release was made in Washington on May 26 by the Army Air Forces that said: "Japanese war industries can expect an even greater volume of air attack than was accomplished against Hitler's fortress Europe. General Doolittle is now prepared to help finish the job he started on Japan on April 18, 1942, when he hit Tokyo with the carrier-based B-25s, but now he'll be using land-based bombers with plenty of fighter cover."

A London newspaper, in announcing my departure, had a story under an attention-getting headline: "Doolittle Tells of Plans to Win Other Half of War." The reporter told how 3,000 Superforts would soon smash the Japs and implied that Doolittle would lead the blitz on the Japanese until they were brought to their knees.

Another headline read: "Doolittle and 8th to Finish Job in Pacific."

Anyone who knows me would not believe I had anything to do with these announcements. The newspapers obviously needed some sensational copy for my departure and assignment to the Pacific. I don't know for certain where the story originated, but Bruce Johnson did a little sleuthing and wrote in his memoirs that a certain general officer had a few too many drinks one night and talked nonsense to a reporter.

There were a number of widely circulated cartoons published that announced my assignment to the Pacific. One of them showed a terrified Japanese naval officer rushing to tell his superior, "O, disaster! O, so veery unpleasantness! DOOLITTLE coming back!" A servant is shown running behind him with a hara-kiri knife, saying, "Now?"

These distorted press notices implied that after more than three years of hard fighting and dying in the Pacific by thousands of brave Army, Navy, Air Force, and Marine personnel, Doolittle was now going to end the war singlehandedly. The reactions of General MacArthur and Admiral Nimitz, two men who had shared the burden of the Pacific war, can be easily imagined when their staffs put those press clippings before them. Both were graduates of their respective service academies and had spent their entire adult lives in the military. Naturally, they would resent a reserve officer who, apparently, if you believed the news reports, thought he was a savior.

I was already off on the wrong foot on the other side of the world, and I hadn't even left England yet. I was now in the same situation with those two top leaders as I had been with Ike after I arrived in England and tried to brief him about my plans for the invasion of North Africa.

I didn't want to think about the reception I might get in the Pacific. For the first time in too many months I was going home. Jim, Jr., and I left England together and were reunited with Joe and John in Washington.

There is no grander feeling in the world than to return to the comfort of one's hearth and family. Joe and I went to Miami for a little R&R (rest and recreation) and caught up as best we could on what each had been doing during our long forced separation. I was amazed and very proud to learn of the many selfless activities to which she had devoted herself, and continued to devote herself, in a self-imposed schedule that was at least as demanding as my own. Joe was always a total participant and an independent contributor. Certainly this was a situation where she sought out and created functions for herself that helped the all-out effort that the nation and, most particularly for her, the men in her family were making. We talked much of our sons and their prospects, and some of what I intended to do after the war.

Meanwhile, in Washington, the War Department public relations folks had a speaking itinerary planned for me before I could go to the Pacific. Winning the war in Germany had caused many Americans to become apathetic. There was a visible letdown that was very damaging to our continuation of hostilities with Japan. A number of general officers who had served in Europe were put on the road to make public appearances and radio speeches. The objective was to have the American people thoroughly realize that the war was not over yet and we had to continue to make whatever sacrifice was necessary in order to bring it to a quick conclusion.

General Spaatz and General Eisenhower were teamed as senior ground man and senior airman in Europe and gave speeches in the Washington area. General Omar Bradley and

General Hoyt Vandenberg gave joint talks around the New York area. Since Georgie Patton and I were both Californians, the War Department issued orders for us to make appearances and speeches together on the West Coast. With our wives accompanying, we met in Denver. As could be expected, Georgie, replete with shiny steel helmet, ivory-handled pistol, large round belt buckle, highly polished boots, battle jacket, swagger stick, and jodhpurs, was a hit with the public and press photographers wherever we went.

We arrived in Los Angeles and were given a generous welcome by what the *Los Angeles Times* said was a million people. We were decked out in all our ribbons, which Georgie said "our dead won," and were driven in a large motorcade to City Hall. I had on my summer uniform and, as all Air Force pilots did in those days, wore my floppy "crushed" cap without the grommet. Pilots always liked to take the grommet out to give the impression we had to do that so we could wear a headset over the cap. It was the only deviation I would make from Army uniform regulations. General officers are authorized to wear different uniforms from their officers, but I never liked to set myself apart uniformwise from the rest of the officer corps. Such variation was Patton's style. To do otherwise wouldn't have been Georgie.

As could be expected, Georgie was his usual blunt self in public. He could not be muzzled, and he made off-the-cuff remarks about our Allies, the Soviets, politicians, and even the next war. When we appeared on a stage where we used a microphone, the Army public relations people who followed us around had a switch on the mike so they could cut him off if he got too candid or coarse with his remarks. They couldn't always catch him in time.

We would take turns speaking first. If he talked first, it was always a typical fire-and-brimstone Patton speech using words that I thought were often too soldierly, especially before mixed audiences. I would follow and try to give a quieter pitch for balance. If I talked first, he would invariably liven it up with his colorful oratory. The *Los Angeles Times* reported, accurately, that Patton peppered his speech with profanity "mild to those who have soldiered with him." He called upon those at home "to provide money . . . provide labor . . . provide sweat . . . so the sacrifices made by your relatives, your friends have not been in vain. You must not sell short the Air Forces, the ground forces, and the Navy. You must produce the sweat and the money to destroy those people whom modesty prevents my describing.''

In typical Hollywood style, a mock tank battle was staged in the Coliseum, after which Georgie said, ''What you have just seen is phantasma but damn near reality, and, God forgive me, I love that kind of war!'' He always got the most applause.

Besides the Coliseum show, another appearance was held at the Hollywood Bowl. Joe and Beatrice Patton were seated on the stage with us. I spoke first and reminded the audience that the war wasn't over and that we had to bring that same spirit and determination that had ended the war in Europe to bear against the Japanese. In conclusion, I acknowledged the presence of our wives, saying, ''If General Patton and I have achieved any success in fighting the war, these two lovely ladies are responsible for that success because of their constant support, understanding, and affection.''

Joe and Beatrice stood up and the applause was deafening. It was Georgie's turn and as I turned to take my seat, he passed me. Not realizing that the mike would catch his every word with glorious amplification, he said, ''You son of a bitch, I wish I'd said that!''

Georgie and I parted soon after. Both of us were scheduled to go to the Pacific and he was anxious to ''get out there and kill Japs'' before the war was over. He was sent back to Europe instead. We lost a genuine national war hero when he was killed the following December in a Jeep accident while serving in the Army of Occupation. I have often wondered how he would have tolerated retirement in peacetime.

After visiting several aircraft factories in California, I went to Seattle to talk with the employees of the Boeing Company and get a good look at the B-29 Superfortresses the 8th would be flying. Meanwhile, Bruce Johnson had preceded me to the States and was now at Peterson Army Air Field, in Colorado Springs, organizing our headquarters unit for the transfer to Okinawa. He selected a B-29 crew for my personal airplane, and I joined him during the first week in July 1945. Pat Partridge, Bruce, my longtime aide Major Tom Barrineau, and I, along with two crews, proceeded to Washington in two planes; I flew the B-29, and Bruce and Pat followed with parts and supplies in a B-17.

After conferring with Hap and others, we took off for Britain minus Pat, who was to return to Colorado and then join us later on Okinawa. One engine of the B-29 swallowed a valve just as we were landing in Britain and it had to have an engine change. I'm sure Pat got a chuckle out of our difficulty because he had wanted us to take two B-17s in the first place.

We stayed a couple of days and I made a quick trip to France to pick up cases of champagne for General MacArthur and General George Kenney, and a bottle of Napoleon brandy for Admiral Nimitz. I thought perhaps that might ease the way for me into their good graces.

We flew in the two planes to Cairo and Kharagpur, India, where we had more trouble with the B-29. A vagrant wind blew a steel barrel into one of the B-29's props, so I proceeded in the B-17 and arrived in the Philippines to meet George Kenney. Bruce, Tom, and I then flew to Kadena Air Base, on Okinawa, where we officially established the presence of the 8th Air Force in the Pacific theater with our lone B-17 on July 17, 1945. We had no way of knowing that on that same day, a new type of bomb had been detonated at Los Alamos, New Mexico.

The happenings of the next three weeks or so while we tried to get established with all the necessary creature comforts for the many men who were to follow were detailed in my letters to Joe. Things were much more primitive than the relatively luxurious life we had led in England. We lived in tents again, just as we had for a long time in North Africa. Bruce established our headquarters about 10 miles northeast of Kadena in an area that was full of Okinawan burial mounds. One of his first acquisitions for us was a refrigerator; I never inquired where he got it. Here are some excerpts from my letters to Joe.

July 19, 1945:

> Rained last night. Blew so hard everything in the tent including me got wet. We had been warned of the blow so put down additional tent stakes and checked hold-down ropes. The wind was blowing so high that the rain was blowing nearly horizontally. Also shifted direction rapidly, so with these "ventilated" tents, it came in one side and out the other—except for a considerable percentage which stopped en route.

July 26:

It is still raining. Have to drive my Jeep in low-low gear and four-wheel drive due to the slick mud. (Some difference between a muddy Jeep self-driven and a Cadillac with chauffeur.)

July 26:

Had quite an impressive flag-raising ceremony in the rain this morning. I hoisted Old Glory up on our new flagpole, and the chaplain solicited divine sanction and aid for our project. We are now officially in business but won't be bombing until next month.

Had a press conference today. Am hopeful that they don't put out too much baloney. Had a press conference in Guam the other day and they quoted me as saying that we would start bombing on August 1. I said, "in August." I wasn't so worried about press errors when my superiors thought more kindly of me. Now I may have serious consequences.

July 28:

Three batches of letters arrived today, one of them with the usual run of—

a. Autograph and send picture.

b. Invention to win the war. Comment requested.

c. Please send dope on so and so, who is MIA [missing in action] and was with your outfit.

d. I want to be with the 8th in the Pacific.

e. Answer following questions:

f. Give speech at ———

g. Put in a plug for me or my friend who wants

1. In the Army
2. Out of the Army
3. Transfer to another outfit
4. A job

I've been thinking we should stake out our claim

someplace in the Monterey Bay area pretty soon. We may not be settling down for some years yet, but ought to be keeping our eyes open for the right spot from now on. We will need a home for the grandchildren as they grow up and come to visit us and get spoiled.

July 31:

Last day of the month and I've been here two weeks. Seems longer somehow—probably because so much construction work has been accomplished and one sees such substantial changes in the camp daily. My temporary tent-office now has a floor in it and Tom [Barrineau] rigged up a salvaged parachute for a ceiling yesterday. The double roof makes the tent much cooler.

August 2:

Still raining. The weatherman predicted clearing for today, yesterday. Now he predicts better weather for tomorrow. Afraid the meteorological crystal balls are no more accurate here than they were in England.

August 7:

Am afraid I'm in a little press trouble. My P.R.O. [public relations officer], a young captain, gave out some dope that was highly controversial and has gotten me in the middle. Gave a talk to the ground force officers here. Talked "off the record." My P.R.O., either misunderstanding my desires or not realizing the implications, gave some dope on "unity of command" to the press. They immediately applied it to the Pacific command setup. If one only had time to write out everything he gave to the press it would be great.

A gang is coming in in about an hour. They will want sensational statements on the new bomb and on Russia's entry into the war. I'll be noncommittal and then pray for the best when their articles come out. The American public wants sensationalism, and the press dishes it out. All of which is dandy when it is not at my expense.

Later. Had a pleasant visit with the publishers. Talked "off the record" but was still very careful—I hope.

August 13:

Have quite a few of the old Rockwell Fielders here now. Could have a swell reunion—or set up an old soldiers' home.

August 22:

There was, I understand, something of a furor over an "off the record" talk I gave to officers of the 10th Army on August 14. I said, "I believe, unreservedly, in unity of command—one supreme commander to control all arms and services. The principle of unity of command was proven in North Africa, Sicily, and Italy and on the Continent. We had divided control at Pearl Harbor."

I then went on to tell how we had operated in Europe and advised that all air would probably be under one commander for the assault phase (against Japan). Didn't even mention the present command in the Pacific. After the meeting a P.R.O. came up and asked if any of the talk could be printed. I stated I had no objection provided controversial subjects were avoided, no mention made of command, particularly in the Pacific and on Okinawa, and nothing I had said restated in a way that could possibly be twisted to represent a criticism of the Pacific command setup. No matter how I felt about it I was not in a position while still in the military service to go outside of military channels.

The story was given to United Press International and Associated Press, and what I thought and said was exaggerated to make a story. The final dope came out, "Doolittle states war in Pacific can't be won unless a supreme commander is appointed now."

One cable and then an ominous silence from home. The clippings are coming in. It's interesting to read the comments. Many analysts ask or try to explain why Doolittle said this or that. Not one questions if he said it. Through the years we have marveled at this trait in human nature—odd but very real—and dangerous.

September 1:

Took a Jeep ride up to the north end of the island and looked over the military government installations. They are handling over 200,000 natives. Many are still coming in from the hills and most of these are in pretty bad shape from malnutrition. Quite a few are "nonreversible" and even with the best of medical care soon succumb. Horribly infected battle casualties are still being brought in. Many of these are children and most are the handiwork of bombardment. It's distressing to realize that only two military services are constructive—the medics and the engineers. All of the rest of us are destructive.

I saw a little six-year-old with his hand blown off by a bomb fragment and a little sock over the stump. He was all alone, an orphan, leaning against a fence post. As I met his eye I know that my glance showed guilt as well as pity. And that guilt is not only of us killers in the war, but it is on the American people at home, unless steps are taken now to see that we don't promptly have another war.

Those steps are:

1. A firm national policy directed toward fair dealings with all nations, and the establishment, not only of a better America, but of a better world.

2. A sound national defense establishment, capable of rapid expansion and equipped with the most modern equipment available. It should be small but

mobile, and this means prepared, equipped, and supplied bases throughout the world.

3. Universal military training as a means to rapid expansion if required.

4. A continuation of all-out scientific development so we lead the world in technology as well as tactics. This technological development will have commercial as well as military applications and will therefore assure our own position and place in world trade.

We want peace, and the only way we can assure peace—human nature being what it is—is to have the means of imposing our will on any misguided minority who want war.

In the meantime we should try to improve the world spiritually. Get away from the "Law of Expediency" and back to the "Golden Rule." This, however, is a long process and may well take decades, generations, or centuries.

. . . I saw another little Okinawan kid with his entire right side in a plaster cast—but ambulatory—holding on to the index finger of a medical sergeant with his good hand, and looking up to him with a look of consummate confidence in his new-found friend and protector. They were both just standing there. It might have appeared to the unobservant that the sergeant wasn't getting his work done, but he was. He was doing the finest job that a human can do—being kind and fair and friendly in the truest sense of the terms. He had no possibility of reward, except that he knew, subconsciously perhaps, that he was making the world just a tiny bit better and war just infinitesimally a bit more remote.

We must realize that nations are just groups of individuals and if individuals will fight so will nations—more readily, in fact, if incited by mass hysteria (which can be induced by carefully arranged and controlled propaganda).

We no longer have geographic isolation from Europe and Asia. Scientific development of the future will bring all parts of the world relatively still closer together.

Someday, I hope, we can disband our military

> establishment and devote ourselves wholly to truly constructive pursuits, but until that time comes, let's do everything possible to so train our children and so direct our nation as to give them both the highest possible degree of security in the world in which they find themselves.

Looking at this last letter to Joe from Okinawa nearly a half century later, I realize now that I had, for the first time, expressed my thinking about the nation's future in writing. Those thoughts were to be declared in many different ways in the months and years to come.

Chapter 18

At 2:45 A.M. on August 6, 1945, Colonel Paul W. Tibbets, commander of the 509th Bomb Group, departed Tinian as pilot-in-command of the *Enola Gay*, a B-29 Superfortress loaded with a single bomb weighing four and a half tons. Called "Little Boy," the bomb had an explosive power equal to 20,000 tons of TNT.

Inside the knee pocket of Paul's flying suit was a small box containing 12 cyanide capsules, one for each member of the crew. Only Paul and the group flight surgeon knew he had them. These were to be used if they were captured, because of the many atrocity stories, some of them authenticated, that had been reported. As the Superfort approached the designated target in Japan, 1,500 miles from Tinian, Navy captain William S. Parsons, weaponeer and ordnance officer, armed the special mechanism of the bomb and reported it ready.

At 8:15 A.M. Japanese time, the first atomic bomb to be dropped in warfare exploded over Hiroshima. Within a few hours, the best-kept secret of World War II was no longer a secret. President Truman, en route home by Navy ship after meeting with Winston Churchill and Joseph Stalin at Potsdam, had made the decision to use the atomic bomb on two cities after an ultimatum sent to Japan was rejected.

In his quarters at Fort Myer, Virginia, Hap Arnold received the message from Tooey Spaatz on Guam:

> HIROSHIMA BOMBED VISUALLY WITH ONE-TENTH [cloud cover] AT 052315A [August 5, 7:15 P.M. in Washington]. THERE WAS NO FIGHTER OPPOSITION AND NO FLAK. PARSONS REPORTS 15 MINUTES AFTER BOMB AS FOLLOWS: "RESULTS CLEAR-CUT SUCCESSFUL IN ALL RESPECTS. VISIBLE EFFECTS GREATER THAN IN ANY TEST. CONDITION NORMAL IN AIRPLANE FOLLOWING DELIVERY."

I was not privy to the secret before we received word on Okinawa that an atomic bomb had been dropped. Since the 8th Air Force wasn't involved, I had no need to know what it was all about, but I certainly followed the news closely and received intelligence briefings on the bomb's effects on Hiroshima quickly thereafter.

When Japan refused to surrender, thousands of leaflets were dropped by the 20th's B-29s during the next three days. They carried this message:

> To the Japanese people: America asks that you take immediate heed of what we say on this leaflet.
>
> We are in possession of the most destructive explosive ever devised by man. A single one of our newly developed atomic bombs is actually the equivalent in explosive power to what 2,000 of our giant B-29s can carry on a single mission. This awful fact is one for you to ponder, and we solemnly assure you that it is grimly accurate.
>
> We have just begun to use this weapon against your homeland. If you still have any doubt, make inquiry as to what happened to Hiroshima when just one atomic bomb fell on that city.
>
> Before using this bomb to destroy every resource of the military by which they are prolonging this useless war, we ask that you now petition the Emperor to end the war. Our President has outlined for you the thirteen consequences of an honorable surrender. We urge that you accept these consequences and begin work of building a new, better, and peace-loving Japan.
>
> You should take these steps now to cease military

resistance. Otherwise, we shall resolutely employ this bomb and all our other superior weapons to promptly and forcefully end the war.

Evacuate your cities now!

Unfortunately, a few Japanese military diehards did not heed or believe the message. There was no word from the Japanese government. On August 9, a second bomb, this one called "Fat Man," was dropped on Nagasaki by *Bock's Car*, a B-29 piloted by Major (later Major General) Charles W. Sweeney.

Sweeney had been prevented by an overcast from bombing Kokura, the primary target, and dropped on Nagasaki, his secondary. He spent an hour circling and used up so much fuel while he was going back and forth that he thought it expedient to come to Okinawa, rather than go all the way back to his home base in the Marianas. When he landed he came into my office and was debriefed. This was the first direct information I received on the bomb and the whole operation.

I have often been asked if I thought dropping these two atomic bombs was the right thing to do. In my opinion, it was, for one very simple reason: it saved lives. A land invasion of Japan would have cost both sides hundreds of thousands of casualties.

Of the 8th's units scheduled to be in place by August 15, two bomb groups had begun to arrive on August 7, the day after the first A-bomb drop. However, according to the plan, we were not scheduled to be at full strength until February 1946.

Things happened fast after the second bomb drop. The Soviets, seeing the end clearly in sight, had declared war on Japan on August 8. With no word yet from the Japanese, Hap Arnold wanted to have a 1,000-plane raid made against Tokyo. The 20th could put up about 850 bombers, and Hap wanted the 8th to send up the balance for a convincing finale to hostilities.

George Kenney had the Okinawan fields tied up with other operations, so even if I'd wanted to, I wouldn't have been able to send up the 8th's B-29s, which were just beginning to arrive. However, 828 B-29s and 186 fighters were dispatched from the other resources available, so Hap got his wish with a total of 1,104 aircraft airborne. There were no losses.

Just two days before the surrender, Tooey Spaatz told me that if I wanted the 8th Air Force bombers to be in combat with the Japanese, I'd better get an operation going the next day. I told him, "No, if the war's over, I will not risk one airplane nor a single bomber crew member just to be able to say the 8th Air Force had operated against the Japanese in the Pacific." Some of the 8th's long-range P-51s had arrived earlier and were based on Ie Shima, adjacent to Okinawa. They flew several escort missions over Japan for the 20th. That was enough.

V-J Day was declared on August 15, when Emperor Hirohito made a broadcast to his people. Arrangements were made for the Japanese to send emissaries to General MacArthur, supreme commander for the Allied Powers, to arrange for the surrender, which took place on the battleship *Missouri*, Admiral Bill Halsey's flagship, on September 2, 1945. Along with all of the senior flag and general officers in the Pacific, I was invited to witness the signing of the surrender documents. I think we all viewed the event with a great feeling of relief. I know I did.

It was certainly a unique ceremony. We were all practically in fatigue uniforms, and it was a good thing for me we were. When I found out I was going to Tokyo for the ceremony, I immediately got my blouse out of a footlocker where it had been since I arrived on Okinawa. It was moldy and in terrible shape. I didn't see how I was going to get it straightened out to wear to a formal affair.

I had a little Okinawan houseboy who was going to help me, so I asked him to brush the mold off and then press it. I told him to be very careful with the iron and to use a damp cloth so as not to burn it. He apparently forgot and left the iron on. There was no way I could wear *that* uniform. I was greatly relieved when word came that we were to dress in summer khakis.

Major General Ennis C. Whitehead, commander of the 5th Air Force, was visiting me at the time and we flew together to Tokyo. After we landed, Ennis said he wanted to make a quick trip somewhere, and he didn't come back in time for us to board the boat that was to take us out to the *Missouri*. There was only one boat left when we got to the dock. It had been reserved for General MacArthur. We had to ask if we could hitch a ride. We were permitted aboard, but the chill in the air when MacArthur saw me was instantly obvious. I'm sure he thought our tardiness in making our boat was my fault.

Let no one think that I didn't have great respect for General MacArthur. He was an outstanding military leader, strategist, and tactician. Totally self-confident and imperious, he had earned the right to be that way if he were so inclined. If I had served under him, I would have had great confidence in him as my superior. I'm sure he didn't feel the same way about me.

The surrender ceremony was brief and we all wished we could have had more time to meet old friends and chat. Although we were dressed informally, General MacArthur made the ceremony seem formal because of its historical significance. It was brilliantly staged for world consumption. We were marched in and marched out. Afterward, 1,500 Navy carrier-based planes and 462 B-29 Superforts roared by overhead. It was hard to believe that the long months of killing and dying were over.

I returned to Okinawa to see if the 8th were to have any flying assignments while occupation forces moved in. We didn't. However, the 20th flew over 1,000 B-29 sorties dropping food, clothing, and medical supplies to 150 POW camps.

The effort was not without its tragedies. Eight aircraft were lost with 77 casualties. In one instance, a B-29 supplying a POW camp in northern Korea was attacked by Soviet fighters and damaged so badly it had to make a crash landing. The Soviets said it was a "mistake."

One of the supply shortages that marred an otherwise effective effort was that of large parachutes. When they ran out of them, the B-29 crews made free-fall drops. Some American prisoners of war, in their rush to get the supplies before the Japanese got them, were killed by the falling packs.

There is no doubt that the decision to use the awesome power of the atom to end the war will still be debated many years after all of us who served during World War II are gone. It was President Truman's decision and his alone, based on the estimate that from 250,000 to 1,000,000 American casualties could be expected from an invasion, in addition to at least that many of the enemy. The Japanese surrender had come without a single American ground soldier having set foot in Japan. A home army of two million men would have been waiting for them if they had.

I have no regrets whatsoever that 8th Air Force bombers did not fly a single mission to bring the war to an end in the Pacific. As far as I was concerned, we had helped to prove the point in Europe. What was important now was to see that the peace could be sustained and that there would be no more Pearl Harbors.

* * *

Unknown to me until long after, while Americans were celebrating V-J Day, Joe had a brush with death that same day. During her visits to the rehabilitation center at Pawling, New York, she had talked with many of the patients who were having difficulty adjusting and were under psychiatric care. She was always a good listener and many of them confided their fears and worries to her confidentially. Not being trained in counseling, she volunteered to go to Fort Logan, Colorado, for a special course given by the Army.

While at Logan, she thought she saw a psychiatric patient who had been at Pawling, but whenever he saw her, he quickly turned away or covered up his face. This young man had crashed in the Pacific, had evaded capture, and had eventually returned to the American lines. He had witnessed atrocities that he could not shake from his mind. Obviously, he was still having adjustment problems.

Joe confronted him one day and found that he had avoided her because he was ashamed that he was still having difficulty. He was obsessed by the idea of returning to "kill Japs" and had learned that I was now stationed in the Pacific. He asked Joe to have me issue orders so he could be transferred there.

Joe was staying in the officers' quarters while attending the counseling classes, and on the evening of V-J Day was resting in her room while the celebrations were going on at the officers' club. There was a knock on the door and when Joe opened it, this young man, who had been drinking, lunged at her, threw her down on the floor, and threatened to kill her. She screamed and several men rushed to her aid. They subdued the lad and put him in a straitjacket. He later committed suicide. It was ironic that after all the close calls I had had during the war, *she* was the one who might have paid the supreme price for her service.

Just before I was to return to the States in September, I received a message from Hap asking if it would be possible for me to lead three B-29s nonstop from Japan to Washington, D.C., to demonstrate their long-range capabilities. The planes would require extra gas tanks installed. However, there were no suitable fields in Japan long enough and strong enough at the time from which the heavily loaded planes, each with a gross weight of 142,800 pounds, could take off safely.

While flattered to be asked to lead such an attention-getting, significant flight, I felt that Tooey Spaatz, Barney Giles, Curt LeMay, or Nate Twining should lead it. They were clearly identified with the success of the B-29's operations, not me.

Apparently, word about the flight was also relayed to General MacArthur's office as the supreme commander. Barney Giles happened to visit his office on routine business, and MacArthur asked Barney who was going to lead the flight. Barney said Doolittle. Nothing else was said.

Shortly thereafter, orders came from Washington that Barney would lead it, which he did. I had no problem with that decision, but I think it may have been made at MacArthur's insistence and been based on the story in the London paper the previous May that implied I was going to win the war when I arrived in the Pacific. In any event, the three planes were modified and the flight was made from Guam, but the three aircraft, short of fuel, had to land at Chicago before proceeding to Washington. They were piloted by Barney Giles, Curt LeMay, and General Emmett F. "Rosie" O'Donnell.*

Bruce Johnson and I returned to the States in an unmodified B-29, which Bruce called "the baggage plane" for "the boys flying the glory mission." All this bothered Bruce much more than it did me. We flew from Okinawa via Kwajalein, Hawaii, and Sacramento and landed at Washington National Airport on September 19, 1945, where a big crowd met our plane. Best of all, the crowd included Joe.

Joe and I had a quiet reunion with Jim, Jr., a captain then, and John, who was in his final year at West Point. There were a number of parties, receptions, and reunions with old friends during the next few days. At one of them in New York, Alex Fraser, my old mentor and boss at Shell, asked me if I would return to Shell as vice president and as a member of the board of directors. I was flattered, especially when he mentioned that I could come back at three times my salary as a lieutenant general. That was an interesting figure. When I joined Shell in 1930, I was hired at three times my Army pay as a first lieuten-

---

*Two months later, four B-29s, led by General Frank Armstrong, did fly nonstop from Tokyo to Washington. They departed from a base on Hokkaido that had been prepared by the Japanese for the specific purpose of sending bombers on one-way missions from Japan to bomb America. These were not to have been suicide attempts. If the planes were not shot down, they would have landed at some convenient airfield after dropping their bombs, and been impounded or destroyed, and the crews would then have assumed the status of prisoners of war.

ant. When I left Shell to go back in uniform in 1940, my pay as a major was exactly one-third of my Shell wages.

I didn't give Alex an answer then. The pay increase was very tempting, but there was still much immediate postwar work to be done. If there were to be a separate air force, I wanted to help get it started.

There was one very serious matter that I had to take care of before anything else. Eight of my boys had been captured by the Japanese after the Tokyo Raid, and we didn't know what had happened to them except that the Japanese had executed three of them. We didn't know for certain which ones. In late August, we heard the good news that four survivors—Lieutenants Chase J. Nielsen, Robert L. Hite, and George Barr, and Corporal Jacob DeShazer—had been released from prison and were on their way home. They were in very poor physical shape, and we learned that they had been tortured, starved, beaten, kept in solitary confinement, and sentenced to death. The death sentence had been carried out in October 1942 by firing squad on the other three—Dean E. Hallmark, William G. "Bill" Farrow, and Harold A. Spatz. The death sentence had been commuted to life imprisonment for the remaining five. They were never to be released, even when the war ended; presumably they were to be hidden so the sentence could be carried out, no matter which side won. Lieutenant Robert J. "Bob" Meder, the fifth man, died of beriberi and malnutrition in prison in December 1943.

The deaths of my boys hurt me deeply and I awaited the arrival of the survivors in the States. Three of them (Nielsen, Hite, and DeShazer), emaciated and numbed from the months of starvation and inactivity, were returned quickly and recovered in due time. They said George Barr was still in China when they left because he was too sick to be moved. I had every confidence he would be taken care of, but heard nothing about his whereabouts for several weeks after the initial news release.

George had been orphaned at six months of age when his father drowned in a boating accident. When his mother couldn't support him, George spent the years from age nine through high school in a boys' foster home in Yonkers, New York. His sister, four years older, became the special interest of Mrs. Charles A. Towns, a social worker, who had taken her into their home. Mrs. Towns and her husband, themselves childless, "adopted" the Barr children in fact but not legally. They were determined to do what they could to see that these two luckless children were not set adrift without a proper sense of values. George was invited to the Townses' house to be with his sister as much as possible. George had gone to college with the Townses' financial help.

After the raid, when the names of the eight prisoners were known, Mrs. Towns communicated with the other families frequently and became the go-between to relay any information she had that might give them some hope. She continually sought information from the International Red Cross, the Federal Bureau of Investigation, Army Intelligence, and the repatriated Americans from Japan who had been returned to the States in June 1942.

The Townses were overjoyed when it was announced that George was one of the survivors. They met Nielsen, Hite, and DeShazer and sought news about George, but none of the three knew anything about what had happened to him since they had bid him good-bye in China. The Townses felt better, however, when a cryptic note arrived from George saying he would be home soon. But this was followed by weeks of silence.

Mrs. Towns wrote to or called everyone she could think of to find out George's whereabouts. I was on the road giving speeches at that time, but there were telephone call slips and a distraught letter from her waiting for me when I returned to the Pentagon. I dropped everything and started an official search. In my reply I assured Mrs. Towns that "we who love George Barr will do everything we can for him. Our objective, however, is not to reform the Army but to find him and help him recover."

From the time of his release, I found out later, George had been caught up in an inexcusable series of medical administrative foul-ups. The war was over and thousands of veterans were getting out. It was a time of military personnel chaos. Those with sufficient "points" for overseas time and length of war service were given priority for release and brought home as fast as possible to be separated from the service.

George had been kept under medical care in a hotel in Peking, his last place of imprisonment. He was too weak to travel and was experiencing hallucinations and periods of extreme anxiety and depression. He was also too mentally unstable to travel, but as he got stronger and seemed more rational, he was transferred under restraint as a mental patient from Peking to Kunming, then to Calcutta. Then, for reasons never ascertained, he was returned to Kunming. He was eventually flown home across the Pacific with two physicians as escorts. They were given transportation on a priority basis as an incentive to accompany him and were destined for separation as soon as they arrived in the States. Their role was to see that he didn't harm himself. When they arrived at Hamilton Field on the West Coast, the doctors went immediately to the separation center in accordance with their orders.

It was a weekend and George went alone on a military bus to the base hospital. He had no records, could not answer questions put to him by the duty sergeant, was wearing an ill-fitting uniform, and was obviously confused. Nothing could be done for him over the weekend, so the sergeant took his clothes, gave him pajamas, and assigned him a room.

There was no one else around and George was suddenly overcome with a feeling of total abandonment. Freedom after nearly 40 months of solitary confinement was too unreal. He couldn't handle it. Overwhelmed and in desperation, he tried to hang himself from a light fixture, but was unsuccessful. He was immediately placed in a padded room and thereafter treated as a mental patient. No one believed his story about having been on the Tokyo Raid, and he languished for days trying to convince the medics that he was telling the truth.

Although he had named the Townses as next of kin and had designated his "home of record" as Yonkers, New York, George had enlisted in the AAF while a student at Northland College, in Ashland, Wisconsin. When he told the medics this, they assumed that he should be transferred to Schick General Hospital at Clinton, Iowa, the nearest military hospital to Ashland. Along with other patients, he was transported by train in a straitjacket and at night was placed in bed under a restraining sheet.

It took three days to make the trip and when the train arrived at Clinton, George's ability to reason was about gone. He was placed in a locked ward with seven other disturbed patients where he remained in a confused state. George did not recall that any doctor inquired about him or visited to check on his physical or mental condition.

Somehow, Mrs. Towns found out where George was before I did, in November 1945, and went to Clinton to see him. George's brother-in-law, then living in Milwaukee, also visited, as did several girlfriends George had known in college. Although he was confused at how much they had all seemed to age, these visits and a balanced diet helped George recover mentally, and he was transferred to an open ward. However, he still had not seen a doctor, had no money, had only hospital pajamas and robe to wear, and seemingly had no status as a human being. He remained under constant surveillance by medical attendants who would offer him no advice or information on his condition or tell him when he might be released.

I immediately flew out to Clinton when the Army sleuths located him. Not knowing George's true condition, I had to be cautious because I knew he would be surprised to see me. I greeted him like an old friend and George immediately broke into tears. I was the first military person he had seen that he knew since his buddies had left him in China. He seemed very normal to me, so we went for a walk and he tried to tell me everything he could. He was hesitant at first, but then the tears flowed and the words began to pour out. Catharsis was obviously what he needed.

I was shocked and found it difficult to believe that he had not seen a doctor and had no money, no clothes, and no military status except that of "patient." The last of my Tokyo Raiders to come home needed help, and I was going to see that he got it.

I can say unreservedly that I have never been so angry in my life as I was when George told me what had happened to him. I walked with him back to the ward and went immediately to the hospital commander's office, where I unloaded Doolittle's worst verbal fury on his head. I won't repeat what I said because it would burn a hole in this page. I will say that George was quickly outfitted in a new uniform, complete with the ribbons he didn't know he had earned, and was given a check for over $7,000 in back pay, and orders promoting him to first lieutenant. Best of all, he was seen immediately by a psychiatrist and began the slow road back to recovery.

Before I left, I asked George if he remembered that before we left the *Hornet* I had promised the fellows a party in Chungking. He said, "Yes, sir, I do."

"Well, George, we never had that party because you and the rest of the fellows couldn't make it. But I'm going to keep that promise. The whole gang is invited to be my guests in Miami on my birthday on December 14. I want you to come. I'll send an airplane for you."

My visit, George told me later, was a turning point in his recovery. George and others were picked up all over the country by military aircraft and brought to Miami's McFadden-Deauville Hotel. We let our hair down for three days of total carefree relaxation. As I said in my letter to each of them, we would "swap handshakes, yarns, and toasts." In trying to locate everyone who had flown on the Tokyo mission, I learned that four men had become prisoners of war of the Germans. Besides the two who had drowned, the one who died on the bailout, and the four who died in prison, 13 others had made the supreme sacrifice in other theaters of war. "I find it difficult to realize that so many of our buddies have gone," I wrote, "and call this sad condition to your mind in order that we may do them homage."

Some would say we raised hell at that Miami reunion. I wouldn't quarrel with that assessment. When several suggested we have a reunion like that every year, I told them I'd like that, but the party had cost me $2,000 and I couldn't afford it every year. We had shared an unusual life-threatening situation and had formed an unusual bonding relationship. It was understood that we would meet again annually if we could.

We didn't have a reunion in 1946 but met again in Miami in 1947. It could be said that we raised more hell. So much, in fact, that the hotel's night watchman made a report to the hotel manager. It said:

> The Doolittle boys added some gray hairs to my head. This has been the worst night since I worked here. They were completely out of my control.
>
> I let them make a lot of noise, but when about 15 of them went into the pool at 1:00 A.M., including Doolittle, I told them there was no swimming allowed there at night. They were in the pool until 2:30 A.M.
>
> I went up twice more without results. They were running around the halls in their bathing suits and were noisy until 5 A.M. Yes, it was a rough night.

When we checked out, the manager showed us the report and asked us all to autograph it. He said as far as he was concerned, we had earned the right to make all the noise we wanted to in his hotel.

We have held a reunion every year since then, except one

year during the Korean War and one year during the Vietnam War. Of all the men who served with me during World War II, I have been closest to my Tokyo Raiders and treasure the days we have spent together at reunions over the years. I know a commander is not supposed to have any favorites, but these men are mine. I care deeply for them and have always considered them part of my family.

CHAPTER 19

One of the first postwar planning tasks of Hap, Tooey, Ira, and many others at the Pentagon was to push for legislation to set up a Department of National Defense with a separate Air Force on an equal basis with the Army and Navy. General Eisenhower and the Army were 100 percent for it. Our success in Europe had proven to Ike that the Army and the Air Force could work together provided there was a single decision maker in charge. The Navy was only 50 percent in favor. The other 50 percent, representing the official Navy viewpoint, was very much opposed.

If a Department of National Defense were not approved, we thought we might still get a separate and equal Air Force. This would have the advantage of putting the Air Force on a par with the other two services, both operationally and politically. However, the disadvantage would be that there would be three instead of two bickerers if there were no single head of the whole establishment to knock heads together.

To have me do what I could to enlist public opinion in our favor, Hap issued orders for me to travel to New York, Cleveland, Detroit, Chicago, St. Louis, and Los Angeles to give talks urging the public to support the concept of a separate but equal Air Force under a National Department of Defense. I spoke on a number of radio programs and made 18 appearances before civic and veterans' groups between October 1 and December 17, 1945. I had no trouble convincing former members of the Army Air Forces or those who had served in the ground Army about a separate Air Force. However, the Navy's propaganda machine was working full time against a separate Air Force and especially against having a civilian secretary of defense over all three services.

While I was on the road, a curious war of words was going on in Washington. My old friend Marc Mitscher, former skipper of the *Hornet* and now a vice admiral, gave a speech at Annapolis in which he stated, "We must not for a moment lose sight of the fact that our carrier supremacy defeated Japan." A few days later, Admiral Chester Nimitz gave a speech in New York in which he claimed that, "It was our sea power which ultimately compelled Japan to ask for peace." I wondered where they both had been when our Air Force B-29s dropped thousands of tons of bombs on Japan and when two lone B-29s delivered those two atomic bombs.

I was greatly disturbed when I read their statements in the paper and fired off a memo to Hap saying:

> Any statement which ignores or belittles the magnificent contribution to victory in Japan made by the B-29s does not give all the facts and depreciates the sacrifices of the heroic B-29 crews who attacked the Japanese mainland at a time when the Japanese air force was still a potent factor. I believe teamwork won the war, and that each agency—land, sea, and air—did its job well.

Hap released my retort to the newspapers and it was given good play because their editors saw plenty of newsworthy interservice battles ahead. When I returned to Washington, I found the war of words was getting more intense.

In November 1945, along with other general and flag officers, I was invited to appear before the Senate Military Affairs Committee to give my views on equal status for the Air Force with the two other services. I reviewed our heavy bombardment experience against Germany during the war, and then, using slides, I showed the airman's view of the world, with polar projections and great-circle routes. My purpose was to explode some fallacious notions—that land-based air should fly over the land only and sea-based air over the sea; that the distances to potential enemy nations by air were much closer than was generally realized. Those distances could be spanned by the B-29s and the giant, 10,000-mile B-36 intercontinental bombers then being built. I stressed that teamwork had won the war—"teamwork between Allied nations, teamwork between the suppliers and the users, the people at home and the people in the field, and teamwork between the various arms and services, teamwork between the Army, the Navy, and the Air Force."

I also pointed out that America was tired of war and that the people didn't want to think about another one. "The thought is unpleasant and we incline to put unpleasant things out of mind," I said. "In spite of this, one fact remains: The only way we can avoid war is to be prepared for war."

One of the many arguments against unification of the armed services under a single secretary and an equal Air Force was that it would increase the cost of defense. I countered that argument by saying an autonomous Air Force and a single Department of National Defense would eliminate useless duplication and waste. It would cut down the existent war-expanded defense organization and would tend to assure the equitable distribution of available funds according to actual military value. There would be more money spent on new, modern weapon systems, and no unnecessary airplanes, carriers, or battleships would be built. I was confident that through this means America would be secure, the public protected, and every defense dollar properly invested.

During this hearing, one of the senators asked me about the remarks made by Admirals Nimitz and Mitscher that had gotten so much attention in the press. It was a loaded question, possibly meant to make new headlines that day. I replied: "Admiral Nimitz and Admiral Mitscher are very great commanders. I cannot belittle the magnificent job they did—the magnificent job that was done by the people under their commands. I earnestly feel that the war in Germany and the war in the Pacific were won by teamwork—that each of the three agencies did its best. I don't believe any single agency was responsible for winning the war in Europe or the war in the Pacific. I do feel, however, very strongly, that it was not sea power that compelled Japan to ask for peace, and it was not carrier superiority that won the air war. I feel also that our B-29 boys are probably resting uneasily in their graves as a result of those two statements."

In October, I received word that the President had sent to the

Senate my nomination as a brigadier general in the Regular Army. Received a letter shortly thereafter from Lieutenant General George E. Stratemeyer, then commanding the Army Air Forces in China, saying he hoped I would accept the appointment and stay in uniform.

I appreciated Strat's letter and replied that I was doubly delighted to hear from him "because it represents the thinking of an old friend whose opinion I have always admired." Still on the fence about staying in or getting out, I decided to remain for a short time to see what I could do to help persuade the lawmakers to our views.

In the meantime, there was a bit of important business to be taken care of that would also affect our crusade to create a separate Air Force. Hap Arnold was our undisputed leader in the fight, and his foresightedness had been proven during the war. He had established *Air Force,* the official journal of the Army Air Forces, which developed into a fine four-color magazine. It was an in-house effort to spread the word about the Air Force, what it stood for, and its wartime achievements. Anticipating public apathy toward, and, possibly, public opposition to, a separate Air Force, Hap proposed that the three million veterans of the Army Air Forces be organized into an alumni group to form the nucleus for organized public support.

On August 1, 1945, Hap approved a study that set down the objectives and criteria for a civilian organization, comparable to the Navy League and the Association of the United States Army. One of the study's recommendations was that an Army Air Forces veteran be asked to take the initiative in this effort. I was asked, and I agreed to serve as first president until a president could be duly elected by the association's membership at its first national convention.

When officially accepting the presidency of the Air Force Association (AFA) on January 24, 1946, I said there were three points I wanted to make clear. First, the AFA was to be a nonprofit organization, created for the benefit of its members and the Air Force they served so loyally. Second, no attempt should be made to duplicate the legislative and financial benefits that membership in veterans' organizations offered. Neither should the Air Force Association cross the lines of the national organizations operating in the public interest in behalf of aviation and air power, such as the National Aeronautics Association. And third, policy would be determined by the voting members of the association.

The AFA had difficult days getting started. Contributions were sought and annual dues established at three dollars. Colonel Willis Fitch was hired as executive director and for a time was the only staff member. He set up an office in downtown Washington, D.C., with furniture left by a previous occupant, and obtained a typewriter on loan. Funds accumulated slowly as Air Force veterans and others responded to the membership drive.

Another of Hap's foresighted actions was to give the rights to the AAF's wartime magazine he had established to the association, so that *Air Force* magazine became the "official journal of the Air Force Association."

The association grew from that austere beginning and today boasts a quarter of a million members. I am very proud that I had a role in forming it and telling its members and the public at large about the dangers inherent in military weakness and the threats that, from time to time, have confronted the nation.

After completing the chores Hap had asked me to work on, I decided to leave active duty effective January 1, 1946, and go on terminal leave. In my letter, I said it was my intention to associate myself with one of the basic industries vital to the civilian economy in which I hoped my background and experience would be of value to that industry and the nation as a whole.

After I had completed my terminal leave, I was notified that I had been appointed a brigadier general in the Regular Army, with date of rank from May 1, 1946. I replied that I appreciated the high honor that had been bestowed upon me and was delighted to accept the appointment. However, I asked that I be permitted to retire. I guess they didn't know how to handle Doolittle. They had never had anyone accept a regular appointment and then request retirement at the same time.* I was subse-

---

*My request for retirement as a regular officer was a self-protective measure to assure that Joe and I would have some kind of pension coming in if I were incapacitated. Since circumstances turned out favorably for me, I retired from the reserves in 1959 but told General Rosie O'Donnell, the head of Air Force personnel, that I didn't need any retirement pay. However, I thought I'd better reserve the right to claim it if Joe and I should fall on bad times. Rosie said I couldn't do that, so I asked that one half of my retirement pay be sent to the Air Force Aid Society and the other half to the Air Force Academy Foundation. It was the least I could do to repay the nation for all the opportunities I had been given during my military career.

quently notified that doing this would place the Army in an "indefensible position," so I left active duty as a reservist with the rank of lieutenant general. So far as I know, I am the only reserve officer ever to hold and be retired in that grade.

In December 1945, after talking with the top officials at Shell, I decided to accept Alex Fraser's offer. Since Shell already had a good man running its aviation department, they made me a vice president, a director, and a member of the executive committee of the board of directors. In general, I was to "keep an eye on" the aviation department and concentrate on being a senior advisor on all aviation matters. I was also to be given special assignments and would evaluate engineering and scientific advances in relation to the petroleum industry and to Shell.

I reported directly to Alex and presided over meetings of the vice presidents when he was absent. There was no one else over me and no one directly under me. I guess you would call me "a vice president without portfolio." Otherwise, I did odd jobs for the company that might come under the heading of public relations, advertising, and inspection. I believe there was some resentment from some of the other vice presidents because I returned from the service and filled a position above them. Again, as in other positions, I felt I had to prove myself by working harder.

Part of the offer to return to Shell was a very generous provision: If any department of the government requested my services for a project or an ad hoc committee post where my experience would be useful, Shell would allow me to serve with full pay and allowances. I agreed that I would not accept any pay from the government. Alex said I could decide what type of aircraft I wanted the company to buy for corporate use, so I immediately sought out a war surplus North American B-25, which cost the company $8,250. New instrumentation and a plushed-up interior for use as an executive transport cost an additional $23,750. The plane had originally cost the government about $40,000. I used it not only for transportation, but also as a test vehicle for fuels and lubricants.

Joe and I moved to an apartment in New York City and tried to settle into a civilian routine. One of my first trips on Shell's behalf was a visit to South America. As I was getting ready to go, I received an invitation from Secretary of War Robert P. Patterson in March 1946 to chair a "Board on Officer/Enlisted Man Relationships," which immediately became known in the press as the "G.I. Gripe Board" and the "Doolittle

Board." The creation of the board was in response to public complaints about the lack of democracy in the Army, instances of incompetent leadership, the abuse of privileges, and the favorable treatment of officers compared with enlisted men during the war. I promptly accepted the invitation.

The board consisted of four officers and two enlisted men. All of us were former enlisted men, but I was the only member still on active duty, although then on terminal leave. The others were retired Lieutenant General Troy H. Middleton, former commander of the 45th Division in North Africa and Italy, who was comptroller of Louisiana State University; Robert Neville, former sergeant on the staff of *Yank* magazine, who had become an officer and the editor of *Stars and Stripes*; Adna H. Underhill, former paratrooper, then working for the New York State Game Conservation Department; Jake W. Lindsay, the one hundredth infantryman to win the Medal of Honor, then with the Veterans Administration; and Meryll M. Frost, former Air Force sergeant with a bomb group in Italy, who had been badly wounded and was then attending college.

When I convened the board on March 26, 1946, one of the first decisions we made was that the hearings would be closed. In a press conference following that first meeting, I told reporters that we did not expect to cure the ills of the world but hoped that we would correct some of the alleged injustices in the War Department. I said no one was to be on trial; we just wanted to hear all the complaints we could and then recommend improvements.

The reason for holding closed sessions was that we felt that witnesses would talk more openly than they would if they were also talking before the press and public. We also decided to meet in an office building in downtown Washington so there would be no feeling that the board was in any way influenced by anything other than the testimony from witnesses. We also declined to give out a list of witnesses until our deliberations were over and said there would be no interim report issued. These announcements provoked much criticism from some newspaper columnists during the six weeks of our deliberations. We ignored it.

We began hearing witnesses immediately and reviewed over 1,000 letters received after the board was announced. We also reviewed many newspaper, magazine, and military journal articles, and transcripts of radio commentaries.

During our deliberations, we reviewed the historical background of the military services, originally derived from Europe. During the Revolutionary War, one of the difficulties in maintaining a fighting army, as expressed by General Washington, pertained to strained relations between officers and men. Even in the Civil War, some men in the ranks of both the North and the South voiced resentment against the "aristocratic" officers who, being more interested in rank and privilege, failed on occasion to concern themselves with the welfare of their men. A report to the secretary of war during World War I called attention to the bitterness engendered among the enlisted men by special privileges accorded the officer personnel.

I had experienced these privilege differences during World War I as an enlisted man, and had also enjoyed the advantages of being a commissioned officer. But I was always uncomfortable about the invisible wall that had been erected by the Regular Army between the enlisted and commissioned ranks. I have always felt that officers should do their best to earn respect from the enlisted men, not obtain it by government decree; however, I accepted the dichotomy at the time as being necessary to maintain discipline.

In September 1939, the military force totaled approximately 198,000, of whom about 15,000 were officers. This force was composed of individuals who had chosen the military service as a career; none were draftees. Mobilization for World War II saw a rapid expansion of the military services. Selective Service was put into operation; reserve officers were called to active duty; National Guard units were ordered into the service. In effect, thousands of civilians entered the armed forces.

Training and organization were speeded up, and manpower demands were created that resulted in the assignment of untrained or partially trained and, in many cases, unqualified individuals to jobs of great responsibility. Time did not allow the Army to develop among its officers an understanding of their responsibilities to troops. As a result, the peacetime gap based on the difference in caliber between commissioned and enlisted personnel was eliminated; the Army received into its enlisted ranks men who were often far superior by training, education, and work experience to men in the commissioned ranks. Many of these draftees disliked the regimented life they experienced in the Army, and as soon as they returned to civilian status, they said so in no uncertain terms. The criticism had reached its peak when Secretary Patterson invited us to sit on the board.

As we listened and learned, we found that the problem of enlisted man–officer relationships was insignificant among combat troops at the front. I had seen this in North Africa and England at the height of the war and was continually impressed with the high morale of our men when under stress. It was in the rear areas and isolated outposts, such as the Aleutians, and on the home front, where most of the abuses of privileges, irregularities, and poor personnel management took place.

Much to the surprise of the officers on the board, there were many differences in pay and allowances between the enlisted ranks and officers that we were not aware of. For example, officers received a 10 percent pay increase for foreign service or sea duty; enlisted men were authorized a 20 percent increase. Officers were entitled to an allowance for housing ranging from $45 to $120 per month, according to rank; only the three top grades of enlisted men received an allowance when government housing for dependents was not available. Enlisted personnel received a monthly allowance for each dependent; officers received none. Officers received a mileage allowance of five cents per mile when traveling on official business; enlisted men received three cents. Enlisted men could receive from one to five dollars additional monthly pay for special arms qualifications; officers, none.

There was also considerable variance in retirement benefits. Officers could retire after 15 years' service, if approved by the secretary of war. However, requests were not normally approved for those with less than 25 years' service. Enlisted men retired after 30 years' service unless sooner for disability. Officers could be paid for unused leave on termination of service; enlisted men received no terminal leave pay.

Other inequities included the prohibition against enlisted men serving on courts-martial; any sentence levied against an officer had to be confirmed by the President, but there was no comparable provision for enlisted men; officers were authorized transportation for dependents and movement of household goods, while only the top three enlisted grades were so authorized; commissioned personnel had reserved seats in post theaters, while enlisted men and families were segregated from officers.

There were also a number of traditional differences between the commissioned and enlisted ranks: enlisted personnel were used for menial tasks; it was considered demeaning for officers to associate with enlisted personnel; enlisted men were required to salute officers first; officers dined privately in officers' clubs and received individual service in mess halls, usually by enlisted personnel, but enlisted men were not permitted to enter officers' clubs, attend officers' parties, or use officers' facilities. However, officers could use facilities provided for enlisted personnel. Especially galling to the latter was the presence of signs on military bases that said, OFF LIMITS TO ENLISTED PERSONNEL.

The greatest differential, and the one that brought the most criticism, was in the field of military justice and courts-martial procedures, which permitted inequities and injustices to enlisted personnel. Censorship of enlisted men's newspapers was an additional source of extensive comment.

The 42 witnesses we called included a cross section of the Army, from Generals Eisenhower and Spaatz to former low-ranking Army enlisted men. Two of them were personalities well known to the GIs: cartoonist Bill Mauldin, creator of the famous "Joe and Willie" cartoons; and Marion Hargrove, author of a popular book entitled *See Here, Private Hargrove*. Interviewees also included a retired West Point brigadier general, a nurse, a chaplain, an FBI agent, an avowed socialist, and a WAC.

Bill Mauldin talked to reporters after his appearance and was widely quoted. He said the Army should get rid of the "theory that an officer breathes a special kind of air and that he is a gentleman while an enlisted man is not." There was much negative press coverage nationally when an enterprising reporter found that a quartermaster sales store in Washington, D.C., had hard-to-get women's nylons for sale to "officers only."

In late May I presented our unanimous report to Secretary Patterson. Our recommendations included a number of items to improve the leadership of the officer corps, including rigorous screening out of incompetents, and an internal policing system to prevent abuse of privileges. We recommended establishment of adequate pay and allowance scales, equal accumulation of leave or furlough time, and equality of treatment of both enlisted and commissioned personnel in the administration of military justice.

We aroused the ire of Army regular officers by recommending the abandonment of the hand salute off duty and off Army installations, except in occupied territories and "under conditions where the procedure might be deemed necessary to properly convey military dignity to local populations." However, we said that the salute should still be used in all official greetings, on ceremonial occasions, and when the national anthem is played or the colors pass by.

We also endorsed more equitable distribution of decorations and awards; improvement of the system for registering complaints; and abolition of "all statutes, regulations, customs, and traditions which discourage or forbid social association of soldiers of similar likes and tastes, because of military rank."

The report was widely accepted, and in fact, the Army had already been making changes. A Discharge Review Board was created to review discharge procedures, adequate recreational facilities were ordered, and the use of OFF LIMITS FOR ENLISTED MEN signs was completely abolished. A thorough study of the military justice system was ordered. Similarity of uniforms for enlisted men and officers was prescribed, and a rigorous officer screening program was introduced.

Despite this climate of change, the report was bitterly criticized, especially by older regular officers who had spent a lifetime in uniform and enjoyed their special privileges. To this day, the recommendations of the "Doolittle Board" are said by a dwindling few to be the beginning of the end of military discipline in our armed forces.

I cannot agree. I offer no apologies and have had no second thoughts about the board's recommendations. They were valid then and still are. Those who hold enmity for the changes that resulted from our report should remember that the greatest war in history had just come to an end—the second "war to end all wars"—and the general public was fed up with war. Since the majority of those who served were enlisted men, their views were more popular. This does not mean that we were persuaded by this fact, but that their views had much merit and deserved sincere consideration.

Once the report was rendered, I became engrossed in the issue of the reorganization of the defense establishment. The fundamental question was whether or not the Air Force should be separated from the Army and Navy and all three services placed under a Department of Defense. One of the words that was often misused by the press and members of Congress during the debates about reorganization was the word "merger." In January 1946, I was one of the speakers on a radio program called *The American Forum of the Air*. The basic question was, "Should we merge the Army and Navy?"

The question was badly phrased. There was no intention at the time to "merge" the two services. What was in contention on the program, but seemed to be lost in the rhetoric, was the establishment of a Department of Defense and a secretary of defense who would be placed over the two services.

I believed that our immediate objective should be a secure and prosperous America, and that the security should be accomplished with a minimum expenditure of public funds. However, in case we were ever again overtaken by the misfortune of war, our objective should be a quick win with a minimum loss of precious American lives. I told the radio audience that this immediate objective could best be achieved, first through the establishment of an ultramodern, highly mobile, readily expandable military organization, composed of an Army, a Navy, and an Air Force; second, by a continuation of research in order to assure the modernity of our equipment; and third, by a type of organization that would permit economy in time of peace and fast, coordinated effort in case of a national emergency. It was my sincere conviction that efficiency, coordination, and economy could be achieved only through the establishment of three autonomous, equal forces—land, sea, and air—operating under one political and one military head, a secretary of the armed forces and a chief of the combined staffs.

At this time, the Senate Naval Affairs Committee was dealing with the question of land-based aircraft for the Navy and I felt obligated to express my personal opinion on the merits of the Navy's argument. Out of uniform now, I could speak out very strongly against the Navy's viewpoints. I cite the following excerpts of my statement before the committee because they show how hard the Navy was fighting to take on new responsibilities that I believed should be vested in a separate Air Force:

> The sum and substance of the case presented by the Navy in the hearing now in progress is that the Navy must provide and maintain its own long-range, land-based air reconnaissance arm. In support of their demands for the continuation of land-based reconnaissance under the command of the Navy, its spokesmen have urged that the Navy's needs are peculiar, that its problems are peculiar, and that only Navy personnel are competent in these situations.
>
> The Navy has long considered that it represents the first line of defense for America. The air has now

taken the role of the "first line of defense" from the sea. It is obviously in an attempt to perpetuate and validate its contention that it is our first line of defense that the Navy is urging the peculiarity of its long-range reconnaissance needs. The rejection of this false claim to primacy should be made by all thinking people at this moment. Anyone capable of understanding, who is aware of even the most basic truths upon which World War II was prosecuted, is fully aware that the first line of defense and the last frontiers of America lie in the sky.

In the name of common sense, let the Navy go to sea and, if it wishes, carry its carrier-based aircraft with it; but by the same token, let it cease this underhanded effort to extend its role into the sphere of strategic bombardment. That sphere belongs to the Air Force. The ruins of Germany and the burned-out cities of Japan are stark testimony to the ability of the Air Force to use this type of aircraft. To permit a comparative novice to enter this field is not only to authorize unpardonable duplication of tremendously expensive equipment, but it actually jeopardizes our national economy and our national safety.

The chronicles of World War II will show that during the critical months of 1942 and 1943, when the effectiveness of the German U-boats was forever broken, the AAF was providing more than half of all Allied long-range antisub patrols all over the world. I need but recall the Battle of the Bismarck Sea, in which Army Air Forces aircraft alone located and wiped out an entire Jap convoy. I may also recall the fact that the Air Forces contributed mightily throughout the months of the war to the reduction of Japanese shipping. There is, then, little basis for the contention of the Navy that the Air Forces cannot effectively fly at sea.

Where before the naval airplane had served to complement the strength of the battleship and the cruiser and the destroyer, we found that the cruiser and destroyer and the battleship were now employed to convoy and protect naval air power. It was at the battles of the Coral Sea and Midway that this historic milestone was passed, for in these two engagements enemy fleets were employed and so-called tremendous naval battles fought in which surface fleets never made contact. In short, the entire engagement consisted of aerial warfare conducted by air components traveling with the fleet, except for the very effective land-based air power employed from the island of Midway. Nevertheless, the principle was established that fleet actions were determined on the issue of control of the air over the fleets. Without that control no fleet could survive.

The question before us is whether we shall produce and maintain at prohibitive costs and tremendous waste and duplication two separate and self-sufficient air forces. The alternative is a separate, unified, and streamlined Air Force whose command shall have power to range through the skies seeking the enemy wherever he may be, in whatever form.

The recent statement of a senior naval commander that "what is not good for the Navy is not good for the country" is evidence that in their own estimation, and quite sincerely, they place themselves above the people and all other agencies of our great nation. What is good for the United States, as far as our armed forces are concerned, is that the activities of all services should be coordinated and each service should retain full control in its own medium and stay out of the others' medium. The naval type of thinking, which lends itself more to perpetuation of the Navy than to the national interest, does great discredit to the glorious traditions of the Navy, which in the war just concluded attained its full and final stature.

It might be well for the Navy to examine with detachment and candor the military future of this age of atomic bombs, ten-thousand-mile bombers, rockets, and guided missiles, and accept for itself the possibility that science has rendered unnecessary the bulk of the Navy, which operates upon the surface of the sea.

These were strong words and have since been overtaken by events and technological progress. However, they show how strident had become the debate about future national defense needs and requirements.

The pro and con arguments about creating a separate Air Force and a Department of Defense went on for months. Meanwhile, I wanted to be useful to Shell and not just a figurehead. I thought it was my job to visit all of the company's facilities, report what I observed, and make recommendations for the future.

I was convinced that commercial aviation would experience an unprecedented postwar boom, and the company had a big stake in it. The war had caused tremendous technological breakthroughs in every aspect of aviation, especially in aircraft design, engines, navigation equipment, and communications. The introduction of the jet engine in military aircraft promised a new era in speed and convenience that, when applied to commercial aircraft, would enhance world commerce, despite the jet engine's high fuel consumption at the time. In my position at Shell, I encouraged the development of jet fuels because I was firmly convinced that the voracious fuel appetite of jet engines would eventually be eased by engine design improvements.

To carry out my visitation program, I flew the B-25 to Shell offices and facilities in Ecuador, Peru, Costa Rica, Nicaragua, and Mexico. I also made a trip to meet Shell officials in England, Holland, and Germany.

Jet engine and fuel production was one of the items on my agenda when I visited Europe, but I also wanted to see how the devastated areas on the Continent were recovering. During my trip to Berlin I had a strange, ominous feeling about the divided city, which was being occupied and ruled by the four Allied powers. It was a city of gloomy, vanquished people who seemed to harbor deep resentment toward their former leaders at having lost the war. I found no remorse and no regret among the Germans. The Soviets were particularly antagonistic toward the American, French, and British troops occupying the city and were universally hated by the Germans. It seemed like a city ripe for turmoil. I returned home wondering how long it would be before the Soviets would try to drive the other allies out of the old German capital.

Meanwhile, the debate about a separate Air Force continued, growing wilder as the Navy's arguments for maintaining the status quo became more extreme. Nevertheless, by mid-1947, several basically similar military unification bills had been brought forward in the Congress for debate. The concept had the endorsement of President Truman, who believed, as we air proponents did, that unification of the services under one head would bring about economies in the military establishment and provide for a more effective defensive and offensive war machine.

After weeks of interservice and congressional wrangling, a compromise was worked out. The Navy's worst fears seemed to center on the question of the status and powers of the secretary of defense and the fact that future Navy and Marine Corps aviation units would be given to the Air Force. To calm these fears Congress restricted the power of the secretary of defense and spelled out the exact missions of both the Navy and Marine air arms. Both houses of Congress finally approved a bill, and this important piece of legislation was forwarded to the President for signature.

Shortly after noon on July 26, 1947, President Truman waited aboard the *Sacred Cow* at Washington National Airport for a courier. He was going to fly to the bedside of his dying mother, but he wanted to sign three important documents before departure. The first was the National Security Act of 1947, which established the Department of Defense, the Department of the Air Force, and a separate Air Force. The second was Executive Order No. 9877, defining the roles and missions of the armed forces. The third was the nomination of James V. Forrestal as the first secretary of defense.

The official birthday of the Air Force is September 17, 1947, the day when W. Stuart Symington, former senator from Missouri, was sworn in as the first secretary of the Air Force. The first annual convention of the Air Force Association was held in Columbus, Ohio, a few days later. Delegates heard a number of Air Force leaders and national figures expound their support for winning the fight and reviewed all that had transpired.

General Eisenhower gave his blessing. He told the assemblage:

> The creation of the United States Air Force as an independent entity recognizes the special capabilities of air power; the creation of the Air Force Association recognizes aviation problems that require specialized—

> and organized—civilian assistance toward their solution. In this group we have a wealth of military and civilian talent that will devote itself to our defense needs, even as it keeps always in view the potential usefulness of the airplane in bringing the world closer together in purpose as well as in time.

General Billy Mitchell's air-power views had been proven in war. Now his dream had come true. By law, the Air Force was the nation's primary agency for gaining and maintaining general air supremacy, for establishing local air superiority, for conducting air defensive operations, and for operating the strategic air force and strategic air reconnaissance. The President's order also listed other capabilities, such as providing airlift and air support to surface forces, as well as "providing the means of coordination of air defense among all services."

Those who had fought the good fight for air power through the years thought the battle was over and had been won. It wasn't.

CHAPTER 20

Although the roles and missions of the three services were clearly spelled out by the legislation, Navy strategists challenged the capability of long-range bombers, specifically the B-36, to carry out the strategic mission. In their place, they argued for giant "supercarriers." The Navy and its supporters called the Air Force's 10,000-mile intercontinental B-36 a "lumbering cow," a "flying milk wagon," and a "billion-dollar blunder." The Navy League launched a $500,000 propaganda campaign to fight for a big Navy. Behind what the press called "the revolt of the admirals," there was a plan to shift the Navy's primary mission from controlling the seas to delivering the atomic bomb.

One of Secretary Forrestal's first chores in trying to settle the dispute was to call meetings of the Joint Chiefs of Staff at Key West, Florida, and Newport, Rhode Island, in August 1948. Out of these meetings came the "Key West Agreement," or the "Functions Paper." I don't know firsthand what transpired at those meetings, but Secretary Forrestal deserves credit for bringing divergent views together. It is an excellent example of what can come about when reasonable men reason together.

The agreement gave each service primary responsibility for certain jobs and also listed "collateral," or secondary, responsibilities. The service with the primary responsibility was to do the major planning, select the weapons, and give general direction to the functions. The primary functions of the Air Force were not changed, but three secondary tasks were assigned: (1) to interdict enemy sea power through air operations; (2) to conduct antisubmarine warfare and to protect shipping; and (3) to conduct aerial mine-laying operations. The secondary functions of one service were the primary functions of another. To prevent any service from making a primary job out of a secondary, the agreement further stated that such an assignment "shall not be used as a basis for establishing additional force requirements." This agreement made sense to me and I supported it wholeheartedly.

While these understandings were being hammered out, the specter of another war seemed to be looming ahead. It was labeled the "cold war," but it forced the United States to assess its military capabilities as compared with the Soviet Union. The difficulties had begun with the agreement between President Roosevelt, Prime Minister Churchill, and Generalissimo Stalin at the Crimean resort town of Yalta in February 1945. Among other decisions, the three agreed on the terms of surrender that would be offered to the Germans and on the Allied zones of occupation in Germany. The latter split Germany into four occupied zones and placed Berlin, the capital, inside the eastern half of Germany, which was controlled by the Soviets. The city itself was divided into four zones and occupied by French, British, American, and Soviet military forces.

My personal suspicions about Soviet intentions came about initially during our shuttle bombing missions in 1944 when we found ourselves unwelcome at the three bases we were using. My second awareness came when American forces were stopped short of taking Berlin and had to leave it to the Soviets. Georgie Patton had his postwar occupation problems with them and shared his thoughts with me during our West Coast speaking tour in 1945. He was convinced that the Soviet Union would be the enemy in World War III. I did not doubt the possibility.

If proof were needed that the Soviets had world domination in mind as their ideology declared, it came on the morning of June 25, 1948. Late the night before, a teletyped message from the Soviet zone in Berlin announced that "the Transport Division of the Soviet Administration is compelled to halt all passenger and freight traffic to and from Berlin tomorrow at 0600 hours because of technical difficulties.'' These ''difficulties'' were never explained. For weeks the Soviets had been actively harassing the French, British, and American military and civilian authorities in an attempt to force them to withdraw from the city. To them, West Berlin was like an island of democracy in their ocean of communism. It was a thorn in their side that had to be removed.

A land blockade of Berlin began, and all road, river, and rail traffic was halted between the three Allied sectors of Berlin and West Germany. Shortly thereafter, the ultimatum was made clear: the Western powers had to withdraw their military occupation forces from the city promptly. To make their point, the Soviets had decided to starve and freeze the West Berliners during the coming winter. Without food, fuel, and the other necessities, it would only be a matter of time.

What followed was the famous Berlin airlift, where war-weary U.S. Air Force C-47s and, later, C-54s supplied the city of two million people through three air corridors for nearly a year—a tribute to the peaceful potential of air power. They were assisted by a smaller number of British and French aircraft.

On May 12, 1949, the ''technical difficulties'' must have been solved, because the land blockade was lifted. However, the airlift continued, just in case, until September 30, 1949. A total of 2,323,067 tons of supplies, mostly food and coal, had been flown into the city. Seventy-five American and British airmen gave their lives to the cause of freedom.

The Berlin airlift was costly, but valuable lessons were learned. As a proving ground for air transport, it had shown the importance and feasibility of sustained, around-the-clock mass movement of cargo by air. It gave air and ground crews invaluable experience in weather flying, air traffic control, aircraft maintenance, overhaul methods, and operational techniques. More than that, the fact that the airlift was necessary proved that the United States and the other Western powers had a potent, dangerous enemy to face in the years ahead. Nine months later, this same enemy provoked the West again. This time the battleground was thousands of miles east of Berlin, in Korea.

The years between 1946 and 1950 were very busy for me. I served as a member of the Joint Congressional Aviation Policy Board in 1948 and as an advisor to the Committee on National

Security Organization. That same year, I was asked to serve on the National Advisory Committee for Aeronautics (NACA), then chaired by Jerome C. Hunsaker, a professor of aeronautical engineering at MIT. After Tooey Spaatz retired as Air Force chief of staff, General Hoyt S. Vandenberg took his place and appointed me his special assistant for science and technology in a civilian capacity.

Van had been my chief of staff when I commanded the 12th Air Force. His major concern was to effect a smooth transition to independent status from the Army. He asked me to be a go-between and troubleshooter, very much as Hap Arnold had asked me to be before the Tokyo Raid.

Van's memorandum to his staff stated that I would be responsible for dealing with problems involving the reorganization of the Air Materiel Command and the Air Research and Development Command that could not be resolved by mutual agreement between them. I was to study the differences and forward a clear statement of each of the conflicting views and my recommendations to Van.

To put it simply, I was responsible for separating the Siamese twins of the Air Force (Supply, Maintenance, and Procurement on one side, Research and Development on the other), with the cut between them taking place somewhere in the Engineering area, which lay in between, and for seeing that neither patient died. The job required a bit of tightrope walking. I knew I couldn't do it and keep everybody happy and in love with Doolittle, but I accepted the responsibility Van gave me because it fitted my military and industrial backgrounds. But the flying back and forth from my Shell office in New York to Washington was not enough for me to stay proficient as a pilot. I thought I should fly a minimum of 20 hours a month, and I was getting only a fraction of that. My proficiency at flying planes under all weather conditions was decreasing fast, and I knew it. To stay proficient in modern, high-speed aircraft, I believe, piloting must be a vocation, not an avocation. A rusty pilot is not a safe pilot, especially in crowded skies.

Since I couldn't stay competent in the air with so much responsibility on the ground, I decided to quit active flying altogether, and did. I've had no further desire to take the controls. The last entry in my pilot logbook was made on September 21, 1947, when I flew Shell's B-25 from East Hampton to New York. To remove the temptation of getting back in the pilot's seat, I had the plane transferred to the West Coast. I closed out my logbook after 30 years, at slightly over 10,000 hours pilot time in 265 different types of military and civilian aircraft.*

I returned to South America and Europe on Shell business in 1950. That same year, Joe and I made a two-and-a-half-month leisurely trip around the world. I conducted business with our Shell representatives in each country, but also took the opportunity to observe how each nation was progressing in its postwar civil and military aviation. I passed on my observations to the Air Force and other agencies where I thought they might be useful. The trip turned out to be valuable background for later assignments. I had the uneasy feeling that another war was brewing in the Far East, and once again, we weren't ready for it.

After V-J Day in 1945, the nation had hastened its demobilization so fast that its air power became only a memory. In the four months after September 1945, 1,200,000 airmen received their discharges. Within 24 hours after the announcement that the fighting had ceased, aircraft production came to a halt. An $8 billion backlog of production contracts was canceled and only about 1,700 of the 30,000 planes then in various stages of production were actually completed. Fortunately, a few research and development projects were allowed to continue, and a few military jet aircraft were procured. But the aircraft industry went into a depressed state and the predicted boom in airline travel and private flying did not materialize.

President Truman recognized the danger to the nation of a continuing depression in the aviation industry and appointed a commission of outstanding citizens, headed by Thomas K. Finletter, to make recommendations for a national air policy. Its report was entitled "Survival in the Air Age." This commission recommended a 70-group Air Force to be equipped and ready by January 1, 1950, with a reserve of 8,000 modern planes and a manpower total of 400,000. At the same time, a Joint Congressional Aviation Policy Board was formed for the same purpose. I provided input to both of these groups. Both submitted their studies early in 1948 with the same basic conclusions: a strong Air Force was the force most likely to discourage an

*I flew Air Force aircraft many times afterward, including supersonic jet fighters and jet bombers, but always with an experienced instructor pilot. I never flew again as pilot-in-command.

aggressor against attack on the United States, most effective in thwarting an attack if launched, and best able to retaliate to paralyze further attack. These were judgments we all wanted brought to the public's attention. Congress subsequently authorized a 70-group Air Force and appropriated the money for it.

The threat of attack, recognized by both boards, was more serious than most people thought. Intelligence sources reported that the Soviet Union was turning out planes at a rate much higher than was the United States. General Vandenberg said publicly that the United States was taking a "holiday" and that the Soviets were building more planes than we were turning out. The first real indication of great trouble brewing was when the Soviets closed the land access to Berlin in June 1948. The Berlin airlift was proof of the value of having an Air Force with the assets and the stamina to resist this form of aggression.

The need for adequate national defense was further emphasized when the Soviet Union exploded its first atomic bomb, in August 1949. Nevertheless, after the ground corridors leading to West Berlin were reopened and antagonisms subsided, strong public pressure developed to cut defense costs. President Truman, overriding Congress and the recommendations of his own commission, impounded only enough from the 1950 fiscal year funds for a 48-group Air Force, instead of the recommended 70 groups.

Still, Secretary of Defense Louis A. Johnson, successor to Secretary Forrestal, was not impressed by this reduction and was determined to cut the "fat" out of the defense budget. He declared that the military establishment "was still suffering from costly warborn spending habits" and said the Defense Department was "like a fat man—and like a fat man, was in poor condition to run a race until the fat could be transformed into muscle." In December 1949, he assured an audience during a major speech that no enemy could defeat the United States by a sudden "four o'clock-in-the-morning attack" and that the United States could "launch a successful counterattack spearheaded by the Air Force."

Johnson was wrong. In March 1950, a military intelligence report cited a buildup of forces in North Korea, but added, reassuringly, ". . . there will be no civil war in Korea this spring or summer." However, on June 1, Far East Air Forces intelligence officers reported that North Korean forces were now strong enough to invade South Korea "whenever Soviet strategy so dictates."

As if to challenge Johnson's words, a "four o'clock-in-the-morning attack" was launched against South Korea by the North Korean People's Army on Sunday, June 25, 1950. It was a reminder of another Sunday morning eight and a half years earlier at Pearl Harbor on "a date that will live in infamy."

War had come to us once more, and again we were relatively unprepared for a surprise attack. With growing alarm, the free world watched what President Truman called a "police action" in Korea. Not waiting to see if the United Nations would back the United States, he made a momentous decision on June 26. He ordered General Douglas MacArthur to use all the naval and air forces at his command to support the Republic of Korea army. However, he forbade any air or naval operations to be conducted north of the 38th parallel, except under emergency conditions. The next day, the UN Security Council recommended that its member nations "furnish such assistance to the Republic of Korea as may be necessary to repulse armed attack and restore international peace and security in the area."

This resolution, however, did not change the order prohibiting the Air Force from attacking north of the 38th parallel. Units of the Far East Air Forces (FEAF) began around-the-clock operations to halt the thousands of North Korean troops crossing the imaginary borderline, but not being able to pursue enemy fighter planes and bomb their supply and communications lines put them at a disadvantage. It was a no-win situation, and those of us who thought we had proven the offensive capabilities of aircraft during World War II were appalled.

General George E. Stratemeyer, commander of the FEAF, asked General MacArthur that his units be allowed to cross the line and bomb the enemy's home bases in North Korea. MacArthur gave verbal permission and Strat's forces went to work. The first attack was by Douglas B-26s against the main North Korean airfield at Pyongyang.

In the following weeks, Strat's forces were successful in driving the North Koreans out of the sky. But the job of bringing the Air Force back to life after it had been allowed to shrivel to a dangerous degree wasn't an easy one. American air units were shifted all over the world to meet the situation. Reserve units were called to active duty. Tactical aircraft were brought out of mothballs. Since the military aircraft industry was largely shut down, any action taken would have to be fought with the planes on hand, not those on the drawing board. During this period, I sat in on many meetings with industrial and military leaders and put in my two cents when I thought my comments were worthwhile. Time after time, the discussions made me recall similar meetings in 1940 and 1941 when I was working with industry to solve problems of converting from the production of automobiles to airplanes.

The lessons we had learned during World War II were still valid. Strat's first task was to gain air superiority, and this was done without great difficulty. The North Koreans relied on their seemingly endless supply of manpower for their ground forces and did not make a determined effort to counter American air power. As a result, our naval and ground forces could operate without fear of enemy air attacks. However, the success was not without its critics. The Army wanted control of the equipping, training, and operation of our tactical air units. Vandenberg spent an inordinate amount of his time in the Pentagon staving off those who would have liked to take over the Tactical Air Force. Despite the fact that the Air Force had won its independence three years before, Van had to continue to fight against its dismemberment.

I made a trip to Korea in the fall of 1950 at Van's request and talked at length with my old friends, particularly Lieutenant General Pat Partridge, my former deputy in the 8th Air Force, then commander of the 5th Air Force. When I returned home, I made an extensive report to Van and wrote to Pat about his support of the Army units in Korea. I guess I preached a little, but my letter to Pat was indicative of the times. I said the Air Force was faced with a tremendous obligation but had insufficient financial support. Its principal job was to avoid war with the USSR if possible, and to assure that it was won if it became unavoidable.

I advocated a strong force of intercontinental bombers and enough fighters to defend continental America from attack so that an initial Soviet blow would not be decisive. Our offensive strength had to be sufficient to assure that retaliation would be devastating, and all air units should be equipped and trained to support the ground and sea forces as required. It was fundamental that the Air Force not be dismembered but remain sufficiently homogeneous and flexible enough to win the air war. It was my opinion that if the Air Force were broken into separate packets of strategic air, tactical air, defense air, naval air, and marine air, it would not be possible to put all our strength against the enemy because he, if smart, could defeat the pieces one by one.

Despite the job that the Air Force's tactical units in Korea did initially in support of ground actions, completion of this task was not sufficient. A strategic phase was required that sent B-29s to pound enemy supply dumps, troop concentrations, airfields, and war industries deep inside North Korea. Meanwhile, medium bombers and fighters sought out tactical targets of opportunity behind the front, such as vehicles, marshaling yards, trains, and bridges. American aircraft were once again putting into practice the air-power philosophy we had preached and practiced against Germany and Italy.

Despite the best efforts of the UN forces, however, the sheer numbers of enemy ground forces were nearly overwhelming. For a while, in the fall of 1950, it seemed the UN forces might be driven into the sea. However, the North Koreans were eventually outflanked and pushed back beyond the 38th parallel.

On October 7, the UN General Assembly realized that merely clearing the enemy out of friendly territory did not mean that the war was won. A resolution was approved that "all necessary steps [must] be taken to ensure conditions of peace throughout the whole of Korea." The old axiom that drove us in our air campaign against Germany during World War II still held: The enemy must be made to lose the will and the ability to fight.

The whole equation changed on November 1 when six Soviet-built MiG-15 jet fighters jumped a flight of American F-51 propeller-driven fighters close to the Yalu River, which marked the China–North Korean border. Eight days later, the first all-jet air battle in history took place when MiG-15s attacked American F-80s high above the Yalu. It was obvious to me that the day would soon come when there would be an all-jet Air Force, and commercial aviation would soon follow the military's lead. I passed my opinion of the significance of the first all-jet dog fight to the people at Shell and encouraged increased research on and production of jet fuels.

General MacArthur ordered the Far East Air Forces (FEAF) to make an all-out effort "to destroy every means of communication and every installation, factory, city, and village" in enemy territory. However, FEAF pilots were forbidden to cross the Yalu. On November 26, thousands of fresh Chinese troops crossed the river, and the war entered an entirely new phase—a no-win phase.

In June 1951, the Soviet delegate to the United Nations had proposed cease-fire discussions to end the war in Korea. However, while United Nations, Chinese, and North Korean delegates attempted to agree on peace terms, the struggle went on.

I visited Korea in 1952, again in a consultant status, and could see firsthand that it was still a no-win situation as long as our Air Force could not attack the sources of manufacture and supply in China. FEAF forces were successful in sustaining an interdiction campaign against railroads, bridges, and truck convoys, but the supplies were still coming across the Yalu River from China. General Mark W. Clark, then UN commander, remarked in May 1952 that "only through forceful action could the Communists be made to agree to an armistice the United States could consider honorable."

The "forceful action" had to be more than strikes against supply lines. General Otto P. Weyland, then FEAF commander, wanted to attack strategic targets, which had been previously forbidden for political reasons. These targets included a complex of hydroelectric power plants in North Korea, war industries along the Yalu River, and the North Korean irrigation system, which included key dams. Approval was given and these were attacked with success, especially the destruction of the dams. Although it has never been proven that their destruction was the decisive blow, the dam-busting campaign, which caused floods to wash out bridges, rail lines, and roads, seemed to be the deciding factor that eventually brought the North Koreans to the peace table at Panmunjon on July 27, 1953, to sign the cease-fire agreement. The Korean "police action" had lasted three years, one month, and two days.

The war in Korea was not decisive; there was no victor and no vanquished. However, when limited strategic bombing was permitted it allowed numerically inferior UN ground forces to remain in Korea. As Lieutenant General Nam Il, chief North Korean delegate to the truce talks, remarked bitterly, "Without the support of the . . . bombardment by your air and naval forces, your ground forces would have long ago been driven out of the Korean peninsula by our powerful and battle-skilled ground forces."

Although American air units attacked North Korean industry, dams, railroads, and troop concentrations with devastating results, there was a restriction placed on their success. The prohibition against using air power to go after the sources of the enemy's supply and communications in Chinese territory prevented complete victory.

The war in Korea was a "limited" war. There were political, economic, moral, and psychological limitations. Both U.S. and UN policy prohibited the Air Force from unleashing the full power of its resources to bring a quicker end to hostilities. After three years of desperate fighting, the opposing forces ended only a few miles from where they had started in June 1950.

It was not the complete military victory that American air power was capable of gaining. Since all of the enemy's war supplies originated on the far side of the Yalu, I would have destroyed those supplies. There was no reason to fear that the Chinese might come into the war. They were already there. We left the supplies in China untouched, which enabled the North Koreans to keep their troops fighting. We should have shut them off at the points of manufacture and distribution.

The conduct of the war was widely criticized by American journalists and commentators at the time. General Eisenhower told me he had an answer for them: "In only two efforts of endeavor do the amateurs consider themselves more competent than the professionals—in the field of military strategy and the ancient profession of prostitution."

What made me personally angry at the situation was that our two sons served combat tours in Korea. I don't think either of them realized at the time that they were taking part in the first American war in which the goal was not victory but a draw, a goal completely alien to American thinking. Unfortunately, we would begin to be involved in a similar war in another part of Asia only a decade later. John, our youngest son, would once again have to fight in a no-win war in the 1960s.

It is my opinion that we made horrible mistakes in Korea and didn't learn from them. It is very distressing to me that we appear not to grasp the lessons of history. If nothing else, the American public had finally begun to realize that we would be confronted with Communist goals of world domination, at least at that time, for what looked like the indefinite future. The war in Korea did much, but not enough, to awaken Americans to the fact that the price of peace is eternal watchfulness backed by modern military strength.

CHAPTER 21

In February 1952, I received a "Dear Jim" letter from President Truman. He was seriously concerned about a sequence of tragic civilian aircraft accidents in the New York–Northeastern New Jersey metropolitan area. A series of three crashes had occurred at Elizabeth, New Jersey, and forced the closing of the Newark, New Jersey, airport early that year. The fact that these mishaps were confined, by coincidence, to a single community accentuated the fears of many Americans that aircraft represented a serious hazard to residential areas. These accidents also served to increase public awareness that airports were a nuisance because of aircraft noise.

President Truman decided to set up a three-man, temporary President's Airport Commission and asked me to serve as chairman. Charles F. Horne, head of the Civil Aeronautics Administration, and Jerome C. Hunsaker, head of MIT's aeronautical engineering department, were the other two members.

President Truman's letter pointed out that the location of many of our major airports had been determined many years before, when the aviation industry was new and operations were relatively limited. After the war, both civil and military air traffic grew rapidly and city boundaries were continuously spreading out toward these airports.

Meanwhile, there had been great progress in the art of flying and the development of supporting facilities, and striking advances had been made in aircraft and power plant development, in speed and service, in operational control of aircraft, and in their ability to operate under a wide variety of weather conditions. A common system of navigation and landing aids, for both civilian and military use, had been installed and maintained by the federal government on the federal airways and at important airports. Concurrently, the nation's investment in both civil and military airports had undergone tremendous expansion.

In view of these developments, the President felt a need for an in-depth study of airport location and use and wanted our commission to be "objective and realistic." He asked us to complete our study within 90 days and assured us of the full cooperation of all government agencies related to our assignment.

We began our work immediately. The Department of Commerce gave us office space, secretarial help, and telephone service. We sent questionnaires to the mayors of 104 cities, invited all organizations known to have an interest in the airport problem to submit their views, and consulted with 264 individuals and civic associations representing people who lived in the vicinity of airports. The three of us traveled by Air Force aircraft together and singly, and sent staff members to 30 cities to interview aviation management officials and inspect their airports. We submitted our report, entitled "The Airport and Its Neighbors," to the President on May 16, 1952. Of course, the press immediately called it the "Doolittle Report."

We made 25 recommendations. Among them: matching federal aid funds for airport development and improvements; establishment of effective zoning laws; regulations clarifying use of airspace; airport certification; positive air traffic control; acceleration of aids to air navigation; standard requirements for runway length; noise reduction programs; avoidance of test flying and military training over congested areas; and separation of military and civilian flying at congested airports.

To counter encroachment on the airports by property developers, we had two suggestions: construct runway extensions or overrun areas inside the airport boundaries; and restrict by local zoning laws, larger areas outside the airport boundaries to prevent the erection of obstructions that might be harmful to aircraft and to control the erection of public and residential buildings as a protection from nuisance and hazard to people on the ground.*

Sad to say, many city fathers did not heed our suggestions then, and even now still allow an airport to be surrounded too closely by housing, public shopping areas, and tall buildings. Unfortunately, some of these local development decisions are deliberate and are designed to provoke the closing of airports in favor of housing and office building development and thus increase the local tax base.

We held a press conference when we released our study, knowing full well that we could not please everyone and that no one would be entirely happy with all of it. I told reporters that we had dealt honestly with the complicated and controversial problems involved and, with due modesty, felt that the summary and the supporting recommendations should be accepted and implemented. Better airports, adequately supported by community, state, and federal government, were needed. This meant the expenditure of a substantial sum of public money.

We recommended that existing laws be clarified with respect to the navigable airspace, the inclined flight pattern leading to and from the airports, and the certification of airports. There must be adequate air traffic control and prompt development and installation of more aids to navigation; improved airport layouts; reduced aircraft noise; additional training in emergency procedures for flight crews; and a more rapid means of ground transport between cities and airports, which we considered one of the greatest deterrents to the further rapid development of transport aviation.

Our recommendations were considered "drastic" by some factions. At a meeting of aviation organizations in Kansas City the following March, a reporter asked a spokesman what the industry was going to do about our report. He replied that the general agreement was to "let buried dogs lie and do little about the Doolittle Report" so far as discussion of its most controversial parts was concerned.

One of the controversial items was our recommendation that airports be certified in the interest of public safety by the federal government. Our reasoning was that pilots had to be licensed by the federal authorities; aircraft had to be certified before they

---

*In 1955, the Federal Aid to Airport Program called these clear areas "Doolittle zones."

were considered safe; and mechanics, tower operators, and others working in the airport environment had to pass certain federal examinations to assure their competence. However, airport authorities did not see why airports should have to meet any standards, especially standards dictated by the federal government. After years of wrangling and resistance, airport certification finally became a fact in the mid-1970s. It was the pressure applied principally by the Air Line Pilots Association to the Federal Aviation Administration that mandated federal certification of airports—a quarter century after we had recommended it.

A bit of partisan politics surfaced in the middle of our deliberations. We had decided early that we would not pinpoint any airport by specific mention as an example of good or bad planning or procedures. At the time, there was a controversy about whether Washington National Airport or Friendship Airport near Baltimore (now Baltimore-Washington International) should be the airport serving the nation's capital. Congressmen and other high federal officials liked their reserved parking spaces at Washington National, and the airport is just a few minutes ride from their Capitol Hill offices. I don't know if congressional pressure was the reason, but Major General Robert W. Burns, President Truman's advisor on aviation matters at the time and former group commander of one of my World War II bomb groups in England, called on me to deliver a message from the President. He said the President wanted one of the commission's recommendations to state that Washington National Airport should be the choice for the nation's capital airport.

I was surprised and very disturbed at this request. I told Burns that we wanted to be completely objective and would frame our recommendations in general terms that would apply across the whole spectrum of airport problems. We would not mention any airport to prove a point, use as an example, or take sides in a controversy. "If the President wants me to change that philosophy," I said, "then I'll turn in my suit and he can find another chairman."

Bobby Burns was surprised at my reaction and asked if I really wanted him to give that answer to Mr. Truman. I expressed myself in a very strong affirmative and he left. Never heard another word about it.

In November 1952, General Eisenhower was elected to the presidency. Despite the controversy I seemed to raise whenever I was party to a government study and its resultant report, someone was pushing my name with the planners of the incoming administration to become the next secretary of the Air Force. I was not and am not a politician. My identity has always been with aviation technological progress, and I do not like partisan politics to enter into the equation when it comes to issues affecting aeronautical developments. Being active in the Air Force Association at that time, I realized that politics entered into many basic technological decisions affecting the future of our defense establishment, but I was never comfortable when I felt the nation's survival depended on technical decisions made solely to satisfy biased political ends.

I did not feel that accepting a political appointment as the civilian head of the Air Force fitted my nature or my desire to serve in a nonpartisan capacity. Perhaps my feelings became known. I was never offered the appointment, but I would have refused if it had been. When a good friend wrote to me in December 1952, congratulating me on hearing that I was to be nominated, I replied, "My spies tell me that the decision has just about been made and that another and better man has been selected." That man was Harold E. Talbott.

The year 1953 marked the fiftieth anniversary of the Wright brothers' triumph at Kitty Hawk. I was asked to serve as the chairman of the national committee to celebrate their accomplishment. In 1954, President Eisenhower asked me to chair a committee to study the Central Intelligence Agency. Senator Joseph McCarthy had loudly claimed that communists had infiltrated the agency, and he had raised such a fuss that the President had no choice but to have a committee appointed to look into his accusations. Concurrently, he appointed General Mark Clark to head another committee to study the possible reorganization of the agency. I traveled to Japan, Korea, and other foreign locations during this period.

We could not reveal the details of our CIA investigation, but our committee found the agency was doing a creditable job and was "exercising care to insure the loyalty of its personnel." I so reported to the President. In my cover letter I noted that there were important areas in which the CIA's organization, administration, and operations could and should be improved. The agency was aware of those problems, and steps were being taken toward their solution. Only one copy of that report was made and I handed it personally to the President. He wrote me a thank-you letter saying, "Both the report itself and the discussion I was privileged to have with the group when the report was presented here were of unusual value in providing an appraisal and stocktaking of those operations."

My appointment had its detractors. Westbrook Pegler, a nationally syndicated columnist, called our study a "whitewash" and wrote:

> I see no reason to place any value on the report which James H. Doolittle has made for President Eisenhower, on the mysterious, secretive, and sinister agency of our government called the Central Intelligence Agency.
>
> To begin with, I know a little about Doolittle's career but absolutely nothing which seems to qualify him as a competent man in this field. . . .
>
> He was a friend of Ike and a protégé of Roosevelt and he was favored by an overload of rank which presents him to history as a Lieutenant General. Altogether, this inflation, or dilution, of rank has worked to the popular discredit of the titles of Admiral and General in their several degrees.

Naturally, this column made me furious but I knew there was nothing I could do about it. It was his opinion and he was privileged to render it in print, but I have often wondered what the basis was for it. I cannot recall ever meeting or having been interviewed by Pegler. I do recall reading some of his columns but always had difficulty understanding his verbiage. I never realized that anyone could possibly imagine that I was a protégé of President Roosevelt, whom I met only once. Whether or not I was "favored by an overload of rank" is an opinion, hopefully, not shared by many others.

The technological superiority of the Soviets, first apparent in the Korean War, had become a major concern by 1955. Once more, I was asked to help out. I began serving as chairman of the Air Force Scientific Advisory Board, which concerned itself solely with Air Force weapons and equipment. Its function was also to advise the Air Force on the latest aerospace developments and to evaluate its long-term planning. I followed Theodore von Karman, a world-renowned aerodynamicist and missile expert, and Mervin J. Kelly, a prominent industrial engineer, as the third chairman. Concurrently, I served on the President's Foreign Intelligence Advisory Board and was appointed chairman of the National Advisory Committee for Aeronautics (NACA), predecessor of the National Air and Space Administration (NASA). I was also chairman of the President's Task Group on Air Inspection of the Stassen Disarmament Committee. To round out my activities, I joined the advisory board of the Smithsonian's National Air Museum (later the National Air and Space Museum). These assignments were in keeping with my background and interests, and I spent many days away from Joe carrying out my responsibilities. Typically of jobs like that, whatever input I had is buried in the minutes of the many meetings I attended, and many of our deliberations were and still may be classified. Suffice to say, the fifties were busy years for me. I like to think they were also worthwhile as far as my contributions were concerned.

Joe and I were invited to visit Australia in 1956, where I was to serve as a U.S. representative to the commemoration of the Coral Sea naval battle of May 1942. Another representative was Admiral William F. "Bull" Halsey, a delightful companion on this trip with whom I had many interesting conversations.

In the Coral Sea battle the Japanese were prevented from landing troops at Port Moresby, New Guinea. It was historically noteworthy because the battle was fought between carrier-based planes; no shots were exchanged between surface ships. It was a very pleasant and restful visit "down under," after which Joe and I continued around the world.

When we returned to the States, President Eisenhower had another assignment for me. At the beginning of his second term, he appointed me to the President's Science Advisory Committee. As the name indicates, this group was formed to recommend national research and development policies and programs for the future; it consisted of some of the most competent scientists in the United States. However, he must have forgotten my name was on his list of appointees. At a White House reception for the committee, he shook hands with each member and when he came to me, he said, "Why, Jimmy! What the hell are you doing here with this group?"

I guess, after all my years of trying to shake my "dare-devil" image and my service under him as one of his top World War II airmen, he apparently still thought of me as a "flyboy" who could only operate airplanes. However, I overlooked his brief memory lapse and we continued our friendly relationship. I enjoyed responding to his calls for my services because they were always a challenge.

CHAPTER 22

One benefit that World War II gave us as a nation was an unprecedented number of scientific and technical developments. Among them were nuclear weapons, radar, jet engines, data-processing technologies, air-to-air and air-to-ground missiles, and improved navigation and communication capabilities. All of these improved the effectiveness of the military services, especially the Air Force, but it should be noted that all of them also provided "spinoffs" for peaceful purposes. In one way or another, they also led to what we call the Space Age and eventually allowed us to put satellites in orbit, men on the moon, and probes deep into outer space.

None of these technical breakthroughs just happened. They were inspired by the demands of war and planned by men and women who not only foresaw future needs but filled them.

One of the leaders who had uncommon foresight was Hap Arnold. As chief of the Army Air Forces during World War II, he felt that he had another task besides winning the air war:

> That [job] was to project myself into the future; to get the best brains available, have them use as a background the latest scientific developments in the air arms of the Germans and the Japanese, the R.A.F., and determine what steps the United States should take

> to have the best Air Force in the world twenty years hence.[1]

Hap Arnold asked his friend Robert A. Millikan at CalTech to recommend the best man to head a committee of practical scientists and engineers experienced in sonics, electronics, radar, aerodynamics, and other phases of science that might influence the development of aircraft in the future. Millikan decided on Theodore von Karman, a member of Millikan's staff at CalTech. Millikan didn't want to let von Karman go, but Hap's requirements were overriding, so von Karman was given a leave of absence and went to Washington. It was the right choice.

Shortly after von Karman arrived, men who understood the advanced theories behind the new developments began to appear. Hap told them he wanted them to think ahead 20 years, forget the past, and regard the equipment then available only as the basis for their boldest predictions. Hap wanted them to think about supersonic and pilotless airplanes; improvements in bombs; defenses against modern and future aircraft; communication systems; television; weather; medical research; atomic energy; and any other factors that might affect the development and employment of air power in the years to come. He wrote:

> I assured Dr. von Karman I wasn't interested in when he submitted his report. He was to go ahead, wherever he wanted and whenever he wanted; to pay no attention to tomorrow's airplane, or the day-after-tomorrow's airplane, but to look into the future twenty years and determine what we would have to have then, and make a report that would be a guide to the commanders of the Air Force who would follow me. I gave him and his associates free rein—to go to England, Germany, Japan, Italy—even to Russia if they could get in.[2]

The appointment of von Karman was one of the many extraordinarily wise personnel decisions that Hap Arnold made during the war. Born in Budapest, Hungary, in 1881, von Karman was educated in Germany and became an internationally renowned research aerodynamicist. He came to the California Institute of Technology as a guest lecturer in 1926 and was persuaded to remain as director of the university's Guggenheim Aeronautical Laboratory in 1929. During the 1930s, von Karman exerted a considerable influence over aeronautical research and development in this country. In the late 1930s, at Hap's invitation, he sat on a special committee for Air Corps research of the National Academy of Sciences. Among the problems that Hap wanted advice on was rocket-assisted takeoffs for aircraft and other "Buck Rogersish" ideas. Thus began the formal part of the relationship between this brilliant man of science and the dedicated military man who was soon to lead his fledgling service into a major war. It was during this period that I first met von Karman.

On December 1, 1944, Hap formed the Army Air Forces Scientific Advisory Group (SAG) as "an office attached to the commanding general, AAF." Von Karman was its director; Hugh L. Dryden was the scientific deputy.

Although science and technology were mobilized during World War II, the war was fought with and decided by conventional weapons. In 1940, Hap had wisely decreed that priority would be given to "the continuing production of current types of airplanes." Although some new aircraft were designed, tested, and produced during the war, care was exercised to avoid interference with our mass-production programs.

We fought the war without advancing the frontiers of aeronautics very far, but basic new breakthroughs were at hand. Jet aircraft, guided missiles, and rockets did not influence the war to a major extent, but they showed great promise.

In 1944, the atomic bomb was about to become a reality. Clearly, in any future conflict, we would not have time for mobilizing and training forces, and building weapons. We would have to fight with what was on hand. Therefore, our force in being had to be both modern and adequate.

General Arnold recognized these facts and was determined not to let the Air Force lapse into obsolescence after the war by ignoring new scientific knowledge. He knew that vast amounts of scientific data existed and were in danger of being lost unless assembled, interpreted, and stored for easy access. These data were to be found scattered throughout the United States and Great Britain and in the soon-to-be-defeated Germany. He also knew that great improvements would have to be introduced into the Air Force and that we could not continue to depend upon the British for new inventions like radar and the jet engine.

Thus, it was imperative to our continued air-power development that all available information be consolidated and a long-range plan developed.

Just before V-E Day in 1945, von Karman and six colleagues made a very timely trip to Europe and were able to save a great amount of valuable German data that might otherwise have been lost to us. In August 1945, they produced a paper entitled "Where We Stand," which highlighted areas that they felt were fundamental for future Air Force planning. Among the factors they considered nearly a half century ago were that there would be aircraft that would fly at speeds beyond the velocity of sound; that missiles would be developed that could transmit destruction to targets at distances of several thousand miles, as well as smaller missiles for defense against enemy aircraft; and that there would be improved communications for the control of aircraft in the air and with fighter controllers on the ground. The group predicted that only aircraft or missiles moving at extreme speeds would be able to penetrate enemy territory protected by such defenses, and that the location and observation of targets, the takeoff, navigation, and landing of aircraft, and communications would be independent of visibility and weather. They foresaw that fully equipped airborne task forces would be able to strike at far distant points and be supplied by air.

Von Karman's group also concluded that the considerable achievements of the German scientists had come about not because the Germans were better or brainier people, but largely as the result of encouragement and adequate support from the German government. This is a valid conclusion, which we would do well to remember.

Once the Air Force's position in regard to the future was thus defined, the Scientific Advisory Group started to make a long-range blueprint for the future. When the war was concluded in August 1945, the future of Air Force research and development faced another challenge. The bulk of military research during the war had been controlled by the Office of Scientific Research and Development, reporting to the White House. In 1945, Vannevar Bush, the director of the agency, proposed that military research henceforth be entirely under civilian control. Von Karman reacted with anger to this proposal. Only some diehard academicians with no military experience agreed with Bush.

In December 1945, the Scientific Advisory Group produced

a study entitled "Toward New Horizons." It was an excellent in-depth look into the future, and officially declared that a vigorous research program was vital to the military and that no one person or agency should act as the Army Air Forces' only source of scientific information. A very significant statement from that report applies fully today: "Problems never have final or universal solutions, and only a constant and inquisitive attitude toward science and a ceaseless and swift adoption of new developments can maintain the security of this nation through world air supremacy."

In the introduction to this study, von Karman dismissed the argument, current at that time, that atomic weapons would negate the need for large military forces in the future. This was an idea that has lingered for years and has certainly hurt us. The individual reports included in the study not only produced large numbers of technical proposals and predictions, but also pointed the way for the Army Air Forces to organize for the conduct of research and for producing scientifically trained officers.

The report was about a half inch thick and was backed up with a two-foot stack of supporting materials. It made some interesting predictions:

- Over the next decade (1945–1955), air power would become increasingly important. Atomic weapons would increase destructive capabilities over a thousandfold.

- Improvements in aerodynamics and propulsion would lead to supersonic flight. (In 1947, Captain Charles E. "Chuck" Yeager broke the "sound barrier" in the X-1 rocket plane.)

- There would be improvements in guidance, navigation, and radar that would lead to all-weather flying and the ability to recognize a target and hit it accurately.

- We would have long-range pilotless aircraft. (In 1953, eight years after the report was published, a pilotless winged bomber called the Snark flew for the first time.)

- We would have intermediate-range and intercontinental ballistic missiles. (Twelve years later, in 1957, we had the Atlas and the Thor.)

- We would have earth satellites. (The Soviets had them in 1957; we had them in 1958.)

As happens so frequently in advisory work of this kind, no great or immediate reaction to the report was apparent. Military appropriations were very meager in 1946 and action was difficult to obtain. In addition, when these reports came out, Hap Arnold had retired and his absence may have affected subsequent events, illustrating the saying that, "Advice is only helpful when someone wants to take it." A corollary is, "A person is much more likely to accept, and act on, advice if he asks for it." However, many of the specific proposals became a point of reference for all the Air Force research efforts that followed.

It was not until 1948, after the Air Force became a separate service, that a more workable situation evolved. The name of the Scientific Advisory Group was changed to the Scientific Advisory Board (SAB), and it was placed directly under the Air Force chief of staff. As administrative procedures improved to permit the SAB to become more useful, the quality and extent of its recommendations increased.

One of the first major tasks was to expand the influence of the research and development staff at the Pentagon. At this time, a committee chaired by Lewis N. Ridenour, dean of the Graduate College of the University of Illinois, was formed to help the Air Force organize its research and development (R&D) efforts. I was asked to serve, along with George P. Baker, of the Harvard Business School; James B. Fisk, of Bell Telephone; Carl Overhage, of Eastman Kodak; Ralph Sawyer, of the University of Michigan; Raymond Woodrow, of Princeton University; and Frank Wattendorf, the Air Force Air Materiel Command's principal aeronautical engineer. Meanwhile, I had been a member of the National Advisory Committee for Aeronautics since 1948 and was its chairman from 1956 until 1958, when it was renamed the National Aeronautics and Space Administration. This association enabled me to keep abreast of vital activities in those scientific domains, a very useful exposure to what was going on in the pure aerospace sciences.

Our SAB report called for the establishment of the Air Research and Development Command in the Air Force with strong ties to the Air Materiel Command. It also advised, in forceful words, that adequate resources would have to be devoted to building the future Air Force. We recommended that a small but significant percentage of the Air Force's R&D budget be allocated for R&D contracts with educational institutions. We also recommended that future R&D be on a "system" basis and that task forces of specialists be assigned to particular weapon systems or components.

Introducing systems engineering was one of the SAB's more far-reaching and successful recommendations. It was the necessary interim step toward the establishment of the present Air Force Systems Command.

Systems engineering was an important managerial concept for the military. In the early days of aviation, the practice was to design an airplane structure and attach it to an available engine. When we got the airplane, we said, "Here is an airplane; we will now see what it can do." We would test it and agree that it was a magnificent plane with great maneuverability, speed, and climbing capability. Then we would say, "Now we will put on the necessary military equipment." We would then begin to install the guns, bombs, cameras, and navigation and communication gear. All too often, by the time we got through satisfying all the military requirements, the airplane had turned into a clunker that could not perform as originally intended.

This process was the absolute opposite of systems engineering, which enabled us to start many things at the same time and have them all come to the stage where they could be introduced into the complete vehicle ready to go at just the right time. Of course, this concept was a tremendous gamble and it took people with courage to pull it off.

Much credit must go to Trevor Gardner, John von Neumann, and General Bernard A. "Benny" Schriever for furthering and implementing the systems engineering concept and making it work. They took a number of new weapons, aircraft, and missiles and developed each of them in parallel, not in sequence, as had been customary in the past. This greatly shortened the time required and was probably the one thing that brought our missile program into actual operational use as rapidly as possible.

Another organization that owes a similar debt to the SAB is the Air Force medical R&D complex, which was recommended by an SAB committee chaired by Dr. Randolph Lovelace. Still another was the establishment of the Lincoln Laboratory, from which our modern air defense system developed.

After the United States got involved in Korea, the SAB was asked to review the Air Force guided missile program. With Louis N. Ridenour as our chairman, this committee emphasized that the use of guided missiles was the natural next step in air warfare and the Air Force should quickly add them to the inventory.

Selling our recommendations was not easy. General Hoyt Vandenberg, my former 12th Air Force chief of staff in North Africa, now had four stars and was Air Force chief of staff. Our recommendations, made by a group of civilian scientists and industrialists, called for fundamental structural changes in Air Force organization. Some members of Van's staff vigorously resisted such changes; therefore, Van was not fully convinced.

Since we were such good friends and I totally agreed with our recommendations, I was asked to brief Van informally. Instead of talking with him in his Pentagon office, I invited him for a few days of duck hunting, a favorite sport of both of ours. While we sat in the duck blinds, I carefully reviewed the rationale for our recommendations and told him we were convinced that the Air Force was woefully deficient in its ability to develop a future Air Force that could win wars if we were ever challenged again. I managed to convince him that the changes were necessary. By the time he went back to the Pentagon, he was "sold."

As a result of Van's subsequent decisions, there was an increase in R&D funds when the Korean War started in June 1950. However, the increase in emphasis on R&D created a great demand for scientific personnel. The SAB was asked to help find ways to attract the right kind of people; Ridenour accepted the chairmanship of a working group to recommend ways to make the Air Force scientific program more attractive and viable.

A recommendation of major significance was that the Air Force should create more weapon systems laboratories to integrate new developments in aircraft and missile components. This recommendation generated Project Vista, a CalTech study of tactical atomic warfare and the atomic defense of Western Europe. An offshoot was a study by the Cornell Aeronautical Laboratory on ways to modify tactical aircraft so that tests of various concepts could be conducted. Other recommendations led to a study at Harvard University of Air Force transport and logistics problems, and armament activities. The eventual result was the establishment of the Air Force Armament Development and Test Center at Eglin Air Force Base, in Florida.

A significant and useful SAB study was a forecast of

weapon weights and yields by class and the prediction of thermonuclear possibilities. This panel, chaired by John von Neumann, had a key influence in getting the initial intercontinental ballistic missile program under way. This panel also provided further guidance during the early years in the development of the nuclear weapons stockpile, for manned aircraft as well as ballistic missiles, and for tactical as well as strategic uses.

In all, 342 reports were produced by eight technical panels after "Toward New Horizons" was first published in 1945. Von Karman was replaced as chairman by Mervin J. Kelly in January 1955; I replaced Kelly the following November and served until December 1958.

The need for maintaining an emphasis on Air Force R&D was spurred by unsettling intelligence reports beginning in 1952 of Soviet weapons development. On August 12, 1953, a shocked world learned that the Soviets had detonated a hydrogen bomb, a weapon with far higher yield for its mass than the atomic bomb. At this time, Soviet scientists were also wrestling with the problem of projecting thermonuclear weapons over vast distances, reducing warhead friction upon reentry, and providing more accurate guidance mechanisms.

Postwar interviews with over 200 German scientists captured by the Soviets during World War II and repatriated to the West revealed the possibility that by 1956 the USSR might have 2,000-pound nuclear warheads in their arsenal that could be launched from two-stage rockets and could reach the northwestern United States. The German scientists estimated that by 1958, the Soviets would be able to launch 8,000-pound weapons that could reach any American target.

During my tenure as chairman of the SAB, I felt it was imperative that another "new" look at Air Force R&D be undertaken. The German scientists were very accurate in their predictions. The Soviets launched an intermediate range ballistic missile (IRBM) in April 1956 and an intercontinental ballistic missile (ICBM) in August 1957. As a climax, the Soviets sent *Sputnik*, the world's first artificial satellite, into earth orbit on October 4, 1957.

Until that time, the American public and government officials had discounted the progress and capabilities of the Soviets. We had for a long time thought rather disparagingly of the Soviets as, perhaps, agrarians with their shirttails out and whiskers. But we came to realize that they had a very fine technological capability. The launching of *Sputnik* really brought this forcibly to our attention and indicated the necessity for us to go all out if we were going to catch up and then surpass them.

Once again, the country had been lured into complacency, and our political, military, and scientific leaders were castigated for their apparent inability to foresee these outstanding scientific achievements.

The Air Force had given priority to the ICBM, and its leaders did not want satellites or any other projects to divert resources from ballistic missiles. However, the American public demanded to know how the Soviets, considered backward by most, could make such awe-inspiring technological breakthroughs.

A group of distinguished scientists, some of them members of the SAB, assembled at Woods Hole, Massachusetts, in 1957. They eventually produced the "Woods Hole Summer Studies." These studies represented an update of "Toward New Horizons" and recognized the international impact of the Soviet accomplishments in space and of their ICBMs, as well as their nuclear capability.

Unfortunately, the Woods Hole report did not have much impact. The leaders of the Air Force's R&D community, pressed by Congress for action to close the space gap revealed by *Sputnik*, had to concede that satellite technology should be given some priority. There was concern in the Air Force that the Strategic Air Command's primary role might be infringed upon.

Seven technologies had to come together to bring about space systems, satellites, and ballistic missiles: servomechanisms, radar, the digital computer, space communications, transistors, the fusion bomb, and rocket propulsion. These seven technologies evolved and accelerated during the 1950s and were bound together by systems engineering. By carefully integrating these technologies, the complexities of manufacturing satellites, missiles, and space vehicles could be brought under control.

The integration of these technologies offered great managerial challenges to our free society engaged in a cold war against an antagonist of surprising scientific capability. As chairman of the SAB, I set forth three chores for us to accomplish: try to solve some of the day-to-day R&D problems of the Air Force; try to answer complex scientific questions of the secretary of the Air Force and the Air Force chief of staff; and generate new ideas. The last is always the most difficult and the most prone to be sacrificed because of involvement in day-to-day operations. However, I believe it is the most important. My views have not changed with the passing years.

I retired as chairman of the Scientific Advisory Board in 1958. Lieutenant General Donald Putt, who had retired in 1957 from the Air Force and was then president of United Technologies Corporation, succeeded me. I subsequently served as a member of the SAB's Ad Hoc Consultant Group for several years.

The SAB made later contributions, one of the most important being participation in the Air Force's Project Forecast during the early 1960s. This project enlisted almost 500 people, balanced between R&D experts who understood the requirements of war, and some of the nation's top civilian scientists, from universities, industry, "think tanks," and government. The man who masterminded the project was Major General (later General) Benny Schriever, brilliant commander of the Air Force's Air Research and Development Command, later the Air Force Systems Command.

The result of this project was a 25-volume compilation of studies, each of which dealt with some aspect of aeronautical or military science. It was a masterful effort that took a long look at the Air Force in the light of a presumed status quo in strategic nuclear relations between the superpowers. The study recommended the continued development of small conventional weapons as well as small nuclear weapons for tactical use on the battlefield. It represented a blueprint for the next decade of the Air Force and has since been followed with other studies designed to keep us ahead technologically. Its value and success can be measured by the fact that we have not been engaged in a nuclear war.

I had become interested in rocket development in the 1930s when I met Robert H. Goddard, who laid the foundation for most subsequent U.S. developments in long-range rockets, missiles, Earth satellites, and spaceflight. While with Shell, I worked with him on the development of a type of fuel that would have a sufficiently high vapor pressure so that the vapor would be completely consumed without a pump, thus simplifying some of his early experiments.

My interest in rocketry was revived while commanding the 8th Air Force. The Germans were using the V-1 rocket against British targets, but we were able to cope with it because its performance was not much greater than that of our better airplanes. We could hear a V-1 coming; a pilot could either shoot it down or fly alongside and tip it with a wingtip, causing the gyro to spill and send the V-1 down before arriving in England.

It was different with the V-2, which was the first practical supersonic rocket. It came and exploded before you saw or heard it. It was a much more effective weapon because of its psychological effect. I thus became aware of the effectiveness of rockets and missiles as weapons. However, there were many who did not then give much credence to the tremendous potential of rocketry; some of us in the airplane business looked with a slightly raised eyebrow at those rocket people, who seemed to be unduly enthusiastic about its possibilities.

After World War II, I gave a talk about Goddard's life and work and the future of rocket power at the preview opening of the Goddard Rocket Exhibit, sponsored by the Daniel and Florence Guggenheim Foundation. As a result, I came in close contact for the first time with the people of the American Rocket Society. While there were undoubtedly geniuses among them, most of us probably looked upon them as somewhat starry-eyed.

This meeting led to my taking over the chairmanship of the National Advisory Committee for Aeronautics from Hunsaker in 1956. He had been chairman for quite a few years and he, even more than I, considered the rocket people way ahead of their time. I did not see the realization of the potential of rockets as imminent at the time, but coming. He asked me to succeed him as chairman because he thought I was more sympathetic to the rocket. He told me, "I know in my heart that the rocket is coming, but I am just not in the mood to give up everything we are doing with the airplane, which badly needs further development, in the interest of going off into the wild blue yonder." He recommended to the members that I be appointed to succeed him. My field of scientific interests thereafter expanded to include all manner of space activities.

Through my various advisory roles to the Air Force and to other agencies of the government while working for Shell, I came to know the organization and functioning of the Air Force's ballistic missile program. I was privileged to see many of the official status reports of the program and acquired some knowledge of the role played by the Ramo-Wooldridge Corporation and later by the Space Technology Laboratories (STL) as the scientific-technical member of the ballistic missile program management team for the Air Force. I studied STL's relationship with Ramo-Wooldridge, its financial structure, its management, and its plans for the future, and I decided that it was a unique organization that was accomplishing a very useful function. It was for these reasons that I accepted the chairmanship of the STL board on January 1, 1959, when I retired from Shell. Before that happened, however, Joe and I would have to cope with the most severe and lasting shock we have ever faced together.

NOTES

1. Arnold, Henry H., *Global Mission*. New York: Harper & Row, 1949, p. 532.
2. Ibid., pp. 532–533.

CHAPTER 23

In December 1955, I had become 59 years old. It was Shell's policy to retire its senior executives at age 60 to make way for younger men. I had no quarrel with that. Since Joe and I wanted to retire on the West Coast, I had asked for a transfer to the Shell office in San Francisco for the remainder of my tenure as senior vice president. My request was granted and we moved to an apartment in San Francisco. It was our plan to build our dream house at Pebble Beach, near Monterey, on the lot we had purchased several years before, and settle into a life of relative tranquility.

I have always thought of life in terms of activity plateaus related to age. As one nears the end of an active life, one should plan to step down gradually. Shell had other ideas. The company asked me to stay on a while longer to continue and complete several projects that I had started in New York. I dislike leaving any project uncompleted and so remained on the job.

Meanwhile, I was asked to continue as a consultant to the Air Force to assist in getting its missile program going, and found myself traveling almost as much as before. In April 1958, I was attending a meeting of Air Force officials at Ramey Air Force Base, in Puerto Rico, when I got the shattering news that our son Jim, Jr., then a major, had taken his own life at Bergstrom Air Force Base, in Austin, Texas.

Young Jim had accepted a regular Air Force commission

after World War II. He had served in the Pacific and in Europe flying medium bombers during that war and had been a fighter pilot during the Korean War. He became a fighter instructor and, for a time, was a test pilot at Wright-Patterson Air Force Base, in Ohio, and Edwards Air Force Base, in California. At the time of his death, he commanded the 524th Fighter Bomber Squadron of the 27th Fighter Bomber Wing.

It is difficult to describe the mental anguish one goes through when a loved one takes his or her own life. You ask why, over and over, knowing you may never learn the complete answer.

Jim left no note, but was believed to have been despondent about his situation in life. His first marriage had dissolved after the birth of his son, James H. Doolittle III. He remarried, and Joe and I knew of no marital problems. However, Jim always seemed to have a difficult time pleasing his superiors and had recently been passed over for promotion to lieutenant colonel. Still, this seemed an inadequate immediate cause.

Jim may have suffered personal stress all his professional life from being easily identified as my son because of his name. Other sons of military men who have been in the news over a period of time, as I was, had self-identity problems. Jim and I never talked about this as a problem, but it could have been a factor during his Air Force career. There may even have been commanders senior to him who saw it as a way to get back at me for imagined injustices, or it could have been his struggle to make his own way in the Air Force that put him at cross-purposes with a few of his superiors.

In the investigation of his death, several of his brother officers stated that for the previous six weeks or so, he had appeared depressed, but they didn't know why except for his failure to make the promotion list. His wife substantiated their observation of his growing despondency and depression.

Joe dealt with her grief in her own way. She knew that it had always helped her in times of personal stress to keep busy. She made it a point to try new things—things she had always put off doing. She went for long walks by the seashore and read a number of books. She tidied up her scrapbooks and wrote long letters to friends who had sent condolences. We tried to comfort each other as best we could.

As I have done several times in my life when I wanted to think things through, I spent some time alone after the funeral and wrote what I titled "philosophical thoughts" about our loss. Those thoughts are repeated here for whatever value they may have to others:

> When a person takes his own life, it is probably because the load of living has become so heavy that it doesn't seem worthwhile to continue to carry it.
>
> In some cases, the cause is readily apparent. More frequently, it is difficult to see exactly what made the load so onerous. It may be one thing or a very few things. It is more apt to be many things, none of which, in themselves, are crucial. It may be triggered off by a final event, which, while the "final straw," may be even smaller than any of the others.
>
> It seems to me that the sum total of the load results, in large part, from three primary causes: personal, people, and environment.
>
> Among the most critical of the personal conditions are frustration, fear, finances, health, and misconduct. These causative elements will, of course, affect different individuals differently—according to their character and personality.
>
> The people who are more instrumental in determining our destiny and therefore contributing to our peace of mind, or lack of it, are family, friends, superiors—particularly immediate superiors—associates, subordinates, and others. Among others, the public and the press are particularly important.
>
> The environment in which an individual lives and operates may vary from very pleasant to extremely unpleasant. It may be stable or unstable. An agreeable environment would certainly lighten the load. A disagreeable environment would as surely make it heavier.
>
> The basic environmental requirements are food, shelter, clothing, and heat. We have come to require comforts and luxuries and are inclined to be unhappy without them.
>
> If we were to put the individual items in the three primary causes in three vertical columns, it would be immediately apparent that some items, such as fi-

nances, may affect all three primary causes in a horizontal manner. Also, in general, one might expect the last two (people and environment) to be largely instrumental in determining the real or fancied conditions that cause the first (personal problems).

Only when someone very near and dear to one leaves does one appreciate the stark tragedy of death. Even then nature tends to cushion the initial shock, and the thought, "He is gone," does not carry the later realization of finality and permanence that comes only with the final indisputable understanding that "we will never see him again."

Actually there is a strong tendency to plan the future including the departed until the unpleasant realization of the complete permanence of death—on this earth—takes over. This realization may be driven home through cold mental analysis, through the eye (realizing the significance of the vacant slot in a fly-by), or through the ear ("Taps").

It does us no good to speculate why our firstborn took his irrevocable step. He left no clues and never discussed his personal feelings or problems with anyone in our family or with friends.

I can think of no greater misfortune for parents than when a child dies out of sequence in the natural order. It is something that I don't think one ever fully recovers from. Fortunately for Joe and me, we had Jim, Jr.'s son, "Double Junior" (James III), who is an Air Force colonel at this writing; young Jim's second wife, Shirley, and her son, Eric; our son John, a career Air Force officer who retired as a colonel; and his wife, Priscilla, their five children, and our great-grandchildren to sustain us over the years.

As great as the loss was to us, Joe and I knew we had to go on living. We buried ourselves in our respective activities and maintained contact with our large circle of friends. We seldom talked about our loss, but we never got over it.

I retired from Shell in 1958, but despite my theory about personal activity plateaus, I was not really looking forward to inactivity in any permanent form. I had seen men in their early sixties retire to a life of golf and fishing who had many years of contributions left in them but who died at an early age from boredom. I believe as long as a man is able to accept new concepts, he can continue to be useful. He is old only when his mind atrophies; then he lives in the past and is no longer in tune with the present and looking into the future.

I was delighted when Fred Crawford, head of Thompson Products of Cleveland, said he wanted to talk with me about my future. I had known Fred since my racing days at Cleveland, and we had kept in close touch through the years. His company made all kinds of aviation and automotive products and I suspected that he wanted me to join that company. Instead, he said he was going to start a new company, to be known as TRW Incorporated. Always a forward-looking man, he said the company was the result of a brainstorm by Dean Wooldridge and Simon Ramo, two brilliant scientists. Both had been formerly employed by Howard Hughes and had left Hughes in 1953 to form the Ramo-Wooldridge Corporation to manage the Air Force's ballistic missile development programs. Their company would be heavily involved in the burgeoning aerospace industry and they had persuaded a number of competent people to go with them. They needed a financial backer and Fred was their man, hence the Thompson-Ramo-Wooldridge team, which became TRW.

I first served on TRW's board of directors. In 1959, TRW established a subsidiary called Space Technology Laboratories (STL) to conduct investigations in the fields of space and missiles. They asked me to be chairman of its board, an assignment much to my liking because of my belief that space was a natural extension of aeronautical thinking and planning. I accepted the invitation, left Shell one day in San Francisco as senior vice president, and was at work the next day in Los Angeles at STL. However, I remained on Shell's board of directors until 1967.

Since many of the programs I would be involved in were government funded and TRW was making products that were aviation related, I thought it prudent to resign from several of the government advisory boards on which I was then serving. I wanted to avoid any accusations of conflict of interest or even the appearance of a conflict. However, I saw no conflict in remaining a member of the President's Foreign Intelligence Advisory Board and the advisory board of the National Air Museum. I also continued to serve on the Plowshare Committee of the Atomic Energy Commission.

Accepting the job with STL, located in Los Angeles, meant a move for Joe and me. On New Year's Day, 1959, we drove to Los Angeles, where we rented an apartment and later bought a beautiful, modest home in Santa Monica. It was located very close to the ocean and right next door to Bill Downs, our lifelong friend from Manual Arts High School days. We were also close to Joe's sister Grace and her husband, Andy Andrews, whom she had married during our stint on the Mexican border, and my cousin Emily. Retired Colonel Jerome Simson, a school classmate of mine in Alaska, lived nearby in Arcadia.

For the first time in our married lives, Joe and I could really spread out and unpack furniture and memorabilia stored since 1940! It was good to have all those things in one place again.

To take a respite from a busy work schedule I always tried to schedule time out for my favorite sports—hunting and fishing—and my hobby—puttering in my workshop. The latter has produced no lasting contributions to society or my family, but I've always had a yearning to do things with my hands, which probably came from my father's side of the family. I usually set up a small workshop wherever we lived so I could take care of household requirements and auto repairs. Both our boys were blessed with the same inclinations.

I am a sportsman-hunter and ardent conservationist. I believe firmly in abiding by the letter and spirit of the law. Poachers are not sportsmen. They operate outside the law and destroy wildlife, so that, eventually, no one will be able to enjoy it. Their actions and, in some cases, the market hunters, have contributed greatly to the depletion or complete loss of important species. Oddly enough, in the minds of many people, the sportsman is the culprit. Unfortunately, all hunters are not sportsmen.

My hunting and fishing, beginning with my boyhood in Nome when I shot my first duck and fished through a hole in the ice, always provided relief from the cares and tensions of the workaday world. Wherever I found myself, I tried to engage in both these sports, albeit very briefly during the World War II days, and have had more than my share of rewarding experiences hunting big game at many locations around the world.

There is always an element of danger when you hunt for big game—danger from the standpoint of the animal you hunt and danger from the point of view of the terrain in which you hunt. One of my desires as a hunter was to score a "big four grand slam," which is to shoot all four species of bighorns—the Dall; the stone sheep found in British Columbia; the Rocky Mountain bighorn of Wyoming and Colorado; and the sand-colored desert sheep seen in Arizona, New Mexico, and Baja California. Only a very few have ever done this. I became one of those few when I finally bagged a Rocky Mountain bighorn ram in the Jackson Hole area of Wyoming in 1970.

Next to the bighorns, my favorite game animal is the bear, especially the great Alaska brown, the famous grizzly, and the polar bear. Although they are found elsewhere, only Alaska can boast of all of these, plus moose and caribou. That's why Alaska is my favorite hunting ground.

One of my memorable bear hunting experiences took place on the Alaskan Peninsula near Cold Bay. I was walking a bear trail in mushy tundra that was only about six inches wide. It was a matter of walking one foot over the other.

I came over a small rise and met a female brown bear head-on. She was followed by a cub that weighed about 250 pounds. Ordinarily, a bear will leave when it sees and smells you, but there wasn't time for either of us to run. She charged instantly, protecting her cub. I had to shoot her.

Bear cubs are like children and will follow their mother through the spring and summer. When the mother gets tired of the responsibility, she eliminates them from her life. Besides, if she meets a new mate, he refuses to accept a ready-made family and will run them off himself. This one was certainly big enough to fend for itself and ran off quickly. Nevertheless, I have always felt bad about this.

Another time, I went bear hunting in the Talkeetna area near Mount McKinley with Bob Shelton, a pilot and well-known Alaskan guide. It was late May, but there was still deep snow all around. We landed on a flat area and I stalked a large brown bear for an hour or so before I got him. Bob and I skinned it and packed it to the plane. Meanwhile, the snow had softened and Bob couldn't take off with the two of us and the heavy bearskin on board.

Bob said he had a plan that he had used many times before. I was a little dubious but had no alternative. We tramped the snow down for about a quarter mile ahead of the plane to make a runway and he took off, leaving me on the ground. He flew a traffic pattern around the spot and came in at low speed toward me. I grabbed a wing strut and stepped on a ski as he sped by. He climbed as slowly as he could while I struggled to get inside. I finally made it. When we got on the ground, I asked Bob what other alternatives there were if I couldn't have grabbed that strut. His reply: "You'd have had to stay there 'til summer."

It was also in Alaska that I had another one of my many embarrassing experiences. While stalking a bighorn alone, I had to cross a freezing glacial stream. I walked in with my waders on but slipped, fell in, and went under. I climbed out and went ashore. I dried out my clothes and rifle by a campfire before continuing. When I dressed, I suddenly realized what I had done. I was still on the same side of the stream. This was proof of my consummate stupidity.

The most unique hunting experience I've had was in the jungles of Venezuela trying to get a jaguar. These are hunted at night. The hunter and his guide sit in a jungle blind in an area where *el tigre,* as the natives call him, is known to hunt for his own game, such as their cattle.

I recall settling down one night with my .300 Weatherby magnum equipped with a spotlight clamped on the barrel. Wires connected the light to a battery in my pocket. The guide blew on a gourd called a *coronto*. The sound was supposed to imitate a jaguar's howl, which I translate as saying, "I am a strange jaguar. I have come into your territory and I can whip you."

Responding, a jaguar, most of the time, will come toward the sound. What you hope is that you will see him when he is still some distance away. Then you flick on your light, sight in on his foreshoulder, and shoot. I didn't see this one, but one of my fellow hunters did and bagged him. I never did get a jaguar.

Another goal of big game hunters is to bag the "big five" of Africa: an elephant, a Cape buffalo, a rhino, a lion, and a leopard. These are the five most dangerous animals on that continent; they are big, strong, and fearless.

I was able to make the grand slam by getting all five of the African animals. The first rhino I tried to bag gave me a problem and chased me up a thorn tree three times. In a case like that, you don't realize that a thorn tree has thorns until you start down.

The leopard is a beautiful animal to watch because of its ability to stalk, its grace, and its cunning. Seminocturnal, it isn't easy to get within rifle shot of one. The best way to hunt them is to put out some bait, such as a dead antelope, in a tree and wait in a nearby blind. When a leopard leaps on the bait and starts to eat, it loses its caution. That's when you can get it.

It is illegal to shoot female leopards, but one night while I was on a one-shot hunt, a leopard approached the bait. The guide whispered that it was a male because it was so large. I accepted his judgment. It wasn't. I shot it and when we went over to it and found it was a female, I felt sad. We reported it to the game warden, who thanked us and said that, from its size, the mistake was understandable.

I don't think that elephant hunting is great sport. It is very distressing to learn that poachers are decimating the African elephant herds only for their ivory. The elephant I got was a rogue that had been terrorizing native villages in Nairobi, so I have always felt I was doing the populace a favor by killing it. An elephant is so huge that it's hard to miss. However, when wounded, they can crush you to death easily if you haven't taken proper precautions.

As a former hunter now, I am greatly concerned that the world is losing all of these magnificent animals to poachers and the encroachment of civilization. Humans are taking away the territory most of them need for survival. I think each country that is a habitat for all these wonderful wild creatures must take every measure possible, including strict enforcement, to protect them from extinction. They should not be hunted just for the private exhilaration a hunter may feel, but killed only if they are overnumerous and endanger humans. When their numbers reach a predetermined minimum, they should be declared "endangered" and protected until their numbers increase to a point of overpopulation.

Bird hunting is different from hunting four-footed creatures in that it is usually not as rigorous. I have enjoyed the companionship of many men who love the sport as much as I do. We have spent many relaxing hours in blinds waiting for the ducks and geese to come in, and those hours have strengthened our friendship. Similarly, the many times stalking grouse, doves, turkeys, and pheasant with longtime friends are some of the most pleasant memories of my life. One of my favorite spots is Slater, Colorado, where I especially enjoyed the hours of happy reflections around a campfire with wise friends who always provided me with a rejuvenated spirit to take back to work.

Bird hunting not only has given me periods of relaxation,

it has given me an appreciation of the wonders of nature and the need for conservation of all the world's creatures. It is a crime against nature to have any animal or bird become extinct through the excesses and selfishness of people.

I have always believed anyone who enjoys hunting must keep himself in good physical condition; otherwise, he will be a handicap to himself and to his companions instead of an asset. It is also very important to maintain proper blood pressure. That's why I do about 15 minutes of calisthenics every morning and do as much walking as I can. Before a hunt in the mountains, I always trained by taking brisk 10-mile hikes to get in shape.

I have never smoked and hold my weight steady simply by eating foods that give me energy and not obesity. By doing this, I have been able to keep my weight at about 145 pounds almost all my adult life. For preventive maintenance, I have a complete physical examination once a year.

Fishing is also a sport I have enjoyed greatly ever since those early days when I dropped a line through holes in the ice on the Snake River at Nome. I have been deep-sea fishing off the coast of Baja California a few times, but most of my fishing has been in the lakes and streams of the 48 states and Canada.

I am reminded of what President Herbert Hoover, an ardent fisherman, once said: "Before a fish in a brook, all men are equal." I agree. Just as with hunting, fishing is a personal challenge, and I have taken that challenge fishing for Dolly Varden trout, steelheads, rainbow trout, grayling, and silver salmon. One of my favorite fishing spots is Miramichi Bay, in Canada, going for the Atlantic salmon. Another is near Creede, Colorado, where I have gone fly-fishing many times with several of my Tokyo Raiders—Jack Hilger, Bill Bower, Dick Cole, Bobby Hite, Dick Joyce, and Dick Knobloch.

One of my treasured nonaviation awards was being named Winchester-Western Outdoorsman of the Year in 1974, the year I reached 78. The award was a new Winchester Super-X Model 1 autoloading shotgun bearing the serial number 1942, a year of special significance to me.

Conservation of all the world's resources is a subject that has concerned me for many years. The most important problem is control of human population growth and consequent overcrowding. How population growth is controlled is a sensitive social problem for which I have no answer, but we must seriously study the consequences of nothing being done.

Technology has also had a profound effect on the environment. We have for a long time accepted the "good life," which has been made possible through technological advances, without guarding against technology's undesirable by-products. I refer to stripping the land in mining for ore and coal and not restoring it after use; careless exploitation of the forests, including complete removal of undergrowth, which eliminates animal habitats and encourages erosion; and the use of pesticides that destroy not only noxious insects but also fish, birds, and small land animals. In addition, we have not paid enough attention to the proper treatment of industrial and human waste.

While it is encouraging to have many organizations warning us about the dangers we face for our carelessness and failure to conserve our natural resources, it is not enough. We must have strong federal and state laws that are enforced with great intensity. If we don't, our planet will slowly destroy itself through our wastefulness. Evidence that this is happening now can be seen in almost every town and city in America.

Back in 1957, I was asked to make predictions about the future. Predictions are always risky, but from what I had observed was going on with space research at that time, I said, among other things, that before the end of the century, a rocket would be landed on the moon with scientific instruments; a manned satellite would orbit and return to earth; men would land on the moon; a space platform would be established; and instruments and then a man would be landed on Mars or Venus. I also said that it would be possible to travel from San Francisco to New York or New York to London in half an hour. I softened this thought by saying: "The determinant as to whether people travel this fast will be not technology, but economics."

I was right about most of my predictions, except that my timing was off; several occurred long before the end of the century. The rest *can* come about if we really want them to.

If I weren't a conservative, I would say that before the end of this century two more events will take place: a permanent observation station will be established on the moon, and interplanetary travel will be a common undertaking. It was my opinion in 1957, and still is now, that if we do not expend the thought, the effort, and the money required, then another and more progressive nation will. What we have witnessed in aeronautical and astronautical progress during the last three decades is only the beginning. What will happen next, I cannot even conceive. I'm only sure that the rate of scientific progress will continue to increase.

In the early 1960s, I was concerned that the United States was failing to maintain its military dominance and its leadership in world economic affairs. I felt that the nation's "middle of the road" stance had, for some time, been sliding farther and farther to the left. The American news media, in my opinion, had begun to lose their objectivity and were biased too much in favor of liberalism. One example comes to mind: *The New York Times*'s early support of Fidel Castro and his procommunist dictatorship of Cuba. It was and is a splendid newspaper, but in that case its editorial position disturbed me.

In addition, I felt there were too many intellectuals in important places in government who had had no previous experience in management and decision making. They were making vital decisions in the areas of military requirements, tactics, and strategy that I thought should be made by the professionals in uniform. When President Lyndon Johnson inherited the presidency after the assassination of President John F. Kennedy, he announced he would campaign in 1964 to keep the job. I thought his liberal views, especially those regarding our national defense, were not realistic. Someone of a more conservative viewpoint was needed to oppose Johnson in the 1964 election.

During this period, I was impressed with the views of Senator Barry M. Goldwater, Republican from Arizona, who announced he would seek the presidential nomination of his party. He was a pilot and a major general in the Air Force Reserve. I had met him on several occasions and found him to be honest, courageous, and blessed with good common sense. He abhorred war but believed that we could maintain peace only through strength—moral, economic, industrial, and military strength. He also believed that we must *earn* national prestige and world respect. He was for a balanced budget and was opposed to deficit spending. He advocated hard work and, if necessary, personal sacrifice in order to have a balanced budget along with a strong defense. He believed we should encourage constructive effort on the part of individuals and nations and should not stifle initiative;

he said we stimulated laziness and greed by putting either on the dole. He did not believe we should promote individual or national shiftlessness and so help it to become a way of life.

These were also my views. Neither of us has ever changed our minds.

I had a man-to-man talk with Barry for several hours after he had declared his intention to run for the presidency in 1964 and was very favorably impressed. Outspoken and honest, he did not come across in the press very well. Some critics accused him of being "too" honest in his views, something I find difficult to comprehend. Many liberal pundits felt that he often "shot from the hip" with his conservative convictions. The Democratic opposition was well financed and determined to dominate public thinking in those days with the promises of Lyndon Johnson's "Great Society."

I had made only two political speeches before in my life backing a candidate for public office. Both were for General Eisenhower, once in Washington when he ran for president the first time, the other in Michigan during his second campaign. In my years in the service, I didn't vote because I believed that my loyalty belonged to the administration in power—whether I agreed with their policies or not. But in 1964, I decided to take sides more actively in a political contest because I believed in what Barry stood for: integrity, courage, ambition, fiscal responsibility, Americanism, and a government that is the servant, not the master.

To help Barry and Representative Bill Miller of Pennsylvania get elected, I agreed to cochair, with Clare Booth Luce, a national Citizens for Goldwater-Miller Committee to solicit contributions. Concurrently, I agreed to chair Pilots for Goldwater, an organization formed in Washington for the same purpose, but aimed solely at pilots. In a letter to 375,000 active, licensed pilots, we asked for donations "to put Barry on TV where millions can and will be moved by his message." We prepared a winged "G" lapel pin and a "Pilots for Goldwater" membership card, which we sent to anyone who donated five dollars or more.

We all know the outcome of the election. The Goldwater-Miller ticket carried only six states. The Johnson-Humphrey ticket prevailed by 43 million to 27 million popular votes. It was a great personal disappointment to me.

After the election, I went elk hunting in the mountains of

northern New Mexico because I have always found that I think more clearly in the mountains, on the water, or by field or stream, than in the office. It gave me a chance to think about why Barry had not been elected. When I returned, I wrote him a long, brutally frank letter analyzing the defeat.

I concluded that Barry himself was the reason for the defeat because he was honest and courageous and said exactly what his conscience dictated. People who wanted sugar-coated pills and not facts didn't like this. It was something of an indictment of our body politic, but it appears that a more adroit and less straightforward man would have pleased more voters. Personally, I believe in absolute honesty. I therefore wholeheartedly approved of his approach.

I recommended that we should do everything possible to help President Johnson and assure the success of his administration. Since the nation was in his hands we, as loyal Americans, had to help him to preserve and improve it. I wrote:

> At the same time those of us who believe in the smallest government that can carry out the necessary functions of government, sound fiscal policies, national prestige, and enhanced national security, must continue to strive to educate the people of our great nation to the dangers of socialism and deficit spending, and the importance of national prestige and national morality. Some day we, or our successors, will prevail.

CHAPTER 24

Although, at 65, I looked forward to more leisure time, I still wasn't really ready to sit and ponder the past. I had met V. J. Skutt, CEO of the Mutual of Omaha Insurance Company, in 1958 and been tremendously impressed with him.

The company had been founded by Dr. C. C. Criss in 1909 and presented an award in his name to honor outstanding contributions to health, safety, education, and/or public welfare. The recipient in 1959 was Dr. Thomas A. Dooley, who was doing some wonderful humanitarian work in Southeast Asia. He had lived in our neighborhood in St. Louis. Someone found out about this, and Skutt invited Joe and me to attend that year's C. C. Criss Award ceremony in Omaha.

In 1961, I was asked to fill a vacancy on his board. I checked on the company very carefully before joining it and found that it was truly a first-class organization operating in accordance with the highest legal and ethical standards. However, I did not want to be just a figurehead and agreed to join the board with one stipulation: I would serve only if my efforts would contribute in a meaningful and significant way to the protection, safety, and well-being of the American public. My stipulation was accepted and I subsequently worked on several committees to develop health insurance plans for Mutual's overseas installations and to draft travel insurance for possible spaceflights and astronaut coverage. I saw my role as contributing to the company's expressed mission of helping others to help themselves. I was especially interested in the company's aggressive programs of fostering travel, accident, and health insurance.

In the years following, I served on the boards of eight of Mutual's companies and was given a number of assignments that fitted into my background in aviation and the military. I made several trips overseas when the company was expanding into international markets.

I was determined never to miss a board meeting, and I never did. But on one occasion in 1965, I had to travel to Omaha by dog sled from a camp in the Yukon to civilization, where I rode a Jeep to an airport, and flew in five different types of planes with five changes to get there. Nearly got trapped by weather in Chicago, but made it to Omaha on time. I vowed never to cut it so close again.

In 1968, I turned 72 years old and was past retirement age for most corporations. I thought the time had come for me to move aside for younger men and women. By that time I had retired from the boards of Shell, TRW, and Aerospace Corporation. However, I was asked to remain as a director on the boards of the several Mutual of Omaha companies and agreed to stay as long as I could be useful to each.

When I reached the age where I was considered a very senior citizen, I remembered a promise I had made to Joe in 1913 while we were still in high school. At that time, I had told her that if she would marry me I would take her on a voyage up the beautiful inside passage of Alaska some day. It's a good thing I didn't tell her when I would do this. In 1973, sixty years later, we flew from Los Angeles to Seattle, boarded a ship, and made a leisurely trip to Skagway, Alaska, then took a train to White Horse, Canada, and returned home by air.

I didn't realize how patient Joe had been, waiting for me to carry out my promise. When we boarded the ship and it seemed certain that she was finally going to get her trip to Alaska, she turned to me and said, "Doolittle, you're a man of your word."

After many years of comfortable living in Santa Monica, Joe and I decided in 1978 to move to a retirement community in Carmel, California. Although we had purchased property at Pebble Beach, a few miles away, we decided that the advantages of moving into a facility that would allow us to maintain our privacy, yet have access to meals and medical facilities, should we need or want them, outweighed the problems inherent in designing and building a house to our specifications. We deeded the Pebble Beach property to our son John and his wife, Priscilla.

Meanwhile, the company graciously offered me the opportunity to continue to serve, so I commuted to Los Angeles for the next two years. As anyone knows who tries it, commuting by commercial airline and living in a hotel away from one's family is very wearing. In 1980, the company opened an office for me in nearby Monterey.

In keeping with my theory about gradually lowering one's plateaus of activity as one grows older, I gradually resigned from committees and the directorships of all of Mutual's companies during the 1980s. However, the company elected me as a director emeritus and consultant for the major company in 1985. The year before, Joe and I were greatly honored by being presented with Criss awards. It was a night to be remembered for us. President Ronald Reagan, Dolores and Bob Hope, Florence Henderson, George Gobel, Charlton Heston, and others paid us tribute. I was especially pleased at what Dolores Hope said about Joe:

> As we know, Jimmy has flown millions of miles and for good reasons was away from home and his dear family for ages at a time. He spent 45 years in the air. Joe Doolittle spent 45 years waiting for him to land—at military bases, at civilian airports—and sometimes at the end of a runway that didn't exist until he landed.
>
> Those of us whose husbands also travel learned from her. For years, Joe was the national distributor of patience. But the Doolittles worked out a special arrangement beyond waiting. When Jimmy began setting records for passenger aircraft, Joe became his official passenger. She flew with him on more than one record flight. She didn't crave the honor. She took the job because her husband needed her. She's an amazing lady.

When Delores presented the award to Joe, she added that Joe

had shared her courage with women everywhere and therefore deserved a Criss Award of her own.

I was doubly honored that night.

Several weeks later, the Society of Experimental Test Pilots paid Joe an unusual tribute. For some time, the society has given a scholarship annually in my name to some deserving young engineering student. In 1984, they decided that one should be given in Joe's name to honor her for taking my place and making many of the annual presentations while I was off somewhere on business, hunting, or fishing. It was also a recognition of her as a test pilot's wife who quietly bore the agony of living with the constant threat of widowhood because of her husband's profession. Once more I was honored by the thoughtfulness of those who realized her important role in my life.

As I complete these memoirs, the world is witnessing a tremendous pro-democracy movement in the Soviet-dominated Eastern Bloc countries and in the Soviet Union itself. The Berlin Wall has come down; the small nations of Eastern Europe that had been swallowed up by Communist regimes are throwing off the yoke of totalitarianism; *perestroika* and *glasnost* have become household words and have come to mean political and economic freedom for millions.

It is a time to rejoice for those who are experiencing democracy, many for the first time, but it is not a time for us to become complacent and cut our military strength to a point of weakness. The Soviets have a long history of broken promises; we have a long history of dismantling our military services too soon after a threat subsides. Over the years, we have never properly prepared for demobilization. No one debates that the military forces can be smaller—they can—but any such reduction must be made in accordance with a well-thought-out plan.

No one expected World War II to end so quickly; too little thought had been given to the demobilization process. General Marshall recalled that the "confused and tumultuous" demobilization was very injurious to our military capability. This was proven when we entered the Korean conflict and found our tactical forces without proper radios or adequate photo reconnaissance, and we were unable to deploy our forces quickly to the Far East.

When we withdrew our forces from Vietnam, we promptly reduced our Air Force fighting strength and the number of aircraft in the operational inventory. Flying hours per pilot fell dramatically; Strategic Air Command pilots, for example, flew only two or three times a month, certainly not enough to retain their flying skills.

Research and development and procurement programs have also been cut drastically after each war. Our post-Vietnam malaise produced the "decade of neglect" of the 1970s and invited a period of "Soviet adventurism" that was scaled back only by the buildup during the Reagan administration from 1981 to 1986. In the 1980s, our inability to react strongly to the hostage situation and the invasion of Afghanistan resulted directly from the conscious underfunding of our forces, the inadequate training they received, and the creation of a "hollow force" incapable of protecting our national interests.

As long as the Soviet Union maintains its awesome military forces and other nations, like Iraq, threaten the peace, we must be prepared for possible conflict. It was especially gratifying to observe the wise use of air power in the 1991 war against Iraq, as the air forces of the international coalition fought a tyrant bent on dominating the Middle East. Following the principles of military leadership, properly employing air power, and using highly sophisticated weapon systems, all developed because of our experience during World War II, Korea, and Vietnam, resulted in early air supremacy for the coalition. I think military analysts and historians will record that thousands of American lives were saved because of our preparedness for such an action. Special tribute must be reserved for those decision makers in power during the 1980s who realized the declining state of our military forces and rebuilt them to a high degree of readiness, thus enabling President Bush to take the actions he did with confidence and assurance of a military victory.

We should always pray for peace; to maintain it, we must remain so strong militarily that no nation will dare to attack us. We must always be able to deter an all-out war and be prepared to cope with the small wars that may from time to time be forced upon us. In order to have that capability, we must have the continuous support of science, technology, and industry because over a period of time what we have on hand is going to become obsolete.

It is possible that at some point, the world situation may permit and encourage us to reduce the size of our forces. If so, I hope we can avoid the problems associated with the previous cutbacks, when all seemed peaceful. If the experience of four wars during my adult lifetime gives me any license to dispense advice, it is to remember how unprepared we were before each of those conflicts. We should never allow this to happen again.

Since the calendar and I have turned into the nineties, I have become a member of the thumb-twiddling society. Several years ago, when I was inclined to take on more extracurricular jobs than I could do well, I deliberately cut down on my workload. I found that when you can't do a job well, you don't enjoy doing it. There's no satisfaction in doing a poor job.

One of the privileges of age is the opportunity to sit back and ponder what you've seen and done over the years. In my nine-plus decades, I've formed some views about life and living that I have freely imposed on trusting audiences, both readers and listeners. I have concluded that we were all put on this earth for a purpose. That purpose is to make it, within our capabilities, a better place in which to live. We can do this by painting a picture, writing a poem, building a bridge, protecting the environment, combating prejudice and injustice, providing help to those in need, and in thousands of other ways. The criterion is this: If a man leaves the earth a better place than he found it, then his life has been worthwhile.

The move to Carmel gave me more time for occasional hunting and fishing expeditions with old, dear friends and to take trips with Joe whenever the spirit moved us. Joe, never one to sit idle, continued to write her daily postcards and letters to each of our friends who was ill, either at home or in the hospital. She continued doing this for "my shut-ins" until she could no longer hold a pen.

On December 24, 1988, after a stroke, followed by months of steady physical deterioration, my precious Joe passed away. It was our seventy-first wedding anniversary. She rests forever in Arlington National Cemetery, where I will join her one of these days.

In February 1990, I moved to Pebble Beach, California, where John and Priscilla built their dream house on the property Joe and I had bought in the 1940s. They had a large addition constructed that is now my final residence and office. As I watch the many bird species scramble for position to get the seed I put out each day, I realize my life has gone full cycle. I'm home and I'm content.

Luck has been with me all my life. Fortunately, I was always able to exploit that luck during my flying years and at each turn in my career. The best thing I ever did was to convince Joe that she should marry me; the luckiest thing that ever happened to me was when she finally did. That's why, whenever I'm asked, I say that I would never want to relive my life. I could never be so lucky again.

Thanks, Joe. I couldn't have done it without you.

Appendix 1

Proposal for the Bombing Attack on Tokyo

Subject: B-25 Special Project
To: Commanding General, Army Air Forces

The purpose of this special project is to bomb and fire the industrial center of Japan.

It is anticipated that this not only will cause confusion and impede production but will undoubtedly facilitate operation against Japan in other theaters due to their probable withdrawal of troops for the purpose of defending the home country.

An action of this kind is most desirable now due to the psychological effect on the American public, our allies, and our enemies.

The method contemplated is to bring carrier-borne bombers to within 400 to 500 miles (all distances mentioned will be in statute miles) of the coast of Japan, preferably to the south-southeast. They will then take off from the carrier deck and proceed directly to selected targets in the Tokyo-Yokohama, Nagoya, and Osaka-Kobe areas.

Simultaneous bombings of these areas is contemplated, with the bombers coming in up waterways from the southeast and, after dropping their bombs, returning in the same direction. After clearing the Japanese outside coastline a sufficient distance, a general westerly course will be set for one or more of the following airports in China: Chuchow, Chuchow (Lishui), Yushan, and/or Chienou. Chuchow is about 70 miles inland and 200 miles to the south-southwest of Shanghai.

After refueling, the airplanes will proceed to the strong Chinese air base at Chungking, about 800 miles distant, and from there to such ultimate objective as may, at that time, be indicated.

The greatest nonstop distance that any airplane will have to fly is 2,000 miles.

Eighteen B-25B (North American medium bomber) airplanes will be employed in this raid. Each will carry about 1,100 gallons of gasoline, which assures a range of 2,400 miles at 5,000 feet in still air.

Each bomber will carry two 500-pound demolition bombs and as near as possible to 1,000 pounds of incendiaries. The demolition bombs will be dropped first and then the incendiaries.

The extra gasoline will be carried in a 275-gallon auxiliary leakproof tank in the top of the bomb bay and a 175-gallon flexible rubber tank in the passageway above the bomb bay. It is anticipated that the gasoline from this top tank will be used up and the tank flattened out or rolled up and removed prior to entering the combat zone. This assures that the airplane will be fully operational and minimizes the fire and explosion hazard characteristic of a nearly empty tank.

In all other respects the airplanes are conventional. The work of installing the required additional tankage is being done by Mid-Continent Airlines at Minneapolis. All production and installation work is progressing according to schedule and the 24 airplanes (six spares) should be completely converted by March 15.

Extensive range and performance tests will be conducted on airplane number 1 while the others are being converted. A short period will be required to assemble and give special training to the crews. The training will include teamwork in bombing, gunnery, navigation, flying, short takeoff, and at least one carrier takeoff for each pilot.

If the crews are selected promptly from men familiar with their jobs and the B-25B airplane, the complete unit should be ready for loading on the carrier by April 1.

General operational instructions will be issued just before takeoff from the carrier.

Due to the greater accuracy of daylight bombing, a daylight raid is contemplated. The present concept of the project calls for a night takeoff from the carrier and arrival over objectives at dawn. Rapid refueling at the landing points will permit arrival at Chungking before dark.

A night raid will be made if, due to last-minute information received from our intelligence section or other source, a daylight raid is definitely inadvisable. The night raid should be made on a clear night, moonlight if Japan is blacked out, moonless if it is not.

All available pertinent information regarding targets and defenses will be obtained from A-2, G-2, and other existing sources.

The Navy has already supervised takeoff tests made at Norfolk, Virginia, using B-25B bombers carrying loads of 23,000 pounds, 26,000 pounds, and 29,000 pounds. These tests indicate that no difficulty need be anticipated in taking off from the carrier deck with a gross load of around 31,000 pounds.*

The Navy will be charged with providing a carrier (probably the *Hornet*), with loading and storing the airplanes, and with delivering them to the takeoff position.

The Chemical Warfare Service is designing and preparing special incendiary bomb clusters in order to assure that the maximum amount that limited space permits, up to 1,000 pounds per airplane, may be carried. Forty-eight of these clusters will be ready for shipment from Edgewood Arsenal [Maryland] by March 15.

About 20,000 U.S. gallons of 100-octane aviation gasoline and 600 gallons of lubricating oil will be laid down at Chuchow and associated fields. All other supplies and necessary emergency repair equipment will be carried on the airplanes.

First Lieutenant Harry W. Howze, now with the Air Service Command and formerly with the Standard Oil Company of New Jersey, will be charged with making arrangements for the fuel caches in China. He will work through A-2 and A-4 and with Colonel Claire Chennault, a former Air Corps officer and now aviation advisor to the Chinese government. Colonel Chennault should assign a responsible American or a Chinese who speaks

---

*I did not know until years later that the third airplane had not participated in the trials.

English to physically check and assure that the supplies are in place. This man should also be available to assist the crews in servicing the airplanes. That the supplies are in place can be indicated by suitable radio code signal. Work on placing supplies must start at once.

Shortly before the airplanes arrive, the proper Chinese agencies should be advised that the airplanes are coming soon, but the inference will be that they are flying up from the south in order to stage a raid on Japan from which they plan to return to the same base.

Radio signals from the bombing planes immediately after they drop their bombs may be used to indicate arrival at gassing points some six or seven hours later.

Care must be exercised to see that the Chinese are advised just in time, as any information given to the Chinese may be expected to fall into Japanese hands and a premature notification would be fatal to the project.

An initial study of meteorological conditions indicates that the sooner the raid is made the better will be the prevailing weather conditions. The weather will become increasingly unfavorable after the end of April. Weather was considered largely from the point of view of avoiding morning fog over Tokyo and other targets, low overcast over Chuchow and Chungking, icing, and strong westerly winds.

If possible, daily weather predictions or anticipated weather conditions at Chungking and the coast should be sent, at a specified time, in suitable code, in order to assist the meteorologist on the carrier in analyzing his forecasts.

Lieutenant Colonel J. H. Doolittle, Air Corps, will be in charge of the preparations for and will be in personal command of the project. Other flight personnel will, due to the considerable hazard incident to such a mission, be volunteers.

Each airplane will carry its normal complement of five crew members: pilot, copilot, bombardier-navigator, radio operator, and gunner-mechanic.

One crew member will be a competent meteorologist and one an experienced navigator. All navigators will be trained in celestial navigation.

Two ground liaison officers will be assigned. One will remain on the mainland and the other on the carrier.

At least three crew members will speak Chinese—one on each of the target units.

Should the Soviets be willing to accept delivery of 18 B-25B airplanes, on lease-lend, at Vladivostok, our problem would be greatly simplified and conflict with the Halverson project avoided.

APPENDIX 2

REPORT OF JOHN M. BIRCH

The Chinese officials at Chuhsien told me that outright purchase of a burial plot was prohibited by existing international law, but that Major Y. C. Chen, representing the Chinese air force, would like to present to the U.S. Army Air Corps the free use of a plot for 100 years or so long as the Air Corps wanted it. I thanked them for their kind expressions and asked them to wait until May 5; meanwhile (May 2), I sent the following telegram to the Military Mission:

> COLONEL DOOLITTLE'S INSTRUCTIONS TO BUY PLOT RECEIVED. MAJOR CHEN CHUHSIEN AIR STATION OFFERING PLOT NOT FOR SALE BUT FOR FREE AMERICAN USE. SHALL ACCEPT IF NOT OTHERWISE INSTRUCTED BEFORE MAY 5. BIRCH.

. . . No contrary instructions came, so I accepted Major Chen's offer on May 5. He offered to supply the labor connected with the burial, and asked me to instruct the workmen. Hindered by constant air raid alarms and air raids, the workmen failed to have the grave and stone ready until May 19, on which date Faktor's body was buried. . . .

As to information gathered: . . . Concerning those who

came down outside of free China—unofficial and uncertain reports locate them as follows: In Siberia, five men, condition and identity unknown here; near Nanchang, five men, probably those of Captain York's plane, two reported dead, two captured, and one rumored to be safe in free China; in Hsiang Shan Bay, five men, two reported dead and three captured, identity unknown to me.

On May 18, a telegram came to Chuhsien from Dr. White at Linhai, just as his party was leaving there for Chuchow (Chuhsien). He expected to reach us at Chuhsien by May 22. On May 20 I wired the Military Mission, asking whether or not I should accompany him to Chungking; at that time I could not anticipate the subsequent change of his route, which kept him from coming by way of Chuhsien. The reply calling me to Chungking reached me on May 23. Also on that date the Chinese air force officers at Wan Tsuen turned over to me a number of personal articles salvaged from the B-25 which crashed near Shuei Chang, Chekiang, these articles to be carried to the Military Mission at Chungking.

The funds I received . . . are untouched; as regards board and lodging, I was the guest of the Chinese air force from April 28 to May 26, 1942.

Appendix 3

Bombing Attack on Tokyo: Post-Raid Crew Summary

CREW NO. 2: Lieutenant Travis Hoover was the pilot and had followed us all the way to the Japanese coast. His copilot was Lieutenant William N. Fitzhugh; Lieutenant Richard E. Miller, bombardier; Lieutenant Carl R. Wildner, navigator; Sergeant Douglas V. Radney, engineer-gunner. After deviating to his target area and bombing two factory buildings and storehouses, Hoover sighted us again and trailed us west toward the Chinese coast. As with everyone else, they encountered a stiff headwind and didn't think they were going to make it to the mainland. However, the headwind lightened and then, providentially, turned into a nice 25-knot tailwind. We all could tell when the wind shifted by observing the whitecaps on the waves. When the weather worsened, Hoover had to leave us and go his own way. Instead of bailing out when his gas was about gone, Trav elected to belly into a rice paddy. No one was injured; after hiding out and walking for about three days his crew was taken into custody by about 30 armed guerrillas who fed them and bedded them down.

Beginning on April 22, they traveled by boat to Sungyao where they met Tung-sheng Liu, a young English-speaking Chinese engineering student, who had just come through the Japanese lines disguised as a merchant. He guided them by ricksha, bus, train, and on foot to Chuhsien where they met Captain Davey Jones and Lieutenant Everett "Brick" Holstrom. They had remained there to intercept gathering crews. Hoover's crew arrived in Chungking on May 14.*

CREW NO. 3: When Hoover's plane cleared the *Hornet*'s deck, Lieutenant Robert M. "Bob" Gray took off. Their three explosive bombs were dropped on industrial targets; the incendiary landed on a dock area. They experienced some antiaircraft fire but were not hit as far as they knew. Arriving over China, Gray ordered his crew to bail out; Corporal Leland D. Faktor, the gunner on this crew, was the one who was killed. Lieutenant Charles J. Ozuk, navigator, injured a leg on landing; and Lieutenant Jacob E. "Shorty" Manch, copilot, cut himself with his knife trying to make a water bag out of his parachute's rubber cushion. Bob Gray and Sergeant Aden Jones, the rear gunner, were not injured; all four made their way to Chuhsien with the help of friendly Chinese.

CREW NO. 4: Pilot of this crew was Lieutenant Everett W. "Brick" Holstrom; his copilot was Lieutenant Lucian N. Youngblood. Shortly after takeoff, Corporal Bert M. Jordan, the rear gunner, reported that the gun turret was out of commission. This meant they had no defense against enemy fighters except the .30-caliber gun in the nose. They made landfall south of Tokyo and were fired on by four Japanese fighters. When the fighters appeared, Holstrom explained what he did:

"I told the navigator (Lieutenant Harry McCool) to tell Corporal (Robert J.) Stephens, the bombardier, to try to use his nose gun. I had given him (McCool) previous instructions to have Stephens salvo the bombs if we were intercepted, so the bombs were salvoed [into Tokyo Bay] from about 75 feet."

This crew also bailed out over China when their gas ran out. McCool was injured slightly when he landed on a steep slope.

CREW NO. 5: Captain David M. "Davey" Jones piloted this

---

*After the war, Liu came to the States and received his doctorate in aeronautical engineering from the University of Minnesota in 1947. He became a citizen in 1954 and was employed by the Air Force as an aeronautical engineer at Wright-Patterson Air Force Base, in Ohio, until his retirement.

plane. Lieutenant Ross R. Wilder was copilot; Lieutenant Denver V. Truelove, bombardier; and Lieutenant Eugene F. McGurl, navigator. Corporal Joseph W. Manske, the gunner, had tried to top off the tanks at the last minute before takeoff, but because the carrier was in "battle condition," the fuel supply had been turned off. Consequently, the tanks were not full. After bombing an oil storage tank, a power plant, and a large manufacturing facility, they escaped. This crew bailed out and joined up next day. No one was injured.

CREW NO. 6: The pilot of this crew was Lieutenant Dean E. Hallmark, a husky six-footer. Copilot was Lieutenant Robert J. Meder; Lieutenant Chase J. Nielsen was navigator; Sergeant Donald E. Fitzmaurice, engineer-gunner; Corporal William J. Dieter, bombardier. Their target was a large steel mill in northeast Tokyo. They escaped without being intercepted. When they got close to China and were nearly out of gas, Hallmark elected to ditch the B-25 close to the beach. The landing was very hard. Hallmark was cut and bruised and, with some difficulty, made it to shore where he was joined by Meder and Nielsen. Dieter and Fitzmaurice were badly injured and drowned. Assisted by friendly Chinese, the surviving trio buried the bodies. They were later apprehended by Japanese soldiers and became prisoners of war.

The Japanese slaughtered many of the Chinese who helped this crew and others. We did not know what happened to these men until the war was over.

CREW NO. 7: This crew's story has been widely told in a book and motion picture under the title of *Thirty Seconds Over Tokyo*. Written by the pilot, Lieutenant Ted W. Lawson, with Bob Considine, Lawson tells of his crew's experience from takeoff to eventual recuperation from injuries received when they ditched after bombing factories in Japan's capital city. Lawson, his copilot, Lieutenant Dean Davenport; Lieutenant Charles L. McClure, navigator; and Lieutenant Robert S. Clever, bombardier, all badly hurt, somehow made it to shore. Corporal David J. Thatcher, the gunner, was unhurt. He assisted the others and prevented their being captured. He stayed with them until they began their recovery at a hospital run by Chinese doctors and English missionaries.

Lawson, the most seriously injured of the crew, nearly died. He was saved after Lieutenant T. R. "Doc" White, the gunner on the fifteenth plane, caught up with them. It was very fortuitous that the only physician on the raid was near enough to render assistance. Doc had to amputate Ted's leg to save his life; in the process Doc gave him two pints of his own blood. The second donation made Doc awfully woozy for several days and could have caused him serious problems. I later made sure that Dave Thatcher and Doc White received the Silver Star for their gallantry and dedication to their crews at great risk to themselves.

CREW NO. 8: Captain Edward J. "Ski" York piloted this plane. His copilot was Lieutenant Robert G. Emmens; Lieutenant Nolan A. Herndon, navigator-bombardier; Sergeant David W. Pohl, gunner; and Sergeant Theodore H. Laban, engineer. Apparently, their plane had been dogged by engine problems from the days at Sacramento when the ground crews there fiddled with the carburetors. Both engines burned fuel excessively, which was all too evident on the run into their target area. After they dropped their bombs, York had to make a difficult command decision. They could not make it if they followed the escape route south and then across the China Sea to the mainland. Making a forced landing in Japan was unthinkable. York believed the only option was to head for Soviet territory and, against orders, headed in that direction. They landed at a field near Vladivostok and naively hoped to refuel and be on their way to Chungking.

Although the State Department had been negotiating with the Soviets to allow us to land there after bombing Japan right up until our departure from Alameda, permission was never granted. In their view, they had good reason. Totally engaged in a war with Nazi Germany in the west, they could not afford to have to battle the Japanese in the east. The Soviets declared their neutrality. To preserve this status, York, his crew, and their B-25 had to be interned. Although the Soviets were our allies, these men were virtual prisoners for the next 14 months, until they escaped into Persia (now Iran). For many months, the Soviet government sent us monthly bills for 30,000 rubles for their keep. For some time afterward, I received irate telephone calls from Secretary of the Treasury Henry Morgenthau each time a bill arrived from the Soviet embassy. I recommended he ignore them. I assume he did.

CREW NO. 9: Lieutenant Harold F. "Doc" Watson piloted this plane. His crew dropped their eggs on the Tokyo Gas and Electric Co., on the shore of Tokyo Bay, south of the city. His crew consisted of copilot Lieutenant James M. Parker; Sergeant Wayne M. Bissell, bombardier; Lieutenant Thomas C. Griffin, navigator; and Sergeant Eldred V. Scott, engineer-gunner. As did most of the others, they bailed out in the darkness and rain; Watson was the only one injured and had to be carried to Hengyang by Chinese porters. He was picked up there and eventually evacuated to the States. In the wake of this crew's escape, Japanese forces killed thousands of Chinese peasants for assisting the Americans. It was later estimated that 250,000 innocent Chinese paid with their lives for helping us.

CREW NO. 10: Lieutenant Richard O. "Dick" Joyce's main target was the Japan Special Steel Co., located in southern Tokyo. A secondary target was a nearby precision-instrument factory. Both were hit. Joyce's copilot was Lieutenant J. Royden Stork; Lieutenant Horace E. "Sally" Crouch, navigator-bombardier; Sergeant George E. Larkin, gunner; and Sergeant Edwin W. Horton, engineer-gunner. This plane encountered heavy ack-ack fire but escaped without damage. As Horton received the order from Joyce to bail out the rear hatch of the aircraft, he replied, "Here I go. Thanks, sir, for a swell ride." None of this crew had any serious injuries.

CREW NO. 11: Captain C. Ross Greening headed this crew; with Lieutenant Kenneth E. Reddy, copilot; Lieutenant Frank A. Kappeler, navigator; Sergeant William L. Birch, bombardier; and Sergeant Melvin J. Gardner, engineer-gunner. Their targets were the docks, oil refineries, and warehouses between Tokyo and Yokohama. Intercepted and fired on by enemy fighters, they dropped all four bombs on a large refinery and tank farm, which immediately exploded. When the weather worsened upon arrival over the Chinese coast, Greening elected to have his crew bail out. All did successfully, although Reddy suffered a slight concussion when he hit. He carried a piece of rock in his scalp for several days until he received treatment in Chuhsien.

CREW NO. 12: Lieutenant William M. "Bill" Bower headed this crew. His copilot was Lieutenant Thadd H. Blanton; Lieutenant William R. Pound, navigator; Sergeant Omer A. Duquette, engineer-gunner; and Sergeant Waldo J. Bither, bombardier. When they arrived over Japan, they were trailed by Japanese fighters but not fired on. Barrage balloons had been erected over their target—the Yokohama dockyards—so they dropped one demolition on the Ogura refinery, two on factories, and the incendiary on a large warehouse.

This crew also bailed out; Sergeant Duquette broke a bone in his foot on landing. The Chinese made sedan chairs out of parachute harnesses and carried this crew to a joinup with Dick Joyce's crew.

Sergeant Bither had a serious problem before the bailout. As he made his way from the nose of the B-25 toward the flight deck, he inadvertently sprung his parachute open and had to repack it in the crawlway. Of all the men on the raid, he was the only one who had ever had any training in parachute packing. When I asked him years later if he was worried about it opening, he replied, "Well, I was a little concerned, but if it didn't open, I didn't have anybody to blame but myself."

CREW NO. 13: Being the thirteenth B-25 off the carrier didn't bother this crew. It was piloted by Lieutenant Edgar E. McElroy; copilot was Lieutenant Richard A. Knobloch; Lieutenant Clayton J. Campbell, navigator; Sergeant Robert C. Bourgeois, bombardier; and Sergeant Adam R. Williams, engineer-gunner. After bombing ships in dry dock and nearby workshops at Yokohama, this crew bailed out successfully. They were rounded up by Chinese guerrillas and proceeded on ponies and sedan chairs to Poyang, a city of about 300,000, where they were greeted and feted by hundreds of townspeople. Banners fluttered from windows; a large one read: WELCOME BRAVE AMERICAN FLYERS. FIRST TO BOMB TOKIO. UNITED STATES AND CHINA RULE THE PACIFIC.

CREW NO. 14: My deputy, Major John A. "Jack" Hilger was the pilot of this aircraft. His copilot was Lieutenant Jack A. Sims; Lieutenant James H. "Herb" Macia, navigator-bombardier; Sergeant Jacob Eierman, engineer; and Sergeant Edwin V. Bain, gunner. Their target was a military barracks, an oil and gas works, and the Mitsubishi aircraft facility in Nagoya. They were all hit with precision, especially the last.

This crew bailed out successfully and made their way to Chuchow in two days. Hilger told me later, "I was never so glad to see anyone in my life as I was to see Jones, Greening, Bower, and all their crew members. It was like a homecoming and we were all as happy as kids. There's nothing like a familiar face in a foreign country." He was certainly right.

CREW NO. 15: The target assigned to this plane was located in Kobe, part of an industrial complex southwest of Tokyo. It was piloted by Lieutenant Donald G. Smith; Lieutenant Griffith P. Williams, copilot; Lieutenant Howard A. Sessler, navigator; Sergeant Edward J. Saylor, engineer-gunner; and Lieutenant (Dr.) Thomas R. "Doc" White, gunner and physician. This crew elected to ditch in the ocean off the coast; fortunately, no one was hurt. However, Doc White lost his medical supplies when their life raft overturned in the rough surf. The crew traveled for several days on a Chinese junk, successfully evading Japanese search parties.

As they progressed toward Chuchow, they learned that Lawson and his crew were injured and headed toward a hospital at Linhai. Smith decided to detour to see if they could help out. When they arrived, Doc found that Lawson, Davenport, McClure, and Clever were in no shape to travel. He elected to stay with them while the other members of Smith's crew and Dave Thatcher of Lawson's crew went on to Chuchow.

CREW NO. 16: This crew was earmarked for trouble from the beginning. The pilot was Lieutenant William G. "Bill" Farrow; copilot was Lieutenant Robert L. Hite; Lieutenant George Barr, navigator; Corporal Jacob DeShazer, bombardier; and Sergeant Harold A. Spatz, engineer-gunner. Just after Farrow started the engines, a sailor slipped into the spinning left propeller and his left arm was cut off. He was quickly carried away by his buddies.

Last off the carrier, Farrow followed two other planes to their target area in Nagoya. While under attack by fighters, they bombed oil storage tanks and an aircraft factory. They arrived over the Chinese coast at dusk in rain showers and climbed on top of the overcast. As they plodded on and the gas gauges neared the empty mark, there was a break in the overcast and Barr identified the city lights below as Nanchang. Although they knew the city was occupied by the Japanese, they had no choice and bailed out. All were quickly captured. We knew nothing more about what happened to these five men until after the war.

Career Summary

U.S. Army Air Service and Air Corps, 1917–1930
Major, U.S. Army Air Corps Reserve, 1930–1940
Major, U.S. Army Air Corps, 1940
Lieutenant Colonel, 1942
Brigadier General, 1942
Major General, 1942
Lieutenant General, 1944
General, 1985
Commanding General, 12th Air Force, North Africa, 1942
Commanding General, 15th Air Force, Italy, 1943
Commanding General, 8th Air Force, England, 1944
Commanding General, 8th Air Force, Okinawa, 1945
Vice President, Shell Union Oil Company, 1946–1947
Director, Shell Union Oil Company, 1946–1967
Chairman of the Board, Space Technology Laboratories, 1959–1962
Director, Space Technology Laboratories, 1959–1963
Director, Thompson-Ramo-Wooldridge Company, 1961–1969
Consultant, TRW Systems, 1962–1965
Director, Mutual of Omaha Insurance Co., 1961–1986
Director Emeritus and Consultant, Mutual of Omaha Insurance Co., 1986–
Trustee, Aerospace Corporation, 1963–1969
Vice Chairman, Board of Trustees, and Chairman of Executive Committee, Aerospace Corporation, 1965–1969

Director, United Benefit Life Insurance Company of Omaha, 1964–1980
Director, Tele-Trip Company, 1966–1980
Director, Companion Life Insurance Company of New York, 1968–1980
Director, Mutual of Omaha Growth & Income Funds, 1968–1980

Military Decorations

Medal of Honor
Distinguished Service Medal, with Oak Leaf Cluster
Silver Star
Distinguished Flying Cross, with two Oak Leaf Clusters
Bronze Star
Air Medal, with three Oak Leaf Clusters
Order of the Condor (Bolivia)
Yon-Hwei, Class III (China)
Knight Commander, Order of the Bath (Great Britain)
Grand Officer of the Légion d'Honneur and Croix de Guerre, with Palm (France)
Grand Order of the Crown, with Palm, and Croix de Guerre with Palm (Belgium)
Grand Commander (Poland)
Abdon Calderon, First Class (Ecuador)

Education

Manual Arts High School, Los Angeles, California
Los Angeles Junior College, 1916–1917
University of California, Bachelor of Arts, 1922
Massachusetts Institute of Technology, Master of Science, 1924, and Doctor of Science, 1925

Honorary Degrees

University of California, Doctor of Laws
University of Michigan, Doctor of Engineering
Clarkson College of Technology, Doctor of Science

Brooklyn Polytechnic Institute, Doctor of Engineering
Waynesburg College, Doctor of Military Science
Northland College, Doctor of Laws
University of Alaska, Doctor of Science
Pennsylvania Military College, Doctor of Science

Honors and Awards

Schneider Marine Cup, 1925
Mackay Trophy, 1925
Spirit of St. Louis Award, 1929
Harmon Trophy, Ligue des Aviateurs, 1930
Bendix Trophy, 1931
Thompson Trophy, 1932
Guggenheim Trophy, 1942
International Harmon Trophy, 1940, 1949
Wright Brothers Trophy, 1953
Fédération Aéronautique Internationale Gold Medal, 1954
Silver Quill, 1959
International Aerospace Hall of Fame, San Diego, California, 1966
Aviation Hall of Fame, Dayton, Ohio, 1967
Thomas D. White National Defense Award, 1967
Horatio Alger Award, 1972
Conservation Hall of Fame, 1973
Wings of Man Award, Society of Experimental Test Pilots, 1973
Bishop Wright Air Industry Award, 1975
Sylvanus Thayer Award, U.S. Military Academy, 1983
C. C. Criss Award, 1984
Motorsports Hall of Fame Award, 1989
Grand Cross of Honour, Supreme Council of Scottish Rite, 1989
Presidential Medal of Freedom, 1989

Appointments

Member, Army Air Corps Investigating Committee (Baker Board), 1934
Chairman, Secretary of War's Board on Officer/Enlisted Men Relationships, 1946
Member, Joint Congressional Aviation Policy Board, 1948

Advisor, Committee on National Security Organization, 1948
Chairman, President's Airport Commission, 1952
Chairman, 50th Anniversary of Powered Flight, 1953
Chairman, President's Task Group on Air Inspection, Stassen Disarmament Committee, 1955
Chairman, Air Force Scientific Advisory Board, 1955–1958
Member, President's Foreign Intelligence Advisory Board, 1955–1965
Chairman, National Advisory Committee for Aeronautics, 1956–1958
Member, Advisory Board, National Air Museum, Smithsonian Institution, 1956–1965
Member, Defense Science Board, 1957–1958
Member, President's Science Advisory Committee, 1957–1958
Member, National Aeronautics and Space Council, 1958
Member, Plowshare Committee of the Atomic Energy Commission, 1959–1972
Member, National Institutes of Health Study, 1963–1965
Member, Air Force Space Systems Advisory Group, 1963–1967

Associations

Honorary Fellow, American Institute of Aeronautics and Astronautics
Fellow, Royal Aeronautical Society
Fellow, American Astronautical Society
Member, American Petroleum Institute
Member, Society of Automotive Engineers
Founding President and Member, Air Force Association
Member, National Aeronautic Association
Member, Order of Daedalians
Member, Explorers Club

Aviation "Firsts"

First cross-continental crossing in less than 24 hours, 1922
First to execute outside loop, 1927
First "blind" flight, 1929
First cross-continental crossing in less than 12 hours, 1932

BIBLIOGRAPHY

Arnold, Henry H., *Global Mission*. New York: Harper and Brothers, 1949.

Coffey, Thomas M., *Hap*. New York: The Viking Press, 1982.

Copp, DeWitt S., *Forged in Fire*. New York: Doubleday & Co., 1980.

Copp, DeWitt S., *A Few Great Captains*. New York: Doubleday & Co., 1982.

Cray, Ed, *General of the Army: George C. Marshall, Soldier and Statesman*. New York: W. W. Norton & Co., 1990.

Freeman, Roger A., *The Mighty Eighth: A History of the U.S. 8th Army Air Force*. Garden City, N.Y.: Doubleday & Co., 1970.

Frisbee, John L., ed., *Makers of the United States Air Force*. Washington, D.C.: Office of Air Force History, U.S. Air Force, 1987.

Glines, Carroll V., *Doolittle's Tokyo Raiders*. Princeton, N.J.: D. Van Nostrand Co., 1964.

Glines, Carroll V., *Four Came Home*. Princeton, N.J.: D. Van Nostrand Co., 1966.

Glines, Carroll V., *The Compact History of the United States Air Force*. New York: Hawthorn Books, 1973.

Glines, Carroll V., *The Doolittle Raid: America's Daring First Strike Against Japan*. New York: Orion Books, 1988.

Goldberg, Alfred, ed., *A History of the United States Air Force, 1907–1957*. Princeton, N.J.: D. Van Nostrand Co., 1957.

Gorn, Michael H., *Harnessing the Genie*. Washington, D.C.: Office of Air Force History, U.S. Air Force, 1988.

Hallion, Richard P., *Legacy of Flight: The Guggenheim Contribution to American Aviation*. Seattle, Wa.: University of Washington Press, 1977.

Hallion, Richard P., *Test Pilots*. Washington, D.C.: Smithsonian Institution Press, 1988.

Hansell, Haywood S., Jr., *The Air Plan That Defeated Hitler*. Atlanta, Ga.: Higgins-McArthur/Longino & Porter, 1972.

Johnson, Bruce, *The Man with 2 Hats*. New York: Carlton Press, 1968.

Maurer, Maurer, *Aviation in the U.S. Army, 1919–1939*. Washington, D.C.: Office of Air Force History, U.S. Air Force, 1987.

Meilinger, Philip S., *Hoyt S. Vandenberg*. Bloomington, In.: Indiana University Press, 1989.

Mets, David R., *Master of Airpower: General Carl A. Spaatz*. Novato, Ca.: Presidio Press, 1988.

Parton, James, *"Air Force Spoken Here."* Bethesda, Md.: Adler & Adler, 1986.

Straubel, James H., *Crusade for Airpower*. Washington, D.C.: Aerospace Education Foundation, 1982.

Index

Note: Certain kinds of information are grouped under the following headings: Aircraft instruments; Airfields and air bases; Airplanes; Air shows, meets, and races; Military units; Ships of the U.S. Navy. The abbreviation "JD" (referring to James H. "Jimmy" Doolittle) is alphabetized as if spelled "Doolittle, James H. 'Jimmy.'" Other names appearing first name first in subheadings are also alphabetized by last name. An italic n *attached to a page number means that the reference is to a footnote.*

D

G

H